Tribal Land, Forest and Identity Issues

ABOUT THE AUTHOR

Prof. K. Gopal Iyer hailed from Tamil Nadu. But his interest in popular movements took him to Andhra Pradesh, Bihar, Haryana, Punjab and other parts of the country. A gold medallist from Patna University, he retired from Department of Sociology, Panjab University, Chandigarh in 2002, where he had been teaching since 1978. He was not just an academic as he has been relating himself with people's movements all over the country. His contribution to the understanding of land reforms in India after five decades of the land reforms law in various states in India is the first of its kind and has vividly described the fallacy in the conceptualisation of land reform legislations and inactive implementation of the laws across the country. He took interest in understanding the problems of rural poor and his published studies are on the bonded labour system, human rights violation of migrant workers, peasant movements, farmer's movements, and land reforms and so on. A prolific writer he has authored a number of outstanding books, research papers, project report etc.

He passed away at the age of 75 in Chandigarh on 19th October 2017.

Tribal Land, Forest and Identity Issues

A Study of Jharkhand and Odisha

K. Gopal Iyer

CONCEPT PUBLISHING COMPANY PVT. LTD.
NEW DELHI-110059

ISBN-13: 978-93-86682-58-1

First Published 2020

Published and Printed by

Concept Since 1974

Concept Publishing Company Pvt. Ltd.
A/15-16, Commercial Block, Mohan Garden
New Delhi-110059 (India)
T: 91 11 25351460, 91 11 25351794
E: publishing@conceptpub.com, *W*: www.conceptpub.com

Cataloging in Publication Data--Courtesy: D.K. Agencies (P) Ltd. <docinfo@dkagencies.com>

Iyer, K. Gopal, 1942- author.
Tribal land, forest and identity issues : a study of Jharkhand and Odisha / K. Gopal Iyer.
pages cm
Includes index.
ISBN 9789386682581

1. Tribes—India—Jharkhand—Politics and government. 2. Tribes—India—Odisha—Politics and government. 3. Tribes—Legal status, laws, etc.—India—Jharkhand. 4. Tribes—Legal status, laws, etc.—India—Odisha. 5. Ethnicity—India—Jharkhand. 6. Ethnicity—India—Odisha. 7. Forced migration—India—Jharkhand. 8. Forced migration—India—Odisha. 9. Land tenure—Law and legislation—India—Jharkhand. 10. Land tenure—Law and legislation—India—Odisha. 11. Community forestry—Law and legislation—India—Jharkhand. 12. Community forestry—Law and legislation—India—Odisha. I. Title.

LCC GN635.I4I94 2020 | DDC 305.800954127 23

Foreword

There is ample evidence to justify that Social Development in India had a setback due to process of liberalization and globalization. Its direct consequence has been the sharp deterioration in the conditions of the marginalized, particularly the Scheduled Castes, the Scheduled Tribes, Women and the pauperized masses.

"Development Induced Displacement" is one of the most serious issues which the marginalized have been facing both during the Colonial and Post-Colonial era. Several experts have considered the sheer magnitude of the problem as staggering because the estimates of the displaced number more than 6 million. The policy of land acquisition today of the Central and State Governments have been seriously condemned by the Activists, Intellectuals, as also by the grassroots movements and they have also been critical of the resettlement and rehabilitation policy carried out so far. Forcible displacement has been the worst form of violence which is being perpetrated during the era of liberalization. Several research studies have observed that "Development Induced Displacement" has led to impoverishment of vulnerable sections.

According to the international standards including the World Bank involuntary resettlement of the India's displaced people have not resulted in their better economic conditions. In the face of massive displacement, the tribals are putting determined resistance to vacate their agricultural land. Such resistance is exemplified particularly in the tribal dominated regions of Jharkhand, Odisha and Chhattisgarh both during the period of Colonialism and Economic Liberalization. These States are also the most poverty-stricken states in the country. They are also among the severely Left Extremist affected States in the country. The Institute of Social Sciences, New Delhi provides encouragement and impetus to such challenging research studies.

I am quite convinced that the present research study sponsored by

ICSSR which tries to establish strong linkage of land and forest with the Cultural Identity of Tribals in Jharkhand and Odisha would throw deeper light on such contemporary and live issues.

20 March, 2017

Dr. George Mathew
Chairman
Institute of Social Sciences
New Delhi

Preface

I am deeply appreciative of Prof. K. Gopal Iyer for undertaking research in an area which is not only of contemporary relevance but also examines the interface between Globalization and its impact on the most vulnerable sections of Scheduled Tribes and Scheduled Castes. The field of research covers basically the tribal areas of Jharkhand and Odisha which are the most intensely affected Maoist region. The Project Director has tried to analyse the symbiotic relationship between Land and Forest not only as a Prime Livelihood Issue, but also as vital to their cultural identity. The research study has an interdisciplinary focus with historical, anthropological and sociological vigour. It is also addressing the contemporary live issues of Land Acquisition, Forest Rights, Forest Produce as a source of Livelihood and the Pauperization Thesis. The study in particular highlights the impact of Naxalite Movement on the Tribals and also explores the Autonomous Tribal Movements in the context of the ongoing predicament and ignominy faced by the Adivasis.

I sincerely hope that this piece of research work is adjudged as useful research report for the entire gamut of stakeholders involved in livelihood promotion of the marginalized sections and would also actively contribute to the policy formation in the area of Development Induced Displacement and access of Forest Rights to the Adivasis and Forest Dwellers.

20 March, 2017

Dr. Ash Narain Roy
Director
Institute of Social Sciences
New Delhi

Acknowledgements

First of all I would like to thank Indian Council of Social Science Research (ICSSR) for sanctioning the present research project on "Land, Forest and Identity Issues in Jharkhand and Odisha". I am equally thankful to Dr. Revathy Vishwanathan, Assistant Director (Research), ICSSR, who has been very helpful in carrying forward the project at the appropriate juncture. I would like to express my gratitude to Dr. George Mathew, Chairman, Institute of Social Sciences, New Delhi, for his overwhelming support at every stage of the research work including constant morale boosting whenever I faced difficult times. I warmly acknowledge the help extended by Dr. Ash Narain Roy, Director, Institute of Social Sciences, New Delhi to facilitate the completion of project in spite of strenuous situation faced intermittently.

I would fail in my duty if I do not thank my field investigators who have been instrumental in data collection both in the states of Jharkhand and Odisha through the difficult situation. It is impossible to give adequate recognition to grassroots social activists like Shri Sanjay Basu Mallick, Jharkhand, Shri P.V. Rajgopal and Shri Ramesh Sharma of Ekta Parishad, Johar (Chaibasa) who were the driving force in providing insight into the land and forest issues in Jharkhand and Odisha. I am equally indebted to many officials in the states of Jharkhand and Odisha without whose cooperation and assistance, it would have been difficult to get the needed official research data relevant for the present study. Important among such officials are the Deputy Commissioners-*cum*-District Magistrates of various districts of Jharkhand and Odisha, subject matter specialist including the technical experts.

Last but not the least, I owe my sincere thanks to the staff of the Institute of Social Sciences like Shri P.K. Krishnan Namboodiri, Shri P. Nandakumar, Ms. Vidya, Shri Josy Jose and Shri Lalit Prasad whose trust, friendship and forbearance have immensely contributed to successful completion of the present research work.

I am very thankful to Ashok Kumar Mittal, Managing Director, Concept Publishing Company (P) Ltd., New Delhi to publish my present research work.

20 March, 2017

Dr. K. Gopal Iyer
Project Director
Institute of Social Sciences
Vasant Kunj
New Delhi

Executive Summary

The thrust of the present research work is to highlight the significance of Land and Forest as basic Cultural Identity Issues for the Adivasis of Jharkhand and Odisha.

Impact of Globalization on Tribal Society and Economy

Globalization and ruthless operation of unbridled market forces are the key formations of new paradigm of development. The specific impact of globalization on tribal society in India can be specified as follows:

- The tribal areas came to occupy the central place due to their rich natural resource endowment.
- The exploiters consisting of the industrialists, the contractors, the middlemen and host of outsiders have descended in the tribal areas in search of new opportunities.
- The tribal people have been reduced to a minority status due to the new migrant population.
- Globalization would prove to be the anti-thesis of the existence of a functioning *'Gram Sabha'* with full control over the habitat and the community and also to the provisions of Fifth Schedule of the Constitution.
- The over-riding importance of individual rights in total disregard of thc community rights, had placed the tribal people in predicament about their basic rights over land, water and forest resource; this makes the position of tribals most vulnerable to crafty manipulations of vested interest.
- Land Acquisition Act of 1894 with minor amendments from time-to-time, is being indiscriminately used to alienate and acquire the tribal lands at throw away price.
- The Central and Eastern India are becoming the theatre of the vulnerability of the Adivasis and they are placed in a predicament

to face the violence perpetrated by the Corporate Groups, State and the Maoist.

- Globalization, privatization and free market have been forced on the tribals in collusion with the national ruling elite to violate the community rights of the tribals.
- The State has taken recourse to repression in the face of the resistance by the tribals against the imposition of forceful industrialization; the police administration has not been viewed by the tribals as their protector but as an ally of the non-tribal groups [Sharma, B.D., (1995), *Globalization: The Tribal Encounter*, Har-Anand Publication, New Delhi].

Few Dimensions of the Subject

- The most important aspect of social injustice caused to the tribals by actions of state agencies in the era of globalization is the failure to effectively implement laws which protect their interests such as those preventing Alienation of Tribal Land, PESA Act, 1996, Forest Rights Act, 2006 and other developmental policies which are favourable to the tribals.
- Mining is the largest component of extractive growth which has attracted large foreign investment and providing impetus to land acquisition of the tribals.
- Land Reforms, the classical plank of Maoists for peasant mobilization is not the prime issue today for which the tribals are agitated, but much greater salience is to be placed to the question of land, forest and cultural identity.
- Movements are rooted in resistance against land and forest rights during colonial period which also continues during present globalization era.
- Nature and variety of present mobilization by marginalized sections for enforcement of their rights ranges from autonomous tribal movement, civil society initiatives and the Maoist movement.
- The spread of left radicalism in the states of Jharkhand and Odisha is a political movement which needs to be analysed in the overall current situation of land, forest and water rights in particular.

Areas of Enquiry on Study of Jharkhand and Odisha

- The State Policy with respect to Land and Forest would be

examined in the Colonial and Post-Colonial period in the States of Jharkhand and Odisha.

- The inextricable linkage between Land, Forest and Identity, during the Colonial and Post-Colonial period would be examined in a comparative frame with respect to Jharkhand and Odisha.
- To examine the adverse impact of *development induced displacement* among the tribals in Jharkhand and Odisha during the colonial period and also in the globalization era in the context of New Industrialization Policy.
- The role of S*ocial Movements* led by tribals, civil society groups and by the Left Extremist Organizations on agrarian issues and corporate land grab would be.
- The role of Non-Timber Forest Produce in the livelihood of the Adivasis in Jharkhand and Odisha.

The anthropological and sociological writings in the States of Jharkand and Odisha are replete with discussions on the militant resistance of the Adivasis movements to protect their land and forest both during the Colonial and Globalization era. They have invariably resisted the Land Issues like transformation of Communal Property as Private Property, Land Acquisition and conversion of Forest as State Property. The present research work is essentially an empirical study for which the field data have been collected mainly from tribal districts of Jharkhand and Odisha as also from two coastal districts of Odisha.

Most of the districts and villages selected for the field study were affected by Left Extremism (Maoist Affected Area). The findings of the research work revealed that one of the basic reasons for the marginalized in the States of Jharkhand and Odisha supporting the Left Extremist Activists was the denial of *social justice*. In both the States of Jharkhand and Odisha the welfare policies like PESA Act, 1996, Constitutional Provisions of the Vth Scheduled Area, Forest Rights Act, 2006, Social Atrocities Act, 1989 etc. were severely violated. The agricultural land of the Adivasis and marginalized were forcibly acquired. Development Induced Displacement rendered them impoverished resulting in landlessness and houselessness. In the face of forcible acquisitions, the marginalized tribals and scheduled caste stood their own ground solidly and sacrificed their life instead of land. Their agriculture lands were acquired by the Government of Odisha at very cheap rate and rehabilitation measures did not improve their economic conditions. The Forest Rights Act, 2006 recognized that the denial of the Forest Rights have been an historical injustice. The present research study has shown that the Government of Odisha has implemented the provisions of Forest Rights Act, 2006 more seriously than the State of Jharkhand. In order to minimize the influence of Left Extremist the State Governments of Jharkhand and Odisha have implemented District Action Plan in the Naxlite affected areas with the help of the Central Government. The principal thesis was that the development initiative would change the mindset of Adivasis from being drawn closer to the Left Extremist. Such attempt was in particular undertaken in the district of West Singhbhum in Jharkhand and known as Saranda Action Plan. In this district several developmental measures like Forest Rights Act, 2006, homestead rights to all the households, watershed programmes, rural development programmes, MNREGA programmes, health programmes to all and similar other benefits were extended to the Adivasis. Apart from this there was heavy security deployment to drive out the Maoist from the area. The Government of Jharkhand claims the Saranda Action Plan as a success. Now this model has been extended also to other Left Extremist affected Districts like Khunti, Saraikela, East Singhbhum, Palamau, Latehar and several other districts. Even in the State of Odisha it has been extended to the tribal dominated districts like Rayagada, Koraput, Kalahandi, Sundergarh etc. In the different districts of Odisha still the grassroots activism of Left Extremist is quite strong and they had played very effective role against the state repression in Kalinganagar, POSCO, Kalahandi, Niyamgari, Kashipur etc. It may be mentioned here that in the Saranda Action Plan in West Singhbhum district in Jharkhand many of the educated youths were provided vocational training and engaged in technical occupations in the States of Karnataka, Andhra Pradesh etc. and it has diverted their attention from Left Extremism. As a consequence the incidence of Left Extremism has drastically declined in the West Singhbhum district.

However, the situation in Khunti district is worsening because of high incidence of Maoist activity. This is also a traditional district of Birsa Munda where the traditional Khuntkatti rights of Adivasis are still kept intact. In Odisha initially the forcible land acquisition accentuated militant struggle. The Development Induced Displacement tremendously aggravated the tensions in areas like Kalinganagar, POSCO, Kashipur etc. The autonomous tribal movements both in Jharkhand and Odisha have played significant role in strengthening of grassroots movement during the globalization era. The role of women in these land struggle has been exemplary. In Jharkhand the land and forest issues prevented the implementation of large number of MOU's and Land Acquisition because of the militant Adivasis grassroots movement which is deeply rooted in the traditional cultural identity. In the State of Odisha acquisition of bauxite was prevented in Niyamgiri hills which is the abode of Niyamgiri Raja and cultural habitat of Kond primitive tribe.

It would be desirable to outline few policy related outcome which emerge from this study. The existing statutory provisions and constitutional provisions which protect the interest and welfare of the Adiviasis need to be properly implemented. These are PESA Act, 1996, Constitutional Provisions of Schedule V, prevention of Adivasis land alienation, proper implementation of MNREGA Act etc. Besides this the land acquisition process should be preceded by obtaining prior consent of Adivasis and marginalized, completing the social impact assessment, avoiding acquisition of agricultural land, and effective Rehabilitation Policy.

Contents

List of Tables

1

Theoretical Framework of the Research Study

1.1 Concept of Globalization

Agrarian Political Economy offers an understanding of the process surrounding and subsuming land transfers that are predicated on the socially embedded character of such transfers, especially through the concept of enclosure (Akram-Lodhi, 2007). The tribal agrarian economy today can also be characterized as peasant economy super-imposed by globalization and market-led agrarian reforms. An understanding of land and forest issues are located within a determinate set of social, political, economic, ecological and cultural relations; and *as a consequence land is woven into the construction of identity.*

Land is the principal agrarian means of production, and is thus a key determinant of social, political, economic, ecological and cultural relationships. Resistance to Market-led Agrarian Reforms (MLAR) has come from various movements of peasants, tribals and the landless. The present challenge is not just limited to securing land for the land-less but also to prevent the alienation of tribal land and protecting the forest rights of the indigenous people.

Globalization and ruthless operation of unbridled market forces are the key formations of new paradigm of development. The specific impact of globalization on tribal society in India can be specified as follows:

- The tribal areas came to occupy the central place due to their rich natural resource endowment.
- The exploiters consisting of the industrialists, the contractors, the middlemen and host of outsiders have descended in the tribal areas in search of new opportunities.
- The tribal people have been reduced to a minority status due to the new migrant population.

- Globalization would prove to be the anti-thesis of the existence of a functioning 'Gaonsabha' with full control over the habitat and the community and also to the provisions of Fifth Schedule of the Constitution.
- The over-riding importance of individual rights in total disregard of the community rights, had placed the tribal people in predicament about their basic rights over land, water and forest resource; this makes the position of tribals most vulnerable to crafty manipulations of vested interest.
- Land Acquisition Act of 1894 with minor amendments from time-to-time, is being indiscriminately used to alienate and acquire the tribal lands at throwaway prices.
- With the increase of industrial and mining activity, the scarce water resources of the tribal areas are being exploited by the industrialists and multinationals. This has happened on a large scale in the State of Jharkhand and is also now taking place in Odisha (Sharma, B.D., 1995).
- The Central and Eastern India are becoming the theatre of the vulnerability of the Adivasis and they are placed in a predicament to face the violence perpetrated by the Corporate Groups, State and the Maoists.
- Globalization, privatization and free market have been forced on the tribals in collusion with the national ruling elite to violate the community rights of the tribals.
- The State has taken recourse to repression in the face of the resistance by the tribals against the imposition of forceful industrialization; the police administration has not been viewed by the tribals as their protector, but as an ally of the non-tribal groups [Sharma, B.D. (1995), *Globalization: The Tribal Encounter*, Har-Anand Publications, New Delhi].

1.2 Few Dimensions of the Subject

- The most important aspect of social injustice caused to the tribals by actions of State agencies in the era of globalization is the failure to effectively implement laws which protect their interests such as those preventing Alienation of Tribal Land, PESA Act, 1996, Forest Rights Act, 2006 and forcible acquisition of tribal lands and other developmental policies which are favourable to the tribals.
- Mining is the largest component of extractive growth which

has attracted large foreign investment and providing impetus to land acquisition of the tribals.

- Land Reforms, the classical plank of Maoists for peasant mobilization is not the prime issue today for which the tribals are agitated but much greater salience is to be placed to the question of land, forest and cultural identity.
- Movements are rooted in resistance against land and forest rights during colonial period which also continues during present globalization era.
- Nature and variety of present mobilization by marginalized sections for enforcement of their rights ranges from autonomous tribal movement, civil society initiatives and the Maoist movement.
- The spread of left radicalism in the States of Jharkhand and Odisha is a political movement which needs to be analysed in the overall current situation of land, forest and water rights in particular.

1.3 Areas of Enquiry on Study of Jharkhand and Odisha

- The State Policy with respect to Land and Forest would be examined in the Colonial and Post-Colonial period in the States of Jharkhand and Odisha.
- The inextricable linkage between Land, Forest and Identity, during the Colonial and Post-Colonial period would be examined in a comparative frame with respect to Jharkhand and Odisha.
- To examine the adverse impact of *development induced displacement* among the tribals in Jharkhand and Odisha during the colonial period and also in the globalization era in the context of New Industrialization Policy.
- The role of *Social Movements* led by tribals, civil society groups and by the Left Extremist Organizations on agrarian issues and corporate land grab would be.
- The role of Non-Timber Forest Produce in the livelihood of the Adivasis in Jharkhand and Odisha.

1.4 Proposition to be Examined in the Context of Jharkhand Identity

- Non-tribal immigrants are changing the demographic profile of the States in the scheduled area reducing them to a minority in the very territory where they are concentrated. As a result, the tribal identity and the protection that goes with it is also jeopardized.

- The roots of alienation of the tribals from the existing policy are much deeper which relate to dispossessing them from their lands, restricting access to forest resources which destroy their culture and identity.
- The resistance to the adverse impact of globalization is severe both in Jharkhand and Odisha.

1.5 Areas of Enquiry on the Study of Jharkhand and Odisha

- The inextricable linkage between Land, Forest and Tribal Identity, during the Colonial and Post-Colonial period is being examined in a comparative frame with respect to Jharkhand and Odisha.
- The adverse impact of *Development induced displacement* among the marginalized sections with special emphasis on Adivasis in Jharkhand and Odisha in the globalization era in the context of New Industrialization Policy.
- The role of *Social Movements* led by Tribals, Civil Society Groups and the Left Extremist Organizations on agrarian issues and corporate land grab in Jharkhand and Odisha.
- The struggle on Forest Issues and the Role of Forest Rights Act, 2006 in addressing the livelihood concerns of the tribals and the forest-dwellers and in enhancing their dignity and identity issues.
- The role of Rural Development and Livelihood issues in ameliorating the socio-economic condition of the tribals and other marginalized sections.
- The role of Minor Forest Produce and Agriculture in addressing the poverty concerns among the tribals in particular and the special role of Self-Help Groups (SHGs) in this context.
- Poverty, migration and predicament of rural labour in Jharkhand and Odisha.
- Status of Adivasis and the marginalized in Jharkhand and Odisha today.

1.6 Objectives of the Study of Jharkhand and Odisha

It is in this background that the following objectives have specifically been examined in Jharkhand and Odisha:

- The role of tribal movements during the colonial period on Land and Forest Issues in establishing the Tribal Identity.
- Continuity of the Tribal Movements during Post-Independence period with the primary focus of Land and Forest Issues as the Centre of Tribal Discontent.
- The role of the Maoist Movement in Jharkhand and Odisha and its impact on the tribals.
- The spate of Land Acquisition during the globalization era and *militant resistance* of the tribals both in Jharkhand and Odisha.
- The strong resistance of the tribals in alienating Forest Rights of the Adivasis in the Globalization era and the struggle for the Implementation of Forest Rights Act, 2006.
- Poverty, migration and predicament of rural labour in Odisha.
- Status of Adivasis and the marginalized in Jharkhand and Odisha today.

1.7 Methodology of Study in Jharkhand

Method of Data Collection

- The exploitation of the tribals based on Land, Forest and Land Acquisition during the colonial period and post-independence would be primarily analyzed through Historical Method, Case Study Techniques and secondary by published literature.
- The exploitation of the tribals on Land, Forest and Land Acquisition during the Globalization era would be studied both through the secondary materials and primary method of data collection.
- The issues of Tribal Identity pertaining to their traditional social institution, community based property and the operation of Wilkinson's Rule in Jharkhand and of persistent suppression of tribal movement in Odisha will be basically examined through qualitative techniques, like non-directive interview, focused group interview, participant and non-participant observation method and data from secondary sources.

- The study of Tribal Agrarian Movements during the Colonial period and Globalization era would be mainly analyzed both through secondary literature and qualitative techniques, like Non-directive Interview, Focused Group Interview, Case Study Method.
- The issues pertaining to the impact of Globalization on Development, Displacement and Rehabilitation would be examined mainly through Secondary Data, and Primary Research Techniques, like Structured Interview Schedule supplemented by the qualitative interview technique, e.g. Focused Group Interview, Case Studies.
- The issues pertaining to the role of Minor Forest Produce, Tribal Development and Rural Development would be examined through secondary data and primary sources.
- The role of poverty, migration and predicament of rural labour would be analyzed both through the secondary literature, secondary data and primary data collection techniques.

Universe and Sample for the Study of Land, Forest and Tribal Identity Issues in Jharkhand and Odisha

The sample districts in Jharkhand are Khunti (separated as a district from Ranchi in the year 2007), Saraikela-Kharsawan, West Singhbhum, and East Singhbhum. These districts represent the two distinct cultural regions of Jharkhand representing Kolhan, Birsa Munda, *Dharti (comprising the Ho and Munda Region) Districty*. Khunti District has majority of Munda population; Saraikela-Kharsawan and West Singhbhum districts are predominantly populated by Ho Tribals and located in the heart of Kolhan Region. In the district of East Singhbhum the Santal, Oraon and Ho tribes are mainly inhabiting.

Demographic Characteristics of the Sample Districts in Jharkhand

Khunti district is located at a distance of 40 kms from Ranchi on Ranchi-Chaibasa Road. It has 148 villages. It is a predominantly Khunt-Katti area. It is a tribal dominant district. The most sensitive circle is Adiki with intense activities of the Maoist group. Out of the total Khunt-Katti area of 1,26,234 acre the whole Khunt-Katti village area is 40,833 (32.35%) acre, the wholly Mundary Khunt-Katti village area is 39,115 (30.99%) acre and the Khunt-Katti + mixed Khunt-Katti area is 46,286 (36.66%) acre. The penetration of the Naxalites in the district was high during 2014-15. During 2014-15 one Maoist was killed and one was arrested in Adiki Police Station. The arrested *Naxal* leader belonged to PLFI Group. Several PLFI persons were arrested between February 2014 and July 2014. The number of Maoist arrested were three. Lands were acquired mainly for knowledge city up to 404 acre, Jharkhand State Housing Board 89 acre, 44 acre for CRPF battalion, 8.40 acre for Cobra Battalion and 125 acre for religious school.

The major area of enquiry in Khunti District are the following:

- Khunt-Katti villages in Khunti district is the most sensitive tribal issue which needs in-depth investigation.
- Implementation of individual Forest Rights in the Blocks of Khunti, Torpa, Adiki, Karra, Rania and Murhu.
- Role of Lac and MFP in the livelihood of the Marginalized People.
- Maoist movement and its impact on the tribal development in Khunti District.

In the Khunti District, there are six Blocks, namely: Rania, Murhu, Torpa, Karra, Arki and Khunti. The names of the villages selected for the empirical study are Siladon, Urikel, Arki, Birbanki, Madhata, Muruhu, Korakel, Khatanga, Diyakel and Torpa. The objectives Stated above for Khunti District have been studied in these villages empirically.

The district of Saraikela has 9 blocks and 136 Gram Panchayats. The major thrust of data collection in Saraikela-Kharsawan District is the following:

- Impact of Land Acquisition/Land purchased on Project Affected and Displaced Families.
- Strength and weakness in the implementation of Forest Rights Act, 2006.
- Development initiatives in tackling Left Extremist forces.

The thrust of data collection in this district is Land Purchase/Land Acquisition, Forest Rights in the livelihood of marginalized people and importance of development initiatives in tackling the activity of Left Extremist Forces.

The names of the blocks in Saraikela-Kharsawan District are: Chandil, Gamharia, Ichagarh, Kharsawan, Kuchai, Kukdu, Nimdih,

Rajnagar and Saraikela. The selection of the villages were confined to the blocks of Chandil, Kharsawan, Kuchai, Rajnagar and Saraikela. The names of the villages selected for the study from different blocks are the following:

Table 1.1: Villages Selected for the Sample Study from different Blocks of Saraikela-Kharsawan District

Sl. No.	*Name of the Blocks*	*Name of the Villages*
1.	Chandil	➢ Pata ➢ Asanboni ➢ Kihauihidih ➢ Makulakocha ➢ Kadamjhor ➢ Katjhor
2.	Gamharia	➢ Mahtabeda ➢ Salampathal
3.	Kuchai	➢ Rolahatu* ➢ Gomiadih ➢ Barulatri ➢ Rugudih ➢ Chotasagoi ➢ Dalbhanga
4.	Rajkharsawan	➢ Buruldih ➢ Raijama ➢ Riding
5.	Saraikela	➢ Kope ➢ Kandarbeda ➢ Ghatduni
6.	Rajnagar	➢ Rajnagar and adjacent villages

*Area affected by Left-Extremism

The Dalma Wildlife Sanctuary is spread in 2 districts, namely—Saraikela-Kharsawan and East Singhbhum. The area of Eco-Sensitive Zone is spread to 377.89 sq. kms in East Singhbhum and 145.09 sq. kms in Saraikela-Kharsawan district. *The Dalma Wildlife Sanctuary was declared as Eco-Sensitive Zone on 29th March, 2012 by Government of India*. The total Eco-Sensitive Zone consist, of 377.89 sq. kms of East Singhbhum district and 145.09 kms of Saraikela-Kharsawan district. As per the Notification of 2012, the industrial units creating pollution will not be permitted within Eco-Sensitive Zone and mining activities will also be strictly prohibited. There would also be no construction work within 300 metres of Dalma Wildlife Sanctuary. Immediately after notification there was lot of commotion and fear among the tribals on displacement of habitations located within the sanctuary area, but after clarification by the sanctuary authorities and the district administration, the people were calmed down. Inhabitants within the Dalma Wildlife Sanctuary are also dependent on the resources of sanctuary for most of their requirement for grazing their cattle, fuel wood, small timber and forest produce.

The study would examine the following issues in the Sanctuary:

- The restrictions in the livelihood activities of the people inhabiting the sanctuary.
- The status of tribals, marginalized and the non-tribals located in the sanctuary.
- The discontent among the people inhabiting the sanctuary.
- The welfare and development activities of sanctuary for the marginalized people.

Table 1.2: Villages Selected for the Study from East Singhbhum District (including Dalma Sanctuary)

Sl. No.	*Name of the Blocks*	*Name of the Villages*
1.	Patamda	➢ Bonta-Dalma ➢ Laylam ➢ Jhunjhaka ➢ Somadih ➢ Kaira ➢ Bankucha ➢ Kherwa
2.	Gulmuri	➢ Kadhong-Dalmi
3.	Jamshedpur	➢ Palashini-Dalma ➢ Villages have also been selected from Subanrekha Project for displaced persons.

The total population of West Singhbhum district is 15.02 lakh. The percentage of rural population is 84.51 lakh and percentage of literacy as per 2011 Census is 59.54 per cent. It is one of the large district consisting of 18 blocks and 216 Panchayats. The tribal population consists of Ho Tribal Community covering two-third of total population. There are also PTG families mainly consisting of Birhor tribe. Koel-Karo, Baitarni, Brahmani and Sanjay are the principal rivers of the district. About 70 per cent of the net cultivated area of the district is upland where productivity is very low. Besides that 40 per cent of the land is forested. The dense forest of this district is known as Saranda Forest. It has 13 Elephant corridors. One of the most important features of this district is that it is one of the strong Maoist Areas and the Central and State Governments have implemented *Saranda Action Plan* to minimize the impact of Naxalite Groups.

West Singhbhum is one of the premier Mineral Producing district in Jharkhand and occupies a prominent place in the Mineral Map of the country. Nearly 47 per cent of the total land under mining of Jharkhand lies in West Singhbhum. Most of Mineral deposits are located in forest area that are intensely inhabited by the tribals. It also produces 99 per cent of Iron Ore in the State. The Forest has displaced large number of tribals dependent on forest and has generated social conflict and discontentment. Saranda has the largest Sal forest in Asia. The *Chiria* Mines in Saranda is the largest iron ore deposit. The total number of Jharkhand Mineral licence is 450 of which the iron ore, Manganese, lime stone etc. are the prominent once. The revenue collection annually from the mining lease is Rs. 205 crorer.

This district is heavily affected by the Maoist Extremist and their major location is the Saranda Forest. This has been one of the major extremist rooted area in the country. This district is also surrounded by 3 States, namely—Odisha, Chhattisgarh and West Bengal. There is strong corridor linkage of the areas linked with forest and hills which are primarily habited by the Ho tribals. This area has provided links to the extremist in Odisha, Chhattisgarh and West Bengal. In order to minimize extremist influence, the Government of India introduced the Saranda Action Plan during the year 2010-14 by incorporating major development programmes, which included MNREGA, Forest Rights, IAY Houses, Ration Cards, Schools, Road connectivity, Watershed etc. The area was also cleared of the Maoist by the security forces. The impact of the implementation of Saranda Action Plan on the Maoist influence in the area will be analyzed in the present study. This Saranda Action Plan has influenced the Jharkhand Government to introduce similar action plan in other tribal districts as well.

The prominent industries like Jindal Steel, Arcelor Mittal and other big corporate agencies faced strong resistance from the tribals for acquiring lands for their industries. The only corporate agency which could derive some success was SAIL which had established good rapport among the local villagers by extending favourable need-based rural development programmes in the surrounding villages.

The major objectives of the study in West Singhbhum District are the following:

- The significance of Militant Land Based Movement during the colonial and Post-Independence period.
- The Role of Forest Based Movement in establishing the identity of the tribals.
- The role of development initiative, like Saranda Action Plan in minimizing the impact of Left Extremist Movement in Saranda Forest Area.
- Forest Rights, and Minor Forest Produce in promoting the livelihood of the tribals.

Table 1.3: Villages Selected for the Study from West Singhbhum District

Sl. No.	*Name of the Blocks*	*Name of the Villages*
1.	Saranda Forest Range	➢ Samta (Jaraikela)* ➢ Tirilpisi ➢ Digha ➢ Bitkalsoy
2.	Goilkera Block	➢ Tatibeda* ➢ Chirungbada ➢ Sirka ➢ Birka ➢ Boripoto ➢ Karodia
3.	Sonua Block	➢ Sasanbeda* ➢ Sakoda ➢ Gangubasa ➢ Ruadiri ➢ Mothrabeda ➢ Saruda
4.	Manoharpur	➢ Dukudih ➢ Sargidih ➢ Patharbeda ➢ Dimbuli ➢ Kolpotka

*Left-Extremist Area.

1.8 Specific Objectives of the Study in Odisha

- To study the adverse impact of Land Acquisition and Development Induced Displacement in Kalinganagar Industrial Complex, POSCO in Jagatsinghpur District would form a major objective of the study. Apart from this the impact of Land Acquisition in Lanjigarh and Niyamagiri Hills in Kalahandi and by MCL in Sundargarh district would also be analysed.
- In the context of Social Movements, the interface amongst the grassroots peasant movements, civil society organizations and the left extremist groups would also be examined during the era of globalization, specifically pertaining to Kashipur, Vedanta and Niyamgiri and Kalahandi district, MCL in Sundargarh district and resistence to land acquisition in Niyamgiri by Dongaria Kond habitation.
- The implementation of Forest Rights Act, 2006 in the State of Odisha and in few selected districts will be empirically studied.
- The role of Non-Timber Forest Produce in the Livelihood of the Adivasis based on the empirical study in the sampled districts.
- The migration of tribal and marginalized laboures from KBK districts to southern States of India.
- The emergence of pan-tribal identity in Odisha will be juxtaposed with the Jharkhandi identity in a comparative perspective.

1.9 Data Collection in Odisha

The data collection both in Jharkhand and Odisha were initiated simultaneously from February to March 2014. Initial three months from February to April 2014 were spent in establishing rapport with the Government Officials and field functionaries in both the States. The preliminary data collection in both the States were collected through qualitative techniques like Focused Interview, Non-Directive Interview and Participant Observation. The secondary data collection from different districts was a continuous process and the sampled interviews of the key respondents continued from November 2014 to February 2016. The sample districts in Odisha are Sundargarh, Kalahandi,

Koraput, Rayagada, Jajpur (Kalinganagar Indsutrial Conflict) and Jagatsinghpur.

Sample Districts in Odisha

In Odisha, the districts of Jajpur (Kalinganagar), Jagatsinghpur (POSCO), Kalahandi, Koraput, Sundargarh and Rayagada have been selected for the study of Land Acquisition, Forest Rights, Social Movements and Rural Livelihood issues. The districts of Jajpur and Jagatsinghpur are coastal districts, whereas the districts of Kalahandi, Koraput, Sundargarh and Rayagada are within the Scheduled Area and predominantly populated by the tribals.

The following issues will be analyzed with respect to Sundargarh District:

- The impact of Land Acquisition and Rehabilitation in the social, cultural and economic life of the tribals and other marginalized sections in the district.
- The implementation of Forest Rights Act, 2006 and its role in the livelihood of the indigenous people.
- The Role of Minor Forest Produce in sustaining the livelihood of the Tribals and other marginalized communities.
- The role of Rural Development Schemes in the livelihood activities of the marginalized people.

Table 1.4: Villages Selected for the Empirical Study in Sundargarh District

Sl. No.	*Name of the Blocks*	*Name of the Villages*
1.	Hemgir	➢ Gopalpur (Land Acquisition for MCL Company) ➢ Sardega ➢ Tiklipara ➢ Gajranbahar ➢ Bankibahar ➢ Bangurkele
2.	Rourkela Forest Division	➢ Birmitrapur (Study of Forest Rights, VSS and SHGs) ➢ Kuarmunda ➢ Bisra ➢ Rourkela

Data Collection in Kalahandi District (Odisha)

In Kalahandi District data has been collected on the following items:

1. Land Acquisition for Vedanta Limited, Lanjigarh and other industries.
2. Role of Minor Forest Produce in the Tribal Livelihood.
3. Migrant workers in Kalahandi District including Koraput and Rayagada district.

Table 1.5: Villages selected for Empirical Study from Kalahandi District

Sl. No.	*Name of the Blocks*	*Name of the Villages*
1.	Lanjigarh	➢ Lanjigarh (Land Acquisition Villages for M/S Sterlite) ➢ Kothduar Company and Vedanta ➢ Rengopali
2.	Th. Rampur	➢ Kharkangigudu (Tribal Scheduled Area) ➢ Bhejligudu ➢ Bhatuguda
3.	Karlapat Sanctuary	➢ Kiapadar (Study of Forest Rights and NTFP) ➢ Sapamundi ➢ Baterliana ➢ Gobardhanpur
4.	Dharmgarh Block	➢ Saisurni (Study of Forest Rights and NTFP) ➢ Kaniguna ➢ Biswanathpur ➢ Ampani

Objectives of the Study in Koraput District

The major objectives of the study in Koraput District are the following:

1. The impact of Land Acquisition on effective rehabilitation of the Project Affected Families.
2. The impact of Forest Rights on the Livelihood and Culture of the indigenous people.
3. The role of SHGs and Rural Development Schemes in the livelihood of the indigenous people.

Table 1.6: Villages Selected for the Empirical Study from Koraput District

Sl. No.	*Name of the Blocks*	*Name of the Villages*
1.	Semliguda	➢ Charangul ➢ Mantriput ➢ Putsil
2.	Koraput	➢ Mundar ➢ Devighat ➢ Dumripada
3.	Narayan Patna	➢ Balipeta ➢ Borigi ➢ Kumbhai
4.	Jeypore	➢ Ambaguda ➢ Anta ➢ Badajuna
5	Kundra	➢ Asana ➢ Bagderi ➢ Banuguda

Table 1.7: Villages Selected for the Empirical Study from Rayagada District

Sl. No.	*Name of the Blocks*	*Name of the Villages*
1.	Bissam Cuttack	➢ Kurli ➢ Chancharguda ➢ Hata Mani Guda ➢ Munikhal-Maniguda ➢ Sibapadara-Maniguda
2.	DKDA-TSP Area	➢ Parsali ➢ Sunakhandi

Objectives of Data Collection in the Study of Kalinganagar Industries, District Jajpur

- Extent of social, cultural and economic damage to the families due to Forcible Land Acquisition and the adverse impact of State Repression on the Adivasis.
- The dissatisfaction among the displaced persons due to differentiation in the compensation paid by TATA Steel and other companies.
- Provision of employment to the displaced persons by different industries.
- The level of satisfaction due to the rehabilitation measures and the grievances still nurtured by some of the displaced.

Table 1.8: Villages Selected for the Empirical Study from District Jajpur

Sl. No.	*Name of the Blocks*	*Name of the Villages*
1.	Kalinganagar Industrial Complex	➢ Trijanga (Rehabilitation Villages) ➢ Kantipur ➢ Gobarghati ➢ Khurunti ➢ Baragadia ➢ Jakhapura (Danogadi Tehsil, Land Acquisition Villages) ➢ Chandia ➢ Kacherigan ➢ Champakoila ➢ Chandia ➢ Gadapur ➢ Siara ➢ Maikosh ➢ Sarangpur

Objectives of the Study of the POSCO Project, District Jagatsinghpur

- Resistance of the villagers of the three Panchayats in preventing the acquisition of land by the State Government and POSCO.
- The extent of violence and police atrocities perpetrated on the protesters.
- The socio-economic condition of the Project Affected Persons and the displaced families subsequent to land acquisition and displacement.
- The present status of POSCO Project and its impact on the socio-economic situation of the displaced.

Table 1.9: Villages Selected for the Empirical Study from District Jagatsinghpur

Sl. No.	*Name of the Block*	*Name of the Villages*
1.	Erasma	➢ Dhinkia ➢ Gobindpur ➢ Nuagaon ➢ Noliasahi ➢ Polango ➢ Bhuyanpal

1.10 Socio-economic Profile of Jharkhand

Poverty is the core issue in the State with more than 2 out of 5 persons unable to meet their basic needs and one of eight going to bed hungry. Approximately 54 per cent of the State population lives below the poverty line and 20 per cent of its people depend on industry, mining and service sectors for their livelihood and the remaining survive on agriculture, forestry and manual labour. Agriculture is characterized by low productivity and mono-cropping. The net sown area is only 37.5 per cent of the arable area. Only 8 per cent of the area is irrigated, 92 per cent of the crop area is used for foodgrains and only 3.50 per cent is under cash crops. *The percentage of ST population in the State of Jharkhand is 67 per cent and percentage of SC population is 8.08 per cent. There is a major gap in the literacy rate of male (67.94%) and female (39.34%).* The percentage of ST households as per Socio-Economic Caste Census of 2011 in Jharkhand is 29 per cent and SC households is 18.45 per cent.

Table 1.10: Poverty in Jharkhand

Percentage below the Poverty Line (BPL) in Rural Areas	*Districts*
75% (BPL)	Dumka, West Singhbhum, Palamau, Chatra
70-75% (BPL)	Sahebganj, Ranchi, Gumla, Garhwa
60-70% (BPL)	Hazaribagh
50-60% (BPL)	Deoghar, Godda, Pakur, East Singhbhum, Giridih, Koderma
40-50% (BPL)	Lohardaga
Less than 40% (BPL)	Bokaro, Dhanbad

Source: Census 2011.

Women constitute 48.5 per cent of the total population; the female literacy is 39.38 per cent and their representation in legislature is as low as 2 per cent. In Jharkhand STs constitute about 26.30 per cent of the total population of the State. The four numerically major tribes are Santhal (35.5%), the Oraons (18%), the Mundas (14.6%) and Hos (9.2%). There are nine primitive tribes in the State. The status of women in the tribal society is better than those in the non-tribal society. The tribal community have been continuously facing the problem of land alienation, displacement due to development projects as also lack of proper rehabilitation and compensation which have been the major casuality. STs are in majority in the districts of Simdega (72%), Gumla

(70%), West Singhbhum (66%), Lohardaga (56%) and Khunti (73.25%), whereas, Rajkharswan-Saraikela (35.18%) and East Singhbhum (28.5%) have slightly lower tribal population. The districts selected for the present study in the State of Jharkhand are West Singhbhum, East Singhbhum, Saraikela-Kharsawan and Khunti.

Table 1.11: Top 5 Districts having Highest Scheduled Tribe and Scheduled Caste Population in Jharkhand

Top 5 districts having highest ST Population	*Percentage of the total population in the district*	*Top 5 districts having highest SC Population*	*Percentage of the total population in the district*
Khunti	73.25	Chatra	32.65
Simdega	70.78	Palamau	27.65
Gumla	68.94	Garhwa	24.19
West Singhbhum	67.31	Latehar	21.31
Lohardaga	56.89	Hazaribagh	17.50

Source: Census 2011.

Table 1.12: Major Source of Income of the Deprived Communities in Jharkhand

	% Households with casual income source				*% Households with salaried income source*			*Landless Households*
	Cultivation	*Manual Casual Labour*	*Part-time or Full-time Domestic Service*	*Others*	*Govern-ment*	*Public Sector*	*Private Sector*	*Percentage*
Scheduled Tribe	42.55	44.68	4.13	8.17	3.49	0.95	1.64	13.23
Scheduled Caste	15.59	68.25	3.71	11.86	5.08	1.62	1.46	29.77

Source: Census 2011.

The long debated marginalization and deprivation of the above said communities is well substantiated by the results of the Caste Census 2011. It can be seen that about 80 per cent of the scheduled tribe households and about 82 per cent of the scheduled caste households have an income less than Rs. 5000 per month. Only 6.07 per cent of the ST households and 8.2 per cent of SC households have a salaried job, cultivation and manual labour being the dominant sources of livelihood. In other parameters of well-being too the scheduled caste and scheduled tribes are found at the bottom rungs. Among SCs housing amenity was found to be poorer than the STs in rural Jharkhand. About 20 per cent of the SC households and 16 per cent of the ST households were found to be living in one room *kuccha* house. The overall literacy among STs of Jharkhand is 57.1 per cent in 2011. Still, 33.95 per cent households are such where no adult above 25 years of age is literate. This number is even poorer among SC households where about 41 per cent households have no literate adults. Of the total 5 million households, about 50 per cent spend less than Rs. 35,000 per year. The lower middle classes and above are less than 0.8 million. It tends to be concentrated in the manufacturing area connecting the cities of Dhanbad–Jamshedpur–Ranchi. India is a major producer and exporter of Lac contributing to about 60 per cent followed by Thailand. Jharkhand, Chhattisgarh, West Bengal, Maharashtra, Odisha and Andhra Pradesh are the lac producing states in the country. Jharkhand contributes to more than 50 per cent of country's production of lac. Lac cultivation is one of the important secondary source of income for villagers in backward districts.

The State of Jharkhand has three possible zones of thrust areas of 'development'. The 6 districts of Zone-1 are: Ranchi, West Singhbhum, Saraikela-Kharsawan, Bokaro and Dhanbad. This area has large manufacturing industries due to the availability of raw-materials and abundance of manpower. *Zone 2* covers 10 districts—Hazaribagh, Chatra, Kodarma, Giridih, Deoghar, Jamtara, Dumka, Godda, Sahib Ganj and Pakur. This area has sufficient green cover, rainfalls and road connection to the rest of India. *Zone 3* is a challenging area covering Chhattisgarh, consisting of 6 districts of Garhwa, Palamau, Latehar, Lohardaga, Gumla and Simdega. *The core challenge in this area is to control over the development agenda from the forces of extremism.* There are three regions in the State such as Palamau, South Chhotanagpur and Santhal Pargana where per capita income is much lower than the State average. In contrast regions of Central and Chhotanagpur are relatively well off. The districts selected for empirical study in Jharkhand are mostly located in Zone-1.

Agriculture sustains a large rural population in the State but the present carrying capacity of the sector is restricted due to high land fragmentation, poor quality of inputs and low levels of irrigation. The per capita availability of foodgrains in Jharkhand is only 230 grams per day as against 523 at the national level; in vegetable consumption the State has got a better position (246 grams per capita) as compared to national per capita daily availability of 230 grams. Within agriculture the important commodities for focus are paddy, pulses, oilseeds and horticulture crops. Forests are a major part of the land mass of Jharkhand. The State has 29 per cent of its total area in forest and 27 per cent of the State population are tribal. Bhuians and Chamars in Palamau, the Malpaharias in Santhal Pargana and the Santhal in Chhotanagpur are placed in economically vulnerable position. *Overall more than 2 out of every 5 people cannot make their basic needs in Jharkhand. The percentage of households not getting two square meals per day in Jharkhand is higher than Bihar.* Jharkhand has the maximum percentage of households who live without sufficient food. More than half of the households in Jharkhand do not have access to safe drinking water. A large part of Jharkhand residents continue to depend upon water for drinking needs. Jharkhand fares very poor in terms of irrigation of its agriculture land. Less than 10 per cent of the total sown area in the State is under irrigation. The relatively low irrigated area for the State continues to be constraint on agriculture development. Jharkhand has the highest proportion of industrial workers as compared to Bihar, Uttarakhand and Chhattisgarh. Only about one-fifth of the total households in Jharkhand own television.

The State of Jharkhand is endowed with a variety of minerals ranging from iron, coal, copper, mica, bauxite, fire clay, graphite, kyanyte, sillimanite, and limestone. It has also small deposits of uranium. *It is thus one of the leading producers of mineral in the country. It has 32 per cent share of the total coal reserve in the country, 23.32 per cent of iron ore, 25 per cent of copper, 91 per cent of pyrite, 9.61 per cent of fire clay and 8.40 per cent of graphite.* The mineral deposits are a very conducive factor for industrial and mining activities in the State. *The State has one of the best* sal *forest in the country*. Tasar culture plays an important role in the upliftment of weaker sections in the society. Jharkhand is the leading producer of tasar silk in the country and accounts for nearly 65 per cent of the total production in the country. *Lac* is a major forest produce in the tribal areas of Jharkhand. Jharkhand State is characterized by Chhotanagpur Plateau and consist of series of Plateau such as Ranchi Plateau, Ramgarh Plateau and Hazaribagh Plateau.

There are 54 literate females for every hundred literate males. The literacy rate for Jharkhand is 54.13 per cent in 2001. Female literacy is highest in East Singhbhum (57.95%) followed by Dhanbad (52.93%) and Ranchi (52.77%). The least female literacy rate have been recorded in Latehar (13.14%) followed by Jamtara (16.63%), Saraikela-Kharsawan (18.77%), Pakur (20.44%), Garhwa (22.91%) and

Sahibganj (26.78%). Out of the 252 blocks in the State of Jharkhand, 111 fall under the 5th Scheduled Areas (spread across 15 districts out of 24 districts).

The districts where ST population in Jharkhand is more than 50 per cent are Khunti, Simdega, Gumla, and West Singhbhum. The distrticts where the ST population in the State is between 25-50 per cent are Latehar, Dumka, Ranchi, Saraikela-Kharsawan, Jamtara and Sahibganj. The tribes with substantial population of tribals in the State are Santhal, Oraon, Munda, Kol, Ho and Bhumij.

Table 1.13: Scheduled Areas in Jharkhand

Districts	*Blocks*	*Gram Panchayats*	*No. of Blocks*
Garhwa	19	193	1
Purbi Singhbhum	11	231	9
Dumka	10	206	10
Khunti	6	86	6
Saraikela-Kharsawan	8	120	8
Palamau	13	283	–

Source: Census 2011.

Among the 32 notified STs, the Santhals are the most popular tribe with a population of 2.41 crore constituting 34 per cent of the total ST population of the State. Other major tribes are Kharia, Bhumij, Lohra and Kharwar together with Santhal, Oraon, Munda and Ho constituting 89.1 per cent of the total tribal population. The Chero, Bedia, Mal Phararia and Mahli Tribes account for another 5.6 per cent; the remaining 18 tribes constitute the balance 5.3 per cent of the total ST population. The 8 tribes fall under primitive tribal group (PTG). Malnutrition, malaria and dysentery are rampant in PTG villages and access to social welfare programmes are also difficult. According to Census 2011, the total population of Jharkhand was 32.96 million with a density of 414 persons per sq. km. The high proportion of ST population of the State at 28 per cent against the All India average of 8 per cent is a notable feature.

The State has five administrative divisions, namely:

- South Chhotanagpur comprising five districts—Ranchi, Khunti, Simdega, Gumla and Lohardaga.
- North Chhotanagpur comprising 7 districts—Hazaribagh, Ramgarh, Chatra, Koderma, Giridih, Bokaro and Dhanbad.

- Kolhan comprising 3 districts—East Singhbhum, West Singhbhum and Saraikela-Kharsawan.
- Palamau comprising three districts—Palamau, Garhwa and Latehar.
- Santhal Parganas comprising 6 districts—Sahebganj, Pakur, Jamtara, Deoghar, Dumka and Godda.

The districts selected for the empirical study from Jharkhand are mainly located in South Chhotanagpur and Kolhan Region. Basically four forms of traditional governance system exists in different tribal regions of Jharkhand:

- Munda-Manki system in Ho areas.
- Parha system in Oraon villages.
- Munda-Manki system in Khunt-katti Munda dominated areas.
- Manjhi Pradhan system in Santhal.

Among Mundas and Hos the headman is known as *Munda* and the priest is known as *Pahan;* among Oraon, the headman is called Mahto. The cluster of 10-12 villages is headed by a *Manki* who used to solve disputes arising between different Mundas. The introduction of *zamindari* system by the British brought tremendous resistance from the Adivasis of Kolhan Region, Munda Region and Santhal Pargana Region resulting in the Kol Rebellion of 1831-32, Santhal Rebellion of 1855 and Birsa Munda Insurrection of 1895-1900. The revolts had shocked the British who brought favourable land legislations in Jharkhand area known as Chhotanagpur Tenancy Act of 1908, Santhal Pargana Tenancy Act of 1949 and the Wilkinson Rule. One of the most important provisions of Wilkinson Rule was that it prohibited transfer of any landed property without the British Agent's consent on any account whatsoever and it also demarcated the jurisdiction of Civil Court in the areas. These rules are still valid during post-independence period. The purpose of Chhotanagpur Tenancy Act was to consolidate certain enactments relating to the law of landlord and tenant and settlement of rents in Chhotanagpur. The CNT Act classified four categories of tenants namely, tenure holders, Raiyats (occupancy raiyat, non-occupancy raiyat), raiyats having Khut-katti rights, under raiyats and Mundari Khut-Kattidar. The CNT Act, 1908 define rights and duties of all classes of tenants and tenure holder. It gave protection of occupancy raiyat, Mundari Khut-Katti rights and *Bhuinas* who are considered to be settled raiyats of their village raiyats could use land authorized by local custom or usage which does not harm the value of land or render unfit the purpose of tenancy.

The Santhals had no security in the possession of land which they made fit for habitation and cultivation by clearing the forest. The *Dikkus* (outsiders) are Non-Santhal settlers gradually acquired large area of land from the Santhals through mortgages from them in return for loans. The *Mahajans*, the police, the revenue officials etc. combined to extort and oppress exactions and creating tyrannies amongst the Santhals. The creation of the district of Santhal Pargana was the direct result of Santhal Rebellion of 1855. The Regulation III of 1872, Regulation III of 1908, the Santhal Pargana Tenancy Act, 1949 recognize some of the customary laws of the districts. The Santhal Pargana Tenancy Act, 1949 codifies some of the customary laws relating to the exchange of raiyati lands, subletting of raiyati lands, rights of raiyats etc. After 1949 the Bihar Act of 1949 was further amended by a series of amendments through the following notable legislations.

(a) The Bihar Scheduled Areas Regulation, 1969 (Regulation of 1969).
(b) The Bihar Scheduled Areas Regulation, 1972 (Regulation of 1972).
(c) The Santhal Pargana Tenancy (Supplementary Provisions) Amendments Act, 1975 (Bihar Act, 17 of 1976).

The resistance of the tribals was also continuous during post-Independence period. Jharkhand Mukti Morcha led by Triumvirate leaders, A.K. Roy, Shibu Soren and Binod Bihari Mahto also fought militant struggle to restore alienated tribal lands from Dikus (Non-Tribals).

The Jharkhandi Panchayati Act, 2001 provides for the constitution of Panchayati Raj in the State of Jharkhand. The three-tier panchayat elections were conducted in the State generating tremendous enthusiasm and participation at the grassroots level. It also saw the enthusiastic participation of the backward classes and specially the tribal people in the scheduled regions. The elections took place in Nov-December, 2010 and all the results were declared by 30th December, 2010. It was a history of sorts when the first Panchayat elections in the State witnessed 58 per cent seats being bagged by women in which 34,750 women candidates were declared successful.

With the strength and support of PESA Act, 1986, the PRI bodies at the district and village level have been vested special powers and responsibility to ensure effective participation of the tribal people in their own development. This Act also helps preserve and conserve traditional rights over natural resources. Under the PESA Act the Gram Sabha have been empowered specially to take care of the village money lending, land alienation, land acquisition, minor forest produce, leasing minor minerals etc.

The Jharkhand Resettlement and Rehabilitation Policy, 2008 was brought due to strong tribal agitation and Naxalite Movement to remove some of the conflict between the displaced persons and the land acquiring authorities; the Adivasi prevented the acquisition of lands for the big corporate. This industrial policy tried to prescribe the following provisions under the industrial policy:

- Industrial Area Development Authority Area (IADA) will be responsible for land acquisition and infrastructure facilities such as roads, drainage, parks, water supply and public utilities for industrial areas.
- Land/sheds in these authorities would be allotted to entrepreneurs for setting up their industrial units on lease for 30 years on annual rent with the facility for renewal.
- Efforts to create land bank in each district for acquiring of 200-250 acre of land for industrial purposes with provision of industrial infrastructure.
- For land acquisition voluntary or involuntary or direct purchase from raiyats as per Chhotanagpur Tenancy Act (CNT) and Santhal Pargana Tenancy Act, Jharkhand Voluntary Land Acquisition Rule, 2010 and Scheduled Area Act (PESA) will be applicable.
- Gair Mazura or government land will be transferred to the investing company only when raiyat and other land availability have been ensured. Government common land to be leased for 30 years. However, the land should be used for the purpose allotted within 5 years of the date of transfer.

1.11 Latest Amendments to Tenancy Laws in Jharkhand

On May 21, 2016 Jharkhand Government issued two ordinances—The Chhotanagpur Tenancy Act, 1908 (Amendment) Ordinance, 2016 and The Santhal Pargana Tenancy Act, 1949 (Amendment) Ordinance, 2016. The main amendment is that the agricultural lands of Scheduled

Tribes (STs), Scheduled Castes (SCs) and Other Backward Classes (OBCs) can be changed for the use by the corporate and land mafias for industrial, commercial, real estate and, after grabbing the lands, for speculative marketing purposes for profiteering. The provision for change in land use was introduced with amendments to Section 21 of the Chhotanagpur Tenancy (CNT) Act, 1908 and Section 13 of the Santhal Pargana Tenancy Act, 1949. The two earlier laws were considered deterrent by the corporate for the growth of Chhotanagpur and Santhal Regions of Jharkhand. Under the proposed amendment, a Scheduled Tribe member with agricultural land can use that land for commercial purposes after following due procedure of the law. By these ordinances, in one stroke, the lands of STs, SCs and OBCs are being made freely transferable and marketable through backdoor. Both the ordinances incorporated a provision in 21(B) in CNT Act and as 13(A) in SPT Act. By these amendments, entire power of deciding the use of the agricultural lands of ST, SC and OBC peasants in Jharkhand is being usurped by the government. The government will frame rules followed by executive orders to serve the purpose of their foreign and *desi* (Indian) corporate masters.

Panchayats (Extension to Scheduled Areas) Act, 1996 (PESA) was enacted with special features for the protection of tribal lands. The Act says, "the Gram Sabha or the Panchayat at the appropriate levels shall be consulted before making the acquisition of land in the Scheduled Areas for development projects...". Instead, by the above two ordinances, the Jharkhand Government is permanently changing the character of the land in scheduled areas and acquiring sweeping power to decide these land use through rules and executive order subverting the above provision of PESA. As per these ordinances, hereafter, the Gram Sabha and the panchayat in Scheduled Areas shall have no role on their land use. The PESA also States that the panchayats and Gram Sabhas are empowered with authority "to prevent alienation of land in the Scheduled Areas and to take appropriate action to restore any unlawfully alienated land of a Scheduled Tribe". The Jharkhand Government's two ordinances permanently removed the role of the panchayats and Gram sabhas in respect of alienation of adivasi lands. In essence, by these two ordinances, the Jharkhand Government subverted the Constitutional direction and main provisions of PESA regarding the necessities of Gram Sabhas consent for acquiring land only for "developmental purposes". Virtually, the two ordinances are contradictions of Part IX of the Constitution.

Already, Adivasi Adhikar Manch (AAM), Jharkhand and some other tribal organizations, Jharkhand Kisan Sabha and other peasant organizations and several opposition political parties have been agitating against these ordinances. They have urged upon the President of India not to give approval to the above two ordinance-related bills. Thousands of Adivasis under the leadership of the Adivasi Adhikar Manch, Jharkhand marched through the streets of Dumka to protest against the anti-tribal land grab amendments to the Chhotanagpur and Santhal Parganas tenancy laws by the BJP Government. Adivasi leaders like Praful Linda and Subhash Hembrom led the rally which was joined by comrade Brinda Karat who also addressed the meeting.

There are 84 Left Wing Extremist Districts (LWED) in the country. Out of them 8 are from Andhra Pradesh, 8 from Bihar, 9 from Madhya Pradesh, 3 from Maharashtra,18 from Odisha, 3 from Uttar Pradesh, 3 from West Bangal, 14 from Chhattisgarh and 18 from Jharkhand. Many of the habitations are severely affected by Left Wing Extremism. Potential conflict between traditional tribal leaders, elected panchayat and Gram Sabha leaders often take place which need to be handled through negotiations and persuasions. The Report of the Expert Group to Planning Commission (2008) entitled "Development Challenges in Extremist Affected Areas" have made significant observation for the persistence of Left Wing Extremism. One of the reason pointed out is the high distress among SCs and STs with highest rural poverty and most of the poor are located in the LWE affected States. Another reason highlighted is the denial of justice, human dignity and alienation resulting in the conviction that relief can be obtained outside the system by violating the current order. The unresolved land disputes, tensions on account of non-payment of minimum wages and atrocities against the tribal communities in the Central Belt of Madhya Pradesh, Chhattisgarh, Odisha and Jharkhand are also attributed as important reasons for promoting Naxalite violence. The conflict pertaining to tribal and forest dwellers' land and forest produce is also reckoned as a major source of unrest in the tribal areas of the country. Another major causative factor is noted as Land Acquisition, Development and Displacement which has given rise to widespread protest in various parts of the country. According to Dr. Walter Fernandes, around 60 million marginalized people have been displaced between 1947 and 2004 and the tribals account for 40 per cent of the total displaced and affected persons. As tribal areas are also rich in mineral resources, the mining projects in Odisha, Jharkhand and Chhattisgarh threaten the very existence of tribal people. The consultations and consent of the tribal community through Gram Sabha which is mandatory under PESA Act is often violated by the ruling elite. Landlessness, unemployment and insecurity of livelihood are other major inbuilt reasons for growing source of dissatisfaction and anger among youth. The development paradigm pursued after independence has accentuated the prevailing discontent among the marginalized sections of the society as they have not taken into consideration their essential ingredients of communal solidarity and cultural identity among the tribals. The PESA Act of 1996 and the Forest Right Act of 2006 are considered to be important steps for minimizing the alienation of the marginalized people which can also minimize the impact of left wing extremism.

1.12 Jharkhand Economy

As per Jharkhand Economic Survey, the Financial Year 2015-16 has been exemplary in many senses. Not only has growth, for the fourth year in succession, remained impressive but also has been widespread across the sectors, regions and societies. The State has been ranked third in "ease of doing business", next only to Gujarat and Andhra Pradesh. This is the fourth consecutive year when the real income of the State, measured, whether in terms of GSDP or NSDP at constant prices, has recorded an impressive growth and is third year in succession when the growth rate has crossed 8 per cent. The per capita income of the State at constant prices (NSDP at factor cost) was Rs. 18,510 in 2004-05 and projected to be Rs. 33,260 in 2015-16. It has grown by 5.47 per cent per annum (CAGR) in the last 11 years. The service sector has been the key performer in the economy. The industrial sector on the other hand has mostly lagged behind. As per the national accounts statistics of the State the agriculture and allied sector, has recorded an impressive average annual growth of more than 8 per cent between 2004-05 and 2015-16. Agriculture and allied sector comprises agriculture (including animal husbandry), forestry and logging and fishing. Between 2004-05 and 2015-16 agriculture grew at an average annual rate of 9.2 per cent and the whole of the agriculture and allied sector at 8.6 per cent. Forestry sector has shown steady growth in this period. According to National Sample Survey Organisation (NSSO), during the reference period of July 2012–June 2013 agricultural households as percentage of rural households was 59.5 per cent in Jharkhand, which is marginally greater than the national average of 57.8 per cent. In Jharkhand, Haat Bazars (Rural Markets) play an important role in the marketing of agricultural produce.

1.13 Socio-economic Profile of Odisha

Odisha is one of the major States of India both in terms of land area and population. The State is ranked at eleventh position in terms of population in India. Census 2011, covered 30 districts in the State. As per census 2011 the total population of Odisha during 1st March, 2011 was 4,19,74,218. In percentage terms the rural population constitutes 83.3 per cent and urban population 16.7 per cent of total population. There has been an increase of 1.7 per cent in the proportion of urban population in the last decade. Population density in Census 2011 worked out to be 270 persons per sq. km. showing an increase of 34 points from 2001. The total SC population during 2011 was 7,188,463 and in terms of the proportion, the SC population constitutes 17.1 per cent of the total population. The total ST population in the State during 2011 was 9,590,756 constituting 22.8 per cent of the total population. The effective literacy rate in Odisha works out to be 72.9 per cent (rural 70.2% and urban 85.7%). The male literacy rate of the State works out to be 81.6 per cent (rural 79.6%; urban 90.7%) and the female literacy rate of the State works out to 64 per cent (rural 60.7%; urban 80.4%). The female literacy rate has increased significantly by 13.5 per cent points during the last decade (rural 14% point and urban 7.5% points). The literacy rate in the State of Odisha also varies by region. The percentage of literacy rate in the Coastal Region is 81.54 per cent, Northern Region 72.21 per cent, Southern Region 57.58 per cent and for the State of Odisha it is 73.45 per cent. *The literacy rate in KVK Region is 57.17 per cent and in non-KVK region it is 77.54 per cent.*

The percentage of main workers among the male workers is 73.9 per cent and female workers is 33.9 per cent. As per Census 2011, 61.8 per cent of the workers are engaged in agricultural activity compared to 64.8 per cent during Census 2001. About one-in-two males and two of every three females were engaged in agricultural activities either as cultivators or agriculture labourers. During the decade 2001-2011, there has been a fall of 1,43,672 cultivators and an increase of 1,74,0889 of agriculture labourers. During the decade 2001-2011, there was a fall among the female cultivators and among the males the number of cultivators have increased by 3,375,350 in Census 2011. The religious distribution of population in Odisha consists of 94.35 per cent Hindus, 2.44 per cent Christians, 2.07 per cent Muslims and 1.14 per cent others.

From geographical, ecological and agro-climatic consideration Odisha has two separate regions, i.e. Coastal Region and High Land Region. The tribal communities reside by and large in the high land region. The areas populated by tribals are concentrated in forest, mountains and undulated plains. These are located in the remote pockets which are generally isolated and inaccessible. The tribals usually live in mono-ethnic or multi-ethnic villages. *The tribal people of the State are considered as autochthones due to their cultural identity.* In the State of Odisha there are 62 tribal communities. With respect to ST population it occupies the third position in India and regarding concentration of STs (22.13%), it occupies the 16th rank in our country among the various States. *The decadal growth rate of STs during 1991-2001 was 24.5 per cent as against 21.4 per cent in India.*

The district-wise population for the present study indicates that they have substantial percentage of tribal population except Jagatsinghpur.

Table 1.14: District-wise Population of Odisha in 2011

Sl. No.	*District*	*Population in 2011*	*Literacy Rate*	*Tribal Population in 2011*	*Percentage of Tribal Population*
1.	Sundargarh	2,080,664	74.13	918903	50.19
2.	Jagatsinghpur	1,136,604	87.13	8640	0.82
3.	Jajpur	1,826,275	80.44	125989	7.76
4.	Kalahandi	1,573,054	60.22	382573	28.65
5.	Rayagada	961,959	50.88	463418	55.76
6.	Koraput	1,376,934	49.87	585830	49.62
	Odisha	**41,947,358**	**67.12**	**41974218**	**32.14**

Source: Census 2011.

Most of the tribal districts are having lower literacy rate. The STs population constitute 32.14 per cent of the total population in the State. The districts with higher percentage of STs population as compared to the State average are Debgarh (33.60%), Gajapati (50.78%), Jharsuguda (31.34%), Kalahandi (28.65%), Kandhamal (51.96%), Keonjhar (44.50%), Koraput (49.62%), Malkangiri (57.43%), Mayurbhanj (56.60%), Nabrangpur (55.03%), Nuapada (34.71%), Rayagada (55.76%), Sambalpur (34.50%) and Sundargarh (50.19%). These figures are important because the thrust of the present study is focused on the tribals of Odisha. The scheduled areas in the State of Odisha include the districts of Mayurbhanj, Balasore, Keonjhar, Sambalpur, Sundargarh, Gajapati, Kalahandi, Koraput, Rayagada, Nabrangpur, Malkangiri, Khondhmal (Phulbani) and Ganjam. The scheduled areas consist of six whole districts, six part-districts and hundred eighteen whole blocks.

Odisha has the largest number of tribal communities in India consisting of as many as 62 tribes. The Kandha, Gond, Santhal, Kolhar, Munda, Saora, Shabar, Bhottada, Kisan, Pareja are among the 18 numerically major tribal communities having population of over one lakh each. Out of the 62 tribals of Odisha 13 tribal groups have been identified as PTGs and they are Bonda, Birhor, Chuktia Bhunjia, Didayi, Dungaria Kandho, Hill Kharia, Juanj, Kutia Kandhe, Lanjia Saora, Lodha, Mankirdia, Paudi Bhuyan and Saora. They are characterized by low level of literacy, subsistence level of economy, shifting cultivation and relative physical isolation. The PTGs are located mainly in the Northern Plateau and Eastern Ghats regions in Odisha. They are found in five districts such as Kalahandi, Nuapada, Sundargarh, Devgarh, Angul and two districts of Northern Odisha such as Mayurbhanj, Keonjhar and in five districts of South Odisha, namely: Malkangiri, Rayagada, Phulbani, Gajapati and Ganjam. The female literacy rate is below 10 per cent. Poverty is very acute among them and the BPL households constitute 79.08 per cent and 37.02 per cent of them are landless households (CCD Plan Survey, SCSTRTI, 2007).

1.14 Poverty among the Tribals in the State of Odisha

Most of the tribals of Odisha suffer from chronic poverty. Overall poverty among them remained very high in 2004-05 and 2009-10. As per Tendulkar Approach the extent of poverty among them was as high as 82.8 per cent in 2004-05 and 62.70 per cent in 2009-10. There is wide rural, urban and regional disparity in the incidence of their poverty. The rural poverty among the tribals of the State was about 37 per cent higher than the urban poverty in 2004-08. This gap has further widened to about 47 per cent in the year 2009-10. There is difference in the incidence of poverty between the coastal and non-coastal Odisha. Among the three major NSS Regions of the State, the poverty is highest in Southern Odisha and lowest in coastal part. The Southern Odisha comprises districts inhabitated by a large proportion of tribal population while the coastal region has a high proportion of non-tribal population. While about 77 per cent of the tribals living in the Southern Region were BPL in the year 2009-10, but only 31 per cent of those living in coastal areas suffered from such acute poverty. The incidence of poverty in Northern Odisha is much higher than that prevailing in coastal area though it is less than in the Southern Region. In the last two decades, i.e. between 1993 and 1999-2000, poverty in Odisha declined only by 28 per cent and that of the tribals of the State by only

16 per cent. In the five year period between 2004-05 and 2009-10, it has declined by about 35 per cent and 24 per cent respectively.

1.15 State of the Odisha Economy

Odisha economy has grown at a modest rate of 5.60 per cent at 2004-05 prices in 2013-14. The State economy experienced severe drought which cost negative growth of agriculture and allied sectors during 2011-12. The severe cyclone *'Phailin'* followed by heavy flood adversely affected coastal Odisha during 2013-14. This cost heavy damage to agriculture crops and very adversely impacted the agriculture sector during 2013-14. *The consequence was that more than 100 farmers committed suicide till November 2015 of which more than 70 per cent have been from Western Odisha alone.* The scourge of their suicide (*Indian Express* dated 16-11-2015, Bhubaneshwar) has enveloped the entire State. But the recent deaths of farmers in Odisha show that all is not well in the States as farm sector is mostly paddy centric [*HT*, Priya Ranjab Sahu, October 20, 2015 (BBSR Edition)]. The present suicide in Odisha is also directly linked to the tenancy system particularly in Western Odisha where farmer suicide has taken place. The tenants had to develop specialized relations with various types of individuals and institutions which fail them by throwing them into the dark dungeons of deaths. The crop sharing arrangement in Western Odisha and mostly in the Hirakud Command Area have taken a new dimension. The dependence on credit depends on local village money lenders to the formal and informal financial institutions. *The marginal farmer is more distressed comparative to the small farmer and stands as a category between the agriculture labourers and small farmer.* The land reforms did not permit the recording of tenancy arrangement and hence most of the tenants are recorded as agriculture labourers in the revenue record. In the Bargarh district 19 farmers who committed suicide during 1st January, 2015 were marginal farmers and dependent on tenancy with crop sharing. Most of the farmers committed suicides were from the unirrigated areas who had taken loan from private and non-government agencies and they were exclusively dependant on agriculture. *All the 100 suicides reported in Odisha were paddy cultivators and 90 per cent of them were tenant farmers.* Due to the verbal agreement the entire tenancy put the real peasant in jeopardy. It is a well known fact that Western and Southern Odisha is home to the 62 tribal categories out of whom 12 are PVTGs. None of the reports of the suicide deaths brings the complex Agrarian distress coupled with social upheavals from natural resources gap (land, water forest, mining etc.) by the multinational corporations with the collusion of local bureaucrats and politicians in power. The Odisha economy has undergone a structural change during the decades of 1990-01 to 2001-11. The industry and service sectors have emerged as the main drivers of growth. *The KVK districts have been adjudged as the worst victim of poverty in the entire State* and hence, the Government of Odisha along with the Central Government have taken special measures for the development of this region. *It is also affected by left extremism. The families below poverty line constituted 85.77 per cent, 86.59 per cent and 86.04 per cent in the districts of Kalahandi, Koraput and Rayagada during 1992 Census and as per 1977 Census the respective BPL per cent had only marginally reduced to 62.7 per cent in Kalahandi, 83.81 per cent in Koraput and 72.0 per cent in Rayagada.* These districts have also higher percentage of ST population than the State overall figure (22.8%) and their literacy-level is also much lower than the State average.

The land for Muchkund Hydro Power Project was acquired between 1947 and 1959 and the total land acquired was 23,155 acre from 274 villages. The multipurpose Hirakud Dam submerged 1.67 crore acre of land which was acquired under Land Acquisition Act, 1984. It affected 249 villages from the Sambalpur district of Odisha and 36 villages of adjoining Rayagarh District of Madhya Pradesh. The Upper Kola Multipurpose Project in Koraput district on river Kolab (1984-85) had submerged 3216 acre of land. The Upper Indira Hydro Electric Project acquired 32,530.87 acre of land. It affected 97 villages comprising 53 villages from Kalahandi and 44 undivided Koraput district. The displaced people hardly have had prior informed consent on whether they would like to support or oppose the land acquisition. The Salandi Irrigation Project (1960-1981) affected 589 families in Keonjhar District of Odisha. The Rengali Dam Multipurpose River Project built on the river Brahmini in Angul district of Odisha affected 11,289 families. The extent of private land acquired for NALCO Project at Damanjodi during 1981-83, was 4,534.95 acre of private land and 3,192.54 acre of government land. The private land acquired was 299.08 acre from the SS, 22,148 acre from STs and 2021.06 acre from other communities. The NALCO Industry has also acquired land at Angul district. Among the displaced persons in Odisha between 1947 and 2001, 35 per cent among them belong to ST categories. The promulgation of the industrial promotion resolution 2001 by Government of Odisha, a large number of industrial houses have signed MOU with the State Government. Many of the industrial houses undertaken projects are mineral-based industries and 90 per cent of the mineral reserves in the State are lying in the thickly concentrated tribal pockets. *In some of the important completed projects, tribals in large number have been displaced from Upperkola, Muchkund, Balimeda, Upper Indrawati, Hindustan Aeronautics Limited, Rourkela Steel Plant, Subarn Rekha, Deo, Kanasbhal, Hartabangi, Badanala, Upper Jonk etc. The empirical study have revealed that majority of the displaced tribal families have failed to regain their pre-displaced economic living standards in the post-displacement period.* In this scenario, the Odisha 2006 R&R Policy is regarded as one of the best in the country and this has some salient provisions for the displaced tribals. Another outstanding issue relates to the acquisition of land by Vedanta Company from the ecologically sensitive area like Niyamgiri Hills which was not permitted by the Supreme Court of India and it revoked the environmental clearance dated 22nd September, 2004 granted by the MoEF and directed them to start further work on the project. *This was a great victory for the vulnerable groups consisting of the Dongaria Kondh, one of the PVTGs of Odisha.*

The extent of displacement caused by development projects in the State of Odisha during the post-Independence period may be divided into five categories (OTA, 2010):

- Thermal Power Projects
- Industrial Projects
- Mining Projects
- Irrigation and Hydel Power Dam Projects
- Other Projects.

The commissioning of various Thermal Power Projects in the State of Odisha has led to displacement of around 1500 families and acquisition of around 2155 hectares of cultivable and homestead lands. The Thermal Power Project account for 2.60 per cent of the total displacement in the State (OTA, 1999). The total number of families affected by *industries* in the State of Odisha is 10,704 which accounts for 11.47 per cent of the total displacement in the State. *It is clear that the industry has been the second biggest region for displacement in Odisha.* Among *various kinds of mining operation in Odisha, Coal Mining has caused the maximum displacement.* The operation of 79 mining projects in the State during the period 1950-1993 caused displacement of 3,143 families accounting for 3.37 per cent of total displacement in the State. The total land acquired for this purpose was 2427.03 hectares of land. The overall picture of displacement in the

State reveals that till 1995, around four lakh people have been displaced by development projects. Dam projects have alone displaced around 70,000 families which constitute 75 per cent of the total displaced population (OTA, 1999). SCs and STs constitute over 50 per cent of the total displaced people while STs alonge constitute 35 per cent of the total population (OTA, 2010 : 32).

Table 1.15: Magnitude of Displacement due to Various Developmental Projects in Odisha during 1950-1993

Types of Project	*No. of Villages Displaced/ Affected*	*No. of Families displaced/ affected*	*Total Land Acquired (in Hactres)*
Mines	79	3143	2427.03
Industries	113	10704	21963.00
Thermal Power	73	2426	3155.31
Irrigation and Hydel Dams	1181	64903	595918.60
Total	**1446**	**81176**	**623463.94**

Source: Balaji Pandey (1998) *Depriving the Underprivileged for Development*, ISED, Bhubaneswar, p. 116 (Quoted from OTA, 2010 : 28).

Satyaprakash Dash (2008, *Social Change*) in his study on "Upper Indiravati Hydro-Electric Project" has observed that majority of the displaced persons took the compensation amount in cash but spent it in unproductive ways. They also became victims of manipulative local elite who exploited them. However, one of the positive outcome of the project as observed by Mr. Dash is that after the completion of the project, the lands have been irrigated to a great extent. The project has checked the migration of the poor people of the relatively undeveloped districts of Kalahandi and Koraput. Further, the district of Kalahandi is now not facing acute food shortage as it was in the past. He also provides the data on the dimension of displacement from the State of Odisha which is reproduced below.

Table 1.16: Human Displacement due to Multipurpose and Other Projects in Odisha

Name of the Project (Multi-Purpose)	*Displaced Families*			
	General	*SC*	*ST*	*Total*
Hirakud	NA	NA	NA	22144
Balimela	NA	NA	NA	1200
Salandi	32	5	352	389
Rengali	8015	1710	1172	10897

(Contd.)

Table 1.16—(*Contd.*)

Name of the Project (Multi-Purpose)	*Displaced Families*			
	General	SC	ST	Total
Upper Indiravati (Not Final)	1557	338	1630	3525
Upper Kolab	1308	442	1421	3171
Total	**10912**	**2495**	**4575**	**41326**
Major Projects not final	2246	416	6382	9044
Medium Projects (Not final)	2041	567	2284	4894
Grand Total (not final)	**15199**	**3748**	**13241**	**55262**

Source: Dalua (1993: 25) Quoted from Satya Parkash Dash, *Social Change*, December, 2008, p. 667.

In Odisha during the post-Forest Conservation Act, 1980, 41,891.25 hectares of forest area has been diverted for mining, irrigation, power, roads, railways, industries, and defence till March 6, 2013 (*Business Standard*, March 29, 2013, Bhubaneswar). In Odisha, nearly 60 per cent of the one million hectare and used for development during 1951-1955 were CPR (Farnandes and Asif, 1977). The prevailing situation in the ground shows very high encroachment of government lands and village common lands. In the otherwise dark scenario, the STs and other traditional Forest Dwellers (Recognition of Forest Rights Act) 2006 is a friendly and important act recognizing the forest rights. It secures individual or community rights for the STs and other traditional forest dwellers. It also recognizes that historically the Adivasis were denied their legitimate forest rights. It is a big step in the struggle to reverse the historical injustice done to them.

The inaccessible hilly terrains, forest and lack of proper implementation of development projects have been conducive to the spread of extremist activities in Odisha. The extremist movement in the State emerged in the early 1960s as a peasant movement in Gunpur sub-division of the then undivided Koraput district. The left extremism has now influenced over 12 of the 30 districts of the State. In the early stage the tribals were used as couriers and foot soldiers by the extremists. The continuity of the left extremist thrust has been embedded in feudal exploitation and oppression of the marginalized section among whom the majority have been the tribals. All these extremists are living in side hills and forest. The incidence and persistence of poverty, particularly in Southern Odisha, in districts like Kandhamal, Gajapati, Koraput, Bolangir, Kalahandi etc. (KBK district) have alarmingly increasing extremist movements.

Amidst the adverse circumstances the Government of India enacted PESA Act in 1996 which is grounded on the principle of participatory democracy in which the basic unit of governance are Gram Sabha and Gram Panchayat. In fact Gram Sabha is the core grassroots level institution of PESA Act. Some of the salient provisions of the Central PESA Act recognizes the traditional rights of the tribals over natural resources which is empowering the Gram Sabha adequately. The PESA Act also recognized the role of Gram Sabha in protecting the tribals alienation of their land including acquisition of land for developmental projects. The consent of Gram Sabha is essential for land alienation and land acquisition. The State laws in the implementation of PESA in Odisha has not achieved a significant result as it has been amended more in a routine way. *In fact in most of the post-21st century land acquisition, the PESA Act has been virtually violated without taking the actual consent of the tribals.*

1.16 Methodology

In the present study on Odisha Tribal situation, six districts were selected for empirical study, namely—Jagatsinghpur, Jajpur, Kalahandi, Koraput, Rayagada and Sundargarh. Among them, five are tribal districts, namely—Jajpur, Kalahandi, Koraput, Rayagada and Sundargarh and Jagatsinghpur is a non-tribal district. All these districts have very high percentage of rural population as well.

Table 1.17: District-wise Population and their Proportion in Odisha as per 2011 Census

Sl. No.	*Name of the Districts*	*Rural*	*Urban*	*Proportion of Rural and Urban*	
				Rural	*Urban*
1.	Jagatsinghpur	1020991	115980	89.8	10.2
2.	Jajpur	1692095	135097	92.6	7.4
3.	Kalahandi	1454882	121987	92.3	7.7
4.	Koraput	1153478	226169	83.6	16.4
5.	Rayagada	820945	146966	84.8	15.2
6.	Sundargarh	1355340	738097	64.7	35.3
7.	Odisha	34970562	7003656	83.3	16.7

Source: Census of India, 2011.

Table 1.18: District-wise SC and ST Population as per 2011 Census

Sl. No.	District	Percentage of SC Population	Percentage of ST Population	Percentage of Literacy to Total Population
1.	Jagatsinghpur	21.8	0.7	86.6
2.	Jajpur	23.7	8.3	80.1
3.	Kalahandi	18.2	28.5	59.2
4.	Koraput	14.2	50.6	49.2
5.	Rayagada	14.4	56.0	49.8
6.	Sundargarh	9.2	50.7	73.3
7.	Odisha	17.1	22.8	73.45

Source: Census of India, 2011.

The percentage of ST population is more than the State average (22.8%) in the districts of Rayagada, Sundargarh, Koraput, Kalahandi and lower in the districts of Jajpur and Jagatsinghpur. The literacy rate in the district of Jagatsinghpur (86.6%) and Jajpur (80.1%) is much higher whereas it is below 60 per cent in the district of Kalahandi, Koraput and Rayagada but similar to State average in Sundargarh district (73.3%).

Table 1.19: Industry and Mining in Odisha, 2010-11

Sl. No	District	Name of the Ores/Minerals	No. of Working Mines	Area Covered	No. of Workers Employed	Quantity Exported (in Thousand Tonnes)
1.	Jajpur	Chromite	14	4011.88	6857	422
		Iron Ore	1	1812.99	609	48
2.	Kalahandi	Quartz	10	178.30	22	Nil
3.	Koraput	Bauxite	3	4915.43	564	Nil
		Lime Stone	2	1586.22	85	Nil
4.	Rayagada	Graphite	13	574.29	53	Nil
5.	Sundargarh	Iron Ore	29	5899.18	7957	3994
		Manganese Ore	17	2688.89	1053	Nil
		Lime Stone	16	3618.16	1936	4
		Dolomite	18	4019.02	128	Nil
		Coal	2	1631	1405	Nil

Source: District Statistical Hand Book 2011, Kalahandi.

Each of the tribal districts have high deposit of minerals, like Chromite, Iron Ore, Quartz, Bauxite, Lime Stone, Graphite, Manganese Ore, Dolomite and Coal. The reason for the selection of the tribal districts of Sundargarh, Koraput, Rayagada, Kalahandi and Jajpur was because these districts have large percentage of tribal population, higher deposit of minerals, highly affected by left-extremism and high incidence of area under forest. These districts have relatively lower percentage of literacy than the State average and the literacy level of Scheduled Tribes is further lower. Besides this, these districts have also been the victims of forceful land acquisition by Government of Odisha and as a consequence the tribals had shown militant resistance. The reason for the selection of Jagatsinghpur is because it had also land acquisition and witnessed heavy police repression as also strong women resistance, though it was not a part of tribal district. The incidence of poverty and percentage of BPL is also high in these districts.

References

Akram-Lodhi, A. Haroon, (2007) "Market-led agrarian reform: Trajectories and contestations", *Third World Quarterly*, Vol. 28, No. 8, pp. 1437-1456, Taylor & Francis.

Akram Lodhi, A. Haroon, *et al.*, (2006), "The political economy of land and the agrarian question in an era of neo-liberal globalization", *op. cit.*, pp. 214-238.

Dash, Satya Prakash (2008) "Resettlement and rehabilitation in Odisha: A study of the Upper Indirawati hydro electric project", *Social Change*, Vol. 38, Number 4, pp. 661-688.

Fernandes, W. (2002) "Displacement and the Land Acquisition Act 1894", *Combat Law*, Vol. 1, Issue 1.

Pandey, Balaji (1998), "Depriving the underprivileged for development", *ISED*, Bhubneswar, p. 116, quoted in Ota (2010), *op. cit.*, p. 28.

2

Identity and Ethnicity in Jharkhand and Odisha

2.0 Jharkhand Identity: Its Formation During the Colonial Period: Major Formulation

2.1 Introducing the Concept of Private Property in Land

The British introduced the concept of private property in land through *Zamindari* system in Jharkhand which has been instrumental in the destruction of their communal land ownership system. Apart from the British imperialist, the new class of indigenous exploiters were moneylenders, landlords, liquor contractors, traders, bureaucrats and their ilk, called in local parlance as Diku. The tribals strongly resisted the imposition of the private property in land through three major tribal movements in the colonial history of India, which are known as Kol Rebellion of 1832-33, Santal Hul of 1855, and Birsa Munda Movement of 1895–1900 (MacDougall, John, 2008). The militant movement led by the different tribal groups in Jharkhand, namely Ho, Munda, Santal, Oraon, Kharia etc. made the British to realize the ingenuity of the traditional land system of the Jharkhandi tribals and accordingly they introduced the Chhotanagpur Tenancy Act, 1908, Wilkinson Rule of 1833 in Kolhan Area, the recognition of Manjhi system of the Santhal Pargana Settlement (Amendment) Regulations of 1908. These legislations not only provided legitimacy to the tribal land tenure system, but also recognized the communal land ownership system like the Mundari Khuntkatti Dari System (Areeparampil, 2002) which are still preserved in the districts of Khunti, Saraikela along with the traditional Munda Manki system among the Ho and Munda community, Parha system among the Oraon and the Manjhi System among the Santhals. These have become the symbols of the tribal and Jharkhandi Identity in Jharkhand and are the strength for the continuing militant resistance against the exploiters whom they term as Dikus. The hypothesis emerging from this historical, secondary and primary analysis is that the conflict on the land issue strengthens the identity of Jharkhandis to resist the Distorted Developmental Paradigm of the colonial period.

2.2 The Tribal Resistance for Land and Forest in Kolhan Area

The tribal resistance for land and forest during the 19th century has remained unparallel in the Indian history as also in the history of Jharkhand. In this section, it is proposed to analyse the integrity of this trinity. One could find its manifestation also in the Sardari movement in which the participants were the members of Munda and Oraon who lived in Ranchi district. They sought to restore land which they considered that they were entitled to hold on nominal rents. They adopted the main techniques of refusal to pay rents, land seizures and written petitions to British officials. The other movement was called the Kherwar movement. They also pressed for lower land rents which were accompanied with open disobedience of the British authority. In the Kherwar movement they were mainly concerned with religious revitalization. The experiences of agrarian struggles led by different tribes had similar objectives. The Munda, Oraon and Santhal believed in hierarchy of deities and their devotion were directed to various spirits.

The major feature of Adivasi society was isolated, egalitarian villages. Among the Munda Oraon and Santhals there were headmen who possessed authority over whole group of villages Maharaja was their chief head men who was paid nominal rents by Adivasi villages. Mundas and Oraons revolted against the domination by the Dikus, consisting of moneylenders, traders, landlords and their ilk. The most important Adivasi insurrection was the Kol Rebellion of 1832. After the repression of this movement the British initiated agrarian and political reforms so that further alienation of Adivasi lands and use of village assemblies for routine judicial business involving Adivasi could be made effective. It was as a result of this that the British Government came out with a unique legislation for the Chhotanagpur area known as Chotanagpur Tenancy Act, 1908. In this Act the raiyati rights remain intact. The landlord has only the right to claim rent from the raiyat. This Act in particular recognized the Khunt-Katti rights, (1) "Raiyat having Khunt-Katti rights" means a raiyat in occupation of or having any subsisting title to land reclaimed from jungle by the original founders of the village or their descendants in the male line, when such raiyat is a member of family which founded the village or a descendant in the male line of any member of such family. This Act also ascribes a special meaning for the word "Mundari Khunt-kattidar". Mundari Khunt-kattidar means a Mundari who has acquired a right to hold jungle and for the purpose of bringing suitable portions thereof under cultivation by himself or by male members of his family, and includes the heirs in the male line of any such Mundari when they are in possession of such land. The rent of a tenure holder or village headman is liable to enhancement during the continuation of his tenancy; such enhancement shall be made only by an order of the Deputy Commissioner. The Act also defines who is a "settled raiyat". Every person who for a period of 12 years after the commencement of the Act has continuously held a raiyati land situated in any village shall be deemed to have become on the expiry a settled raiyat of that village. The Act also recognizes under section 18 that Bhuinhar and Mundari Khunt-khattidar are to be settled raiyats in certain cases. Every person who is a settled raiyat of a village have a right to occupancy in all land held by him as a raiyat in that village. When the immediate landlord of an occupancy holding is a proprietor or permanent tenure holder, such person shall hold the land as a proprietor or permanent tenure holder as the case may be. The provisions of the Act relating to occupancy raiyats shall also apply to a Khunti-katti raiyat. The Act also make specific as to who is an occupancy raiyat; once a raiyat is admitted in the occupation of such land, he becomes liable to pay such rent as may be agreed between himself and the landlord. The Act also specifies the conditions under which the land can be converted into a Korkar with the Deputy Commissioner's permission and such right extends to every cultivator.

The Deputy Commissioner may hold a court for hearing and determining suits and applications under this Act in any place within the local limits of his jurisdiction. When any land is located in more than one district then the district or sub-division in which greater part of such land is situated shall be deemed to be the deciding factor. The Act also recognizes restrictions of transfers of Mundari Khunt-kattidari tenancies. No mortgage of Mundari Khunt-kattidar tenancy or any portion thereof shall be valid, except a *bhugut bandha* mortgage for a period, expressed or implied, which does not exceed or cannot in any possible event exceed seven years.

One of the most important provision is to protect the alienation of tribal land; it is the incorporation after Section 71, the following "A power to restore possession to member of the Scheduled Tribes over land unlawfully transferred. The Act also gives unusual powers to the Deputy Commissioner to evict the transferee from such land without payment of compensation and restore it to the transfer or his heir. It is important to mention that many of the provisions of the Chhotanagpur Tenancy Act, 1908 have also been incorporated in the Santhal Pargana Tenancy Act. It needs to be mentioned that the British made a very significant contribution to the Scheduled Tribes/Adivasi within the Jharkhand State by recognizing the traditional inalienable right to land including the communal property as Khunt-kattidari tenure which has been protecting the tribal interest on land till today and has become an important part of the tribal identity. They stand as one man to protect their interest on land at any cost even if it necessitates sacrificing life as could be evinced in the militant land struggles of Kol Rebellion of 1833, Santhal Hul of 1855 and Birsa Munda uprising of 1899-1900. These are very important reminiscences in the minds of the Adivasis. One can see the continuity of such struggle even in the 20th century which was noticed in the *Jharkhand Multi Morcha* agrarian movement conducted from 1973 to 1976, the *Jangal Kato Movement* in the Saranda Jungles (one of the thickest forest in India), *Koel-Karo movement, resistance shown in the prevention of land acquisition which led to the martyrdom of one of the heroic ho-tribal leader named Kalundia.* Apart from this the tribals in Kolhan and Santhal Pargana areas have continued resisting the acquisition of land in the wake of globalization by corporate sector and multinational agencies. This is stunning message to the policy makers of the State of Jharkhand not to forcefully acquire land of the tribals. In the new industrial policy the Government of Jharkhand has signed memorandum with several corporate agencies for acquiring land particularly from the mining sector which is an anathema for the tribals.

As a part of the struggle of the Kol Rebellion of 1832, the British Government formulated a special Wilkinson's rules for the administration of Civil Justice within the jurisdiction of the agent to the Governor-General under regulation XIII of 1833. It gives special powers to the Munsif or the native chiefs to monitor civil rules of whatever value which is instituted in the court of the Assistant within the limits of whose division of the jurisdiction, the cause of action may have originated, the senior administrative officials are authorized at their discretion to refer suits to decisions to Panchayats. The person to compose the Panchayat shall not be nominated until the plaintiff; defendant and witnesses have been assembled. The Deputy Commissioner cannot nominate himself as one of the panches but it is mandatory for him to accept nominations of panches as made by the plaintiff and defendant. In matters of inheritable right, Munda and Oraon communities are similar and it is also applicable to the whole community. When the matter at issue is a boundary dispute between two villages within the same estate the Panchayat shall be selected from amongst the Head, most influential and respectable men from the adjacent villages, who shall proceed to the boundary and decide the dispute after careful investigation and fix such boundary marks which will leave no room for further disputes.

2.3 Khuntkatti Rights

The tribals consisting of Hos, Santhals, Oraons, Mundas and Kharwas cherish the Khuntkatti right, Wilkinson's rules, Chhotanagpur Tenancy Act, 1908 and Santhal Pargana Tenancy Act as significant achievement in protecting their cultural, social and political rights and is considered as part of Tribal Identity.

During the recent field visit the author had been to the districts of Khunti, Saraikela, West and East Singhbhum and adjoining regions; we could still find the evidences of Khuntikatti system being preserved in its pristine form. The tribals are protecting the community land rights and preventing any form of intervention or land acquisition with full determination even during the globalization era. We could notice this in the Kuchai Tehsil of Saraikela district wherein the panchayats of Dalbhanga (8 villages), Kasudi Panchayat (7 villages), Goipadhi Panchayat (10 villages), Ralahatu Panchat (14 villages) located in revenue circle Kuchai are still functioning as Khuntkatti villages where the tribals have strongly protested the acquisition of lands by the corporate industries. Similarly, in the Khunti district the Mundari Khuntkatti villages and forests are preserved and maintained as a part of the traditional system. Even today the names of the original Khuntkattidars are recorded in the revenue records of the district Ranchi, Kharsawan, Saraikailla and Khunti districts and through this provision the tribal right to community forest and community land is preserved for generations. The Bihar Land Reforms Act, 1960, under Section 2(O) has defined the Khuntkattidars as *bhooswamies* (*Swatvadhari*) meaning thereby that the villagers can protect their natural resources including land and forests and the inheritance right is limited to the descendents. They have also retained the right of communal property to the community forest. The Chottanagpur Tenancy Act, 1908 protects the rights of the traditional descendents of the original settlers (Sanjay Basu Mullick "Jungle ki Jang", Birsa, 2006, Jharkhand, ID Publishing, Ranchi).

Praveen Kumar/Sanika Tuti in their book (*Munda People's History: Khuntkatti Village and Culture*, ID Publishing, Ranchi, Jharkhand, 2011) have traced the historical origin of the Mundas and the Khuntkatti village as one of its glorified reminiscences. They list out 60 Khuntkatti villages as the surviving memory of the village governance of community ownership. They have also provided the population of each Khuntkatti villages. They have covered the case studies of some of the Khuntkatti villages like Totada, Salgadih, Chondor, Gadamada, Jojahatu, Sodag, Maranghada, Setagada. The present author had the occasion of visiting Khuntkatti villages of Marangada and adjacent villages where the community land rights and forest rights are being managed under the village head men who enforces traditional rights. During our field visit, we could witness a massive awakening and mobilization of tribals to prevent the acquisition of natural resources of adivasi and also preventing land acquisition by the multinational corporations. They hold the colonial policy of the British period and its continuation during the post-independence period as solely responsible for the destruction of the natural resources and acquisition of tribal land rights. The Government of Jharkhand has provided the figures of the implementation of forest rights under the Forest Act, 2006 for the districts of West Singhbhum and Saraikela where the author had undertaken his field visit. As per the figures of District Welfare Officer, West Singhbhum, 2475 claim petitions were accepted of which all the 2475 were given authorization in respect of 10,643.09 acre in the entire district of which the maximum extent is from the developmental blocks of Goelkera, Manoharpur, Sonua and Bandhgaon located in Chakradharpur Sub-Division covering almost more than 80 per cent of the total claims. It would be necessary to point out that these areas were the *epi-centre* of the *Jungle Kato* movement during 1969 to 1974 when the local tribals had deforested massive teak plants which the Forest Department had undertaken as part of their afforestation programme. For the tribals Sal Trees are part of their survival needs and symbol of culture. The Adivasis of these forest areas converted the forests into agricultural land and since then local tribals have been cultivating these lands. The Jharkhand Government did not have the guts to evict the tribals as encroachers. Hence, under the dispensation of the new Forest Right

Act, 2006, the District Administration provided legal *pattas* to the tribals by providing the joint land rights to husband and wife. This again reminds us of the strength of the tribal movement to protect their land and forest rights. Similarly, in the Saraikela district forest rights were distributed to 210 tribals during the year 2011-12, another 54 tribals were distributed forest lands in Khunti district during 2012-13.

2.4 Economic Base of the Jharkhandis

The tribals in Jharkhand consider land and forest as twin plinth of their economy which is also an important source of their identity. The British had made forest as the property of the State thereby seriously violating the forest rights of the tribals. This has also promoted discontent and conflict among the tribals. They also led militant struggles against the British occupation of their forest and waged militant struggles in Singhbhum district of Jharkhand during 1978-1985 and led one of the most Militant Forest Andolan; one of the reason was converting the Khuntkatti villages into Reserve Forest. The hypothesis emerging from this is that violation of forest rights by the State would incur the tribal wrath in the form of resistance and militant forest movement. The tribals in the Singhbhum district led one of the most Militant Forest Andolan [Areeparampil, Mathew, 1992) in Narayan, S. (ed.), *Jharkhand Movement: Origin and Evolution,* Inter-India Publications, New Delhi, pp. 144-189].

2.5 Cultural Ingredients of Tribal Identity

The tribal identity is also manifested in the ethnic ingredient of *revenge* which has been amply demonstrated in their struggles and resistance movement against Dikus and find adequate mention in the scholarly analysis of the Anthropological writings (Jha,1987). It has also been adequately documented that for the tribals land and forest is not only a source of economy and livelihood but also embedded in their culture and religion which provides adequate mooring of strong identity and basis for resistance and struggle. The forests are also associated with the concept of sacred grove which are important landmarks of historical and religious symbols for the tribals which they strongly identify and any destruction of the sacred place also enrages the tribals with the feelings of vengeance.

2.6 Land Acquisition of 1894—Internal Colonialism

The British also seriously violated the tribal land rights by promulgating the colonial land legislation known as the Land Acquisition of 1894 which gave unrestricted power to the British colonialists (eminent domain) to acquire tribal lands which were covered with mines and other natural resources. The British acquired huge areas of tribal lands covered with minerals like Coal, Iron, Manganese which were mostly located in tribal lands of Chhotanagpur. Even during the colonial period, the tribals were displaced from these lands without adequate compensation and rehabilitation. The land acquisition thus became a distinct marker of tribal discontent and cumulative resistance (Ekka and Asif, 2000). Due to the liberalization policy foreign companies have been allowed 100 per cent participation in mining projects (Ekka, Alex, 2003). The strong roots of tribal identity are facilitating the Jharkhandis to resist land acquisition for mining and industrial purpose in the liberalization era. The hypothesis of resistance to internal colonization in the shape of Land Acquisition is being resisted in the districts of Saraikela, East and West Singhbhum of Jharkhand where the corporate sector is trying to acquire land with the help of State Administration, but also the tribals are strongly resisting such land acquisition.

The development since the British period has been rooted in the capitalist production system which has also been continuing during the post-Independence period culminating in the liberalization era in the form of Market-led Capitalism. The studies on development induced displacement have been conducted by several scholars at the All India level (Fernandis and Asif, 1997) and in Jharkhand by (Ekka and Asif, 2002); they have shown that mining industries, dams, reservoirs, power plants etc. have led to large scale displacement which is estimated to be 1.5 million people of whom 41.27 per cent are Adivasis, 14.16 per cent dalits and the rest 44.57 per cent are from other communities. Between 1951 and 1995, nearly 155 lakh acre of land belonging to the marginalized, have been alienated to various development schemes. The Land Acquisition Act of 1894 introduced the concept of 'public domain' (eminent domain) concept of State ownership of land resources based on land acquisition measures. *Involuntary displacement has become a human rights issue leading to impoverishment, landlessness, houselessness and marginalization.* Liberal economic policy has further accentuated land acquisition and displacement. The Act of 1894 promulgated during the colonial period continues to be used during the liberalization era as well which smacks of "internal colonialism'. There was strong resistance to land acquisition in Jharkhand for various developmental projects like Swaran Rekha Project, Koel Karo Project etc. during post-Independence period. It also led to resistance by people, in which adivasis were killed in the Bahra Gora area of Singhbhum district on 6th November, 1978. It also led to large scale arrest, beatings and molestation of women (Report of the Delhi unit of PUCL, March 1979).

2.7 Tribal Autonomy Movements in Chhotanagpur and Formation of Jharkhandi Identity

Chhotanagpur tribes had a tradition of militant and organized struggles going back to over two hundred years, centred around land and forests. The Christian Missionaries pioneered temperance movements to check the evil of drinking among tribals and formed cooperative societies to free them from the clutches of moneylenders. They constituted the matrix of the political movement which was spearheaded by the educated Christians later. The second phase, which lasted from 1920 to 1938, was dominated by the revived activities of the Chhotanagpur Improvement Society (Chhotanagpur Unnati Samaj). The third phase, from 1938 to 1947, saw the rise of a militant movement under the Adivasi Mahasabha. A series of violent incidents occurred during this period which signified the militant nature of the movement. The fourth phase, from 1949 to 1963, saw the rise of the Jharkhand party. The Census of 1951, like the Census of 1931, showed that the tribals were not a majority in Jharkhand Area. *There was thus a transition from ethnicity to regionalism.* Initially, the areas inhabited by the Chhotanagpur tribals formed parts of Bengal, Odisha and Madhya Pradesh.

2.8 Formation of Jharkhandi Identity during Post-Colonial Period

The years from 1952 to 1957, which cut across the two elections after independence were in many ways the peak period for the Jharkhand Movement. The late 1950 saw the decline of the party, which can be attributed to many factors. There was a distinct radicalization of politics which came about largely as a result of the articulation of the agrarian factor in the tribal situation by Jharkhand Mukti Morcha. The incidence of alienation of land belonging to tribals increased more and more during the globalization era. Construction of industrial complexes resulted in the displacement of tribals from the land, and their absorption into industrial culture was gradual. The percentage of the scheduled tribes in the population of the districts of tribal Bihar had fallen sharply in the decade 1961-71: in Ranchi from 61.61 per cent to 58.08 per cent, in Singhbhum from 47.31 per cent to 46.12 per cent, and in the Santhal Parganas from 38.24 per cent to 36.22 per cent. This was in fact largely due to the heavy influx of people from other parts of Bihar. The radicalization of Jharkhand movement can also be attributed to the influence of the Naxalite movement, the infiltration of extremist element in tribal organizations and the entry of the leftist parties in the region. However, as the political character of the Jharkhand Movement was diluted and the agrarian aspects came into prominence.

We may conceptualize the developments during this phase in terms of:

- Fragmentation of the tribal party and fractionalization of tribal politics;
- Rise of urban pressure groups; and
- Political extremism, agrarian radicalism and cultural revivalism.

The merger of the Jharkhand Party with the Congress in 1963 shocked the hard core of the Jharkhandis, who were keen to maintain a separate political identity, and sections of the dominant Christian elite and missionaries feared loss of the leverage they exercised. The Jharkhand factions were in disarray.

2.9 Forest as State Property—Forest Based Movement

The British had made forest as the property of the State thereby seriously violating the forest rights of the tribals. This has also promoted discontent and conflict among the tribals. They also led militant struggles to occupy the community forests in Singhbhum District of Jharkhand during 1978-1985 and also termed as *Jangal Kuto Andolan* (Areeparampil, Mathew, 1992, in Narayan, S. (ed.), *Jharkhand Movement: Origin and Evolution*, Inter-India Publications, New Delhi, pp. 144-189). Another precipitant to this struggle was also the British converting several Khuntkatti villages into Reserve Forest. The proposition emerging from this is that the violation of forest rights by the State would incur the tribal wrath in the form of resistance and militant movement. In the year 1978 the Sadar sub-division of Singhbhum district witnessed the outbreak of a well organised and formidable *Andolan* known as the "Tree War" or Forest *Andolan* started by the adivasis of this area. The Sadar sub-division consists of the old Kolhan Government Estate (a reserve created by the British for the special administration of the Hos by their traditional Mund-Manki system) and the area which was under the Porahat Raja. This area is covered with some of the best forest trees in the country. The *Andolan* took the form of felling of trees in these forests by the Adivasis as a symbolic protest against the threat to their livelihood and identity. It spread like wildfire in the whole sub-division and vast areas of forests were cut down by the adivasis. Their argument was that these lands once belonged to them and were illegally taken away by the Forest Department. The State's reaction against this movement was one of increased repression. During the nine years of the Andolan there were more than eighteen police firings on Adivasis in which many innocent people were killed. Hundreds of Adivasi houses were looted and burnt down by the police and the forest officials. Thousands of adivasis were implicated in false cases just for the purpose of harassing them. This reinforces the proposition that the violation of forest rights would kindle the emotion and identity of the tribals and would precipitate militant movement. The causes of Forest Andolan in Singhbhum were the following:

- Encroachment by the Forest Department on Adivasi Forest Land.
- Exploitation and Harassment of Adivasis by Forest Officials.
- Commercialization of Forests and the Resultant Pauperization of Adivasis [cf. Areepaparampil, Mathew, "Forest Andolan in Singhbhum," in Narayan, S. (ed.) *Jharkhand Movement: Origin and Evolution*, Inter-India Publications, New Delhi, 1992, pp. 144-183].

The tribal identity is also manifested in the ethnic ingredient of revenge which has been amply demonstrated in their struggles and resistance movement against Dikus and finds adequate mention in the scholarly analysis of the Anthropological writings (Jha, 1987). It has also been adequately documented that for the tribals land and forest is not only a source of economy and livelihood, but is also embedded in their culture and religion which provides adequate mooring of strong identity and basis for resistance and struggle. The forest is also associated with the concept of sacred grove which are important landmarks of historical and religious symbols for the tribal which they strongly identify and any destruction of the sacred place also enrages the tribals with the feelings of vengeance. (Areeparampil, S.J., 2002).

According to A.K. Roy (1982), uneven development in the different segments of society in Jharkhand has created problems of inequity and discrimination. The first ingredient of internal colonialism is the caste system. The second ingredient is the uneven development of the different regions of the society. The third ingredient is the economic unevenness based on deformed capitalism (Roy, A.K.) "Jharkhand: Internal Colonialism", *Frontier*, April, 17 and 24, 1982). Basu, Sajal (1994) has also highlighted additional ingredients of internal colonialism like:

- Land and Forest Alienation of the Tribals.
- Development induced Displacement of the Indigenous People.
- Victims of Conquest, Colonization and Development: Ethnocide/Cultural Genocide.

2.10 Political Extremism, Agrarian Radicalism and Cultural Revivalism

Agrarian radicalism was also witnessed among the Santhals who were more sensitive to the agrarian question. The Jharkhand Mukti Morcha (JMM) launched an undeclared movement to recover alienated land from moneylenders and landlords in North Chhotanagpur consisting of the tribal pockets of Girdih, Dhanbad and Hazaribagh districts an area which was not the stronghold of the Jharkhand Party. There were 120 violent incidents including looting of crops or forcible harvesting of crops standing on lands in illegal possession of moneylenders, attacks on exploiters, arson and murder. The largest number of incidents (69) occurred in 1974.

The Kurmi Mahtos' alliance with Santhals gave the JMM an extra-ethnic dimension; there was the possibility of the Santhal movement developing into a pan Santhal awakening cutting across the Santhal areas of Bihar and West Bengal. The Hul Jharkhand supported it. The Santhals of Hazaribagh, Giridih and Dhanbad formed a common front with those of the Santhal Parganas. Cultural revivalism is also to be seen in overall working of the JMM. This movement laid to the revival elements of the ancient tribal self-government called *Baisi* (assembly village governance) in the Santhal Pargana.

In the course of this phase of the movement there were 46 incidents from October 1977 to June 1978 as a sequel to the formation of a separate State with South Chhotanagpur as a epi-centre. The issues against which the leaders of the movement agitated were: (a) acquisition of land for large irrigation projects and army firing ranges; (b) survey and settlement operations; (c) collection of loans, rent and cooperative dues, which were resisted; (d) nationalization of forest produce and collection of kendu leaves; and (e) boycott of Panchayat elections.

This phase of the movement for a separate State reached its culmination in Ranchi on 12 May, 1978. To add fuel to the fire, the tribals were also instigated by the forest contractors to agitate against the Forest Development Corporation to destroy the teak trees which were planted by the Forest Department in place of *sal* trees. Munda Christians obstructed to felling of trees and plantations by the Forest Department in the Porahat region of Singhbhum district. They *gheraoed* and assaulted the forest officials, burnt down godowns of Kendu leaves in it. The Jharkhand Party launched the direct action programme by observing a day of mourning to make the point *that independence was not complete without tribal autonomy. Bandhs* were also organized in towns of the Chhotanagpur Division.

An important trend that emerged towards the end of 1978 centred round the activities of the extremists in the Munda-Ho areas of the Singhbhum district bordering Ranchi. JMM projected a radical ideology—*the Jharkhandi is a producer irrespective of caste, tribe or nation residing in Jharkhand.* The Jharkhand must, therefore, turn into a lalkhand that is, the movement of political separatism and struggle of the working classes should go together. The militant movements in Chhotanagpur were led by the Kolarian tribes, the Mundas, Hos and Santhals, who were the dominant communities. Its appeal to the non-tribal sections of the Chhotanagpur is were still at a nascent stage. Thus, tribal ethnicity in a multi-ethnic society characterized by cultural independence among different communities struck out a different course of development in Chhotanagpur unlike the North-East.

The link between extreme class exploitation and tribal oppression was revealed in the united struggle of tribals working class and the Kurni Mahtos. Land has been closely associated with the political struggle in Jharkhand. All in all, the conjunction of class and community interests in Jharkhand pushed closely connected communities to the ethnic (nationality) aspirations. The movement for socio-cultural regeneration was propagated by intellectuals like Ram

Dayal Munda, Nirmal Minz, B.P. Kesari, and others. There has been an almost parallel discussion on the present and prospective status of women in tribal society. The role of women in tribal society and the changes therein have not received much analytical attention. It is significant that a radical account of Jharkhand ethnoregionalism emerged with the support of the Jharkhand Mukti Morcha which also actively involved in the women question.

The mafia in the coal mines Dhanbad was drawn from the notorious ABC—Arrah, Ballia, Chapra—districts of Bihar. The aggression of these immigrants was unleashed on tribal workers and peasants. The dikus hold sway not only over employment in industry but also monopolise trade and commerce. Till recently, even the middle class, as it existed in the region, was essentially non-tribal.

The emergence of an enlightened middle class among the adivasis also qualitatively altered the Jharkhand Movement. Indeed tribal resistance to domination and exploitation was legendary. The political and ethnic assertiveness of the tribals, in particular that of the Mundas, had been facilitated by several factors. The economic dualism of Bihar is matched by cultural and social dualism.

2.11 Political Participation of Jharkhandis

Prakash, Amit (2001) in his book on *Politics of Development, Identity and Autonomy* observed that the overall consequence of this model of development was that the local communities became passive beneficiaries of the State's Development Policy or even object of exploitation instead of being active partners. The political economy of development was lopsided consequently, the discontented tribals began to resort to agitational politics which was essentially premised on tribal heritage and culture, but the leadership of the movement was quick to include the non-tribal population of the Jharkhand region (locally termed as Sadans in the category of Jharkhand because of the overall numerical minority of people of tribal origin). All those people who are living here for years have the same claim to the region as the original residents. *Thus, the concept of identity were broadened to include Adivasi and Mulnivasi.*

Clearly, the identity of being a Jharkhandi was bolstered by this attitude since it defined yet another aspect of the "we" and "them" division. Tribal heritage and culture was seen as the foundation stone for this politically self-conscious community/identity. Only about 36 per cent of the population of the region was of tribal descent by 1951, and by rationalizing the inclusive policy indicates an astute political understanding. The political context gave different emphasis to Jharkhand identity as it evolved during the first general election held in 1952, the issue of the Jharkhand region had acquired some degree of mass appeal. Shri Jaipal Singh and Jharkhand Party had begun to highlight the question of an autonomous territory for the Jharkhandis. The issue of a separate State of Jharkhand had mass support among tribals which was also substantiated by the results of the Lok Sabha election. *Concept of 'identity' was also sharply developed into through political participation in various general elections.*

In the first general election, the Jharkhandi parties managed to win three of the eight Lok Sabha seats in the Jharkhand region securing 65 of the votes cast. Overall, the Jharkhandi parties polled 43 per cent of the total valid votes cast in the Jharkhand region. Most of the support was restricted to tribal pockets. Shri Jaipal Singh and Jharkhand Party had been emphasizing the tribal characteristics of the region in the run-up to the elections. It is hardly surprising that other issues such as tribal identity were taking precedence over the development issues. Their concern was to preserve the uniqueness and separateness of the tribal way of life, as is evident in the arguments in their memoranda to the States Reorganization Commission. They emphasized the linguistic, cultural and ethnic difference of the region. This point of view was reinforced by the large scale demonstrations of the tribal population and tribal symbolism, such as bows and arrows and the cock in order to impress upon the SRC the need to create a tribal State based on tribal separateness. The Jharkhandi groups managed to win more seats in the 1957 general election, though there was a slight decline in the percentage of votes that they polled. Also noticeable in this election was the rising support for the leftist politics in the region. The perpetual divisiveness among the leaders had an important role to play in this failure of the Jharkhandi groups. From 37 per cent in 1951, the population of Scheduled Tribes in the region diminished to 34 per cent in 1961. There was also an increase in the percentage of population residing in Jharkhand from Bihar.

The third general election was held in 1962. Consequently, it became clear that the issue of tribal identity and a separate State based on it (the main plank of the Jharkhandi groups) was to be relegated to the political backwaters of the region. Jharkhandi groups were still a minority in the Central and State Legislatures. The Jharkhandi groups managed to win only three of the thirteen seats in the Jharkhand region, with an average of 49 per cent of the votes in these three seats. Two important reasons for this decline in political performance were the growing percentage of the non-tribal population in the electorate of the Jharkhand region and in 1962 general election, the Jharkhand Party merged with the Congress. The second pattern, which is quite clear from the results of the 1967 electron is that the days of single-party rule in the Jharkhand region was disappearing from the fact that the Indian National Congress (INC) did win nine of the thirteen seats. The fourth general election, thus, marked the emergence of multi-party politics in Jharkhand; there was also growing distrust and disenchantment of the electorate with the Jharkhandi leaders. Another important factor was the decline of ST component of the Jharkhand population; it was reduced to 29 per cent from 34 per cent in 1961. The faction ridden Jharkhand groups also dismayed the tribal population as is evident from the election results of 1971. The Jharkhandi political groups were able to win only one of the thirteen Lok Sabha seats from the Jharkhand. A new trend was the emergence of leftist political groups in election which was more pronounced in the Jharkhandi political formations. The AIJP emerged as a new Jharkhand formation which won the Singhbhum seat with a majority (73). However, this was the only seat which the Jharkhandi groups won out of a total of fourteen Lok Sabha seats in the region. Thus, the declining support for Jharkhandi groups, which started in the 1960s, was noticed in the 1977 election as well. In the 1980 Lok Sabha election, the Jharkhandi parties once again won only (Khunti) out of the fourteen Lok Sabha seats in the region, polling 36 per cent. Sibhu Soren, the head of JMM won the Dumka seat with 38 per cent of the votes, and A.K. Roy was successful in Dhanbad, polling 34 per cent of the votes. Soren and Roy won their respective seats due to their roles in the left politics in the Jharkhand region during the late 1960s and also l se they subscribed to Jharkhandi ideology.

The electorate had shifted their political support from the Jharkhandi groups to the national parties in the hope of being able to derive policy initiatives from them. Clearly, there was an overwhelming support for the INC in the region in the Eighth General Election. In the period between the Eighth and Ninth General Elections, the JCC was active, but failed to secure any long term gains for the region. The successful economic blockade by the JCC and AJSU in the late 1980s increased the political legitimacy of the Jharkhandi political groups which resulted in the revival of their electoral fortunes. One feature which started emerging in this period was that a number of parties were gradually adopting Jharkhandi stances of supporting autonomy for the region. Unsuccessful in the 1984 elections, the JMM won three of the fourteen Lok Sabha seats in the region in 1989. In the Lok Sabha elections, however, BJP found political support in the Jharkhand region because it was the only national party that had promised and later created the State of Jharkhand. This was manifested in the support for the agitational politics (economic blockades, general strikes, and so on). As a result, a Committee on Jharkhand Matters (COJM) was appointed and by 1995, Bihar Vidhan Sabha had legislated to create the Jharkhand Area Autonomous Council (JAAC). After the creation of the State in November 2000, the BJP became the single largest party in the newly constituted Vidhan Sabha. It formed the government, headed by Chief Minister Babulal Marandi, with the support of its other National Democratic Alliance (NDA) partners.

2.12 Fluctuations in the Trend of Formation of Jharkhand Identity

The process of evolution of Jharkhandi identity has also traversed through an uneven course. The Jharkhandis have actively associated themselves in the electoral politics at All India and State Level. It needs to be examined as to whether the interface with electoral politics has contributed to the strengthening of Jharkhandi identity and Jharkhandi movement or it had the reverse effect. After the State Re-organization Commission in 1956 rejected the demand for Jharkhand autonomy, the Jharkhand party led by Shri Jaipal Singh received tremendous support. However, the Jharkhand party merged with the Congress Party in 1963 which was a tremendous setback to Jharkhandi identity.

Subsequently, several political parties emerged within the Jharkhandis which brought division and factionalism within the Jharkhandi Identity Formation. Besides this, party system of democracy has divided the tribal voters from within. The electoral politics has also placed the tribals in the open fray politics with Sadans and other non-tribal groups. In Jharkhand apart from the Scheduled Tribes, there are also various other indigenous groups who have been sharing similar culture and language with the tribals. These communities are grouped under the generic category of Sadans especially during the Post-Independence period (Kesri, V.P., 1992). Hence, in the process of identity formation of Jharkhand, the Jharkhand identity consist of the following:

- Scheduled Tribes known locally as adivasis who are the autochthons.
- Sadans also called in local parlance as *Mool Niwasis*, co-terminus with the indigenous people of Jharkhand.

- Exploited classes of peasants, working class and other deprived and discriminated communities (Sengupta, Nirmal, 2003 : 338-339).

Jharkhandi Identity is thus inclusive which not only subsumes Adivasi and indigenous groups but also incorporates others who are also exploited in Jharkhand. Apparently the category of Dikus are Excluded from the category of Jharkhandi Identity which has a special connotation within the Jharkhandi culture and *lingua franca.* During the colonial period, the landlords, moneylenders, contractors, petty bureaucrats, police officials and their ilk were termed as Dikus by the Adivasis as it was these categories who alienated the adivasi land. They mostly belonged to upper caste-class during the British period and also continue to be so during post-Independence period as well. The alienation of the lands of Jharkhandis were done not only by the upper class but also by the class of industrialists who acquired the tribal land for the mining and industrial purposes. This also included the immigrants from Bihar, North Bihar and other parts of India. Thus, the exploiters and land-grabbers not only constituted of the landlord but also incorporated the capitalists class.

The process of internal colonialism of the tribals and *sadans* continued during the post-Independence period and the liberalization era. It needs to be specially mentioned here that the gradual penetration of outsiders into the tribal areas of Jharkhand reduced the position of the tribals into a minority and today they are only 27 per cent of the total population. This has not only weakened the process of Jharkhandi Identity, but also led to a transformation of Jharkhandi Identity from ethnicity to regionalism (Singh, K.S.; Alloysius, G., 2003).

2.13 Adivasis and Moolniwasis in Jharkhandi Identity

It is of great salience and significance to understand the changing ingredients of the Jharkhandi identity in the era of globalization. There are several numerically preponderant tribal groups in Jharkhand, e.g. Ho, Munda, Oraon, Santhals, Kharias etc. Yet the process of exploitation and discrimination has been common to all the groups and they are equally endowed with the ethos of resistance and militancy which has shaped the Jharkhandi identity during last over two centuries. It has sharpened the ethnic identity of tribals. However, one of the dilemmas facing the tribals in Jharkhand today is their minority status. The tribals today constitute only 27 per cent in Jharkhand which places them in disadvantaged situation with the formation of the new Jharkhand State. *The BJP which has been instrumental in the formation of Jharkhand State has conceived of Jharkhand State based on developmental deficit and not on the cultural identity ingredient.* Thus, this poses a predicament to the tribals by restricting Jharkhandi identity to the tribals only. It needs to be emphasized here that in the State of Jharkhand, *there are also other indigenous groups known as Sadans who are also the indigenous inhabitants of Jharkhand often designated as moolnivasis and identify themselves with Jharkhandi.*

2.14 Demand for Autonomy in Jharkhand

There were submission before the Simon Commission which had pleaded for the creation of a new province in the Jharkhand region. However, the Commission did not advocate this course of action. The question of a separate administrative structure for the region was taken seriously and the JAAC was created, followed by the creation of the State of Jharkhand in November 2001. Murmu one of the distinguished Jharkhandi leaders criticized the opportunism of the leaders of the Jharkhand movement, their inability to put forward a creative agenda before the Jharkhandi population and the absence of any ideal or principle in the movement. He relates the unrest in the region to its development problems. Political and intellectual figures active in the movement tried to create and sustain a politically significant ethnic identity with the help of such historical legitimization. The leaders were quick to point to the development deficit to add to the legitimacy of the movement. The States Reorganization Commission dealt with the issue comprehensively and reported against the creation of a State in the Jharkhand region. It recommended creation of new States on linguistic lines only, rather than on principles such as tribal cultural identities.

JMM was not ready to give up the cultural and tribal identity based articulation of the Jharkhandi identity. JMM saw the issue of administrative autonomy for Jharkhand and to the nationality question. JMM thus emphasized the relationship between under development and the lack of administrative autonomy. Report of the Committee on Jharkhand Matters 1990 (COJM) constituted by the Union Ministry of Home Affairs is an attempt to find a solution to the issue.

The COJM report defined the Jharkhand movements in terms of development problems. The report also examined the process of conversion of the Jharkhand movement premised on ethnic factors into one that is primarily premised on the relative underdevelopment of the region. The committee thus felt that there was a political consensus about regional autonomy in the Jharkhand region due to widespread neglect or the region in development terms. It did not, however, recognize the significant ethnic tribal components in the movement.

Underplaying of the tribal heritage aspects of the movement and highlighting of the regional aspect became the emerging conceptualization of the Jharkhand movement. This definition of the nature and character of the movement became the dominant point of view across the political spectrum. Committee recommended the creation of a cultural development authority, with possible autonomous powers, for the overall cultural development of the region, the introduction of tribal languages in school syllabi, and the development of a composite culture. The COJM, however, found it salient to preserve and promote the cultural uniqueness of the region. In sum, from being the foremost political force in the Jharkhand region, the Jharkhandi groups became increasingly marginalized. Hence, the Jharkhandi leaders sought to involve themselves in parliamentary politics in order to make their point heard.

The direct correlation between autonomy and development was further emphasized in the Resolution regarding Creation of New States of Uttaranchal and Vananchal tabled. The BJP was the first national party that offered a practical alternative to the demand for a Jharkhand State. It postulated that the region of Santhal Pargana and Chhotanagpur was in some way the real Jharkhand, dwelling upon the separateness and uniqueness of the region. Clearly, a direct link was constructed between the creation of a Jharkhand State and improvement of the development profile of the region.

Even the left parties emphasized that there was no basic question of ethnicity, language or culture for the demand of creation of Jharkhand State. The basic issue or the basic emotion or the basic sensitivity for the demand of creation of Jharkhand State is a regional disparity of development. Such an emphasis on the development problems in the region by the Jharkhandi groups, the government and political parties across the political spectrum altered the character of the demand for economy itself. JMM was trying its best to put forward the points of view of the Jharkhandi people in the highest forums of power. The issue of poor rate of development in the region within an existing State seemed to have been accepted as this objective criterion.

Besides, the creation of a separate State in the Jharkhand region falls within the domain of Parliament. Consequently, the opinions expressed in the political manifestos of national parties are relevant.

Moreover, it was only after the early 1980s that the Jharkhand movement became politically volatile in terms of economic blockades. When the JCC, the JMM and the AJSU were successful in holding-up transportation of minerals from the region, national attention was forced on to the problems of the Jharkhand region.

Thus, the whole question of the autonomy of the Jharkhand region came to acquire more geographical, regional and development related overtones. The issue of the tribal identity of the region was lost in the emphasis on the development problems both by the government agencies as well as the political groups of the region.

2.15 Role of Bharatiya Janata Party

In fact the BJP (Bharatiya Janata Party) proposed some fresh alternatives to the demand for the creation of a new State of Jharkhand which found increasing political support in the Jharkhand region. The BJP election manifesto for the midterm Lok Sabha poll in 1991 stated a clear policy towards the region of Jharkhand, as part of its policy of smaller States. It is significant that in the BJP manifesto, the thrust was on the regional imbalances borne out of the large sizes of the existing States. The manifesto made no mention of the identity aspect of the Jharkhandi region and sought to emphasise the development deficit line of argument.

The 1996 manifesto of the BJP went one step further and promised to "carve out Uttaranchal, Vananchal, Vidarbha and Chhattisgarh and give them full Statehood and consider setting up a commission to examine the formation of smaller States". BJP had established its views about the Jharkhand region in the national political life. The fact that the BJP had consistently clubbed together the Scheduled Castes and Scheduled Tribes since their first manifesto indicates that they did not see any question of a tribal identity existing in the region of South Bihar or elsewhere. The incessant struggle on the part of the Jharkhandi political parties and social groups and the accompanying economic blockades of minerals in the South Bihar region in the 1980s and 1990s succeeded in bringing the necessity of new politico-administrative arrangements for the Jharkhand region onto the national agenda.

The 1999 election resulted in the BJP-led National Democratic Alliance (NDA) coming to power. Creation of the Jharkhand State did partially satisfy the aspiration of the Jharkhandi identity, but the degree to which this will improve the performance of development policy in this new State as also promote Jharkhand Identity was a futuristic issue.

2.16 Scenario of Tribal Situation during Globalisation Era

The Jharkhand Government has signed well over 100 MoUs with corporate sectors during the globalization era notable among them are International and Indian Corporate giants, namely—Arcelor Mittals, Jindal, Essar, Tata, Hindalco, Abhijit Group etc. Among the MoUs signed by the State Government 74 are for setting up steel plants and 24 for power plants with the estimated investment of Rs. 4,67,24 crore requiring approximately 2 lakh acre of land. The new corporates venturing for fresh Industrialization was regarded as a colonial enterprise by the Adivasis. They expressed strong discontentment which took the form of resistance; in this process, the adivasis attacked the Kohinoor Steel Plant near Jamshedpur, seized 70 trucks and stopped the work. The Jindal Steel, Essar, and CESE were forced to leave the area and as a result, the Government of Jharkhand were unable to execute large number of MoU at the grassroots levels; as a consequence due to the strong resistance by the tribals in the liberalization era, process of land acquisition has become difficult in Jharkhand. The Jharkhandis are very sensitive to forcible acquisition of land for mining and developmental purpose. It would be of interest to point out here that the during the period of 1986-90, the two newly formed organizations, namely—Jharkhand Coordination Committee (JCC) and All Jharkhand Students Unions (AJSU) initiated militant action by giving call to boycott elections and socially boycotting the political leaders, committed to electoral politics. They also forged links with other indigenous people's movement across the country to strengthen the demands for autonomy, identity and Jharkhand nationality.

It also needs to be emphasized here that the Naxalite Movement (now termed as Maoist movement) has been growing in Jharkhand since 1967 with the active involvement of MCC which has now spread to 16 out of 22 districts in the State. The Maoist movement is not limited to armed operation but it has also established parallel system of governance that includes Jan Adalats and People's Police. *Denial of justice is emerging as one of the important reasons for the spread of the Maoist Movement and it also attract the tribals faith in the Maoist Movement*. Economic blockades and *bandh* call given by the Maoist, are some of the examples indicating the helplessness of the State. The penetration of left extremism in Jharkhand is minimizing the space for autonomous Jharkhandi Movement and also of other civil society organizations.

The independent Government of India has also followed same land, forest, and land acquisition policy initiated by the British with all the consequences which the tribals suffered during the colonial period due to the distorted developmental model. The liberalization and globalization era from 1990s onward accentuated the process of exploitation, pauperization and impoverisation during the new colonial period. The only weapon available with the Jharkhandi tribals was their cultural source of resistance which they also used during the post-colonial period in struggles against land alienation, displacement from the forest and development induced displacement. This weapon they have been utilizing even in the era of globalization which is amply demonstrated in the resistance of the land acquisition and land purchase by the corporate groups who have entered into MoUs with various corporate groups. The tribals in Jharkhand are showing their resistance against such land acquisition in the districts of East and West Singhbhum, in the district of Saraikela and elsewhere in Jharkhand.

The hypothesis emerging from this is as follows: The land acquisition by the State and corporate agencies in the era of globalization would be met with stiff resistance in areas imbued with strong Jharkhandi Identity.

It is of great salience and significance to understand the changing ingredients of the Jharkhandi identity in the era of globalization. There are several numerically preponderant tribal groups in Jharkhand, e.g. Ho, Munda, Oraon, Santhals, Khairas etc. Yet the process of exploitation and discrimination has been common to all the groups and they are equally endowed with the ethos of resistance and militancy which has shaped the Jharkhandi identity during last over two centuries. It has sharpened the ethnic identity of tribals. However, one of the dilemmas facing the tribals in Jharkhand today is their minority status. The tribals today constitute only 27 per cent in Jharkhand which places them in disadvantageous situation with the formation of the new Jharkhand State. The BJP has been instrumental in the formation of Jharkhand State based on developmental deficit and not on the cultural identity ingredient. Thus this poses a predicament to the tribals by restricting Jharkhandi Identity to the tribals only. It needs to be emphasized here that in the State of Jharkhand, there are also other indigenous groups known as *Sadans* who are also the indigenous inhabitants of Jharkhand and identify themselves with Jharkhandi identity. Hence, the Jharkhandi identity has led to the formation of two distinct cultural identity groups known as Adivasis and *Moolnivasis*. During the 70s there was a combined struggle of the tribals along with the *Sadans* and the working class of collieries and industry in Jharkhand which led to the formation of a new concept of Jharkhandi identity namely: Jharkhandis are producers and hence all those who are exploited form the essence of Jharkhandi Identity. *Hence, the inclusion of Sadans and other exploited classes widens the concept of Jharkhandi identity and transforms it from ethnicity to regionalism* (Alloysius, G., 2003). This also provides strength to the argument that conflicts strengthen the identity and provides indomitable strength to resist against the distorted path of development (in collusion between the State, corporate group and vested interest in imposing forcible land acquisition and developmental model against the tribals of Jharkhand).

2.17 Tribal Movement and Identity Issues in Odisha

For the adivasi's in Odisha Land and Forest issues are part of Cultural Ingredients and Life sustaining issues. The present Section deals with the Tribal Movement and Identity Issues in Odisha in the Past and in the Contemporary Scenario several authors have drawn our attention to this intensity of life sustaining and cultural essence of the Land and Forest question in Odisha.

Professor S.N. Tripathy (2016) has dealt with "An Analysis of Tribal Movements during the British period in Odisha". He mentions that "Indeed, nothing could be more inspiring and edifying than saga of heroic struggle and sacrifice of galaxy of tribal personalities" (Panigrahi, 2011). He traces the tribal movement in Odisha during the British period and also relates it to the contemporary tribal movement in the State. He particularly mentions about the heroic struggle of the *Khonds* of Ghumsur against the British who launched Guerilla warfare by the Khonds Chief Dora Bisoyee who was the main target of the English Soldiers. The Khonds had killed a group of British Soldiers: similarly Chakra Bisoyee, another indomitable tribal leader of Ghumsur also used Guerilla tactics against the British Soldier. Such tribal resistance movement had taken place in different parts of Odisha during the British period. The author also mentions about the great tribal leader Laxman Naik of Koraput who belongs to Bhuyan tribe of Malkangiri who vehemently fought against the British with great courage and strength: he also fought for the cause of national freedom and also led the *Satyagraha* Struggle in 1941 in Mathili Police Station area and was distinguished as "Gandhi of Malkangiri". The Bonda tribes were violent and belligerent and seized Mathili Police Station under the leadership of Laxman Naik. He was ultimately sentenced to death under section 302 of IPC and on 29th March, 1943. He gallantly marched towards the gallows. In this way Laxman Naik heroically resisted against the British imperialism. *Alienation of land ownership of tribal ryots and eviction of tribal tenants was the direct and inevitable outcome of this process of invasion of crafty and unscrupulous traders and moneylenders and prosperous peasants from the plains into tribal areas and forced induction of the tribes into their ways.* He mentions that the most dominant characteristics of the tribal resistance movement was that it was fundamentally an uprising against the foreign rulers and in that sense could be considered to be precursor of the national liberation movement.

According to Dr. Tripathy if alienation of tribal lands in favour of non-tribal immigrants constituted an important factor of tribal unrest and uprising in the early part of the nineteenth century, it is no less today. It has no doubt enacted laudable legislative enactments like the Tribal Land Alienation Regulation of 1956 to arrest the process of grabbing of Tribal lands by non-tribals but the process is going on unabated and often unnoticed. The crafty and resourceful members of the non-tribal community are responsible for such land-grabbing. Land alienation coupled with denial of a fair and equitable return on the products of their hard labour have been responsible for misery and alienation of lands of members of the scheduled tribe community on an increasing scale.

S.N. Tripathy further discusses the tribal movement in Contemporary Odisha which includes the analysis of Resistance of the Tribals in Niyamgiri Hills (Kalahandi). He mentions that the laws like Land Acquisition Act and the Indian Forest Act etc. legitimize the continuing decline in access and control over forest resources that are considered as the basis of their subsistence economy. The experience in Odisha shows that tribal people's protest movements, however, well organized, have to take cognizance of the powerful interests of economic elite and industrial capital—both domestic and foreign—that wield considerable political power. In essence the problem is the marginalization of tribes and their access of failure to natural resources, especially land, forest and water. Low productivity, dispersed habitation, shifting cultivation, weak cooperative and marketing infrastructure, continued tribal land alienation leading to their dispossession and exploitation, physical complications etc. are some of the manifest feature which characterize the tribal area. The symbiotic relationship between the forests and the local dwellers was not recognized and the forest became property of the State. The tribes have a lifelong relationship with the forests—which are their very homes, their religion and their culture. The author mentions about the contemporary Forcible Eviction of project affected communities in Lanjigarh area of Kalahandi district for development of bauxite deposits and alumina processing by the British Vedanta Group in collaboration with the Odisha Mining Corporation. This area is populated by Dongria Kondh who worship Niyam Raja for their very survival particularly pertaining to Niyamgiri hills and its forest.

The Hon'ble Supreme Court of India imposed conditions on Vedanta Aluminium Project to make comprehensive plan for rehabilitation and all-round development of project affected tribal families before their displacement, which are to be monitored by the Government of Odisha. It was around this time that the MoEF refused forest clearance for Vedanta's phase II. In February 2010, steeping up their resistance to the controversial project, hundreds of Dongria Kondhs tracked to the abode of their presiding deity Niyam Raja on the Niyam Dongar (hill slopes) and designated it as inviolate. They carried out religious rituals and then put up a totem pole in the area. Since then, over a two-year period, the Government has tried to hasten the process and finalize individual claims under the FRA. In the light of the above discussion the author concludes that the factors which have contributed to the tribal unrest stems from the realization that they have not benefited from development projects.

The Dongaria Kondh tribal people of Niyamgiri said an emphatic no to the proposed mining in the Niyamgiri hills which is spread over in the tribal-dominated districts of Kalahandi and Rayagada in Odisha. Taking part in the first Gram Sabha that was held at Sherkapadi village in Sibapadar gram panchayat in Rayagada district during the day, as many as 36 out of the 38 adult residents of the village who attended the hearing vehemently opposed the proposed mining in the Niyamgiri hills. The Gram Sabha was conducted by Ward Member Shriram Gardia in the presence of Panchayat Extension Officer Pradhani Sabar. District Judge of Rayagada Sarat Chandra Mishra was present as an observer in the meeting as per Supreme Court Order. The villagers, who rejected an inter-departmental inquiry report that detailed the land used by the residents of Sherkapadi, said that they worshipped the entire Niyamgiri hill range as 'Niyamraja'. The 20 men and 16 women of the village who took part in the Gram Sabha hearing and spoke in Kui and Odia language said the proposed mining will affect their religious rights as well as the rituals. *According to sources, two resolutions were passed in the Gram Sabha. While in one resolution the villagers completely opposed the proposed bauxite mining project, in the second resolution they claimed religious rights over the whole of Niyamgiri which has as many as 112 tribal villages.* The Gram Sabha was conducted amid tight security. The hearing that lasted for several hours passed off peacefully. *Meanwhile, Prafulla Samantara, National Convener of National Alliance of People's Movements, congratulated the tribal people for their determination to protect Niyamgiri.* The Gram Sabha at Sherkapadi was the first in a series of Gram Sabhas to be conducted in 12 villages in Kalahandi and Rayagada districts as announced by Odisha Government. In its judgement passed on April 18, the Supreme Court had ordered that Gram Sabhas should take a final view on the proposed bauxite mining in Niyamgiri hills to source bauxite for the existing alumina refinery of Vedanta Aluminium Limited at Lanjigarh in Kalahandi district. As per the Odisha Government's decision, Gram Sabhas will be conducted in seven villages of Rayagada district from July 18 to August 19 and five villages of Kalahandi from July 23 to July 30. The Niyamgiri Suraksha Samiti, however, had opposed the Odisha Government decision and demanded that Gram Sabhas be held in all the 112 villages of Niyamgiri instead of only in 12 villages chosen by the authorities. *The Hindu,* July 18, 2013 (Tribal's Emphatic 'no' to Mining in Niyamgiri Hills).

Mohanty, R.K. (2016) in his paper, "*Sources of Deprivation and Styles of Mobilization—Contextualizing the Issues of Dispossessed Tribals in Contemporary Odisha*" first outlines his basic conceptual frame based on P.N. Mukherji's (1977) *Theoretical Framework consisting of the basic ingredients of discrimination* (D1), *deprivation* (D2), *dispossession* (D3). Mohanty adds another ingredient as *development displaced inducement* (D4). On this basic theoretical framework Mohanty looks at the ground level four D's suffered by the tribals due to the historic conditions of core problem faced by them which have manifested in some form of response (style of mobilization) articulated by themselves and for them in due course. *Deprivation and discrimination are deeply historical and acutely perennial in case of the tribes in Odisha. Dispossession (D3)* relates to the action by government, corporate and/or their agents to take out the tribal's land, home, heart, forest, and resources thereon which give meaning to their life and living. *Displacement (D4)* understood as the socalled cost of development, refers to the forced movement of tribal people from their locality or environment and occupational activities leading to loss of livelihood and consequent impoverishment. He has analyzed the nature of tribal movements in the ten tribal populated districts of Odisha, namely—Malkangiri, Mayurbhanj, Nawarangpur, Kandhamal, Rayagada, Sundargarh, Koraput, Keonjhar, Kalahandi and Bolangir. The KBK region which is considered as one of the poorest region is located within the above eight districts. Generally, the literacy rate in the tribal districts are low as compared to the non-tribal districts. The female literacy is also the lowest of all social groups in terms of literacy. The author analyzes the roots of Resistance and Mobilization of five contemporary tribal movements, namely—Kashipur Movement in Rayagada District, Niyamgiri Movement in Kalahandi District, Anti-POSCO Movement in Jagatsinghpur District, Kalinganagar Movement in Jajpur District and Narayanpatna Movement in Koraput District. *In fact these tribal movements are based on Land Alienation and Land Acquisition.* It is necessary to State in this context that Schedule V of the Constitution of India enjoins the government to respect and uphold the land rights of Scheduled Tribes. The two districts of Jagatsinghpur and Jajpur are the two coastal districts not covered under Schedule V Area. *According to the author, poverty, unemployment, illiteracy, land deprivation and exploitation of tribals were the common triggers of all the above cited movements into one.* The author gives a brief highlights of the five contemporary movements in Odisha.

The Kashipur Resistance Against ALCAN-HINDALCO began in 1993 by the tribal and dalit people in the area when they came to know that Utkal Alumina India Ltd. (UAIL) is being established in mineral rich Kashipur and adjoining area of Rayagada District (undivided Koraput) for the purpose of bauxite mining in the Baphlimali hills and setting up of a factory for processing the same in a big refinery at a Kondh village, named Ramibeda for producing the alumina. In the wake of persistent resistance against the UAIL between 1998 and 2000, Tata quit the venture. It has now become a joint venture of the mining giants HINDALCO (of Aditya Birla group) (55%) and ALCAN of Canada (45%). The plant site is at Doraguda in Kuchiepadar Panchayat. The UAIL project acquired 2,865 acre of land in Kashipur block in 1995. This includes 1,000 hectares of land presently under cultivation. All these developments *added to people's fear of loss of land, livelihood and culture terminating in violent resistance*. The Kashipur Block of Rayagada district is the land of primitive tribal communities like Kondh, Paraja, Penga and Jhodia. On 15th December, 2000, UAIL tried to forcibly organize a meeting in support of the bauxite mining at village Maikanch. The people in Maikanch protested vigorously against this. The people drove these outsiders. *Next day, on 16th December, three tribal men were shot dead and dozens of people suffered bullet injuries in police firing.* Women and children who remained behind the protesters and tried to stop the violent Police were not spared. The protest in the Kashipur block started against the UAIL as the chief target, and was later carried further against other bauxite mining projects. Over 500 arrests were made against anti-mining villagers in Kashipur up to 1999 alone (Mahapatra, 1999), and villagers attending the court every few weeks for these cases say they have to pay fees or bribes to a large range of lawyers and court officials.

A summary of Mishra's report was finally released to the media on 10 October, 2003, when Dharitri published an account under the title "Maikanch firing was justified". Basically, according to the extracts released, the report reached the contradictory conclusions that grossly excessive force was used, but that the firing was justified. It singles out the OIC (Officer In Command) of Kashipur Police Station "for continuing with firing beyond requirement", after the Magistrate had given the order to fire, and also admonishes this Magistrate, for giving an open–ended order to fire. The excerpts release mention the 19 rounds fired as excessive, and question the prior intent of the police visit to "investigate" and "maintain law and order", but they do not highlight the height at which bullets were fired (i.e. with intention to kill), nor the live ammunition in the guns, which implies a prior intension to cause harm. The report accepted the villagers' account that the incident was provoked when police laid their hands on two of the women. But critics of Utkal had hoped Mishra's inquiry would reveal the collusion between politicians and ministers, police, and company officials. The fact that the report did not apparently touch on the question of who called out the armed police, or how this decision was reached, implies to critics that the whole exercise was basically a whitewash. Most controversially, the report went beyond its brief to justify the alumina project, stating that "the State cannot afford to remain backward for the sake of so-called environmental protection"— an ideological Statement.

Prafulla Samantra (2000) in his write-up on "People's Struggle for Rights to Livelihood" has also highlighted the agitation in Kashipur against Gopalpur Steel Plant on the eve of Globalization. According to him the movement in Kashipur in the district of Ganjam has been continuing since 1995 after the Government of Odisha signed the MoU with TISCO for establishing and export oriented steel plant in the area. The Plant is to acquire more than 6,000 acre of agricultural land destroying the whole complex of socio-economic life of the people of

25 villages. About 25,000 people are being forced to vacate the area and sacrifice their homes and livelihood. Another steel plant is also being proposed in the neighbourhood by the Larsen & Toubro (L & T). This plant is to snatch away 5,000 acre of land where another 20,000 villagers are to be displaced from their land. The agitation at Gopalpur attained a feverish pitch when the villagers including women and children faced the in human police action in the month of August 1996. Two old women, named Laxmiama and S. Yerrama, died after being injured by police teargas and *lathi* charge. Till now the villagers successfully obstructed the administration to have survey work for acquisition of land by TISCO from the affected villagers in Gopalpur area. On March 19, 1997 the district administration resorted to police firing on unarmed villagers to enter into the villages for survey work. But the determined village agitators did not allow the survey staff to proceed with their work. In the police firing 5 villagers were severely injured by bullets and hundreds of women and children were injured by police *lathi* charge.

The second contemporary Movement analysed by R.K. Mohanty is *Lanjigarh Niyamgiri* movement against Vedanta Alumina Limited (VAL) which is an associate company of the London Stock Exchange. The company's original name was Sterlite Industries (India) Ltd. (SIIL). In December 2003, it was launched in the London Stock Exchange as a subsidiary of Vedanta Resources (VRP) in order to build Lanjigarh refinery in Kalahandi district. Tribal people like Dongaria Kondh, Kutia Kondh and Desia Kondh have lived in the Niyamgiri mountain range of Lanjigarh area from time immemorial. While the Kutia Kondh inhabit in the foothills, the Dongaria Kondh live in the upper reaches of the Niyamgiri hills. Vedanta started mining bauxite from the Niyamgiri hills jointly with OMC in October 2004. For this purpose, 723.43 hectares of land was required by Val, out of which 232.75 hectares land was private and most of this land belonged to the Kondhs. Most of the land is categorized as forest. According to the office of the Collector, Kalahandi, 12 villages of the Gram Panchayat Lanjigarh and Batelima was affected by the proposed alumina refinery at Lanjigarh. *From these villages, 60 families were to be displaced and 302 families will be affected where their land will be acquired for the project.* But in reality, the plant displaced 102 families from their homes. Another 1,220 'Project Affected' families lost all, parts, of their farmland. *Four tribal villages, Borobhota, Kinari, Kothdur, Sindhabahali and their agricultural fields, in South East Kalahandi district, were razed by VAL, and the villagers were forcibly evicted.*

Apart from large scale displacement of tribal people, Lanjigarh Movement countered the violation of environmental laws/forest conservation laws including Panchayats Extension to Scheduled Areas (PESA) Act of 1996 as its extensive mining in Niyamgiri mountains threatened an entire ecosystem, implying even drying up of rivers flowing from the mountains.

The 8,000 strong Dongaria tribe residing in the foot hills of the Niyamgiri hill in Kalahandi district have been carrying out resistance movement against the mining of bauxite from the hill top on the ground as their tribal diety Niyamraja resided there and any mining activities would destroy their God and ecology and deprive them of their main source of livelihood. People across the globe have resisted the protests against Vedanta. The Supreme Court of India while adjudicating a case on mining in Niyamgiri hills of Odisha directed the Odisha State Government on 18th April, 2013 to place issues concerning individual, community, cultural and religious claims of STs and TFDs before the Gram Sabha which would take decision on the project. *The seventh Gram Sabha was held on 29th July, 2013 at Phuldumer village in Trilochanpur Panchayat under Lanjigarh Block and passed a resolution rejecting the proposed bauxite mining in Niyamgiri hills as happened in six Gram Sabhas held earlier.* Mohanty, R.K. (2016) has also discussed—Three other important movements, namely—Anti-POSCO Movement in Jagatsinghpur District, Kalinganagar Movement in Jajpur District and Narayanpatna Movement in Koraput District.

POSCO signed a memorandum of understanding in June 2005 with the State Government of Odisha to construct a mega-integrated steel plant and modernization of Odisha's iron ore mines. This is an area of betel farming done mostly on forest land belonging to the State. Of the 1,620 hectares needed for the project, 90 per cent, or 1,440 hectares, is confested forest land. On 23 March, 2008, the Gram (*palli*) sabha of Dhinkia village [the statutory authority to initiate the process of recognition of rights under section 6(1) of the Forest Rights Act] passed resolutions initiating the process of claims for rights, and further demarcating the boundaries of the village's "community forest resource" and declaring its intention to protect it, including its resolve to deny consent to any diversion of this land. *The Anti-POSCO activist Dula Mandal was killed by pro-POSCO goons in this village of Govindpur on 21 June, 2008*, dredging the Jetadhari river mouth. After completing the dredging on 30th June, they held a memorial for Dula attended by 3,000 villagers and supporters. A few days later, villagers captured several goons who had used violence, along with six boxes of home made bombs and other weapons', from the school in Govindpur (*Statesman*, 26.6.2008). When serious violence erupted before this, on 29 November 2007, and bombs had been thrown by goons at a crowd consisting largely of women, Priyabrat Patnaik had made a Statement on TV that "those people have been taught a lesson". As per MoU signed on 22 June, 2005, between the Government of Odisha and M/s POSCO having its registered office at Koldang-Dong, Pohang City, Republic of Korea, the latter had planned to set up an Indian company. The company needed 4,000 acre of land for steel plant and associated facilities, and 2,000 acre of land for township development (1,500 acre near steel plant and 500 acre near mining project). There were massive protests and agitations in Odisha by different groups and activists on various grounds against the installation of the POSCO plant, its mining and other activities. Most of the villages in Nuagaon, Gadakuango, and Dhinkia Gram Panchayats were affected due to land acquisition. The people in these villages mainly depend on fishing, shrimp culture, betel vine (*pan baraj*). The POSCO Company has now closed its establishment in Jagatsinghpur District.

Narayanpatna block is a hilly tract of land on the Odisha-Andhra Pradesh border. Almost 90 per cent of the 45,000 people who live in the block are tribals. For several years, according to the police, the block has witnessed violent attacks by Maoists informers and contractors have been declared anti-people agents of the State and murdered with impunity and even police stations have been blown-up. The November 20, 2009 police firing took place in an extremely troubled condition. The undivided Koraput district in Western Odisha has acquired notoriety because of the Maoists literally taking over the dense hilly and forest areas, inhabited by the tribal communities, still trapped in the vicious traps of infinite poverty, injustice and underdevelopment. *The Maoist's presence stretch across the landscape and beyond to Ganjam, Malkangiri, Rayagada, and across the tense border zones of Jharkhand, Odisha and Andhra Pradesh. Few years later upper caste landlords grabbed the land of three tribals after giving them petty amount as loans. The tribals protested,* by using every form of democratic means. They submitted a memorandum to the Tehsildar, the District Magistrate and the Superintendent of Police of Koraput. *They demanded that the "arrack trade" and land-grabbing should be stopped.* The tribals have also 'recovered' thousands of hectares of agricultural land from the landlords and redistributed them among the tribal community. They have categorically claimed that this land belonged to the indigenous people who have inhabited this land

and forest since centuries, and mostly outsiders, with the help of police, bureaucracy and politicians, have captured their land. Under the Chasi Mulia Adivasi Sangha (CMAS) the struggle is led, under the leadership of Nachika Linga with support from veteran CPI-ML leader Ganantha Patra. It is led and controlled by tribals and has support base running into thousands, sometimes external support from Maoists. The police could not move even as thousands blocked their way with bows, arrows and sickles, albeit peacefully, even while others actually started tilling the 'recovered' land. *The movement has spread and acquired huge support base in the Koraput region, where scattered tribal communities share a strong chord of unity and angst with the tribals of Narayanpatna.* The tribals, after years of condemnation, have refused to accept the logic of injustice any more. More than 45,000 forest cases are pending against these poor tribals. The tribals are to fight the entrenched State machinery and this vicious nexus of the landlords, officials and [police police].

Table 2.1: Support base and the Continuity of Movements from 1990 onwards in Odisha

Sl. No.	*Name of the Movements*	*Core Issues*	*Duration*
1.	Kashipur Movement Rayagada District (Scheduled V Area)	Displacement due to bauxite mining and refinery; loss of land, livelihood and culture environmental degradation	(1994-2008)
2.	Niyamgiri Movement Kalahandi District (Scheduled V Area)	Displacement; loss of livelihood; environmental pollution; mining and crushing of sacred Niyamgiri; Damaging impact on Vamshadhara	(2003-Ongoing)
3.	Kalinganagar Movement Jajpur District (Non-Schedule V Area)	Against TATA's Kalinganagar Steel Plant, displacement due to industries; protect land and livelihood; justice for the killing of 13 tribals in police firing	(2005–Ongoing)
4.	Anti-POSCO Movement Jagatsinghpur District (Non-Schedule V Area)	Displacement; loss of way of life and livelihood; destruction of betel vine and fishery based economy	(2006–Ongoing)
5.	Narayanpatna Movement Koraput District (Non-Schedule V Area)	Tribal Land Alientation	(2006–Ongoing)

2.18 Predicament faced by the Marginalized Groups in Odisha

According to Professor A.B. Ota (June 2010), since Independence a large number of projects have been taken up in Odisha to usher in economic growth and development. The projects undertaken include dam/irrigation, industrial, mining, urban infrastructure development and wild life sanctuaries projects, besides linear project like roads, railways and so on. *As per conservative estimates, more than 10 lakh people have been displaced while over 50 lakh have been affected adversely in varying degrees without getting rehabilitated by development project so far.* Empirical studies reveal that most of the people displaced by development projects have failed to retain their pre-project living conditions in the post-project period. Many of the displaced have actually slipped below the threshold of poverty. Displaced tribals, who constitute more than 35 per cent of the total displaced population in Odisha, are the worst sufferers. The major development projects undertaken in the fifties were the Rourkela Steel plant and Hirakud Dam Project, Hindustan Aeronautics Limited (HAL), Talcher Thermal Power Stations (TTPS) and the Balimela Dam Projects followed in the sixties. During the Seventies, several multi-purpose dam project like Rengali, Upper Kolab, Upper Indravati and Subarnarekha were started in the State. The Thermal Power Station (ITPS), Talcher Super Thermal Power Projects (TSTP) and the National Aluminium Company (NALCO) came up in the Eighties. These projects were established in the resource rich highland districts of the State, which are predominantly inhabited by the tribals and other marginalized sections of the society. These large projects left trail of unintended adverse effects at the local level. Besides massive displacement, they also led to myriad economic and socio-cultural problems for the oustees.

The extent of displacement caused by development projects in Odisha were from:

(a) Thermal Power Projects,
(b) Industrial Projects,
(c) Mining Projects,
(d) Irrigation and Hydel Power Dam Projects, and
(e) Other Projects.

A total of 1463.16 hectares of land has been acquired for the Thermal Power Projects, affecting 940 families in 53 villages in and around Talcher (NTPC, 1993). According to another report, the number of families affected by TSTP at Kaniha is 1632. The Talcher Thermal Power Projects (TTPS), set up in 1964, was the First Thermal Power Project in Odisha. It required the acquisition of 205.67 hectares of land and displaced 157 families spread over 17 villages in and around Talcher town in Angul (then Dhenkanal) district. The Thermal Power Station (ITPS) at Banharpali in Jharsuguda District (formerly Sambalpur) was started in the early 1990s. The project acquired 486.48 hectares of land from three villages, affecting 329 families. Around 3,29,169 families were fully displaced and evacuated for the commissioning of the project at its present site. Together, the commissioning of various thermal power projects in the State has led to the displacement of around 1,500 families and acquisition of around 2,155 hectares of cultivable and homestead land.

The major industries in Odisha include the Rourkela Steel Plant, National Aluminium Company's plants functioning at Angul and Damanjodi, Fertilizer Corporation of India Plant at Talcher, Paradeep Phosphates Limited at Paradeep, Aluminium Plant at Hirakud, Refractories at Belpahar, Hindustan Aeronautics Limited at Sunabeda and the Ordnance factory at Saintala. The setting up of these large industries has led to large-scale acquisition of land and displacement of marginalized and downtrodden people—mostly in the backward but mineral rich highland districts of the State.

The Rourkela Steel Plant, set up in the fifties, acquired 7,917.84 hectares of land and displaced 2,464 families from 30 villages in Sundargarh district. According to an estimate by Mahapatra, 1231 (50.37%) out of the 2464 families displaced were tribals and 733 families (30%) were scheduled castes (Mahapatra,1990). Further, 2741 hectares of land had to be acquired in Damanjodi in Koraput district for the aluminum plant, mining activities and township of NALCO. The number of project affected people were 17,678, out of which tribals constituted 52.44 per cent, Scheduled Castes 10.84 per cent and other castes 36.72 per cent. NALCO also further acquired 3877.81 hectares of land in Angul for its smelter plant, captive power plant and township. This affected 3,997 families in 40 villages. Out of the affected families, 12.76 per cent belonged to scheduled castes and 2.78 to Scheduled Tribes (Fernandes *et al.*, 1992).

The Hindustan Aeronautics Limited (HAL) set up the MIG factory at Sunabeda in Koraput District in 1963. The project acquired 3,764 hectares of land and displaced 468 families from 10 villages (Reddy, 1993). The ordnance factory at Saintala in Bolangir district, established in 1984, displaced 1200 families from 14 villages. The total number of families affected by industries in Odisha is 10,704, which accounts for 11.47 per cent of the total displacement in the State (Ota, 1999). Clearly, industry has been the second biggest reason for displacement in Odisha.

Among the various kinds of mining operations in Odisha, coal mining has caused the maximum displacement. Though mining of iron ore has displaced a large number of people in North Odisha, the exact magnitude of displacement has not been fully documented. Odisha coal deposits are concentrated in two areas—Talcher area in Angul district and Valley area in Jharsuguda district. Coal mining operations in Odisha are carried out by Mahanadi Coalfields Limited (MCL), a subsidiary of Coal India Limited (CIL). By 1994, MCL has acquired 2,576 hectares of land in Talcher area. Twenty three villages in the area are affected by the five open cast mines (MCL) which acquired 929.58 hectares of land by 1993. These five open cast mines affected 17 villages and 130 families from two of these affected villages.

There are around 600 mines all over Odisha; located mostly in the tribal pockets of the State. It is common knowledge that exploration of minerals through open cast mines results in displacement of human settlements, felling of forests and acquisition of agricultural land. There is no official record of the magnitude of displacement caused due to mining projects in the State. But going by the thumb rule that one mine affects the livelihoods of an average of around 50 to 100 families in the project area, *the number of people displaced by the 600 mines in the State must have been around 50,000.*

Development of urban infrastructure, creation of wildlife sanctuaries and construction of roads and railways have also contributed in no small measure to the problem of displacement in Odisha. So far, a total of 12,000 slum dwellers have been displaced from various parts of Odisha. The two wildlife sanctuaries—Similipal Tiger Reserve and Chandaka Elephant Sanctuary—have displaced 42 and 100 families respectively. Various kinds of development projects in the State have together displaced 81,176 families and led to the acquisition of 6.22 lakh hectares of land between 1950 and 1993 in the State of Odsiha. Apart from this, major and medium dam projects have caused the lion's share of displacement in the State. Construction of river dams also required the acquisition of around 6 lakh hectares of land.

The multi-purpose hydel dams taken up in Odisha before and in the immediate aftermath of Independence were Machhkund, Hirakud and Balimela, Rengali Upper Kolab and Upper Indravati. Machhkund dam, started in the 1940s on River Dumduma in Koraput district, was the first major river dam project in Odisha. It displaced 2,938 families, out of which 51.00 per cent belonged to Scheduled Tribes and 10.21 per cent to Scheduled Castes. The construction of the Hirakud multipurpose dam project on River Mahanadi in Sambalpur District started shortly after Independence and was completed in 1957. The project affected 249 villages of Odisha and 36 villages of Madhya Pradesh (Baboo, 1992). About 1,10,000 persons belonging to 22,144 families were affected by the project (Government of Odisha, 1968). The project submerged an area of 74,300 hectares, which included 23,988 hectares of forest land and 49,888 hectares of agricultural land.

The Balimela Multipurpose Dam Project, constructed in the Koraput district in 1962-63, was an inter-State project of Odisha and Andhra Pradesh. It submerged 17,496 hectares of land in Odisha and 648 hectares in Andhra Pradesh and affected nearly 2,000 families, most of them being tribals. The estimated number of tribal families displaced by the project was 1,507 (79.31%). The Rengali multipurpose dam project on River Brahmani in Angul district of Odisha (erstwhile Dhenkanal) was started in 1973 and was completed in March 1991. The project submerged 4,23,000 hectares of land in the undivided districts of Sambalpur and Dhenkanal. A total of 263 villages from Deogarh, Pallahara and Talcher sub-divisions of the said districts were submerged under water. The total number of families affected by the dam was 10,897, out of which 1,710 (15.69%) belonged to Scheduled Castes and 1,172 (10.75%) to Scheduled Tribes. The rest belonged to general Caste Hindu category. Many in the latter category were from the cultivator caste, popularly called *Chasa* in Odisha. The Upper Kolab multi-purpose dam project on River Kolab in Koraput district was initiated in 1976 and was completed in 1991. It submerged 16,258 hectares of land and displaced 3,180 families from 53 villages (Status Report on Upper Kolab Irrigation Project, August 2005). Out of the displaced families 1,442 (13.90%) belonged to the Scheduled Caste category and 1,421 (44.70%) were from the Scheduled Tribes (Government of Odisha, 1993).

Work on the Upper Indravati Multipurpose Dam Project, which envisaged the creation of a composite reservoir by damming Indravati, Padagoda, Muran and Kapur rivers in undivided Koraput and Kalahandi districts, started in 1978-79. It submerged 11,000 hectares of land in 99 villages. A total of 5,301 families from 99 villages were displaced by the project, out of which 2,223 families (41.94%) were

Tribals and 796 families (15.02%) were Scheduled Castes (Government of Odisha, 1993). The number of people affected by the dam was around 20,000 in 105 villages going by the World Bank Staff Appraisal Report. The Subarnarekha multi-purpose project is an inter-State project of Odisha, Bihar and West Bengal on the River Subernarekha. The project aims at construction of two major dams, namely—Chandil and Ichha Dam, which are expected to affect 3,830 families in 36 villages of Odisha. A whopping 3152 (82.3%) of the affected families are STs, 116 families (3.0%) SCs and 562 (14.7%) families belong to other castes (Government of Odisha, 1990). Together Ichha and Chandil dams will submerge 2,600 hectares of land in Bihar (now Jharkhand) and around 4,000 hectares in Odisha. The number of families to be affected will be 10,000 in Bihar (Jharkhand) and 1,000 in Odisha.

Besides multi-dams, people are also displaced by irrigation projects. The Salandi Irrigation Project at Hadagarh on River Salandi in the district of Keonjhar was completed in 1976. The project submerged 1,229 ha. of land affecting 589 families. A study on the project reports that out of the 589 displaced families, 552 (93.23%) were Tribals. The Samal barrage known as a Rengali Irrigation Project in Angul district submerged 2,888 ha. of land affecting 8 revenue villages including 3 uninhabited villages. Agricultural lands in 30 villages were also affected by the barrage and around 828 families were affected by the barrage and around 828 families were affected due to submergence caused by the water reservoir. In other major irrigation projects like Kanput, lower Indra, Lower Suktel etc. the total number of villages to be affected is estimated to be 122, the land area to be submerged about 30,233 ha. and families to be affected by displacement 9,221. The overall picture of dis[illegible] Odisha reveals that till 1995, around 4 lakh people had [illegible] by development projects while dam projects alone have displaced around 70,000 families, which constitutes 75 per cent of the total displaced (Ota, 2010).

2.19 Commissioning of Special Field Research Studies by Experts

In order to prepare an appropriate policy response to resettlement problems as they presently exist on the ground, six field-based research studies were especially commissioned. The studies were conducted by well-known experts familiar with the local situation on the following areas of major concern: (1) Water Resources Development, (2) Coal mining, (3) Industrial projects, (4) National Highway Projects,

(5) Tribal rights, and (6) Gender Issues (Hari Mohan Mathur, 2008, *Social Change*, December 2008).

The lower Suktel Irrigation Project aims to provide irrigation and drinking water to Bolangir, a predominantly drought prone district. Starting in late 1990s, upon completion it is expected to submerge 16 villages fully and 10 partially, involving 4,160 families, out of which 1,222 belong to Scheduled Tribes. The project is moving at a slow pace; it is particularly slow on land acquisition and compensation payment. Meanwhile, resistance to the project has rapidly grown, due to the lack of information among the people on project impacts and the absence of a planned approach to their resettlement concerns. The research team by Agnihotri (2005), the author of this study could not even enter certain villages, because people were up in arms against this project as they see nothing good coming from it. The findings of this study also confirm that the project is going to produce largely negative impacts and given the present intervention methods, people expect a definite decline in the quality of their life.

It is acquired mainly by the Mahanadi Coalfields Limited, a subsidiary of the Coal India Limited. This study, conducted by the team led by Pandey (2005) in Angul and Jharsuguda, the two districts with most coal deposits, found the impact of mining to be entirely disruptive and impoverishing. The tribal people and women are among the groups that have lost most from displacement triggered by the mining. The conflicts between resettler and host populations are on the increase. What adds to the woes of displaced people is the Coal Bearing Area Act is much harsher than the Land Acquisition Act and the team suggests that it is be scrapped.

Stimulated by the globalization of the Indian economy, Odisha is now on the threshold of rapid industrial growth. Its vast natural resources, especially mineral, forest, hydrologic and marine, give it an added advantage.

Odisha has a component of about 444 kms length road expansion under the larger National Golden Quadrilateral Project being implemented by the National Highway Authority of India (NHAI). It is for the first time that a linear project affecting a sizeable population is under construction in this State. The Project is likely to directly affect 11,152 persons, out which 2,188 will lose structures of both residential and commercial kinds. The rest 8964 will lose only strips of land. This study, carried out by Ota (2005) reports that while some affected persons have not only regained but also improved their living standards; some of them have either failed to maintain their standards or even slipped below the poverty line. Another finding is that people doing well are those who were well to do to begin with. It is the poor who have got poorer. A major area of concern brought out by the study is that there is no national highway policy on resettlement; all that exists is a draft and that too seems not to be receiving due consideration.

As a result of development projects, the tribal people in Odisha have become poorer than before, maintains Mahapatra (2005). Partly this is to due to a process of alienation of their rights over land, forest, water bodies and other resources, which started during the colonial times but continues even to this day. *Odisha has also not conceded the rights of the tribal people to be consulted on matters concerning the acquisition of land for project purposes, which the Panchayats (Extension to Scheduled Areas) Act, 1996 (PESA) has specifically offered on them.* As a result, whenever projects come up in tribal territories, people even in permanent possession of lands all through the centuries are often dispossessed without compensation in the absence of legal rights.

Professor A.B. Ota (2010) analyses the risk factor under study and states that Development-induced displacement has resulted in widespread and traumatic psychological, social and cultural consequences. The "Impoverishment Risk Model" captures (Cernea,1997), the eight sub-processes listed below:

1. Landlessness,
2. Marginalization,
3. Joblessness,
4. Homelessness,
5. Food Insecurity,
6. Loss of Access to Common Property,
7. Social Disarticulation, and
8. Increased Morbidity and Mortality.

He suggests some of the minimizing risk factor include:

1. 'Land for land' should be the sole guiding principle in the rehabilitation of the displaced so as to prevent the emergence of landlessness.
2. Marginalization also occurs through the loss of income from extra agricultural sources in the locality, which again are disrupted by the acquisition of the entire area (i.e. the village, or the neighbourhood) by the project authorities.

3. Out of the four projects surveyed, there was no rehabilitation policy. As a result, all those who were ousted by HAL lost their old sources of the income, but did not get any alternative means of livelihood as none among them was provided either with a job in the project or land for cultivation. In Upper Kolab Project, oustees who had owned land were benefited by the rehabilitation policy. However, artisans, share-croppers, landless labourers, those employed in service, and small businessmen, who lost their occupations and means of livelihood because of displacement, were not recognized as displaced persons eligible for rehabilitation benefits under the resettlement and rehabilitation policy of the project authorities.
4. *Homelessness is also placelessness,* loss of a group's cultural space and identity, or cultural impoverishment. It gives a sense of belonging, social and psychological security and an assurance of togetherness in times of difficulty. In all the four projects under study, compensations was paid for the house which the oustees complained that it was by no means the replacement value. In HAL, the displaced persons have encroached on government land to build houses on their own in the absence of any rehabilitation policy. They have no private homestead land. The quality of these houses is far from satisfactory.
5. Land acquisition in the project areas has destroyed self-sufficiency. After displacement, they now have to spend money to procure foodgrains and vegetables. They also have to cope with the high prices of essential commodities.
6. No compensation has been provided under the Land Acquisition Act, 1994 for common properties in any of the four projects. In the absence of any policy measure, the displaced persons of HAL did not get any replacement for the common property they lost.
7. Production systems are dismantled, kinship groups and family systems are often scattered, local labour markets disrupted and the *cultural identity of the people is under threat.* Social disintegration also takes place because of the lack of linkages with others and the loss of economic status. Social disintegration has been a major impoverishment risk in all the projects studied.
8. Social-economic inequalities among the mining oustees households are widespread due to the unavailability of

> remunerative and well-paid occupations in the place of resettlement and the virtual collapse of the traditional agrarian economy. They now have to purchase the same minor forest produce, which they used to collect free of cost from the jungles earlier. Oustees have shifted to other sectors of employment due to displacement and loss of agricultural land (which was not fully replaced by "land for land" policy). More and more households are found to be engaged in agricultural labour and non-agricultural labour activities.

Felix Padel and Samarendra Das (2008) in their write-up "Odisha's Highland Clearances: The Reality gap in R & R" have attracted our attention to the fact that what is happening in terms of *Cultural Genocide is the extinction of people's communities and social structure which largely explains why they fight so strenuously to resist displacement. Displacement arises out of a clash of ideologies.* On one side, the value systems of traditional cultures, where relationships with land and community are more important than money. On the other, an ideology of industrialization as development, in which market forces and swift financial profit override other values. The police firing that killed tribal people at Maikanch village in December 2000, and Kalinganagar Industrial Area in January 2006, are key symbols of this struggle in Odisha. *The divide and rule legacy of British colonialism is bearing fruit now, in internal colonialism carried out through large scale privatization of resources, and takeover of huge tracts of cultivated land, by mining and construction companies, in Odisha and neighbouring States.*

In Odisha, hundreds of communities have ceased to exist, and hundreds more are threatened with extinction. Local tribal and non-tribal politicians and landlords in Kashipur and Lanjigarh have sold out their communities. Around the upper Indravati reservoir, displaced people cut down the remaining forests, because they have lost their land along with their traditional forest-based livelihood system. Selling the timber as firewood is all that saves them from starvation. The Aluminium Companies are entering the Kond region of Western Odisha after the bauxite deposits which are cited on the summits of the biggest mountains, they erode the water-bearing capacity of the mountains, and thereby threaten the local Konds cultivation of millet, maize, turmeric, ginger, orange pineapple and dozens of other food crops which they depend on for sustenance and income. *Mining bauxite from these mountain tops is also an assault on their religion, because Kond religion recognizes mountains as prime sacred entities and source of life;* geologists recognized this fact when they named the base rock of these bauxite-capped mountains as Khondalite (Padel and Das, 2007).

According to R & R policies formulated by the World Bank, DFID and UNDP, as well as the Governments of Odisha and India, people's standard of living is supposed to go up, not down. It is generally acknowledged that this hardly ever happens in practice (Mathur, 2008). According to Padel and Das (2007), *one set of issues involves Cultural Genocide and the sacrificing of people's quality of life, along with all the non-measurable factors that make-up their culture and community.* Another basic problem is that in most, if not all, the project areas, various forms of intimidation and coercion appear to be standard procedure towards people unwilling to be displaced, by police and administrative authorities, as well as by a mafia network of goondas. Most of Odisha's first wave of industrial projects have been notorious for their lack of adequate R & R, such as the Rourkela Steel Plant, the Hirakud, Upper Kolab and Indravati dam projects, and also NALCO in Koraput, sometimes cited as a model of good practice. *So the present situation in Odisha involves several high profile struggles of people opposing displacement in Odisha.* Three companies in particular face protracted opposition; Tata at Kalinganagar and Gopalpur (steel plants), Naraj (thermal power plant near Cuttack), Dhamra (port), and North Odisha (iron-ore mines), POSCO at Jagatsinghpur (steel plant and port) and North Odisha (iron ore mines), and Vedanta at Lanjigarh (Alumina Refinery), Niyamgiri (planned bauxite mine), Jharsaguda district (smelter and giant power plant) near Puri (university-*cum*-business–centre), and Gandhamardan (another bauxite deposit).

Where people have taken a strong stand resisting displacement, include the Utkal Alumina Refinery, numerous Steel Plants and sponge iron factories by Bhushan, Jindal and other companies, and the Lower Suktel dam, the protestors are holding-up foreign investments worth many crores of rupees. *From the viewpoint of protestors threatened with displacement, they are being treated with a fundamental injustice.* Most of the people faces with displacement do not see the projects as development at all. Since 1995, the Kashipur Movement has been at the forefront of questioning what is meant by "development," (Lingaraj 1995, Pradhan 1995). Defined in purely material and economic terms, "development" loses all connection with the original aim of improving people's actual well-being. NALCO-dominated Koraput is the poorest of all, with 78 per cent of the population below the poverty line (CSE, 2008 : 254, 322).

2.20 Cultural Genocide

Cultural genocide is the least recognized but perhaps most painful aspect of the drastic drop in the quality of life of people who are displaced (Padel & Das, 2008). The economy is completely changed when people who have been essentially cultivators are removed from the land and turned into an industrial labour force. Food security vanishes, and money assumes far greater importance in defining relationships between people. People's identity is also radically altered. *Their fields and houses were often made by their forefathers, so losing their land and ancestral village creates a traumatic break with previous generations.*

Women's position is often particularly badly affected, even where education, health centre's and Self-Help Groups (SHGs) are provided for oustees. The reason for this is that in a tribal village, women often retain a large degree of control over their own labour, working essential for themselves and their own families, at times of their own choice. Tribal women who retain their land go to market to sell their own produce. *The dignity from this self-sufficiency is destroyed by displacement.* Religious life is also transformed. *People's sense of sacredness in nature lies at the heart of traditional tribal religion.* For example, a woman who had just been removed from Kinari village to make way for refinery said *"Amora deveta bhi nasht kole"*. Similar testimony is given by people displaced by the Indravati reservoir, who says "Our deities were drowned". *Cultural Genocide applies most clearly to tribal cultures*, which differ markedly from mainstream orientation in their lifestyle's groundedness in nature. So, the various people in Odisha and other States who are striving to protect their land from corporate takeover are actually campaigning for much more to preserve India's cultural integrity and independence against the forces of global finance.

In Odisha one of the outstanding areas is the forested mountain: summit in Niyamgiri where Vedanta plants to mine bauxite. The reason is the Dongria Konds and their religion, which centres on Niyam Raja, Lord of the law, whose abode is the, mountain summit. The tribes maintain a taboo on cutting trees up there in Niyam Rajas name out of the recognition that the natural vegetation conserves the fertility of their land through an abundance of streams. *So mining bauxite from Niyamgiri and other Khondalite mountains in South Odisha is bound to cause an erosion of Kond spiritual values* as well as an erosion of Odisha natural environment and fertility (Dash, 2008). Sudden release of water by the Hirakud Dam caused widespread displacement and loss of life and property in 1980 and 1999 as well as 2008. The Hindu-Christian issue was sparked in December 2007 by the application of certain Panos (the main Scheduled Caste) in Kandhamal district to change their status from Scheduled Caste to Scheduled Tribe on the basis that they speak the Kond tribal language, Kiu-an application that angered Konds, and fanned the flames of double split in society that broke out in violent attacks: SC (Pano)–ST (Kond), and Hindu-Christian. The split broke out with renewed ferocity in August 2008 following the murder by Maoists of the VHP leader Laxmananda Saraswati, whom they held responsible for instigating communal violence in December. August-October 2008 has been the burning of countless villages and churches, and the displacement of tens of thousands of Christians. The Kandhamal violence demonstrates the power of several related polarizations—Hindu-Christians, and SC-ST conflicts highlights the positions of the Maoists in this process.

Increasingly, people who resist displacement are being branded as Maoists, especially in the Kalinganagar and POSCO areas (as also at Singur and Nandigram). To what extent Maoist influence is penetrating these areas is often difficult to gauge. What is clear is that these movements against forced displacement are primarily motivated by the farmers who wish to retain their land and communities, and if Maoist influence enters, the main reason for this is people's exasperations at the injustice they face, and the Maoists readiness to capitalize on this, since supporting fights against injustice are at the core of their ideology. It is also apparent that labelling protestors as Maoists makes it easier to justify repressive measures against them. So, one aspect of social evolutionism, and therefore of the mainstream values promoting industrial development in India and Odisha today, involves a set of negative stereotypes about tribal people and other small-scale farmers: as "primitive", "backward", "uneconomic", "unsustainable" etc. This has actually been the dominant view of tribal cultures since European moderns first encountered them and causes an immense undervaluation of tribal culture. Neo-liberal economics gives prime importance to a belief in "market forces" on the view that if everyone follows their own interests, market forces will produce the proper adjustments in society.

A blatant double set of values is apparent in the application of law. While protestors against the Utkal, POSCO and Tata projects are harassed by countless "false cases" that tie them into a drawn out and highly exploitative process at the local law courts, the big corporations are seen to wriggle out of legal injunctions with ease, e.g. in the notorious bribes paid by the mining companies to ministers, and in the way that Utkal and Vedanta proceeded to build their factories without having first acquired proper environmental clearance for the mines they were depending on. Vedanta/Sterlite's clearance for mining Niyamgiri came after the Norwegian Government Council on Ethics released a report that delayed long list of transgressions of law by the Sterlite-Vedanta group, and abuse of the environment and human rights in India and other countries (2007). The use of goondas (hired thugs) by mining companies is particularly blatant example of double legal standards.

In the Kalinganagar area, leading activists of the *Bisthapit Birodhi Jan Manch* (People's Platform Against Displacement) have been attacked, and one murdered, while another activist was killed in the POSCO area. Amin 'Shyam' Banara was gunned down on 1 May, 2008 by goons—a crime for which gangster Arbind Singh was later arrested a month before, another activist, Jogendra Jamuda, was shot in the back while driving his mother and wife on the motorbike past the Kalinganagar police station. The Anti-POSCO activist Dula Mandal was killed by Pro-POSCO goons in his village of Govindpur on 21 June, 2008, after a day's work alongside hundreds of others, dredging the Jetadhari river mouth. After completing the dredging on the 30th June, they held a Memorial for Dula attended by 3,000 villagers and supporters. A few days later, villagers captured several goons who had used violence, along with six boxes of home made bombs and other weapons, from the school in Govindpur (*Statesman*, 26.6.08). When serious violence erupted before this, on 29 November, 2007, and bombs had been thrown by goons at a crowd consisting largely of women, Priyabrat Patnaik had made a statement on TV that "those people have been taught a lesson". Similar intimidation, by goons as well as police, took place at a Public Hearing for a Tata Thermal Power Plant at Naraj, near Cuttack on 10 March, 2008, that would displace several villagers. POSCO's invitation of Journalists to Korea, and Vedanta's invitation of Journalists to Lanjigarh, and the money offer to journalists who promote positive news for these companies, is well known. Manufacturing of consent by corporate interests making use of the media plays a significant part (Chomsky and Herman, 1988). Tata and POSCO followed Vedanta's example of trying to construct their factories before getting mining clearance. Sukinda adjacent to Kalinganagar, has been named one of the ten most polluted spots on earth.

The difference in values and beliefs between corporate attitudes to law and those of Adivasis could not be starker. *The Kond concept of*

Niyam Raja as upholder of law unites a universal with human conceptions of law, like the ancient Indian concept of dharma. Indeed, if it is true that Maoists' appeal is on the rise, village people's despair of getting justice at the courts should be counted as a significant factor. The call to armed struggle appears as radical and progressive empowerment for oppressed people who lack legal redress for their grievances.

Over 200 arrests were made against anti-mining villagers in Kashipur (Mahapatra, 1999), and villagers attending the court every few weeks for these cases say they have to pay fees or bribes to a large range of lawyers and court officials. Kashipur Police Station continued with firing beyond requirement, after the Magistrate had given the order to fire, and also admonishes the Magistrate, for giving an open-ended order to fire. The report accepted the villagers' account that the incident was provoked when police laid their hands on two of the women. The whole exercise was basically a whitewash. Most controversially, the report went beyond its brief to justify the Alumina Project, "stating that the State cannot afford to remain backward for the sake of so called environmental protection" —an ideological Statement.

Much of what is being called "development" is essentially destructive of the removal of unrenewable resources (in the case of Odisha's minerals), and dangerous overuse of water, as well as destruction of communities living basically in harmony with nature. Most studies of R & R agree that oustees had rarely regained their previous standard of living, let alone raise it. Odisha's 3 million oustees, and people faced further displacement now are bound to be cynical about the new R & R policies, when many areas often mentioned as positive examples of resettlement, such as NALCO Damanjodi area, prove anything but positive. "Land for land" is the minimum requirements to safeguard indigenous people's quality of life, and this provision is not there in the recent R & R policies. The UN Declaration, like the Extractive Industries Review. Insists that people faced with displacement have the right to free prior informed consent and this too is not in the R & R policies; it cannot be said that these R & R policies are generous. When company people say of a tribal area where they have erected a factory "there was nothing here before—only mud huts", this shows how the dominant mindset equates development with modern, material constructs, such as roads and buildings. Most R & R schemes assess traditional tribal house as without any economic value. *The contrast between houses before and after displacement demonstrates a far-reaching difference in values and culture.*

The following are the some of the areas of life where displaced people generally see a marked decline in their living standards:

1. Food security loss.
2. Self-employment replaced by humiliating dependency on a supply labouring jobs.
3. Egalitarian social structure replaced by a low place in an extreme hierarchy.
4. Splits in the community between people for and against a project/company.
5. Access to fresh stream water ends, replaced by pump water, often polluted and unreliable.

In this context, the specific problems with the new R & R policies are that:

1. They say it is best to avoid displacement, but there is no serious or publicly transparent process or pursuing alternatives.
2. The promise of one job per family has often been made (e.g. at Rourkela and Damanjodi) but has rarely if ever been kept in practice.
3. Land is often bought for absurdly low prices, a major factor of discontent at Kalinganagar, where land was resold by IDCO to Tata for ten times the price paid.
4. People without *patta* are classed as "encroachers on government land" even though they have often farmed this land over generations.
5. The value of houses is grossly underestimated by classing them as "mud huts".
6. Cash compensation is the norm, and accepted uncritically in the R & R policies, even though it has been shown repeatedly that business sharks invariably pursue those in receipt of cash and new bank accounts, with offers of vehicle or schemes that enmesh oustees immediately into debt.
7. Even recent suggestions that mining companies should give 5 per cent of their profit for local area development, or make displaced people shareholders are unenforceable and likely to compound the exploitation.
8. The very fact that the displaced persons have spelt-out their options and preferences for their relocation, resettlement and

rehabilitation indicates that they are willing to accept the project. It also indicates that they are mentally preparing themselves to get displaced to give way for the project. POSCO, like Tata, has spent a lot of money studying the people resisting displacement, and a visit to the POSCO office in Bhubaneswar revealed a site map where resisting households were marked with red dots, Pro-POSCO households with green and fence-sitters with blue.

Balaji Pandey (2008) in "*The Kalinganagar Tragedy: Development Goal or Development Malaise*" states that on January 2006, the police in Kalinganagar, Odisha opened fire against a group of tribal people protesting against Tatas constructing a steel plant on their lands and not paying them adequate compensation. This tragedy killing 14 persons on the spot shocked the whole nation. The area has high concentration of Scheduled Tribes and Scheduled Caste population. The two blocks—Sukinda and Danagadi—under which Kalinganagar falls have 36.06 per cent and 28.19 per cent Scheduled Tribes and 11.89 per cent and 22.31 per cent Scheduled Caste population respectively. It is significant to note that the Scheduled Tribes population in the acquired area is much higher than the block average. Of the tribes, people belonging to Ho community constitute nearly 80 per cent of the population, and the rest of them belong to Munda and Santal communities.

Table 2.1: Socio-economic Profile of the Three Villages displaced by the Tata and the Maharashtra Seamless Company

Name of the village/ Panchayat	*No. of Households*	*% of ST population*	*% of SC population*	*Literacy rate*	*% of cultivator*	*% of ST agricultural labour*
Chandia	331	85.9	0.2	37.6	41.0	36.2
Gobaraghati	558	88.8	2.1	53.5	16.0	37.7
Gadapur	140	97.8	0.0	46.7	43.0	13.5

Source: Census 2001.

While developing Kalinganagar the people of the area were never taken into confidence. The State Government had acquired around 12,000 acre of land in Kalinganagar during 1992-94 for allocation to steel projects. Those who owned these lands were compensated at Rs. 37,000 per acre with some additional compensation later on when a tide of protests rose. Two companies implemented their projects, but neither met the promise of providing employment to one person in every household displaced from the land. Then, in 2004-05, the government allotted 1,960 acre of Tata Steel, reportedly at nearly 10 times the rate at which the landowners were originally compensated. There were serious grievances: extremely inadequate compensation for the land acquired, gross failure in resettlement and rehabilitation, and major shortcomings in the provision of jobs. *The tribals in the area have been cultivating mostly non-patta land in the absence of proper land records*, though they have been dependent on these lands for their livelihoods, they were neither offered compensation nor land in lieu of the land cultivated by them.

Tribals in Kalinganagar instead of becoming panicky after the killing became more determined to oppose any construction in that area. They resorted to roadblock and immobilized the traffic movement in one of the busiest routes of the State, which they are continuing till date. They made it clear to the government that under no circumstances would they withdraw unless their demands are fulfilled. The demands are:

- No fresh displacement on grounds of industrialization;
- Five acre of land in lieu of land acquired;
- Rights over possessed land;
- Action against State Finance Minister and four senior officials directly responsible for the killings;
- *Ex-gratia* of Rs. 20 lakhs each for families of the dead and Rs. 10 lakhs for each of the injured;
- Ban on multinational units entry into the area; and
- Withdrawal of cases slapped against tribals.

They formed a Visthapan Virodh Jana Manch (People's Forum to Oppose Displacement) to lead their agitation. In the wake of the Kalinganagar killings, the State Government announced compensation of Rs. 5 lakh for each of the victims' families. In addition, the Centre also agreed to offer Rs. 5 lakh to each family.

The Kalinganagar tragedy is the expression of the overwhelming domination of the corporate sector to the extent that the State everywhere has turned to be almost executor of the will of the Corporate Sector. A significant fallout of the tragic incident is that the State Government promptly (May, 2006) came out with an R & R policy, which has some very progressive feature. The policy on the contentious issue of land acquisition is quite liberal. It States, "The project proponent may opt for direct purchase of land on the basis of negotiated price after issue of notification requiring acquisition of land under the relevant Act. If acquisition of land through direct purchase fails, other provisions of the relevant Act may be invoked. Land not utilized by the project within the prescribed limit and for the required purposes shall be resumed".

There are massive protests and agitations in Odisha by different groups and activists on various grounds against the installation of the POSCO plant, its mining and other activities. Most of the villages in Nuagaon, Gadakujanga, and Dhinkia Gram Panchayats will be affected. The people in these villages depends on fishing, shrimp culture, betel vine, cashew nut plantation and paddy cultivation. There are around 5,000 betel vine (*pan baraj*). The police is very cautious in using force. This is one of the outcomes of brutal police firing at Kalinganagar on January 2006. In the case of the Maikanj police firing, the quantum of force was grossly in excess of the requirement. The overzealousness of SP and Collector of Rayagada district in deploying a huge number of police force and 19 round firing on that day show that the firing in Maikanj was pre-planned and motivated. On 1 December, 2004, there was a conflict between the Collector and the local people on the issue of opening a police *phandi* near Kashipur. There were Public Hearings for the Utkal Alumina project, one at Tikiri and on 25 May, 2008, the displaced and affected families of the alumina project of the UAIL at Kashipur threatened to cultivate the ceded agricultural land for the alumina project if the compensation amount is not increased.

2.21 Resume of Odisha Tribal Identity

Professor S.N. Tripathy while analysing the tribal movements in Odisha during the British time observes that alienation of land ownership of tribal raiyats and eviction of tribal tenants was the direct and inevitable outcome of the process of invasion of crafty and unscrupulous traders and moneylenders as also prosperous peasants from the plains into the tribal areas and forced induction of the tribes into their ways. According to Professor Tripathy if alienation of tribal land in favour of non-tribal immigrants constituted an important factor of tribal unrest and uprising in the early part of the 19th century, it is no less today. In essence, the problem is the marginalization of tribes and their access of failure to natural resources, especially land, forest and water. One of the major shortcomings of the recent agitations in Tribal pockets of Odisha has been that Gram Sabha—Palli Sabha consent was not taken and *Social Impact Assessment* was not properly carried out. It was a forcible acquisition by the State of Odisha followed by intense State repression. The silverlining were the Saxena Committee Report in case of POSCO and Niyamgiri which brought some element of social justice to the marginalized communities in these areas. The decision of Niyamgiri Gram Sabha-Palli Sabha was unique in as much as the cultural ingredients of the tribal communities were recognized and given effect. The Supreme Court Decision in favour of the Dongaria tribal community also deserves appreciation. The Kashipur, Kalinganagar and POSCO resistance are examples of militant peasant movement initiated by the tribals which resembles the Tribal Identity Movement in Jharkhand. The worst scenario has been the protest of the tribals in Kalinganagar in which 14 tribals including few women were killed and despite such a gruesome massacre, the tribals of Kalinganagar renewed their agitation more vigorously for another one year. Similarly, Narayan Patna Movement in Koraput district is also a militant tribal struggle against the local triumvirate consisting of traders, money lenders and dominant caste landlords. R. K. Mohanty in his theoretical framework of Discrimination (D1), Deprivation (D2), Dispossession (D3), and Development Induced Displacement (D4) has analyzed the continuity of movements of the Tribals and the Marginalized from 1990 onwards to 2010. He has also stressed the basic point that land alienation and land acquisition have been the basic cause of tribal discontent.

Professor A. B. Ota has systematically analyzed the wide ranging Development-Displacement Project taken up in the State of Odisha since Independence and till recently. It includes dam/irrigation, industries, mining, urban infrastructure development, wildlife sanctuaries and others. As per his conservative estimates more than 10 lakh people have been displaced while over 50 lakh have been affected adversely. Empirical studies revealed that most of the people displaced by development projects have failed to retain their pre-project living conditions. Many of the displaced have actually slipped below the threshold of poverty. Displaced tribals who constitute more than 35 per cent of the total population of Odisha are the worst sufferers. The extent of displacement caused by development projects in Odisha include Thermal Power Projects, Industrial Projects, Mining Projects, Irrigation and Hydel Dam Projects and other development projects. The Rourkela Steel Plants set up in the fifties acquired 7917.84 hectares of land and displaced 2464 families from 30 villages in Sundargarh district. Of them 50.37 per cent were tribals and 30 per cent were

Scheduled Caste. Damanjodi in Koraput district displaced 52.44 per cent of tribals and 10.84 percent of Scheduled Castes. The total number of families affected by industries in Odisha is 10,704 which accounts for 11.47 per cent of the total displacement in the State. The number of people displaced by mines would be around 50,000. Various kinds of development projects in the State have together displaced 81,176 families and led to the acquisition of 6.22 lakh hectares of land between 1950 and 1993. Professor A. B. Ota quotes Cernea (1994) citing the *Impoverishment Risk Model* to suggest empirically that development induced displacement has resulted in landlessness, marginalization, joblessness, homelessness, food insecurity, loss of access to Common Property, Social Disarticulation and increased morbidity and mortality.

Felix Padel and Samrendra Das (2008) have characterized tribal killings and massacre as "*Cultural Genocide*" which indicates the extinction of people's communities and social structure which largely explains why they fight strenuously to resist displacement. *Displacement arises out of a clash of ideologies*. The divide and rule legacy of British Colonialism is bearing fruit now in internal colonialism, through privatization of resources by mining and construction companies in Odisha. In the State of Odisha hundreds of communities have ceased to exist and hundred more are threatened with extinction. Mining bauxite from Niyamgiri Hills is also assault on their religion. Cultural Genocide and the people's quality of life along with all the non-measurable factors is the essence of the tribal culture and community. According to Padel and Das, "Cultural Genocide" is the least recognized but perhaps most painful aspect of the drastic drop in the quality of life of people who are displaced. People's sense of sacredness in nature lies at the heart of traditional tribal religion. "Cultural Genocide" most clearly applies to tribal culture. *This section on Tribal Movement in Odisha essentially highlights Land Aquisition and Land alienation which lies at the core of the Tribal Struggle and Identity in Odisha and in this respect it is similar to the ingredients of cultural identity of the tribals of the Jharkhand.*

It is necessary to point out here some of the similarities and differences in the formation of Cultural Identity in Jharkhand and Odisha:

- The roots of the Jharkhand Identity Formation goes back to the beginning of the 19th century when property rights and *zamindari* system were introduced by the British and continued to perpetuate and forced on the tribals of Jharkhand.

- The communal ownership rights and land rights of the village chiefs were principally affected. It arouse the wrath of the tribals and had manifestation of militant tribal autonomous movement in the form of Kol Rebellion of 1833, Santhal Uprising of 1855 and Birsa Munda Rebellion of 1895-1900 which had ignited the tribal identity to the core.
- The impact of Militant Tribal Movement in Jharkhand shook the edifice of the British Rule in Eastern India and they were *ipso facto* had to promulgate Chhotanagpur Tenancy Act, 1908 and Santhal Pargana Act, 1947 which *institutionalized* the Adivasis Movement in Jharkhand and provided it a fundamental institutional shape which is also revered as the identity symbol of the Adivasis in Jharkhand.
- The history of tribal movement in Odisha also shows an uninterrupted continuity during the 19th century which forms the essence of the formation of tribal identity in Odisha.
- It was, however, the massive land acquisition during the globalization era in Odisha which shook the tribal conscience in different parts of the State, like Kalinganagar, Kashipur, Niyamgiri, POSCO etc., where the tribals and the marginalized people manifested their grassroots militancy which had its severe impact on the governance of Odisha.
- One could witness the strength of tribal identity in the Kalinganagar, Kashipur and POSCO struggle which has presented an enormous cultural strength to the Adivasis and marginalized people against any form of exploitation of land rights and forest rights.

References

Agnihotri, Anita (2005). "Resettlement and Rehabilitation in Suktel Irrigation Project", Prepared for the Government of Odisha, UNDP/DFID Resettlement Police Project (MIMEO).

Alloysius, G. (2003). "Ideology and Hegemony in Jharkhand Movement", In: R.D. Munda and S. Bosu Mullick (eds.), *Jharkhand Movement: A Historical Analysis*, Copenhagen: IWGIA and Birsa, Document No. 108, pp. 206-15.

Areeparampil Mathew (1992). "Forest Andolan in Singhbhum", In: S. Narayan (ed.), *Jharkhand Movement: Origin and Evolution*, New Delhi: Inter-India Publications, pp. 144-89.

Baboo, Bal Govind (1992). *Technology and Social Transformation: The Case of Hirakud Multipurpose Dam Project in Odisha*, New Delhi: Concept Publishing Company.

Basu, Sajal (1994). *Jharkhand Movement: Ethnicity and Culture of Silence*, Shimla: Indian Institute of Advanced Study.

Cernea, Michael M. (1997). *Poverty Risk From Population Displacement in Water Resources Development*, Harvard University, H.I.I.D., Cambridge, M.A., Harvard University.

Chomsky, Noam and Edward Herman (1988). *Manufacturing Consent*, New York: Pantheon.

Das, Arvind N., (1989) "Jharkhand's Roots: Tribal Identities in Indian History", published in P.C. Chatterji (ed.), *Self-Images, Identity and Nationality*, Shimla: Indian Institute of Advanced Study.

Dash, Suryashankar (2008). "Niyamgiri, The Mountain of Law", *Documentary Film*, Bhubaneswar : Samadrushti, TV.

Ekka, Alexious and M. Asif, (2002). "Development-Induced Displacement and Rehabilitation in Jharkhand: A database on its Extent and Nature (Mimeo)", New Delhi: Indian Social Institute.

Felix, Padel and Samrendra Das (2008). "Odisha's Highland Clearance: The Reality Gap" in R & R: *Social Change: Journal of Council for Social Development*, Volume 38. No. 6, December 2008.

Fernandes, W. and M. Asif. (1997). "Development-Induced Displacement in Odisha, 1951 to 1995: A database on its Extent and Nature (Mimeo)", New Delhi: Indian Social Institute.

Iyer, K. G. (1993). "Tribal and Forest Question in Bihar", *The Administrator*, 38 (April–June 1993), pp. 73-101.

Jha, J.C. (1987). *The Tribal Revolt in Chhotanagpur* (1831-32), Patna: Kashi Prasad Jayaswal Research Institute.

Justice Bhargava (2006). *Highlights of Justice S.N. Bhargava Committee (IPTT) on Kashipur.*

Kesri, Visveshwar Prasad (1992): *Jharkhand Ke Sadan*, Ranchi: Chhotanagpur Sanskritik Sangh.

MacDougall, John (2008). "Tribal Resistance", New Delhi: Critical Quest.

Mahapatra, L.K. (1999). *Resettlement, Impoverishment and Reconstruction in India: Development for the Deprived*, New Delhi: Vikas Publishing House Pvt. Ltd.

Mahapatra, L.K. (2005). "Tribal Rights and Entitlements in Land", Forest and Other Resources, Prepared for the Government of Odisha, UNDP/DFID Resettlement Policy Project (Mimeo).

Mahapatra, Richard (1999). "Confrontation" in *Down to Earth*, Delhi 15th April, 1999.

Maharaj, R.N. and K.G. Iyer (1982). "Agrarian Movement in Dhanbad", In: N. Sengupta (ed.), *Fourth World Dynamics: Jharkhand*, Delhi: Authors Guild Publications.

Mathur, Hari Mohan (2008). "A New Deal for Displaced People: Odisha's Involuntary Resettlement Policy", *Social Change*, December 2008, Vol. 38, No. 4, pp. 533-575.

Mathur, Hari Mohan (ed.) (2008). "India Social Development Report 2008", *Development and Displacement*, New Delhi: Oxford University Press/Council for Social Development.

Mohanty, R.K. (2016). "Sources of Deprivations and Styles of Mobilization: Contextualizing the Issues of Dispossessed Tribals in Contemporary Odisha" in S.N. Choudhary (ed.), *Social Movements in Tribal India*, pp. 144-201.

Mullick, Bosu, S. (2003). "The Jharkhand Movement: Indigenous People's Struggle for Autonomy in India", In: R.D. Munda and S. Basu Mullick (eds.), *op. cit.*

Mullick, Sanjay Basu, "Jungle Ki Jang", *Birsa*, 2006, Jharkhand: ID Publishing, Ranchi.

Munda, R.D. (1988). "The Jharkhand Movement: Retrospect and Prospect". *Social Change*, 18, 2:28-42.

Munda, R.D., and Keshri, B.P. (1992). "Recent Developments in the Jharkhand Movement". *India International Centre Quarterly*, 19, 1 and 2, 71-89.

Narayan, S. (1992). *Jharkhand Andolan, Udgam Ewam Utthan,* Delhi: Inter Alia Publications. Coordination.

Ota, A.B. (2005). "Impact of Land Acquisition in NHAI Projects", Prepared for the Government of Odisha, UNDP/DFID Resettlement Policy Project (Mimeo).

Ota, A.B. (2010). *Development Projects and Displaced Tribals: An Empirical Study*, SC and ST Research and Training Institute, Government of Odisha, Bhubaneswar.

Pandey, Balaji (2005). "Displacement From Coal Mining in Odisha", Prepared for the Government of Odisha, UNDP/DFID Resettlement Policy Project (Mimeo).

Panigrahi, N.P. (2007). "Tribal Leader Laxman Naik of Koraput and His Uprising", the *Quarterly Journal of The Mythic Society*, Vol. XC, VIII, No. I, January-March, p. 84.

Panigrahi, N.P. (2011). "Tribal Resistance Movement in Odisha: Some Reflections", *Odisha Review*, August 2011.

Prakash, Amit (2001). *Jharkhand: Politics of Development and Identity*, New Delhi: Orient Logman.

PUCL (1979): "Repression in Singhbhum, New Delhi: Report of the Delhi Unit of People's Union for Civil Liberties and Democratic Rights", Delhi in Bihar, March.

Roy, A.K. (1981). *Jharkhand or Lalkand*, Dhanbad: Markswadi Coordination.

Roy, A.K. (1982). "Jharkhand: Internal Colonialism", *Frontier*, April 17 and 24.

Sengupta, N. (ed.) (1982). *Fourth World Dynamics: Jharkhand,* Delhi: Authors Guild Publications.

Sengupta, Nirmal, (2003). "Jharkhand Movement and Tribal Identity", In: R.D. Munda and S. Basu Mullick (eds.), *op. cit.*, pp. 333-47.

Sengupta, Nirmal, (2004). "Development, Identity and Development of Identity", In: Rajiv Balakrishnan, *Jharkhand Matters—Essays on the*

Ethnicity Regionalism and Development, Konark Publishers, New Delhi, pp, 143-161.

Singh, K.S. (2003). "Tribal Identity Movement in Chhotanagpur", In: R.D. Munda and S. Basu Mullick (eds.), *op. cit.*, pp. 88-107.

Singh, K.S., (1982). "Tribal Identity Movement in Chhotanagpur", In: Singh, K.S. (ed.), *Tribal Movement in India*. Delhi: Manohar Publishers, pp. 1-30.

Singh, K.S., (2004). "Ecology, Ethnicity, Regionalism and State Formation: An Exploration of the Jharkhand Movement", In: Rajiv Balakrishnan, *Jharkhand Matters—Essays on the Ethnicity, Regionalism and Development*, New Delhi: Konark Publishers, pp. 116-142.

Tripathy, S.N. (2016). "An Analysis of Tribal Movement in Contemporary Odisha", In: S.N. Choudhary (ed.), *Social Movement's in Tribal India*, pp. 76-99.

3

Development Induced Displacement in Odisha and Jharkhand

3.1 Background

The Report of an Expert Group to Planning Commission, Government of India, New Delhi entitled *Development Challenges in Extremist Affected Areas* has observed that Displacement is a multi-dimensional trauma, with far reaching impact. As tribal areas are also rich in mineral resources, the mining projects initiated in Odisha, Jharkhand and Chhattisgarh include the very existence of tribal people. Protest action becomes an inevitable consequence of displacement, such as in Kalinganagar and in Kashipur people's movement against Utkal Alumina Rayagada district, Odisha. The consultations leading to consent of the tribal community/Gram Sabha as required under PESA are mandatory. A policy guiding the Rehabilitation and Resettlement (R&R) should ensure that none of the displaced be worse off after the project. Even though consultation before land acquisition and rehabilitation became a Constitutional mandate under Section 4(i) of PESA, there is no appreciation that consultation, without placing a clear picture about their future before the concerned people, has no meaning. The National Rehabilitation and Resettlement Policy (NRRP) 2007 seeks to involve the people, especially the tribal people, in the rehabilitation and resettlement. Internal displacement caused by irrigation/mining/industrial projects, resulting in landlessness and hunger, is a major cause of distress among the poor, especially the adivasis. Landlessness, extremes of poverty and social oppression can also be causes of displacement (pp. 15-17). The Ministry of Home Affairs (MHA)'s *Annual Report* for the year 2006-2007 mentions the spread of Naxal movement across 12 States of the Union. The profile of violence during the last few years has been given in Table 3.1.

Table 3.1: Profile of Naxal Violence in India

Head	*2003*	*2004*	*2005*	*2006*
Number of Incidents	1597	1533	1608	1509
Number of Civilians killed	410	466	524	521
Number of Policemen killed	105	100	153	157
Number of Naxalites killed	216	87	225	272

Source: The Ministry of Home Affairs (MHA), *Annual Report, 2006-07*, Government of India.

Ground reality in the Maoist conflict theatres may be different. While the level of violence orchestrated in 2010, so far the worst year of Maoist violence, resulting in the deaths of over 900 civilians and security forces would possibly remain unmatched, an upswing in violence, albeit marginal, was recorded in 2013 over the previous year. 270 civilians and security forces were killed in 2013 in various States compared to 250 deaths in 2012. In spite of the killing of 151 Maoist cadres in 2013, the outfit's level of violence did not show much signs of abatement. States like Chhattisgarh, Jharkhand, Bihar and Odisha remained affected by significant amount of extremist mobilization as well as violence.

The NSCN-IM purchased arms from a Chinese company intended for the Maoists. ULFA Chief Paresh Baruah has congratulated the Maoists for their successful ambushes in Chhattisgarh and sent condolence messages following the killing of Maoists in encounters.

However, following two Maoist attacks within a fortnight in Chhattisgarh that killed 20 security force personnel in February and March 2014 in Dantewada and Sukma districts, the narrative shifted and the potency of the extremists was reconfirmed. The Maoists, who appeared to have previously weakened, have resurfaced as a real threat to the 2014 Lok Sabha elections in certain States.

The 1 December, 2014 killing of 14 Central Reserve Police Force (CRPF) personnel in Chhattisgarh's Sukma district by the Communist Party of India-Maoist (CPI–Maoist) should invariably go down as one of the country's worst security force operations in recent times. In terms of the killing of trained personnel, looting of their weapons, and the follow up response of a well established security establishment in the State, the attack surpasses even the far bigger extremist attacks of the past in which the force had lost far larger number of personnel. The incident further gives rise to the question whether a victory over the Maoists is at all possible under a CRPF–State Police Force combination formula?

The Report of the Planning Commission further says that there has been an effective implementation of protective legislation. The State's response to continued unrest and social dissension in areas predominated by Scheduled Castes and Tribes was to formulate protective laws and a major policy decision. These Acts are the Provisions of the Panchayats (Extension to the Scheduled Areas) Act, 1996, the National Rural Employment Guarantee Act, 2005, the Scheduled Tribes and Other Traditional Forest Dwellers (Recognition of Forest Rights) Act, 2006, and the National Rehabilitation and Resettlement Policy, 2007.

Walter Fernandes (2008) has presented a Sixty Years of Development-induced Displacement scenario in India. He mentions that in the 1980s the struggle against the Koel Karo Dam in Jharkhand and the Hirakud in Odisha attracted wide public attention in India. He examines the number of displaced persons in different States in India during 1951 to 1995 and mentions that there is an absence of official data base and the researchers carried out their own studies on development induced displacement and the deprivation for the period 1951 to 1995 in Odisha (Fernandes and Asif, 1997) and Jharkhand (Ekka and Asif, 2000). According to him between 1951 to 1995 the total number of displaced persons in Jharkhand was 15.48 lakh and in Odisha it was 14.66 lakh. The displacement were mostly from the mines, dams, industries, defence establishment and environment related developmental projects. Dr. Walter Fernandes provides social group-wise figures of displaced persons indicating that in Jharkhand the total number of displaced persons was 15.48 lakh of which 40 per cent were tribals and 13.75 per cent were dalits. On the other hand, in Odisha out of 14.66 lakh displaced persons during this period, 40.38 per cent were tribals and 11.64 per cent were dalits indicating a very high percentage of tribals and dalits involved in displacement. The extent of private land acquired in Jharkhand was 55.11 per cent and common land acquired was 22.56 per cent; on the other hand in Odisha the private land acquired was 41.81 per cent and the common land acquired was 27.99 per cent. The data of Dr. Walter Fernandes indicate that in both the States of Odisha and Jharkhand the percentage of tribals and dalits displaced were equally high.

Felix Padel and Samarendra Das (2008) has characterized the real impact of Development Induced Displacement as "Cultural Genocide". According to them Cultural Genocide is the least recognized but perhaps most painful aspect of the drastic drop in the quality of life of people who are displaced (Padel and Das, 2008). They have also examined the social impact of a number of current industrial projects particularly in Odisha and its adverse effect. In Lanjigarh (West Odisha), Vedanta's new 'Greenfield' alumina refinery has displaced several tribal villages, and threatens to displace more (Padel and Das, 2004). If the company starts mining bauxite from the top of Niyamgiri, this will also seriously impinge on the Dongria Kond tribe who live throughout this mountain range. Niyam Dongar is a mountain sacred to the Dongria and other Konds, who are fiercely opposing its acquisition by Vedanta. A recent detailed report by World Bank Anthropologist Robert Goodland (2007) catalogues numerous human rights violations against the regions' adivasis; their non-violent protests have been purely in defence of their land and culture against a real invasion of their area by the company, backed-up by excessive use of force by police, including the notorious Maikanch firing that killed three in December 2000.

Plans for a steel plant by POSCO (Pohang Steel Company of South Korea) in Jagatsinshpur district would again displace numerous non-tribal villages from a fertile area of coastal Odisha. Just as the Lanjigarh and Kashipur projects have been forced through with heavy-handed police intimidation, Jagatsinghpur is the scene of great tension between protesting villagers and police platoons. The same is true of Kalinganagar, where Tata is trying to construct another huge steel plant on tribal land in the face of determined resistance by the villagers who cultivate this land. This is where, on 2 January, 2006 attempts to force construction of Tata's plant were the cause of people's protest that left a constable and 14 tribals dead, followed by a high profile blockade of the main highway to North Odisha by the Bisthapan Birodhi Janmanch (People's Platform Against Displacement). Though, they agreed to dismantle this in March 2007, villagers still say they would die rather than leave their land. Several companies have already built steel plants at Kalinganagar, and more are planned. The company Maharashtra Seamless Steel caused similar violence through a police lathi-charge when it tried to start construction in June 2005, after which the company withdrew. The deaths at Maikanch and Kalinganagar are taken as symbolic of a collective death. According to Felix Padel *physical genocide means the extermination of all members of a tribe often accompany cultural genocide, i.e. the killing of cultures.* People's identity is also radically altered. Women's position is often particularly badly affected. Religious life is also transformed. *Cultural genocide applies most clearly to tribal cultures which differ markedly from mainstream orientation.* The deaths in Maikanch and Kalinganagar are taken as symbolic of a collective death.

Vedanta plans to mine bauxite. This is an example of project that may not cause direct displacement, *but strikes at the heart of a cultural heritage* that is also the heart of one of Odisha best preserved forests areas. The reason is the Dongria Konds and their religion which centres on Niyam Raja, Lord of the Law, whose abode is the mountain summit. The tribes maintain a taboo on cutting trees up there in Niyam Raja's name, out of a recognition that the natural vegetation conserves the fertility of their land through an abundance of streams. *So mining bauxite from Niyamgiri and other Khondalite mountains in South Odisha is bound to cause an erosion of Kond spiritual values as well as an erosion of Odisha natural environment and fertility* (Das, 2008).

Prof. A.B. Ota (2010) has analyzed the development-displacement scenario in the State of Odisha since independence up to the present. According to him the developmental projects undertaken include dam/irrigation, industries mining urban infrastructure development and widelife sanctuary projects. *As per conservative estimates more than 10 lakh people have been displaced and over 50 lakh have been adversely affected in various ways. Most of the people displaced by developmental project have failed to retain their pre-project living conditions in the post-project period. Displaced tribals constitute more than 35 per cent of the total displaced population in Odisha and they are the worst sufferers.* During the 1970s several multi-purpose projects were established which are predominantly inhabited by tribals and other marginalized sections. These large projects left a trail of unintended adverse effect at the local level. The extent of displacement caused by the developmental projects in Odisha are due to thermal power projects, industrial project, mining projects, irrigation and hydal dam power projects and other development projects. Immediately after Independence the Rourkela Steel Plant in the 1950s acquired 7,917.84 hectares of land and displaced 2464 families from 30 villages in Sundargarh district (Roy-Burman, 1966). The magnitude of displacement due to various developmental projects in Odisha during 1950-1993 involved 1,446 villages covering 81,176 families comprising 6.22 lakh hactares. The cumulative effect of all these has been impoverishment through landlessness, joblessness, homelessness, marginalization, food insecurity, loss of common property, increased morbidity and destruction of social fabric and local economy.

3.2 Profile of Koraput District

The population of Koraput district was 13.80 lakh during 2011. Most of the towns are very small and the important ones are Koraput, Sunebera, Damanjodi and Jeypore. The ST population as per 2011 Census was 6.98 lakh and the SC population was 1.79 lakh. The district of Koraput had the Zamindars of Jeypore and Kashipur Zamindars. The district has a number of mountain and hill ranges; the important rivers are Indrawati, Kolab and Machkund. In 1768, the district was occupied by the British. The district also witnessed freedom movement by the tribals against the British Authority. The important Scheduled Tribe communities in the district are Gadaba Omantya, Soura, Bhumia and Bhotadas.

The Koraput district came into existence on 1st April, 1936, but it was further divided into four districts, namely—Koraput, Rayagada, Malkangiri and Nevrangpur w.e.f. 2nd January, 1992. The district of Koraput is adequately endowed with significant mineral deposit like bauxite, black granite, limestone, dolomite, mica etc. The Machkund river has been dammed at Jalaput to form the Jalaput reservoir. Machkund Hydro Electric Project with a joint scheme of Government of Odisha and Andhra Pradesh has full right to the use of 50 per cent of the ultimate power generated by the project. Upper Kola Hydro Electro Project was taken up in 1976 providing irrigation facilities to 48,985 hectare by the lift canal irrigation and supplying drinking water to Damanjori, Koraput, Sunabeda and Jeypore Town. Middle Kolab Small Hydro Electric Project has installed capacity of 25 mega wt and the entire power generated from the project is sold to West Bengal. The refinery unit of NALCO at Damanjori has coal operated thermal power plant with installed capacity of 74 MW.

The important mines of Koraput district are Panchpatmale bauxite mines, of MS National Aluminium and Company Limited, Mali Porbat Bauxite Mines of MS Hindal Limited, Ampavally Lime Stone Mines of M.S. Odisha Minerals Limited and NALCO Aluminium Company Limited established on 7th January, 1981. The Hindustan Aeronautics Limited, Sunabeda was established during March 1964 for manufacturing MIG 21. Toshali Cement Private Limited started its operation in the year 2004. The Bilt Graphic Paper Products Limited Jeypore was commissioned in the year 1984.

There have been a number of large scale industries in Koraput District like Hindustan Aeronautics Limited, Sunabeda, NALCO, Damanjodi, BGPPL Unit, Sewa, OHPC, Bariniput, Machkund Hydro

Electro Project, Toshali Cement Ltd., Ampavali. The Damanjodi unit comprising Refinery Complex and Mining at Panachapattamali Hill employs 5350 regular and contractual Executives and workers. The labourers of the Mining Division and the Refinery Unit have got registered trade unions to look into the interest of workers. Currently the plant has got 15 numbers of registered trade unions. The company has developed integrated township for its employees along with amenities.

The Hindustan Aeronautics Limited has around 3,000 executives, non-executives and contract labour employed in the Engine Division and SU-30 division of Hindustan Aeronautics Limited. The company has three Registered Trade Unions. The company provides all statutory benefits to its employees.

The first major displacement occurred in the district after it was envisaged to construct Machkund Hydel Dam. The displacement began in the late 1940s. Given the scarcity of record those days, collection of exact data is not possible relating to actual displacement. According to sources, 2,938 families were displaced by the project, out of which almost half were from tribal community. Most of them were rehabilitated to Dandakaranya area of Malkangiri.

The Upper Kolab Multipurpose Project was constructed to harness the water potential of River Kolab. Displacement and rehabilitation started during 1970s. From 53 fully displaced villages, 3,318 families were identified for rehabilitation. Out of those family, 2,792 families opted for cash based rehabilitation and rest 526 families were rehabilitated on land basis. Those who opted for land based rehabilitation were each provided with 2.5 acre of land and a house.

The NALCO operation in Damanjodi and Panchapattamali Hills has affected 600 families. More than 10,000 acre of land was acquired for mines, refinery unit and township. During the initial stage of establishment of projects of the Company at Koraput District, total 600 families were identified as the Land Displaced Persons (LDPs) and all have been provided with houses in two specifically constructed rehabilitation colonies having all infrastructural facilities. One able bodied man from 599 LDP families have been provided with regular employment in the Company. Besides, recently 235 families have been identified as Substantially Land Affected Persons (SAPs), i.e. whose one-third or more of their total landholding has been acquired for the Company and based on their nomination, rehabilitation benefit will also be provided to one nominee each from these identified families.

The Engine Division of HAL at Sunabeda initially gave regular employment to 138 Land Displaced Persons as per the recommendation of State Administration. Additionally, it provided those displaced facilities like health free medical treatment in HAL hospital, Sunabeda, vocational training in mushroom cultivation, beauty parlours, making of *agarbati*, candle, phenyl, soft toys and pickle making, tailoring with free distribution of sewing machines, mobile repairing, driving etc.

The year of land acquisition for NALCO (M&R Damanjodi) was 1981-83. The extent of private land acquired for NALCO Project at Damanjodi was 4,534.95 acre and 3,192.40 acre of Government land was alienated for this project. The total number of villages affected were 25 of which 13 were from Koraput Tehsil, 5 villages were from Semiliguda Tehsil, 2 villages from Laxmipur Tehsil and 5 villages were from Dasmanthpur Tehsil. The number of displaced families were 600. The area of lands acquired from the Scheduled Caste was 299.08 acre, from Scheduled Tribes 2,214.81 acre and from other communities 2,021.06 acre were acquired. Out of 600 displaced families, 598 nominee of displaced persons have been provided employment in NALCO and rehabilitation measures have also been undertaken for them. Houses have been provided to all displaced families. 12 persons among Scheduled Tribes have been claiming employment in NALCO, but the NALCO officials consider it as non-tenable. In Damanjodi NALCO Scheduled Tribes affected persons (PAPs) who have lost more than 1/3rd of their agriculture land/house site have not yet been provided rehabilitation measures. The authorities are maintaining that it is difficult to obtain the figures of actual PAPs after lapse of more than 25 years. It was decided by the NALCO authorities to provide the rehabilitation for widows of diseased LDP employees at the rate of Rs. 5,000 each but the employees are demanding regular employment to widows/ nominees of LDP employees. The NALCO industry has also acquired land at Angul District, where 1,528 persons have lost their land out of which 1,340 persons have been rehabilitated and they have received better deals than those displaced at Damanjodi. The Labour Union of the displaced persons of Damanjodi have been demanding the same rehabilitation benefits as their counterparts in Angul district. The District Collector of Koraput also identified 416 families of land losers and recommended for the rehabilitation to NALCO Management. However, the NALCO authorities decided to provide rehabilitation benefits to only 235 land losers out of 416.

Land Acquisition for MS Aditya Aluminium Project in Koraput District

Lands were acquired for Aditya Aluminium Project in Koraput district from five villages by IDCO during the years 2005-2008 to the extent of 439.45 acre. Out of the total land acquired from 106 land owners belong to Scheduled Tribe, 21 to Scheduled Castes and rest to other Castes. The area of land acquired from Scheduled Tribe land owners was 400.67 acre, 37 acre from Scheduled Castes family and 1.69 acre from others. The lands acquired were primarily agriculture land. Out of the total number of affected 306 families most of them belong to Scheduled Tribes. The total amount of compensation paid by IDCO was Rs. 15.76 crore.

Land Acquisition for HAL Sunabeda in Koraput District

The total area of private land acquired by IDCO for HAL Sunabeda was 2,315.72 acre and government land alienated was 379.45 acre. The lands were acquired from five villages, namely—Kaki Gaon, Chikapar, Thalaput, Kodigaon and Chakarliput. The number of persons affected and displaced due to acquisition of land were 397 out of which majority of them were Scheduled Tribes. Number of persons not provided employment yet by HAL Sunebeda is 159. The compensation has been provided for the affected families which includes hospital, medical camps, free concessional education to the children of affected villages, provision of drinking water and facilities for sports for the youth. *The unused private land by the company is 551.58 acre and as per Provisions of the Land Acquisition Act, its resumption can be initiated by the government. There is also 379.45 acre of Government Land which is unused and it can also be resumed by the Government.*

Land Acquired for Aero Engine Project

The total land acquired for Aero Engine Project, HAL includes 2,315.72 acre of private land, 805.43 acre of government land; it also includes 5,354.97 acre of private land under the control of Revenue Department and Government Land 422.94 acre; *thus the total land allotted inclusive of private and government land is 8,476.12 acre*. The lands have been acquired from village Kaki (2416.62 acre), Chikapar, (1,474.38 acre), Chakarliput (318.22 acre), Thalaput (993.44 acre), Kodigaon (854.21 acre), Chulapari (1,215.91), Rajpallama (334.94 acre), Charanguli (141.55 acre), Bodengam (627.75 acre), Kumriput

(100.907 acre), Pitaguda (97.55 acre) and Charagaon (174.93 acre); *The vacant site of the acquired land as on date is 1,499.54 acre (28 % as reported by Tehsildar, Semiguda).*

Land Acquired by Machkund Hydro Electrical Project

The land for Machkund Hydro Power Project was acquired between 1947 to 1959 in two phases—the first phase was during 1947-1950 and the second phase during 1952-1959. The total land acquired is 23,155 acre from 274 villages. As per the information submitted by the authorities of the project, the compensation to the displaced persons have been paid as per their entitlement according to the prevailing rate at that time. The displaced persons have been rehabilitated in 13 villages. The MHE (J) scheme is a joint hydro electric generation project owned by Government of Andhra Pradesh and Government of Odisha in the ratio of 70 : 30 respectively. An amount of Rs. 85.50 lakh has been received from Andhra Pradesh Power Generation Corporation Limited towards peripheral development. The amount has been spent by the District Administration towards College Building at Lakshmipur, CC Road in different villages, protection wall, bridge and culvert, *mandap* and community centres. The number of displaced persons rehabilitated include 3318 of which 1483 are Scheduled Tribes 417 are Scheduled Castes and 1364 belong to other Castes. The land based resettlement has been undertaken for 526 displaced persons of which 199 are Scheduled Tribes, 30 are Scheduled Castes and 297 belong to other Castes. The land based resettlement and area allotted for them is 1,674.99 acre.

HAL Koraput Division has adopted 14 surrounding villages for the socio-economic development in line with companies CSR and SD policy. The total families in these 14 villages are 2,089 and total population of 7,912 under the CSR activity. The company has undertaken health care, education, infrastructure, development, sports, skill development and training activities.

The Government of Odisha in Resolution No. 5503 dated 31-3-2000 of the Department of Forest and Environment had entrusted Gram Panchayat the authority to regulate, purchase, procure and trade 69 Minor Forest Produce. The policy resolution demands that the persons purchasing MFPs from the primary collectors or traders will need to register with the Gram Panchayats on payment of fee.

Large Industries: The Koraput district has 4 large industries as shown in Table 3.2.

Table 3.2: Employment generated by Large Scale Industries in Koraput District

Name of the Industry	*Location*	*Products*	*Investment (Rs. in crores)*	*Employ-ment (No.)*
HAL, Sunabeda	Sunabeda	Aero Engine	4033.00	3206
NALCO Damanjodi	Damanjodi	Aluminium	2095.23	3985
Ballarpur Industries	Jeypore	Paper	315.92	942
Snehadhara Industries	Ampavalli	Portland Cement	17.57	250
Total			**6,461.72**	**8383**

Source: Potential Linked Credit Plan: 2012-13.

These industries have been responsible for enhancing the per capita income of the district and employment opportunities in the State as well as in the country.

3.3 Land Acquisition in Sundargarh District (Odisha)

The total population of Sundargarh in its 17 blocks is 14.67 lakh. The percentage of Scheduled Tribes population in the district is 61.25 per cent and SC constitute 11.4 per cent while others comprise 27.31 per cent. There are 17 Panchayats in Sundargarh District and in 14 Panchayat, Scheduled Tribes constitute more than 50 per cent.

The mandatory powers of PESA are mentioned below:

- Management of community resources,
- Approve all plans/projects,
- Identification of beneficiaries, and
- Issue certificate of utilization of funds.

The discretionary powers of PESA are the following:

- Prior mandatory recommendation for acquisition of land and rehabilitation and reconstruction of scheduled areas.
- Prior mandatory recommendation for grant of prospective licence or lease for mining minor minerals.
- Prior mandatory recommendation for grant of concession for exploitation of minor minerals by auction.
- Planning and management of minor water bodies.
- Prior mandatory recommendation for acquisition of land and rehabilitation and reconstruction in scheduled areas.

- Prior mandatory recommendations for grant of prospective licence or lease for mining minor minerals.
- Prior mandatory recommendation for grant of concession for exploitation of minor minerals by auction.
- Planning and management of minor water bodies.

While mining in the area causes the great hardship, it is also their source of sustenance. Iron Ore Mining in Kandodhar has existed since 1946-47; mining in Kandodhar began in 1940s with the Odisha Mining Corporation, but since then there is influx of private companies as well. There is influx of private companies in mining since 1980s; of a total of 633 metallic mines in the country, 76 per cent are owned by the private sector and only 28 per cent by the public sector. Of three major mines two are private companies (named Arion and Rungta and one of them is owned by the Odisha Mining Corporation in Barsuan. Iron ore and Manganese and Lime Stone are the main minerals that are found in the Sundarnagar side of the Kandodhar while coal is found in the Keonjhar side. In December 2006 the Odisha Government recommended granting of prospecting license to POSCO for an area of about 6,200 hectares but it was challenged by Odisha High Court by Kudremakh Iron Company. There have been some conflicts in the year 2014. Some of the villagers had complaint that one of the mining companies tried to bribe the villagers to allow them to continue minor operations, but the community refused. The Paudibhuyam community is resisting the development of extractive industries in their area. The Lohanipoda Block has several mining affecting villages which is located in Bhutude Panchayat.

3.4 Land Acquisition in Sundargarh District

Most of Odisha's first wave of industrial projects have been notorious for their lack of adequate R&R, such as the Rourkela Steel Plant, the Hirakud, Upper Kolab and Indravati dam projects, and also NALCO in Koraput, sometimes cited as a model of good practice.

So, the present situation in Odisha involves several high profile struggles of people opposing displacement in Odisha. Three companies in particular face protracted opposition, in a series of projects some of which have already caused displacement or are currently causing agitation, while others, e.g. iron ore mines have yet to be finalized. Tata at Kalinganagar and Gopalpur (steel plants), Naraj (thermal power plant near Cuttack), Dhamra (port) and North Odisha (iron ore mines), and Vedanta at Lanjigarh (alumina refinery), Niyamgiri (planned bauxite mine), Jharsaguda district (smelter and giant power plant), near Puri (university-*cum*-business centre), and Gandhamardan (another bauxite deposit) have also been facing resistance from people.

In Hemgir Block of Sundargarh District land was acquired for Dulingakur Mines project (NTPC Limited) and Manoharpur Coal Block (OPGC Limited). For the NTPC Limited the total land acquired was 177.57 acre private land and 1.570 acre government land. Another 159.96 acre of government land is yet to be given to the NTPC. In the Manoharpur Coal Block for OPGC Limited the private land acquired is 869.90 acre and the area of government land handed over to the industry by IDCO is 592.60 acre.

Land has also been acquired by Land Acquisition Officer, Sundargarh Sadar for Ultra Mega Power Project Sundargarh, four-laning of Sambalpur Road and also for widening of Bolinga-Toparia Road. *The area acquired for 4000 Ultra Mega Power Project Sundargarh is 2,731.04 acre of Private Land and 405.05 acres Government Land.* Similarly, for the four laning of Sambalpur Road 193.74 acre of private land and 145.80 acre of government land have been acquired; for widening of Balinga Toparia Road 21.39 acre of private land have been acquired.

In Sundargarh Sub-Division, maximum lands have been acquired for NTPC Darlipali consisting of 1306.78 acre of private land and 348.37 acre of Government land. Besides this 110.55 acre of private land and 63.60 acre of Government land have been acquired for South Eastern Railway Jharsuguda Subrega Railway Line and another 36.40 acre is being acquired for South-East Railway Jharsuguda Sardega line. Apart from this for NH 215 83.42 hectares of private land 168.49 hectare of Government land is also being allotted. Land is also being acquired by Special Land Acquisition officer, UMPP Sundargarh for 4000 MW UMPP covering private land 2731.04 acre and for the power project.

Acquisition of Land by MCL in Sundargarh District

One of the major Land Acquisition project in Sundargarh district which was acquired by MCL *vide* Notification U/S 9 (1) of the CBA (A&D) Act, 1957, on 10-07-1989 and 29-10-1990, the Central Government Project acquired 8030.053 Ha (19,842.261 acre) of land in village Gopalpur, Sardega, Tikilipara, Balinga, Bankibahal, Garjanbahal, Siarmal, Kulda, Karlikachhar, Bangurkela, Tumulia, Jhupurunga,

Ratansara, Kiripisira and Lalma RF (14 villages and 1 Reserved Forest) in the district of Sundargarh, Odisha. It remained a major source of discontent with the displaced families.

Subsequently *vide* notification under section 11(1) of the CBA (A&D) Act on 13-9-1990 and 30-3-1993, the above land was vested with the MCL for Baundhara and Garjanbahal Area. From the date of 11(1), all the lands of village Gopalpur and 13 other villages with Lalma RF became the property of MCL and the land owners of those villages lost their legal rights over the acquired land. Though, these lands were acquired and vested with MCL, the land losers except the village, Gopalpur (Part), Sardega, Tikilipara (Part), Balinga and Bankibahal were never paid any compensation for their lands. The land losers were paid compensation where the projects were approved and became operative.

After waiting for a number of years, one Sri Mathias Oram and 32 others of village Gopalpur filed a writ petition bearing No. W.P. © No. 11463 of 2003 before the Odisha High Court for grant of compensation and other benefits in lieu of their acquired lands. The Odisha High Court after hearing the Counsel for those petitioners, *passed order dated 13-11-2006* directing the MCL to pay compensation and other benefits to the petitioners in accordance with law as expeditiously as possible preferably within a period of six months from the date of receipt of order.

Challenging the order of the Hon'ble High Court, the MCL filed SLP © *vide* No. 6933 of 2007 before the Hon'ble Supreme Court of India. The Solicitor General of India assisting the Court in this matter in consultation with Ministry of Coal placed a scheme before the court to facilitate payment of compensation to all the land losers of 15 villages.

The scheme is to set up a Commission for the purpose:

(a) A former judge of the High Court of Odisha (Chairman).
(b) An Officer equivalent to the rank of Secretary to the GoI (Member).
(c) An Officer to be nominated by Chairman, Coal India Limited (Member).

The Claims Commission has carried out necessary exercise and submitted its report on the compensation payable and the persons to whom it should be paid, within a period of six months. Hon'ble Supreme Court approved the scheme *and the Claims Commission was formed by the court in July 2010.* The Claims Commission recommended that the compensatory value of the acquired land of village Gopalpur be assessed on the average market rate as indicated below:

Table 3.3: Average Market Rate of MCL Land Acquisition in Gopalpur

Nature of Land	*Approximate value of the land per acre*
Gharabari	Rs. 12 Lakh
Mal and Goda	Rs. 8.5 Lakh
Behal and Berna	Rs. 10 Lakh
Others categories	Rs. 3.5 Lakh

Source: Claims Commission Report.

The largest land acquisition in Sundargarh district is for Basundra Gajan Bahal Area of MCL in which land is being acquired from the land owners of 14 villages as indicated below:

Table 3.4: Village-wise Land Acquired for MCL in Sundargarh District (Odisha)

Sl. No.	*Name of the Villages*	*No. of Land Owners*	*Remarks*
1.	Sardega	99	The rehabilitation package includes a plot of 10 decimals or Rs. 3 lakh house building assistance, of Rs. 2.55 lakh maintenance allowance for 12 months @ Rs. 3,400 per month, assistance for temporary shed Rs. 17,000 and transportation allowance of Rs. 3,400. Besides this, the rate per acre ranges from Rs. 11,779 per acre to 43,582 per acre varying on kisam of land. The claim commission increased the land compensation from Rs. 8.50 lakh per acre to Rs. 12 lakh per acre. Compensation has already been assessed by claims Commission.
2.	Gopalpur	42	
3.	Tikilipara	142	
4.	Bolinga	199	
5.	Bankibahal	55	
6.	Gopalpur	545	
7.	Tikilipara (P)	167	
8.	Garjanbahal	202	
9.	Kuida	49	
10.	Karlikachhar	69	
11.	Sarmal	92	
12.	Bangarkela	88	
13.	Jhupiranga	501	
14.	Kiripsira	216	

Note: The rates for different *kisam* of private land was assessed as follows for the purpose of land acquisition for KOCP and Basundhara.

Source: Claims Commission Report.

Table 3.5: Market Rate of Different Assets fixed by MCLs Sundargarh

Sl. No.	*Name of the Villages*	*Rate of different kisam of land*
1.	Sardega and Gopalpur (P) (Two Villages)	Goda–11,779.00
		Masa–15,313.00
		Besa–21,202.00
		Basa–24,736.00
		G.B.–43,592.00

(*Contd.*)

Sl. No.	*Name of the Villages*	*Rate of different kisam of land*
2.	Tiklipara (P), Balinga and Bankibahal (Three Villages)	Goda–15,227.00 Masa–19,795.00 Besa–27,409.00 Basa–31,977.00 G.B.–36,957.00
3.	Gopalpur, Tikilipara (P), Garjanbahal, Kuida, Karlikachhar, Siarmal, Bangurkela, Jhupurange, Kiripsira, Tumulia and Ratansara (Eleven Villages)	Goda–8.50 lakh Masa–8.50 lakh Besa–10 lakh Basa–10 lakh G.B.–12 lakh Others 3.5 lakh

Source: Claims Commission Report.

Table 3.6: Status of Land Acquisition of B.G. Area of MCL in Sundargarh District (ib block–viii under B.G. Area)

		Notified Land in Acre				
Sl. No.	*Villages*	*Forest*	*GNF*	*Tenancy*	*Total*	*Total Acquired*
1.	Sardega	328.77	240.51	290.90	860.18	Full
2.	Gopalpur (P)	382.41	1549.84	1127.97	3060.22	Part
3.	Ratansara	472.25	370.33	1007.17	1849.75	Full
4.	Jhupurunga	133.97	344.71	1384.10	1862.78	Full
	Sub Total	**1317.40**	**2505.39**	**3810.14**	**7632.93**	**3089.00 Ha**

Source: Claims Commission Report.

Table 3.7: Lands Acquired and Leased Out to MCL—IB Block–VIII under B.G. Area

		Notified Land in Acre				
Sl. No.	*Villages*	*Forest*	*GNF*	*Tenancy*	*Total*	*Total Acquired*
(1)	(2)	(3)	(4)	(5)	(6)	(7)
1.	Tiklipara	1056.87	204.83	482.15	1343.85	Full
2.	Siarmal	423.45	198.02	240.87	862.34	Full
3.	Gopalpur (P)	—	125.59	15.08	140.67	Full
4.	Tumulia	312.58	436.62	1632.12	2381.32	Full
5.	Karlikachar	102.41	90.65	318.88	511.94	Full
6.	Kulda	149.01	162.15	231.66	542.82	Full
7.	Bankibahal	435.93	159.19	241.21	836.33	Full

(Contd.)

(1)	(2)	(3)	(4)	(5)	(6)	(7)
8. Balinga	236.18	451.25	547.21	1234.64	Full	
9. Garjanbahal	135.92	255.55	406.88	798.35	Full	
10. Bangurkela	279.29	246.01	530.66	1055.96	Full	
11. Kiripsira	505.91	395.73	779.47	1681.11	Full	
12. Lalma RF	420	0	0	420	Full	
Sub-Total	**4057.55**	**2725.59**	**5426.19**	**12209.33**		
TOTAL IB BLOCK–VII and XI IN AC	**5374.95**	**5230.98**	**9236.33**	**19842.26**		
TOTAL IB BLOCK–VII and XI IN HA	**2175.212**	**2116.949**	**3737.892**	**8030.053**		

Source: Claims Commission Report.

Table 3.8: Summary of Employment and Resettlement under B.G. Area in MCL (as on 31-3-2015)

Sl. No.	*Project Head*	*Villages*	*PAF's Category (A to E)*	*Eligible for Employ-ment*	*Employ-ment Provided*	*Eligible for Resettle-ment*	*Plot Provided and shifted*	*Remarks*
1.	KOCP	Banki Bahal	153	87	72	118	67	Balance under Process
		Balinga	289	187	187	272	NA	Balance under Process
2.	BWOCP	Gopalpur	58	31	29	39	—	Balance under Process
		Sardega	240	133	127	159	124	Balance under Process
3.	BEOCP	Tiklipura	258	186	179	132	132	Balance under Process
		Grand Total	**998**	**624**	**594**	**720**	**323**	

Note: An alternative to employment is also cash compensation and some of the workers are opting for this alternative. Similarly, for resettlement also there is provision of cash compensation instead of opting for plot.

Source: Claims Commission Report.

Summary of the Report of the Claims Commission of Gopalpur

1. Survey of all the landholdings and measurement of all houses and structures was done by five survey teams and 715 case records for the land holders were prepared. The family genealogy of all land holders were prepared in presence of witnesses and age and marital status of each family member was prepared.

2. For each landholding, person in possession and nature of possession were ascertained.

3. Except Ac. 73.19 decimal of land for which compensation has already been paid by the MCL, all other lands of Gopalpur were found to be in possession of the land holders. These land holders were found residing in their respective houses and cultivating their lands, enjoying the usufructs thereof.

4. Though the MCL took plea in the writ petition before the Odisha High Court and in S.L.P © No. 6933 of 2007 before the Apex Court that they do not want all the acquired lands of village Gopalpur, during survey and objection hearing, they expressed that they want all the acquired lands and do not want denotification of any land. In that situation, there was no scope to recommend any denotification of any part of the acquired land.

5. After publication of the compensation offer made by the MCL, 650 Numbers of objections were filed by the land holders demanding higher monetary compensation and better resettlement and employment packages.

6. During policy hearing and individual objection hearing, the land holders demanded the implementation of the Odisha Rehabilitation and Resettlement Policy, 2006 and not the Rehabilitation and Resettlement Policy, 1998 which was followed by MCL in awarding the compensation to the land holders. They demanded that the cut-off date to be September, 2010.

7. Taking note of abnormal delay of 24/25 years and the sharp rise in the price of the land in the area as well as the diminishing value of money, it is recommended that *the cut-off date be taken as September 2010* when the Claims Commission published the notice in Gopalpur for survey of the lands and properties of the landholders and that date be hypothetically taken as date of acquisition notification.

8. It is recommended that the monetary compensation for the lands, houses and properties of the landholders be assessed on the market value prevalent in 2010 in the relevant area:

(a) The recommended market value of the land after necessary scrutiny is as follows:

Table 3.9: Market Value of Gopalpur Land fixed by Claims Commission

Nature of Land	*Approximate value of the land per acre*
Gharabari	Rs. 12 Lakh
Mal and Goda	Rs. 8.5 Lakh
Bahal and Berna	Rs. 10 Lakh
Others categories	Rs. 3.5 Lakh

Source: Claim Commission Report.

(b) The recommended plinth area value of structures are as follows (this includes the finished structure with all E.I. and P.H. fittings):

Table 3.10: Market Value of Rates fixed for other Assets

1.	*Pucca* building with RCC column structure and RCC Roof	Rs. 1000 per sq. ft.
2.	*Pucca* building with wall support structures and RCC Roof	Rs. 900 per sq. ft.
3.	*Pucca* house with asbestos/G.I. Sheet roof	Rs. 700 per sq. ft.
4.	Brick walls with nuria tile roof houses	Rs. 600 per sq. ft.
5.	Other type of residential, commercial houses with thatched roof.	Rs. 400 per sq. ft.
6.	*Pucca* portico, garage etc.	Rs. 500 per sq. ft.
7.	*Pucca* compound wall 10 thick and 5ft high	Rs. 400 per running ft.

Source: Claims Commission Report.

- For marble floor and granite floor further Rs. 79 and Rs. 190 per square feet respectively to be added.
- For industrial structures additional 15 per cent rate be added.
- The recommended flat rate for ancillary structures are as follows:

Septic tank (usable by 10 persons)	Rs. 10,000
Tulasi Choura	Rs. 1,000
Gobar Gas Plant	Rs. 10,000

- For structures where plinth area valuation is not possible, it is recommended that those structures be valued as per the schedule of rates of the PWD Department of the State prevalent at present.
- For tubewell and borewell, the recommended compensations are as follows:
  - Tubewell 125mm × 100 mm size—Rs. 44,400
  - Borewell 200 mm × 150 mm size—Rs. 78,600
  - Cost will be proportionately reduced if the size is smaller.
- Standing trees be valued as per unit rates provided by the Divisional Forest Officer, Sundargarh.

9. Recommended that interest @ 9 per cent for the 1st year and @

15 per cent thereafter be awarded on the compensation amount from September 2010 till the date of payment.

10. Solacium @ 30 per cent on the compensation recommended.

11. Compensation for price escalation @ 12 per cent per annum be awarded on the compensation amount subject to a maximum of 36 months.

12. Recommended that all employment and re-settlement of the displaced families be done as per the Odisha Rehabilitation and Resettlement Policy, 2006.

13. Recommended that the MCL be directed to keep ready the rehab centres, i.e. plots, houses etc. so that the displaced families can shift there soon after physical displacement and not be destitute.

14. Recommended that the MCL should undertake periphery development of Basundhura area and must spend at least 10 per cent of the net profit it makes from its project in the area. Also recommended for a direction to the State Government of Odisha and the periphery development committee to formulate the development plans and supervise its execution.

15. Part-I report contains the details of the exercise undertaken by the Claims Commission and recommendations of the policies on each subject.

16. Part-II of the report, which is under process, contains the recommended monetary compensation, rehabilitation and resettlement packages of each landholders of Gopalpur and will be submitted by 15th of February, 2012, as verification relating to some new structures have become necessary in view of the cut-off date being moved to September 2010 and detailed calculation to work out the individual compensation of each land holder is involved.

Survey is now completed not only for Gopalpur but for all the 14 villages from which lands have been either acquired or leased out to MCL.

Table 3.11: Village-wise Number of Awardees and Area Acquired by MCL Sundargarh

Sl. No.	*Villages*	*Sanctioned Amount*	*Gross Paid Amount*	*No. of Awardees paid*	*Area Acquired in Acres*	*Remarks*
1.	Balinga	Included in the total Amount	Included in the total Amount	57	–	Survey for all the villages completed; compensation
2.	Bankibahal	-do-	-do-	39	—	paid and
3.	Garjanbahal	-do-	-do-	868	406.88	employment given. Re-

(Contd.)

Sl. No.	Villages	Sanctioned Amount	Gross Paid Amount	No. of Awardees paid	Area Acquired in Acres	Remarks
4.	Gopalpur	-do-	-do-	1791	1127.00	settlement will
5.	Karlikachhar	-do-	-do-	294	318.88	be done after
6.	Kulda	-do-	-do-	289	231.66	development
7.	Sardega	-do-	-do-	3	—	of R&R Sites.
8.	Tikilipara	-do-	-do-	418	105.00	
9.	Siarmal	-do-	-do-	281	240.87	
10.	Bangurkela	-do-	-do-	0	530.66	
11.	Gopalpur (Forest Land)	-do-	-do-	18	–	
12.	Gopalpur (Lease case)	-do-	-do-	10	–	
13.	Jhupurunga	-do-	-do-	–	–	Award is in objection hearing statge by Claims Commission
14.	Kripsira	-do-	-do-	–	–	Award is in objection hearing statge by Claims Commission
15.	Tumulia	-do-	-do-	–	–	Assessment of compensation is in process
16.	Ratansara	-do-	-do-	–	–	Assessment of compensation is in process
	Total	***976.72 crores**	***616.79 crores**	**4068**	**2960.95**	

• Includes sanctioned amount and gross paid amount for all the Sixteen Villages.
Source: Claims Commission Report.

Table 3.12: Summary of Employment and Resettlement under B.G. Area as on 31-3-2015

Sl. No.	Project Head	Villages	Eligible for Employment	Approved Employment	Eligible for Re-settlement	Plot Provided for Resettlement
1.	KOCP	Bankibahal	87	72	118	67
		Balinga	187	150	272	Nil
2.	BWOCP	Gopalpur	31	29	39	Nil
		Sardega	133	127	159	124
3.	BEOCP	Tiklipara	186	179	132	132
	Total		**624**	**557**	**720**	**323**

Source: Claims Commission Report.

Table 3.13: Data related to Land Acquisition Rehabilitation and Resettlement for the 4000 MW UMPP Behedabahal Power Project Project (Data as on 18-4-2015)

Sl. No.	Date of Acquisition under Land Acquisition Act 1984	Total Area Acquired in Hac	Multi-cropped Irrigated Land (In Ha)	No. of Displaced Families	No. of Affected Families	Amount of Compensation Paid	Rehabilitation Amount in Rupees
1.	2010	1093.73	25.59	1937	843	42.46 crore	13.78 crore

Source: Special Land Acquisition Officer, UMPP, Sundargarh.

Table 3.14: Lands Acquired for Dulinga Coal Mines Project (NTPC Limited)

Sl. No.	Land	Total Land Applied	Land Acquired	Possession of Land handed over to IDCO	Balance	Remarks
1.	Private Land	199.44	177.57	173.426	21.87	
2.	Government Land	161.66	1.70	1.70	159.96	

Source: Special Land Acquisition Officer, UMPP, Sundargarh.

Table 3.15: Lands Acquired for Manaharpur Coal Block (OPGC Limited)

Sl. No.	Land	Total Land Applied	Land Acquired	Possession of Land handed over to IDCO	Balance	Remarks
1.	Private Land	1116.58	869.90	670.36	246.68	
2.	Government Land	1073.04	994.89	592.60	78.15	

Source: Special Land Acquisition Officer, UMPP, Sundargarh.

Table 3.16: Land Acquisition for 4000 MW UMPP, Bhedabahal (Position as on 7-4-2015)

Sl. No.	Villages Name	Total Award		Paid		Cases Referred to Civil Court		Percentage of Achievement	
		No. of Khata	Area in Acre	No. of Khata	Area in Acre	No. of Khata	Area in Acre	No. of Khata	Area in Acre
1	2	3	4	5	6	7	8	9	10
1.	Kopsingha	370	909.95	298	644.29	27	185.59	91.20	91.09
2.	Lankahuda	186	652.10	134	413.67	16	137.49	84.52	84.52

(*Contd.*)

1	2	3	4	5	6	7	8	9	10
3.	Bhedabahal	58	161.65	38	68.88	14	79.18	91.59	91.59
4.	Kirei	106	296.76	73	185.07	14	86.84	91.62	91.62
5.	Rupidihi	279	511.22	242	408.35	18	79.42	95.41	95.42
6.	Khdabahal (P)	75	126.17	57	85.10	11	31.67	92.54	93.01
7.	Kandabahal Colony	96	73.19	82	60.18	4	8.92	94.41	94.41
	Total	**1170**	**2731.04**	**924**	**1865.54**	**104**	**609.11**	**90.61**	**90.60**

Note: The total amount of award for the 1170 Khatedar is Rs. 620.78 crores the amount paid to the 924 Khatedar is Rs. 423.95 crores. 104 cases have been referred to Civil Court comprising 609.10 acre covering the total amount of Rs. 138.45 crore.

Source: Special Land Acquisition Officer, UMPP, Sundargarh.

3.5 Land Acquisition in Rayagada

Rayagada district was first constituted as a separate district out of erstwhile Koraput district on 2-10-1992. As per Census 2011, the total population of the district is 9.68 lakh with a population growth of 15.74 per cent between 2001 and 2011. The ST population is 4.63 lakh which forms 56 per cent of the total population and the SCs constitute 1.16 lac comprising 14.28 per cent. It is an extremely poverty-stricken district with 72 per cent BPL families. The agriculture labourers comprise 18.7 per cent of the total population. The sex-ratio during 2011 was 1048 as compared to 1028 during 2001. The total literates were 43.50 per cent to the total population. There is gender gap in literacy with 53 per cent male literates and 34 per cent female literates. The maternal mortality rate is 31 per thousand and the infant mortality rate 70 per thousand. The geographical area is 7073 sq. km. and the forest area is 3197 sq. km. (45.20%). There are 1399 primary schools out of which 56 are exclusively under SC and ST department. Similarly, the number of upper primary schools is 589 and the SC/ST department has 48 upper primary schools. The number of high schools for the general category is 37 and 27 are exclusively under ST/SC development department. There are 22 colleges in the district out of which 3 are under SC/ST development department. There are 2 Government ITIs, 5 private ITIs, while there is one polytechnic. The number of financial institutions are nearly 70, which are the branches of various banks.

Prafulla Samantara (2000) in his write-up on "People's Struggle for Right to Livelihood" has discussed the People's Movement against Gopalpur Steel Plant located in the district of Ganjam in the South

Eastern Part of India since 1995 after the Government of Odisha signed the MoU with TISCO for establishing an export-oriented steel plant in the area. The plant was to acquire more than 6,000 acre of agriculture land destroying the whole complex of socio-economic life of the people of 25 villages. About 25,000 people are being forced to vacate the area and sacrifice their homes and livelihood. The agitation at Gopalpur attained a feverish pitch when the villagers including women and children faced inhumane police action in the month of August, 1996. Two old women, named Laxmi Amma and S. Yerramma died after being injured by police tear gas and lathi charge. Till then the villagers successfully obstructed the administration to have survey work for acquisition of land for TISCO from the affected villages in Gopalpur area. On March 19, 1997 the district administration resorted to police firing on unarmed villagers to enter into the villages for survey work. But the determined village agitators did not allow the survey staff to proceed with their work. In the police firing 5 villagers were severely injured by bullets and hundreds of women and children were injured by police *lathi* charge.

Land Acquisition Information in Rayagada District

The District Administration of Rayagada had submitted a note on Land Acquisition and R & R Matters of Utkal Alumina International Limited to the members of Odisha Assembly House Committee on 16th November, 2016. As per the requisition filed by M/s. Utkal Alumina International Ltd., the Government of Odisha has acquired private land measuring an area of 2,153.93 acre from 24 villages of Kashipur Tehsil of Rayagada district under applicable provisions of Land Acquisition Act, 1894 during 1995-96. After taking over possession of said acquired land, Government of Odisha through its nodal agency Odisha Industrial Infrastructure Development Corporation (IDCO) leased out the said land of Ac. 2,153.93 through registered lease deeds in favour of Utkal Alumina International Ltd. and handed over the possession of the aforesaid land for establishment of Alumina Refinery at Doraguda. All the land owners have already taken their land compensation from the Collector, Rayagada through the Special Land Acquisition Officer.

Subsequently, on the request made by the land losers for giving some more *ex-gratia* amount, Utkal Alumina International Limited has paid the *ex-gratia* amount to the beneficiaries as indicated below:

Table 3.17: Compensation paid by Utkal Alumina International Limited, District Rayagada

(Amount in Rs.)

Kisam (Type) of Land	*Compensation under LA Act*	*Ist Ex-Gratia*	*2nd Ex-Gratia*	*3rd Ex-Gratia*	*Total Payment*
1	2	3	4	5	6
Atta	21,300	78,700	1,00,000	1,44,000	3,44,000
Mala	32,660	87,340	1,00,000	1,44,000	3,64,000
Berna	39,050	90,950	1,00,000	1,44,000	3,74,000
Bahai	50,410	99,590	1,00,000	1,44,000	3,94,000
Ghar (Homestead)	71,000	729,000	1,00,000	1,44,000	10,44,000
Bahalpani	58,220	91,780	1,00,000	1,44,000	4,66,000
Bahalpani Do Fasli	66,030	83,970	1,00,000	1,44,000	5,38,000
Patita	10,650	89,350	1,00,000	1,44,000	3,44,000
Bagayat	21,300	78,700	1,00,000	1,44,000	3,44,000
Kachar	33,370	86,630	1,00,000	1,44,000	3,64,000
Rasta	21,300	78,700	1,00,000	1,44,000	3,44,000
Total	**425290**	**1,594,710**	**11,00,000**	**1584000**	**4920000**

Source: Industrial Infrastructure Development Corporation.

As per the applicable R & R Policy, the Company has provided homestead land of Ac. 0.10 and *pucca* houses with all amenities to each displaced family in two constructed Rehabilitation Colonies. The Government of Odisha has already issued homestead RORs (*Pattas*) to all 183 displaced families resettled at the said colonies. The families were displaced from the villages of Kendu Khunti, Ramibeda, D. Koral and the total number of displaced families were 183. Employment was provided to 145 displaced families, five of the educated youth are pursuing higher studies, 11 physically challenged DPs have been provided subsistence allowance, 10 per cent of displaced have been provided one time cash assistance in view of employment. Besides R&R benefits have been provided to the displaced families consisting of 0.10 acre of homestead lands, provision of *pacca* house with individual land, RoR for the homestead land, land compensation with *ex-gratia* amount, maintenance allowance, transportation allowances, cattle shed assistance and provision of electricity and street lighting. In the R&R colony pipe water supply through overhead tank, drainage facility, free health care service, funeral ground, barbed wire fencing of homestead land, place for worship, community centre and school building have been provided.

The number of displaced persons from Kansarigura village is 119, from Pohundi village 22. Of the total number of displaced families consisting of 183, the number of STs families are 41 the number of SC families are 139 and number of OBC families is 3. The number of displaced persons provided employment is 1455 persons who have opted for employment but few are pursuing higher studies, 11 persons are receiving monthly subsistence allowance for old age and physically challenged, 13 persons took one time cash assistance and 3 persons and 8 persons have expired and their legal heirs would get the employment. Every displaced family have been provided 0.10 acre of homestead land, *pacca* houses and individual toilet; RoR for homestead land, *Ex-gratia* grant, maintenance allowance, transportation allowance, cattle shed assistance and street lighting. Besides this, they have been provided piped water supply through overhead tank, free health care service, ephemeral ground place for worship, community centre and school building.

Another industry which has taken land on land acquisition basis is UAIL near Doraguda (Tikri). It consists of 41 families from Ramibera village, 55 families from Kendu Khuti village and 87 families from Koral village. The name of the villages coming under project area are Podapadi, Phulajuba, Kansariguda and Pohandi. The area acquired from Podapadi is 36.10 acre, from Phulajuba 170.77 acre, from Kansariguda 495.59 acre and from Pohandi 197.65 acre, i.e. 904.11 acre overall. The total number of affected families is 626 out of which the largest number is from Kansariguda (265), Pohandi 175, Phulajuba 138 and Korapadi 48. The number of affected families is 626 and the total number of displaced is 141; the number displaced is 119 from Kansariguda and 22 from Pohandi. Till date the DPs have not yet been physically displaced from their own places.

3.6 Land Acquisition for Vedanta Limited, Lanjigarh—MOU of Government of Odisha with Sterlite Industry Limited, Kalahandi

Private Land from the tribals and other marginalized sections were acquired by Industrial Development Corporation Limited (IDCO), Odisha for Alumina Refinery Project, Vedanta Limited, Lanjigarh, measuring an area of 1518.03 acre of Private Land and 453.73 acre of Government Land. The MoU for this Industry was signed on 7th June, 2003 between Government of Odisha and Sterlite India Limited. Lands were acquired from 25 villages in which the Project Affected Persons (PAPs) were 1532. Compensation were paid to 1217 PAPs and 315 PAPs have refused to accept the payment of compensation as they are demanding higher rates of compensation.

The Memorandum of Understanding (MoU) was made on 7th day

of June, 2003 at Bhubaneswar between Government of Odisha and Sterlite Industries (India) Limited, (hereinafter referred to as S.I.L. SIL has been desirous of setting up an Alumina Refinery Complex at Lanjigarh, Kalahjandi District in Odisha State which would include setting up of a one million tonnes per annum Alumina refinery, 3.0 million tonnes per annum of Bauxite Mining facilities as well installation of a 4 × 25 MW Captive Power Plant at an aggregate investment of approximately Rs. 4,000 (Four thousand) crore. The Government of Odisha agreed to provide all help, prevailing incentives and facilitate clearances necessary for the aforesaid project in the State of Odisha consistent with the various constitutional and statutory provisions relating to the area of the said project.

The major areas of cooperation between the Government of Odisha and SIL are listed below.

The Government of Odisha shall provide all necessary assistance in procuring land for the proposed project in Lanjigarh, District Kalahandi, including land for the Bauxite Mining and other requirement of the project. Odisha Industrial Infrastructure Development Corporation (IDCO) shall take immediate steps to facilitate land acquisition and other requirements such as rehabilitation of the displaced persons/project affected persons at Lanjigarh, District Kalahandi. The Government of Odisha agreed to hand over the land free from all encumbrances to SIL through IDCO for construction of the plant and allied facilities. SIL agrees to pay IDCO/Revenue authorities the cost of the land and other charges.

The Odisha Mining Corporation will take necessary steps in executing an Agreement with SIL with approval of the Government of Odisha in Steel and Mines Department for all matters related to Bauxite Mining Lease.

The Government of Odisha will permit withdrawal of water from a suitable source for construction/operation for the aforesaid project and housing colony as per the prevailing rates under appropriate terms and approval of the Water Allocation Committee. The requirement of water is approximately 30,000 m^3/day.

The Government of Odisha will permit implementation of the water supply scheme to be prepared by SIL and Water Resources Department.

SIL plans to set up a captive power plant of 4 × 25 MW capacity to meet their own captive load. SIL will make application to OBRC for this purpose, which shall be recommended by the Government of Odisha to OERC. Government of Odisha would assist SIL in getting operational power on payment from WESCO. SIL will also approach GRIDCO for suitable PPA for sale of excess power to GRIDCO at mutually agreed rate subject to approval of OERC. In case of sale of surplus power to outside the State, separate agreement for wheeling will be made with GRIDCO on payment of wheeling charges approved by OERC. Government of Odisha would facilitate permission from GRIDCO and/or OERC.

- The Government of Odisha agrees to assist SIL in obtaining NOC through the State Pollution Control Board for mining, construction of the plant, the housing colony, pipeline, power project etc.
- Government of Odisha agrees to assist SIL in obtaining all clearances from the Central Government.

SIL will arrange to conduct Rapid Environment Impact Assessment (RELA) and detailed EIA, prepare Environment Management Plan (EMP) for the project. The Government of Odisha agrees to assist SIL in this regard during the time when EIA is being conducted and EMP is being prepared. "Government of Odisha appreciate that SIL is fully committed to the proper resettlement and rehabilitation of the project affected households. The Government of Odisha appreciate that SIL is a responsible corporate house with a high involvement in employee's welfare and social development. The Government of Odisha appreciate that SIL will be entitled to induct suitable foreign and/or Indian Joint Venture partners, choose appropriate financial options, suppliers, credit options and technologies in the best interest of the project. SIL may assign the rights and obligations under this Agreement to a group of company where SIL holds a controlling interest. *The MOU shall remain valid for a period of two years from the date of signing.* In the event of non-implementation of the project or part thereof, the corresponding support/obligation of the Government of Odisha indicated in the MoU with regard to Bauxite Ore Mines, incentives and concessions of the State Government shall be deemed to be withdrawn.

3.7 Land Acquisition for Alumina Refinery Project Vedanta Limited, Lanjigarh, Kalahandi

The MoU was signed on 7th June, 2003 between the Government of Odisha and Sterlite Industries Limited for establishment of Alumina Refinery Project at Lanjigarh in Kalahandi district of Odisha. The area of land acquired was 1,518.03 acre of private land and 453.73 acre of government land in the district of Kalahandi. There are 918 cultivators from whom land has been acquired from 25 villages. An amount of Rs. 15.08 crore has been paid in compensation to the land losers. The total number of project-affected persons are 1,532 of which compensation have been paid to 1,217 persons and 3,151 *persons have not been paid compensation as they have been demanding Rs. 5 lakh per acre.* The socio-economic survey of the PAPs was undertaken by the District Administration during the year 2003 along with VDO and Tehsildar of Lanjigarh including local NGOs (CHARM Bishvanathpur) wherein 121 number of displaced families and 1,532 of PAPs were identified. Each displaced family has been given 0.10 acre of land for homestead purpose free of cost in a resettlement colony covering 116 number of families. Each of the displaced families who have opted for self-relocation have been given one time cash assistance of Rs. 50,000. The company has provided employment benefit to the eligible displaced persons in the industry and ancillary units to a total of 3015 persons within Kalahandi, Rayagada, Odisha and also some to outside Odisha. One time cash assistance has been paid to 1217 PAPs out of 1532 PAPs leaving a balance of *315 PAPs who have not been paid one time cash assistance due to the demand for higher compensation @ Rs. 5 lakh per family* is held by the Government of Odisha as beyond R & R Policy, 2003. A Resettlement Colony has been established by Vedanta Limited, Lanjigarh in village Jagatnathpur and named as Niyamgiri Vedanta Nagar in an area of 11.42 acre. They have been provided a primary school, hospital, temple, crematorium market complex, pipe drinking water supply, electricity, boundary wall and child care centre.

The proceeding of the 6th RPDAC meeting of Vedanta Aluminium Limited, Lanjigarh was held on 26th June, 2015 at Collectorate Kalahandi at Bhawani Patna. According to this proceeding an area of 2,063.87 acre of both private and Government land in Kalahandi and Rayagada district have been acquired and handed over to Vedanta Limited, Lanjigarh as per details furnished below:

- Total Private Land Acquired 1610.14 Acres
- Private Land–Kalahandi 1518.03 Acres
- Private land–Rayagada 92.11 Acres
- Total Government land 453.73 Acres.

Villagers of Rengopalli, Bonduguda and Kothudwar were left out while acquiring the land for the existing plant as most of their lands were already acquired and the rest of the lands were surrounded by the plant land. The villagers were suffering from TB diseases due to dust from the plant, also from eye diseases due to air pollution and malaria due to water pollution; besides this some of the cattles were also suffering from many types of unknown diseases due to red-mud pond. *Hence, the villagers were insisting to acquire rest of the land also. A copy of the proceedings of the Gram Sabha/Palli Sabha along with meetings of 5th RPDAC was sent to Managing Director, IDCO to acquire the total land of 200 acre consisting of both government and private lands.* It was decided in the 5th RPDAC meeting to extend all rehabilitation benefits to the displaced persons of these 3 villages with payment of due compensation, for supply of electricity to the rehabilitation colony from the power grid of VAL. *From the Rayagada district 56 cases of left out PAPs have to be paid compensation and rehabilitation.*

Supreme Court Decision in Writ Petition Civil No. 180 of 2011 between Odisha Mining Corporation and MOEF, GOI

Odisha Mining Corporation (OMC) a State of Odisha Undertaking, has approached the Supreme Court seeking a Writ of Certiorari to quash the order passed by the Ministry of Environment and Forests (MoEF) dated 24-8-2010 rejecting the Stage-II forest clearance for diversion of 660.749 hectares of forest land for mining of bauxite ore in Lanjigarh Bauxite Mines in Kalahandi and Rayagada Districts of Odisha and also for other consequential reliefs.

Vedanta, however, filed an application I.A. No. 1324 of 2005 before this Court seeking a direction to the MoEF to take a decision on the application for forest clearance for bauxite mining submitted by the State Government on 28-2-2005 for the Refinery Project. The question that was posed by this Court while deciding the above mentioned I.A. was whether Vedanta should be allowed to set up its refinery project, which involved the proposal for diversion of 58.943 hectares of forest land. CEC had, however, objected to the grant of clearance sought by Vedanta on the ground that the Refinery would be totally dependent on mining of bauxite from Niyamgiri Hills, Lanjigarh, *which was the only vital Wildlife habitat, part of which constituted elephant corridor and also on the ground that the said project would obstruct the proposed wildlife sanctuary and the residence of tribes like Dongaria Kondha. Further, it was also pointed out that if Sterlite was allowed to mine in the Niyamgiri Hills, it would affect the identity, culture and other customary rights of Dongaria Kondh. Review Petition was, however, dismissed by this Court on 7-5-2008. This project was also challenged in the Hon'ble Supreme Court of India on the ground that it violates the provisions of the Scheduled Tribes and other Traditional Forest Dwellers (Recognition of Forest Rights) Act, 2006 WP (C) No. 549 of 2007 was filed in the Hon'ble Supreme Court of India by one Sri Siddharth Nayak challenging the project on the above issue.*

The recommendations of the FAC dated 23-8-2010 and Saxena Committee Report were considered by MoEF and the request for Stage-II Clearance was rejected on 24-8-2010. The blatant disregard displayed by the project proponents with regard to rights of the tribals and primitive tribal groups dependent on the area for their livelihood, as they have proceeded to seek clearance is shocking. Primitive Tribal Groups have specifically been provided for in the Forest Rights Act, 2006 and this case should leave no one in doubt that they will enjoy full protection of their rights under the law. *The narrow definition of the Project Affected People by the State Government runs contrary to the letter and spirit of the Forest Rights Act, 2006.* Simply because they did not live on the hills does not mean that they have no rights there. The Forest Rights Act, 2006 specifically provides for such rights but these were not recognized and were sought to be denied.

Moreover, the fate of the Primitive Tribal Groups need some emphasis, as very few communities in India in general and Odisha in particular come under the ambit of such a category. Their dependence on the forest being almost complete, the violation of the specific protections extended to their "habitat and habitations" by the Forest Rights Act, 2006 are simply unacceptable.

One also cannot ignore the Dalits living in the area. While they may technically be ineligible to receive benefits under the FRA 2006, it would be impossible to disentitle them as they have been present for over five decades. The Committee has also said on p. 40 of their report that "even if the Dalits have no claims under the FRA the truth of their *de facto* dependence on the Niyamgiri forests for the past several decades can be ignored by the Central and State Governments only at the cost of betrayal of the promise inclusive growth and justice and dignity for all Indians". This observation rings true with the MoE&F and underscores the MoE&F's attempt to ensure that any decision taken is not just true to the law in letter but also in spirit. *The Saxena Committee's evidence as reviewed by the FAC is compelling.* The violations of the various legislations, especially the Forest (Conservation) Act, 1980, the Environment (Protection) Act, 1986, and the Scheduled Tribes and Traditional Forest Dwellers (Recognition of Forest Rights) Act, 2006, appear to be too egregious to be glossed over. Whether STs and other

TFDs, like Dongaria Kondh, Kutia Kandha and others, have got any religious rights, i.e. rights of worship over the Niyamgiri hills, known as Niyamgiri, near Hundaligali, which is the hill top known as Niyam Raja, have to be considered by the Gram Sabha. Gram Sabha can also examine whether the proposed mining area Niyama Danger, 10 km away from the peak, would in any way affect the abode of Niyam Raja. *Needless to say, if the SMP, in any way, affects their religious rights, especially their right to worship their deity, known as Niyam Raja, in the hills top of the Niyamgiri range of hills, that right has to be preserved and protected. This aspect of the matter has not been placed before the Gram Sabha for their active consideration, but only the individual claims and community claims received from Rayagada and Kalahandi Districts, most of which the Gram Sabha has dealt with and settled.*

The Gram Sabha is also free to consider all the community, individual as well as cultural and religious claims, over and above the claims which have already been received from Rayagada and Kalahandi Districts. Any such fresh claims be filed before the Gram Sabha within six weeks from the date of this judgement. State Government as well as the Ministry of Tribal Affairs, Government of India, would assist the Gram Sabha for settling of individual as well as community claims. The Supreme Court gave a direction to the State of Odisha to place these issues before the Gram Sabha with notice to the Ministry of Tribal Affairs, Government of India and the Gram Sabha would take a decision on them within three months and communicate the same to the MoEF, through the State Government. *On the conclusion of the proceeding before the Gram Sabha determining the claims submitted before it, the MoEF shall take a final decision on the grant of Stage 11 clearance for the Bauxite Mining Project in the light of the decisions of the Gram Sabha within two months thereafter.* The proceedings of the Gram Sabha shall be attended as an observer by a judicial officer of the rank of the District Judge, nominated by the Chief Justice of the High Court of Odisha who shall sign the minutes, of the proceedings, certifying that the proceedings of the Gram Sabha took place independently and completely uninfluenced either by the Project proponents or the Central Government or the State Government.

With this, the projects' tracks changed. Vedanta rightly became unworthy of clearance for several compelling reasons, including illegally increasing the capacity of its aluminium refinery sixfold and violating the FRA. In contrast, Vedanta stands accused of numerous anti-environment and callously anti-people practices and is boycotted by ethical investment funds, including the Norwegian Pension Fund, and the Church of

England. As the Odisha Government put it, POSCO would bring unprecedented "prosperity and well-being to its people" without causing unconscionable destruction. *However, the perseverant resistance by the Niyamgiri Surakhya Samiti and allied civil society groups, in August 2010, the Ministry of Forest and Environment had stopped VAL from its plants to mine bauxite at the top on the Niyamgiri Hill for processing in the nearby large Lanjigarh factory.* After nominating a special committee of enquiry, the Saxena Committee, the Minister had agreed to its findings that Vedanta Limited had infringed he Forest Rights Act, 2006 that protect especially the Kondh's forests. In a precedent setting decision in April 2013, the Supreme Court applied the Forest Rights Act for the first time saying that it was up to the local communities to decide whether the project should go forward through public consultations and votes in each of the surrounding villages. *Keeping in view the directives of Supreme Court of India, the Government of Odisha was bound to organize Pallisabha in 12 villages, and majority of Pallisabhas have voted against the VAL mining project unanimously in the presence of judicial officers. Now, it seems that the 12 years long "Save Niyamgiri Movement" against bauxite mining in the Niyamgiri Hill will finally be won by the Kondhs of Kalahandi.* [Tapas Kumar Dalapati, 2016, in S.N. Chaudhary (ed.), Rawat Publications, Jaipur].

The Dongaria Kondh tribal people of Niyamgiri said an emphatic no to the proposed mining in the Niyamgiri hills which is spread over the tribal dominated districts of Kalahandi and Rayagada districts in Odisha. Taking part in the first Gram Sabha that was held at Sherkapadi village in Sibapadar gram panchayat in Rayagada district as many as *36 out of the 38 adult residents of the village who attended the hearing vehemently opposed the proposed mining in the Niyamgiri hills.* The Gram Sabha was conducted by Ward Member Shriram Gardia in the presence of Panchayat Extension Officer Pradhani Sabar. *District Judge of Rayagada, Sarat Chandra Mishra, was present as an observer in the meeting as per Supreme Court Order.* The villagers, who rejected an inter-departmental inquiry report that detailed the land used by the residents of Sherkapadi, said that they worshipped the entire Niyamgiri hill range as 'Niyamraja'. The 20 men and 16 women of the village who took part in the Gram Sabha hearing and spoke in Kui and Oria languages said *the proposed mining will affect their religious rights as well as the rituals.* According to sources, two resolutions were passed in the Gram Sabha. While in one resolution the villagers completely opposed the proposed bauxite mining project, *in the second resolution they claimed religious rights over the whole of Niyamgiri which has as many as 112 tribal villages.* The Gram Sabha was conducted amid tight security. The hearing that lasted for several hours passed off peacefully.

Meanwhile, Prafulla Samantarta, National Convener of National Alliance of People's Movements, congratulated the tribal people for their determination to protect Niyamgiri. The Gram Sabha at Sherkapadi was the first in a series of Gram Sabhas to be conducted in 12 villages in Kalahandi and Rayagada district as announced by Odisha Government. In its judgement passed on April 18, the Supreme Court had ordered that Gram Sabhas should take a final view on the proposed bauxite mining in Niyamgiri hills to source bauxite for the existing alumina refinery of Vedanta Aluminium Limited at Lanjigarh in Kalahandi district. As per the Odisha Government's decision, Gram Sabhas will be conducted in seven villages of Rayagada district from July 18 to August 19 and five villages of Kalahandi from July 23 to July 30. The Niyamgiri Suraksha Samiti, however, had opposed the Odisha Government decision and demanded that Gram Sabhas be held in all the 112 villages of Niyamgiri instead of only in 12 villages chosen by the authorities.

3.8 Land Acquisition of POSCO Project in Jagatsinghpur District

The Government of Odisha executed an MoU on June 22, 2005 to assist the (formerly Pohang Iron and Steel Company) renamed as POSCO India is a multinational steel-making company headquartered in Pohang, South Korea attempted to obtain all clearances including Forest and Environmental Clearance, approval of the State Pollution Control Board; the Ministry of Environment and Forest, GoI to provide permission for opening up the Iron Ore Mines and expeditious clearance of applications relating to mining lease and related matters such as Forest, Environment etc. It was also expected that employment opportunities generated by POSCO India would eliminate the entire backlog of current unemployment in Odisha. The LCAER study also estimated that POSCO Steel Plant would generate 1,59,734 additional jobs in the trade sector, 5809 additional job in the Animal Husbandry Sector, 10,912 jobs in Food Crop Sector and 6,394 jobs in other sectors.

1. The Government of Odisha and POSCO signed a MoU on June 22, 2005 to set up an integrated Steel Plant with the total capacity of 12 million tonnes per annum.
2. The integrated plant includes a Captive Power Plant and a Captive Minor Port.
3. The project requires about 1621 hectares of land of which about 1253 hactres is Forest Land and rest 386 hectares is private land.

4. The Environmental Clearance for the captive minor port was granted by MoEF on May 15, 2007.
5. On September 28, 2008 one clearance for Diversion of Forest Land was granted by MoEF and final clearance was granted by MoEF on December 29, 2009.
6. On January 8, 2010, MoEF demanded clarification from Government of Odisha that the final approval of Diversion of Forest Land is conditional on the settlement of rights under the Forest Rights Act, 2006.
7. On March 16, 2010 the Forest and Environment Department of Government of Odisha wrote to the MoEF conveying that there are no tribal people or traditional Forest Dwellers Residing in the Forest Area being acquired by POSCO.
8. The MoEF wrote on 5th August, 2010 to the Principal Secretary, Forest that the Committee set up by MoTA and MoEF brought the following facts to the attention of MoEF:
    (a) There are OTFDs in the area.
    (b) The FRA process has not yet been completed.
    (c) Some Pallisabhas have given resolutions refusing to consent to the Diversion of Forest land on which they are dependant.
    (d) Any work related to the project in this area is a violation of FRA and hence handing over the Forest and Non-Forest land of the project shall be stopped herewith.

There was stiff resistance from the local people about the forcible land acquisition from 2005 to 2010 continuously. Men, women and children all opposed tooth and nail the land acquisition by POSCO in spite of heavy police engagement. They also pointed out to the importance of betel vine cultivation which sustain a large population in this area. They also raised the issue of poor rehabilitation of previous development project oustees in Odisha. The village people also had blocked the entry of any Government or POSCO official to the 3 Panchayat areas of Dhinkia, Gadokujonga and Nuagaon consisting of 9 villages earmarked for the POSCO project. There were also violent action initiated by the unruly elements and the deployment of police to break the blockage created by the village people. An Activist Dula Mandal was also killed on June 20, 2008. The social activist Abhey Sahoo was first arrested on October 12, 2008 and was also arrested several times later. The total land required for the POSCO Project was 4,004.24 acre spread over 8 villages as per particulars given below:

Forest Land	2958.82 Acres
Non-Forest Government Land	607.74 Acres
Private Land	437.68 Acres
Total	**4004.24 Acres**

Table 3.18: Lands required for POSCO Project in Jagatsinghpur

Name of the Village	*Forest Land*	*Gochar Land*	*Communal Land*	*Leasable Land*	*Total*	*Private Land*	*Total (Column 6+7)*
1	2	3	4	5	6	7	8
Dhinkia	803.88	2.05	2.70	129.23	937.56	284.97	1222.53
Gobindpur	854.55	10.58	2.09	24.30	891.52	73.24	964.76
Polanga	325.8	2.54	0.49	0.30	328.41	53.85	382.26
Nuagaon	666.55	0.00	0.00	69.56	736.11	3.42	739.53
Bayanal Kandha	52.03	0.00	0.00	0.00	52.03	2.41	54.44
Bhuyanpal	29.79	9.31	5.14	5.31	49.55	2.02	51.57
Noliasahi	37.70	1.57	1.57	9.62	51.79	17.75	69.54
Jatadhar	189.24	0.00	322.55	7.50	519.29	—	519.29
Total	**2959.54**	**26.05**	**334.54**	**245.82**	**3556.26**	**437.66**	**4003.92**

Source: Government of Odisha, Department of Revenue.

Diversion of 1,253.225 hectares of forest was sanctioned by GoI on 4th May, 2011 with certain conditions: However, the approval of the Pallisabha was not obtained by the Government of Odisha but still the forest land was handed over to POSCO by Government of Odisha and the non-forest Government land of 561.41 acre was acquired by IDCO. The local community people had articulated their voice relating to the livelihood dependence on the forest land and also the betel vine in which their survival was dependant. The local people also raised the issue of daily wages on which the agriculture labourers were dependent. Besides this, it was estimated that about 25,000 small fishermen operating in the Jatadhar area will be affected by the project. The local people have been strongly resisting the acquisition of land, but the State Administration have forcibly acquired the forest land from the two Panchayats of Nuagaon and Noliasahi but the villagers of Dhinkia were dead set to resist the land acquisition process. Hence, the local administration including the POSCO authorities were ultimately reconciled to the area of existing land acquisition and to go ahead with the implementation of their plan.

Table 3.19: The Displaced Family, Area under Betel Vine, Trees and Prawn Ponds in POSCO Project

Name of the Village	*Displaced Families*			*Displaced from*				
				Betel Vine		*Trees*	*Prawn Ponds*	
	Original Family	*Extended Family*	*Total*	*No*	*Area in (Acres)*	*No.*	*No.*	*Area in Acres*
Gobindpur	100	69	169	689	93.11	55796		
Nuagaon	12	6	18	432	82.63	17813	1	0.29
Nolisahi	164	76	240	4	1.38	10560	—	—
Polang	54	23	77	278	56.98	18164	—	—
Bhuyanpal	12	—	12	17	2.79	843	3	15.27
Bayanal Kandha	—	—	—	83	16.31	1948	—	—
Jatadhar	—	—	—	—	—	—	27	254.40
Dhinkia	124	78	202	374	50.87	—	—	—
Total	**466**	**252**	**718**	**1877**	**304.07**	**105124**	**31**	**269.96**

Source: Government of Odisha, Department of Revenue.

The total area required for this project is 4,004.00 acre. 6(1) notification has already been made for acquisition of 437.68 acre of private land. Stage 1 Forest Diversion Proposal for an area of 3097 acre has been approved by the Hon'ble Supreme Court of India. From remaining 607 acre of non-forest government land, 193 acre of leasable land has already been leased out to the company and rest of the non-forest land is under different administrative process for sanction.

Table 3.20: Displaced Families from Different Villages for POSCO Project

Sl. No.	*Village*	*Total Families*	*Displaced Families*	*% DFs*
1	Dhinkia	871	124	14.23
2.	Govindpur	587	100	17.03
3.	Trilochanpur	588	0	0
4.	Nuagan	1064	12	1.12
5.	Gada Kujang	514	0	0
6.	Noliasahi	164	–	100.00
7.	Polang	106	54	50.94
8.	Bhuinyapal	97	12	12.37
9.	Bayanalkandha	55	0	0
	Total	**4046**	**302**	**21.74**

Source: Government of Odisha, Department of Revenue.

Socio-economic Profile of People in Project Affected Villages relating to POSCO Project

The demographic profile of the 8 affected villages based on the Socio-economic study conducted in September-December 2007 reveals that:

- There are altogether 4044 families residing in the affected area, of whom 466 families will be displaced by the project.
- In the affected villages, out of the total population 29.09 per cent belong to SC community, whereas 15.04 per cent are SC. In contrast to Scheduled Caste population, concentration of Scheduled Tribe is less in affected villages (0.16%). Only 3 out of 466 DFs are STs.
- Overall literacy rate in the affected villages is 81.62 per cent which is little higher than the district average (79.61%) and much higher than the State average (63.61%). The male literacy is 84.44 per cent whereas the female literacy is 78.51 per cent. The literacy rate of DFs is considerably low (Overall 71.96%, Male—75.79% and female—65.08%).
- *The overall occupational pattern shows that cultivation of betel vine is the major livelihood generating activity, where 62.84 per cent persons of the affected community are engaged. The other major occupations are Agricultural Labourers (13.17%), Fishing and Shrimp culture (6.95%), Business (4.91%), Non-Agricultural labourers (4.16%), Salaried Job (3.53%) and surprisingly less in Agriculture (1.76%).* There are also 28 families depending solely upon allied activities whereas 3 families on collections from CPRs.
- Only 29.20 per cent of the total population in affected villages are workers. Female workforce participation rate is very low in the affected villages. It is only 6.65 per cent as against 50.50 per cent in the male population of affected villages.
- Average wage earning per family from agricultural labour, which is Rs. 10,454 is much more than the average annual income from cultivating land. Therefore, the loss of livelihood for the wage earners is more than that of the land owners.
- Income from wage earning in non-farm sector is almost twice as much as the farm sector.
- Cultivating betel leaves is far more remunerative than cultivating crops, as can be seen from the net income levels, where the average family income for betel vine operators is nearly 5.6 times as that from cultivation of crops.

- Although only 341 persons from PAP families are salaried, the annual income from salary happens to be the highest among all occupations.
- Therefore, altogether 82 per cent families are found to earn an annual income between Rs. 25,000 and Rs. 1,00,000. While 8 per cent are in the creamy layers of economic status (more than Rs. 1,00,000) and at the bottom 10 per cent of families, who earn an annual income of Rs. 25,000 or less.
- Similarly, nearly 100 Women Self-Help Groups are linked to local banks to operate income generation activities.
- One of the major hurdles the project faces, is with respect to large number of encroachments in the Government Land. The provisional figures of encroachment of land of 600 acre (except Dhinkia), is primarily utilized for growing betel vines, paddy cultivation fields, raising trees (horticultural and energy plantations), fish farming tanks and residential houses.

Some Economic Profile of People Specific to Displaced Families

- As many as 611 out of 718 displaced families are from Dhinkia, Govindpur and Noliasahi villages. It forms about 85 per cent of the total displaced families. It indicates that the displacement is mostly concentrated in these three villages. As many as 703 out of 718 families (nearly 98%) have been living in these villages since their forefathers' time.
- *As per the R&R Policy (2006) of the Government of Odisha, 65 women DPs are belonging to the category of widow/women divorcee. Among the male DPs, out of 653, two physically/mentally challenged boys become eligible as separate families.*
- *Nearly 80 per cent, a vast majority of the DP families, belong to other backward communities*; 15 per cent belong to the scheduled caste; and a negligible proportion of the families belong to either the general caste or the scheduled tribe communities. Only three displaced families are from the scheduled tribes.
- Total population of the 718 DP families covered works out to be 2201, comprising 1144 male and 1057 female, a ratio of 924 female per 1000 male. Out of 718 DPs, 65 are *women who being widows/woman divorcee are considered as a separate category*. Out of the balance 653 DPs, 520 men are married.

Therefore, it leaves 133 (18.28%), who are unmarried sons but chosen as separate DP families on account of being major.

- *Primary source of occupation for the displaced families reveals that while 301 out of 466 DP families pursue betel vine as major occupation, for 20.5 per cent, it is fishing and for 11.7 per cent it is wage earning in the agricultural sector.* All the other occupations occupy relatively a minor position. There is village-wise concentration of livelihood activities. While for maximum number of families growing betel leaves is the major occupation in Dhinkia (94 out of 202), Govindpur (90 out of 169), Polanga (26 out of 77) and Nuagaon (11 out of 18), it is fishing for the families of Noliasahi (110 out of 240) and Bhyanpal (7 out of 12). Only 13 out of 718 families perceive agriculture to be the major occupation pursued by them.
- The data reveals that strangely, the average income for a family from working for wages in the agricultural farms is Rs. 14,500.
- Those who are earning wages as agricultural labourers category of affected population will have to be compensated.
- Possession of productive assets for the purpose of cultivation is found to be restricted only to plough and the power sprayer. The only economic activity, where the ownership of productive assets dominates is the fishing. Noliasahi, one of the villages where the fishermen community and fishing activities are concentrated, has large number of families owning (either individually or jointly) fishing boat and nets.
- Except 17 displaced persons all the other remaining DPs confirmed that they hold voter's identity card.

The RPDAC after a prolonged deliberation undertook the following decisions:

1. It approved the list of the displaced families for its publication of the project affected villages and inviting claims and objections.
2. The list of betel vine owners of the POSCO project area prepared by the Tehsildar Kujang and Erasama was approved in principle with due regards to the sentiments of the people and their emotional attachment with betel vine.
3. The rate of compensation for betel vine was increased from

Rs. 6 lakh to Rs. 11.5 lakh per acre and allocated 20 per cent of such compensation for labourers who would be rendered jobless.

4. RPDAC also approved unemployment allowance of Rs. 2250 per month to each labourer upto one year.
5. It approved the beneficiary list of fruit bearing and non-fruit bearing trees standing on the government land and authorized the Collector to make payment for such trees.
6. It enhanced the compensation for Prawn Ponds development on the Government land from Rs. 1 lakh to Rs. 2 lakh per acre.
7. It also enhanced the compensation for Government Land from Rs. 75 thousand to Rs. 1 lakh per acre.
8. It approved a uniform rate of Rs. 17 lakh per acre of private land anywhere in the project area.
9. It enhanced the transportation allowance from Rs. 2300 per family to Rs. 5000 for carrying the luggage to Rehabilitation Colony.
10. A three room house with verandah, kitchen, bathroom and toilet with the plinth area of 743 sq. ft and cattleshed plinth area of 203 was approved.

POSCO has deposited Rs. 10.6 crore with Government of Odisha for aforestation. The Non-Forest land consisting of 561.41 acre was released out in favour of IDCO. The private land comprises only 10 per cent of the total project area. The GoI had issued final clearance for acquisition of land to POSCO *vide* letter No. 8-63/2007FC dated 4-5-2011.

Present Status of POSCO Industry

Recently, the POSCO Industry asked for detailed expenditure receipts for Rs. 30.34 crore it had given to the Government of Odisha towards land acquisition. It also sent another letter asking for refund of Rs. 11.21 crore out of Rs. 13.52 crore it had paid towards acquisition of 438 acre of Private land for the forest. The private land was not acquired after an interim order from Odisha High Court in 2012. Odisha Government has managed to acquire over 2,700 acre of land of which 1703 acre of land is officially with the Company. IDCO has reportedly made it clear that POSCO would not be given possession of the rest 1000 acre unless it pays the outstanding dues towards the 1703 acre that it has been handed over. Odisha Government has also asked POSCO to make it clear whether it is still keen to set up its Steel Plant.

In a case where POSCO was defending the revised environmental clearance it had received in 2014, the court recorded the Korean giant as stating the "environmental clearance is valid only up to July 19, 2017, and they would not be able to do any work because the land has not been handed over to them and therefore, the project cannot proceed any further". The company asked for its environmental clearance to be cancelled, saying it would not be able to complete the project by the deadline of the environmental clearance in 2017.

The formailities of a final pull-out by POSCO from its proposed 8 million tonne steel plant in Odisha's Jagatsinghpur district may have started with both the State Government and the South Korean major hardening their stance on payment of acquired land. In a recent letter to Industrial Infrastructure Development Corporation of Odisha, the land acquisition agency of the State Government. POSCO asked for detailed expenditure receipt for the Rs. 30.34 crore it has given towards land acquisition.

It sent another letter asking for refund of Rs. 11.21 crore out of the Rs. 13.52 crore it had paid towards acquisition of 438 acre of private land for the project. The private land was not acquired after an interim order from Odisha High Court in 2012. Sources said POSCO was miffed after IDCO sent it a letter asking it to pay its outstanding dues of Rs. 54 crore towards the 1703 acre of land already handed over to it and an additional Rs. 19 crore for net present value of de-reserved forest land. POSCO has also withdrawn from the special purpose vehicle for the laying of the Haridaspur-Paradeep railway line, which would facilitate transport of iron ore from the mines to its plant. Though no POSCO official was willing to respond to the development, sources said the company is weighing its option on getting mining rights through auction route. The Union Mines Ministry had made it clear that all companies including POSCO have to bid for mines. Meanwhile, Odisha Government asked POSCO to make it clear whether it is still keen to set up its steel plant.

3.9 Land Acquisition in Kalinganagar Industrial Complex

Kalinganagar Integrated Industrial Complex (KNIIC) comprising 30 villages comes under Sukinda and Danagadi Tahasils of Jajpur district of Odisha. It is about 100 km. from the State Capital, Bhubaneswar and about 40 km from the district headquarters. The NH-200, connecting the iron ore/chromite belt of Jajpur and Keonjhar districts with the Paradeep Port, runs through the area. Brahmani, one of the major rivers of Odisha, runs nearby KNIIC. As there is no significant irrigation facility, the area is largely rain-fed and mostly rice is cultivated. The idea of the Kalinganagar Integrated Industrial Complex (KNIIC) was conceived in the early 1990s with an aim of rapid industrialization of harnessing the rich mineral resources of the State.

Table 3.21: Basic Information of Danagadi Block

Name of Block	*Geographical Area in Sq. Km*	*Total Area in Hectare*	*Total Villages*	*Population*			
				ST	*SC*	*Others*	*Total*
Danagadi	481.24	11,923	115	29,009 (28.72%)	22,488 (22.27%)	49,490 (49.01%)	10,0987

Source: Government of Odisha.

For setting up of industries in KNIIC, 8111.75 acre of private land have been acquired and 6382.38 acre of Government land have been alienated and leased out to IDCO for industrial purpose. For acquisition/alienation of above land, the acquisition/alienation process started in the year 1990-91 and it is an on-going process basing on the requirement of land from time to time for setting up new industries and for the purpose of other ancillary development work in the KNIIC area.

Table 3.22: Compensation Paid in Kalinganagar to Displaced Persons

No. of L.A. Case	*Area Involved*	*Estimated amount of Compensation*	*Compensation Paid*		*Balance Pending*	
			Area Paid (in acre)	*Amount paid in Rs*	*Area in acre*	*Amount in Rs.*
1	2	3	4	5	6	7
39 old L.A case	6961.61	35,10,84,318	6094.23	25,29,58,232	867.38	9,81,26,086
21 New L.A. Case	1150.14	16,70,33,257	440.97	4,36,63,084	709.17	12,33,70,173
32 old Land Acquisition Case	6954.16	39,32,03,000	5257.54	30,11,55,071	1696.62	9,20,47,929
22 New Land Acquisition Cases	1150.14	6,38,86,149	436.08	2,17,49,871	714.06	4,21,38,278
Total	**16216.05**	**975208724**	**12228.82**	**619528258**	**3987.23**	**355682859**

Source: Government of Odisha.

In 1st, 2nd and 3rd Phase 6961.61 acre of private land in 20 villages of Kalinganagar Integrated Industrial Complex area has been acquired through 39 Land Acquisition cases. Possession of the land has already been handed over to IDCO.

During the period of 2005 onwards, 21 L.A. proposals for an area of 1150.14 acre in 16 villages are under acquisition. This land is required mostly for development of KNIIC, Township, Ash pond, water pipe line and Railway line etc. These acquisition proposals also cover some interspersed land of 1st and 2nd phase acquisition area.

Government of Odisha had allowed the payment of *ex-gratia* over and above the compensation to all the land losers of KNIIC in difference phases. The up-to-date *Ex-gratia* Payment status is described below:

The major impediments to land acquisition has been—

- Some land owners are reluctant to part their land.
- The land losers are demanding higher compensation.
- They are also demanding employment for each land losing family.
- In some of the cases the land records have been too obsolete for rightful tenant to produce the relevant document.

Ex-gratia Payment

1. In 1997, Rs. 10,000 per acre was fixed as *ex-gratia* payment for all the lands acquired in Duburi Industrial Complex.
2. Again during 1997, additional grant of Rs. 5000 in addition to Rs. 10,000 was fixed as compensation after 1st April, 1997 who lost their land for M/s. NINL Ispat Limited.
3. During 2004 rate the *ex-gratia* ranged from Rs. 10,000 to Rs. 15,000.
4. During 2005, the *ex-gratia* was increased at the rate of Rs. 25,000 per acre over and above the compensation. This was applicable to all lands acquired in KNIIC except for NINL and MISL.
5. Government of Odisha has further decided to revise the quantum of *ex-gratia* overall amounting to Rs. 50,000 per acre including *ex-gratia* amount already received which cumulatively becomes Rs. 1,00,000 per acre. These are to be paid by IDCO.
6. *Ex-gratia* amount paid so far includes Rs. 28,00,17,466 covering an area 4957.05 acre.

Tribals from the Ho and Munda communities predominantly inhabit the villages near Kalinganagar. These villages were part of former Sukinda State during the colonial period. The tribal people in this area are mainly immigrants from Saraikela-Kharsawan in Jharkhand. The ruler of Sukinda brought the Ho community from Saraikela-Kharsawan to clean the forest and make the land cultivable. The land settlement was taken up and completed between 1922 and 1928. In the last 78 years there has been no land settlement in the area. The land records also continued to be in the name of the grandfathers of the present tenants in all tribal villages. Some tenants were given independent land rights but their number was very low. The immigrant Ho/Munda community in the Sukinda Valley cleared the wild forest and developed the land into fertile agriculture fields. The main land owning dominant caste in the district are Khandayats and their main occupation is agriculture. The loss of livelihood and insecure future has created tension among the displaced tribals. *Roughly 20 per cent of the tribal households owns some land. The remaining 80 per cent are engaged as wage labourers. The tribals have been cultivating and living on this land for generations.* In Kalinganagar area considerable number of them are left homeless and destitute.

Table 3.23: Land allotted to Industries in Kalinganagar

Sl. No.	*Name of the Industry*	*Government Land Allotted in Acres*	*Private Land Acquired through IDCO (In Acres)*	*Total in Acres*
1.	M/s. Neelachal Ispat Nigam Limited, Kalinganagar	2052.88	447.12	2500.00
2.	M/s. Mid-east Integrated Steel Ltd. Kalinganagar	102.53	428.15	530.68
3.	M/s. JSL Stainless Ltd. Kalinganagar	829.45	410.55	1240.00
4.	M/s. VISA Steel Ltd., Kalinganagar	91.30	468.70	560.00
5.	M/s. Rohit Ferrotech Ltd., Kalinganagar	4.60	45.40	50.00
6.	M/s. K.J. Ispat Ltd., Kalinganagar	16.97	33.03	50.00
7.	M/s. Maithan Ispat Ltd. Kalinganagar	1.37	123.63	125.00
8.	M/s. Dinabandhi Power and Steel Ltd., Kalinganagar	78.21	21.79	100.00
9.	M/s. Brahmani Rivers Pellect Ltd., Kalinganagar	52.27	36.73	89.00
10.	M/s. TATA Steel Ltd., Kalinganagar	571.89	2468.50	3040.39

(Contd.)

Sl. No.	*Name of the Industry*	*Government Land Allotted in Acres*	*Private Land Acquired through IDCO (In Acres)*	*Total in Acres*
11.	M/s. Apeejay Logistic Ltd. Kalinganagar	26.99	3.01	30.00
	Grand Total	**3828.46**	**4486.61**	**8315.07**

Source: Government of Odisha, Department of Revenue.

There was militant struggle by the tribals to prevent acquisition of land by the different industries particularly by the TATA Steels. The Government and the police also strongly repressed the protest launched by the tribals. The police also resorted to indiscriminate firing in Kalinganagar town and industrial complex particularly in the area meant for TATA Steel. The brutal firing by the police personnel resulted in the tribal youths, both boys and girls being killed in the police encounter. The list of the tribals, who were victims of police firing, are reproduced below.

Table 3.24: List of Persons Died in Police Firing in Kalinganagar, District Jajpur on 2nd January, 2006

Sl. No.	*Names*	*Father's/Husband's Name*	*Villages in P.S. Kalinganagar*
1.	Rama Gagarai	S/o Bisa Gagarai	Gadapur
2.	Ati Jamuda	S/o Uppan Jamuda	Chandia
3.	Landu Jarika	S/o Bagam Jarika	Gobarghati
4.	Bhagban Soy	S/o Badan Singh Soy	Gobarhati
5.	Mukuta Bankira	W/o Udaya Bankira	Candía
6.	Bana Badra @ Jagat Badra	S/o Routa Badara	Gadapur
7.	Jurga Jarita	W/o Surendra Jarita	Gobarghati
8.	Dagi Tiria	W/o Sarita Tiria	Champaakoila
9.	Gobinda Laguri	S/o Sitaram Laguri	Gobarghati
10.	Subam Barla	S/o Sada Charan Barla	Gobarghati
11.	Ramgalal Mundela	S/o Chandra Mundela	Baligarh
12.	Rama Chandra Jamuda	S/o Gpramga Jamada	Gobarghati
13.	Shyam Jambira	S/o Jambira	Baligarh
14.	Kiran Bandibuli (died on 2-4-2007)	S/o Sikur	Candía

Source: Government of Odisha Police.

Large number of families were protesting against Land Acquisition by the Government of Odisha for the Corporate Sector on the 2nd January, 2006 out of which the 14 families were killed in the course of police firing. *The tribals also established a Memorial in Kalinganagar to pay their obeisance to the Martyrs who sacrificed their lives for the cause of the tribal identity and land as a source of livelihood.* They also followed it up with one year long Rasta Roko of the important Highway which ultimately resulted in the Government of Odisha enacting the Odisha Rehabilitation Policy-2006 to enhance the compensation package. Being unnerved by the killing of tribals, the Government of Odisha hurriedly promulgated the Odisha Rehabilitation Act 2006. The Tata Steel Company also announced the enhanced rehabilitation package based on the new rehabilitation policy of Government of Odisha for the year 2006.

Rehabilitation and Re-settlement in Kalinganagar

Most of the acquisition of land in KNIC area was done before enactment of Odisha Resettlement and Rehabilitation Policy, 2006. As such Rehabilitation and Resettlement in Kalinganagar is done as per 2005 Guidelines of Revenue and Disaster Management Department.

The number of displaced persons rehabilitation is as follows:

Table 3.25: Displaced Persons provided Employment in Kalinganagar Industries

Sl. No.	*Name of the Industries*	*Total No. of families enumerated for displacement*	*No. of families physically displaced*	*Family resettled in the colony*	*Self-Relocated family*	*Employment Provided*	*Cash paid in lieu of employment*
1.	MISL	172	147	153	Nil	103	7
2.	NINL	668	645	158	491	436	167
3.	VISA Steel	39	39	3	36	29	10
4.	JSL Stainless	252	211	204	19	144	23
5.	K.J. Ispat Limited	8	8	Nil	8	6	2
6.	Rohit Ferro-tech	12	12	Nil	12	11	1
7.	Tata Steel	1234	993	786	36	Nil	162
8.	Apeejay Logistic	8	3	1	Nil	Nil	Nil
9.	BRPL	30	8	20	Nil	1	Nil
	Total	**2423**	**2066**	**1325**	**602**	**730**	**372**

Source: Information Sheet provided to Hon'ble Sub Committee-1 of the House Committee on Environment of Odisha Legislative Assembly during their visit on 10-01-2013 to District Jajpur.

The Hon'ble Sub-Committee of the Odisha Legislative Assembly was also provided with the figures of number of displaced families who were provided plots in different villages of Jajpur district:

Table 3.26: Resettlement Colony in Kalinganagar

Villages	*Area (in acre)*	*No. of plots allotted to the displaced families**
Gobarghati-1	140.00	465
Gobarghati-2	98.00	216
Trijanga-1	68.15	374
Trijanga-2	34.75	156
Sansailo	19.00	96
Kantipur	3.00	24
Total	**362.90**	**1331**

*Most of the amenities have been provided in the resettlement colony.

Source: Government of Odisha, Department of Revenue.

The different industries in Kalinganagar have also taken up Corporate Social Responsibility (CSR) activities since 2009-10 onwards. It is necessary to make a special mention of *Tata Steel Project* since the major violence in Kalinganagar Complex in 2006 had arisen due to the administration providing massive police support to the Tata Steel Project. The major reason was the land acquisition for the Tata Steel Project both for the Plant Site as also for the Rehabilitation Colony. The lands acquired and alienated by Tata Steel Plant both for the plant site and the rehabilitation colony village-wise is given in Table 3.27.

Table 3.27: Lands acquired and leased out to Tata Steel Plant in Kalinganagar

Sl. No.	*Revenue Village*	*Total Area*	*Private Land*	*Government Land*	*Status of the Land*
1.	Chandia	1408.970	1146.750	262.220	Land Registered in favour of Tata Steel
2.	Gobaraghati	934.110	759.410	174.700	
3.	Nuagoan	122.716	90.130	32.586	
4.	Gadapur	505.320	391.160	114.160	
5.	Khurunti	140.282	127.842	12.440	
6.	Baragadia	360.410	240.520	119.890	Land yet to be registered
	Grand Total	**3471.808**	**2755.812**	**715.996**	
	Land acquired for Rehabilitation Colony				
	Gobaraghati	238.00	182.750	53.250	Land Provided by IDCO
	Trijanga-II	19.200	0.000	19.200	
	Sansoila	19.200	0.000	19.200	
	Baragadia	45.000	21.000	24.000	
	Total	**321.400**	**203.750**	**117.650**	

The figures in the above table indicate that the total area involved for the plant for the Tata Steel Project was 3,471.808 acre of which 2,755.812 acre was acquisition of private land and 715.996 acre was leased in land of the Government. All these plant site lands were part of the inhabitated villages of the tribals consisting of Chandia, Gobarghati, Nuagaon, Gadapur and Khurunti and Baragadia. For rehabilitation purpose lands were provided by IDCO from the villages of Gobarghati, Trijanga-II, Sansoila and Baragaria.

Table 3.28: Resettlement of Displaced Families of Specific Industries

Sl. No.	*Name of the Colony*	*Industries Concerned*	*No. of Families*
1.	Gobaraghati-I	TATA	364
		NINL	135
2.	Gobaraghati-II	TATA	236
3.	Trijanga-I	TATA	43
		JSL	138
		MISL	154
		NINL	26
		VISA	03
		Apeejay	01
		BRPL	20
4.	Trijanga-II	TATA	118
		JSL	46
		MISL	1
		NINL	1
5.	Sansailo	TATA	101
6.	Kantipur	JSL	26
7.	Self-relocated families	NINL	491
		TATA	36
		VISA	36
		JSL	14
		Rohit-ferrotech	12
		K.J. Ispat	8
		Total	**2010**

Source: Government of Odisha, Department of Revenue.

Position on Resettlement

The total number of displaced family in the seven major industries are 2211 in which 745 families have been resettled in the colony, 600 are self-relocated family, 463 have been in transit camp. Employment has been provided to 681 and 343 were paid cash in lieu of employment. Besides, 1,345 families have already been resettled or self-relocated and 403 were in the process of shifting among whom majority belongs to TATA Steel.

The industrial complex in Kalinganagar was established by acquiring 83 revenue villages in Sukinda and Danagadi block of Jajpur district. In Jharkhand the activist of Jharkhand Mines Areas Coordination Committee stage a demonstration on 3rd January, 2006 in Ranchi against the firing. The situation continued to remain tense in Kalinganagar. The road blockage continued along the Paradip-Daitri express highway as more than a thousand tribals armed with bows and arrows sat near Madhuban in Ambagadia village where the mass cremation of tribals were carried out. Over 15,000 tribals from across different parts of the country gathered at Kalinganagar on 30th January, 2006 to pay their homage to the 14 tribals who died in the police firing. The Bisthapan Birodhi Manch (peoples form against displacement) was leading the agitation. The palms of at least five of the 14 tribals killed were chopped off by the doctors to prevent identity of the victims. The doctors responsible for chopping the victim's hands off had been placed under suspension. The opposition sponsored dawn to dusk Odisha Bandh Call which was a success with a normal life paralysed across the State. This was a continuous call which was supported by all opposition parties. The State Government had announced a judicial probe into the Kalinganagar incident by the sitting High Court Judge as a commission of enquiry. The National Commission for Scheduled Tribes also sought a report from the State Government on the Kalinganagar firing. *The bows and arrows for tribals are symbols of solidarity and assertion.* The media also linked the tribals resistance with the Naxalite Movement. In case of Kalinganagar the Gram Sabhas were not consulted on the question of land acquisition. In case of NINL out of 634 displaced families who were given small plots of lands at Gobarghati rehabilitation colony to move away to other areas instead of settling down there.

The Odisha High Court took objections to the road blockage for one year and asked the State Government to lift it. The State Government of Odisha accordingly had removed the road blockage. The Tata Steel Company also started training some local people to work for the company. *In case of Kalinganagar, the Odisha Government never consulted the tribal Gram Sabhas before land acquisition. The tribal communities have been depending on land and forest for their livelihood. Taking their land away and uprooting them from their habitat is a cultural genocide. Their social, economic, kinship, political institutions and cultural identity are related to land and sacred forests.* The country has several policies in relation to land, forest, mines, education and environment to protect tribes. However, the displacement of tribes from their ancestral land is a mockery of all this safeguard measures (Nayak, Ramesh C. and Kujur, Joseph Marianus, 2007, New Delhi).

Tata Steel provided employment to 730 displaced persons from the villages of Ambagaria, Baidubri, Baligotha, Bamiagotha, Bandaragadia, Champakoila, Chandia, Gadapur, Gobarghati, Kalamatia, Sanachandia and Sasagotha. They were shifted from the villages during the year 2005, 2006, 2007, 2008, 2009, 2010, 2011 and some were also shifted during 2012. All the displaced families were included as part of Tata Pariwar. They were rehabilitated as per the comprehensive R&R Policy of Government of Odisha which was renamed as Revised Kalinganagar Policy, the main features of which were as follows:

- Additional *Ex-gratia* announced to increase the land compensation to Rs. 1 lakh per acre from Rs. 37,500 per acre disbursed in 1992-94.
- A 1/10 acre plot of land in the rehabilitation colony to each extended family.
- House Building Assistance increased from Rs. 0.5 lakh to Rs. 1.5 lakh.
- Temporary Shed Assistance increased from Rs. 5,000 to Rs. 10,000.
- Introduction of Maintenance Allowance of Rs. 2000 per month.
- Employment of one nominated family member or Cash in lieu, on their choice.
- Equal benefits to landless encroachers.
- Cut-off date for enumeration revised to 1st January, 2005.
- Revised Family definition for entitlement to R & R benefits.

The revised rehabilitation policy for Kalinganagar Tata Steel Limited had some beneficial provisions which gave positive incentive to the newly displaced and rehabilitated families. A typical case study of rehabilitation of a displaced Tata Steel Family would exemplify this.

Table 3.29: Case Study of the family of Late Sukura Soren, Hamlet—San Chandia, Mouza Chandia

1.	Land owned including House Site	2.79 acre
2.	Compensation for two Houses	Rs. 0.74 lakh
3.	Land compensation	Rs. 2.79 lakh
4.	8 Nos. of 1/10th Acre plot in the Rehabilitated Colony worth	Rs. 4.0 lakh
5.	Total House Building Assistance	Rs. 12.0 lakh
6.	Temporary Accommodation Assistance	Rs. 0.80 lakh
7.	Transport Allowance	Rs. 0.16 lakh
8.	Maintenance Allowance	Rs. 1.92 lakh
9.	Cash in Lieu of Employment for 3 persons	Rs. 6.0 lakh
10.	Employment	5 No.

Source: Field Study.

Late Sukura Soren had 3 sons, namely—Late Abhiram Soren, Madhu Soren (Male 71) and Sinu Soren (Male 60). Late Abhiram Soren had his surving wife Tulsi Soren (Female 56), Son Mansingh Soren (Male 33), Son Malaram Soren (Male 30 years), Son Manika Soren (Male 25 years) Son Rajen Soren (Male 43 years) and Son of Rajan Soren named Ghana Soren (Male 19 years). The displaced family of Late Sukura Soren became 8 expanded families and all the adult members were entitled for compensation and rehabilitation. All together they receive cash benefit of Rs. 28.41 lakh, five adult members got employment and their family income increased considerably. This is just a similar case study to point that in the aftermath of rehabilitation by Tata Steel several displaced tribal families could construct *pacca* houses and in this respect the rehabilitation package of Tata Steel Company was much better than other Steel companies of Kalinganagar Complex.

3.10 Odisha Government Rehabilitation and Resettlement Policy, 2006

K.B. Saxena (2009), has highlighted the positive features of the Odisha Government Rehabilitation and Resettlement Policy 2006 brought out in May, 2006. The Odisha Government brought out a rehabilitation and resettlement policy in May, 2006 (Government of Odisha, 2006). It applies to persons displaced on account of the acquisition of land carried out through negotiations also and not merely those affected as a result of compulsory acquisition by the Government. The definition of 'family' is more inclusive in the Odisha Policy than in the National Policy. It recognizes unmarried daughters and sisters more than thirty years of age, a widow or a women divorcee as a separate family for the benefit of rehabilitation and is, thus, gender neutral. Additionally, it empowers physically and mentally challenged persons and minor orphans by conferring the status of a separate family. The National Policy continues to show bias against these social groups. The Odisha Policy clearly stipulates that no physical displacement shall be effected before the completion of resettlement work while the National Policy is less equivocal on this issue. Multiple displacement does not even attract the attention of the National Policy. The Odisha Policy recognizes the harassment involved to the affected persons who have gone through the experience before and therefore, provides for least additional 50 per cent compensation over and above the normal compensation to mitigate it. In terms of concrete benefits, this provision is as valueless for the displace to get a job as in the National Policy. The only difference is that one time cash compensation ranging from 5 to 1 lakh where employment cannot be provided has been added in the Odisha policy.

A mandatory provision has been made for allotment of 2½ acre of irrigated agricultural land or five acre of non-irrigated agricultural land to each ST displaced family in type (c) projects while the displaced families of all other social categories would be provided with two acre of irrigated or four acre of non-irrigated agricultural land. On the provision of homestead land and house building assistance, the Odisha Policy is more liberal than the National Policy. It provides for at least 1/10 of an acre for this purpose along with a house building grant of Rs. 1,50,000 for projects in rural areas and 1/25 of an acre with a house building grant of Rs. 1,50,000 in urban areas. It is in respect of benefits to the landless and the homestead less encroachers that the Odisha Policy shows greater sensitivity than is to be found in the National Policy. The landless encroachers will get *ex-gratia* equivalent compensation admissible under the Land Acquisition Act. The entitlement, however, would be restricted to one standard acre of encroachment. The homestead less persons would similarly get cash compensation against encroached homestead of 1/10th of an acre in rural and 1/25th of acre in urban areas subject to the a above conditions.

It can be stated as a concluding note pertaining to the Development Induced Displacement in Odisha that:

- The tribals in Odisha have a prolonged history of militant resistance against land alienation and land acquisition.
- They have again demonstrated this in the contemporary land acquisition process and particularly during the globalization era.

- The noteworthy militant resistance have been demonstrated in Kalinganagar Episode and in POSCO struggle.
- The Activists including the radicals have actively supported the tribal movements in different parts of Odisha.
- The women have played a crucial role in resistance movement everywhere and their participation in POSCO Movement have been exemplary.
- The environmental experts like Shri N.C. Saxena have played significant role in clearly pointing out that the Forest Rights Act, 2006 were violated in case of POSCO Project and Acquisition of Land by Vedanta from Niyamgiri Hills.
- The Dongaria Konds could adequately resist their sacred and religious significance of Niyamgiri Hills and even the Supreme Court pronounced positive decision protecting the land rights, forest rights and religious rights.
- The State Government of Odisha violated most of the protective legislations like the PESA Act of 1996, provision of Scheduled V Area, Forest Rights Act, 2006, role of Gram Sabha and liberally used Brutal Police Force to protect the Corporate Interest.
- The tribal and the marginalized sections amply demonstrated that the militant protest movement, their collective solidarity, their cultural identity with land and forest are their major strength.
- On the aftermath of the Kalinganagar Massacre the Government of Odisha was compelled to enact the Odisha Resettlement and Rehabilitation Policy, 2006.
- The Land Acquisition and Land Alienation Policy is a continuity of Colonial and Post-Colonial policy.
- Felix Padel and Samrendra Das (2008) have rightly characterized the police firing in Maiknch Village in December 2000 and in Kalinganagar Industrial Area in January, 2006 as "Cultural Genocide, the extension of people community and social structure". They have also termed it as "Internal Colonialism" carried out through large scale privatization of resources and takeover of huge tracks of cultivable land by corporates.
- They have also significantly observed that mining bauxite from Niyamgiri Hills is an assault on Kond Religion as they recognize mountains as sacred entities and source of life. "Cultural Genocide" and the sacrificing people's quality of

life make-up their cultural and community life. According to Felix Padel and Samrendra Das, the present situation in Odisha involves sacred high profile struggles of people opposing displacement in the State. "Physical Genocide" meaning the extermination of all members of a tribe often went alongside "cultural genocide": "The Killing of Cultures", "Cultural Genocide" most clearly applies to tribal cultures which differ markedly from mainstream orientation in their lifestyle groundedness in the nature.

3.11 Development, Displacement and Land Acquisition in Jharkhand

No region in the world is gifted with such a vast occurrences of varieties of minerals as in Jharkhand. The State occupies first position (30% of total coal reserve) in coal reserve in the country with 73,897 million tonnes of deposits which are located in Dhanbad, Bokaro, Ramgarh, Hazaribagh, Dumka, Pakur Deoghar, Godda, Giridih, Ranchi. The State holds second position (28%) in iron ore reserve in the country. The future of steel production in the country will largely depend upon exploitation of iron ore deposit of these areas. The State has reserve of 117.54 million tonnes of bauxite in the plateau area of Gumla, Latehar and Lohardaga districts which is presently catering to the need of one alumina and another aluminium plant located at Muri, Ranchi and Renukut. The State occupies 17th position in limestone deposit in the country with 745.77 million tonnes of reserve which is distributed in Hazaribagh, Ranchi, Ramgarh, Godda, Palamau, Latehar, Bokao and East Singhbhum districts of the State. Singhbhum Thrust Zone (STZ) is situated in the south western part of State has potential of rare earth metal and minor metals. The area near Bahragora Kond and Gohakle to Darhaul and between Ramchandra Pahar to Duorpuram-Karaikela Bentanagar have good prospect for exploration and development of these minerals. (Mineral Resources, "the Opportunity in Jharkhand", Ministry of Mines and Geology, Government of Jharkhand, 2003).

Damodar is a small rainfed river originating from the Khamerpet hill near the trijunction of Palamau, Hazaribagh and Ranchi districts. It flows through the cities of Ramgarh, Dhanbad, Asansol, Durgapur, Burdwan and Howrah, before joining the lower Ganga (Hooghly estuary) at Chayampur, 55 km. downstream of Howrah. Today this river is considered a sacred river by the local people, looks like a sewage canal, shrunken and filled with filth and rubbish, emanating obnoxious odours. Damodar basin is the repository of nearly 46 per cent of the coal reserves of India. Seven coalfields are presently located along this river. Because of the easy availability of coal in this belt, many coal based industries like coal washeries, coke oven plants, coal fired thermal power plants and steel plants are located on this river. The huge quantities of untreated industrial wastewater that is discharged by these industries into the river, often containing toxic metals, are the main source of contamination of the river. It is obvious that due to extensive coal mining and vigorous growth of industries in the area, water resources have been badly contaminated. The people living in this area are forced to use this contaminated water as there is no alternate source of drinking water. Therefore, a sizeable part of the population suffers from water-borne diseases. The most common diseases in this area are diarrhea, dysentery, skin infections, work infections, jaundice and typhoid. Dysentery and skin infections are exceptionally high.

The women are thus forced to lead unhygienic lives by not bathing daily, not washing clothes regularly and not drinking water adequately. It has been found out that due to water contamination the villagers avoid taking bath everyday, and that there is a gap of 5 to 10 days. Clothes are kept unclean and washed infrequently. Children are the most affected due to living in such unhygienic conditions and filth. The water scourge also leads to social ill-health as tensions build up among the women everyday.

Chhotanagpur Tenancy Act, 1908 and Santhal Parganas Tenancy Act, 1949 are protective legislations designed to protect Adivasi lands from alienation. Similarly, the Fifth Schedule in the Constitution gives special emphasis on the protection of the lands, culture, livelihoods and social values of the Adivasis. But it is ironical that despite all these constitutional safeguards and protection, it is the Adivasi people who have been displaced the most for development projects in Jharkhand. *Out of this, 40 per cent of the total displacement has been for mining purposes*. The PESA is an important legislation acknowledging the rights of the Adivasis over natural resources and giving Gram Sabhas powers to prevent land alienation. But, unfortunately, the Jharkhand Panchayat Raj Act, 2000 has overlooked all the clauses devolving such important powers to Gram Sabhas.

The health hazards related to mining have not yet received any serious attention as a serious public health issue. The damaging effects of radiation on the health of miners and their families as well as the villagers living in surrounding villages of the uranium mine in Jadugoda is an issue that has been constantly pushed under the carpet by the company as well as the government. Safety regulations and norms are flouted with impunity, whether it is in Jadugoda or Roro or in any mine dealing with hazardous minerals and chemical substances. Occupational health of mine workers, especially in the unorganized sector is an area that is totally untouched.

Table 3.30: Total Number of Tribals displaced in Jharkhand (1951-1995)

Sl. No.	*Project Name*	*Total Displaced*	*Scheduled Tribes*	*Percentage*
1.	Water Resources	2,32,968	1,75,127	75.2
2.	Industries/	66,087	22,473	34.0
	Quasi Industries	21,809	7,415	—
3.	Mining, coal/non-coal	2,68,588	79,568	29.6
4.	Defence establishment	2,64,353	23,7147	89.7
5.	Wildlife/national park	5,09,918	80,867	15.8
6.	Infrastructure development	50,000	13,800	27.6
	Grand Total	**14,13,723**	**6,16,397**	**45.32**

Source: Ekka, Alexius and Mohammed Asif, 2000. *Development induced Displacement and Rehabilitation in Jharkhand: A database on its Extent and Nature*, New Delhi: Indian Social Institute.

The estimated displacement by major dams in Jharkhand include 26,046 hactare from Damodar Dam, 12,805 hectare from Icha Dam (30,800 number of displaced persons out of which 80% are tribals) from Chandil Dam the area of displacement is 17,683 hectare comprising 37,600 number of displaced persons covering 87.92 per cent of tribal population and from Koel-Karo Project estimated displacement is 17,764 hectare and the total number of displaced persons is 37,600 and covering 87.92 per cent of the tribal population.

3.12 Law for Acquisition of Land in Coal Bearing Areas

British East India Company had started mining of coal in India for the first time at Ranigunj in Bengal in 1774. In the 1800s, many private individuals and companies obtained coal mining leases from the colonial government and started mining. The coal mines were concentrated in Bengal on the banks of river Damodar. By 1891, there were 91 companies involved in coal mining. There were 725 coal mines operating in India by 1942. With Independence in 1947, the mineral rights in all the areas, with the exception of the permanently settled areas of Bengal and Bihar, vested in the Government. The Coal Bearing Areas (Acquisition and Development) Act, 1957 was passed by the Parliament primarily to enable the State to take control over the mineral rights of private owners. This Act had special provisions for acquiring mineral rights, which had been granted earlier by private land owners to individuals or companies.

Acquisition of Land for Mining

The procedure for acquisition of land for prospecting and extraction of various minerals is governed by the following Acts:

- Land Acquisition Act, 1894.
- Coal Bearing Areas (Acquisition and Development) Act, 1957.
- Atomic Energy Act, 1962—in the case of atomic minerals. (Ms Ajita Susan George).

It may be necessary to mention that the Tata Steel Project (TISCO) displaced 3,564 acre of tribal people during 1907, the Heavy Engineering Corporation acquired 9,200 acre from 25 villages during 1958 displacing 12,990 tribals, Bokaro Steel Plant acquired land from 46 villages in which the number of tribals displaced were 12,487 and between 1981-1985 the lands acquired for Coal Mining was 1,50,300 acre. *Here some of the empirical studies conducted by Ajita Menon* a social activist in Jharkhand is being briefly reviewed to get an understanding of the situation as it exists today.

- Coal Mine at East Parej, Hazaribagh district.
- Proposed Coal Mine at Pachwara in Amrapara block, Pakur district.

Case Study of Parej

Parej is a village that is situated to the east of the North Karanpura valley and on the western boundary of the West Bokaro Coalfields. It comes under Mandu block of Hazaribagh district. Tata Steel has their captive collieries very close to Parej. In fact, one of the tolas of Parej had partially been acquired by Tata Steel, for their coal mine. CCL started acquisition proceedings in this area in 1983, when they issued the first notification under section (4) of CBAA. East Parej open cast coal mine is one of the 25 mines supported by the World Bank under the Coal Sector Environmental Social Mitigation Project (CSESMP) of Coal India. Mining started here in 1993, though the World Bank Project was initiated only in 1997. Two villages had to be completely relocated for the project, East Parej and Duru Kasmar, which involved 227 families.

World Bank Support to Coal Sector Reform in India

The CSESMP was designed to assist Coal India's efforts to mitigate the environmental and social impacts of the mining expansion to be undertaken in 25 mines under the proposed CSRP. In May 1996, World Bank informed that the CSESMP and CSRP would be linked by cross-conditionality. In the same month, the IDA granted a credit of US $ 2 million was approved for financing CSRP. Because of implementation difficulties, this loan was cancelled in July 2000. Coal India, however, decided to continue with the mitigation programmes started under the CSESMP. On April 20, 2001 it requested and the Bank agreed to extend the CSESMP closing date for one year from June 30, 2001 to June 30, 2002.

The first tola that had to be relocated under East Parej O.C. mine was that of Turis, traditional basket-makers, classified by the government as Scheduled Caste. The Turis were earlier living in Sonaghuttu, one of the tolas of Parej and nearly 30 years ago, were displaced from there by Tata Steel Company. The Turis demanded from CL that they would move out of their houses only after the rehabilitation site at Pindra was ready in all respects. CCL has also filed a civil suit for the eviction of the villagers of Turi tola, in the district court, saying they were squatters on CCL land. This case went on for nearly 2 years and finally, a compromise was reached between the two parties on the advice of the judge. The compromise formula included withdrawal of criminal charges against the 4 persons, provision of plots of land with ownership titles at the rehabilitation site of their choice, Prem Nagar, provision of facilities like, drinking water, school, community centre, at the site. CCL agreed to provide two jobs, one for Rameswar Turi, against a land area of 2.08 acre and another for Pano Devi. a widow whose husband had died in jail arrested in an excise related case.

Chhotanagpur Adivasi Sewa Samiti (CASS), had brought to the World Bank's notice many times, that the standards or targets set by the

World Bank for the CSESMP were not being met by CCL, the enforcing agency. Actually, this was the most supervised project under CSESMP. These included inadequate compensation for land and for houses, Resettlement sites lacking basic facilities like potable water, schools, availability of casual labour opportunities, Title to house plots not made available to PAPs, Inadequate compensation for PAPs' traditional land rights, No compensation for loss of access to forest produce, failure to restore incomes, failure to provide land for land, failure to provide subsistence allowance during transition period, non-functioning of the Public Information Centre, failure to disclose important information to PAPs, Lack of consultations with local villagers and NGOs among others.

Coal India's R & R policy "underscores that the subsidiaries have a responsibility towards the landless, whose livelihood is often taken away" and includes landless labourers, sharecroppers, land lessees, tenants and tribals dependent on forest produce, into the ambit of Project Affected Persons (PAPs). At present, the only jobs that the displaced persons get, is of loading coal into the trucks at the coal dump. For that job also, there are too many candidates, so a person will have to wait for days, before his/her turn comes up. Some of them are doing their traditional jobs, but many have disappeared.

Women—Compensating their Losses

One section of society, whose losses due to displacement and relocation are the least discussed or understood, is women. They are often counted with their husbands and minor children along with widows and unmarried daughters, if any, as one unit, for purposes of rehabilitation. Each major son (married or unmarried) will constitute a separate family. When it comes to getting jobs, it is the men who get jobs, as heads of households or as sons. A very small percentage of women, widows or unmarried daughters, where there are no sons, get jobs. In Parej, where 595 families were displaced, about 25 jobs were given to the PAPs, out of which only one woman, Bilaso Devi got a job. What happens to the women after displacement? They become homebound and thrown out of the production process. The incidence of violence or atrocities on women is high in mining areas. Cases of rape, murder, molestation are reported frequently from mining areas, where people from different ethnic and cultural backgrounds come together. Domestic violence is also high in mining areas.

One of the serious problems that the displaced people in the coal mining areas experience is that they are not given title deeds for the land that has been allotted to them at the rehabilitation sites. This is because, most of the time, they are rehabilitated on land which the CCL has taken on lease from the government and CCL cannot give ownership rights to people on that land. In Parej, the question of *patta* (title deed) for allotted house sites was raised first when the people of Turi Tola, the earliest tola to be displaced, demanded that land *pattas* be issued in their names before they would move to the rehabilitation site.

Sunil Minj and Gladson Dungdung (2013) in his book "*Vikas Ke Kabragah*" has brought our attention to three important displacement before independence and immediately after independence in Jharkhand. These relate to: Tata Steel which acquired land during 1907, Heavy Engineering Corporation, Ranchi which acquired land immediately after independence during 1956 and Bokaro Steel Company during the 1960s. The Tata Steel Company had acquired 12,708.59 acre all of which were Raiyati Land (belonging to tribal and non-tribals), Heavy Engineering Corporation acquired 7,199.71 acre of which 6,355.82 acre land belong to the land owners and rest of the lands were government and forest lands; Bokaro Steel Limited had acquired 26,908.565 acre of private land and the rest were government and forest land, i.e. a total of 31,287.24 acre. The authors also mention that the Tata Steel Limited has still kept 31.54 per cent of the total land unused; HEC has kept 2910 acre of lands unused and Bokaro Steel Limited has kept 20.1 per cent of the total land unused. This is also the common practice of land acquisition in most of the projects for which lands are acquired.

3.13 Pachwara Coal Mining Project

It was reported in the local media, around May 2002, that a coal-mining project was granted to the Punjab State Electricity Board (PSEB) in the Scheduled Tribal area in Amarapara Block in Pakur District in Jharkhand, Eastern India. The PSEB is a "public utility service" wholly owned by the Government of Punjab. By a letter of the Ministry of Coal and Mines (Department of Coal), letter No. 47011/1(4) 2000-CPAM dated 26th December, 2001, Pachwara Central Block was allotted to the PSEB for captive mining for supply of coal on an exclusive basis to its own power plants. According to Gazette notification, by the Ministry of Coal and Mines (Department of Coal) F.No. 38011/4/2002 CA dated 22 February, 2002 the Central Government specified "as an end use the supply of coal from the Pachwara Central Block by PANEM Coal Mines Limited on an

F.No. 38011/4/2002 CA dated 22 February, 2002 the Central Government specified "as an end use the supply of coal from the Pachwara Central Block by PANEM Coal Mines Limited on an 00exclusive basis to the power plants of Punjab Electricity Board for generation of thermal power. Pachwara Coal Mines area covering 41 square kilometres with demarcated divisions such as North, South and Central Blocks. Pachwara Central Block is given to PSEB. This Block measures approximately 13 square kilometres covering nine revenue villages (*mouzas*) such as Singhdehri, Taljhari, Kathaldih, Chilgo, Bisupur Dangapara, Amjhari, Liberia and Pachwara.

The following descriptions of land will be affected/utilized by the Central Block:

- Raiyati land: 640 hectares
- Forest: 360 hectares
- Homestead: 2 hectares
- Wasteland: 15 hectares
- Nala River: 34 hectares
- Road: 28 hectares
- Grazing land: 22 hectares.

The Central Block envisages 44 years of open cast mining to extract 289 million tonnes of coal. The Jharkhand Government is expected to get annual royalty at the rate of Rs. 100 crore. It is also estimated by official figures that within next 10-15 years 250 families will be displaced and afterwards possibly more.

The PSEB has worked out a Rehabilitation Package. The details are as follows:

- Monetary compensation calculated on the basis of prevailing legal norms.
- The company may consider employment against land in exceptional circumstances' only to fill vacancies subject to the land losers meeting the eligibility criteria.
- Employment may be offered to one member of a family who has lost three or more acre of land subject to vacancy and eligibility criteria.
- It is not possible to offer employment due to lack of vacancy; one time cash grant/monetary compensation in lieu of employment for acquisition of land on following basis shall be applicable.

- Rs. 50,000 only for the first acre of land on *prorata* basis subject to a minimum of Rs. 20,000 only.
- Rs. 30,000 only on *pro rata* basis for 2nd and 3rd acre of land.
- Rs. 20,000 only on *pro rata* basis for land beyond three acre.

These conditions were not acceptable to the PUCL and also to the local people. The PSEB incited some of the local youths to support the starting of the mine by giving them money and other incentives. Several of the local agitating tribals were arrested and subjected to humiliation. The village leaders strongly felt that this was an instance where the law and order machinery was being used by the PSEB Company with the support of the State Government and the local administration to stifle the voices of the Adivasi people demanding their legal rights.

Apart from these land acquisition the Subarnrekha Dam Project also displaced a large number of tribals and other marginalized people from the villages of the district of Saraikela, East Singhbhum and West Singhbhum. The total area acquired by them for the entire Subarnrekha Project was 8,222.20 acre comprising 76 villages. The process of rehabilitation for this project is almost in the process of completion. (Special Land Acquisition Officer, Subarnrekha Project, Adityapur, 4-10-2016).

3.14 Displacement during Globalization Era

During the Globalization era the Government of Jharkhand passed the Jharkhand Industrial Policy, 2001 under the Chief Ministership of Shri Babulal Marandi. The Industrial Policy of 2001 proposed to optimally utilize the available resources of the State in a planned manner and to accelerate the industrial development of the State. This industrial policy envisaged that land/sheds in growth centres and industrial areas would be allotted to entrepreneurs for setting their industrial units on lease of 30 years. The State Government shall constitute a "Land Bank" at district level to make available the required land to intending entrepreneurial to overcome the delay in land acquisition process. Waste land/Degraded forest land will be made available by the State Government on long term basis after taking prior approval from the GoI under Section 2 of Forest Conservation Act, 1980. The State Government will assist the entrepreneurs in providing land and also in acquiring land for locating industrial units outside industrial areas/growth centres. The Chhotanagpur Tenancy Act, 1908 has been land bank out of which the collectors would authorize to lease up to 5 acre of Government land for industrial purposes and government land in excess of 5 acre would be least to entrepreneurs by the collector with the approval of high level empowered committee headed by Members Board of Revenue. Government would encourage establishment of private industrial estates by acquiring and making available such land at the acquisition cost. The Government also will provide infrastructure facilities such as water, electricity and road at the doorstep of such private industrial State. The area of such private industrial estate shall not be less than 100 acre. (Jharkhand Industrial Policy, 2001).

It is necessary to mention here that some of the major industrial concerns like Jindal, Arcelor Mittal and other corporate industries wanted to acquire land in the district of East Singhbhum but the local Tribal Activists strongly resisted which was a big setback to them and as a result of that many of the corporate industries cancelled their MoU with the Government of Jharkhand which was a big setback to the newly formulated industrial policy of Government of Jharkhand. In this process 38 corporates cancelled their MoU with the Government of Jharkhand amounting to Rs. 1.24 lakh crores. Thereafter, the Government of Jharkhand made modifications in the land acquisition process and proposed that the corporate should directly purchase the lands from the Raiyats instead of Government acquiring lands for them. *Still the State Government helped by leasing out of Government lands to the Corporate.* For example in the district of Saraikela-Kharsawan, the Abhijit Company was provided with *167.25 acre of Government land* and the company had purchased 57 acre of land from the tribals and non-tribals. The Adhunik Alloy was allocated 299.28 acre of government land and besides that it also purchased land directly from the Raiyats in Gamharia Tehsil of Saraikela-Kharsawan District. In the same manner Tata Power Ltd. Trirudih was also leased out government land in the Saraikela District. M/s Rungta Limited was leased out Government land in the Rajnagar Tehsil of Saraikela District; it also purchased private land from large number of private land owners.

The Government of Jharkhand again passed an Industrial Policy during 2012. This Industrial Policy states that land acquisition for industrial enterprise, i.e. voluntary or involuntary shall be done as provided under Indian Land Acquisition Act and Jharkhand Voluntary Land Acquisition Rule, 2010. Direct purchase of land for industrial enterprises shall be done as provided under CNT/SPT Act. Provision of Scheduled Area Act and PESA shall be applied wherever applicable. GM land or Government land may be transferred to the investing industrial enterprises only when most of the Raiyat and other types of land availability is ensured. GM land may be leased out to the investing industrial enterprises for 30 years with a provision of renewal of lease twice on specified terms and conditions notified by the Department of Revenue and Land Reforms. All efforts shall be made to avoid use of double crock or rich agriculture land to minimize displacement. Wasteland/degraded forest land may be made available by the State Government on long term lease basis after taking approval from Government of India. Government will try to acquire land in new suitable location and ensure infrastructure development for specific and general industries. Cases of industries which have been allotted mines but not set up their plans or where reserve of the leased mines is an excess requirement of the plan are proposed to be reviewed and if required the steps will be initiated for cancellation of the allotted mines or curtailment in the least quantity of raw-materials.

Jharkhand Industrial Policy, 2012 made specific provisions for Land Allocation to the Corporate Sector as indicated below:

- Efforts will be made to create land bank in each district by acquiring minimum of 200-500 acre of land and demarcating them as industrial estates with provision of basic industrial infrastructure.
- A comprehensive exercise will be undertaken to identify and utilize land that is owned by the Government or common land, mostly waste and fallow land in different parts of the State.
- Land acquisition for industrial enterprises, i.e. voluntary or involuntary shall be done as provided/applicable under Indian Land Acquisition Act and Jharkhand Voluntary Land Acquisition Rule, 2010.
- Direct Purchase of Land for Industrial Enterprises shall be done as provided under CNT/SPT Act.
- Provision of Scheduled Area Act (PESA) shall be applied as above, whenever applicable.
- GM land or Government land may be transferred to the investing industrial enterprises only when most of the raiyat and other types of land availability is ensured.
- GM land may be leased out to the investing industrial enterprises for 30 years with a provision of renewal of lease twice on specified terms and conditions notified by the Department of Revenue and Land Reform. However, the land shall be used for the purpose it has been allotted within 5 years from the date of transfer.

- In case of conversion of agricultural land for industrial purpose the prevailing revenue rules pertaining to rent and transfer will be applicable.
- All efforts shall be made to avoid use of double-cropped or rich agricultural land and to minimize displacement.
- Waste land/degraded forest land may be made available by the State Government on long term lease basis after taking prior approval from the Government of India under Section 2 of Forest (Conservation) Act, 1980, wherever required, for plantation development/tourism purposes which will encourage forest based tourism industries.
- Government will try to acquire land in new suitable location and ensure infrastructure development for specific and general industries.
- It is proposed to allot mines/captive mines on preferentially viable sick units which have previously generated adequate employment and revenue resources for the State Government will be preferred over industries situated outside the State.
- Cases of industries which have been allotted mines but not set up their plants or where reserve of the leased mines is in excess of the requirement of the plant are proposed to be reviewed and, if required, the steps will be initiated for cancellation of the allotted mines or curtailment in the leased quantity of raw material.
- Efforts will also be made to allot more iron ore and coal mines etc. to Jharkhand State Mineral Development Corporation (JSMDC) to enable the industrial units including group of MSMEs with adequate financial viability to enter into joint venture with other companies for taking up the development of these mines for supplying raw materials to the needy industries of the State.

Subsequent to the Industrial Policy of 2012, around 55 companies have been provided lands for various kinds of mineral, like Graphite, Limestones, Gold, Coal, Iron Ore, China Clay, Kynite, Bauxite, Uranium etc. in the districts of Palamau, Giridih, Chaibasa, East Singhbhum, Kodarma, Jamtara, Palamau, Latehar, Ranchi, West Singhbhum, East Singhbhum, Saraikela Kharsawan, Deoghar, Gumla, Bokaro, Lohardaga and Pakur. The corporate groups like Abhijit Group, NTPC, JVK and some other corporate groups also acquired land during the globalization etc. The Government of Jharkhand is facing lot of constraints due to the agitation and movement of the militant tribal groups as also due to the Naxalite Movement. (*See* Appendix-I for details).

The tribals in Jharkhand are still sanguine to their traditional leadership of *Munda, Manjhi, Manki, Baisi, Parha* System which are the traditional source of their identity and strength. These traditional ingredients still continue to be the major source of strength for the tribals to preserve and protect their land, forest and identity.

List of Mines granted during the Globalization Era in Jharkhand

Sl. No.	*Name of Company*	*District*	*Area*	*Date of Grant*
1.	Jharkhand State Mining Development Corporation	Latehar	100.47 acre	12-8-2003
2.	Sri Hemant Kr. Poddar	Palamau	78.47 acre	12-9-2003
3.	M/s. Rungta Mines Limited	Chaibasa	138.84 acre	01-10-2004
4.	M/s. Jagnath Cement Works Private Ltd.	Saraikela	33.715 acre	06-12-2004
5.	M/s. Ganga Engineering	Saraikela	77.49 acre	15-12-2004
6.	M/s. Mangilal Rungta	Chaibasa	226.81	17-12-2004
7.	M/s. Bheli Refractories Limited	W. Singhbhum	674.86 acre	31-5-2005
8.	Usha Martine Limited	W. Singhbhum	155.08 ha	23-3-2005
9.	M/s. Panem Coal Mines Limited	Pakur	2556.74 ha	16-1-2004 & 30-3-2005
10.	M/s. Jindal	Gumla	388.88 acre	19-8-2005
11.	Sri Bachhan Pd. Singh	Latehar	106.59 acre	10-9-2005
12.	UCIL	East Singhbhum	1128.32 acre	24-6-2005
13.	M/s. Indal	Gumla	471.84 acre	13-3-2006
14.	Tata Steel Limited	Bokaro	2700 acre	07-11-2006
15.	Usha Martine Limited	Palamau	687.93 ha	07-3-2007
16.	M/s. Electro Steel Casting Limited	Bokaro	8.80 Sq km	20-12-2007
17.	UCIL	East Singhbhum	557.18 acre	26-4-2008
18.	UCIL	East Singhbhum	433.42 acre	26-4-2008
19.	UCIL	East Singhbhum	253.44 acre	26-4-2008
20.	UCIL	East Singhbhum	303.14 acre	26-4-2008
21.	M/s. Minerals and Minerals	Lohardaga	270.59 acre	16-5-2008
22.	Tenughat Emta Coal Mines Limited	Hazaribagh	221.00 ha	14-11-2008 & 14-9-2012
23.	M/s. Anandita Traders and Inverstment Ltd.	West Singhbhum	116.50 acre	01-12-2008
24.	GVK Power (Govindwal Sahib) Ltd.	Hazaribagh	584.95 ha	17-1-2009
25.	M/s. Minerals and Minerals	Gumla	332.04 acre	18-7-2009
26.	M/s. Murliwala Partner–Sri Binod Kumar Tiwary	Giridih	9.81 ha	16-8-2010
27.	M/s. Bangal Emta Coal Mines Limited	Pakur	1218 ha	12-9-2012

Source: IDCO.

3.15 The Highlights of Land Acquisition and Displacement in Jharkhand

- The Adivasis in Jharkhand have a militant tradition of land struggle since the Colonial period.
- They have tried to preserve the integrity of Land and Forest issue as an important ingredient of their cultural identity.
- The Private Property Right in Land, the undermining of communal rights, the colonial law of Land Acquisition of 1894 have been the major precipitant to aggravate the land struggle among tribals as a live issue.
- The Land Acquisition has been invariably forced on the tribals as the welfare law like Schedule-V provision, the favourable feature of PESA have never been enacted to safeguard the Land Right of the Tribals.
- One of the important limitations has been that the tribals were reduced to minority status in their State which was a constraint to preserve their cultural identity. In the emerging contest, the Adivasis have rightly united with *Moolnivasis* and the Proletariates.
- The attachment to Chhotanagpur Tenancy Act, 1908, the Santhal Pargana Tenancy Act, 1949, the Khutkatti Rights make them alive to the Traditional Cultural Identity and Traditional Ingredient.
- Dr. Hari Mohan Mathur an expert on Development and Displacement has commented that "Project Induced Displacement is one of the most serious issues of social development causing widespread concern and demanding immediate attention". Prof. Upender Bakshi one of the leading intellectuals of the country is critical of the Corporate view of Development who maintain that there can be no Vikas (Development) without *Vinash* (Destruction). In this sort of discourse, the violence of developmental destruction stands presented as fully servicing the means and ends of development. According to him in the distinctive genre of Indian Political culture fully missing the sense of accusation of the human rights-oriented Indian habits of governance. This invites some anxious consideration of human rights cost of insurgent and ungovernable forms of constitutional insurgency as well.

- According to Usha Ramanathan, displacement is based on the colonial the Land Acquisition Act, 1894 that has survived generations, seeing three centuries, and thrived when India was a colony and rather through independence. The LAA, 1894 is an expression of doctrine of eminent domain, which invest power in the State to take over private land for a public purpose. This appropriation is converted into acquisition and the cosine nature of the taking over is toned down by compensating persons with interest in the land. There is a presumption of morality and a notion of the greater good attaching to "public purpose" that has acquired axe-rated validity. The LAA 1894 is a significant element in effective mass displacement.
- Another expert in this field Shri Shekhar Singh has observed that forcible displacement is perhaps among the worst forms of violence that innocence can be legally subjected to.
- Michel M. Cernea one of the authority in this field has commented that the experience of countless development projects and recurrence of impoverishment despite the payment of compensation and has generated from opposition to displacement like the killing of people and there is growing resistance at Kalinganagar, Singur and Nandi Gram during 2006-07.
- Another distinguished person in the field Dr. Walter Fernandes has estimated that over six million people have been displaced in the country between 1951 and 2004 in which the tribals account for 40 per cent of the displaced followed by Dalits who constitute another 16 per cent of the displaced. Women and children feel the ill effects more than men.
- Felix Padel and Samarendra Das had resulted in 'genocide' which essentially means the killing of people culture by approaching them from their ancestral lands. The killings of the tribals and the marginalized people at Mikinch and Kalinganagar have been enumerated as symbolizing a psychic death for the Adivasis. According to Ritu Diwan, a Professor in Bombay University, the first and most profound impact of development induced displacement is their grammatical increase in the germination of poverty and the overall decline in the economic and extra-economic status of women. [Mathur, Hari Mohan (2008), "India Social Development Report 2008: Development and Displacement", Council for Social Development, Oxford University Press, New Delhi].

- The massive resistance to land acquisition throughout the country created an atmosphere for the Central Government to enact the Land Acquisition Amendment Act of 2013 which has brought some positive dimension to the Forcible Land Acquisition Act of 1894. "The Right to Fair Compensation and Transparency in Land Acquisition, Rehabilitation and Resettlement, 2013" has provided higher compensation for land acquisition (at least four times of market prices in rural areas and twice the market price in urban areas) and makes consent of 80 per cent and 70 per cent of affected land owners as imperative for acquiring land for private and public-private partnership projects.
- It has compensation provisions for landless households like tenants, farm workers, who depend on farming activity on acquired land, and automatic rehabilitation and resettlement (R&R) package is applicable if the acquired land is more than 100 acre in rural areas and 50 acre in urban areas. Further, irrigated and multi-cropped land can be acquired only as the last resort and only up to a small percentage of total such land in a given areas, for example, not more than 5 per cent in multi-crop districts. It also includes annuities, land for land, transportation allowance, a portion of capital gains from resale and construction of alternative housing and communal amenities in the even of loss of homestead, tightens the definition of public purpose, and provides for social impact assessment (SIA) (Ghatak & Ghosh, 2011; Raghuram & Sunny, 2015). For the first time, land acquisition and R&R provisions have been brought together in one law RECTLARRA, 2013 (Nielsen & Nielsen, 2015). [Sukhpal Singh (2016), "Land Acquisition in India: an Examination of the 2013 Act and Options", *Journal of Land and Rural Studies*, Special Issues—Land Acquisition, Rehabilitation and Resettlement in India (LARR), Vol., IV, Issue 1, January, 2016, pp. 66-78].
- The Land Acquisition Act, 1894 was comprehensively amended in 2013 which, among others, provided for prior consent of land owners in cases of acquisition for private companies and public partnerships, social impact assessment of all projects requiring land acquisition and restrictions on acquisition of irrigated agricultural land to accommodate some of the concerns of people affected by land acquisition.

Chapter II of 2013 Act deals with determination of SIA and public purpose. The insertion of SIA in Chapter II in the 2013 law was amended to achieve certain objectives. The first of such objectives was to ensure that the entire document could be weighed against the benefits that were claimed to accrue to the people in the project report so that the overall utility of the project to the people could be realistically and objectively assessed while taking a decision on acquisition of land. The second objective of carrying out an SIA was to examine whether the activities to be undertaken by the project would qualify for being called "Public Purpose".

- The Principal Act, 2013 changed this arbitrary exercise of power and democratized it by providing for scrutiny by the people as well the courts. The third objectives of this exercise was to examine whether the extent of land to be acquired is necessary and, if so, is the barest minimum needed for the project and whether it can be met from the unutilized land already available with the government either from its own pool of owned land or from the unutilized land acquired for other projects so as to avoid acquisition of land and consequent displacement of people. This exercise would also deliberate on whether alternative land other than the one proposed for acquisition would not serve the purpose which may reduce the quantum of acquisition and consequent displacement and entail less disruption of people's lives and livelihood.
- The fourth and the most important objective of this chapter was to introduce a paradigm shift in the process of land acquisition from an exclusively bureaucratically handled process to a participatory one where the people likely to be affected could be involved in different stages of land acquisition, rehabilitation and resettlement. The fifth objective was to identify the extent of displacement it would cause of those dependent on agricultural land which is proposed to be acquired.
- It was particularly intended to identify the livelihood losers who are usually ignored in any scheme of rehabilitation and resettlement. This is because such schemes are based on rights holders inserted in the land records which do not even record the names of tenants far less other livelihood losers such as

agricultural labourers. Thus, the most vulnerable group among the displaced would get left out. This right to compensation, rehabilitation and resettlement for livelihood losers was inserted for the first time and after a sustained advocacy by civil society.

- Chapter III in the 2013 Law deals with measures to safeguard food security. It puts checks on the acquisition of irrigated multi-cropped land by banning it except in special circumstances and also introduces a caveat that if such exceptional circumstances are made out to justify its acquisition, the total acquisition of such land would not exceed the limit specified for a district or State by the State government. These measures were inserted so as to protect agricultural land in general and irrigated and multi-cropped land in particular from diversion for non-agricultural purposes.
- The shrinking area of agricultural land has been a cause for concern as it affects food security. But the exemption from application of Chapter III granted by the ordinance has a negative impact on this too. Section 46 of the Principal Act (2013) deals with provisions relating to rehabilitation and resettlement of persons affected by purchase of land through private negotiation. It obligates the purchaser to apply to the collector with necessary information about his transaction so that the obligation to provide rehabilitation and resettlement is cast on him as a condition for obtaining permission to change in land use [Saxena, K.B. (2015), "The Ordinance Amending the Land Acquisition Law (2013): Farmers Lose out in the Unequal Contest of Power", *Social Change*, 45(2), pp. 324-336, CSD 2015, Sage Publications, New Delhi].
- The proposed amendment removing SIA was aimed at completely doing away with the SIA. It is important to recall that there were several reasons for which SIA was brought in, which included ensuring that both positive and adverse impacts of the proposed project could be investigated and documented to establish the overall utility of the project to the people while taking a decision on acquisition of land; examining whether the activities to be undertaken by the project qualified for being called "Public Purpose"; ascertaining whether the extent of land proposed to be acquired was necessary and, if so, was the barest minimum needed for the project and, whether it could be met from the

unutilized land already available with the government or an alternative land so as to avoid acquisition of land and consequent displacement of people.

- The 2013 Act had excluded private hospitals and private educational institutions from the ambit of infrastructural projects for which land could be acquired without the consent of the affected persons. The ordinance omitted these exclusions implying that there two purposes have also qualified for being considered 'infrastructure' for which compulsory acquisition could be undertaken by the State, and therefore, the obligation for obtaining a prior consent of the affected people for such acquisition would not have been necessary.
- The 2013 legislation also had land acquisition provisions only for government or private companies while the amendments from ordinance made it for any entity by replacing private company with private entity (Ramesh, 2015a). This change had extended the facility of acquisition of land by the State even to registered societies, cooperatives, trusts, proprietorships, partnerships, non-profit organizations etc and enormously expanded the ambit of acquisition and therefore, had potentially increased the displacement of people manifold (Saxena, 2015) although this kind of definition of public or State was there in the LAA of 1894 as well (Verma, 2015) and, therefore, the new Act (2013) is as regressive as the LAA of 1894.
- The National Democratic Alliance (NDA) Government proposed amendments in 2014 (enforced through an ordinance which now stands withdrawn) in the 2013 Act which included removing land owner consent clause and the mandatory SIA for projects in five areas, that is, defense, rural infrastructure, housing, industrial corridor and social infrastructure. It also changed the term "private company" to "private entity" and definition of public purpose to include private hospitals and education institutions.
- A new chapter was proposed to be added to the 2013 Act which empowered appropriate government to exempt five categories of projects from the obligation of obtaining consent of the families affected by acquisition of land which include: projects vital to national security or defence of India, rural infrastructure, including electrification; affordable housing for the poor people, industrial corridors and infrastructure, including social and public private partnership projects (Saxena, 2015).

- The 2013 legislation also had land acquisition provisions only for government or private companies while the amendments from ordinance made it for any entity by replacing "private company" with "private entity" (Ramesh, 2015a). The change had extended the facility of acquisition of land by the State even to registered societies, cooperatives, trusts, proprietorships, partnerships, non-profit organizations etc. and enormously expanded the ambit of acquisition and therefore, had potentially increased the displacement of people manifold (Saxena, 2015) although this kind of definition of public or State was there in the LAA of 1894 as well (Verma, 2015) and, therefore, the new Act (2013) is as regressive as the LAA of 1894.
- With Jharkhand Mukti Morcha (JMM) legislators resigned from the Tribal Advisory Council (TAC) on November 21 in protest against the State BJP Government's move to amend age-old tenancy laws, the opposition parties and tribal groups have decided to further intensify their movement against this step of the Chief Minister Raghubar Das.
- While the JMM chief and Leader of Opposition Hemant Soren announced holding of a three-day "fight to finish" Statewide agitation against the amendments, AJSU, ally of the ruling BJP made it clear that it was not a party to the move to "tamper" with Chhotanagpur Tenancy (CNT) Act and Santhal Pargana Tenancy (SPT) Act. AJSU chief Sudesh Mahto said that a legislature party meeting would be held within a couple of days to decide on their strategy.
- Undeniably the BJP government in Jharkhand was pursuing a divisive policy by bringing amendments to the century-old land tenancy acts. The opposition allege that the TAC was being misused to push the government's selective agenda and help the industrialists and big business acquire tribal land in the State. The council in fact was formed to protect the constitutional interests of tribals. But the recent move of the Chief Minister makes it explicit that the government was treating it as a pocket institution to further the business interest of the BJP's friends.
- In the globalization period, the State has signed 74 MoUs with different companies, which include mining and steel plants by Arcelor Mittal, Bhushan Power & Steel, Jindal Steel, and thermal power plant and dam by ECSC. The execution of these projects will result in displacement of thousands of tribals and diversion of rich agricultural land and forestland for non-

agricultural purposes. As these tribal areas are designated as "Scheduled Areas" under the Constitution, the Provisions of Panchayats (Extension to Scheduled Areas) Act, 1996 [The Constitution (73rd Amendment) Act, 1992, commonly known as PESA Act] is applicable; besides several special laws like Chhotanagpur Tenancy Act, 1908 and the Santhal Parganas Tenancy (Supplementary Provisions) Act, 1949 also apply. The prior consultation of Gram Sabha is necessary under the PESA Act for acquiring tribal land (IPA). The Jharkhand Government was forced to put on hold the implementation of new rates notified for land acquisition in Santhal Parganas for power and other industrial projects, after the opposition raised a *hullabaloo* in the assembly on Thursday accusing the government of facilitating land acquisition for Adani Group at throwaway prices.

- Leader of the opposition Hemant Soren said, "What will the displaced do with compensatory amount when they cannot buy land elsewhere in Santhal Parganas as sale/purchase of land is prohibited in region under Santhal Parganas Tenancy Act, 1948". "The government should ban acquisition through law and instead should come up with a rule for leasing of land as in the case of government land so that right of tenant continues perpetually over the land and his interests are protected," Soren added. Apart from Adanis, several private and multinational players are planning huge investment in the power sector considering State's rich coal reserves and other resources.
- The Media is known as the fourth estate of democracy though it has not been mentioned in the Constitutional or legal document. Since the Media plays a role of watchdog (free, fair and fearless), therefore, it has this legitimacy. However, in the era of globalization, the media is in the hands of few vested interest groups. Today, the Jharkhandi media is one of the crucial examples of how it is being used to protect vested interest in the State. It is obvious that since the creation of the State, Jharkhandi Media has been batting hard to protect corporate interests. After the order of the Jharkhand High Court to enforce the CNT Act in the State, there has been upheaval. The pro- and anti-CNT Act movement started in the State and the Jharkhandi Media also became a party to the anti-CNT Act Movement.
- Villagers are protesting against the NTPC in Hazaribagh and against coal mines in Barkagaon. Protests against equal land

acquisition for industries are gaining momentum in Jharkhand and a police firing in Ramgarh has fuelled it further. Former Chief Minister, Babulal Marandi, started a two-day mass fast at Hazaribagh district against land acquisition by the National Thermal Power Corporation (NTPC). The police had opened fire on villagers, who were demanding compensation for land acquired by Inland Power Limited (IPL). Two people were killed and more than 20, belonging to either sides, were injured. The displaced people were earlier called for talks, at the IPL factory, which the management did not attend. This angered the villagers.

- According to opposition parties, the land rate compensation given to villagers this time were much lesser than the 2013 land acquisition provisions. Jharkhand is facing these protest at various places. In Hazaribagh, the villagers are protesting against the NTPC, while in Barkagao the protest is against coal mines. NTPC was awarded coal blocks for thermal power plant at Barkagao in 2010, but mining could not start because of protests.
- Echoing his view, former Chief Minister and Jharkhand Mukti Morcha (JMM) executive president, Hemant Soren, told *IANS,* "The killing of people indicates the ruthless and insensitive approach of the Raghubar Das government". The opposition has also alleged that the State has proposed to form land banks which will lead to the eviction of people living on government land.
- The protest against NTPC had gained momentum in July when opposition leaders went to Barkagaon to extend their support to the movement. NTPC lodged an FIR against them for entering the mining area. On August 4, the opposition even courted arrest. Chief Minister Raghubar Das had assured the villagers earlier this month that agricultural land would not be acquired forcefully.

References

Alloysius, G. (2003). "Ideology and Hegemony in Jharkhand Movement", In: R.D. Munda and S. Bosu Mullick (eds.), *Jharkhand Movement: A Historical Analysis*, Copenhagen: IWGIA and Birsa, Document No. 108, pp. 206-15.

Areeparampil, Mathew (1992). "Forest Andolan in Singhbhum", In: S. Narayan (ed.), *Jharkhand Movement: Origin and Evolution*, New Delhi: Inter-India Publications, pp. 144-89.

Basu, Sajal (1994). *Jharkhand Movement: Ethnicity and Culture of Silence*, Shimla: Indian Institute of Advanced Study.

Chacko, P.A., (2003). "Enquiry Report—PUCL Dumka, Jharkhand Unit—Pachwara Coal Mining Projects", Secretary, PUCL, Dumka Unit, Jharkhand.

Dalapati, Tapas Kumar (2016). "Struggles for Survival and Tribal Assertions in South West Odisha", In: Chaudhary, S.N. (ed), *Social Movements in Tribal India*, Jaipur: Rawat Publications, pp. 244-260.

Das, Arvind (1989). "Jharkhand's Roots: Tribal Identity in Indian History", In: P.C. Chatterji (ed.), *Self-images, Identity and Nationality*, Shimla: Indian Institute of Advanced Study.

Department of Industries, Government of Jharkhand, "List of Cancelled MoU Signed Projects during 2002", Department of Industries, Government of Jharkhand.

Deputy Commissioner, Saraikela-Raj Kharsawan (2015). "Lands Acquired and Leased Out to Abhijit Company in Raj Kharsawan, Saraikela Area", Saraikela.

Deputy Commissioner, Saraikela-Raj Kharsawan, "Lands Acquired and Leased Out to Adhunik Alloy and Power Limited", Gamharia Tehsil, Saraikela.

Ekka, Alexius and M. Asif (2002). "Development-Induced Displacement and Rehabilitation in Jharkhand: A Database on its Extent and Nature", New Delhi: Indian Social Institute.

Ekka, Alexius and Mohd. Asif (2000). *Development Induced Displacement and Rehabilitation in Jharkhand: A data base on its Extent and Nature*, New Delhi: Indian Social Institute.

Fernandes, W. and M. Asif (1997). *Development-induced Displacement in Odisha, 1951 to 1995: A Database on its Extent and Nature*, New Delhi: Indian Social Institute.

Fernandes, Walter (2008). "Sixty Years of Development–Induced Displacement in India: Scale, Impact, and the Search for Alternatives", *India Social Development Report*, 2008, Development and Displacement, Council for Social Development, pp. 89-102.

George, Ms. Ajitha Susan (2012). *Laws Related to Mining in Jharkhand*, Ranchi, Jharkhand.

Jha, J.C. (1987). *The Tribal Revolt in Chhotanagpur (1831-32)*, Patna: Kashi Prasad Jayaswal Research Institute.

Kesri, Visveshwar Prasad (1992). *Jharkhand Ke Sadan*, Ranchi: Chhotanagpur Sanskritik Sangh.

Land Acquisition Officer, Suvarna Rekha Project (2016). *Areas Submerged under Suvarna Rekha Project in Jharkhand*, Adityapur, Jamshedpur, East Singhbhum.

MacDougall, John (2008). "*Tribal Resistance*", *Critical Quest*, New Delhi.

Maharaj, R.N. and K.G. Iyer (1982). "Agrarian Movement in Dhanbad", In: N. Sengupta (ed.), *Fourth World Dynamics*, Jharkhand, Delhi: Authors Guild Publications.

Marandi, Babu Lal, Chief Minister, Jharkhand, (2001). *Jharkhand Industrial Policy 2001*, Department of Industries, Government of Jharkhand.

Munda, Arjun, Chief Minister, Jharkhand, (2012). *Jharkhand Industrial Policy 2012*, Department of Industries, Government of Jharkhand.

Nayak, R.C. and Kujur, M.K. (2007). *State Aggression and Tribal Resistance: A Case of Police Firing at Kalinganagar*, New Delhi: Indian Social Institute.

Ota, A.B. (2010). "Development Projects and Displaced Tribals", Scheduled Castes and Scheduled Tribes, Research and Training Institute, Government of India, Bhubaneswar, June, 2010.

Padel, Felix and Das Samarendra (2008). "Cultural Genocide: The Real Impact of Development-Induced Displacement", *India Social Development Report, 2008, Development and Displacement*, Council for Social Development, pp. 103-115.

Padel, Felix and Samandra Das (2008). "Displacement and Rehabilitation in Odisha", *Social Change*, Vol. 38, No. 4, December.

Prakash, Amit (2001). *Jharkhand: Politics of Development and Identity*, New Delhi: Orient Longman.

PUCL (1979). "Repression in Singhbhum", *Report of the Delhi Unit of People's Union for Civil Liberties and Democratic Rights*, New Delhi.

Report of an Expert Group to Planning Commission (2008). "Development Challenges in Extremist Affected Areas", Government of India, New Delhi, April, 2008.

Roy, A.K. (1981). *Jharkhand or Lalkhand: Markswadi Coordination*, Dhanbad.

Roy, Burman (1966). Quoted in Ota, A.B., "Development Projects and Displaced Tribals: an Empirical Study", SC and ST RTI, Bhubneswar (2010, p. 25).

Samantra, Profulla (2000). "Peoples Struggle for Right to Livelihood", Gopalpur Coast Environment, "*Protection Forum*", New Delhi: Berhampur and Lok Shakti Abhiyan.

Singh, K.S. (2003). "Tribal Identity Movement in Chhotanagpur", In: R.D. Munda and S. Bosu Mullick (eds.), pp. 88-109.

Sinha, Nagendra Nath (2010). "Mineral–Rich Jharkhand State is Well-Recognized as Natural Destination for Future Exploration", *Business Times*, February 2010, pp. 10-17.

Sinha, S.K., (1987). Surveyer-*cum*-Draftsman, "Adityapur Industrial Area Development Authority", Adityapur, Jamshedpur.

4

Implementation of Forest Rights Act, 2006 in Jharkhand and Odisha

4.0 Objectives of the Study

- In this Chapter a comparative attempt has been made to discuss the findings on the implementation of the Forest Rights Act, 2006 in the sampled districts of Jharkhand and Odisha.
- The sampled districts covered in Jharkhand are the Districts of West Singhbhum, East Singhbhum, Saraikela-Kharsawan, Khunti and Dalma Sanctuary.
- The sampled districts covered in Odisha are the Districts of Koraput, Rayagada, Kalahandi and Sundargarh.
- A comparative analysis of the findings of the different districts of Jharkhand are presented including the analysis of Jharkhand State.
- A comparative analysis of the findings of the different districts of Odisha are presented towards the end of the District Analysis of Odisha.
- Finally, a concluding analysis of Jharkhand and Odisha have been undertaken towards the end of the Chapter.

4.1 Neglecting the Recognition of the Rights of the Forest Communities

Traditionally, the access and ownership rights of natural resources were governed by the principles of Community Rights over Common Property. During the colonial rule there was militant confrontation between advasis and the colonial State. The Colonial State took over the control and rights over land and forest forcibly. These were also needed for raw materials for the industrialization. This was followed by legislations and laws to establish the ownership of the State over these resources for long time to come. It also prompted the alienation of advasis from their cultural and historical rights over land, water and forests. During the Post-Colonial period same model of development continued to persist. The continuation of such a policy was also evident in May 2002 when the MoEF directed all States to evict 'encroachers' from forest lands. Based on this order, the Forest Department brutally carried out eviction drives and according to available figures, 1.52 lakh hectares of encroachments from forest lands were removed over a span of 18 months. In 1995, the Godhavarman Public Interest Litigation (PIL) was filed, to stop commercial interests from encroaching upon forests. In 1998, the Supreme Court created the Centrally Empowered Committee to look into what came to be known as the 'forest case', in which a series of interventions were filed, including one on illegal occupants. In response, the Supreme Court ordered a halt to regularization of encroachments. The MoEF interpreted this as an order to evict encroachers, without considering its failure to implement its own 1990 Orders.

This policy continued unabated even during the era of liberalization and privatization. The biggest threat that adivasis and other forest dwelling communities have faced in the last two decades is displacement from their habitats as corporate interests took over land and forest resources for industries and mining projects. It is in this period that the Panchayats Extension to Scheduled Areas Act (PESA) was evolved and introduced to give greater control to Gram Sabhas in adivasi dominated areas.

In this background, the "Forests Rights Act" passed by the Parliament of India in December 2006 is a decisive political shift. For the first time, the Indian State admits and recognizes the "historic injustice" done to the adivasis. However, it is to be remembered that the culmination of several democratic struggles made it possible for the promulgation of such a legislation. The Forest Rights Act is a product of this history. Indeed, it is desirable that the Indian Forest Act, the FCA, and the Wildlife Protection Act is integrated into a livelihood perspective and becomes a part of indigenous people's vision. Had the interests and traditions of forest-dwellers been taken on board in the past few decades, the country would have had several million more supporters of conservation. The preamble text of the Act clearly lays out the context for its operative provisions. It is meant to undo historical injustices meted out to forest dwelling populations in not recognizing their rights to land and resources. But it also stresses that the rights of forest dwelling communities include responsibility for the sustainable use and conservation of biodiversity.

4.2 Rationale behind Forest Rights Act, 2006

It is in this context that the Forest Rights Act [Scheduled Tribes and Other Traditional Forest Dwellers (Recognition of Forest Rights) Act] was enacted in 2006—to undo the historical injustice and address the "issues" related to the forest dwellers. The Act specifically aims at:

- Recognizing and vesting forest rights and occupancy rights to those forest dwellers who have been living in such forests for generations but whose rights were not recorded;
- Providing a framework for recording the forest rights; including the responsibility and authority for sustainable use; and
- Conservation of biodiversity and maintenance of ecological balance, thereby strengthening the conservation regime of forests; and ensuring livelihood and food security of the Scheduled Tribes and other forest-dwellers.

4.3 Classification of Rights under FRA, 2006

No forest dweller can claim user rights over any forest land that he or she was not cultivating before 13 December, 2005 and is not cultivating at present. Those who are cultivating such land but do not have documents to prove continuous land use can claim up to 4 hectares if they cultivate the land themselves only for their livelihood. Those who possess government leases for forest land can claim user rights even if the land was taken by the Forest Department or is the subject of a dispute between the Forest Department and the Revenue Department. However, if those lands are re-conferred on an individual, a household, or a community, they cannot be sold or transferred to anyone except by inheritance.

Community Rights

The FRA restores the forest dwellers' right to collect minor forest produce such as edible herbs and medicinal plants. But the forest dwellers cannot fell trees for sale. This also includes ownership and right to process and sell. The Amended Rules September 2012 even permits the Gram Sabha to issue transit permits. The law also recognises the use of grazing grounds and water bodies by nomadic or pastoralist communities.

Right to Protect and Conserve

Until the FRA was enacted in 2006, only the Forest Department was entrusted with the duty of protecting forests. This legislation for the first time gives the forest-dwelling communities the right to protect and manage the community forest resource within customary boundaries. It authorises forest dwellers to conserve community forest resources by giving the community a general power to protect wildlife and forests. This is vital, as thousands of forest-dwelling communities are trying to protect their forests and wildlife against threats from forest mafias, industries, and land grabbers, most of whom operate in connivance with the Forest Department.

Relief and Development

The FRA Act, 2006 States in Section 4(1) that "notwithstanding anything contained in any other law for the time being in force, and subject to the provisions of this Act, the Central Government hereby recognizes and vests forest rights in (a) the forest-dwelling Scheduled Tribes in States or areas of States where they are declared as Scheduled Tribes in respects of all forest rights mentioned in Section 3; (b) the other traditional forest dwellers in respect of all forest rights mentioned in Section 3". This is a powerful and unambiguous recognition of rights of forest dwellers and an unreserved vesting of such rights on them. (*Source:* Forest Rights Act, 2006).

The FRA empowers holders of forest rights and their Gram Sabhas to:

- Protect the wildlife, forest, and its biodiversity;
- Ensure that adjoining catchment areas, water sources, and other ecological sensitive areas are adequately protected;
- Ensure that habitats of forest-dwelling Scheduled Tribes and other traditional forest dwellers are preserved from any form of destructive practices affecting their cultural and natural heritage; and
- Ensure that the decisions taken in the Gram Sabha to regulate access to community forest resources and prevent any activity that adversely affects the wild animals, forest, biodiversity, and natural heritage are implemented.

Over a period of 4 years between 2008 and 2012 several problems regarding the implementation of the Act, were noticed by the Ministry of Tribal Affairs including recognition of Rights which were addressed by Ministry of Tribal Affairs in their letter No. 23011/32/2010-FRA [Vol. II (Pt.) dated 12th July, 2012] with a view to ensure effective implementation of the Act. The following guidelines were issued by MoTA which are reproduced below:

> The State Governments should ensure that on receipt of intimation from the Forest Rights Committee, the officials of the Forest and Revenue Departments remain present during the verification of the claims and the evidence on the site.
>
> (a) In the event of modification of rejection of a claim by the Gram Sabha or by the Sub-Divisional Level Committee or the District Level Committee, the decision on the claim should be communicated to the claimant to enable the aggrieved person to prefer a petition to the Sub-Divisional Level Committee or the District Level Committee, as the case may be, within the sixty days period prescribed under the Act and no such petition should be disposed of against the aggrieved person, unless he has been given a reasonable opportunity to present his case.
>
> (b) The reasons for not accepting the recommendations should be recorded in writing and a copy of the order should be supplied to the claimant.
>
> (c) On completion of the process of settlement of rights and issue of titles the Forest Department shall prepare a final map of the forest land so vested and the concerned authorities shall incorporate the forest rights so vested in the revenue and forest records.
>
> (d) A question has been raised whether the four hectare limit specified in Section 4(6) of the Act, which provides for recognition of forest rights in respect of the land mentioned in clause (a) of sub-section (1) of Section 3 of the Act, applies to other forest rights mentioned in Section 3 (1) of the Act. It is clarified that the four hectare limit specified in Section 4(6) applies to rights under Section 3(1) (a) of the Act only and not to any other right under Section 3(1), such as conversion of *pattas* or leases, conversion of forest villages into revenue villages etc.

It would be worthwhile to cite the view point of Mr. G. Seetharaman, *ET Bureau*, July 31, 2016 about the major milestone of

Forest Act, 2006 after its enactment to the present, i.e. from 2006 to 2016.

- The Scheduled Tribes and Other Traditional Forest Dwellers Act (Recognition of Forest Rights) Act, 2006, or the Forest Rights Act (FRA), is among India's most important legislation since 2005, along with the Right to Information Act and the Right to Education Act.
- It looks to right the wrongs of government policies in both colonial and independent India toward forest-dwelling communities, whose claims over their resources were repeatedly ignored.
- The biggest game changer in FRA, CFR rights give the Gram Sabha the right to protect and manage their forest. No project can come up in the forest nor can any conservation plan for the forest be carried out without the approval of the Gram Sabha.
- The authority of Gram Sabhas was upheld in a historic ruling by the Supreme Court in 2013, which gave 12 affected Gram Sabhas the right to decide on a bauxite mining project of Vedanta group in Niyamgiri, Odisha. All the Gram Sabha members voted against the project.
- FRA clearly states that CFR rights (Distinguishing Rights) apply not just to village forests, but also to protected forests, reserved forests (which have more restricted access than protected forests), and even protected areas like wildlife sanctuaries and national parks.
- As of April 2016, around 40 per cent of overall claims received have been settled across the country and over 30 per cent of the land distributed is under community rights. Chhattisgarh does not report data separately for CF rights and CFR rights, and therefore, the activists are skeptical about the genuineness of the implementation of CFR rights.
- Activists say that one of the biggest hurdles for FRA is that States like Maharashtra, and Odisha which are among the better performers, are introducing policies which will help the Forest Department retain control of forest resources through joint forest management committees or similar bodies, which will dilute the powers of the Gram Sabha.

4.4 Present Status of Forest in Jharkhand

Jharkhand, the 28th State of the Union of India, carved out from the southern part of Bihar State on 15th November in the year 2000 is a mineral and forest rich State of India. The State has a geographical area of 79,714 km. Of the total population of 32.98 million (Census, 2011), the tribal population constitute 26 per cent; they have symbiotic relations with forests and they have influenced their ecosystems by varying practices of agro-pastoralism over the years. The rural population is quite high in the State constituting about 76 per cent, and the urban population is only 24 per cent despite rapid development in mines related industrial sector in the State over the years. The survival of the majority of the poverty stricken rural and tribal population depends whole lot on the forests as it provides variety of Non-timber Forest Produce (NTFP) to them. The forest vegetation of the State varies from rich *Sal* forests to miscellaneous forests and sparsely covered grasslands. The main species of Jharkhand are *Sal*, *Asan*, *Dhaura*, *Gamhar*, *Mahua* etc. The major forest types of the State include *Sal* forest which has a unique significance for Adivasis livelihood and culture.

Table 4.1: The Recorded Forest Area in the State of Jharkhand

Types of Forest	*Area (sq. km.)*	*Remarks*
Total Recorded Forest Area	23,605 km^2	29 61% of the total geographical area of Jharkhand
Total Area under Reserved Forests	4,387 km^2	18.58% of the total Recorded Forest Area of Jharkhand
Total Area under Protected Forests	19,185 km^2	81.28% of total Recorded Forest Area of Jharkhand
Total Area under Un-classed Forest	33 km^2	0.14% of total Recorded Forest Area of Jharkhand

Source: ISFR, 2013.

"India State of Forest Report 2013" (PDF). Forest Survey of India. Retrieved 1 December, 2015. The Forest Cover in Jharkhand.

The Forest Cover of Jharkhand has increased from 22,531 km^2 in the year 2001 to 23,437 km^2 in 2013 with the net gain of 942 km^2. The increase in Forest Cover is due to the culture of adivasis as also to plantation activities and protection measures carried out by Jharkhand Forest Department over the years.

Table 4.2: Categories of Forest Cover in Jharkhand

Very Dense Forests (VDF))	Density of 70 per cent and above
Moderately Dense Forests (MDF)	Density of 40 per cent or more and less than 70 per cent
Open Forests: (OF)	Density of 10 per cent or more and less than 40 per cent.

Source: ISFR, 2013.

Table 4.3: The Forest Cover (in sq. km.) in India by States and Union Territories (Published by the Forest Survey of India in 2013)

State / UT	*Geographical Area*	*Very Dense*	*Moderately Dense*	*Open Forest*	*Total Forest Area*	*% of Forested Area*
1	2	3	4	5	6	7
Andhra Pradesh	275,069	850	26,079	19,187	46,116	16.77
Arunachal Pradesh	83,743	20,828	31,414	15,079	67,321	80.39
Assam	78,438	1,444	11,345	14,882	27,671	35.28
Bihar	94,163	247	3,380	3,664	7,291	7.74
Chhattisgarh	135,191	4,153	34,865	16,603	55,621	41.14
Delhi	1,483	6.76	49.38	123.67	179.81	12.12
Goa	3,702	543	585	1091	2219	59.94
Gujarat	196,022	376	5,220	9,057	14,653	7.48
Haryana	44,212	27	453	1,106	1,586	3.59
Himachal Pradesh	55,673	3,224	6,381	5,078	14,683	26.37
Jammu & Kashmir	222,236	4,140	8,760	9,638	22,538	10.14
Jharkhand	79,714	2,587	9,667	11,219	23,473	29.45
Karnataka	191,791	1,777	20,179	14,176	36,132	18.84
Kerala	38,863	1,529	9,401	6,992	17,922	46.12
Madhya Pradesh	308,245	6,632	34,921	35,969	77,522	25.15
Maharashtra	307,713	8,720	20,770	21,142	50,632	16.45
Manipur	22,327	728	6,094	10,168	16,990	76.10
Meghalaya	22,429	449	9,689	7,150	17,288	77.08
Mizoram	21,081	138	5,900	13,016	19,054	90.38
Nagaland	16,579	1,298	4,736	7,010	13,044	78.68
Odisha	155,707	7,042	21,298	22,007	50,347	32.33
Punjab	50,362	0	736	1,036	1,772	3.52
Rajasthan	342,239	72	4,424	11,590	16,086	4.70
Sikkim	7,096	500	2,161	697	3,358	47.32
Tamil Nadu	130,058	2,948	10,199	10,697	23,844	18.33
Tripura	10,486	109	4,641	3,116	7,866	75.01
Uttar Pradesh	240,928	1,623	4,550	8,176	14,349	5.96
Uttarakhand	53,483	4,785	14,111	5,612	24,508	45.82
West Bengal	88,752	2,971	4,146	9,688	16,805	18.93
Andaman and Nicobar Islands	8,249	3,754	2,413	544	6,711	81.36
Chandigarh	114	1.36	9.66	6.24	17.26	15.14

(Contd.)

1	2	3	4	5	6	7
Dadra & Nagar Haveli	491	0	114	99	213	43.38
Daman and Diu	12	0	1.87	7.4	9.27	8.28
Lakshadweep	32	0	17.18	9.88	27.06	84.56
Puducherry	480	0	35.23	14.83	50.06	10.43
Total	**3,287,263**	**83,502**	**318,745**	**95,651**	**697,898**	**21.23**

Source: IFSR, 2013

It can be seen from Table 4.3 that the highest percentage of Forest area is mainly located in the North-Eastern States followed by Central Indian States like Odisha, Chhattisgarh, Uttarakhand and Jharkhand etc. Same is the situation with respect to the Intensity of Area under different category of forests, namely highly dense, moderately dense and with low density.

Table 4.4: District-wise Forest Coverage During 2013 and 2015 (*sq.km*).

Sl. No.	*Districts*	*Total Forest Coverage in 2013*	*Forest Coverage in 2015*	*Per Centage to Total forest coverage in the State*
1.	Bokaro	565	565	2.41
2.	Chatra	1780	1781	7.59
3.	Deoghar	203	204	0.87
4.	Dhanbad	202	202	0.86
5.	Dumka	663	660	2.81
6.	Garhwa	1390	1392	5.93
7.	Giridih	885	878	3.74
8.	Godda	408	412	1.75
9.	Gumla	2658	2661	11.33
10.	Hazaribagh	2088	2093	8.91
11.	Koderma	598	598	2.55
12.	Lohardaga	499	499	2.13
13.	Pakur	288	287	1.22
14.	Palamau	3586	3594	15.31
15.	West Singhbhum	3914	3912	16.66
16.	East Singhbhum	1069	1070	4.56
17.	Ranchi	2084	2076	8.84
18.	Sahebganj	593	594	2.53
	Total	**23473**	**23478**	**100.00**

Source: IFSR 2005, 2009, 2011, 2013 and 2015.

The figures in Table 4.4 show that the highest forest coverage percentage is in the district of West Singhbhum (16.66%) followed by Palamau (16.31%), Gumla (11.33%), Hazaribagh (8.91%), Ranchi (8.84%); the percentage of forest coverage in other districts is much lower.

Table 4.5: Forest Area as per Forest Division in Jharkhand

(Area in ha)

Sl. No.	Name of the Forest Division	Reserved Forest		Protected Forest		Un-classed Forest		Total Forest Area
		Area	%age	Area	%age	Area	% age	
1.	Saranda	81808	95.25	3988	4.64	86	0.11	85882
2.	Kolhan	58716	83.83	11258	16.07	68	0.10	70042
3.	Porahat	50628	76.08	15816	23.77	98	0.15	66542
4.	Chaibasa South	631	0.06	50875	99.94	0	0	50906
5.	Chaibasa North	6486	9.53	61540	90.47	0	0	68026
6.	Dhalbhum	53050	50.56	51863	49.44	0	0	104913
7.	Ranchi East	11742	12.77	80182	87.23	0	0	91924
8.	Ranchi West	26290	26.28	73744	73.72	0	0	100034
9.	Gumla	12101	9.25	118717	90.74	16	0.01	130834
10.	Giridih	8776	7.29	113320	92.21	0	0	121796
11.	Hazaribagh West	673	0.38	176524	99.42	340	0.20	177537
12.	Hazribag East	1743	1.68	102055	98.32	0	0	103798
13.	Bokaro	0	0	50901	100.00	0	0	51901
14.	Chatra South	752	0.73	101828	99.27	0	0	102580
15.	Chatra North	0	0	93372	100.00	0	0	93372
16.	Koderma	15630	17.68	13108	82.32	0	0	88738
17.	Dhanbad	10825	41.03	15555	58.97	0	0	26380
18.	Daltanganj South	58081	55.76	46044	44.20	45	0.02	104170
19.	Daltanganj North	3987	3.05	126661	96.95	0	0	130648
20.	Garhna South	549	0.44	123586	99.56	0	0	124135
21.	Garhwa North	0	0	78705	100.00	0	0	78705
22.	Latehar	20648	15.60	111736	84.40	0	0	132384
23.	Deoghar	2866	3.73	73922	96.23	0	0	76788
24.	Dumka	12803	8.61	135389	91.91	420	0.28	148612
25.	Saheb Ganj	50	0.39	10471	81.82	2276	17.79	12797
26.	Giridih Forest station	485	2.89	16318	97.11	0	0	16803
	Total	**438720**	**91.31**	**1918178**	**81.25**	**3349**	**0.00014**	2360547

Source: Forest Department Government of Jharkhand, Ranchi.

The area under reserve forest is relatively high in Saranda (95.25%) Forest division followed by Kolhan (83.83%), Porahat (76.08%) and Palamau (55.76%). Many of the remaining districts have substantial area under protected forest. The Reserve Forest of Saranda, Kolhan and Porhat forest division are also affected by the movements of Adivasis and Left extremists. National Park and Wildlife Sanctuaries are located in the districts of Palamau, East Singhbhum, Hazaribagh, Chatra, Gumla, Giridih, Dhanbad and Sahibganj. The present study includes the Dalma Sanctuary for its empirical study.

4.5 The Status of Implementation of Forest Right Act, 2006 in different States of India

Table 4.6: State-wise details of claims received and titles distributed (for Individual and Community Rights) (as on 28.02.2015) in Major States

Sl. No.	*States*	*No. of claims received*	*No. of titles distributed*	*Extent of Forest land (for which titles distributed) in Acres*
1	2	3	4	5
1.	Andhra Pradesh	411012 (400053 individuals and 5193 communities)	16930 (167263 individuals and 860 communities)	1456542
2.	Assam	131911 (126718 individuals and 5193 communities)	36267 (35407 individuals and 860 communities)	77609.17 for 34286 titles
3.	Bihar	2930	28	(Not available)
4.	Chhattisgarh	817809	336590	701020.98
5.	Gujarat	190051 (182869 individuals and 782 communities)	72625 (68769 individuals and 3856 communities)	1100038
6.	Himachal Pradesh	5692	346	0.3548
7.	Jharkhand	42003	15296	37678.93
8.	Karnataka	260679 (256104 INDIVIDUALS and 4575 communities)	7700 (7604 individuals and 96 communities)	36536.12 (10292.85 individuals and 26242.67 communities)
9.	Kerala	37535 (36140 individuals and 1395 communities)	24599	33018.12
10.	Madhya Pradesh	592643 (552142 individuals and 40501 communities)	198310 (179700 individuals 18610 communities)	1757019.72
11.	Maharashtra	350908 (344834 individuals and 6074 communities)	145469	1045601.00

(Contd.)

1	2	3	4	5
12.	Odisha	609772 (597222 individuals and 12500) communities)	345473 (341999 individuals and 3474 communities)	7723417 (543253.72 and individuals 109391.46 under communities)
13.	Rajasthan	69775 (69123 individuals 652 communities)	34254 (34189 individuals 65 communities)	52022.71 (51542.98 individuals 479.72 communities)
14.	Tripura	182617 (182340 individuals 277 communities)	120473 (120418 individuals and 55 communities)	416555.58 (416498.79 individuals and 56.79 communities
15.	Uttar Pradesh	93635 (92512 individuals and 1123 communities)	18488 (17654 individuals and 834 communities)	140073.483
16.	West Bengal	140309 (137068 individuals and 3241 communities)	34165	17655.4937
Total Claims 1301207 Titles				

Source: Ministry of Tribal Affairs, Government of India.

The comparison of state-wise details of implementation of Forest Rights Act, 2006 indicates that the maximum Forest titles have been distributed in Andhra Pradesh numbering 14.56 lakh, the number of titles given is 169370 and the community rights given is 2107. In Chhattisgarh titles distributed is 336590 and the extent forest land for which titles distributed is 701020.98 acre. Odisha also has good achievement as it has distributed 609772 claims out of which 597222 are individual claims and 12500 are community claims. The number of titles distributed in Odisha is 345473 of which 341999 are individual titles and 3474 community titles; the extent of forest land distributed in Odisha is 7723417 acre of which 543253.72 acre are under individual right and 109391.46 are under community rights. As against this the achievement in the State of Jharkhand, the number of claims is 4200, titles distributed is only 15296 and the forest titles for the land distributed are 37678.93 acre. Since, the present study is a comparative one for Odisha and Jharkhand, the overall claims received, titles distributed and the Forest land for which titles distributed are much larger in the State of Odisha as compared to the State of Jharkhand. This apparently shows that the status of implementation in Jharkhand is much slower as compared to the state of Odisha.

Table 4.7: District-wise Status of Implementation of the Forest Rights Act, 2006 in Jharkhand State (10.10.2014)

Sl. No.	*Districts*	*No. of Claims received by the Gram Sabha*	*No. of claims approved by DLC*	*Total No. of Claims rejected*	*Title deed issued*		*Total No. of claims pending*	*No. of titles distributed*	
					Area	*Vertical %*		*No.*	*Vertical %*
1.	Bokaro	2830	593	2187	344.14	0.78	59	584	3.15
2.	Chatra	638	254	–	200.24	0.45	384	254	1.37
3.	Garhwa	3162	435	955	603.38	1.36	1772	435	2.35
4.	Gumla	1034	503	473	412.97	0.93	58	503	2.72
5.	Hazaribagh	2980	1253	1727	1059.80	2.39	–	1253	6.77
6.	Latehar	3025	1019	21	1428.39	3.22	1985	1019	5.50
7.	Lohardaga	388	148	–	288.30	0.65	240	148	0.80
8.	West Singhbhum	7158	3133	274	13569.22	30.57	3945	2977	16.08
9.	Palamau	1122	661	–	749.67	1.69	461	661	3.59
10.	East Singhbhum	2768	884	1867	502.19	1.13	17	884	4.77
11.	Ramgarh	1087	315	772	143.14	0.32	–	315	1.70
12.	Simdega	5898	1070	626	993	2.24	4202	1070	5.78
13.	Saraikela	1641	571	994	352.17	0.79	76	571	3.08
14.	Koderma	727	203	594	91.80	0.21	–	200	1.08
15.	Ranchi	970	881	31	418.58	0.94	88	881	4.76
16.	Khunti	448	401	43	243.73	0.55	2	401	2.17
17.	Giridih	4126	3303	823	3438.63	7.75	–	3303	7.84
18.	Dhanbad	1396	211	1185	33.92	0.08	–	211	1.14
	Total Ranchi Region	**41398**	**15838**	**12472**	**24871.77**	**56.03**	**13289**	**15670**	**4.63**
19.	Dumka	5102	1412	3690	431.72	0.97	–	1412	7.63
20.	Jamtara	100	63	31	52.45	0.12	–	63	0.34
21.	Sahebganj	779	624	155	315.76	0.71	–	624	3.37
22.	Pakur	156	134	22	64.69	0.15	–	134	0.72
23.	Godda	1030	358	672	18432.50	41.53	–	358	1.93
24.	Deogarh	335	255	80	218.71	0.49	–	255	1.38
	Total Santal Pargana Region	**7502**	**2846**	**4650**	**19515.83**	**43.97**	**6**	**2846**	**15.37**
	Jharkhand State Grand Total	**48900**	**18684**	**17122**	**44387.60**	**100%**	**13295**	**18516**	**100%**

Source: PCCF, Department of Forest, Van Bhawan, Jharkhand.

Within the Ranchi region out of the total claims received by Gram Sabha consist of 41,398; the highest claims have been received in the district of West Singhbhum (7158) followed by Simdega (5898), Giridih (4126), Garhwa (3162), Latehar (3025), Hazaribagh (2980), and East Singhbhum (2768). The number of claims filed in the other districts like Gumla, Palamau, Ramgarh, Koderma, Chatra, Ranchi and Dhanbad are generally below 1000. One more important observation is that the number of claims filed in the district of Saraikela (1641), and Khunti (448) districts which are among the selected sample districts, the number of claims filed is 1641 and 448 only. In the Santhal Pargana Region, the number of claims filed is highest in Dumka (5102) but lower in the district of Deogarh which is only 335. In the entire Ranchi region the total no. of claims filed is 41,398, in the entire Santhal Pargana Region the total number of claims filed is 7502 and the entire State of Jharkhand the total no. of claims filed is 48,900. This figure relates to the period of 10th October, 2014. The number of claims approved by DLC at the entire state-level is only 18,684 (38.21%) of which 15,838 (84.77%) is in the Jharkhand Region and 2,846 (17.97%) is in the Santhal Pargana Region. The No. of claims rejected by DLC in the entire State is 17,122 which is very high comprising 35.01 per cent of the total claims filed in the Gram Sabha. This high state of rejection is a matter of grave concern which needs to be addressed by the Government of Jharkhand. In the Ranchi-Chhotanagpur Region, the total claims rejected by DLC are 12,472 comprising 72.84 per cent of the total rejection in the State; while in the Santhal Pargana Region the total claims rejected are 4650 which forms 27.16 per cent of the total State rejection. The total area for which title deeds have been issued in the entire State is 44,387.60 acre of which 24,871.77 acre, i.e. 56.03 per cent have been issued in the Jharkhand region and 19,515.83 acre, i.e. 43.97 per cent have been issued in the Santhal Pargana Region. In the entire State, the maximum area of Forest title deeds distributed have been in the district of Godda (Santhal Pargana) comprising 18,432.50 acre, i.e. 41.53 per cent followed by the District of West Singhbhum (Ranchi-Chhotanagpur Region), covering an area of 13,569.22 acre, i.e. 30.57 per cent. This may be pointed out that the District of West Singhbhum is an area not only of Militant Tribal Movement but also of Left Extremist Movement. The total number of claims pending in the entire State is 13,925 in which the maximum number of cases pending is in the Ranchi Chhotanagpur Region comprising 99.95 per cent of the total cases pending. The total number of claims distributed so far out of the total claims approved by DLC is 18,516 comprising 99.10 per cent of the total claims approved by DLC.

The overall figures seem to indicate that the total number of claims rejected is 17,122, the total number of claims pending is 13,295 and the area distributed is also only 44,387.60 acre which is a very low figure. This needs to be followed up by the State Government of Jharkhand at the earliest. One of the significant point is that out of the total community rights of 2803 claims recommended by the Gram Sabha at the State-level the highest is in West Singhbhum District covering 264 number; 58 in the district of Koderma, 54 in the district of Khunti, and 230 in the district of Godda. The total number of claims pending is as high as 2,790 in the district of West Singhbhum which is the highest figure in the State. This is also a matter of concern as most of the social activists and also the Ministry of Tribal Affairs, Government of India, have been emphasizing Community Rights as a major thrust area. In this respect, the position of the Government of Jharkhand is quite depressing. However, one of the significant point is that the number of titles given to PTGs in the entire State is 1276 of which 1219 is in the Ranchi Chhotanagpur region and 440 is in the Santhal Pargana region. The Government of Jharkhand have to provide greater stress on the PVTG community which is among the most deprived and vulnerable community. The total number of PVTG families in the entire State is 77,014 out of which 37,851 (49.15%) are in the Ranchi Chhotanagpur Region and 39,163 (50.85%) are in the Santhal Pargana Region.

The District-wise position shows that the maximum claims have been rejected in the district of Hazaribagh, East Singhbhum, Giridih, Dhanbad and Dumka. The number of title deeds distributed is quite substantial in Hazaribagh, Latehar, West Singhbhum, Giridih and Gumla Districts. The number of claims pending is larger in the district of Garhwa, Latehar, West Singhbhum and Simdega. The number of titles distributed is larger in Hazaribagh, Latehar, Simdega, Giridih, Dumka and West Singhbhum district.

The data on forest rights for the year 2014 for Jharkhand indicates that the maximum claims rejected by the Gram Sabha include for the district of Hazaribagh, East Singhbhum, Dhanbad and Dumka. Bokaro district tops the list with respect to the total number of claims rejected followed by the districts of Hazaribagh, Garhwa, East Singhbhum, Dhanbad and Dumka.

The total number of the community claims recommended by Gram Sabha is in Left Extremist-prone district like West Singhbhum. The number of individual titles given are maximum in Hazaribagh followed by Latehar, West Singhbhum, Simdega, Giridih districts. The community rights recommended by Gram Sabha is more in the district of Bokaro, West Singhbhum, Kodarma and Khunti. The number of claims pending with Gram Sabha relates to the district of West Singhbhum. The claims recommended by SDLC are more for Ramgarh, Dumka, and Dhanbad and the community claims are recommended more for Chatra district which is a Maoist infested area. The individual *pattas* given are larger in the district of Hazaribagh, Latehar, West Singhbhum, Palamau, East Singhbhum, Simdega, Ranchi and the district of Giridih. The forest rights individual titles have also been given to the PTGs in the district of Garhwa, Gumla, Hazaribagh, Latehar, Palamau, East Singhbhum, Ramgarh, Saraikela, Kodarma and Ranchi.

4.6 Implementation of Forest Rights in the Sample Districts of Jharkhand

It may be mentioned here that the sample districts for the present study are West Singhbhum, Saraikela-Kharsawan, Dalma Sanctuary, Khunti and East Singhbhum.

Table 4.8: Status of implementation of Forest Rights Act, 2006 in West Singhbhum District (Jharkhand State for the month January 2012)

Sl. No.	*Item of Information*	*Number*	*Remarks*
1.	Gram Sabha Meeting organized in February 28, 2008 onwards for explaining the Provisions of the Act and Rules. Responsibilities of PRIs, Gram Sabha, PRCs etc.	1207	
2.	Constitution of Forest Rights Committees by the Gram Sabha	1207	
3.	Number of Claims filed at Gram Sabha level (20+21+30+31) (break-up given below)	6661	
4.	Number of Claims verified by the PRCs And submitted to Cram Sabha for Consideration	6661	
5.	Number of claims recommended by the Gram Sabha to SDLC (22+23+32+33)	2716	40.77 per cent of claims were recommended by Gram Sabha and the rest 59.23 per cent not recommended.

(Contd.)

Sl. No.	*Item of Information*	*Number*	*Remarks*
6.	Number of claims recommended by SDLC to DC	2486	
7.	Number of Claims rejected by SDLC	230	9.25 per cent of claims were rejected by SDLC.
8.	Number Claims approved by DLC for Title	2475	
9.	Number of titles distributed (28+29+38+39)	2475	
10.	Extent of forest land for which titles deeds issued (in acre)	10643.0 9	4.30 acres per titles were distributed
11.	Number of claims rejected by DLC	11	
12.	Total number of claims rejected (11+13+17)	241	9.69 per cent of claims were rejected by SDLC and DLC.

Source: Dy. Commissioner, West Singhbhum District, Jharkhand, January 2012.

The number of claims filed at Gram Sabha-level was 6661 out of which 2716 claims were recommended to SDLC in the District of West Singhbhum which was only 40.77 per cent of the total claims and 59.33 per cent were not recommended. However, the SDLC rejected 230 claims (only 9.25%) of the claims. The DLC also approved most of claims which were filed. In all, 10,643.09 title deeds were issued and individually 4.30 acre lands were assigned. The rejection rate by Gram Sabha was relatively high. It would be worthwhile to mention here that the District of West Singhbhum is seriously affected by Left Extremism as also by Militant Tribal Movement on Forest issues. The Tribals during 1980s had launched of their social movement, and also forcibly converted the Forest Land into agricultural land. Large area of such land were included under forest title and assigned to the tribals under the Forest Rights Act, 2006. It can be noticed that on an average area per beneficiary of forest land assigned in West Singhbhum District is one of the highest amongst the districts in Jharkhand State.

It can be noticed in the above Table 4.9 that most of the claims filed at the Gram Sabha Level in West Singhbhum district is 4970 for the Scheduled Tribes and the number of claims recommended by Gram Sabha to the SDLC is 2677 (53.86%) and number of title given is 2436 (91%) of the claims recommended by SDLC.

Table 4.9: Break-up of the Number of Individual and Community Claims filed at Gram Sabha Level (West Singhbhum District)

	Forest Dwelling Scheduled Tribes	
Sl. No.	*Individual Rights*	*Number*
1.	Total number of claims filed at Gram Sabha level	4970
2.	Number of claims Recommended by Gram Sabha to the SDLC	2677
3.	Number of claims rejected by the Gram Sabha	0
4.	Number of Claims pending with the Gram Sabha	0
5.	Number of titles given	2436
	Community Rights	***Number***
1.	Total number of claims filed at Gram Sabha level	1691
2.	Number of claims Recommended by Gram Sabha to the SDLC	39
3.	Number of claims rejected by the Gram Sabha	0
4.	Number of Claims pending with the Gram Sabha	0
5.	Number of titles given	39

	Other Traditional Forest-Dwellers	
	Individual	***Number***
1.	Total number of claims filed at Gram Sabha level	Nil
2.	Number of claims recommended by Gram Sabha to the SDLC	Nil
3.	Number of claims rejected by the Gram Sabha	Nil
4.	Number of claims pending with the Gram Sabha	Nil
5.	Number of titles given	Nil
	Community	**Number**
1.	Total number of claims filed at Gram Sabha level	Nil
2.	Number of claims recommended by Gram Sabha to the SDLC	Nil
3.	Number of claims rejected by the Gram Sabha	Nil
4.	Number of claims pending with the Gram Sabha	Nil
5.	Number of titles given	Nil

Source: Dy. Commissioner, West Singhbhum District, Jharkhand, January 2012.

The number of community claims filed at the Gram Sabha level is 1691, but those recommended by the Gram Sabha to SDLC is only 39 (2.31%) reflecting that still large number of community claims are pending at the Gram Sabha level. This needs to be probed by the West Singhbum District Administration. On the other hand, there is total neglect of OTFD both at the level of individual and community rights.

Table 4.10: Implementation of Forest Rights Act, in the Villages of West Singhbhum District (with very high Left Extremist Movement)

Sl. No.	*Name of the block*	*Name of Villages*	*Name of Pancha-yat*	*Area in acre*	*Forest rights titles*	*Nature of claims*	*Date of approval of claims*	*No. of patta holders*	*Average area per patta holder (in acre)*
1.	Tonto	Tumbahaka	Regad Hatu	8.67	Titles given	Community rights	13.08.09	54	2.1675
2.	Golkera	Tatibeda	Bara	465.84	-do-	Individuals Rights	13.08.09	57	8.1763
3.	-do-	Chirugbere	Bara	193.72	-do-	-do-	09.09.09	41	4.7249
4.	-do-	-do-	-do-	118.65	-do-	-do-	17.04.10	29	4.0914
5.	-do-	Chhatomadli	Gamaria	134.15	-do-	-do-	17.04.10	41	3.2720
6.	-do-	Bidi poto	Bara	317.20	-do-	-do-	25.02.10	28	11.3286
7.	-do-	Sirka	Saragada	513.22	-do-	-do-	29.03.10	57	9.0039
8.	-do-	Korodeya	Kebra	547.45	-do-	-do-	29.03.10	61	8.9746
9.	-do-	Sakoda	Boy keda	56.54	-do-	-do-	13.03.10	16	3.5339
10.	-do-	Jatisereng	Kebra	154.04	-do-	-do-	01.04.10	20	7.702
11.	-do-	Bunmaoli	Bara	329.41	-do-	-do-	12.05.10	35	9.4117
12.	-do-	Masuri beda	Kebra	162.88	-do-	-do-	14.05.10	23	7.0817
13.	-do-	Karowa	Kebra	251.99	-do-	-do-	03.05.10	28	8.9996
14.	Sonua	Barubeda	Boykela	22.20	-do-	-do-	03.03.12	10	2.220
15.	Goilkera	Rubadiari	Gulkeba	12.46	-do-	-do-	04.02.11	4	3.011
16.	Goilkera	Sajanpide	Kebra	107.06	-do-	-do-	22.03.11	15	7.1373
17.	-do-	Tikibeer	Arahasa	176.62	-do-	-do-	22.03.11	44	4.0141
18.	-do-	Chirugbda	Arahasa	41.81	-do-	-do-	17.04.11	24	1.7421
19.	-do-	Rubbayee	Bara	431.45	-do-	-do-	18.04.11	85	5.0759
20.	-do-	Bara	Bara	30.00	-do-	-do-	13.08.09	3	10.000
21.	-do-	Hotro beda	Boykeda	24.21	-do-	-do-	11.08.10	9	2.690
	Total			**4099.57**				**643**	**6.3757**

Source: Dy. Commissioner, West Singhbhum District, Jharkhand, January 2012.

The Goilkera block is located deep inside the Saranda Forest Division which is part of West Singhbhum district. This area is one of the epicentre of Jangal Kato Andolan (of Adivasis) during 1979-1985 and presently the primary theatre of Left Extremist movement. The tribals had launched a militant movement during 1980-86 in which the forest lands were felled and transformed into the cultivable land. Those felled forest areas have also been included in the assignment of forest rights to the local tribals mostly comprising the tribal community of Mundas and Hos. The average area of land assigned per beneficiary is 6.56 acre which is one of the highest area assigned in any Jharkhand Block. This is also part of the area of Saranda Action Plan formulated by the Government of India during UPA Government. Even in the villages of Sonua Block the average area assigned per beneficiary is higher than most of the other blocks in the State of Jharkhand. Sonua Block is also part of the Saranda

Action Plan. Hence, the forest rights have been more effectively implemented in the Maoist affected area of Saranda Forest Division as compared to other Forest Division of Jharkhand.

As per the Forest Reserve Survey, 2006 the Adivasis had forcibly occupied 2770.79 hectare land between 1980 and 1988 which constituted 3.24 per cent of the total Saranda Forest area. In Saranda Forest the individual *pattas* accepted claims is 416 and the distributed *pattas* are 394 covering 315.74 acre and the average land per family is 75.8 decimal (Letter No. 594, DC West Singhbhum). The Total Community Pattas distributed in Saranda Forest is 3558.32 acre (*Source:* Letter No. 594, DC office West Singhbhum). The total lease area given to different Companies like SAIL, Rungta Mines, Usha Martine, Tata Steel, and other Companies include 14,410.09 acre (Answer given by the Steel Minister on Rajya Sabha Unstarred Question No. 436 on 15th March, 2012). Besides this, another 9337.54 acre have been given to Mining Companies in 2012 to 22 Companies.

4.7 Implementation of Forest Right Act, 2006 in the District of Saraikela-Kharsawan (Figure up to January, 2012)

Table 4.11: Claims Approved in Saraikela-Kharsawan District

Sl. No.	*Description of item*	*Number of claims*
1.	Number of claims filed at Gram Sabha	1641
2.	Number of claims recommended by Gram Sabha	1641
3.	Number of claims recommended by SDLC to DLC	743
4.	Number of claims rejected by SDLC	898
5.	Number of claims approved by DLC for the titles.	558
6.	Number of titles distributed	558
7.	Extent of Forest Land for which title deeds issued (in acre)	348
8.	Number of claims rejected by DLC	96
9.	Total Number of claims rejected	994

Source: District Forest Officer, Saraikela, 2015.

It can be discerned from the above figures that at the Gram Sabha level no claims were rejected but at the SDLC level 898 claims were rejected and at DLC level another 96 cases were rejected and thus the total number of claims rejected in the Saraikela-Kharsawan district was 994. The average extent of Forest Land assigned per beneficiary was

0.62 acre. Besides this, no claims were recommended for Other Traditional Forest Dwellers. Further, only 2 claims were filed at Gram Sabha level for community rights and out of this only one title was recommended, but the area of the title has not been mentioned. This shows that the implementing authorities are not adequately concerned towards Community Rights issue; it is one of the important issues highlighted in the Forest Rights Act.

Table 4.12: Implementation of Forest Rights in Saraikela-Kharsawan District (Jharkhand)

Sl. No.	*Name of the Block*	*No. of Benefi-ciaries*	*Total Area*	*Average area per Benefi-ciary*	*No. of Villages in which Forest Rights given*	*Average area per village (in acre)*	*Area per beneficiary in villages (in acres)*
1.	Chandil	109	55.10	0.50	8	6.88	0.28 to 0.80
2.	Gamharia	150	99.06	0.66	4	24.77	0.44 to 1.03
3.	Kharsawan	145	245.86	1.70	6	40.98	0.80 to 1.63
4.	Kuchai	111	119.61	1.07	1	119.61	1.08
5.	Rajnagar	116	37.44	0.32	12	3.12	0.10 to 0.84
6.	Saraikela	67	29.15	0.43	9	3.24	0.12 to 1.49
	Total	**698**	**586.22**	**0.78**	**40**	**33.10**	**0.63**

Source: District Forest Officer, Saraikela, 2015.

In the district of Saraikela the number of beneficiaries are larger in Gamhariya and Kharsawan blocks, followed by Rajnagar, Kuchai and Chandil and the lowest is in Saraikela block. The area assigned to the beneficiaries is maximum in Kharsawan block followed by Kuchai block, but still lower in other blocks. The average area assigned is also highest in Kharsawan block (1.70 acre) followed by Kuchai block (1.07 acre) and much lower in other blocks. This area is also affected with extremist and activist influence. The average area per beneficiary is higher in the Kharsawan and Kuchai block where it is possible for the individual beneficiary to use the assigned land for cultivation purpose and in the remaining block the average area is so low that it can be used either for kitchen garden or homestead purpose. The overall situation of the assigned forest land in Saraikela-Kharsawan District indicate that only few beneficiaries can utilize the land for cultivation purpose and still fewer can utilize it for kitchen garden and rest for homestead purpose. There is no effort on the part of District Administration to increase the productivity of the assigned Forest land through irrigation and through other rural development convergence programme.

The implementation of Forest Rights Act, 2006 in the Dalma Sanctuary Area located in the District of East Singhbhum and Saraikela Kharsawan District are produced below:

Table 4.13: Implementation of Forest Rights Act in Dalma Sanctuary located in East Singhbhum and Saraikela-Kharsawan District (Jharkhand)

(Area in Acres)

Sl. No.	*Item*	*District*		*Dalma Sanctuary (Total)*	*Remarks*
		East Singhbhum	*Saraikela Kharsawan*		
1.	Number of claims received at Sub-divisional level	180	158	338	The Dalma Sanctuary is spread to the districts of East Singhbhum and Saraikela.
2.	Number of claims rejected at SDLC level	107	57	164	59.44% of the claims were rejected at the SDLC level for East Singhbhum and 36.07% for Saraikela-Kharsawan district.
3.	Number of claims forwarded to District level Committee	80	101	181	No
4.	Number of claims approved	80	101	181	No
5.	Number of claims approved for cultivable land.	19	101	120	No

(Contd.)

Sl. No.	*Item*	*District*		*Dalma Sanctuary (Total)*	*Remarks*
		East Singhbhum	*Saraikela Kharsawan*		
6.	Number of claims approved for area covered with bushes	61	Nil	61	No
7.	Area of Forest rights given in *Patta* lands	6.43	6.53	12.96	No
8.	Area of Forest rights given in bushes	49.29	NIL	49.29	No
	Total area of Forest Rights given	**55.72**	**6.53**	**62.25**	**0.34 acre only were allotted as titles to each beneficiary.**

Source: District Forest Officer, Saraikela, 2015.

The Dalma Sanctuary Area is spread to both East Singhbhum district and Saraikela-Rajkarswan district. Of the total 338 claims received at SDLC level, 59.44 per cent of the claims were rejected in East Singhbhum and 36.07 per cent rejection were in the Saraikela-Kharsawan district. Further of the total 181 approved claims, 120 beneficiaries received forest land and the remaining 69 were assigned rights within bushes. The *patta* land assigned is only 6.43 acre in East Singhbhum and 6.53 acre in Saraikela-Kharsawan district. The net result has been that out of 62.25 acre of assigned land, only 12.96 acre were forest land and the rest 49.29 acre have been provided within bushes. Further, only 6.43 acre of Forest Land (without bushes) were assigned in East Singhbhum District and in Saraikela District it was 6.53 acre. Thus in sum and substance, the Forest rights cultivable land assigned is limited to only 12.96 acre inclusive of both the districts which is only 0.11 acre per beneficiary. It is indeed a very miniscule area which can hardly be used for cultivation and can only be used for homestead purpose.

Forest Title to the Adivasis and other Forest Dwellers in the District of Khunti-Jharkhand. (Forest Rights Act, 2006)

Table 4.14: Claims of Forest Dwellers in District Khunti (Report upto 31.7.2014)

(in acres)

Sl. No.	*Description of item*	*Number*
1.	Number of claims filed at Gram Sabha level	443
2.	Number of claims recommended by Gram Sabha to SDLC	425
3.	Number of claims rejected by the Gram Sabha	18
4.	Number of claims recommended by SDLC to DLC	425
5.	Number of claims approved by DLC for title	421
6.	Number of titles distributed	421
7.	Extent of forest land for which title deeds issued	257.33
8.	Total Number of claims rejected	18

Source: District Welfare Officer, Khunti.

The number of claims recommended by the Gram Sabha in Khunti district is 425 and the number of rejection of claims by the Gram Sabha is limited to only 18. The number of claims recommended by SDLC to DLC is 425 indicating that no claims were rejected by SDLC. Further, DLC recommended 421 cases for approval by DLC and for all this claims titles were distributed and the area of forest land assigned was 257.33 acre. Each beneficiary was assigned 0.61 acre which is a small plot suitable marginally for the purpose of agriculture and more suitable for kitchen garden and homestead purpose. The number of community claims filed at the Gram Sabha level was four and all these 4 community claims were recommended by Gram Sabha to the SDLC for which the titles are yet to be assigned.

It is necessary to mention that the District of Khunti is also a very intensely affected area by Left Extremist Movement and continues even today. Fieldwork was undertaken in the district of Khunti from January 2014 to December 2016 to collect the data on Forest Rights implementation both from the official sources, NGOs and individual Adivasi beneficiaries in order to have a more in-depth understanding which can be discerned from the figures in Table 4.15.

In the District of Khunti 84 villages have been assigned Forest Rights Title and the number of beneficiaries is 412. The total area assigned is 326.43 acre for the 412 title holders. The average area assigned per village is 3.89 acre and per beneficiary it comes to only 0.79 acre. The average area per beneficiary is highest in Rania Block

Table 4.15: Implementation of Forest Rights Act, 2006 in Khunti District (For the period 2010-11 to 2013-14)

Sl. No.	*Name of the Block*	*No. of villages*	*No. of Beneficiaries*	*Area assigned (in acre)*	*Average area per village*	*Average area per beneficiary*
1.	Karra	30	112	48.46	1.62	0.43
2.	Khunti	18	118	102.21	5.68	0.87
3.	Torpa	17	81	50.32	51.32	0.62
4.	Murhu	4	12	27.76	6.94	2.31
5.	Adki	7	77	56.67	9.52	0.74
6.	Rania	5	12	41.01	8.20	3.42
	Total	**81**	**412**	**326.43**	**3.89**	**0.79**

Source: District Welfare Officer, Khunti.

(3.42) acre, followed by Murhu (2.31 acre), Khunti (0.87 acre), Adki (0.74 acre), Torpa 0.62 acre and the lowest area per beneficiary is in Karra Block (0.43 acres). It is necessary to mention here that Khunti District is the home of Khuntkhatti area where the tribals regard their land and forest to be part of their communal ownership and forms an important ingredient of their cultural identity. Therefore, even the forest area within the Khuntkhatti villages are under the control of the Khuntkhatti Raiyats the Adivasis manage even the forest area as within their community rights. As such they do not allow the Government or the Forest Department to interfere with their Khuntkhatti land and forest. Hence, the adivasis do not allow the Forest Rights Act, 2006 to be implemented in the Khuntkhatti villages for which the adivasis are even prepared to sacrifice their life as well as launch militant struggle.

Table 4.16: Individual Forest Right Titles Allotted to Tribals in Khunti District (Sampled Villages included in the present study).

Sl. No.	*Block*	*Village*	*No. of Beneficiaries*	*Area of titles (in acre)*	*Average area per Village (in acre)*	*Average area per beneficiary (in acre)*	*Remarks*
1.	Khunti	Knadih	01	0.15	0.01	0.15	In Khunti District under community Rights Khunt-katti area are major traditional rights and hence
		Chituramu	10	16.69	0.98	1.67	
		Kalamati	09	1.34	0.05	0.15	
		Irood	03	7.00	0.27	2.33	
		Rayee	05	2.89	0.11	0.48	
		Kathartoli	06	0.66	0.02	0.13	
		Chhotabaru	13	6.24	0.24	0.48	

(Contd.)

Sl. No.	Block	Village	No. of Benefic-iaries	Area of titles (in acre)	Average area per Village (in acre)	Average area per benefic-iary (in acre)	Remarks
		Chala`m	01	0.96	0.04	0.96	non-khuntkatti area is very less for allotment of forest rights. Very few villages In Khunti distrect do not have enough of non-Khuntikatti lands.
		Chandidih	03	0.85	0.03	0.38	
		Murhi	01	2.00	0.08	2.00	
		Tilma	01	0.30	0.01	0.30	
		Chitrnu	16	21.87	0.84	1.37	
	Total		**69**	**25.98**	**2.17**	**0.38**	
2.	Torpa	Mamrauf	04	1.76	0.10	0.01	
		Patrotoli	02	1.20	0.07	0.60	
		Churgi	14	8.93	0.53	0.64	
		Sundari Bhusatoli	13	13.13	0.77	1.01	
		Huseer Pahartoli	06	6.40	0.25	1.07	
		Chandarpur	08	3.40	0.13	0.43	
		Kocha	08	5.39	0.21	0.67	
		Karanj Toli	01	2.00	0.08	2.00	
	Total		**56**	**42.21**	**5.28**	**0.75**	
3.	Rania	Dahutamari	01	2.80	0.17	2.80	
		Khudibir	04	1.54	0.09	0.39	
	Total		**05**	**4.34**	**0.26**	**0.86**	
4.	Adki	Purtu	10	2.10	0.12	0.21	
		Gamharia	01	8.99	0.53	8.99	
		Telangadhi	01	3.10	0.18	3.10	
		Tirdih	10	5.00	0.19	0.50	
		Sargeta	14	21.29	0.82	1.52	
	Total		**36**	**40.48**	**8.10**	**1.12**	
5.	Karra	Sipulot	01	0.06	0.01	0.06	
		Bamraoa	06	2.55	0.15	0.43	
		Hansbedas ahnatoli	02	0.35	0.02	0.18	
		Bankuti Pipertoli	01	0.10	0.01	0.10	
		Setarahu	05	0.25	0.01	0.05	
		Manpur	08	1.70	0.07	0.21	
		Lota	06	1.70	0.07	0.28	
		Kuhuta	03	1.40	0.05	0.47	
		Gunni	09	1.33	0.05	0.15	
		Changatoli	02	1.80	0.07	0.90	
		Jiputoli	20	1.36	0.05	0.07	
	Total		**63**	**12.06**	**1.10**	**0.19**	
6.	Fudi	Kalamati	01	4.00	4.00	4.00	
	Total		**01**	**4.00**	**4.00**	**4.00**	
7.	Murhu	Kudki	01	23.40	23.40	23.40	
	Total		**01**	**23.40**	**23.40**	**23.40**	
	07 blocks (Khutti district)	41 villages	231	152.47	3.72	0.66	

Source: District Welfare Officer, Khunti.

The above figure of Forest Rights implementation in the individual sampled villages indicate that the area assigned per beneficiary is 0.66 acre which is very inadequate for cultivation purpose. However, along with the traditional Khuntkhatti land it can be used both for homestead and cultivation purpose.

A comparative analysis of the Forest Right assignment in the different studied district of Jharkhand indicate that maximum title was given in the district of West Singhbhum comprising 10643.09 acre. It has been very low in East Singhbhum district (707.46 acre) and in Saraikela Kharsawan district (626.22 acre). The lower extent of distribution in these two districts could be attributed to lower level of grassroots mobilization as compared to West Singhbhum district. The task of forest rights assignment was at the lowest ebb in the district of Khunti and Dalma Sanctuary area. The district of Khunti, however, needs to be placed at a different level of analysis, as it is predominant Khuntkhati area where the tribals have preserved the traditional Khuntkhatti rights against the onslaught of the forces of globalization and land acquisition. The symbolic exhibition of the traditional Jharkhandi identity is still intact in the minds of the tribal and particularly the intense sacrifice of Bhagwan Birsa Munda in land and forest struggles during the nineteenth century.

4.8 The Number of Individual and Community Claims filed in East Singhbhum District

Table 4.17: Implementation of Forest Rights in East Singhbhum District (For the Period Ending 30th May, 2016)

Sl. No.	*Period*	*Total No. of claims filed at Gram Sabha Level*	*No. of claims recom-mended by Gram Sabha to SDLC*	*No. of claims reject-ted by the Gram Sabha*	*No. of claims pending with the Gram Sabha*	*No. of titles given*		*Total No. of titles given*	*Extent of forest land for which titles needs issued (in acre)*
						Indivi-dual	*Comm-unity*		
1.	Total for East Singhbhum District	6131	3430	2320	381	2900	5	2905	1267.00

Source: District Forest Officer, East Singhbhum, Jhamshedpur.

The district of East Singhbhum is also one of the sampled districts of Jharkhand State in the present empirical study. The above data of implementation of Forest Rights in East Singhbhum District represents the latest figure covering the year 2016. The data indicate that the total number of claims filed at the Gram Sabha level in the District of East Singhbhum is 55.95 per cent and the number of claims rejected by Gram Sabha is very high representing 37.84 per cent of the total claims filed. All these relate to the individual land rights. The number of titles given is 2900 beneficiaries cover 47.30 per cent of the total claims filed at the Gram Sabha level. The total land assigned is 1267 acre which is 0.43 per cent acre per beneficiaries'. This is indeed a small plot of land suitable either for homestead or kitchen garden. Those families who have also individually owned land can use it more usefully for agricultural purpose. The number of community claims approved is only 5 but the area assigned is not indicated. The Gram Sabha cases of rejection is pretty high which needs to be probed further.

Table 4.18: Consolidation of Implementation of Forest Rights in the Five Districts of Jharkhand (Sampled Districts for the ICSSR Study)

Sl. No.	*Name of the sample district*	*No. of claims approved by DLC*	*No. of beneficia-ries given titles*	*Total Area Titles given (in Acres)*	*Average area per beneficiary (in Acres)*	*Remarks*
1.	West Singhbhum	2475	2475	10643.09	4.30 acre	Intense Left Extremist affected area
2.	Saraikela-Rajkharsawan	571	571	626.22	1.09 acre	Moderately affected Left Extremist area.
3.	East Singhbhum	3430	2900	- 1267.00	0.44 acre	
4.	Khunti	231	231	152.47	0.66 acre	Large part of the district is covered by Khuntkhanti community rights.
5.	Dalma Sanctuary Area	181	181	62.25	0.34 acre	This sanctuary is located both in East Singhbhum and Saraikela Rajkharswan district.
	Total	**6888**	**6358**	**12748.03**	**6.83 acre**	

The figures in Table 4.18 indicate a gist of the implementation of Forest Rights Act, in the sample districts of empirical study of Jharkhand. From the consolidated figure, it can be evinced that the approved claims by DLC in these five districts are 6888 out of which 6358 beneficiaries have been given titles which constitutes 92.31 per cent of the total claims approved. The total area of titles given in the Five district is 12748.03 acre which comprises 2 acre per beneficiary. However, the figures also clearly indicate that the average area per beneficiary assigned is 4.30 acre in West Singhbhum district followed by 1.09 acre in Saraikela-Rajkharsawan district and is much below 1 acre in the District of East Singhbhum and Khunti. The highest average area assigned to the beneficiaries in the West Singbhum District can be attributed to the impact of Left Extremist Movement in the district. The beneficiaries in the West Singhbhum district can much more usefully utilize the assigned land for cultivation purpose than in district of East Singhbhum and Khunti. The lessons learnt from the Saranda Action Plan which has been successful in controlling the Naxalite movement in the area has set an example to other districts in Jharkhand to follow the example of Saranda Action Plan.

4.9 Implementation and Outcomes of FRA in Jharkhand State

Implementation of the FRA only began in Jharkhand in October 2008, because there were no elected panchayats in the State. The State Government claimed that it was not able to implement the Act, since the Act requires elected members in the SDLCs and the DLCs, while the rules require the panchayats to summon a Gram Sabha. The Ministry of Tribal Affairs was requested for a clarification on this and had, in July 2008, informed the Jharkhand Government that the State Government can, in consultation with the Gram Sabhas, appoint members to fill these positions. Thus, in the Latehar, West Singhbhum, and East Singhbhum districts, Gram Sabhas were called at the end of November 2008 and Forest Rights Committees were elected, though in some areas the Forest Department tried to impose JFMC members as the FRC members.

Initially, most Gram Sabhas were held at the revenue village level, though hundreds of settlements submitted resolutions seeking constitution of hamlet level Gram Sabhas. In Latehar, the Collector agreed to hold Gram Sabhas as per the provisions of the Panchayati Raj Act in Jharkhand. Thus, the process of recognising hamlet-level Gram Sabhas was initiated in the district of Latehar. During early 2009, there were also intensifying efforts to remove people from their lands for plantation purposes. For instance, in Latehar District, in the second week of February 2009, false cases were filed against people who resisted plantations and two people were arrested. Even in August 2009, cases were filed against people occupying forest land for decades, and they were jailed. Likewise, many villagers were evicted since 2005 in the name of undertaking plantations.

Since 2010, the process of implementation of the FRA in Jharkhand has comparatively picked-up, largely due to State Government's pressure for results. About 18,516 titles were already distributed as on 10th October, 2014 (PCCF, Jharkhand). However, in many cases, the titles are for lesser area than that claimed by the beneficiaries for which no reasons have been given. Besides, the claims filed by other Traditional Forest Dwellers are being grossly ignored, and there have been very limited reported claims for community forest rights. The figures given by PCCF Jharkhand (as on 10th October, 2014), indicate that the number of community claims filed at the Gram Sabha Level were 769 in the entire State of Jharkhand of which 514 were from the Ranchi-Chhotanagpur Region and another 255 claims were from Santhal Pragana Region. The total community claims filed were 264 which was recommended by Gram Sabha in the West Singhbhum district, 59 in the district of Koderma, 54 in the district of Khunti, 11 in Sahebganj and 230 in Godda district. The total number of community claims pending with the Gram Sabha at the State-level was 2803 of which 2790 claims were pending in the district of West Singhbhum alone. The actual number of community rights title given was 356 of which 230 were from the district of Godda, 16 were from West Singhbhum district and 21 were from Chatra district. It is essential to State here that the Adivasi activist organization in the State of Jharkhand have been consistently demanding the implementation of community claims and community rights, but the district administration as well as the State Administration including the Forest Department are not showing keen interest in the implementation of community rights claims which has also been part of essential right in the Forest Rights Act, 2006. As per the facts mentioned by Gladson Dung Dung (2016) the total Forest land diverted for development work between 1980 to 2015 was 20,778.72 acre.

There are complaints from the Social Activists that the Forest Department is refusing to accept claims in most wildlife sanctuaries, national parks, and tiger reserves on the grounds that rights in reserve forests were recognised during the colonial period. However, some individual land titles were issued in the Hazaribagh Wildlife Sanctuary and Dalma Wildlife Sanctuary. It is essential that the Government of Jharkhand should implement both community rights also individual rights in the wildlife, National Park and Sanctuaries. Besides this, very little effort has been made to convert forest villages (there are 28 forest villages in the State) into revenue villages although individual titles have been issued in some of the Forest Villages. Further, bamboo and tendu leaves continue to be managed as nationalised MFPs by the Forest Department.

Jharkhand is an important State for FRA implementation, with a large forest area and a very large tribal and non-tribal forest-dependent population. However, by 10th October, 2014, the number of individual claims received in Jharkhand was only 48,900; and of these, only 18,516 titles were distributed covering an area of 44,387.60 acre. This is one of the lowest figures among the States of Central and East India which is a cause for concern about the manner of the implementation of the Act. Moreover, very few claims for Community Forest Rights have been received; those listed as CFR claims are mostly for diversion to non-forest activities or minor claims for graveyards and threshing grounds. Hence, the main objective of giving community rights to forest resources has not been achieved.

The reasons for this situation in Jharkhand include:

- A number of potential claimants appear to be left out of the process entirely, due to lack of awareness and information, non-supply of forms etc.
- A large number of applications have been rejected due to wrongful interpretation of the Act.
- A number of cases of inordinate delays in processing claims, providing support to Gram Sabhas to process claims, and tenable allegations of corruption by the implementing staff and village leaders have emerged.
- Several cases of the Forest Department illegally initiating plantation activities in the land for which cultivation claims have been filed (or could be filed).
- Several deviations have taken place from the process of implementation laid down in the law, including less involvement of the Gram Sabha, wrong attribution of rejection made by the officials to the Gram Sabha, no communication of rejection to the claimants etc.
- Where claims have been granted, the process of mutation of land records is incomplete; and in the case of community claims, the titles issued are defective.

- Several communities believe that applying under the Act will weaken their claim for full forest rights as per earlier Acts, for which they have been agitating since a long time.

4.10 Implementation of Forest Rights Act in the State of Odisha

The State of Odisha has a recorded forest area measuring 58,136 sq. km. This includes 26,329 sq.km. (45.29%) of reserve forests, 15,525 sq.km. (26.70%) of protected forests and 16,282 sq.km. (28.01%) of unclassified forests. The total recorded forest area in the State is 37.34% of its total geographical area. (*Source: Odisha Economic Survey Report*, 2011-12). Forest land to the tune of 41,891.25 hectares (or 1,03,515.53 acre) has been diverted in Odisha for non-Forestry purposes till March 6, 2013. The Minister of Forest and Environment, Government of India, March 6, 2013, stated that between 1972-1999 Odisha has lost more than a quarter of its forest cover. The major factors attributed to these trends include massive deforestation for different development projects including mega dams, mines, and industrial hubs.

Bishnu Prasad Mohapatra (2014), states that the factors responsible for deforestation are: (i) Commercialisation of Forest Products; (ii) higher price for agricultural products; (iii) lower wage and non-availability of non-farm jobs; (iv) technical changes that increase agricultural yield; (v) greater access to forest and market through construction of roads; and (vi) absence of well-defined and secure property right of forest dwellers. It is estimated that the forest area diverted for non-forest use in the 1980s and 1990s was 27,466 hectares (Sarap, 2004). During the period from 2005-06 to 2010-11, the extent of diversion of forest land was high, and most forest lands were diverted for mining (471.4 ha) followed by miscellaneous purposes (344.6 ha). *The Economic Survey Report of Odisha*, 2011-12, reveals that the actual forest cover of Odisha in 2007 was 48,855 sq.km., which constituted 31.38 per cent of the State's geographical area in terms of forest canopy density classes. 8.

Kendu Leaves, Forest Policies and Livelihoods in Odisha

Kendu leaves play an important role in the forest economy of Odisha. It is estimated that the annual production of Kendu leaves in the State is around 4.5 to 5 lakh quintals (*Odisha Economic Survey Report*, 2011-12). Under the NTFP, in some districts Kendu leaves collection has been deregularised. The procurement price of the green Kendu leaves has also been enhanced from 29 paise to 35 paise per Kerry (i.e. a bundle comprising 20 leaves) during 2010-11 and the wages of the seasonal staff has also been enhanced by 40 per cent (Odisha Legislative Assembly, 2012).

Since 1988 onwards, the Odisha Forest Policy and legal frameworks witnessed relatively pro-people policy measures such as the JFM Resolution, Odisha Minor Forest Produce Administration Rule, the FRA and the recently-revised JFM Resolution in 2011. In Odisha, over 8,000 villages (Vasundhara, 2005) are actively protecting and managing State appropriated lands in their vicinity. There are 12,000 CFM groups who have been managing 8,50,000 ha forests in the State which is 40 per cent of the total forest area. (Odisha Jungle Manch, 2012). These groups, under the banner of VSS, have formed their own management system, devised a self-management mechanism, and through the process of collaboration among the different groups, have formed district and State-level federations for such purpose. Such democratic and autonomous institutions have become a guiding force for others, especially for the forest bureaucracy, for managing forests effectively. JFM in Odisha has supported the management of the vast forest land, and as per data, nearly 9377 (PCCF, 2005) VSS groups have been formed for managing the 8,17,788 hectares of forest land in the State. Out of the 16,98,065 households involved in JFM, 40 per cent belong to the STs and 15 per cent belong to SCs. The forest areas

Table 4.19: The Status of the Ongoing Forest-based Livelihood Programmes in Odisha

Project	*Project Area*	*Forest Area (Size) Covered under the Project*
Revised long-term Action Plan (RLTAP)	KBK areas (Koraput, Rayagada, Malkangiri, Nalrangpur, Kalahandi, Nuapara, Bolangir and Sonepur Districts)	13,130 ha
National Afforestation Programme (NAP)	27 forestry divisions	10,946 ha
Economic Plantation	22 non-KBK areas	349 ha
Odisha Tribal Empowerment and Livelihood Programme (OTELP assisted by IFAD, WFP and DFID)	Koraput, Rayagada, Malkangiri, Nalarangpur, Kalahandi, Gajapati and Kandhamal Districts)	16,500 ha (target in 3 years)

Source: JBIC, Odisha Forestry Sector Development Project, Odisha.

covered through JFM is 14 per cent of the total forest land in the State. [*Source:* (i) PCCF Odisha Office and DEFOs, (ii) Japan Bank for International Cooperation (JBIC), 2005].

4.11 Status of Implementation of Forest Rights Act, 2006 in Odisha

The Government of Odisha, since the implementation of Act, 2006, has been able to provide land titles to as many as 3,25,449 (Ministry of Tribal Affairs, GoI, 2014) forest dwelling households in the tribal regions of the State. FRA beneficiaries are being linked with different development programmes and schemes such as farm, ponds and land development programmes under MGNREGA, housing through the IAY and *mo kudia* (my hut), plantation of fruit-bearing trees under MGNREGA and Horticulture Mission Programme, OTELP which have helped to strengthen the livelihoods of the tribal people.

The Act prescribes a number of sequential steps for the implementation of the provisions of the Act from the Gram Sabha to the State level committee.

- A meeting of the Palli Sabha is convened by the *Sarpanch* on the request and presence of a representative of the Panchayat Samiti and the Secretary of the concerned GP/village/hamlet panchayat to elect the Forest Rights Committee (FRC) comprising 10 to 15 members including one-third women representation. The role of FRC is to assist the Gram Sabha in its function to collate, verify and approve claims to rights.
- The FRC receives claim forms from individuals and communities on behalf of the Gram Sabha/Palli Sabha. It has to provide reasonable time and opportunity to the FRC and the claimants to prepare maps demarcating the area of each recommended claim as prescribed under the Act. The claim form is to be accompanied by at least two evidences (out of nine given in the Act) authenticating the claim. The Gram Sabha shall, then, pass a resolution on the claims submitted and forward a copy of the same to the Sub-Divisional Level Committee (SDLC). Any person aggrieved by the decision of the Gram Sabha may apply to the SDLC within 60 days from the passing of resolution by the Gram Sabha for a decision on the petition.
- The SDLC consists of the SDO, Tribal Welfare Officer, Forest Range Officer, and three members from the Panchayat Samittee (PS), appointed by the PS. The SDLC examines the resolution/decision of the Gram Sabha, prepares the records of

forest rights and forwards it through the SDO to the District Level Committee for a final decision.

- The District Level Committee (DLC) is composed of the District Collector, District Forest Officer (DFO), District Welfare Officer (in Odisha it is the DRDA/ITDA), and three representatives of the Zilla Parishad (ZP), appointed by the ZP. The DLC is the final authority to decide and approve on the forms (both individual and community) prepared by the SDLC.
- The State Level Monitoring Committee monitors the progress of recognition and vetting of the forest rights (*Source:* Forest Rights Act, 2006). In the State of Odisha the process of implementation of the Act started since January 2008. A number of Departments are involved in the process—namely Tribal, Revenue, Forest and Panchayati Raj which are working in coordination for implementing the Act; the Tribal Welfare Department is the nodal agency. Based on the Forest Rights Act, 2006 the Department of SC and ST, Development Commissioner, Government of Odisha, has written to all collectors of the districts to form committees at District, Sub-divisional, and village levels through the Palli Sabha.
- The Panchayati Raj Department, in consultation with other departments, directed the officials at the district and block levels to hold a Palli Sabha on 16 and 23 March, 2008 to form the FRC at the village/hamlet level after giving proper orientation on the FRA and its rules. The dates of holding the Palli Sabha were published through the local media, and the official to be entrusted for implementation of the FRA at different levels were familiarised through discussion and training on the different provisions of the Act.
- Due to the legal and technical grounds on the control and management of land by both Revenue and Forest Departments, only the maps for the lands occupied and cultivated within the revenue boundary were prepared while the areas under Reserve Forest (RF), Protected Forest (PF), National Parks, Sanctuaries etc., were excluded. This was observed only in case of individual rights over forestland, while the rights over Community Forest (CF) were not given much attention for a long time. The officials have regarded FRA as largely land rights over a piece of forest land negating the Community Forest Rights (CFR). This a major gap in understanding the FRA at the Government level as well as at

the Civil Society level. Besides, there are specific provisions for the PTGs, pastoral, and pre-agricultural nomadic communities displaced under the FRA.

4.12 District-wise Analysis of Forest Rights Implementation in the Sample Districts in Odisha

Koraput District

In 14 Tehsils of Koraput district the number of titles issued is 24,651 covering an area of 30,902.261 acre. There are 1229 number of Village Level Forest Rights Committees in the Koraput Revenue Sub-Division. There are 23,751 individual claims which have been filed and out of this 21,708 claims have been forwarded by the Gram Sabha to the Sub Divisional Committee and 20,567 individual claims have been submitted to the District Level Committee and finally, the DLC has approved 20,471 claims over an area of 28,239.86 acre. The titles of individual claim for 18,067 persons have been given over an area of 26,469.60 acre. Similarly, 149 number of community claims have been approved over an area of 2,239.87 acre which have been issued to different communities by the District Level Committee. The Gram Sabha has approved 21,708 number of claims out of 23,751 claims, i.e. Gram Sabha rejected 2,043 claims constituting 8.60 per cent of the total claims. The SDLC also rejected 1,141 claims constituting 5.26 per cent of the total claims which was submitted to SDLC to Gram Sabha; the DLC also rejected 96 claims constituting 0.47 per cent of the total cases submitted to it by SDLC. This obviously reflect that higher percentage of claims is rejected by Gram Sabha followed by SDLC and miniscule percentage rejected by DLC.

The author visited the village of Doliamba, located in Lakshmipur Panchayat and Lakshmipur Block. In this village, there were 15 beneficiaries; all of them belonged to the Kandha Scheduled Tribes. The type of land in which the title was given included Reserve Forest area and the area assigned to them ranged from 1 acre to 2 acre. The Forest Management has range-wise VSS and the total number of VSS is 766 and the total area of 61,712.68 hectares has been assigned to the VSS. It is interesting to note that the Koraput Division has used MGNREGA grants for plantation which includes 796 hectares and the man-days generated is 25,870 numbers. The payment of wages to the labourers is being done through online payment directly to the accounts of labourers. The Forest Division also undertakes works like Road

Table 4.20: Status of Implementation of Forest Rights Act, 2006, in Koraput District (Individual claims as on 29.10.2015)

Sl. No.	Item of information	Koraput Sub-division	Jeypore Sub-Division	Koraput District	Total Koraput District.
1.	Number of claims received by FRCs	23760	11188	34948	69896
2.	Number of claims approved by Gram Sabha	21281	8629	29910	59820 (85.58%)
3.	Area involved (in acre)				
	(a) Area	31229.67	12632.33	43862.00	87724.00
	(b) Number of families	20963	7206	28169	56338.00
4.	Number of claims rejected by Gram Sabha	64	2434	2498	4996.00 (7.15%)
5.	Number of claims approved by SDLC	20599	7205	27804	55608 (79.56%)
6.	Area involved (in acre)				
	(c) Area	30480.22	12340.32	42820.54	85641.08
	(d) No. of families	20599	7205	27804	55608.00
7.	Number of claims rejected by SDLC	452	Nil	452	904 (1.60%)
8.	Number of claims approved by DLC	20471	7205	27676	55352
9.	Area involved (in acre)				
	(e) Area	30068.12	12340.32	42408.44	84780.88
	(f) No. of families	20471	7205	27676	55352
10.	Number of Certificates of titles distributed	18537	7205	25742	28316
11.	Area in Acres	28090.86	11995.56	40086.42	80092.84

Source: DFO, Koraput, 2015.

repair, culverts, causeways and water bodies. The Forest Division also has allotted and transferred 100 trees to the Corporate HAL Sunabeda during 2013-14 and 190 trees were assigned during 2014-15; similarly some trees have been assigned also during 2015-16 to Telengiry Canal Division Barniput and NH 326 Koraput Rayagada Road have been assigned 423 trees. Thus more than 1300 trees were felled by the Forest Division for industries and irrigation.

The Government of Odisha in Resolution No. 5503 dated 31-3-2000 of the Department of Forest and Environment had entrusted Gram Panchayat the authority to regulate, purchase, procure and trade 68 Minor Forest Produce. The policy resolution demands that the persons purchasing MFPs from the primary collectors or traders will need to register with the Gram Panchayats on payment of Fee.

The total number of claims received by Forest Rights Committee in the entire Koraput district is 69,896 and the number of claims approved by Gram Sabha is 59,820 constituting 85.58 per cent indicating that the Gram Sabha rejected 14.42 per cent of the cases. The total area involved in acre assigned to the beneficiaries is 87,724 acre to 56,338 families. The number of claims approved by SDLC is 55,608 comprising 79.56 per cent of the total claims which suggest that 21.44 per cent of the claims were rejected by SDLC. The area involved in acre is 85,641.08 acre to 55,608 families. The number of claims approved by SDLC is 55,352 comprising 84.780.88 acre to 55,352 families. Finally, the number of titles distributed to 28,316 families consisting of 80,092.84 acre, i.e. 2.83 acre per beneficiary. This is an adequate area to be used for cultivation purpose.

Table 4.21: Status of implementation of Community Rights in the District of Koraput as on 29.10.2015

Sl. No.	*Items of Information on Community Rights*	*Name of the Sub-division Koraput*	*Name of the Sub-division Jeypore*	*Grand Total for the district of Koraput*
1.	Number of claims received	–	–	–
2.	Form B	276	190	466
3.	Form C	131	27	158
4.	Total B+C	407	217	624
5.	Total claims settled (B+C)	–	–	–
6.	No.	149	20	169
7.	Area in Acres	10358.3	685.34	11044.2
8.	Total claims distributed	–	–	–
9.	No.	45	13	58
10.	Area	2239.87	541	2780.87
11.	Claims pending	–	–	–
12.	Form B	139	170	309
13.	Form C	113	27	140
14.	Total	252	197	449
15.	Number of claims settled u/s 3(2)	–	–	–
16.	No.	–	4	4
17.	Area in Acres	–	16.11	16.11

Source: JBIC, Odisha Forestry Sector Development Project, Odisha.

It could be noticed from Table 4.21, that the total claims of Community Rights received is 624 inclusive of (Forms B & C) and the total claims settled is only 169 which constitutes 27.08 per cent of the total claims received indicating that the balance of 62.92 per cent of the claims are yet to be decided. Further, the number of claims distributed is 58 comprising an area of 2780.87 acre amounting to 47.95 acre per single claim. The number of community claims still pending is quite large amounting to 449 cases which needs to be speedily tackled by the district administration.

Rayagada District

The Rayagada Division has 7 Forest Ranges, namely—Rayagada, K. Singhpur, Kashipur, Tikri, Gudari, Maniguda and Gunupur. The area under forest in respect of Rayagada Division is given below:

Table 4.22: Category of Forest in Rayagada District

Sl. No.	*Particulars of Nature of Forest*	*Area in (Hectare)*	*Remarks*
1.	Reserve Forest	77,337.38 (33.61%)	This includes the area under all the seven forest ranges
2.	PRF	1,17,754.74 (51.18%)	-do-
3.	DPF	33,434.69 (14.54%)	-do-
4.	CA	1061.14 (0.46%)	-do-
5.	Village Forest	488.50 (0.21%)	-do-
	Total	**230076.85 (100.00%)**	

Source: JBIC, Odisha Forestry Sector Development Project, Odisha.

The area under reserve forest constitute 33.61 per cent and the Protected Forest comprises 51.18 per cent in Rayagada District.

Table 4.23: Implementation of Forest Rights Act, 2006 (As on 31-10-2015) in Rayagada District

Sl. No.	*Name of the Sub Division*	*No. of Claims Approved by SDLC*	*Area involved (in Acres)*	*No. of Families*	*No. of Claims approved by DLC for Titles*	*Area Involved (in Acres)*	*No. of Families*	*No. of Certificates of Titles Distributed*	*Area (in Acres)*
1.	Rayagada	5709	9146	5709	5701	9133	5701	5504	9133
2.	Gurupur	17574	28506	17574	16376	26552	16376	13994	26552
	Total	**23283**	**37652**	**23283**	**22077**	**35685**	**22077**	**19498**	**35685**

Source: JBIC, Odisha Forestry Sector Development Project, Odisha.

A persual of Proforma One relating to individual claims of Rayagada District indicates that the number of claims approved by SDLC is only 23,283 (69.14%) and the area involved is 37,651.43 acre. Further, number of claims approved by DLC for titles is 22,077 which constitutes 94.82 per cent of the claims approved by SDLC. The number of certificates of titles ultimately distributed is 19,498 amounting to 35,684.43 acre. The area distributed per title is amenable to be used for the purpose of cultivation. The number of claims remanded to Gram Sabha is 2785 which is quite high and similarly, the number of claims remanded to SDLC is 1206 which need to be further probed for providing justice to those who have been deprived of the title and the land rights.

Table 4.24: Status of Implementation of Community Rights in the District Rayagada as on 31-10-2015

Sl. No.	*Name of the District*	*Particular of Items*	*Number*
1.	Rayagada	No. of claims received	
2.	-do-	Form B	405
3.	-do-	Form C	206
4.	-do-	B+C	611
5.	-do-	Total No. claims settled (B+C)	
6.	-do-	No.	178
7.	-do-	Area in Acres	3789.20
8.	-do-	Total Claims disbursed	
9.	-do-	No. (B+C)	146
10.	-do-	Area in Acres (B+C)	3201.6
11.	-do-	Claim pending	
12.	-do-	Form B	288
13.	-do-	Form C	145
14.	-do-	Total	433
15.	-do-	No. of claims settled U/S 3(2)	
		No.	23
		Area in Acres	**9425.8**

Source: Information sheet on presentation of Forest Right Act of Rayagada District as on 31.10.2015.

The total number of claims received in Form B was 405 and 206 in Form C, i.e. a total of 611. Out of this 117 claims were settled under Form B involving an area of 3789 acre; besides this 61 number of Form C claims were also taken up but area involved is uncertain. Inclusive of Form B and Form C the total claim settled is 178 covering 3789 acre out of which 90 claims have been distributed involving an area of 3202 acre. Form C claims have not been settled; all the claims of 146 persons covering an area of 3201.86 acre have been distributed. The number of claims pending includes 288 of Form B and 145 of Form C involving a total of 433 pending claims. It is found that of the total number of claims consisting of 33,677 recommended by the Gram Sabha, SDLC recommended only 23,283 numbers of claims to DLC and rejected 10,394 claims constituting nearly 30.86 per cent of the total claims which needs to be reviewed.

Table 4.25: FRA Beneficiaries Convergence for the Entire District of Rayagada (As on 31.10.2015)

Sl. No.	*District*	*Particular of Items*	*Number*	*Remarks*
1.	Rayagada	No. of Certificates of title distributed	19498	Cover 13 blocks of Rayagada district
2.	-do-	Convergence under various Government schemes		
3.	-do-	IAY	9435	House Construction. (Government of India)
4.	-do-	Mo Kudia	65	State Government Housing Scheme (Government of Odisha)
5.	-do-	Mo Pokhari	313	Construction of Ponds (Scheme of Government of Odisha)
6.	-do-	Land development under MGNREGS	1521	Government of India Scheme on employment to rural poor.
7.	-do-	National Horticulture Mission	164	Government of India Scheme
8.	-do-	Other programmes	1879	Mostly Government of India Scheme on old age pension and Social security.
9.	**District Total**	**All progammes**	**32875**	Innovative attempt.

Source: Information sheet on presentation of Forest Right Act of Rayagada District as on 31.10.2015.

It is a healthy sign that the district of Rayagada has tried to converge different Government Schemes with the forest rights titles because the lands distributed under forest rights are generally bereft of irrigation and other necessary productive input. The convergence shows that 19,498 titles distributed are covered under Government of India

Scheme of House Construction, another substantial number of beneficiaries have been covered under MGNREGS for Land Development and Productivity. Other Convergence programme includes the Odisha Government Schemes of house construction and construction of ponds and social security schemes

Table 4.26: PTG Households and Distribution of Titles Under FRA 2006 in Rayagada District as on 31.10.2015

Sl. No.	Name of the District	Name of the Micro-Project	Name of the Block	Particular of items	Number
1.	Rayagada	DKDA Parsali	K. Singhpur		
2.	-do-	-do-	-do-	Number of Households	615
3.	-do-	-do-	-do-	No. of claims approved by Gram Sabha	532
4.	-do-	-do-	-do-	No. of Claims approved by SDLC	532
5.	-do-	-do-	-do-	No. of claims approved by DLC	532
6.	-do-	-do-	-do-	Certificate of titles distributed	532
7.	-d0-	-do-	-do-	Area in Acres	867
8.	-do-	DKDA Chatikona	Bissam Cuttack	Number of Households	1444
9.	-do-	-do-	-do-	No. of claims approved by Gram Sabha	1363
10.	-d0-	-do-	-do-	No. of Claims approved by SDCL	1363
11.	-do-	-do-	-do-	No. of claims approved by DLC	1363
12.	-do-	-do-	-do-	Certificate of titles distributed	1363
13.	-do-	-do-	-do-	Area in Acres	2221
14.	-do-	LSDA Putasingi	Gunupur	Number of Households	947
15.	-do-	-do-	-do-	No. of claims approved by Gram Sabha	802
16.	-do-	-do-	-do-	No. of Claims approved by SDLC	802
17.	-do-	-do-	-do-	No. of claims approved by DLC	802
18.	-do-	-do-	-do-	Certificate of titles distributed	802
19.	-do-	-do-	-do-	Area in Acres	1307

Distribution of titles to PTG Households under FRA 2006 as on 31.10.2015 in Rayagada District (Addition of Rayagada and Gunupur Sub-Division).

Source: Information Sheet on Implementation of Forest Rights Act of 2006, Rayagada District.

It would be of interest to find that large number of FRA beneficiaries have been included under convergence programme under different Government schemes as on 31st October, 2015. In the entire district of Rayagada there are 14 blocks in which the total number of titles distributed is 19,498 out of which 9435 beneficiaries have been provided IAY houses; 65 beneficiaries have been provided benefits under Mo-Kudia Scheme; 313 beneficiaries have been provided benefits under Mo Pukhri Scheme; 1521 beneficiaries have benefitted in Land Development Programme under MNREGA; 164 beneficiaries have benefited under National Horticulture Mission; and 1879 other programmes mgfly GoI schemes and Social Security.

The PTG households have also been provided titles under FRA, 2006 in Rayagada District. The PTGs are located in 3 blocks of Rayagada District, namely DKDA Parsali (K. Singhpur Block), DKDA Chatikona (Bisam Cuttuck Block), and LSDA Putasangi (Gunupur Block). There are 3006 number of PTG households in the district out of which claims were received by FRC numbering 3131 and all these were sent to Gram Sabha and the number of claims approved by Gram Sabha was 2697; the certificate of titles were also issued to 2697 numbers involving an area of 4395 acre in the entire district of Rayagada. It is quite appreciable that so many individual titles have been conferred to PTG families. It may be mentioned that the total number of individual titles approved in the entire Rayagada District was 19498 and the area assigned was 35,685 acre and the area of titles assigned to PTGs was 4395 acre constituting 22.5 per cent of the total district. This is indeed a good augury in the implementation strategy of Government of Odisha.

4.13 Implementation of Forest Rights Act, 2006 in Kalahandi

The District of Kalahandi has two Forest Divisions, namely North and South Forest Division. The North Forest Division has 1545.91 sq. km of which the Reserve Forest are covered under 826.1400 sq. kms, another 263.6462 sq. kms. are proposed to be covered under Reserve Forest. The total forest area of Kalahandi North Forest Division constitutes 40.15 per cent of the total geographical area. There are adequate natural regeneration in M. Rampur and Narla Range which offers a healthy and comfortable habitat for all types of wild animals. This division comprises five ranges, 20 sections and 94 beats. There are several road construction projects within the forest area which were constructed during 2010-11, 2011-12, 2012-13, 2013-14 and 2014-2015 in Lanjigarh Golamunda M. Rampur, Narala Blocks. There are also developmental activities like tubewell, community centre, water harvesting centre etc. within the left wing affected areas of the district (IAP) which includes Rs. 12.43 lakh. Forest Rights Act, 2006 is implemented in 314 villages and individual titles have been given to 3854 beneficiaries covering 5806 acre and community rights of 7748.29 acre. The Kalahandi district includes the Tehsils of Golamunda, Junagarh, Bhawanipatna, Narla, M. Rampur, Kesinga etc.

Jamguda Gramsabha is harvesting bamboo from 2012-13. Between 2012-13 and 2015-16, nearly 30,114 bamboos have been harvested the value of which includes Rs. 3.59 lakh. Out of this 3.49 lakh major amounts have been spent for wages, silvi-cultural operation, community hall etc. The potentiality of MFP item between October to June each year includes bamboo, *kendu* leaf, tamarind, *mahuva* flower, *siali* leaves, mango kernels, hill brooms, *bahda, amla, sal* seeds, *mahua* seeds, *neem* seeds and *babul* seeds. Proposal for diversion of 359 ha of forest land in respect of three forest villages have been submitted to the GoI.

After reorganization of Forest Department since 1st October, 2003 the Kalahandi Forest division is bifurcated into two forest divisions, namely, Kalahandi North Division and Kalahandi South Division. Kalahandi South Division has approximately 4.70 sq. km. Both the forests division covers the area of two revenue sub-divisions, namely Bhawani Patna and Dharmgarh. Most of the area of Bhawani Patna sub division and a small portion of Dharmgarh sub-division constitute Kalahandi North Forest Division and the rest area is coming under Kalahandi South Division. Bhawanipatna is the district HQ of both the forest division. The total area of Kalahandi north is 1,53,963.72 ha. The area under Reserve Forest in Kalahandi South Division is 62,289 ha and the Protected Forest is 22,186 ha; the Revenue Forest is 9237 hectare. There are several forest roads which have been constructed in Kalahandi South Division extended to 175.1 km.

Karlapat Sanctuary is situated in the South of Bhawani Patna town and it signifies hilly and forested landscape. Six continuous forest blocks with a total area of 175.5 sq. km have been notified as Karlapat Sanctuary. The entire sanctuary area comes under Kalahandi South Forest Division. The sanctuary was notified under Section 18 of Wild Life Protection Act, 1972. It also serves as a crucial corridor for the elephant. The sanctuary came into existence on 15-10-1992. Area of Karlapat Wildlife Sanctuary is 147.66 sq. km. and it consists of 6 forest blocks. It is covered with sal forest. It is an area of excellence with diversity and unique eco-system. It acts as a recreational centre for the local urban dwellers particularly for children, students, businessmen, Government servants and politicians. It acts as watershed for major rivers, i.e. Tel which facilitates irrigation, drinking water supply and electricity. It has presence of animals such as tigers, leopard, bear etc. In recent years the use of herbal medicine, herbal cosmetics and other herbal products has increased substantially. It has a great demand for NTFPs for quite a sizeable population of Kalahandi forest dwellers who depend for their sustenance on forests. The important NTFPs are tamarind, *mahua* flower, hill broom, thorn bloom, *phulo jhadu* (flowery Hill Broom), *kochila* seeds, *Horida, Bahda, Amla Ritha, Bhalla*, Nut, Honey, *Siali* leaf, *Sabai* grass, Mango kernel, Khargrass, *Palua Dhotuki* Flower, *Putrani, Shikakai, Jatropa, Fola* seeds, *Siali* seeds, *Indira Binachir Haldi, Kolathia, Kontapadma, Talmakhna* seeds, Biodanka seeds, *Bhogani* seeds, *Bela, Bhuin Neem, Rohini* fruit etc.

The maintenance of NTFP resource of the forest has gained momentum as the sustainable income from forestry sector. Fruit, flower, seed, leafs etc. are used as NTFP. The area kept under NTFP overlapping working circle is 73,908 ha. These species are almost covering 69 items transferred to GPs for regulating the collection and trade. *Kendu* leaf and processing is done by the State Government while marketing is done through OFDC limited. A sizeable income accrue to the local Adivasi people from NTFP of Kalahandi District from January to June. In Kalahandi South Division there are 377 VSS covering an area of 25,226 ha spread to large number of Panchayat. MGNREGA activities are also carried out in Kalahandi South Division during 2013-14, 2014-15 and 2015-16 covering an expenditure of Rs. 370 to Rs. 447 lakh and generating 1.91 lakh to 1.68 lakh man-days.

The number of claim applications disposed in Kalahandi Sub-Division is 5768 covering an area of 8997 acre. In Kalahandi South Division 6563 individual claims petitions have been approved by DLC covering a total area of 4110.545 ha and 118 community cases covering an area of 5771.456 ha. In the entire district of Kalahandi the number of individual claims approved by DLC for title is 10,520 covering an area of 16,182.34 acre and the number of titles distributed is 10,077 covering an area of 15,299.71 acre. The community rights of Form B have been settled for 185 claims covering an area of 23,720,47 acre and 8 forms have been settled covering an area of 395 acre.

It is significant to note that no claims have been rejected. It is also appreciable that the development agency for the primitive tribes known as Lanjigarh KKDA has 310 claims approved by GS and same number has also been approved by DLC covering an area 313.80 acre. Besides this, the other traditional forest dwellers have not at all benefited from the Forest Rights Act. Till November 2015—8884 certificates of title under revenue forest and 1193 under reserve forest have been distributed covering a total area of 15,299.71 acre in the entire district.

Table 4.27: Forests Rights Act Kalahandi District—For the Month of November—2015

Sl. No.	*Name of the Block/Sub-division*	*No. of claims appro-ved by Gram sabha and sent to SDLC*	*Area in Acres*	*No. of claims appro-ved by SDLC sent to DLC*	*Area in Acres*	*No. of claims appro-ved by DLC for title*	*Area in acre*	*No. of certifi-cate of tiles distri-buted*	*Area in Acres*
1.	Dharmagarh	3296	4430.36	2641	4040.61	2633	4017.06	2425	3712.93
2.	Bhawanipatna	7889	12167.82	7889	12167.82	7887	12165.28	7652	11586.78
	Total	**11185**	**16598.18**	**10530**	**16208.43**	**10520**	**16182.34**	**10077**	**15299.71**

Source: Forest Rights Act of Kalahandi District

The information in the above table relates to the status of implementation of the Forest Rights Act, 2006 in Kalahandi as per the information furnished by the District Administration for the month of November 2015. The district of Kalahandi has two sub-divisions, namely Dharmgarh and Bhawanipatna and the number of villages covered in Bhawanipatna is 19,493 which is much larger than Dharmgarh. In fact Bhawanipatna covers 72.20 per cent of the total number of villages in Kalahandi. It could be noticed from the table that the number of claims approved by Gram Sabha and sent to SDLC is 11,185 and it is heartening to note that there are no claims rejected by Gram Sabha and no claims have been remanded to FRCs. Out of 11,185 no of claims approved by Gram Sabha the SDLC has approved 10,530 number of claims amounting to 94.14 per cent of the claims

Table 4.28: Status of Implementation of Community Rights in the State (Odisha) for the Month of November 2015 for Kalahandi District

Sl. No.	*Name of the District*	*Particulars of Items*	*Number*
1.	Kalahandi	No. of claims received	
2.	-do-	Form B	191
3.	-do-	Form C	8
4.	-do-	Total B+C	199
5.	-do-	Total claims settled (B+C)	
6.	-do-	No. of claim settled	193
7.	-do-	Area in Acres	23720.40
8.	-do-	No. in Acres of claims distributed	
		No.	172
		Area in Acres	**24483.40**

Source: Forest Rights Act of Kalahaandi District.

approved by Gram Sabha. The balance cases has yet to be perused at SDLC level. The number of claims approved by DLC for title is 10,520 which is only 10 number short of the claims approved by SDLC. The area involved in the 10,520 claims is 16,182.34 covering 1.54 acre per title/beneficiary. However, finally, the number of certificates of titles distributed is 10,077 covering an area of 15,299.71 acre covering 1.52 acre per title. This is also a feasible area for cultivation and to be suitably utilized for agriculture. It is noted from the data supplied by the District Administration that out of total area of 15,299.71 acre distributed to the title holders, a majority of 12,153.23 acre out of the total area distributed accounts for 79.43 per cent and the balance 20.67 per cent amounting to 3146.48 acre is covered by Reserve Forests.

The total number of community right claims received in Kalahandi district is 199 out of which 193 claims have been settled and only 6 claims remain to be settled. The total claims settled includes an area of 23,720.40 acre out of which 23,081.35 acre have been distributed to 172 claimants. Which comes to 134.19 acre of community rights per claims. However, the purpose of the community rights have not been cleared by the district administration. It appears that still 21 claims remains to be distributed which needs to be expedited.

Table 4.29: FRA Benefiiaries covered under Convergence for the Month of November 2015 for Kalahandi District

Sl. No	*Name of the District*	*No. of Certificates of Titles distributed to individual claimants*	*No. of rights holders covered under various Government Schemes for their benefit*					
			IAY	*Mo Kudia*	*Mo Pokhari*	*Land Dev. Under MGNREGS*	*+Other Programmes*	*Total*
1.	Kalahandi	10,077	3494	3	38	3200	310 (143-Wadi and 167-Land Leveling by OTELP)	7045

Source: Forest Rights Act of Kalahandi District.

It can be inferred from Table 4.29, that a total of 69.91 per cent of the FRA beneficiaries have been covered under different Government schemes under Convergence programme of which the two major Government Schemes are IAY (Housing Construction) Scheme of Government of India constituting 34.60 per cent of the beneficiaries and land development under MGNREGS which covers 31.76 per cent of the total beneficiaries. It is commendable that the District Administration of Kalahandi has included nearly 69.91 per cent of the total FRA beneficiaries under different Government schemes to lift them from the BPL category.

Table 4.30: District-wise PTG Households for the Month of November 2015 for Kalahandi District

Sl. No.	Name of the District	Name of Micro Project	Name of the Block	No. of House-holds	Particular of Item	Number of Titles
1.	Kalahandi	Lanjigarh KKDA	Lanjigarh	591	No. of claims approved by Gram Sabha and sent to SDLC	310
2.	-do-	-do-	-do-		No. of claims approved by SDLC	310
3.	-do-	-do-	-do-		No. of claims approved by DLC to titles	310
4.	-do-	-do-	-do-		Certificate of titles distributed	310
5.	-do-	-do-	-do-		Area in Acres	313.80
6.	-do-	-do-	-do-		No. of claims non-forest land verified for settlement	31

Source: Field Study.

It is a good achievement of Kalahandi District Administration that they have initiated Lanjigarh KKDA scheme for PTGA Households in Lanjigarh Block numbering 591 households. It is also a promising

Table 4.31: Title Card of Forest Rights signed by the DFO Kalahandi South Division

Name of Range	No. of Blocks	No. of Villages	No. of claims	Total Area
Karlapat	1	41	483 (9.41%)	957.91 (12.32%)
Biswanathpur	1	140	1712 (33.36%)	2139.45 (27.46%)
Th. Rampur North Range	1	50	1894 (36.91%)	2874.35 (36.95%)
Junagarh	1	29	437 (8.52%)	699.52 (9.00%)
Jaipatna	1	21	311 (6.06%)	472.46 (6.08%)
Dharamgarh	1	14	295 (5.74%)	636.51 (8.19%)
Total	**6**	**295**	**5132 (100.00%)**	**7780.20 (100%)**

Source: DFO Kalahandi.

indicator that 562 of the households constituting nearly 95 per cent of the total beneficiaries have applied for claims to FRCs and 310 of them comprising 55.16 per cent of the total households have been approved by Gram Sabha. However, the reasons for not approving the balance claimant of 44.94 per cent is a matter to be investigated so that the left out cases get the benefit of Forest titles. It is again significant to note that the number of claims approved by Gram Sabha have all been approved by SDLC and DLC for title. The total area is 313.80 acre which approximates to almost 1 acre per household.

The implementation of Forest Rights Act in Kalahandi South division indicates that there are 6 ranges out of which maximum area of forest Rights have been extended in the 2 ranges of Th. Rampur North Range and Biswanathpur amounting to 2874.35 (36.95%) acre and 2139.45 acre (27.46%) of the total Forest Rights distributed in the Kalahandi South division.

Table 4.32: Range-wise and Tehsil-wise Information on Individual Claims under Forest Rights Act, 2006, Kalahandi, North Division

Sl. No.	Name of the Range	No. of claims	No. of Title Card issued	Gramya Jungle in Acre
1.	Kegaon	949	949	
2.	Bhawanipatna	700	700	
3.	Narla	319	319	
4.	M. Rampur	669	669	
5.	Kesinga	397	75	
	Total	**3034**	**2712**	**3730.35**

Source: Forest Rights Act 2006.

There are 5 forest ranges in Kalahandi North division and the maximum number of claims have been filed from Kegaon, Bhawanipatna and M. Rampour; it is relatively less from Narla and Kesinga Range. Accordingly, the number of title card issued is highest in Kegaon followed by Bhawanipatna and M. Rampur; it is relatively less in Narla and Kesinga. The village forest (*Gramya Jungle*) accounts for 3730.35 acre. The comparative figures indicate that the number of claims filed in Kalahandi South Division is 5132 and the area of title issued is 7780.20 acre. The per acre title issued is 1.52 acre in Kalahandi South Forest Division and the per acre title distributed in Kalahandi North Forest Division is 1.23 acre. These lands can be utilized both for cultivation, homestead rights and for vegetable gardening.

Table 4.33: Progress of Implementation of Forest Rights Act, 2006 of Kalahandi South Forest Division for the Month of November 2015

Name of the Division/ District	*No. of claim petitions forwarded by Gram Sabha to SDLC*	*No. of claim petitions forwarded by SDLC to DLC*	*No. of claim petitions approved by DLC and the total area involved in ha*	*No. of community claim cases approved by DLC and the total area involved in ha*	*No. of titles issued for invididuals and the area involved in ha*	*No. of titles issued for communities and the area involved in ha*
Kalahandi South	6563 nos.	6563 nos.	6563 nos. =4110.545 ha	118 nos. = 5771.456	6563 nos. =4110.545ha	118 nos. =5771.456 ha

Source: DFO Kalahandi.

Karlapat Sanctuary

The Karlapat Sanctuary is situated in the South of the Bhawanipatna town in Kalahandi District. The land Karlapat signifies the fact of hilly and forested landscape. The Forest blocks adjoining to the sanctuary are Alma, Khandual, Goelkhoj, Karli, Hatimunda, Bamni, Gundi and Benbhatta. The landscape comprises about 300 sq.km. of land area. The sanctuary is located to the Western fringe of Odisha bounded by the Nabarangpur. The entire sanctuary area comes under Karlapat range of Kalahandi South Forest Division whose head quarter is at Bhawanipatna. The sanctuary was notified under section 18 of Wildlife (Protection) Act, 1972 *vide* Notification No. 24498-8F-41/92FE of Government of Odisha. Karlapat boasts for its elephant population and serves as a crucial corridor for the elephants in Kotagarh region of Kandhamal District. There are 19 villages inside the Karlapat Sanctuary and 110 villages in the fringe area. Karlapat Wildlife Sanctuary came into existence on 15.10.1992 *vide* Government of Odisha Forest and Environment Department Notification No. 24498-8F(W)-41/92 dated 15.10.92, published in the *Odisha Gazette*, dated 27.11.1992. This sanctuary is situated 15 kms from Bhawanipatna town in Kalahandi District. The existing sanctuary with its total area comes to 175.503 sq km and with boundary length of 145 kms. This needs a revised *Gazettee Notification* to make it effective. The administrative headquarter of Karlapat Sanctuary is located at Bhawanipatna on NH 201. Six contiguous forest blocks having an area of 175.50 sq.km. constitutes Karlapat Wildlife Sanctuary. The forest of this division contains a number of NTFP species. These species are almost covering 69 items transferred to Gram Panchayats for regulating the collection and trade in phases *vide* Government of Odisha, Forest and Environment Department Resolution

No. 5503 dt. 2.3.2000 (60 items), Resolution No. 13285 dt. 23.8.2000 (7 items). Kendu leaf collection and processing is done by the State Government while marketing is done through OFDC Ltd. A sizeable income accrue to the local Adivasi people of Kalahandi District from January to June through bushy cutting operation, *phadi* and godown repairs, collection of leaves at approved price, drying and storage operation, processing and binding and transportation of bags to the godowns where those are delivered to OFDC Ltd., for marketing. There are some commercially important selected species of NTFP items, prominent among them being *Siali* Leaves, Tamarind, Hill Broom, *Harida Bahada Amla*, *Mohua* Seed-flower, *Neem* seed, *Char* seed, Gum and honey. These NDFP items are available in plenty particularly in the forest range Th. Rampur, Biswanathpur, M. Rampur, Dharamgarh, Jaipatna, Junagarh and other forest ranges. The Kalahandi South Division has 25,226 hectares assigned for 377 VSS of Kalahandi South Division. There are also Convergence activity like MGNREGS in Kalahandi South Division where plantations have been taken up in 54,030 hectares between 2013-14 to 2015-16.

4.14 Implementation of Forest Rights Act, 2006 in Sundargarh District

The three important Forest Divisions in Sundargarh are Bonai, Rourkela and Sundargarh. The geographical area of Bonai Forest Division is 2934.21 sq. mtr. and the total forest area is 2029.95 sq. mtr. constituting 69.18 per cent of the total Bonai Division. In terms of density 43.54 per cent of the total forest area is very dense, 47.76 per cent is moderately dense and 8.07 per cent is open forest. The Reserve Forest constitutes 53 per cent including the proposed Reserve Forest of 16.8 per cent. The area under un-demarcated protected forests is nearly 10 per cent and the area under village forest, unclassified forest and DLC land and projected forest is very marginal.

The Rourkela Forest Division includes 6 forest ranges and it has 174 VSS under OFSDP and 92 VSS under Ama Jangal Yojana; the total number of SHGs are 463 and total 6 SHG clusters. The Odisha Forestry Development Sector Project (OFDSP) was launched during 2006-07 for restoration of the degraded forests and community development based on Joint Forest Management (JFM) meant for the improvement in the livelihood of people living in the forest fringe villages. The problems faced by the local Adivasis are alcoholism, deforestation, exploitation, lack of drinking water, high environmental pollution due to mining and industrial area, non-availability of NTFP and general discrimination. The major intervention of the forest department for improving the livelihood of the tribals and forest dwellers are improving communication network, building community assets providing water for pisci culture, undertaking sanitation measures and minor agriculture irrigation support. The forest department also undertakes other community works like compost pit, VSS building, provision of solar lights, human health camps and non- formal education centre. In order to promote village forest activity it has a developmental fund and revolving fund for the SHGs. The operation area under Ama Jangala Yojana (AJY) is 7347 ha which includes a major area under reserve forest and a small area under productive forest. The total number of villages in the district is 1668. Most of the villages have been covered under Forest Right Act, 2006. In all 2795 Gram Sabha meetings were held. The total number of FRCs constituted by Gram Sabha is 1668. The number of claims received by FRCs in the district is 40,311 of which 15,558 (38.59%) was from Sadar Block 10,381, (25.75%) was from Panposh Block and remaining 14,372 (35.65%) were from Bonai Block. The FRCs verified all the claims and sent them to Gram Sabha. The number of claims approved by Gram Sabha and sent to SDLCs was 26,700 of which 12,726 (47.66%) was from Sadar, 3026 (11.33%) was from Panposh Block and 10,948 (41.00%) was from Bonai Sub Division. The area of Patta given is 53,804.48 Acres of which 31,328.59 (58.23%) was from Sadar, 3288.34 (6.11%) was from Panposh and 19,187.55 acre (35.66%) was from Bonai Sub Division. The total number of families benefited were 26,700 of which 12,726 (47.66%) were from Sadar Sub-Division, 3026 (11.33%) from Panposh Sub-Division, and 10,948 (41%), were from Bonai Sub-Division. The number of claims received was largest from Panposh numbering 7355 and 2832 from Sadar Sub-Division.

The area involved at the District Level Committee was 24,584 acre of which 14,715 (59.86%) was from Sadar Sub-Division, 3090 (12.57%) acre were from Panposh Block and rest 27.57 per cent were from Bonai Block. The number of claims rejected by SDLC was 3629 from Sadar Sub-Division and 1710 was from Bonai Sub-Division. The reason for the rejection have to be investigated. The number of claims approved by DLCs was 7953 from Sadar Block, 2415 from Panposh Block and 4252 were from Bonai Sub-Division. The number of certificates of titles distributed in the entire district was 9390 of which 5284 (56.27%) was from Sadar Sub-Division, 930 (9.90%) from Panposh Block and 3176 (33.82%) was from Bonai Sub-Division.

The Community Rights were filed for 22 claims under Form B and 20 claims under Form C, i.e. a total of 42 in the entire district and all this claims were in Bonai Sub-Division. The claims rejected were 20

Table 4.34: Implementation of Forest Rights Act, 2006 in Sundargarh District

Sub-Division	*No. of Claims recei-ved by FRC*	*No. of claims appro-ved by Gram Sabha and sent to SDLC*	*No. of claims reject-ted by SDLC*	*Area of Patta given*	*No. of families benefi-tted*	*No. of claims appro-ved by DLC*	*Area of Titles distribu-ted by DLC*	*No. of titles distribu-ted*
Sadar	15558	12726	3629	328.59	12726	7953	14715.00	5284
Panposh	10381	3026	–	3288.34	3026	2415	3090.00	930
Bonai	14372	10948	1710	19187.55	10948	4252	6779.00	3176
Total Distt	**40311**	**26700**	**5339**	**22804.48**	**26700**	**14620**	**24584.00**	**9390**

Source: DFO, Sundargarh District.

from Bonai Sub-Division and the claims pending were 22 from Bonai Sub-Division. The number of certificates of titles distributed in the entire sub-division was 9394 and of this 1824 cases were provided IAY rights, 59 were provided Mo Kudia Rights. 293 were provided Mo Pokhari Rights, 638 were provided land development benefits; 45 titled holders were given benefits under National Horticulture Mission and one was given National Bamboo Mission right. Apart from this, 463 titles were distributed under Forest Right Act to PVTGs in Khutgaon Block in Sundargarh district constituting 423.36 acre and 558 were given homestead rights covering 23.43 acre, 459 beneficiaries were given agriculture benefits and 459 titles covering 683.57 acre.

Number of Claimants in Sundargarh District

The total number of claimants under Forest Rights Act, 2006 in Sundargarh District is 9390 of which 8835 (94.09%) are STs and 555 (5.91%) are from other communities. Out of total 9390 claims in the entire Sundargarh District the distribution of claimants in different sub-division is 5284 (56.27%) in Sundargarh Sub-Division, 930 (9.90%) in Panposh Sub-Division and 3176 (33.82%) in Bonai Sub-Division. The total area involved for the total claims is 18,338.05 acre of which 13,066.76 (71.25%) is in Sundargarh sub-division, 122.47 (0.67%) acre in Panposh Sub-division and 4048.82 (22.08%) acre in Bonai Sub-Division. It may be necessary to state here that out of total 18,338 acre for which titles have been given, 17,318.45 (94.44%) acre have been given to STs and 1019.60 (5.56%) acre have been given to other forest dwellers.

Titles to other Traditional Forest Dwellers have been distributed in Sundargarh district in all the three sub-divisions namely—Sundargarh, Panposh and Bonai. Of the three sub-divisions the total claimant is highest in Bonai Sub-Division consisting of 555 claimants and the second in order is Sundargarh Sub-Division with 369 claimants and Panposh Sub-Division has only 7 claimants. Similarly, the area provided to them is highest in Bonai Sub-Division with 906.6 hectares followed by 703.76 acre in Sundargarh Sub-Division and a very low 6.22 acre for Panposh Sub-Division. The forest rights titles under revenue forest is highest in Bonai Sub-Division consisting of 484.45 acre followed by 281.53 acre in Sundargarh sub-division and a very low 6.22 acre in Panposh Sub-Division. However, in respect of forest rights titles provided under reserve forest, maximum area is in Sundargarh sub-division consisting of 422.23 acres.

Table 4.35: Titles given in Rourkela Sub-Division (Sundargarh District)

Sl. No.	*Name of the Blocks*	*No. of Cases in which Forest Titles distributed*	*Area of Forest Titles Distributed (In Acres)*	*Block-wise Forest Pattas Distributed (in %age)*	*Average Area allotted for village (in Acres)*
1.	Birmitrapur	132	156.01	15.02	1.22
2.	Kuarmunda	261	333.30	31.24	1.26
3.	Latikata	302	374.81	36.09	1.25
4.	Koira	128	107.90	10.39	0.86
5.	Lahunipara	32	17.78	1.71	0.54
6.	Bandamunda	50	57.67	5.55	1.13
	Total	**905**	**1047.47**	**100.00**	**1.04**

Source: DFO, Sundargarh District.

In Rourkela Sub-Division 905 beneficiaries have been given forest rights and per acre average area assigned is 1-16 acre. This can be utilized partially for cultivation purpose because of the small extent and more useful utilization can be for homestead and kitchen garden purpose.

It can be noticed from the above comparative table of the three sampled districts that SDLC approved 82.37 per cent of the claims sent by Gram Sabha and DLC approved 97.86 per cent of the claims. The number of Certificate of titles distributed was 55,317 constituting 91.78 per cent of the total claims approved by DLC. The area distributed constitutes 91,070.56 acre, i.e. 1.65 acre per title. The area distributed can be utilized for cultivation purpose with convergence programme.

The SDLC needs to again probe into the 17.63 per cent of the claims which have not yet been approved.

Table 4.36: Consolidated Figures of implementation of Forest Rights Act, 2006 (individual) in the Sample District of in Odisha

Districts	*No. of Claims approved by Gram Sabha*	*No. of claims approved by SDLC*	*No. of claims approved by DLC*	*No. of Certificate of titles distributed*	*Area (in acre) Total*
Rayagada	33677	23283	22077	19498	35684.43
Kalahandi	11185	10530	10520	10077	15299.71
Koraput	29910	27804	27676	25742	40086.42
Total of the Three districts	**74772**	**61617**	**60273**	**55317**	**91070.56**

Source: DFO, Sundargarh District.

Table 4.37: Consolidated Status of Implementation of Community Rights in the Sampled Districts of Odisha

Sl. No.	*Items of information on Community Rights*	*Implementation of Community Rights*			*Remarks*
1.	No. of claims received	Kora-put	Rayaga-da	Kala-handi	In the district of Koraput 309 claims under Form B and 140 Claims under Form C are still pending.
	Form B	466	405	191	
	Form C	158	206	8	
	Total B+C	624	611	199	
2.	Total claims settled (B+C)				
	Number	169	178	193	
	Area in Acres	11044.2	3789.20	2372.40	
3.	Total Claims distributed				
	Number	58	146	172	
	Area	**2780.87**	**3201.6**	**23081.35**	

Source: DFO, Sundargarh District.

It can be seen from the above table that in the three sampled districts of Koraput, Rayagada and Kalahandi, the total number of claims received in Form (B + C) are 624, 611 and 199 respectively. Altogether in the three districts the total number of claims received are 1434 and the total claims settled inclusive of three districts are 540 and the total area in which claims settled in the three districts is 17,205.8 acre. However, the total claims distributed is highest in district

Kalahandi consisting of 23,081.35 acre whereas it is much lower in the district of Koraput (2780.87 acre) and Rayagada (3201.60 acre). In the State of Jharkhand the sampled Districts are West Singhbhum, East Singhbhum, Sariakela, Khunti, and Dalma Sanctuary, but the Community Forest Rights has been located by the District Administration only the District of West Singhbhum where the number of Claims filed at Gram Sabha level is 1691 and 39 of them have been recommended. This is a very low figure as compared to the Community Rights claims settled and distributed in Odisha.

Table 4.38: FRA Beneficiaries under Convergence Schemes during 2015 in the districts of Kalahandi and Rayagada

Sl. No.	*Districts*	*No. of certificates of titles distributed to individual claimants*	*No. of rights holders covered under various Government Schemes for their benefit*					
			IAY	*Mo Kudia*	*Mo Pokhari*	*Land Dev. Under MGNREGS*	*+Other Programmes*	*Total*
1.	Kalahandi	10077	3494	03	38	3200	310 (143-Wadi and 167-Land Levelling by OTELP)	7045
2.	Rayagada	19498	9435	65	313	1521	2043	13377

Source: Government of India, Ministry of Tribal Affairs.

It is a healthy sign that both in the Districts of Kalahandi and Rayagada the Forest Rights titles have been converged with different Government Schemes which includes Government of India Scheme of House Construction, MNREGA programme for land development and productivity State Housing Rights Programme etc. These are input augmentation programmes which will give additional benefit to the FRA beneficiaries; it will not only make the FRA land productive but also generate additional income to the beneficiaries. It may be mentioned that in the State of Jharkhand there is no provision of any convergence programme to be associated with Forest Rights Programme. In this respect the District Administration and State Government of Odisha are trying to take a forward and progressive step relating to the implementation of forest rights programme.

The Scheduled Tribes constitute 22.8 per cent of the total population in Odisha and 26.2 per cent in Jharkhand. The area under forest is higher in the State of Odisha constituting 37.3 per cent of the total geographical area and it is likely less in Jharkhand consisting of 29.6 per cent of the total geographical area. The tribals depend on forest resources for livelihoods is considerable in both the States. These two States are also coming under the Fifth Schedule Area of the Constitution and also covered under PESA Act, 1996.

Table 4.39: Comparative Picture of Forest Situation in Odisha and Jharkhand

Particulars	*Unit*	*Details Odisha*	*Details Jharkhand*
Total Geographical Area	Sq. Kilometres	1,55,707	79,714
Total Forest Area	Sq. Kilometres (%)	58,136 (37.3)	23605 (29.6)
Total Population	Number	4,19,74,218	32,988,134
Total ST Population	Number (%)	95,90,756 (22.8)	86,45,042 (26.2)
Districts	Numbers	30	24
LWE Districts	Numbers	19	21
Tribes	Numbers	62	32
PVTGs	Numbers	13	9

Source: Census of India, 2011 and Forest Survey of India, 2011 (include 2013 figures).

4.15 Implementation and Outcomes of FRA in Odisha

Constitution enjoins certain rights over the land, forests, water bodies, and other resources. In September 1997, the Supreme Court of India delivered a landmark judgement upholding the rights of tribal people to life, livelihood, land, and forests in a case that dealt with issues of mining in tribal land. Samatha, a Non-Governmental Organisation (NGO) in Andhra Pradesh, filed the case on behalf of the affected tribal people. The Supreme Court held that forests and lands in Scheduled Areas, irrespective of their being owned by the government or by a tribal community, cannot be leased out to non-tribal people or to private companies for mining or industrial uses. It restricted the mining activity in these areas to the State Mineral Development Corporation or a cooperative of the tribal people and all leases granted by the State Governments were declared to contravene Schedule V of the Constitution and were declared null and void. The judgement, known as Samatha Judgement, is a significant check to restrain the State from encouraging indiscriminate exploitation of land, forests, water bodies, and other resources, for commercial purposes, especially in tribal areas.

The Committee concluded that the judgement is not binding on the State. The reasoning was that there are enough laws in the State to ensure protection of tribal interests and therefore, Odisha could stay outside the purview of the Supreme Court's ruling. On the basis of this interpretation, the government decided to allow the transfer of land in areas covered by Schedule V of the Constitution for mining and industrial purposes. This is a patently wrong inference because the ruling was applicable to all States. After the Samatha judgement, the Government of India issued executive instructions in 1998 to set up systems for consulting with the Gram Sabhas and detail the procedure for land acquisition in the Schedule V areas. However, in Odisha, the State Government circumvented the Gram Sabhas and gave their power to the Zilla Parishad (Divisional Councils). This was a manipulation of the PESA that undermined its intent and effectively denied the tribal people their rights to be consulted on land acquisition for projects (Mahapatra, 2005).

4.16 Shortcomings in the Implementation of FRA

There have been some procedural bottlenecks in the implementation of the FRA; they arise out of inadequate knowledge of the FRA and its implications. Hence, the pace of implementation has been very slow. The Stay Orders by the courts and the elections to the State Assembly as well as the Parliament have further delayed the implementation and presentation of the members of the Forest Rights Committees (FRCs) and the DLCs, which could have helped the implementation of the Act, Moreover, the FRA does not go along well with the other existing Acts such as the Wild Life Protection Act (WLPA), Forest Conservation Act (FCA) etc. Hence, the restrictions provided in these legislations will continue and may even override the FRA.

One of the biggest challenges for the Act is the issue of multiplicity in policies and institutions. Joint Forest Management (JFM) created under the programme is a key concern. It now has 1,06,482 JFM committees (on paper) throughout the country and it covers 22 million hectare of forests spread across 28 constituent States of India and Union Territories (Bhattacharya *et al.*, 2010). JFM, as a society, has largely been unsuccessful in providing tenure rights or legal status through legislative procedures for forest-dwelling communities. This insecurity has affected collective action, especially on issues of encroachment and illegal logging.

4.17 Why Odisha has better Implementation of Forest Rights than Jharkhand

The number of individual claims filed in Jharkhand was only 42,003 against 5,32,464 filed in the State of Odisha. Obviously, much lower number of claims were filed in the State of Jharkhand as compared to the State of Odisha. Further, 56.57 per cent of the individual claims were approved in the State of Odisha as against only 36.42 per cent in the State of Jharkhand. Hence, until March 2013 the progress of

Table 4.40: Progress under FRA 2006: A Snapshot (as on 31st March, 2013)

States	*No. of claims received*	*No. of titles Distributed*	*No. of claims rejected*	*Extent of forest land for which titles distributed (in acre)*
Odisha	5,32,464 (5,29,160 IFR and 3,304 CFR)	3,01,200 (56.57%) (3,00,321 IFR and 879 CFR)	1,31,970 (1,31,361 IFR and 609 CFR) (24.78%)	5,39,277.45 (4,84,025.80 IFR and 55,251.65 CFR)
Jharkhand	42,003	15,296 (36.42%)	16,958 (40.37%)	37,678.93
All India level	32,45,369	12,80,100 (31,78,608 IFR and 66,761 CFR) (39.44%) 16,226 (Ready for distribution)	15,13,742 (46.64%)	46,93,122.27
Odisha ranks 3rd and Jharkhand ranks 8th in terms of percentage of titles distributed over the number of claims received: (IFR—Individual, CFR—Community)				

Note: Figures in the brackets indicate percentage of the total claim received.

Source: Government of India, Ministry of Tribal Affairs (as on 31st March, 2013).

Jharkhand was much slower in comparison to the State of Odisha. In addition to this, 879 community forest rights were distributed in the State of Odisha as against lack of any such cases in the State of Jharkand. The number of claims rejected in the State of Odisha was 24.78 per cent as against 40.37 per cent in the State of Jharkhand. Obviously, the percentage of rejection of Individual Forest Rights was higher in the State of Jharkhand as compared to the State of Odisha. The number of individual titles distributed in the State of Odisha was 55,39,277.45 acre which constituted 1.79 acre per beneficiary as against 2.46 acre in Jharkhand indicating higher area distributed in Jharkhand as compared to Odisha. The area of individual forest rights assigned per beneficiary is 3.67 acre at All India level which is higher to the States of Odisha and Jharkhand.

As per the latest status report, Welfare Department, Government of Jharkhand, 13th April, 2016 the total number of claims filed at the Gram Sabha level is 89,345 of which individual claims are 86,483 and community claims are 2862. The Gram Sabha has rejected 21,888 claims which constitutes 24.50 per cent of the total claims filed in the Gram Sabha and still 12516 claims are pending in Gram Sabha. The Sub-Divisional Committee has recommended 49,436 claims to district-level committee and the total claims recommended by DLC is 47071 and 2965 claims are still pending at DLC-level. The area of total title provided to the beneficiaries is 91,611.95 acre which comes to an average of 1.98 acre per *patta*.

Table 4.41: Forest Rights distributed in the State of Jharkhand and Odisha for the Period Ending 31.12.2015

States	*No. of claims received*			*No. of titles distributed upto 31.12.2015*			*Extent of Forest land for which titles distributed (in acre)*		
	Individual	*Community*	*Total*	*Individual*	*Community*	*Total*	*Individual*	*Community*	*Total*
Jharkhand	80819	2734	83553	41691	1434	43125	87989.80	NA	87989.80
Odisha	603271	12866	616137	349400	5004	354404	550912.53	179663.50	730576.03

Source: Government of India, Ministry of Tribal Affairs.

The number of claims filed in the State of Jharkhand is 89,345 whereas in the State of Odisha 6,03,271 claims have been filed which is much larger as compared to Jharkhand. The number of community claims filed in the State of Odisha is 12,866 against only 2862 claims filed in Jharkhand. It is clear that both individual and community claims in the State of Jharkhand is much lower as compared to Odisha. The number of titles distributed in Jharkhand is 51.58 per cent of the total claims received indicating a very large number of claims still pending at Gram Sabha, SDLC and DLC level. The figures of Odisha indicate that 57.91 per cent of the total claims received have been distributed up to 31st December 2015 which is likely higher than the figure of Jharkhand.

The extent of Forest land distributed to the individual beneficiary is 87,989.80 acre which is 1.77 acre per title as against 1.58 acre per beneficiary in Odisha. The per acre area distributed per beneficiary is higher in the State of Odisha as compared to Jharkhand. The figures of community rights issued in the State of Odisha is 1,79,663.50 acre but figures of Jharkhand is not provided. The per title community rights distributed in Odisha is 35.90 acre but similar figures for the State of Jharkhand has not been provided. The Eighteenth Report Committee on Petitions (Sixteenth Lok Sabha) mentions that as on 31st December, 2015, 43,125 titles (41,691 individual and 1,434 community titles) covering nearly 88,000 acre of forest land has been granted in Jharkhand. Odisha has implemented some provisions of the FRA, especially those that deal with individual rights and a few community rights. In nutshell it can be stated that the performance of the implementation of Forest Rights Act, 2006 is much better in the State of Odisha as compared to Jharkhand. The highest CFR area has been recognized and distributed in Mayurbhanj district followed by Keonjhar District.

It would be appropriate to provide the latest district-wise status of the Forest Rights in different districts of Jharkhand.

The figures in Table 4.42, indicate that the individual rights have been more in some districts like Simdega, West Singhbhum, East Singhbhum, Latehar, Palamau, Hazaribagh, Giridih, and Dumka. Similarly, the community rights have been assigned more in the districts of Garwaha, Godda, Saraikela, West Singhbhum and Chatra. One of the negative features of implementation in the district of Jharkhand is the rejection of claims in several districts like Simdega, East Singhbhum, Chatra, Bokaro, Dumka and Godda. The non-implementation of community rights and the rejection of claims of such large scale needs to be probed by the Government of Jharkhand and the various officials of the District Administration. The total claims rejected in Jharkhand State is 31.15 per cent which is a very high figure; similarly, the total pending claims constitute 18.66 per cent of the total claims.

4.18 Violation of PESA, Fifth Schedule and other Connected Rights

Out of the total tribal population of India, more than 40 per cent has already been displaced. This is happening when, even by government estimates, more than 60 per cent of the Adivasis are classified as living in extreme poverty with no access to land, adequate food, health facilities, and education. Under such circumstances, even minor

Table 4.42: District-wise Status of Forest Rights in Jharkhand (as on 30th April, 2016)

Sl. No.	Districts	Claims filed			Titles Distributed			Rejected claims	Pending claims
		Individual	Community	Total	Individual	Community	Total		
1.	Ranchi	1141	08	1149	1135	8	1143	–	6
2.	Lohardaga	1277	4	1281	423	4	427	285	569
3.	Khunti	971	79	1050	720	62	782	232	36
4.	Gumla	3375	13	3388	1034	1	1035	300	2053
5.	Simdega	11060	21	11081	7481	21	7502	3481	98
6.	West Singhbhum	6551	83	6634	5058	64	5162	–	1512
7.	East Singhbhum	6190	21	6211	2305	14	2319	2511	1381
8.	Saraikela	3462	112	3574	1630	19	1649	1925	–
9.	Latehar	5619	77	6596	1994	–	1994	277	3425
10.	Palamau	4799	20	4819	2969	–	2969	700	1150
11.	Garhwa	2714	798	3512	1373	798	2171	640	701
12.	Chatra	3903	105	4008	1240	23	1263	2294	451
13.	Kodarma	972	74	1046	330	13	343	703	–
14.	Hazaribagh	4139	48	4187	2572	02	2574	1379	234
15.	Ramgarh	1731	66	1797	536	–	536	863	398
16.	Bokaro	3654	94	3748	748	03	751	2173	824
17.	Dhanbad	2006	44	2752	374	42	416	1619	717
18.	Giridih	6665	36	6701	5987	5	5992	527	182
19.	Dumka	8952	71	9023	2338	6	2344	5258	1421
20.	Pakur	904	4	908	636	–	636	22	250
21.	Deoghar	1020	23	1043	527	2	529	54	460
22.	Jamtara	1191	2	1193	933	2	935	40	218
23.	Sahebganj	1405	114	1519	1400	113	1513	6	–
24.	Godda	2780	245	3025	959	245	1204	1766	55
	Total	**86483**	**2862**	**89345**	**44702**	**1447**	**46149**	**27055**	**16141**

Source: FRA Status Report Welfare Department, Government of Jharkhand, 30th April, 2016.

violations of the law like PESA and other provisions of the Fifth Schedule have an enormous impact on marginalized sections. PESA is one of the biggest element of the participatory democracy that India boasts of.

However, on 18th April, 2013, in a landmark judgement, the Supreme Court has directed the smallest units of local governance, Gram Sabha, to use their powers and take a decision on whether the Vedanta group's $1.7 billion bauxite mining project in Odisha's Niyamgiri Hills can go forward or not. Affirming the decision-making power of the village councils of Rayagada and Kalahandi under the FRA, the court directed the Gram Sabhas to "take a decision...within three months" on any claims of cultural, religious, community and individual rights that the forest dwellers of the region are entitled. In a letter to the Odisha Government on 2nd May, 2013, the Ministry directed the State to facilitate the Gram Sabhas affected by the proposed bauxite mining project on Niyamgiri Hills to decide independently and in a transparent manner the veracity of the religious and cultural rights claimed by the tribal people on Niyamgiri Hills. It has also issued several legally binding directions under the FRA to the Odisha Government and prescribed a timeframe for the entire process.

The Other Traditional Forest Dwellers (OTFDs) have been discriminated in some States and denied their rights under the FRA. The National Committee on the FRA stated that "the misinterpretation of the definition of OTFDs is probably the single biggest source of wrongful rejections and omissions across all States". In Assam, the State Government has been reluctant to provide land rights to the OTFDs under the FRA due to prejudice against these communities.

A critical review of the process and outcome of the FRA implementation clearly highlights the need for closer scrutiny of community rights under the Act, pointing out that State Governments have been paying inadequate attention to implementation. The FRA amendment rules mandate the issue of CFR titles for every forest dwelling village; and in cases where this is not possible to issue the same, and the DLC must give a proper written explanation. Several issues emerge from the review, which are important for designing the study on policy/structural issues and setting objectives. The implementation as well as the operation is crucially linked to grassroots governance, which is possible only by empowering the Gram Sabhas to take control of the implementation thus protecting the rights of tribals and other forest-dwelling communities.

Another implementation problem with the Act is that it marginalises community rights claims compared to individual rights. Applications for community rights are harder to make and few have been granted. On the other hand, granting individual rights to forest plots may undermine the essence of tribal culture and the future growth of forests (Sharma, 2006). Hence, processing community claims over forest is probably the best way to ensure tribal communities' long-term food security. However, it is only in last week of November 2012 that the Government of Odisha issued instructions to the implementing agencies at the district-level (collectors) to emphasise the implementation of community forest rights.

Mr. Sanjoy Patnaik (2008), Director, Research and Advocacy, at the Regional Centre for Development Cooperation (RCDC),

Bhubaneswar, Odisha, conducted a study on "Status Report of Land Rights and Ownership in Odisha", which was jointly sponsored by UNDP, India (Delhi), and MoRD, GoI. The report observes the following unresolved issues in the context of the implementation of the Forest Rights Act, 2006, in Odisha.

- There is an apprehension among forest dwellers, who have been displaced several times because of various development projects; that they might not get the benefit of the Act as proving residence for three generations in the present village would prove difficult, if not impossible.
- Non-functional Gram Sabhas and the ignorance of Panchayat functionaries about the law may make them pass a resolution in favour of those not deserving the benefits.
- Predominance of Government officers in both the appellate committees (Sub-Divisional Level Committee and District Level Committee) may dilute the authority and freedom of the tribal leaders, who may even go unheard.
- Difficulty in collecting caste certificate by the beneficiaries—nobody knows who is going to issue the caste certificate.
- Ensuring the presence of two-third of the members for the formation of the Forest Rights Committee is a tall order.
- There are any number of instances where the forest department is taking up in great haste plantation activities in the forest land earlier cultivated by the tribals and other forest dwellers so that people cannot prove occupation.
- Prospective beneficiaries want forest rights to be alienable and mortgageable, but expect protection under the Odisha Scheduled Areas Transfer of Immovable Property (by Scheduled Tribes) Regulation, 1956.
- It is a moot point whether this land can be acquired under the Land Acquisition Act.
- Recognition and vesting of rights in case of a man who has more than one wife. Processes to draw the traditional boundaries in the forest villages.
- No clear understanding on whether communities would have "community forest resource" rights if it falls within the Critical Wildlife Habitat.

4.19 Study on High Rate of Rejections of Claims under FRA

The process of claim recognition was continuous in Odisha. In order to facilitate the effective and efficient implementation of the FRA Act, orders and circulars were issued by the State Government at regular intervals. These helped in accelerating the claim process, clarifying the ambiguities in the acts and rules, supporting awareness through devising IEC materials and capacity building for the district and sub-district level officials.

With this backdrop, UNDP assigned a study on "High rate of rejection of claims under FRA especially in Jharkhand, Chhattisgarh and Odisha" to Foundation for Ecological Security (FES). The major observation of the study is reproduced below:

- Nearly 60.9 per cent of the claimants have received title in Odisha, which is highest in the study States. The rate of recognition in Jharkhand and Chhattisgarh is 38.7 per cent and 39.1 per cent respectively.
- Nearly 13.1 per cent individual claims in Odisha and 23.1 per cent claims in Jharkhand are pending. 38.2 per cent claims in Jharkhand and 26 per cent individual claims in Odisha are rejected. Rejection is high in Chhattisgarh and pending cases are high in Jharkhand among the study States.
- The average area per individual claim is as low as 0.57 acre in Jharkhand. It is calculated to be 1.97 acre in Chhattisgarh and 1.58 acre in Odisha.
- In Odisha, the rate of recognition of individual claims in Rayagada district (LWE affected) is 55.4 per cent which is highest among the study districts.
- The rate of recognition in LWE affected districts of Jharkhand, Odisha (Rayagada), Chhattisgarh (Dantewada) is found to be higher than that of the non-LWE affected study districts. The trend of average area per claim is also same as rate of recognition. Out of these districts, Kandhamal and Keonjhar tops the list in both claims made and title received.
- In Jharkhand Title has been issued in only few districts. It is noteworthy that more than 90 per cent of the total claims and more than 80 per cent of the titles received in the State is confined to only two districts—West Singhbhum and Godda. It may be stated that the District of West Singhbhum is one of the severely Left Extremist affected Districts in Jharkhand and

special Saranda Action Plan was also initiated in this district to limit the influence of the Maoists.

- In spite of several efforts, the picture depicts the low level of importance given to community claims in comparison to individual claims. More than half of the claimants received community titles in Chhattisgarh, while it is only 28.4 per cent in Odisha and a meagre 15.7 per cent in Jharkhand. Chhattisgarh also have highest proportion (31.1%) of the claims rejected in comparison to other two States i.e., Odisha and Jharkhand, in which the rate of rejection stand at 5.6 per cent and 2.7 per cent respectively. A very high proportion of claims is pending at different levels in Jharkhand and Odisha. Nearly 81.6 per cent of cases are pending in Jharkhand while in Odisha nearly two-third cases are pending at different levels. This implies that pace of settlement of community claims is very slow in Jharkhand whereas it is better in Odisha and in Chhattisgarh more than 80 per cent claims received have been settled.
- The highest number of 3,28,580 titles have been issued from the State of Odisha and titles for the largest forest area of 10,81,426.65 acre have been issued in Madhya Pradesh.
- Some of the major concerns regarding implementation of the Act were related to low level of literacy among the claimants; grassroots level institutions and committees like Gram Sabha and FRCs are not adequately capacitated to initiate the claim process. There is lack of awareness among the grassroots level functionaries as well as claimants. The claimants have no knowledge about the type (*kisam*) of land they possess, non-recognition of unhindered absolute rights over the minor forest produce (MFP) to forest dwellers. There are imposition of several restrictions, non-recognition of some community rights, such as 'nistar rights, conversion of all forest villages, old habitations, not surveyed villages and other villages in forest, whether recorded, notified or not, into revenue villages. Similarly, there is non-recognition of community forest resource rights relating to protection, regeneration or conservation, or management of any community forest resources.
- In some States like Bihar and Jharkhand the implementation is progressing at a very slow pace. In some of the States like Andhra Pradesh, Odisha and Chhattisgarh, the progress is

satisfactory in terms of numbers. Unlike other States, the implementation of FRA was continuous in Odisha. The committees responsible for implementation were formed within a couple of months of notification of FRA rules.

- Out of 5,34,275 individual claims filed in Odisha, 3,25,449 titles have been distributed till January 2014. Of 11,004 community claims filed in Odisha, only 3,131 titles have been distributed so far. The community claims include the claims under developmental rights.
- A total of 45,482 individual claims and 3737 community claims (both ST and OTFD) have been received by Gram Sabha in Jharkhand. Out of these claims, 17,614 individual titles and 587 community titles have been distributed. Only 0.4 per cent of the total OTFDs claims have received title out of the total title distributed in the State till the end of January 2014.
- An analysis of rate of recognition of individual claims reveals that titles have been distributed to 60.9 per cent of the claimants in Odisha, which is highest among the studied States. The rate of recognition in Jharkhand and Chhattisgarh is almost same, which is 38.7 per cent and 39.1 per cent respectively. But in Chhattisgarh, more than 95 per cent individual claims have been settled leaving only 4.5 per cent pending at different levels; 38.2 per cent claims in Jharkhand and 26 per cent individual claims in Odisha are rejected. Nearly 13.1 per cent individual claims in Odisha and 23.1 per cent claims in Jharkhand are pending.
- In Odisha, the rate of recognition of individual claims in Rayagada district (LWE affected) is 55.4 per cent which is highest among the studied districts. The average area per claim in this district is also the highest (1.63 acre) among the study districts. The rate of recognition in LWE affected districts of Jharkhand covered under the study is higher than that of the non-LWE affected study district, Godda. The rate of recognition is 27.8 per cent and 21.2 per cent in Dumka and Bokaro respectively, which is only 16 per cent in Godda. The trend of average area per claim is also same as rate of recognition. The average area per claim estimated to be 0.59 acre in Bokaro and 0.31 acre in both Dumka and Godda.
- Among the districts in Chhattisgarh, Dantewada (LWE affected) tops the list both in terms of rate of recognition and

average area per title. More than three-fourth of the total claims received have been conferred with title with an average area of 2.43 acre. In Kawardha, the rate of recognition is 69.7 per cent, which is 34.1 per cent in Mahasamund. The average area per claim is 1.04 and 0.74 in Kwardha and Mahasamund respectively.

- In Odisha, claim for community rights has been made in 24 districts out of 30 districts where FRA has been initiated. Out of these districts, Kandhamal and Keonjhar tops the list in both claims made and title received. It is noteworthy to mention here that out of the 22 districts where title has been issued on community rights it is restricted only on development rights under section 3 (2) of the Act.
- Though there are certain initiatives to settle community rights in LWE affected districts like Rayagada, it has not received due attention in other studied districts. The status of community claims in Jharkhand portrays a clear distinction between LWE affected districts and district not affected by LWE. Godda, a non-LWE affected district, depicts a brighter picture by giving title to all the 230 community claims received.
- Recognition of both individual and community claim in Jharkhand depicts a dismal picture in comparison to other two studied states. Low claim and recognition rate in Jharkhand may be attributed to following factors.
- There is often confusion among the revenue and forest officials regarding FRA with Chhotanagpur Tenancy Act and Santal Pargana Tenancy Act. Using this as a reason, senior forest officials are opposing claim settlement in reserve forests.
- FRC members and members of Gram Sabha in the LWE affected districts revealed that the officials of revenue and forest department were reluctant to visit the villages for verification due to security concerns.
- Dantewada district is the only exception, where all claims made by OTFDs have been accepted and conferred with title. There is a great degree of variation in rejection of claims as only 16.5 per cent FDST claims are rejected in Jharkhand while the same is 63.4 per cent in case of OTFD.
- It would be apt to peruse through the criticism of implementation of Forest Rights Act, 2006 undertaken by an

All India NGO, "Campaign for Survival and Dignity (CSD), Odisha".

- The very enactment of the historic Forest Rights Act, 2006 by the Indian Parliament in the country after the 71 years of India's independence is a landmark constitutional reform. Campaign for Survival and Dignity (CSD) played a vital role in mobilizing the tribals, forest dwellers and people's representatives at different levels in whole country and successfully got this Act passed by the Indian Parliament which admitted for the first time in the history of India to have done historical injustice to the tribals and forest dwellers before and after India's independence.
- FRA aims at redressal of a number of problems which arose due to the draconian Acts like Indian Forest Act, 1927 and Land Acquisition Act, 1894 which were used to evict the tribals and the forest dwellers from their homes and shelters. The Forest Rights Act, 2006 not only revived the tribal self-governance regime in Schedule 5th area enforced by the Central PESA Act, 1996 but it also extended the provisions of the PESA even to the non-scheduled area (whole State) empowering the Village Council, the Gram Sabha to decide over their fate of their resources which has been upheld by the Supreme Court, the highest Court of the nation in the Niyamgiri case on 18th April, 2013.
- All the State's Apparatus has now to accept that "Gram Sabha" is the lowest unit of "Government" having its own exclusive legislative, executive and judicial power and authority over its stipulated areas like any other forms of Government at Block, District, State and Central level. The FRA has also raised fundamental questions over the ongoing Panchyati Raj Systems; representative system runs in different State and aims at implementation of direct democracy side-lining the over empowered bureaucracy.
- Forest Rights Act, 2006 has also challenged the age-old State hegemony over forest protection and conservation in the name of "Scientific Forest Management" and has strengthened the "conservation regime handing it to the community people who live and die in the forest".
- Tribals and Forest Dwellers in Odisha were denied their rights to appeal as prescribed under Sections 6(2) and 6(4) of Forest Rights Act, 2006. Around 1,37,877 (One lakh thirty seven

thousands and eight hundred seventy seven) tribals and forest dwellers in Odisha were denied rights to appeal against their rejection of claims by SDLC and by DLC mostly putting the blame upon Gram Sabha given under Section 6(2) and 6(4) of the Forest Rights Act, 2006. Even in many cases, the claims rejected and remanded back by the DLCs needs to be reviewed. The progress in considering the remanded individual forest rights claims have been very poor over the period at all levels. Even there are number of discrepancies in thousands of individual Forest Rights Titles duly shown approved and distributed by the DLCs to the tribals in the State which has been commented in the Column 24.

- The Forest area approved for individual forest rights claims were arbitrarily decided by the SDLC/Technical team who dominated the field verification process and not by the FRCs/Gram Sabha.
- In the process of Number of claims approved by SDLC (Sub-Division-wise), in the whole FRA Implementation process the role of SDLC have been very crucial. SDLC's roles have been very crucial in terms of violations of the provisions of FRA and hijacking the authorized and empowered authority, power and role of the Gram Sabha/FRC. The servants have become masters in the whole FRA implementation process.
- It is being shown that around 62,151 individual forest rights claims duly approved and recommended by the Gram Sabha have been rejected by the SDLC. Whose claims are these? Those are the claims mostly of OTFDs which were duly approved and recommended by many Gram Sabhas, but rejected by the SDLC demanding unnecessary documentary evidences of three generations. The requirement of proving three generations is not required for the land occupied and claimed by the OTFDs. It is required under the Act that the OFTD claimant family would be residing in that area for three generations and would have occupied or have depended over forest or forest land prior and would have occupied or have depended over forest or forest land prior to 13th December 2005. But most of the SDLC have rejected the claims of OTFDs wanting documentary evidence of three generations over the forest land occupied and claimed under FRA.

4.20 Unresolved Issues Critical to the Realization of Forest Rights

There are apprehensions among forest dwellers who have been displaced several times because of various development projects that they might not get the benefit of the Act as proving residence for three generations in the present village would prove difficult, if not impossible. Non-functional Gram Sabhas and the ignorance of Panchayat functionaries about the law may make them pass a resolution in favour of those not deserving the benefits.

Predominance of Government offices in both the appellate committees (sub-dividional level-committee and district level committee) may dilute the authority and freedom of the tribal leaders, who may even go unheard.

There is difficulty in collecting caste certificate by the beneficiaries as they are ignorant about who is going to issue the caste certificate. Ensuring the presence of two-third of the members for the formation of the Forest Rights Committee is a tall order. There are any number of instances where the forest department is taking up in great haste plantation activities in the forest land earlier cultivated by the tribals and other forest dwellers so that people cannot prove occupation.

Prospective beneficiaries want forest rights to be alienable and mortgageable, but expect protection under the Odisha Scheduled Areas Transfer of Immovable Property (by Scheduled Tribes) Regulation, 1956.

References

Dungdung, Gladson (2016). *Adivasi and Forest Rights—The Grassroots Status of Forest Rights in Jharkhand*, New Delhi: Prithavi Prakashan.

Mahapatra, L.K., (2005). "Tribal Rights and Entitlements in Land, Forest and Other Resources," Paper prepared for the UNDP Odisha Resettlement Policy Project.

Mohapatra, Bishnu Prasad (2014), "Decentralised Forest Governance, Institutions and Livelihoods in Odisha: A Study of Evolution of Policy Process and Politics", Centre for Economic and Social Studies, Hyderabad, Rural Monograph-19.

Patnaik, B.K. and Brahmachari, A. (1996): "Community based Forest Management Practices, Field observations from Odisha", *Economic & Political Weekly*, April, pp. 969-975.

Patnaik, S., (2013) "Greening Odisha", In: Patnaik, S.R. and Hussain, W. (eds.), Janaki Ballav Patnaik *the March to a Modern Odisha*, Ama Odisha, Bhubaneswar, pp, 392-405.

Poffenberger, Mark and Betsy, McGean (Eds.) 1996, *Village Voices, Forest Choices*. New Delhi: Oxford University Press.

Sangitha, S.N., (2008), "State, Society and Inclusive Governance: Community Forests in Andhra Pradesh, Karnataka and Odisha", Working Paper 200, ISEC, Bangalore.

Sarangi, Tapas Kumar (2013), "Legalising Rights through Implementation of Forest Rights Act, 2006: A Critical Review on Odisha and Jharkhand", Centre for Economic and Social Studies, Hyderabad, Rural Working Paper No. 20.

Sarangi, Tapas Kumar (2014), "Working of Forest Rights Act, 2006 and its impact on Livelihood: A Comparative Study of Odisha and Jharkhand", Centre for Economic and Social Studies, Hyderabad, Rural Monograph-21.

Sarap, K. and Sarangi, T.K. (2009) "Malfunctioning of Forest Institutions in Governance in Odisha", *Economic & Political Weekly*, Vol. XLIV, No. 30, September, pp. 18-22.

Sarin, M. (1996), "From conflict to collaboration: Institutional issues in Community Management", In: Mark Poffenberger and Betsy McGean (ed.) *Village Voices, Forest Choices*, JFM in India, New Delhi: Oxford University Press, pp. 165-209.

Saxena, N.C. (2003), "Livelihood diversification and non-timber forest products in Odisha: Wider lessons on the scope for policy change", Working Paper-223, Overseas Development Institute.

Sundar, N. (2000), "Unpacking the 'Joint' in Joint Forest Management", *Development and Change*, 31:255-279.

Sarap, Kailash, Sarangi Tapas Kumar, Naik Jogindra, "Implementation of Forest Rights Act in Odisha—Process, constraints and outcome", *Economic & Political Weekly*, Vol. xlviii.

5

Study on Land Rights in Odisha and Jharkhand

5.1 Objectives

In this Chapter an attempt is made to understand the following Land Issues in Odisha and Jharkhand:

- Status in Mining and Land Rights of the Tribals and other Marginalized Communities in the States of Odisha and Jharkhand.
- The specific situation of Land Rights in Tribal districts of Odisha and Jharkhand.
- The Implementation of Land Reforms in the States of Odisha and Jharkhand.
- The Land Rights of Women in Odisha and Jharkhand.
- The overall Scenario of the Land Rights of the marginalized communities in Odisha and Jharkhand.

In the first part of the study the Agrarian Situation and Land Rights of Odisha is being discussed and it is followed by the analysis of the Land Situation in the State of Jharkhand.

5.2 Mining and Land Rights of the Weaker Sections in the State of Odisha

Manas Jena conducted a "Study on Mining and Land Rights of the Marginalized Communities in State of Odisha" (2013). The study was conducted by Development Initiative, Bhubaneswar which was supported by Action-Aid. The author has discussed about the Mining and Land Rights in Odisha. Odisha has about 58 varieties of major minerals and above 22 varieties of minor minerals. The four major minerals zones are Coal Belt, Chrome, Iron Ore, Manganese belt, bauxite belt and coastal mineral belt. The coal belt is located in the districts of Angul, Jharsuguda, Sambalpur and Sundargarh. The mineral belt of Coal and iron ore are located in the districts of Jajpur, Keonjhar, Mayurbhanj and Sundargarh district. The bauxite belt is mostly located in South a West Odisha which include Malkangiri, Koraput, Raygada, Bolangir, Kandhamal and Kalahandi. The coastal mineral belt covers the districts of Ganjam, Mahanadi Delta and Puri Brahmagiri belt.

The history of mining dates back to 1898. Presently, there are about 600 mining lease and about 200 companies which include Central Government Undertakings like Steel Authority of India Ltd. (SAIL), National Aluminium Company (NALCO), Mahanadi Coalfields Ltd. (MCL), India Rare Earth (IRE), and Odisha Mining Corporation owned by the Government of Odisha and a number of private mining companies prominent among which are TATA, Birla and IMFA. Minerals valucd worth Rs. 15,317.10 crore was produced in the year 2009-10 in the state. The State contributes 9 per cent to the total value of mineral production of the country and claimed first position among the States.

The National Mineral Policy has been revised in 1994 to permit private (both domestic and foreign) investment in mineral sector. Indian mining sector was opened to foreign direct investment in 1993 and was further liberated in 1997 with automatic approval. Similarly, though land is a State subject as per constitution—there are Central Acts like Land Acquisition Act, 1894, SEZ Act, 2000, Coal Bearing Area Act, 1957, which vest more power with Centre. There has been tendency to take away the power of the State in relation to ownership and control over land.

There have been a number of land struggles in the mining areas of Odisha. Many of the visible struggles are in areas having mineral reserve where mining activities are sure to come up in future. The South-West Odisha Bauxite deposit areas like Kashipur and Niyamgiri have been such struggles where local communities are opposing mining and do not want to leave their land. In North-Odisha and Central West mining areas of Sukinda, Keonjhar, Sudhargada, Jharsuguda and Angul where mining activities have been continuing for the last fifty-sixty years, the struggles are not directly against mining, but to bargain more in terms of compensation.

In the State the extremists as well as the moderates have been playing a crucial role in organizing the poor landless Dalit and Adivasis to launch protests and struggles for settling land questions. The land struggle in South-West Odisha had incidence of caste and ethnic conflict between Dalits and Adivasis in places like Narayanpatna, Kandhamal, Kashipur and Kalahandi. The Dalit communities of these areas are facing land alienation and land grabbing. Thousands of Dalit families at Narayanpatna were forcefully driven out of home. As a result, many Adivasis were involved in police cases rightly or wrongly lodged against them; both the communities were subjected to police atrocities. But the land issues still remain unsolved, which is a very potential threat to peace in these areas. The struggle of Adivasis in non-Scheduled areas like Kalinganagar for land, where 14 Adivasis sacrificed their lives and hundreds of families have been harassed, have suffered all sorts of difficulties. They have lost their lands without compensations and without addressing the basic issues of land like Survey and Settlement of Adivasi and Dalit land.

5.3 Women of Marginalised Communities in Mining Areas in Odisha

Landlessness affects women, as she has to manage all household work, collecting fuel, fodder, fetch water, cook food, take care of children and elders in family. Dalit and Adivasi women share the burden of livelihood in family apart from household responsibility. Women are mostly engaged in agriculture, forestry, minor forest produce collection, animal husbandry work but mining activities have mostly made them work as construction labourers and casual labourers. Lack of homestead land and proper shelter is a major issue which affects women more in providing security to self and family.

Many Dalit and Adivasi women are working in mines as casual labour under contractors in Sukinda, Keonjhar and Sundaragarh mines area. They face all kinds of exploitation like lack of minimum wage, social security, protection against sexual harassment, work place etc. The flow of truckers and migrant workers disturb the normal life of the local people and in particular women are more vulnerable to this situation. It is found that there are single mothers (unwed mothers) in mining areas of Sukinda, Keonjhar, Angul and Jharasuguda. Their socio-economic condition is very bad which needs urgent attention. The condition of women in mining is very insecure. Alcoholism and criminalization of male members of the Dalits and Adivasi families has been a growing menace, which aggravates the plight of the women. The incidence of maternal ill-health and infant mortality is very high in the mining areas. Pollution-related diseases like, TB and Asthma are chief health hazards. Women are participating in all land-related movements and protests in the mining areas, but women leadership is conspicuously absent.

The study conducted by Development Initiative, Bhubaneswar have undertaken an empirical study of 60 villages from ten places in 7 mining districts of Odisha, namely—Angul, Jharsugada, Mayurbhanj, Sundargarh, Keonjhar, Jajpur and Baragarh. These studies have established that Dalit landlessness is more closely linked to food insecurity, distress migration and indebtedness (Prof. Manoranjan Mohanty, Council of Social Development, New Delhi) in Odisha, the poorest State in India, has 40 per cent of its population belonging to SC and ST communities. As per NSS landholding survey of 1992, about 70 per cent of the Dalit households are under category of landless and below one acre holding. They bear the historical burden of untouchability. They are not only socially discriminated but also resourceless. They have no land and only 45 per cent of them are literate. They are historically deprived of resources, and a dignified life. They are being treated as lesser humans and live in sub-human conditions with all human indignities and exploitation. Each year about fifteen hundred cases of atrocities are being registered in different Police Stations of the State of Odisha (White Paper of Home Department, Government of Odisha). The atrocities include rape of Dalit Women, murder, house burning, physical assault, social boycott, mass-attack, forcible possession of Dalit land, false case against Dalits etc. Many of the Dalits are facing difficulties in getting bail in courts due to lack of land "*Patta*". Dalits and Adivasis are suffering in courts and jails. Adivasi land alienation is a major issue in the State. It has been reported by the State Government that under Regulation-2 of 1956, till 2007, total 62, 145 number of cases have been settled in favour of SCs and STs involving an area of 57,240 acre but the physical possession has not been ensured. Similarly, 10,272 number of cases are settled in favour of SCs and STs under the section 23 of OLR Act. (Natural Disaster Management Department, Government of Odisha). The State has mineral resources. Out of 90 major minerals available in the country, Odisha has 35 varieties of minerals. It has 30 per cent of coal, 98 per cent of chrome, 70 per cent of Bauxite, 35 per cent of Iron ore, 38 per cent of Manganese etc. The minerals are exported to countries like China, Japan, South Africa, Korea, Netherland, Singapore, Hong Kong, France, Italy, Australia, UAE, Bangladesh, and Peru etc.

5.4 Mo Jami Mo Diha

As one of the innovative measures for ensuring welfare oriented Revenues Administration for the poor and weaker sections of the society, the State Government has launched a campaign named "Mo Jami Mo Diha", which has started since 2007 to protect the land rights of the poor. The objectives of the campaign are: (a) to protect and ensure the land rights of the poor who were allotted lease of government lands earlier or to restore their lost land; (b) dovetailing the programme with the development schemes to ensure that the land allottees are in a better position to utilize the land; and (c) to assist the poor with major emphasis on those belonging to ST and SC communities, to retain their land and homestead land within the existing legal framework. Up to the end of December 2011, out of 2,33,484 number of cases received for verification, 1,41,808 cases have been disposed. All out efforts are being taken to dispose of the balance cases. (*Source: Annual Report*, 2011-12, Revenue Department Government of Odisha).

Land Alienation in the form of Land Acquisition by the State Agencies and Central Government owned Public Sector companies like SAIL, NALCO, MCL, NTPC, IRE Ltd. have taken huge quantity of land. SAIL possesses 5,999.957 hectares in Rourkela, NALCO has 4647.177 hectares in Simliguda, and MCL owns 17,387.537 hectares in Sundargarh, IRE Ltd. has 2,483.019 hectares in Rourkela, Ganjam for factories and mines. Even many factories like RSP have acquired land far on excess of their requirement. Private companies like TATA, Birla, Jindal, Bhushan, Vedanta, POSCO, Arcelor Mittal, have mines and factories in the State. Many of the private companies have secured lease land for SEZs. Companies like TATAs have not started activities on the acquired land at Gopalpur for last ten years. It was found that mining activities in the state of Odisha has claimed a lease area of 99,430.392 hectares of land covering 600 number of mining of 30 minerals. The highest number of mining activities are in Sundargarh and Keonjhar districts with 128 and 119 mines respectively.

The figures from Table 5.1 indicate that the percentage of ST population is relatively high from the tribal districts of Sundargarh (50.19%), Keonjhar (44.50%), Mayurbhanj (56.60%), and Koraput (49.62%). The percentage of the Scheduled Caste population is highest from Jajpur district. The total leased in area is highest in Sundargarh District (19,889.253 hectares) followed by the district of Angul (10,230.462 hectares), Mayurbhanj (5391.617 hectares) and Koraput (6274.568 hectares). The number of homestead families is highest in Jajpur district (22,653), followed by the district of Bolangir (18,903) and Mayurbhanj (12,765). Landless families is quite substantial in the district of Jajpur (44,646) followed by Bolangir, 23,079), Mayurbhanj (24,155) and Koraput (18,746). As per the available data, there are some lands available for homestead purpose and also for agriculture purpose which can be distributed to both homesteaders and landless.

Table 5.1: Land Available for Distribution and Landless Families in Districts having Major Mining Deposits

Districts	*Total population (2011 Census)*	*Percentage of SC population (2001)*	*Percentage of ST population*	*No. of mines*	*Total lease area (In Hector)*	*Home stead less Family*	*Landless family*	*Land available for Homestead purpose (In acre)*	*Land available for Agri. Purpose (acre)*
Jharsuguda	5,79,499	17.07	31.34	25	7656.547	2479	3014	299.03	5002.35
Sundargarh	20,80,664	8.62	50.19	128	19889.253	2319	3823	3582.70	19274.94
Keonjhar	18,02,777	11.62	44.50	119	31435.255	6784	17553	14009.73	17875.81
Jajpur	18,26,275	22.99	7.76	20	4496.376	22653	44646	4846	14239.38
Angul	12,71,703	17.20	11.67	17	10,230.462	3447	8955	4961.16	25396.65
Bolangir	16,48,574	16.92	20.63	75	1919.316	18903	23079	3862.38	18930.38
Mayaurbhanj	25,13,895	7.68	56.60	45	5391.617	12765	24155	5848	42578.57
Koraput	13,76,934	13.04	49.62	9	6274.568	5005	18476	11267.826	10546.881

Source: Data about mines and lease area from Department of Steel and Mines till 2004.

As per the 1991 Census the districts of Mayurbhanj, Sundargarh, Koraput, Rayagada, Nabarangpur and Malkangiri are wholly Scheduled Area districts where as only one or two tehsils of the districts of Keonjhar, Kondhmal, Gajapati, Ganjam, Kalahandi are Scheduled Areas. Sukinda Valley mines has leased area of 7505.68 hectares covering three tehsil and bordering Sukinda the largest Steel Hub of Asia with 14 Steel Plants is located here at Kalinganagar in Danagadi block. The State Government has leased out 14.666 acre of land to the industries in Kalinganagar. In Sukinda Chrome Valley and Kalinganagar Steel plant area, land has been a major issue for a long time. In the year 2006, fourteen Adivasis were killed by police to suppress the land struggle of the people in Kalinganagar. Land survey and settlement is a major issue in these areas. Many Dalit families had got '*patta*' as Record of rights from the then King of Sukinda before Independence, but later on this has not been regularized by the Revenue Department. Many Adivasi families staying here for generations are not being recognized by the Revenue Administration.

There are 22 mining companies which have diverted 1887.44 hectares of forest land for mining companies; they have also leased in Government land and the total leased area by them is 4579.095 acre. In the Sukinda tehsil of Jajpur district 11 companies have leased in 8870.39 acre and the Government land leased in by them is 4601.18

acre whereas private land acquired by them is 4444.21 acre. The mining activities add more burden to the people in general and marginalized communities in particular, who are more dependent on common property resources for their livelihood and survival. The people of mining areas who are being displaced and affected by mining are losing CPR and on the other hand they are not getting anything as compensation. Dalit and Adivasi livelihood are mostly dependent on CPR like forest, river, canals, pasture where they collect food and firewood but they have been deprived of all these due to mining.

During last 100 years of mining there has been large number of abandoned mines. The coal mining area has leased-up 18,075.983 hectares of land which can be reclaimed and distributed for cultivation purpose. MCL has started a programme called land restoration. It is expected that 10 per cent of the mines land in Odisha can be reclaimed and 10,000 hectares will be available for distribution among the poor and landless families; in the mining areas of Odisha particularly in the district of Angul, Jharsuguda, Sambalpur and Sundargarh have 17,557.842 hectares area covered by coal mines and the SC and ST families are dependent on homestead land and cultivable land. The Scheduled Caste families are mostly agricultural labours and need land for homestead and cultivation purpose which can be distributed to them. Dalit and adivasi women in mining areas are mostly landless, daily wage workers, illiterate and are engaged in domestic work and also contract labour. On the 20th June, 2013 in Lakhanpur tehsil of Jharsuguda about 300 men, landless persons and other people from 33 GPs gathered in the meeting to explain their problem of landlessness.

There are a number of single women in mines areas who need land to have a dignified life, which will ensure them shelter and agriculture-based livelihood. It need to be ensured that the land *patta* and the compensation money should be given to women in the family, so that they can feel secure and play a proactive role in the matters relating to their lives and livelihoods. Land is central to life and livelihood for a family where women play a crucial role along with male. Therefore, both men and women should be recognized equally in asserting their rights over land. The ground water level has gone down in al-most all mining areas. The scarcity of water accompanied with deforestation affect agriculture adversely. The overall process leads to desertification of the area after mining. Minerals like coal, Bauxite and Iron ore attract mineral based industries like Steel, Alumina, Aluminium and Power Plants. Mining projects have displaced two hundred villages in ten Tehsils. Coal mining has been cause of major displacement in Talcher,

Kaniha, Chendipada of Angul district, Hemagiri of Sundargarh district and Lakhanpur and Jharsuguda of Jharsugada district. Most of the Dalit families almost in all mining Tehsils are homestead less and landless. Many families are still on government land. The study team has identified 1200 landless families from 15 villages and they also claimed distributing '*pattas*' for Dalit and Adivasi landless which has been illegally transferred to Non-Dalits and Non-adivasis. Even Non-Adivasis are staying on Adivasi land and the land has been recorded in the name of another Adivasis (narratives by activists from Sundargarh). The steel companies in Kalinganagar have knowingly diverted their boundary wall to avoid Non-Dalit land and occupied land of Dalits, Adivasis and Minorities.

Empirical work was undertaken in some villages to understand the number of homestead families. For example, Ambedkar colony, Talcher in Angul district had 25 homestead landless families. Again in this study the researchers found that in village Malade the number of homesteadless families were around thirty and from Ubuda under Lakhanpur Tehsil the number of homestead landless families were 15 in numbers. In the village of Bansapani under Barbil Tehsil, the number of homestead landless families were 10 in number. Similar, incidence of homestead landless families were found in the Jalahari village under the Barbil Tehsil, Kashia village in Keonjhar district and 14 homesteadless dalit families in Rangamatia village of Sukinda tehsil. Similarly, they found that out of 120 displaced families from the Danagadi Tehsil, 104 families were landless as well as homesteadless. There were a number of other villages in Kalinganagar Industrial Complex where landless and Homestead landless families were located. These were the village of Gadapur, Jakhapura, Manoharpur. The study also found that in Sukinda Tehsil there were 67 families belonging to Mankidia community who were homestead landless families. The study by Development Initiative provides a detail list of 600 companies which have leased in different kinds of mines for their industrial purpose. The study indicates that in the 30 districts of the Odisha the total number of homestead landless families is 2.49 lakh which includes 84,723 Scheduled Tribe, 70,118 Scheduled Castes and 80,215 persons belonging to other castes. Besides this the study also provides the figure of the total number of landless families in the 30 districts as 4.45 lakh of which the Scheduled Tribes are 1.42 lakh, the Scheduled Castes 1.25 lakh and the other caste are 1.63 lakh. The area of Government wasteland, surplus ceiling land available for homestead purpose is 1.23 lac acre and for agriculture purpose 5.41 lakh acre are available. The study gives evidence to the fact that there is sufficient land available for distribution to the houseless and landless households who are affected by the displacement due to mining and also due to other purpose. [*Source:* Sh. Manas Jena (2013), "Study on Mining and Land Rights of the Marginalized Communities in State of Odisha", Development Initiative, Action-Aid, Bhubaneswar.]

5.5 Land Rights Situation in the State of Contemporary Odisha

Mr. Sanjoy Patnaik, Director, Research and Advocacy, at the Regional Centre for Development Cooperation (RCDC), Bhubaneswar, Odisha, has discussed the various land rights issues like Ceiling Surplus land, Homesteadless, Bhoodan Land, Land rights for tribal, land acquisition and land holding among the weaker section.

Table 5.2: Main Provisions and Impact of Land Legislation in Odisha

Name	*Year*	*Provisions*	*Impact*
Odisha Estate Abolition Act	1952	Abolition of intermediaries. Vesting of all land rights in the State. Agricultural landless than 33 acre to remain with the intermediary for personal cultivation	No provision for protection for tenants. Eviction of tenants as the *zamindars* were allowed land, less than 33 acre, for personal cultivation. Abolition of intermediaries could not be completed until 1974.
Odisha Land Reforms Act (Amended in 1965, 1973 and 1974)	1960	Permanent, heritable and transferable rights in land for the tiller. Ban on leasing of land except under special conditions (in 1972). Under adverse possession, land in continuous cultivation for 12 years or more by a person other than its owner shall pass to the cultivator. Rent not to exceed one fourth of the gross produce. Ceiling on individual	Delay in the enactment and actual implementation of the Act provided sufficient opportunities for large landowners to escape ceiling restrictions. By explicitly banning tenancy, the law is unable to address the problem of share-cropping. No provision was made to record concealed tenancies.

(*Contd.*)

Name	Year	Provisions	Impact
		holdings at 33 standard acre—later reduce to 20 (in 1965), and to 10 standard acre (in 1972).	
Odisha Prevention of Land Encroachment Act (Amended in 1982)	1972	Unauthorised occupation of government land prohibited. Penalties on encroachers to be followed by eviction. The 1982 amendment for settlement of two (later amended to one) standard acre of 'unobjectionable' land (i.e. government wasteland) with 'eligible' beneficiaries (e.g. landless).	Disregard of the Act with widespread encroachment on both government and common lands, often by powerful groups. Penalties too low to act as a disincentive to encroachers. The 1982 amendment not a 'proactive' right-encroacher cannot 'apply' to be regularised as act of encroachment is regarded as illegal in the first place. Only Revenue Inspector can initiate regularisation of rights. Considerable scope for rent seeking by revenue officials.

Source: Government of Odisha—Different Land Legislations enacted from time to time.

Ceiling Surplus Land

As per ceiling surplus rules, land up to 0.7 standard acre was allotted to the landless persons for agricultural purpose. The ceiling surplus operation failed to yield the desired result because of lack of actual physical possession by the beneficiary, unavailability of record of rights, and poor land quality making it almost impossible for him/her to cultivate the land and at times even identify it. A number of beneficiaries have *pattas* for ceiling surplus land allotted to them, but the land is still under possession of the previous owners. If the coastal Odisha is facing the problem of increasing landlessness and less land available for distribution with more and more land getting converted to non-agricultural purpose, in tribal Odisha it is the other way around: particularly Government land is available in the tribal district of Scheduled Areas for distribution to the landless and more land for distribution. Land distribution to the landless and ensuring their physical possession has remained a major area of concern. Besides, land of all categories is under tremendous stress because it is being slowly though consistently being acquired for non-agricultural purposes.

Odisha, however, experienced limited success in reforming the land tenure and revenue assessment system, the two major contributing factors being weak revenue administration and lack of updated land records. Similarly, the high ceiling level, fixed at 33 standard acre, enabled eviction of tenants by the intermediaries. As a result, by the time the ceiling limit was reduced to 10 standard acre in 1972, most of the big landowners had already escaped the ceiling limit by transferring the surplus land to their kith and kin, while maintaining actual control

Table 5.3: Land Ceiling Limits under Revised Laws

(in hectares)

State	*Irrigation required for*		*Dryland*
	Two crops	*One crop*	
Odisha	4.05	6.07	12.40-18.21

Source: Government of Odisha—Different Land Legislations enacted from time-to-time.

As per 2005-06 records, there are about 4,45,450 landless individuals in the State, whereas degraded ceiling surplus land available is about 5,40,725 acre.

Mo Jami Mo Diha

The government responded to repeated appeals from tribal and civil society organizations, by coming out with a campaign called *Mo Jami Mo Diha* (My Land and My Homestead land), launched in 2007 to ensure possession within a stipulated time. It is generally believed, however, that the amount of illegal land transfer is much more than what is reflected in government records and this initiating of the government has not been an unqualified success.

The campaign *Mo Jami Mo Diha* (My land—My homestead) has been launched to protect and to ensure land rights of the poor, who were allotted lease of Government lands earlier or restored their lost land. The objective is to achieve convergence with development schemes to see that the land allottees are in a better position to utilize the land; and to assist the poor, with emphasis on those belonging to Scheduled Tribe and Scheduled Caste communities, to retain their land and homestead within the existing legal framework.

5.6 Ownership of Land in Tribal Areas

The ownership of land in tribal areas has remained a complex issue for decades in most parts of India. Tribals living in forest areas are yet to receive legal entitlement over land in many areas they have been cultivating for decades. They face the constant threat of eviction and dispossession. Different categories of land and varied ownership, land use and management patterns make land resource management all the more complex. In tribal areas, concentration of land in a few hands, illegal possession of land by the elite, passing of irrigated land as unirrigated land in land records and use of agricultural land for commercial purposes are some of the stumbling blocks in the individual's rightful access to land.

Similarly, there are about 2,49,334 Homesteadless families for whom land available is 1,22,764 acre. Besides, since 1974-75, government wasteland up to one standard acre is allotted to the landless for agricultural purposes.

Table 5.4: Land Distribution Details (1974-2007)

Allotment Distribution category	*Total Land allotted (acre)*	*Total number of beneficia-ries*	*Scheduled Tribe*		*Scheduled Caste*	
			No.	*Area*	*No.*	*Area*
Ceiling Surplus	159384	142616	52934 (37.11%)	66303 (41.59%)	48794 (34.21%)	51109 (32.06%)
Homestead land lease	–	1213655	462536	–	332706	–
Wasteland	736491	478469	231630 (48.41%)	384364 (52.18%)	104235 (21.79%)	175576 (23.83%)

Source: Government of Odisha, Different Land Legislations enacted from time-to-time.

Distribution of Ceiling Surplus Land

The reasons for non-distribution of land ceiling, range from the area being locked in litigation, being reserved for public purposes and land being unfit for cultivation. This means that tribals still do not enjoy the benefits of land distribution. There are three basic problems that beneficiaries face in such ceiling surplus and wasteland distribution cases:

(a) lack of actual physical possession by the beneficiary;
(b) no records (*patta*-ownership) with the beneficiary; and
(c) poor land quality making it almost impossible to cultivate.

A large chunk of beneficiary families, who have *pattas* for ceiling surplus land allotted to them do not physically possess them as the land is still under the possession of the previous owners. The previous owners still reap the benefits from such land. Although about three decades have passed since allotment, efforts to ensure physical possession of the land to the allottees have been limited. Interestingly, even though most do not have physical possession, they have to pay tax as they are owners as per Government records.

The study reveals that the much talked about re-distribution of ceiling surplus land has remained far from being impressive. Over the years, the poor and landless, especially the tribals, have not been able to benefit much from the ceiling surplus land that has been transferred to them under various schemes. As per the survey conducted in three blocks of Koraput, the landless are not an improved lot even after re-distribution of the ceiling surplus land. For, as much as 16 per cent of the beneficiaries continue to struggle to get physical possession of the land allotted in their favour. Similarly, 30 per cent of beneficiaries have record of rights for land which is not suitable for cultivation. While 42 per cent beneficiaries are cultivating their land, 6.6 per cent have either sold or mortgaged it. This goes on to show that most beneficiaries are not deriving any actual benefit from the land they legally owned by them.

There are large number of families that have been allotted a piece of land, but have not got *patta* implying lacunae in the implementation of land reforms for the last three decades. Moreover, the allotted land is usually far away from the village and adjacent villagers claim rights over the reallocated land. Physical land demarcation is also a major issue and a majority of beneficiaries are unable to identify their plot. As a result, they cultivate land that does not belong to them and are called encroachers.

Prevention of Transfer and Restoration of Land

As per Section 22 of the Odisha Land Reforms Act, any transfer of land that belongs to Scheduled Castes and Scheduled Tribes to people who are not from this group without prior permission of the competent authority is declared void. Under Sections 23 and 23A of this Act, there is a provision for restoration of land to Scheduled Castes and Scheduled Tribes if it has been transferred without prior written permission of the competent authority or if the land has been under unauthorized occupation by those who are not Scheduled Castes or Scheduled Tribes. The details regarding Scheduled Caste and Scheduled Tribe beneficiaries under the provisions of Sections 23 and 23A of the Odisha Land Reforms Act during 2006-07 are provided in Table 5.5.

Table 5.5: Transfer and Restoration of Land under the Odisha Land Reforms Act

Social Category	*Number of beneficiaries Land ordered for restoration (in acre)*	*Land ordered for restoration (in acre)*
Scheduled Castes	1350	1389.923
Scheduled Tribes	229	57.251
Total	**1579**	**1447.174**

Source: Government of Odisha—Different Land Legislations enacted from time-to-time.

Homestead-landless

Since 1974-75, as one of the frontline anti-poverty programmes of the State, the government has provided land up to four decimals to the homesteadless for house-site purpose. About 2,49,334 homesteadless families have been identified in the State, out of which more than 60 per cent belong to the Scheduled Tribe and Scheduled Caste families. As per Government records, from 1974-75 till the end of 2005-06, the State Government had distributed 49,248.117 acre of homestead land to 11,15,000 homeless families including 4,15,000 Scheduled Tribes and 3,07,000 Scheduled Caste families. In 2005-06, homeless families (72,585) have been provided with house sites up to 0.04 acre per applicant—this includes 34,944 Scheduled Tribes, 18,176 Scheduled Castes and 19,465 other poor homeless families.

In 2006, Project 'Vasundhara' was launched as a mission under which all the homesteadless families shall be provided house sites within a span of three years. Intense efforts are being made to expedite its implementation. Till date, 2,49,334 homesteadless families have been identified in the State. For 2006-07, 98,774 homesteadless families, which includes 46,196 Scheduled Tribes, 25,721 Scheduled Castes and 26,857 other families, have been provided house sites under the aforesaid project.

Differences in the Coastal and the Tribal Hinterland

In the coastal districts of Cuttack, Jajpur, Jagatsinghpur, Kendrapada, Nayagarh, Puri, Khurda, Ganjam, Balasore and Bhadrak, the number of landless is more than the land available for distribution. However, in the tribal dominated districts of Koraput, Rayagada, Malkangiri, Nabarangpur, Sundargarh, Mayurbhanj, Keonjhar, Deogarh, Sambalpur, Kandhamal, Angul and Dhenkanal, the number of landless is less than the land available for distribution. In the 10 coastal districts, the per capita land availability for the landless is 0.9 acre whereas in the 12 tribal districts, the per capita land availability for the landless is just double, i.e. 1.8 acre. Therefore, in terms of access to land in both coastal and tribal areas attention needs to be given.

Under the Bhoodan movement, land was distributed to the poor and landless by the first generation of land owners and so necessary records for such transfer of title were not created. As a result of this, in districts like Koraput, Nabarangpur and Malkangiri, the second generation land owners took back this land from the beneficiaries rendering the entire Bhoodan movement futile.

As part of the campaign, Regional Centre for Development Cooperation, an NGO in Odisha facilitated the submission of applications of 33 beneficiaries from its study villages in Koraput Tehsil office during December 2007. After the submission of applications in the Tehsil office, the organization has been following up with the revenue officials on the verification status of the concerned beneficiaries. Subsequently, the revenue officials stated that the verification report reveals no possession problem in the selected villages and there are cases only where a repeat demarcation of the area is required.

In view of this response, the NGO interacted with 46 ceiling surplus beneficiaries, of the seven villages under study, who had attended the first phase of the *melas* in their respective areas. These interactions revealed that 27 beneficiaries had attended the *mela* and all of them had applied for possession, however, none of them had received possession over their land until the beginning of February 2008.

On the one hand, the beneficiaries felt that though they had submitted the applications in the *mela*, there was no provision for follow-up. To add to their misery, the previous land owners in village Podapadar and Gaudaguda of Kakriguma circle threaten the applicants of dire consequences if they continue to ask for their rights. On the other hand, the beneficiaries are unaware of the implications of the campaign and even the decisions taken on legal cases filed on their behalf. The feeling of hopelessness on the part of the beneficiaries leads to the realisation that information dissemination needs to be stepped-up for greater impact. In the coastal districts of undivided Cuttack, Puri and Balasore, a large area of Bhoodan land has been illegally encroached by the rich and the influential (this includes builders). This need to be verified. The Bhoodan Yagna Samiti has been reconstituted *vide* a Revenue Department Notification. According to the report received from this Samiti an extent of 6,38,706.50 acre of land was collected as donation, out of which 5,79,994.21 acre of land have already been distributed amongst 1,52,852 landless persons. The Samiti is expediting the distribution of the balance 58,722.29 acre after verification of the present status of such undistributed land.

Unresolved Issues Critical to the Realization of Forest Rights

- There is an apprehension among forest dwellers, who have been displaced several times because of various development projects, that they might not get the benefit of the Act as proving residence for three generations in the present village would prove difficult, if not impossible.
- Non-functional Gram Sabhas and the ignorance of panchayat functionaries about the law may make them pass a resolution in favour of those not deserving the benefits.
- Predominance of Government officers in both the appellate committees (sub-divisional level committee and district level committee) may dilute the authority and freedom of the tribal leaders, who may cvcn go unheard.
- Difficulty in collecting caste certificate by the beneficiaries—nobody knows who is going to issue the caste certificate.
- Ensuring the presence of two-third of the members for the formation of the Forest Rights Committee is a tall order.
- There are any number of instances where the forest department is taking up in great haste plantation activities in

the forest land earlier cultivated by the tribals and other forest dwellers so that people cannot prove occupation.

- Prospective beneficiaries want forest rights to be alienable and mortgageable, but expect protection under the Odisha Scheduled Areas Transfer of Immovable Property (by Scheduled Tribes) Regulation, 1956.
- Recognition and vesting of rights in case of a man who has more than one wife is a problematic issue.
- Processes to draw the traditional boundaries in the forest villages is also posing problem.
- No clear understanding on whether communities would have "community forest resource" rights if it falls within the Critical Wildlife Habitat and in the mining areas.

5.7 Women and Land Rights

Women and land rights is one of the most crucial issues of equity and justice. As per different land laws, the State Government may distribute all such land under ceiling surplus that is not categorized as commons, *gochar* and *rakshita* and those which are not under the discretion of the WAKF Board to a set of landless people. Among them, landless widows and unmarried women up to 30 years old are listed as beneficiaries who get high priority.

In order to give preference to widows, unmarried women, victimized women and women living below the poverty line, in 2002, the Government of Odisha decided to allot at least 40 per cent of the Government wasteland kept for agriculture and house site purpose, ceiling surplus land and Bhoodan land to the landless women. The government also stressed that at least 40 per cent of this land should be allotted to women belonging to the Scheduled Tribes and Scheduled Castes.

The recent Odisha Rehabilitation and Resettlement Policy, 2006 has some progressive features such as unmarried daughters/sisters more than 30 years of age should be treated as separate families: Physically challenged persons, orphans who are minors, widows and women divorcees are also to be treated as separate families. Though elaborate provisions have been made to ensure land rights to women in the practice this has not always been followed. There are significant gaps between women's land rights and their actual ownership and possession, and between the limited ownership rights and their effective control over land (Bina Agarwal, 1994).

Women's legal rights are in land conflict with deep-seated social norms and customs, and are rarely recognized socially to be legitimate. There are strong pressures, reinforced by social stigma, seclusion practices, and other sanctions, on women to forfeit their legal rights in favour of their brothers. Women tend to internalize the imposed social restrictions because they feel that they may find themselves dependent on their brothers for economic and social support in the event of widowhood or marital break-up. In the context of women's role in agriculture, it would be worthwhile to discuss land rights provision for women in the Odisha Land Reforms Act. The Act allows widows, divorcees, unmarried women to lease their land for cultivation, when leasing is otherwise prohibited. Although this seems progressive, it may have two underlying presumptions (a) women should be protected from cultivation, therefore, they should be allowed to lease their lands; and (b) only female heads of households should have control over land, while the normal married women's control over land is subsumed under 'family'. Due to lack of education and awareness, women invariably do not have record of rights. Agricultural land subject to tenancy is exempt from the Hindu Succession Act, and is governed by State-level acts.

5.8 Tribal Land Alienation

The Odisha Transfer of Immovable Property Regulation 2 of 1956 was further amended in 2002 and rules were made more stringent to check large scale alienation of tribal land in Scheduled Areas. The regulation prohibits transfer of immovable properties belonging to members of Scheduled Tribes in favour of persons not belonging to that category. This regulation provides for penal action in respect of illegal transfer as well as unauthorised transfer. In spite of all these provisions of illegal transfer actual sale of land is a regular feature in tribal areas, and many of these cases remain unreported. An interesting aspect of the Regulation amended in 2002 is that "a member of the Scheduled Tribe shall not transfer any land if the total extent of his land remaining after the transfer is reduced to less than two acre in case of irrigated land or five acre in case of irrigated land". Section 5(2) of the Fifth Schedule refers to land and its ownership as follows:

(a) Prohibit or restrict the transfer of land by or among members of the Scheduled Tribes in such area;
(b) regulate the allotment of land of members of the Scheduled Tribes in such area; and

(c) regulate the carrying on of business as money-lender by persons who lend money to members of the Scheduled Tribes in such Area.

The Gram Sabha or the Panchayats are to be consulted before acquisition of land in the Scheduled areas.

Table 5.6: Progress Achieved under Regulation 2 of 1956 (till March 2007)

No. of cases instituted	*No. of cases disposed*	*No. of Scheduled Tribe beneficiaries*	*Extent of land ordered to be restored (in acre)*	*Extent of land actually restored (in acre)*
1,06,547	1,05,578	65,660	57,162.21	56,519.95

Source: Government of Odisha—Different Land Legislations enacted from time-to-time.

Table 5.7: The present status of the Tribal Land in Scheduled Areas

District	*Total private landholdings (percentage of the total area)*	*Approximate Percentage of landless (less than one standard acre)*	*Percentage of total Government land available on records*	*Percentage of Forest Land*
Gajapati	15.39	89.45	84.61	64.13
Kalahandi	37.13	66.30	64.10	30.34
Keonjhar	19.01	84.93	79.80	37.30
Kandhmal	14.47	88.55	85.53	74.64
Koraput	30.87	59.04	69.13	23.80
Malkangiri	17.88	63.44	82.12	54.21
Mayurbhanj	32.95	88.82	89.38	42.16
Nabrangpur	31.87	73.22	68.13	46.52
Rayagada	18.17	74.08	81.83	37.10
Sundargarh	21.87	70.43	78.13	51.04

Source: Census figure and Government of Odisha.

Recently, the State Government has proposed an amendment to the Odisha Transfer of Immovable Property Regulation 2 of 1956, which would enable transfer of tribal *patta* land to Non-Tribals, in specific cases. It is widely debated and argued that such amendment would completely defeat the purpose for which the regulation was promulgated. Government records reveal that in the tribal dominated districts of Odisha about 84 per cent of the land belongs to the Government under forest and revenue land, and the rest, very small holdings, are private or rayati land. Since in most parts of the Scheduled Areas Tribals depend on forest and other revenue land for which they do not have *patta*, such deregulation might have serious implications on tribal land ownership in the scheduled areas. Odisha presents enigmatic situation.

Where the landlessness of the tribal is very high, but they are not distributed government land which is available in large number in the tribal areas. This is a contradiction in term and indicates the very unfavourable attitude of the government of Odisha, Revenue department and the District Administration. On the other hand, the government land is easily distributed to the corporate entities during the globalization era. This is indicative of the anti-poor attitude of the Government of the Odisha relating to its land rights for the vulnerable Sections inclusive of Scheduled Castes and Scheduled Tribes. Even the implementation of land ceiling and Bhoodan programme are major failures. It is suggested that the government of Odisha should launch a major campaign of distribution of Government land to the Scheduled Tribes and Scheduled Castes.

Table 5.8: Distribution of Operational Holdings and Operated Areas in the Sampled Districts of the based on Agricultural Census, 2010-11

(*Land in Hectares*)

Sl. No.	*District*	*Marginal* (0–1)		*Small* (1–2)		*Semi Medium* (2–4)		*Medium* (4–10)		*Large* 10 +		*All Sizes*
		No.	%	No.	%	No	%	No.	%	No.	%	
1.	Jagatsingh Pur	103018	83.827	16455	13.393	3044	2.49	347	0.29	11	10.013	122896
2.	Jajpur	84439	67.33	30476	24.25	9339	7.45	1147	0.98	70	0.05	125411
3.	Kalahandi	118405	64.24	39457	21.41	19622	10.65	6291	3.41	535	0.29	184310
4.	Koraput	85071	51.02	53743	32.23	22830	13.69	4596	2.76	494	0.30	166734
5.	Rayagada	71599	55.24	38994	30.08	15201	11.73	3486	2.69	334	0.26	129614
6.	Sundergarh	137657	65.48	52454	24.95	15919	7.57	3888	1.85	322	0.15	210240
7.	**State Total**	**3368296**	**72.17**	**918647**	**19.68**	**311261**	**6.67**	**63688**	**1.36**	**5574**	**0.12**	**4667466**

Source: Odisha Agriculture Statistics, 2012-13, pp. 79-80.

In the present empirical study in Odisha the district of Jagatsingh Pur, Jajpur, Kalahandi, Koraput, Rayagada and Sundargarh were selected as sampled districts for field study. The Jagatsinghpur district is coastal district whereas the remaining five districts are tribal districts. Table 5.8 provides the land size information of the farmers in different districts and the present table, describes the overall data of operational holding distributions. The data indicates that as per Agricultural Census, 2010-11, the maximum operational holdings are marginal

(72.17%) followed by small (19.68%), semi-medium (6.67%), medium (1.36%) and large size of ten hectares and above is only (0.12%). The data indicates that agrarian inequality has on the one hand reduced as the large farmers constitute only 0.12 per cent of the total holdings, but the marginalized and small farmers together constitute 91.78 per cent indicating severe marginalization of land holdings. There is the necessity of strengthening the agricultural policy to safeguard and protect the interest of marginal and small farmers in Odisha.

Table 5.9: District-wise operated areas of all Social Groups of Odisha State as per Agricultural Census, 2010-11

(Area in Hectares)

Sl. No.	District	Marginal (0–1)		Small (1-2)		Semi-Medium (2–4)		Medium (4–10)		Large 10 +		All Sizes
		Area	%	Area	%	Area	%	Area	%	Area	%	
1.	Jagat Singh Pur	55293	58.26	27931	29.43	9379	9.89	2059	2.17	238	0.25	94900 100.00
2.	Jajpur	55999	37.87	52225	35.31	28507	19.28	6904	4.67	4247	2.87	147882 100.00
3.	Kalahandi	75739	29.62	68630	26.84	61620	24.10	39811	15.57	9887	3.87	255684 100.00
4.	Koraput	60332	22.26	94488	34.87	71994	26.57	28129	10.38	16039	5.92	270982 100.00
5.	Rayagada	43265	27.40	53725	34.02	38108	24.14	17900	11.34	4891	3.10	157889 100.00
6.	Sundar Garh	93777	135.25	90530	34.04	49832	18.73	23645	8.89	8209	3.09	265993 100.00
7.	**State Total**	**1921842**	**39.61**	**1497752**	**30.87**	**918967**	**18.941**	**381272**	**7.86**	**132201**	**2.72**	**4852014 100.00**

Source: Odisha Agriculture Statistics, 2012-13, pp. 79-80.

The data in the above Table 5.9, indicate that the marginal holdings operate only 39.61 percent of the total holdings, Small holdings operate (30.87%), the semi-medium holdings (18.94%), the medium operational holdings operate (7.86%) and a large holdings operate (2.72%) of the total operated area. The operated area is more equally distributed between the marginal small, semi-medium and medium holdings with concentration of 2.72 per cent with large farmers. The agricultural policy of the State of Odisha should try to protect the existing land size distribution, otherwise, there will be process of pauperization and proletarianization.

As per the Forest Inquiry Committee Report of 1959, about 30,720 sq.km of forest area was under shifting cultivation in the forested and tribal dominated districts of Odisha which is about 20 per cent of the total geographical area of the State. Current estimates reveal that an area ranging between 5298 to 37,000 sq. km comes under shifting cultivation in Odisha. About 31,237.9 sq. km. of forests is affected, in varying degrees, by shifting cultivation. Though shifting cultivation has been an important source of livelihood for the tribals, the Government of Odisha is yet to recognize it as a legitimate land-use and has declared all such cultivation areas, including forest land, as Government land.

Table 5.10: Land Acquisition, Transfer and Alienation

Name	*Area Required (acre)*	*Families expected to be displaced*	*Affected villages*	*Remarks*
POSCO Steel Plant	4100	3700	11	POSCO would displace nearly 22,000 people from Dhinkia, Nuagaon and Gadakujang Gram Panchayats
Kalinganagar	13000	1150	16	The Government had acquired the land at Kalinganagar during 1990 and 1996 and paid compensation of Rs. 35.14 crore for 6895 acre of private land at an average cost of Rs. 51,000 per acre.
Mahanadi Coal Field Ltd., Talcher	13,610	12209.33	77	—
Arcelor-Mittal (Steel Plant)	8000	3000	4	15,000-17,000 people are expected (Steel Plant) to be displaced in Keonjhar district.

Source: District Administration and Field Study.

As per Panchayat (Extension to Scheduled Areas) Act, 1996 land acquisition power has been vested with the Gram Sabha or Panchayat, which mandates that there should be consultation before land acquisition for development projects and before resettling or rehabilitating persons affected by such projects. But in Odisha, the District Collectors and Special Land Acquisition Officers have been asked by the revenue department to submit proposals for the acquisition of land in scheduled areas along with copies of the resolution of concerned Gram Sabha/Panchayat.

Tribal Policy and its Effect on Land Alienation

It is presumed that setting up industrial units, including SEZs, may become more difficult in areas inhabited by the tribal population in the days to come. The New Tribal Policy is all set to provide land ownership rights to the tribal population. This would not only make their eviction process stringent, but also increase the liability for the acquirer to resettle and rehabilitate the tribal families. The move would impact mining, paper and metal-based industries. It would become difficult for a company to acquire tribal land. When the SEZs acquire single crop land, the worst hit would be the marginal and small farmers with fragmented holding as well as limited irrigation infrastructure for the second crop. This affects sharecroppers and agricultural labourers who do not get any compensation as they do not have title to the land. Two notified SEZs in Odisha will come up in the coastal districts of Bhadrakh, Jajpur, Jagatsinghpur where at the moment the number of landless is more than the land available for distribution. With the setting up of SEZs in these districts, the number of land less will increase further and since the barren and cultivable wasteland will be acquired by the SEZs, the available land for distribution will again go down. This will imply further marginalization and change of profession especially for the marginal farmers, sharecroppers and landless labourers.

There are two crucial issues that need attention with reference to the alienation of the small and marginal landholders. If on one hand, the Apex Court in the *Haryana SEZ* case in 2007 has held that farm land cannot be acquired for SEZs, in States like Odisha the relevant land legislations (explained elsewhere) have been amended to convert agricultural land into non-agricultural purpose with prior notice and a premium. The Apex Court conditions will not be applicable, once such conversion process is over. Secondly, with regard to the compensation on land acquisition, evicted people due to SEZ will not get land against land or relative compensation. They will get suitable employment.

In Odisha, cashew plantation has been raised by Soil Conservation Department on 1,20,000 hectares of so-called "Government Wastelands" in Schedule V areas which the tribals had been cultivating for many years even without the record of rights. During settlement, many tribals could not get their possessions recorded, due to their lack of awareness, and thus the land under their possession was recorded as government wasteland and in some cases was transferred to the Forest Department. Therefore, as per subsequent laws, the tribals became encroachers in their own ancestral lands. The Soil Conservation

Department with a view to check soil erosion in big dams like Machkund, Kolab, Chitrakonda and Indravati, undertook massive cashew plantation under different schemes. In order to bring the tribals to do watch and ward, the Department went into an agreement which promised distribution of cashew plantation areas among the landless, marginal and small farmers.

When the Cashew Development Corporation took over the onus of cashew plantation in April 1979, it could not run profitably and so started leasing out the production and marketing of cashew crops to private parties, invariably non-tribals. During the 1980s, there was a mushrooming of such cashew plantations in degraded non-forest lands where invariably rights of the local community existed or which were shifting cultivation areas in districts like Ganjam, Gajapati, Rayagada, Kandhamal and Malkangiri. Thus, lands that were once with tribals were now with private corporations, with the tribals getting no compensation or rehabilitation.

Table 5.11: Violation of Tribal Rights

PESA	*Odisha Government Land Settlement Manual, 1983*	*OSATIP Regulation, 1956*
Traditional rights over land was not recognized in the Schedule V Area—No resolution at the Palli Sabha/Gram Sabha was made.	The Soil Conservation Department had obtained permission from the Revenue Department for cashew plantation—Odisha Cashew Development Corporation did not have land lease permission to go in either for tender or putting the revenue land for long term lease.	In 2005, the Revenue Department gave tree *patta* to 1500 families of 37 villages in 7 panchayats but the *patta* land of Similiput village was auctioned to another party in the year 2006 by Corporation. In 2007, Odisha Cashew Development Corporation gave tender of the Godiput cashew land, where *patta* was already given to 32 families.

Source: Government of Odisha, Revenue Department publication.

There is a growing dispute around a cashew plantation in Kamda village of Tentulikhunti block in Nabarangpur district leading to the formation of two groups. The cashew plantation that spreads over 160 acre of government land in the village was started in 1985-86 under the

ERRP programme of the Soil Conservation Department., Government of Odisha. Out of 160 acre of land, 50 acre has already been distributed amongst the poor families in the village. The dispute exists over the remaining 110 acre of land. The government land on which the cashew plantation exists was long cultivated by a few people in the village. People of the village had lodged complaints and allegation against the people who have forcefully acquired government land for cultivation. However, there has been no action from the government and the group continued to cultivate this land. As per government rules, this land needs to be rightfully distributed amongst the poorest of poor for agricultural purposes. However, due to the problems and disputes the land could not be distributed. All the 110 acres of cashew plantation is now handed over to the Panchayat for protection and safekeeping. The Panchayat has accordingly identified 105 families who rightfully deserve to be the beneficiary of the land out of which 29 acre has been given to Scheduled Tribes, 50 belong to Scheduled Castes and 26 belong to other categories.

It is the coastal districts, the rate of conversion of agricultural land into non-agricultural purpose is high. It is increasing the number of marginal holdings, agri-labourers and the landless.

Table 5.12: The Percentage of Farmers and Agri-Labourers (1981-2001)

Year	*Percentage of farmers*	*Percentage of Agri-labourers*
1981	40.4	23.9
1991	38.7	25.1
2001	36.4	22.04

Source: District Census Handbook.

Table 5.12 indicates that small and marginal holders within the Scheduled Caste and Scheduled Tribe communities are fast losing their land either through outright sale or through leasing. One of the reasons for the increase in the percentage of partial leasing within the tribals could be the growth of informal commercial farming from Gajapati to Nabarangpur district—a huge tribal area that encompasses issues like Naxalism, landlessness, forestland cultivation, high input oriented commercial farming, hunger and malnutrition.

According to Table 5.13, the State loses about 37,000 hectares of agricultural land every year. The loss in agricultural land is about 9 per cent which is alarmingly high. But the loss in the two other categories is about 50 per cent which is worrying.

Table 5.13: Loss of Agricultural Land

Agricultural Land (million hectares)			*Gochar land (million hectares)*			*Cultivable wasteland (million hectares)*		
1990-91	2005-06	Percentage loss	1990-91	2005-06	Percentage loss	1990-91	2005-06	Percentage loss
63.04	57.39	9	8.00	4.00	50	6.00	3.00	50

Source: Land Governance study, Odisha.

Current Issues and Challenges—Suggested Actions

Any loss or decline of village common lands severely affects social and economic systems in rural India. Identification and legal categories of common lands are not clear and there is ambiguity in the allocation of management responsibility and procedures, which may even encourage encroachments. CPRs available to the villagers declined substantially over the years, following the expansion of State control over these resources but resulting in open access situations, as well as due to individualization /privatization, industrialization, urbanization, unauthorized encroachments and illegal regularization etc. Besides, the over-use and over-exploitation of existing common resources has led to deterioration in its quality. The average size of the common village lands per household in Odisha is 0.28 ha in 2014, while the percentage of land under Gochar is 3 per cent and under village forest also 3 per cent. However, Gochar land as per Rules should have been around 5 per cent and village forest around 10 per cent.

'Commons' or Common Property Land Resource (CPR) are with the boundary of the village and commonly used resources like village pastures and grazing grounds, government forests, wasteland, common threshing grounds, watershed, drainage, ponds and tanks, rivers, rivulets, water reservoirs, canals and irrigation channels. Any loss and decline of village common land severely affects social and economic system in rural Odisha. Identification and legal categorization of common land are not clear and there is ambiguity in the location of management responsibility and procedures which may even encourage encroachment. The average size of the common village land per household in Odisha 0.24 hectares as in 2014, why the percentage of land under gochar is 3 per cent and under village forest it is 3 per cent.

Two-thirds of all land in the State, and even 80 per cent in the Scheduled V Areas, is recorded as government land; it is under the ownership of either Revenue or Forest Department. Almost 30 per cent of total rural area in the State was public land under revenue department, varying from 35 per cent in Scheduled districts to 18 per cent in non-Scheduled districts. The government has become the main landholder. In practice, most government lands are used as common resources either *de facto* or *de jure*.

In nearly, nineties, Odisha rode on the economic reforms and liberalization process started in India to attract investments leveraging on its natural resources to unleash State's development (GoO, 2006+) with State according greater priority to industrial and urban development, the land available for the agricultural purposes has been declining over the year owing to unbiased transfer for non-agricultural purposes. While, commitments received by the State is over 2.3 trillion US$ since the turn of the century around land-intensive industries, there has been a sharp reduction of productive public lands (under tree crops and groves, pastures and culturable wasteland) during 1990-2013. Land acquisition process in the State, particularly for industrial and economic development, has been fraught with protest and mistrust by communities and civil society. Repeated audits by CAG have reported irregulatories by the State Government to favour industrialization in the State. While the latest Right to Fair Compensation and Transparency in Land Acquisition, Resettlement and Rehabilitation Act, 2013, have some provisions to address equity, justice and sustainability issue through a more participatory and responsible land acquisition process there has been resistance in adapting to the cumbersome procedures laid out. During the last 50 years a number of laws have been enacted in Odisha in order to establish the legal framework for land reforms (e.g. Odisha Estates Abolition Act, 1952, Odisha Survey and Settlement Act, 1958). Odisha Land Reforms Act, 1960, subsequently, the Odisha Consolidation of holdings and prevention of Fragmentation of Land (OCH and PFL) Act, 1972, (to prevent unauthorized occupation of government land). Odisha, like many other States has enacted legislations to abolish tenancy (Land Leasing), except in the case of the disability (the definition of which includes widows, divorcee, unmarried women etc.).

Out of the total 11,065 Gramdan's made in the entire country by the November 1965. Odisha made a handsome contribution of 2807 Gramdans and thus occupied the second place in the country in that respect. Since 1951 to the year 2012, around 6,38,706.50 acre of land was collected as donation by the Bhoodan Yagna Samiti. So far 5,79,994 acre has been distributed among 1,52,852 landless persons according to the Bhoodan Yagna Samiti (BYS). A special land rights campaign named "*Mo Jami Mo Diha*" was launched by the Government of Odisha since 2007 to protect the land rights of poor.

The objective of the campaign are:

(a) To protect and ensure the land rights of the poor who were allotted lease of government lands earlier or restore their lost land.
(b) Dovetailing the programme with the development schemes to ensure that the land allottees are in a better position to utilize.
(c) To assist the poor with emphasis on those belonging to ST and SC communities, to retain their land and homestead land with the existing legal framework. Under this campaign (up to end of December 2011) out of 2,33,484 numbers of cases received for verification 141,808 cases have been disposed of.

Since inception of OLR Act, 1960 till December 2011, land restored in favour of the STs and SCs families 23 and 23A of the Act, is given in table below:

Table 5.14: Land Restoration to SC and ST

Social Category	*No. of beneficiaries*	*Area of land ordered for restoration (in acre)*
SC	25271	17805.684
ST	14084	13183.432
Total	**39355**	**30989.116**

Source: Government of Odisha.

The implementation of Alienated Land Restoration to the SC and ST is an important provision and its continuous monitoring is very necessary. Even now the status of the cases of illegal transfer of tribal land reported is very large as per the Government record. During 2011-12 (till September 2011) the number of cases instituted is 34,702 involving land areas of 32,824.77 acre aliented to non-tribal persons, of which 27,905 number of case involving land area of 23,641.39 acre have been disposed of. With enactment of new legislations like FRA the habitat rights of PVTGs and Community Forest Resource rights of village community have been at least statutorily recognized.

5.9 Women's Property Rights in Odisha

The relevant land laws which are formulated for the Property Rights of Women are not properly implemented. The Government of Odisha has directed to issue joint *patta* in the name of both husband and wife while setting the government wasteland, house sites and ceiling surplus lands with landless persons (through a series of administrative circulars commencing with letter no. 48425 dated 19th August, 1987). In one of such circulars, i.e. letter no. 73774/R dated 27-12-1989, the Government observed that the tehsildars are not issuing *pattas*/intimation slips jointly in the name of husband and wife. Reiterating the earlier order, the letter emphasized that in case of widow or widower, *patta*/intimation slip may be issued in the name of individual applicant and also directed the Tehsildars to return the application received for the assignment of land to the applicant if the same has not been signed both by husband and wife and also with the instruction that they apply jointly. Further in letter no. LD-25/2008-28733/R&DM dated 03-07-2008, the govt while enhancing the limit of distribution of government land for house site under Vasundhara Scheme from 4 decimal to 10 decimals, the government also have reiterated that the lease of homestead land needs to be made jointly, i.e. in the name of the wife followed by the name of the husband.

In the Settlement of Donger Land exclusively in favour of tribal women, the Government in its letter no. S-23/93-17783/R dated 21st April, 1994, the then Revenue and Excise Department had ordered that the Donger land should be recorded exclusively in favour of Tribal Women in Kashipur Tehsil areas by the Settlement authorities as Settlement of such land in favour of the tribal people has been taken up recently for the first time in the State. The Tehsildar should *suo motu* settle the said land in favour of the tribal women. It also ordered that the aforesaid instruction should be followed in respect of all the Donger lands relating to Tribal Sub-plan area of the State where settlement of such land has to be taken-up in future for the first time by the settlement authorities.

In the year 2008, in the matter of issues of tree *pattas* and Dafayati rights, the Chief Secretary in his letter no. GE (GL)-23/2008/51607/R&DM dated 11-12-2008 has issued a circular for issue of tree *patttas* and recognizing 'Dafayati' Rights of ST persons in Tribal areas to the maximum extent of 2 acre cashew plantations per family, in which the names of both husband and wife of the beneficiary family need to be recorded.

In the Section 2 (f) of Rehabilitation and Resettlement Policy 2006 of Government of Odisha, it is mentioned about family with regard to an unmarried women of 30 years above to be treated as a separate family. Likewise widow and divorced women are also treated as separate family. But there is no mention about giving priority to ensure employment of women. Women specific need assessment and resettlement and rehabilitation provisions is absent in the Odisha R&R Policy. Active role of women in State-level movements for Gandha Mardan, Chilika, Kashipur, Kalinganagar and Dhinkia area of Erasama in Jagatsinghpur district—all reflect the active participation of women. The Gram Sabha or the Panchayats at the appropriate level shall be consulted before making the acquisition of land in the Scheduled Areas for development projects.

The Land Reforms Implementations and its impact so far has been as follows:

- High prevalence of unrecorded tenancy/illegal lease transactions; sharecropping being ubiquitous, its adverse impact on crop production.
- Very limited success of ceiling surplus land distribution strategy.
- Tardy implementation of land regularization and distribution.
- Inaffective implementation of access of government land to weaker section.

Desirable Land Rights Recognitions:

- Identification of concealed tenancy and recognition of rights on tenants.
- Lands above 10 degree slopes not surveyed and settled.
- Further alienation of land settled with STs through private transactions.
- Lack of proper recording of occupation rights through survey and settlements.
- Inadequate survey and demarcation of Particularly Vulnerable Tribal Group (PVTG)'s lands over which rights are not settled
- Once recognized collective use rights such as *kudki patta* not working a ground level.
- Gray areas around recognition and recording of women rights over property; Recognition granted only in Hindu Succession Act, 1956, but not enforceable on ground.

Massive encroachment (by contract farmers, companies' influential individuals) and easy alienation of common lands are taken place by massive encroachment for development projects leading to more vulnerability for the poor who depend upon such lands for their livelihood support. Even they are not protected by the Revenue Department for the purposes for which such lands have been "set-aside". During 1990 to 2009, the lands under permanent pastures and other grazing lands have decreased from 7.2 lakh ha. to 4.9 lakh ha. There is no detailed information available about other categories of common lands at State level.

There prevails complete lack of awareness among the Panchayats/ Gram Sabhas their role in maintaining and protecting the commons. No coordination exists between Revenue Department on one hand and Panchayats/Gram Sabhas on the other on such issues even after the Supreme Court judgement ordered to hand over the common land to Gram Panchayats/ Gram Sabhas management by them.

CAG report on Land Acquisition tabled in Assembly in 2012 reported that, Revenue and Disaster Management Department allotted 20,346 ha., including 13,498 ha. (66%) of acquired private land, to 107 promoters for setting up industries in 16 districts. However, since the lands were acquired by the State by application of "public purposes" to promote industrialization, there was 'legally' no transfer of land for private purposes.

The Odisha R & R Policy, 2006 that was based upon the LA Act as its principal legislation, did also refrain from recognizing the unrecorded rights. The public do not get any compensation against acquisition of the common land they depend upon, against acquisition of forests wherefrom they collect their fuel and NTFP or against acquisition of water bodies which serve the lifeline of people, as their rights over these common property resources are non-recorded.

Table 5.15: Data from IDCO Site about Public Land Allocation

(*in Acres*)

Requirement as per MOU/IPICOL's appraisals/Government	*Extent of land applied*	*Land allotted*		
		Government	*Pvt.*	*Total*
MoU 107,589	96,064	13,536	28,725	42,261
Non-MoU 59,674	49,631	6,894	9,790	16,684
Total 167,263	**145,695**	**20,430**	**38,515**	**58,945**

Source: Government of Odisha, IDCO, Bhubaneswar.

CAG in its audit of IDCO in 2012 on land acquisition rapped the State Government for not maintaining comprehensive and centralized data on acquisition and allotment of land.

Community Claims

Community claims involves a total of 6,62,089.11 acre (5,10,925.00 acre to individuals and 1,51,164.11 acre to community) as per the statistics in the website of Ministry of Tribal Affairs, GoI.

VASUNDHARA (Distribution of House-sites to Homesteadless Persons)

The scheme was initiated to provide homestead plots to the 3,00,000 landless families in the State while 2,49,334 homestead-less families were identified in the State (GoO, 2012).

As per Annual reports of Revenue and Disaster Management Department, GoO, however, till 2012-13, 1,99,904 families were covered including SCs (25%) and STs (45%) (GoO, 2013).

Mo Jami Mo Diha

As of 2012-13, a total of 2,130,410 number of cases were instituted out of which 73 per cent (1,553,253) cases were disposed of.

Odisha Government Land Settlement (Amendment) Rules, 2010

5.3 lakh families benefited (average about 2 decimal per family as per Annual report 2010-11 of RDM Department. Under OGLS, 82,861 homestead-less and 22,634 landless families were provided homestead lands till December 2012 (GoO, 2013).

Distribution of Government Wasteland for Agricultural Purposes

As of 2011-12, 7.45 lakh acre (24% to SC and 52% to ST) of agricultural lands were distributed to 4.88 lakh farmers (including 22% SC and 48% ST farmers) as reported in the Annual Reports (2006-07 to 2012-13) of Revenue and Disaster Management Department, Odisha.

The State Cabinet approved Odisha State Policy for Girls and Women 2014 in July 2014. The Policy would enable women groups to claim their rights over assets, land and housing and ensure inheritance rights. As per the provisions, the Government would provide free land and homestead land to the landless women and widows above the age of 45 years and disabled women. The women SHGs would be provided at least four decimals of Government lease land free of premium.

Besides, stamp duty would be waived for women for registration of land and house and other immovable property, whether bought or obtained as gift.

5.10 Tenancy Situation in Odisha

The abolition of tenancy in order to vest land ownership with the actual tillers of the lands formed the corner-stone of most land reform efforts in India after Independence in 1947. It was predicated on the widely held belief that the tillers of the land were locked in exploitative relationships with intermediaries who had little interest in the land but for the extraction of rent. The Odisha Estates Abolition (OEA) Act, 1952 initially permitted landowners to resume 33 standard acre for personal cultivation (Section 2.3), which led to the large-scale eviction of tenants. No parallel legislation was introduced to protect tenants. Under the Odisha land reforms (OLR) Act, 1960 (as amended in 1972), the leasing of land was explicitly banned, except where lessees fell into certain excluded categories. Under the 'adverse possession' clause in the OLR Act, if it can be demonstrated that a tenant has cultivated a parcel of land continuously for 12 years, permanent occupancy rights to that land may legally pass to the tenant. But the institution of tenancy has proved to be highly resilient on the ground, for reasons outlined below, and attempts to regulate tenancy by legislative means have been counterproductive. It is as widespread in Odisha as it is illegal, though now less exploitative and better concealed from official records.

A substantial literature now corrects many long-standing perceptions that share tenancy is necessarily inefficient or that landlord-tenant relations are necessarily exploitative. Share tenancy represents a second-based response to missing, thin and imperfect markets for land, credit, labour management, information and insurance and performs some very important functions which would otherwise have to be fulfilled by other institutions: tenancy contracts often play an important role in matching land, labour and capital endowments.

There is general agreement that available data on both number of tenants and the acreage under tenancy are underestimates. Both the Census of Land Holdings carried out by the National Sample Survey Organization and the Agricultural Census, tend to underestimate the proportion of land under tenancy. The under-estimation of tenancy stems from reporting bias as lessors tend to understate the leased out area owing to the fear that tenants will stake claims in favour of continued right of cultivation, desire to escape the ceiling on land holdings. The share of operated area leased in is therefore considered to be a more reliable measure of the magnitude of agricultural tenancy than the share of owned area leased out as lessees have fewer incentives to under-report the extent of area leased-in. Nonetheless, land reform legislations designed to prohibit sub-letting regulate rents and confer security of tenure has given many landlords and tenants a common interest in concealing agreements which may be deemed illegal.

It is estimated that on average, 10-20 per cent of households in each village participate in the land-lease market in Odisha, although, this is subject to wide inter- and intra-regional variation. NSS data reported that 17 per cent of households have leased in land in 1981-82. More than 80 per cent of the based-in area is in the size class of less than 10 acre, and the percentage of leased in area to operated area decreases with the increase in size of operational holding. At the same time, 85 per cent of the area leased out is the farmers with less than 10 acre. Together, these results indicate considerable leasing activity by small and marginal farmers. Land leasing or tenancy may take the form of fixed rentals or sharecropping arrangements, in which rents are paid in cash, in kind, or a combination of two, but sharecropping is the predominant, though declining, form of tenurial arrangement in Odisha. About 42 per cent of the leased-in area is under sharecropping as against about 14 and 8 per cent respectively under fixed produce and fixed rent contracts. However, share tenancy seems to be more prevalent in non-irrigated villages than in irrigated villages. More than 40 per cent of the operational area is under share tenancy in dry villages in Dhenkalan district as against 12-19 per cent in irrigated villages in Cuttack district. This is to confirm the persistence of the potential of risk-sharing under sharecropping contracts. Fixed tenancy payment in varieties of cash and kind is common in the irrigated villages in Sambalpur district. Only about 20 per cent of land leasing households were found to participate in sharecropping contracts. They were small landowners and the primary reason for leasing-out land was their inability to cultivate land either with the help of family labour or by hired labour. In leasing out landowners, employ various devices to get around the law banning tenancy. Most contracts are oral and of short duration. Oral contracts help to ensure that tenants are not recognized in the updated land records during survey and settlement operations. At the same time, short-term contracts (typically 2-5 years) prevent tenants from establishing claims to land through adverse possession.

Table 5.16: Typology of Land Tenancy Contracts in Different Parts of Odisha

Form	*Terms of Contract*	*Common among*		*Geographical location*	*Whether limited to particular crops*
		Lessors	*Lessees*		
Share cropping	Gross output divided equally (1:1) between landlord and tenant after deduction of expenditure on chemical fertilizers or HYV seeds.	Small and marginal farmers	Landless, small and marginal farmers	Sambalpur	No
	Gross output divided equally (1:1) between landlord and tenant.	Small and marginal farmers	Landless, small and marginal farmers	Cuttack, Khurda, Gopalpur	Paddy, gram, lentils and jute
	Gross output divided either (1:20) or (1:3) between landlord and tenant respectively.	Small and marginal farmers.	Small and marginal farmers.	Cuttack	Potato
Fixed tenancy in kind	Agreed amount (8-10 bags/acre/crop) to be paid after harvest, tenant responsible for cultivation.	Medium farmers	Small and marginal farmers	Sambalpur	Paddy
Fixed tenancy in cash	Agreed amount of cash paid to landlord before getting access to land .	Medium farmers	Small and marginal farmers	Sambalpur	Paddy

Source: Swain, M. (1998) *Peasant Agriculture and Share Tenancy in Odisha.* New Delhi: Commonwealth Publishers.

The common reasons for leasing out land in Odisha are the lack of supervisory labour, lack of bullock power, small uneconomic holdings and poor quality of lands. The reasons for leasing-in are limited to non-farm employment opportunities, availability of bullocks and increase in operational holdings. In practice, land owners are easily able to ensure that the record-of-rights in land do not get mention and tenants also have good reason to conceal tenancy because of their personal interest. The tenancy in Odisha is mostly share-cropping and it is considered as illegal. The rent paid by the lessee in almost in excess of the legally stipulated one-fourth of the gross produce. Many of those seeking to lease-in land are either the landless or the small and marginal farmers both land owners and tenants have their own reasons to conceal tenancy arrangement.

Ramya Ranjan Patel (2015), in his study of "Practice of Tenancy in an Irrigated and Unirrigated Regions", has given his analysis of the extent and types of tenancy in the unirrigated and irrigated villages. In the backward unirrigated villages of Nuapara district the land lease market is largely dominated by the small holders. Marginal and small farmers who have a relatively larger presence in the village together account for 60 per cent of the total households leasing-in: they also account for 37.84 per cent of the total area leased-in. The only other groups farmers constituting 40 per cent of semi-medium operations leased in 48.65 per cent of the operated area. In these villages there is neither a single large farmer, nor the existing medium farmers leasing in any land. Thus, it is clearly evident that leasing-in purely continues with the small farmers. In the irrigated developed villages 31.25 per cent of the households leasing-in land belong to the marginal and small categories, while they lease-in only 15.39 per cent of the total area in the semi-medium category. However, the top few categories which accounts for 68.75 per cent of households leasing-in land and the area leased in is 84.61 per cent of the total area leased-in. In total 39 per cent of the leased-in household under small and marginal farm size groups leased-in 65.87 per cent of the area. Thus, in these villages both the small and the large size classes of holders are leasing in land for the upper size group is higher than the lower farm size groups. In the irrigated villages though there is higher incidence of leasing-out households among the small and marginal categories, the area leased-out is much lesser than the higher farm size groups. The percentage as well as the number of household leasing-out is higher at the small categories and higher at the large categories. Another important point that comes out is that the incidences as well as the area of leasing out is much lesser in the unirrigated rainfed villages in comparison to the developed irrigated villages. This reflected the fact that a proportionately higher percentage of the marginal, small and other lower category farmers were on leased-in land for augmenting the low size of their operational holding. But a new phenomenon of reverse tenancy has started since 1981-83. But, in 1992 for the first time, this trend got reversed. And the percentage of tenant farmers was higher than the lower class categories. The pattern of tenancy has drastically changed from the small and marginal farmers leasing-in large area of land in backward rainfed agriculture from large farmers to large farmers leasing-in more numbers in advanced irrigated agriculture from the small farmers. The phenomenon of reverse tenancy was especially strong in the agriculturally advanced States. All the leasing-in under share-cropping are dominant by small marginal category of farmers. Fixed produce is more prevalent in the irrigated region. The comparison shows that in the unirrigated villages sharecropping is the dominant mode of leasing-in and in the irrigated villages fixed produce and fixed cash is the dominant mode. The most important region for leasing-in as reported by majority of tenant is non-availability of alternative job opportunity (Swain, 1999).

Table 5.17: Incidence of Tenancy in Different States Based on NSSO Reports

NSSO Reports	*Report 36 (8th round)*	*Report 215 (26th round)*	*Report 330 (37th round)*	*Report 388 (48th round)*	*Report 492 (59th round)*	*Report NSSO Key Indicators (70/18.1) (70th round)*
States	*1953-54*	*1972-73*	*1981-82*	*1992-93*	*2002-03*	*2012-13*
Andhra Pradesh	21.2	9.0	6.2	9.6	9.97	35.70
Assam	43.0	16.7	6.4	8.9	5.06	4.20
Bihar	12.4	14.5	10.3	3.9	11.76	22.67
Gujarat	19.4	3.9	2.0	3.3	5.08	5.82
Haryana	39.8	23.3	18.2	33.7	14.38	14.82
Himachal Pradesh	n.a.	15.9	3.2	4.8	2.87	5.33
Jammu & Kashmir	22.1	8.1	2.5	3.7	0.32	0.20
Karnataka	21.5	15.9	6.0	7.4	3.68	6.90
Kerala	20.2	8.6	2.1	2.9	4.18	8.93
Madhya Pradesh	19.8	7.5	6.6	6.3	2.83	5.14
Maharashtra	19.7	6.2	5.2	5.5	4.59	3.44
Odisha	12.6	13.5	9.9	9.5	13.15	16.96
Punjab	39.8	28.0	16.1	18.8	17.84	24.42
Rajasthan	21.0	5.3	4.3	5.2	2.81	7.11
Tamil Nadu	27.0	13.1	10.9	10.9	6.10	13.54
Uttar Pradesh	11.4	13.0	10.2	10.5	3.49	7.89
West Bengal	25.4	18.8	13.4	10.4	9.42	14.73
All India	**20.6**	**10.6**	**7.2**	**8.3**	**6.60**	**10.41**

Source: NSSO Reports: Report 492 (59th round) for 2002–03, and NSS Key Indicators (70/18.1) (70th round) for 2012-13 data.

The data (in Table 5.17) of NSSO provides the area leased-in by different States. At the all India level the area leased-in has declined from 20.6 per cent during 1953-54 to 10.41 per cent by 2012-13. There is considerable variation in area leased-in different States. It is highest in the State of Andhra Pradesh (35.70%) followed by Punjab (24.42%), Bihar (22.67%), Odisha (16.96%), West Bengal (14.73%) and Tamil

Nadu (13.54%). The leasing in percentage in Odisha during 2012-13 is as high as 16.96 per cent. However, the incidence of tenancy increased from 13.15 per cent during 2002-03 to 16.96 per cent during 2012-13. It also assumes criticality as during the Odisha drought year of 2014 in the rural suicides, the tenants were one of the major victims.

Landesa (2017) had conducted a study on 152 tenants undertaking tenancy cultivation and found that there were two primary types of tenancy being practiced—*Kata* (lease) and *Sanja* (sharecropping). Neither involved a written agreement. In both, the period of tenancy was frequently annual, but was dependent on the relationship and level of trust between the tenant and the land-owner. Sharecropping continues to be the dominant cropping pattern, but in irrigated area it is transforming to fixed crop tenancy. It is estimated that on average, 10-20 per cent of households in each village participate in the land lease market in Odisha, although this is subject to wide inter- and intra-regional variation. Most sharecroppers lack access to formal institutional credit and borrow money from informal lenders for cultivation. Due to lack of valid documents, sharecroppers lack access to government minimum support price. As they lack recognition by the government, sharecroppers lack access to any government benefits. Sharecroppers lack the sense of security due to short-term arrangements and lack of written agreement. All the sharecroppers interviewed (100%) supported a formal written agreement with copies kept by sharecropper, landowner and a third person. Most of the sharecroppers support concept of landlord resuming or sell land in extraordinary circumstances. They preferred that Revenue Department provide identity cards to sharecroppers to facilitate access to loans and other benefits. In case of crop loss, 60 per cent believed government compensation should be shared as per sharing agreement and 40 per cent believed it should be shared equally. They also believe that government should extend input subsidies directly to sharecroppers. Keeping in mind the input cost most (98%) believe that sharecroppers should be able to rent in up to 4 acre. The land owners cited that the major concerns they face currently for farming is lack of irrigation facilities which is a major issue. They cited that one reason for short-term arrangements is to avoid conflicts. Sharecroppers sometimes do not abide by verbal agreement and increasing labour costs contribute to leaving up to 20 per cent of land fallow. Out of the land owners interviewed, 80 per cent prefer not to have registered written agreement as they fear this will lead sharecroppers to claim ownership of land as per existing law in the State. This 80 per cent is ok with short-term, annual agreements on plain paper, with R.I. and PRI members as witnesses. About 20 per cent of the land owners interviewed are ok with registered, written agreements on stamp paper. Sharecropper should be able to use land only for cultivation and not demand ownership of the land. Landowners said that they should have unilateral right to terminate agreement at any time and 80 per cent believe government compensation for crop loss should go to landowners. An expert group consultation was held in Bhubaneswar to come up with a set of accommodation to be submitted to Niti Aayog in consonance with the Model Agricultural land leasing Act formulating by Niti Aayog. Country Director, Landesa, suggested for an alternative framework that addresses tenant insecurities and apprehensions of the land owners resulting into a win-win situation for both. The experts agreed on creating a mechanism to record tenants through engagement with the local community-level organisations, Panchayats, SHGs, Government institutions and financial institutions with a progressive intention of increasing visibility of the tenants. This exercise will help the tenants to access credit from the financial institutions; however, the experts suggested for an appropriate procurement policy to enable tenants to get a fair price for their produce. The solution to the entire gamut of problems that tenants are facing and recording tenancy will address the input level barriers, credit, protective measures including insurance against crop loss as well as increase market linkages. This is important in the context that the Odisha Government has recently formed a High level Committee to visit Andhra Pradesh and Telangana to study its implementation and submit recommendations.

Gyanendra Mani (2016) has made some observations on the Model Agricultural Land Leasing Act particularly about its Inherent Limitations. The Model Leasing Act, if adopted in the proposed form, may encourage the diversion of agriculture land from crop cultivation to commercial use because it allows leasing of agricultural land for activities like plantation crops, animal husbandry and dairy, poultry farming, stock breeding, fishery, agro-forestry, agro-processing and other related activities in addition to crop cultivation. Once agricultural land is transferred to allied activities, it will not only reduce the total land stock available for crop cultivation with an adverse impact on production of field crops but will also change the land-use pattern, if not permanently, at least for a very long period. This will be particularly true if land is used for plantation crops, agro-forestry and agro-processing activities. It is very likely that the transferred land may not remain suitable for growing field crops once it is resumed to the lessor. This fear is further compounded by the lack of clarity on the definition of lessee cultivator. The Model Leasing Act defines a lessee cultivator as a "person who leases in agricultural land". It is not clear whether corporates and absentee landlords willing to manage cultivation through their employees/representatives can be allowed to lease-in agricultural land or the leasing should be restricted to farmers/group of cultivators (self-help groups/joint liability groups/farmers producers organisations) including landless cultivators. Further, whether contract farming, particularly by corporates, should also fall under the purview of the proposed Model Leasing Act. There should not be any problem in leasing of agricultural lands by corporates if land use is restricted to cultivation of agricultural crops only since the leasing-in by corporates may lead to increased flow of investment to the agriculture sector. However, such contracts would affect the food security in the country, if choice of crops is solely motivated by profit. Perhaps what is more worrisome is allowing lease contracts between the parties for an indefinite period and that the "government shall not fix a minimum or maximum lease period". Prescribing ceiling on lease period, say for a maximum of five or six years, will not only help the lessee to complete one life cycle of agricultural allied activities (animal husbandry, etc.) but will also help the lessor to resume the cultivation if he/she had quit the cultivation in search of an alternative income opportunities but failed to succeed. Further, it would also reduce the risk of any influence/pressure on the lessor to lease out the land for a very long period and it might become very difficult for the survivors in the family to resume operating the land from an influential lessee. Thus, if the government does not fix maximum lease period, it will increase the risk of losing the contracted land permanently from food crops. He further points out that the ceiling on ownership holding must also be taken into account in the lessor-lessee relationship.

It would be useful to analyse the tenancy situation in Andhra Pradesh and the protection to tenant farmers in the context of Rural Suicides. In this background the government of Andhra Pradesh has come out with "Land Licensed Cultivators Act, 2011" with a view to provide legal security and "loan eligibility card" to the tenant farmers. In the principle, it will also safeguard the rights of land owners and the card is issued by the concerned revenue officer to the tenants. If there is any objection to the landowners, he/she has to report the same within 15 days. The card will enable tenant farmers secure institutional credit through banks, crop loss to the tenant farmers. The tenant will have a right over the harvest but not on the land. The banks are supposed to extend loan on the basis of the loan eligibility card without linking to the land records. At the same time, the land owner can get all types of loans except crop loan. The land owner can pledge the property while availing the loan though in effect it is the tenant who is cultivating.

It was revealed that the constraints faced by tenant farmers in continuing agriculture are due to the fact that there is no guarantee: that the banks would give loans on the basis of loan eligibility card. In fact, it has been proved that very few tenants are given loans till today, Further tenants are afraid of eviction, if they take loan in Godavari districts land owners have taken back the leased out lands by giving same excuses. Landowners are saying to tenants that they need card or land, let them decide. Moreover, land owners are not interested in furnishing survey numbers and signing on the applications. It clearly shows that the interest of land owners is only for obtaining harvest but not for tenants' welfare. There have been apprehensions by land landowners expressed in view of the Land Licensed Cultivators Act that are not seriously taken by the government. They are as follows:

- In case of non-repayment of loans availed by tenants, what will be our situation? If the government confiscates our land, who will come to our rescue?
- Why there is a condition that the land owner has to sign and provide survey number for issuing loan eligibility card? In principle, when the State Government has decided to issue the tenant recognition cards, they should issue the same without any condition.
- There is an apprehension that, in future, if the tenant goes to court claiming occupancy rights as evidence of written consent to record the same.
- If the tenants are provided loans against the same land what will be our fate? We may not be able to get the loans based on the same land.

It is clear from the study that the land licensed cultivators, though given LEC, were not able to access institutional credit leave alone crop insurance, input subsidy and various programmes of the government. It was noticed that the apathy of bankers is another important problem in accessing agricultural credit by the majority tenants. It was revealed that both the tenants and the landlords should get the credit and other benefits irrespective of ownership of the land. Many landowners have an apprehension that the tenants may eventually claim the ownership/occupancy rights over the land and they may lose land in the process. Therefore, the State Government should amend the Act which enables the government machinery to identify the tenants from the field based on the evidence of actual cultivation of land, issues them identity cards without linking it to the land and finally provide them benefits at par with the land owners.

Mamta Swain, in her empirical study on tenancy situation in Odisha has shown that the major manifestation of tenancy in Odisha is sharecropping. The break-up of total leased-in area into different types of tenancy reveals that in Odisha sharecropping is more pervasive than fixed produce and fixed money tenancy. In 2012-13 nearly 45 per cent of leased-in area was under sharecropping. The coverage under fixed money and fixed produce was only 6.9 per cent and 24.3 per cent respectively. Proportion of area under share tenancy was showing an increasing trend during 1971-2002. In 1971-72, 41.8 per cent of leased-in area was under sharecropping which increased to 73 per cent in 2002. The percentage of area under fixed produce has increased significantly from 13.6 per cent in 1971 to 24.3 per cent in 2012. Subsistence Tenancy is more widespread than commercial or capitalist tenancy (Swain, 1999). As per the N.S.S. 70th round report, in 2012-13 the number of leasing-in households in Odisha was 13.9 lakh whereas the number of leasing-out households was only 3.6 lakh. Thus, on an average for one lessor there were more than three tenants willing to lease in land. Due to large scale under-employment and unemployment in rural Odisha, the demand for leased-in land outstrips its supply. The terms and conditions of tenancy arrangements in Odisha are found to be inimical to tenant's interest. The predominant form of tenancy in Odisha is share tenancy and most of the tenants are marginal and small farmers. Also, it is found that marginal and small land owners are mostly sharecropping. But the big farmers are leasing on land on fixed produce or fixed money basis as they can bear the risk of making a fixed payment. Due to the fear of tenancy legislation, the durations of leases are being shortened. It is most unlikely that they share in input cost and take interest in actual cultivation. The tenant's major objective of leasing in land is to meet subsistence needs and not to cultivate land commercially. Thus, prevalence of non-legalised leasing by small peasants with high rents, no security of tenure and absence of cost sharing has been detrimental to agricultural growth of the State, as it adversely affects the use of yield enhancing inputs and investment in durable capital by the tenants. In spite of being prohibited, tenancy is quite widespread in Odisha and shows an increasing trend over the last five decades. The most important reason for such pervasiveness of tenancy is that there is no alternative job opportunity available for the tenants in the non-farm sector. Marginal and small farmers are leasing in land to produce crops to meet their consumption needs. In Odisha subsistence tenancy as a survival strategy is more observed than capitalist or commercial tenancy on profit motive. Landowners are increasingly leasing out land due to emigration of family members to urban areas for employment, unprofitability of self-cultivation, increase in wage cost and difficulty in labour supervision. Thus, tenancy seems to persist as a means of earning livelihood of the landless, land-deficient and labour-surplus households. Tenancy needs to be legalised and the restrictions on leasing out of land need to be revoked. Tenancy contracts need to be documented and recorded. Legalisation of tenancy will help in unearthing the large scale concealed tenancy existing in today's Odisha. (Mamta Swain, "Changes in Incidence of Tenancy in Rural Odisha: Implications for Second Generation Tenancy Reforms", Paper presented in NIRD Hyderabad, National Workshop held in 2016).

Land to the Landless

1. How much land is available in Odisha for distribution:
    - *Ceiling Surplus Land*—Ac. 17,664.380 (*Source*—Revenue Dept.)
    - *Bhoodan Land*—Ac. 58,722.58, (*Source*: Revenue Dept.)
    - *Waste Land*—Ac. 5,40,725.461, (*Source*: Revenue Dept.)
    - *Land to the tribal landless in Scheduled Areas*—government land in revenue records.
    - *Temple Land*—16,000 (Sixteen thousand temples) has huge land.
    - *Matha Land*—600 Matha (In an average minimum 10 acre per Matha).
    - *Jagannath Temple Land*—Ac. 56,653.29 (and Temple Office, Puri, Odisha Review).

    In the State of Odisha, Ceiling Surplus Land, Bhoodan Land, Waste Land and Temple Land, Matha Land and Jagannath Temple Land are available for distributions.
2. In 2007 the State Government has instructed to all the collectors under a programme "*Mo Jami and Mo Diha*" to physically verify the actual possession of ceiling surplus land and wasteland of 8,95,875 acre which are distributed to 6,21,085 beneficiaries who have only *Patta* without physical possession. Out of the total beneficiaries 2,84,564 were ST,

1,53,029 were SC and 1,83,452 are others. Similarly, Bhoodan Yagya Samiti has distributed 5,79,984 acre out of the total donated land of 6,38,706 acre to 1,52,852 number to land less persons. The Revenue Department Source says that with a view to improve the economic status of the weaker sections of the society and to boost agricultural production, the Government land up to one standard acre (2.5 acre) is being allotted to landless persons of the State since 1974-75. During the year 2011-12 till end of December 319.729 acre of Government waste land were distributed among landless families which need to be verified.

According to the latest information 6,58,230 number of applications have been received under the campaign "*Mo Jami Mo Diha*", out of which 621,751 number of cases of physical possession have been restored in favour of the beneficiaries as on 30-04-2013. The limitation of distribution of Government land under the 'Vasundhara' had been enhanced to 10 decimals from 4 decimals *vide* Revenue and Disaster Management Department Notification No. LD/25/2008-28733 dated 3-7-2008. After independence nearly 0.7 million acre of government wasteland has been provided to the landless in Odisha. In addition 5,80,000 acre of Bhoodan land has been distributed to the poor in Odisha (Pattnaik, 2008).

3. The Rights to common land and common property resources are owned by the Government but used by people. So, people have user rights over it. The community cannot sell or purchase commons. It has been observed that many communities are deprived of using such commons because of lack of such space in their locality Even the Government land under use of the communities are not being converted to CPR. It is often the dominant caste in a village that has almost monopolized their authority over commons. Whenever they aspire to access community land under the hegemonic control of caste-Hindus it results in caste conflicts and eventually atrocities of grievous nature against Dalits. Mostly the CPR, waste land, forest, water-bodies pasture and temple land are being given to private companies in the name of Government land, mining and industrial areas and seacoast, urban areas of the State. The private companies are using the CPR without respecting the need of the local community. It is suggested that the Government should adequately allocate common land

for use of common people and restrictions should be imposed on grabbing of common land.

4. The natural resource management policies in the State including access to and control over land, water and forest are now being decided from a mining and industrial perspective. For instance, recently released State Forest Policy is an IPR 2001 requirement, changes in the Odisha Land Reforms Act for making agricultural land conversion into non-agricultural purpose easier. Proposal has gone for making land transfer from tribals to non-tribals possible through amending the 1956 Regulation 2, besides, all the reforms supporting industrialization are primarily for easier forest clearance, simplified revenue laws etc.
5. Land distribution to the landless does not seem to have made much headway as a large number of people who had got land under various schemes and under ceiling surplus are still languishing in abject poverty due to lack of access to land. Issues that stand in the way are continuance of control by the previous owner, underdeveloped land, lack of record of rights etc.
6. As regards settlement of tribal land, figures reveal that though tribal areas have less number of landless as compared to the land available for distribution, majority of the development induced displaced in these districts are still not given land. This raises doubts about the actual availability of land provided in government records and the amount of land encroached by the rich and influential.
7. Joint *patta*, though an official necessity for land distribution, has not been very successful. One of the main reasons for this is that below poverty line have to deposit a processing fee that acts as a disincentive in applying for a joint *patta*.
8. Due to lack of necessary records, the land distributed under Bhoodan either has gone back to the people who distributed them or the government. Due to lack of records, in the coastal districts, a large chunk of Bhoodan land is being illegally encroached by the rich and the influential.
9. One of the crucial issues in land distribution in the State is the lack of records on different *kisam* (category) of land in different tehsils. This is the reason for which incorrect data on actual land possession and distribution is being given to the revenue headquarters. The scheme *Mo Jami Mo Diha* has only

remained as a scheme of promise and very limited actual field level verification is going on. Besides, the lack of proactive involvement of the field level revenue officials and resultant limited action has helped the encroachers in continuing illegal possession of ceiling surplus land. Moreover, most of the tehsils do not have correct records on the actual number of revenue villages, boundaries, *kisam* of land etc. There are either no or conflicting records on the amount of reserve forest areas at the district level for which the revenue authorities have even leased out forestlands.

10. The amendment to the Section 8A of the Odisha Land Reforms Act to facilitate conversion of agricultural land for non-agricultural purpose will certainly address population growth, check urban sprawls and habitation. But the associated danger could be that such easier ways to convert agricultural land into non-agricultural purpose could only end up promoting industrialization at the cost of farming. Such apprehensions seem to have a strong basis as the move for industrialization and the said legal changes have come almost during the same time. The amendment prescribes for 50 per cent and 100 per cent conversion fee for those who have done the conversion before and after 1993 respectively. The Central Government has directed the State Governments not to get involved as middlemen in the purchase of land and leave that to industries and farmers. Similarly, the Odisha Resettlement and Rehabilitation Policy of 2006 propose that industries may opt for direct purchase of land on the basis of negotiated price after issue of notification requiring acquisition of land. However, this may lead to the non-recognition and the dilution of the welfare role of the State and further exploitation of the tribals both by the project proponents and the emergent local land *dalals* (middlemen).
11. As per the SEZ provisions, up to 75 per cent of the area under large SEZs can be used for non-industrial purposes. This facility for the SEZs violates the provisions of the Resettlement and Rehabilitation Policy of Odisha, which says that land not utilized by the project within the prescribed time limit and also for the required purpose shall be resumed. This loophole is likely to be taken advantage of by private developers and property dealers. The Scheduled Tribes and Other Traditional Forest Dwellers (Recognition of Forest

Rights) Act, 2006 states that forestland rights can be vested to Scheduled Castes and Scheduled Tribes. These are visible contradictions to the SEZ provisions.

12. The State Government has taken a decision to strictly implement all rules and orders meant for overall development of tribals for which Task Forces at three levels have been formed—at the State level, at the district and at the sub-divisional level. The objective of the task force is to monitor the actual possession of land distributed under various schemes. While this is a positive move, the effectiveness of the task force committees is hampered as there is no regular meeting, no demand for action taken, and no data available on actual implementation.
13. Though many families have received land passbooks they do not have actual possession.
14. The Gram Sabha now have a limited role in the settlement of rights nor its consent is mandatory in diversion of forest land for non-forest purposes. This authority now lies with the sub-divisional committee. Similarly, as regards deciding the critical wildlife habitat in a protected area, Gram Sabha will have a smaller role. In cases of eviction or relocation, the Gram Sabha will only give its informed consent on the resettlement package. It will not have the right to disagree.
15. The small and marginal holders within the Scheduled Caste and Scheduled Tribe community are fast losing their land either through outright sale or through lease.
16. Odisha is getting a 'Mines Unlimited' identity which means that the check on the extent of forest and farm land diversion for mining will be minimal.
17. Large tracts of land leased out to companies are lying unused and no subsequent cancellation of lease has taken place.
18. Major conflicts that have taken place during land acquisition are because of the superseding of the decision of the Gram/Palli Sabha. Though the "informed consent" of the concerned Gram Sabha(s) is mandatory, more often than not this process follows unfair means.
19. In the undivided Kalahandi-Bolangir-Koraput area and other tribal districts like Kondhamal and Keonjhar, formal and informal forms of contract farming are going on without the knowledge of the government authorities. The terms and conditions of production and trade including price, inputs,

procurement, are heavily in favour of the traders or farming institutions.

20. State loses about 37,000 hectares of agricultural land every year. Such loss in agricultural land is about 9 per cent but with Gochar and cultivable waste the loss is about 50 per cent.
21. Agricultural area and holding size is decreasing on a gradual basis, which has impacted production. The small and marginal holders within the Scheduled Castes and Scheduled Tribes community are fast losing their land either through outright sale or through leasing.

Suggested Future Action

1. State Governments that have a sizeable acreage of land surplus due to the enforcement of ceiling limits, but that are not able to allot it due to litigation may immediately undertake an exercise to identify and segregate such cases.
2. Fallow land should be compulsorily taken over for allotment to Scheduled Caste families on a priority basis, making necessary provision in the existing laws, where necessary.
3. Land acquisition by Government for 'public purpose' should be minimized to the extent possible; for the provision of basic infrastructure.
4. The alarming rate at which agricultural land is being converted to non-agricultural land needs to be stopped.
5. All new homestead land distributed to landless families should be only in the woman's name.
6. The State should consider not proposing amendment to the Odisha Scheduled Areas Transfer of Immovable Property Regulation, 1956 that would enable transfer of tribal land to the non-tribals. On the contrary, it should strengthen the Odisha Scheduled Areas Transfer of Immovable Property Regulation, 1956 in lines with Samata Judgement and tribal land protection laws in Andhra Pradesh.
7. Survey of the hill slopes up to 300 should be mandatory and done in the States with Schedule areas and such lands should be settled in favour of tribals doing shifting cultivation and subsistence agriculture. This will not only confer land rights on the tribals occupying such lands, but also help improve the forest cover.
8. The government land in the Scheduled Districts to the Tribal Landless families need to be expeditiously distributed.

9. The Surplus Ceiling Land, Government Land and Bhoodan Land which are not under the possession of beneficiary should be entrusted in possession to them.
10. "*Mo Jami Mo Diha*" needs to be implemented with all seriousness.
11. The landlessness of the Scheduled Caste should be distributed ceiling surplus land and Bhoodan Land on priority basis.
12. The land to the homeless should be given top priority.
13. The Land Rights to women have been taken up as an important issue of land reforms in Odisha. The Government of Odisha has issued instructions to the District Collectors to earmark 40 per cent of ceiling surplus land for distribution among women including women of disadvantage groups, including SCs and STs. This needs to be implemented immediately.
14. There are large number of women landless labourors in the Mining areas of the State of Odisha. Land Rights should be extended to them.

Balic Land Rights in Jharkhand

Mundari-Khunt-kattidari

Section 8 of Chhotanagpur Tenancy Act, 1908 –Mundari-Khunt-kattidari means a Mundari, who has acquired a right to hold for the purpose of bringing suitable portions thereof under cultivation by himself or by male members of his family and includes:

(a) The heir male in the male line of any such Mundari when they are in possession of such land or have any subsisting title thereto; and
(b) As regards any portions of such land which has remained continuously in the possession of any such Mundari and his descendants in the male line, such descendants.

Section 4 of Chhotanagpur Tenancy Act, 1908 specifies following classes of tenants, namely:

1. Tenure-holders, including under-tenure-holders;
2. Raiyat, namely:
   (a) Occupacy-raiyats, that is to say, raiyats having a right of occupancy in land held by them;

(b) Non-Occupacy-raiyats, that is to say, raiyats not having such a right of occupancy; and

(c) Raiyats having Khunt-katti rights;

3. Under-raiyats, that is to say, tenants holding, whether immediately or mediately, under raiyats; and
4. Mundari khunt-kattidars.

[*Source*: Roy, R.N., Panday, (2009), *Handbook on Chhotanagpur Tenancy Laws*, Allahabad: Rajpal & Company, pp. 8-11].

Security of Tenancy under CNT Act

CNT Act defined rights and duties of all tenants and tenure holder. It gave protection to occupancy raiyat under Section 16 of CNT Act by ensuring the continuance of their occupancy in the land. Under Section 17 of CNT Act they defined settled raiyat (and their heir) as someone who has been holding land since last 12 years before the enactment of CNT Act. Under section 19 all the settled raiyats were granted occupancy rights of the land that was settled to them. These provisions have solidified the position of raiyat against unjust alienation from their ancestral land which was the major source of strife between them and government.

Under Section 18 of the Act, Mundari-Khunt-kattidari and Bhuinhars (surveyed in 1869 as discussed above) demand to be settled raiyats of their village and their occupancy right is guaranteed.

Raiyats can use land in any manner authorized by local custom or usage or in any manner which does not materially impair the value of land or render it unfit for the purpose of tenancy. It further defines what does not impair the value of land. Following use of land are deemed to not impair the value of land materially or to render it unfit for purpose of tenancy.

1. Manufacture of the bricks and tiles for domestic or agricultural purposes of the raiyats and his family.
2. Excavation of tanks or the digging of wells or the constructions of *bandhs* and *ahars* intended to provide a supply of water for drinking, domestic, agricultural or piscicultural purposes of the raiyats and his family.
3. Erection of building for the domestic or agricultural purposes of for the purposes of trade or cottage industries of the raiyats and his family.

Raiyats can plant, cut down and appropriate trees and bamboos, cut down and appropriate any trees standing on such land, appropriate the flower, fruits and other products of such land, rear lace cocoons subject to the provisions made in records of right. [*Source*: Jharkhand State Team, (2004) "Report on Local Governance Assessment Framework, Jharkhand", Ranchi: National University of Study and Research in Law, (pp. 39-40)].

Best Practices and Strength of Chhotanagpur Region

1. Section 46 of CNT Act, 1908 puts restriction on transfer of Scheduled Tribes (ST), Backward Class (BC) or Scheduled Caste (SC) land. An occupancy raiyat who is a member of ST may transfer with the previous sanction of Deputy Commissioner, his rights in his holding or a portion thereof by sale, exchange, gift or will to another person who is a member of Scheduled Tribe and who is a resident with a local limits of the area of a police station within which holding is situated. Similarly previous sanction of Deputy Commissioner is required for a member of SC or BC. These restrictions are immensely beneficial to the member of Scheduled Tribes, Scheduled Castes and Backward Classes.
2. No transfer in contravention of the above provisions shall be registered or shall be in any way be recognized by any court, whatever, in exercise of its civil, criminal or revenue jurisdiction.
3. The Deputy Commissioner shall be a necessary party in all suits of civil nature related to any holding or portion thereof in which one of the parties of the suits is a member of Scheduled Tribe and the other party is not a member of a Scheduled Tribe.
4. The Deputy Commissioner on his own motion or on application filed by a tribal raiyat, for annulling an illegal transfer, hold an enquiry and of he finds the transfer as illegal, he shall annul the transfer and evict the transferee from such holding or portion thereof and put the transferor in possession thereof.
5. Section 48 puts restriction on the transfer of Bhumihari tenure, the manner and extent of the restrictions are same as is in the case of an aboriginal raiyat and Deputy Commissioner is empowered to evict unlawful transferee.

6. Section 49 allows and raiyat to transfer his land for industrial, mining purpose and for other purposes subsidiary thereto. Sec. 71 "A" provides immense power to restore member of Scheduled Tribes over land unlawfully transferred. It is the most ideal law in the country. This section broadens the definition of transfer. It removes time bar regarding filing in of application. It provides for restoration of the transferor or heir of any other *bonafide* tribal raiyati of the village.
7. Section 72 of the CNT Act provides for the surrender of land a raiyati only with a previous sanction by Deputy Commissioner in writing (As amended in 1947).

[*Source:* Jharkhand State Team, (2004) "Report on Local Governance Assessment Framework, Jharkhand", Ranchi: National University of Study and Research in Law (pp. 43-44)].

Santhal Pargana Tenancy Laws

The Santhals had cleared the forest lands for which they held no security in the possession of the land which they made fit for cultivation. The outsiders who were non-santhals settlers gradually acquired more-and-more land from the Santhals through the instrumentality of the mortgeaes from them in returns from the loans. The Santhals were easily amenable to mortgages and loans. Once they took a loan it was difficult to return and so they were subjected to land alienation by the non-tribals who were designated as *Dikku* (exploiters). They were victim of land grabbing by *Mahajans*, the police, the revenue, and court officials. This process of land grabbing continued unabated from 1810-55 which resulted in the famous Santhal Insurrection of 1855. It was a marathon agrarian struggle led by the Santhal collectively leading to direct confrontation with the British Armed personnel resulting in bloodshed of thousands of Santhals, but the Santhals were not deterred by the heavy repression by the colonial State. It not only led to the formation of the district of Santhal Parganas but led to the separate land regulation for the Santhal Pargana areas. The Act 37 of 1855 and later on Santhal Settlement II of 1872 were promulgated. It declared the non-transferability of raiyati land and empowered the Deputy Commissioner to interfere with illegal land alienation. In 1949 the tenancy laws of district was further supplemented by Bihar Act XIV of 1949, the Santhal Pargana Tenancy (Supplementary Provisions) Act, 1949 it incorporated some of the customary laws of the district which included exchange of raiyati land, sub-letting lands, specifying the Rights of raiyats and so on. The important officials of the Santhals became the *Manjhi* (headman), the *paramanik*, the *Jog Manjhi*, the *Nayak* and the *Gorait*. The *Manjhi* is the headman of the village. He collects rent and holds rent-free land for his services and also settles village disputes according to the tribal system of the governance. The Headman or *Manjhi* is also called as *Pardhan* and is appointed with the consent of two-thirds of *Jamabandi raiyats* by the Deputy Commissioner.

Section 27 of the Regulation III of 1872 prohibits any transfer of land holdings by a raiyat either by sale, gift, mortgage or lease or by any other contract or agreement. Sub-section 2 of Section 27 in clear terms enjoin upon the court not to recognize any transfer of such land by sale, mortgage, lease etc. or by under any other agreement or contract whatsoever.

On the application of a raiyat or of landlord of any *khas* village and with the consent of at least two-thirds of the *jamabandi raiyats* of the village ascertained in the manner prescribed, the Deputy Commissioner may declare that a headman shall be appointed for the village and shall then proceed to make the appointment in the prescribed manner.

During the currency of his lease the headman is entitled:

(a) To enjoy the official holding, where such exists, on payment of rent.

(b) On a raiyat's absconding or dying without heirs, to settle his holding with one or other of the following, giving preference in the order mentioned below:
- With a resident *jamabandi raiyat* of the same community.
- With himself, if resident, or with a resident *jamabandi raiyat* of a different community.
- With himself, if non-resident *jamabandi raiyat.*
- With a non-*jamabandi raiyat.*

Prior to the passing of the Santhal Pargana Tenancy (Supplementary Provisions) Act, 1949, there was no self-contained codified law of tenancy for the areas. Some of the tenancy laws were contained in Regulation III of 1872. Some were to be found in the record of rights and duties as contained in Settlement Report, in the ruling of the Commissioner Bhagalpur and the Deputy Commissioners and the decisions of civil and revenue courts and also in the executive instructions of the Government and Revenue authorities issued from time-to-time.

The Santhal Pargana enquiry in its report in 1938 felt that the codification of various laws, ruling and executive orders should be taken up at the same time, it was conscious that straight codification might result in rigidity and inflexibility. The Santhal Pargana Tenancy (Supplementary Provision) Act, 1949 tends to amend and supplement the existing tenancy laws of Santhal Pargana. It codifies some of the customary laws of relating to exchange of raiyati lands, subletting of raiyati lands under certain circumstances, settlement of vacancies and abandoned holdings, rate of the landlords fees on transfer, rights of raiyats relating to tanks and water reservoir, razing land and *jaherthan* and rights of raiyats on trees on his land etc.

After 1949, the Bihar Act of 1949 was further amended by a series of amendments through the following notable legislations:

(a) The Bihar Scheduled Areas Regulation, 1969 (Regulation 1 of 1969).
(b) The Bihar Scheduled Areas Regulation, 1972 (Regulation 1 of 1972).
(c) The Santhal Pargana Tenancy (Supplementary Provisions) Amendments Act, 1975 (Bihar Act, 17 of 1976).

The following are some of the distinctive features of tenancy situation on Santhal Pargana.

1. Those who have acquired title under Regulation III of 1872 could not be evicted.
2. Raiyati rights have never been transferable in Santhal Pargana. Regarding the prohibition again transfer, after incorporation of Section 27 in Regulation III of 1872, 1908 by the matter State concluded by the decision of Supreme court in the *Ram Christo Mendal* vs. *Dhen Ksito Mendal* (AIR, 1964 SC 204) that no incidence of transferability attended to raiyats in Santhal Pargana and were inalienable. The relevant portion from the said decision are quoted here:
   - "The language of section 27 is clear and unambiguous. It prohibits any transfer of any holding by a raiyat either through sale, gift, mortgage or lease or by any other contract or agreement. Sub-section 2 of Section 27 in clear terms enjoin upon the court not to recognize any transfer of such land by sale, mortgage, lease etc. or by under any other agreement or contract whatsoever.

3. Restriction on transfer in the Santhal Pargana region are reasonable ones and fully justified in the interest of the Village Community and for the protection of the Scheduled Tribes residing therein as it will be they who will have preferential right of getting those lands in the event of any *jamabandi raiyats* aboriginal or non-aboriginal becoming extinct or abandoning any holding.

Best Practices and Strength in Santhal Parganas Region

- Section 20 of the SPT Act bar transfer by all raiyat.
- Section 20(5) is common with section 71 'A' CNT Act; both 71 'A' 20(5) were incorporated following Scheduled Area Regulation, 1969.
- Section 42 of the SPT Act provided for ejectment of a person in unauthorized possession of agricultural land.
- Section 64 outlaws limitations for an application under section 42.
- Section 69 puts a bar to land held or acquired in contravention of the provision of Section 20.
- Section 46 of the Chhotanagpur Tenancy Act, 1908 deals with restrictions on transfer on the rights by raiyat. (1) No transfer by a Raiyat of his right in his holding or any portion thereof—
  (a) By mortgage or lease for any period expressed or implied which exceeds or might in any possible event exceed five years, or
  (b) By sale, gift or any other contract or agreement, shall be valid to any extent:

Provided that a raiyat may enter into a 'bhugut bundha' mortgage of his holding or any portion thereof for any period not exceeding seven years or if the mortgage be society registered or deemed to be registered under the Bihar and Odisha Co-operative Societies Act, 1935 (B&OAct VI 1935) for any period not exceeding fifteen years:
Provided further that:

(a) an occupancy-raiyat, who is (a member of the Scheduled Tribes) may transfer with the previous sanction of the Deputy Commissioner his right in his holding or a portion of his holding by sale exchange, gift or will to (another person, who is a member of the Scheduled Tribes and), who is a resident within the local limits of the area of the police station within which the holding is situated.

(b) An Occupancy-Raiyat, who is a member of the Scheduled Castes or Backward Classes may transfer with the previous sanction of the Deputy Commissioner his right holding or a portion of his holding by sale, exchange, gift, will or lease to another person, who is a member of the (Scheduled Castes or, as the case may be, Backward Classes) and who is a resident within the local limits of the district within which the holding is situated.

Development of Land Issue in Santhal Pargana after 1887

After 1887 two fresh principles gradually began to assert themselves in the administration and case law of the Santhal Parganas: (1) that alienations contrary to custom and the record-of-rights were not only voidable at the suit of the zamindar, headman or village community, but were *ipso facto* null and void; (2) that it was the duty of the Deputy Commissioner and Officers subject to his control, as guardians of the settlement, to interfere with all unauthorized alienations that came to their notice. The view of the Courts that alienations were voidable at the suit of interested parties was in course of time found to be an inadequate safeguard. The *zamindar* had very little inducement to interfere in matters of village economy. The settlement had left him little more than a rent receiver dealing with the village headman.

In the Pakur sub-division Mr. McLeod Smith had done an excellent piece of work between 1887 and 1890. He called together alienors and alienees and by providing to them that the former had abandoned their rights while the latter had acquired none, he induced them to make an amicable settlement of account and thus got back for Santhal raiyats 16,856 *bighas* of land which had passed into the hands of their *mahajans*. The amount to be repaid was Rs. 48,394 or less than Rs. 3 per bigha. In order No. 2017 L.R., dated 4th August, 1876, Government had laid down in a clear and unmistakable manner that the rights of headmen were not transferable.

Khunt-katti Rights in Singhbhum and Ranchi Districts

The intimate relationship of the Adivasis between land and forest in the undivided Singhbhum district were similar to the heritage of Forest Rights in Jharkhand. Hos and Mundas have been the autochthones of this territory known as Kolhan where the British had introduced the

Wilkinson Rule which had Munda-Manki system of traditional governance. Porahat Pargana consisting of Anandpur, Bandgaon, Kera and Champa had dense forest located in Kolhan Government Estate. During the colonial rule, the forest policies were exploitative of the traditional community owned forest rights of the adivasis. It aroused the anger of indigenous people which led to major revolts like Kol Insurrection of 1832 and Birsa Ulugulan (Revolt) of 1895-1900 as the communal property system of Khunt-katti was transformed by the Colonial Forest Policy in the form of Reserve Forest and Protected Forest. Several Khunt-katti villages were subsumed within this frame. In Bandgaon 34 Mundari Khunt-katti villages, in Porahat proper 176 Mundari Khunt-katti villages, 35 villages of Anandpur got submerged within Reserved Forest and Protected Forest. Generally, a single clan decided in a village with whom the Khunt-katti rights vested. The Khunt-katti rights were also located Saraikela-Kharsawan area and Dalbhum States. The Colonial Forest Policy was based in the Indian Forest Act, 1875 and 1927. Such forceful displacement from the traditional Khunt-katti rights characterized by internal colonialism were bereft of any compensation. The Reserved Forest were out of bounds for the adivasis. One instance of such forceful displacement was from Chirkubeda village of Porahat estate. The Zamindars and Forest Officials had imposed Begari (forced labour) in the forest area. In village Kundrugutu the adivasis even refused to follow the Begar system of carrying the Forest officials on their shoulders. The densest Saranda forest was also converted into reserved forest. In the process 7 Khunt-katti villages were also converted into Forest Villages. As per 1971 District Census Handbook there were still 27 Forest villages. The author in the present empirical study during 2015-16 found evidence of Khunt-katti villages in the districts of Khunti and Singhbhum districts. In the district official records there were 129 Khunt-katti villages in Adki circle comprising 2040.15 acre, Karra circle had 1145.26 acre, Torpa circle had 95,385.12 acre of mixed Khunt-katti area, Rania circle had 29,221.65 acre and Khunti circle had 36,932.42 acre. Similarly, there were several Khunt-katti villagers in Saraikela district. [*Source:* Mathew, Areeparampil, (1988), "Forest and Adivasis: Victims of Exploitation", Tribal Research and Training Centre, Chaibasa.]

5.11 Land Alienation in Jharkhand

The land alienation in Jharkhand comprises the colonial form of land and forest exploitation and also the land grabbing by the non-tribals upper caste. It is the Adivasi people who have been displaced the most due to development projects in Jharkhand. Out of this, 40 per cent of the total displacement has been for mining purposes.

Table 5.18: Total Number of Displaced Tribals in Jharkhand (1951-95)

Sl. No.	*Project name*	*Total Displaced*	*Scheduled Tribes*	*Percentage*
1.	Water Resources	232968	175127	75.2
2.	Industries	66087	22473	34.0
3.	Quasi industries	21809	7415	–
4.	Mining, coal/non-coal	268588	79568	29.6
5.	Defence establishment	264353	237147	89.7
6.	Wildlife/national park	509918	80867	15.8
7.	Infrastructure development	50000	13800	27.6
	Grand Total	**1413723**	**616397**	**38.85**

Source: Ekka, Alexius and Mohammed, Asif, (2000). Development induced Displacement and Rehabilitation in Jharkhand: A database on its Extent and nature, New Delhi: Indian Social Institute.

The total number of persons displaced in Jharkhand between 1951-1995 was 15.03 lakhs out of which 41.27 per cent were tribals. The estimated displacement by major dams in Jharkhand include 26,046 hectare from Damodar dam, 12,805 hectare from Icha Dam (30,800 number of the displaced persons out of which 80 per cent are tribals), from Chandil Dam: the area of the displacement is 17,683 hectare comprising 37,600 number of displaced persons covering 87.92 per cent of tribal population and from Koel-Karo Project estimated displacement is 17,764 hectare and the total number of displaced persons is 37,600 covering 87.92 per cent of the tribal population.

There were 725 coal mines operating in India by 1942. With Independence in 1947, the mineral rights in all the areas, with the exception of the permanently settled areas of Bengal and Bihar, vested in the Government. The Coal Bearing Areas (Acquisition and Development) Act, 1957 was passed by the Parliament primarily to enable the State to take control over the mineral rights of private owners. This Act had special provisions for acquiring mineral rights, which had been granted earlier to private land owners to individuals or companies.

It would be now appropriate to discuss about the land alienation due to Tata Steel Limited, Heavy Engineering Corporation Ltd. and Bokaro Steel Limited. The Tata Steel Ltd. in Jamshedpur was established in 1907 which displaced adivasis from 18 villages without any iota of compensation. The total land acquired for Tata Steel Ltd. is 12,708.59 acre and all these were raiyati lands. The total land acquired for Heavy Engineering Corporation Ltd., Ranchi was 7199.71 acre of which 6355.82 acre were raiyati land and rest were Government and Forest land. The total land acquired for Bokaro Steel Limited was 31,287.24 acre of which 26,908.56 acre were raiyati lands. It would be necessary to highlight that Tata Steel, Jamshedpur sub-leased 33.75 per cent of the land to the private handlers, and 31.54 per cent of acquired land is still lying vacant. The Heavy Engineering Corporation, Ranchi has sub-leased 793.68 acre and 2910 acre are lying vacant. The Bokaro Steel Limited has sub-leased 417.66 acre and 9435.63 acre is kept vacant. In this process the adivasis were rendered landless. The land were acquired from 51 villages for the Bokaro Steel Plants. [*Source*: Sunil Minz and Gladson Dungdung, (2013), *Vikas ke Kabragah–Grave of Development*, Ranchi: Deshag Publisher].

S.L. Batra, Ramesh Sharan and Amar Kumar Singh have analysed tribal land alienation by private land owners. One of the form of land alienation is through collusive title suits by circumventing the Chhotanagpur Tenancy Act which prohibits transfer of tribal land to a non-tribal. They were one of the important means by which land was alienated in and around the city of Ranchi. Conversion of agricultural land to *chapar-bandi* (homestead land, which can be transferred without contravening the provisions of the Chhotanagpur Tenancy Act), was another mode of land alienation, with mortgage and even outright sale also occurring. The Author had conducted study in the district of Ranchi and Dumka.

Out of the reported loss of 467.73 acre by the households of the Ranchi sample, forms of transfer were specified only in the case of 401.21 acre or 85.78 per cent of the total lands transferred. In the acre of the households from Dumka district, details of the form of land transfer were available in the case of 39.48 acre or 95.98 per cent of the total transfer.

In Ranchi, as much as three-fourths of the alienated tribal land (76.2%) was lost through *sada patta*. A tenth was transferred through collusive title suits, with title suits accounting for another 2.60 per cent. Tribal land sold to a tribal with the permission of the Deputy Commissioner (a legal category under the CNT Act) accounted for 5.76 per cent of the transfers *dan patra* for 3.49 per cent and ante dated *hukumnama* for 1.31 per cent. In Dumka, as in Ranchi, *sada patta* accounted for a large share of transferred land. Though marked by

Table 5.19: Transferred Land of Sample Households by Category of Land Transfer: Ranchi and Dumka (1994)

Category of Transferred Land	*District*			
	Ranchi		*Dumka*	
Dan patra (gift)	14.00	(3.49)	20.28	(52.74)
Badlanama	–	–	3.48	(8.81)
Land sold to a tribal with DC's permission	23.10	(5.76)	–	–
Title Suits	10.43	(2.60)	–	–
Registration (Collusive Title Suits)	46.66	(11.63)	0.66	(1.67)
Ante dated hukumnama	1.25	(0.31)	–	–
Sada patta	305.77	(76.21)	14.52	(36.78)
Total of Reported Transfers	**401.21**	**(100.00)**	**38.94**	**(100.00)**
Total of Reported Forms	**467.73**		**41.13**	

Source: Based on Field Study.

elements of encroachments as well as forcible eviction, in a majority of cases, it was based on consent. However, it was *dan patra*, which accounted for as much as 52.7 per cent of the land transfers and has been popular way of land alienation in both urban as well as rural areas, that accounted for the lion's share of the land transfers in Dumka. *Sada patta* and *dan patra* accounted for close to 90 per cent of all land transfers in the Dumka. *Badlanama* was the next most important mode of land alienation in Dumka, with 8.8 per cent of the transferred land of the sample households alienated through this process. Collusive title suits, whose share of alienated land was high as 11.6 per cent in Ranchi accounted for a mere 1.7 per cent of in Dumka.

State acquisition of tribal land for public use of the 168 sample households from Dumka reveals that 158 lost their lands to an irrigation project which alienated 501.39 acre of their land and accounted for 99.54 per cent of the total land alienation for public purposes.

5.12 Land Rights in Mining Areas in Jharkhand

In India especially, Jharkhand, the history of both industrial mining of coal and that of exploitation and oppression of tribals have always gone together, since the mode of production associated with coal mining was not in tandem with the lifestyle and practices of the Jharkhandi people. Industrialization began with the establishment of the first coal mining industry in Raniganj in the year 1775. In the year 1843, the first Joint Stock Company M/s. Bengal Coal Company was formed. Chains of

Table 5.20: Tribal Land Alienated by the State: Dumka and Ranchi Districts (1996)

Land Taken over for/by	*Dumka*		*Ranchi*	
	Area (Acres)	*Household Affected*	*Area (Acres)*	*Households Affected*
Irrigation Project	501.39	158	182.53	63
Industrial project	–	–	140.90	43
Airport, Railway, Road	–	–	144.14	71
Army/BMP/Bazaar/Dairy	2.51	8	59.62	19
Voluntary Organization	0.20	2	–	–
Total	**504.10**	**168**	**527.19**	**196**
Average per Household	**3.00**		**2.68**	

Source: S.L. Batra, Ramesh Sharan and Amar Kumar Singh (2004), "Alienation of Tribal Land in Jharkhand Region of Bihar: Process and Pattern" in Rajiv Balakrishan, "*Jharkhand Matters*", New Delhi: Konark Publishers, Council for Social Development.

other establishments also followed. Mining is a major activity in Jharkhand. The State possesses 37 per cent of the total minerals of India and in 2000-01 had an annual production of Rs. 4,997 crore (GoI, 2003). Among these came up huge number of establishments on Damodar River basin and the famous Jharia Coalfield in Dhanbad district, one of the richest treasure house of India's metallurgical coal. The working of Jharia, Bokaro and Kanpura Coalfield started in 1846. The opening of coal mining in Dhanbad area during the second half of the nineteenth century and the establishment of the Tata Iron and Steel Company in Jamshedpur in Singhbhum district marked the beginning of the large scale exploitation of mineral and other resources in Jharkhand.

These hydel-power projects, as roughly estimated has a total of 5,07,952 acre of land occupation in the State. It has displaced as many as 2,32,968 persons. An additional 6026.87 acre of land has gone against setting up of Thermal power stations. Damodar River is the fourth most polluted river in the world. The contribution of the coal industry in bringing the river to such a pitiable state is very huge. Today, the water in that river can neither be used for human consumption, nor for the use of animals.

Table 5.21: Displacement and Rehabilitation by Coal Mines, 1981-85

Sl. No.	Name of the Company	No. of persons displaced	Number of jobs provided to one member of the family and (% of displaced families)	
1.	Eastern Coal Fields Ltd.	81,100	4,195	(33.32%)
2.	Central Coal Fields Ltd.	43,600	3,984	(50.25%)
3.	Western Coal Fields Ltd.	34,300	2,250	(36.10%)
4.	Bharat Cooking Coal Ltd.	21,000	752	(19.58%)
Total		**1,80,000**	**11,181**	**(34.81)**

Source: *Vikasman* (undated), Bulletin Number 2, Ranchi: Tribal Resource Research and Training Centre.

Table 5.22: Land Rights Affected due to Mining in Jharkhand

Sl. No.	Name of the Project	Area Covered	Number of Displaced Persons	% of Tribals among Displaced Persons
1.	Icha (Kharkai river)	4,268.29 (hec)	30,800	80.00
2.	Cahndil (Swarnrekha river)	17,683.00 (hec)	37,600	87.92
3.	Netarhat Field Firing Range (245 villages)	4,368.17	1,50,000	90.00
4.	North Koel Palamau	20,000	6,000	72.00

Source: *Vikasman* (undated), Bulletin Number 2, Ranchi: Tribal Resource Research and Training Centre.

Damodar river basin is very important because of the coal mining industry; 46 per cent of the total reserves of coal in India lie in this region. The estimated reserves of coal in the region come to 71.86 billion tonnes. There are 311 coal mines, 182 non-coal mines, 78 urban centres and 82 industrial centres on the banks of Damodar River.

5.13 Radical Agrarian Movement on Land and Forest Questions during the 1970s

The Jharkhand Mukti Morcha started the struggle against all usurers, renters and land grabbers between 1972-78. The forcible harvesting operations in 1973 were conducted under the leadership of the Jharkhand Mukti Morcha. They were organized but were limited to villages where adequate mobilizations was feasible. The activists conducted surveys to identify target villages, target plots and the nature and magnitude of resistance likely to be encountered. Over twenty such villages were selected. To ensure that the balance of forces was in its favour the Morcha mobilized the tribals from the district of Giridih also. In the village of Maniadih in Tundi block powerful Bhumihar moneylenders used firearms against the tribals. The latter replied with their arrows. Both sides suffered injuries. Another notable features of the paddy harvesting movement (Dhan Katti Andolan as the Morcha Christened it) was its extension to the neighbouring development blocks of Govindpur and Baliapur.

The *dikus*, in their panic made liberal use of firearms involving loss of several lives. In a village of Topchanchi block a village *mukhia* (headman of village Panchayat) bribed the police to arrest participants in the harvesting movement. A posse of police consisting of two constables, an assistant sub-inspector and headed by Mr. Ghatak, Inspector of police visited the village to arrest them. In the face of resistance mounted by the villagers the sub-inspector and the constables took to their heels. The inspector, however, could not be traced in spite of massive combing operations conducted jointly by Dhanbad and Giridih police. Giridih witnessed a phenomenal rise in the incidence of forcible paddy harvesting. Villages in as many as six blocks of the districts were affected. *The Indian Nation*, an important Patna daily reported that 1.2 lakh maunds of paddy were forcibly harvested from Pirtanr P.S. alone during the first fortnight of November. Around fifty tribals were arrested. The administration was forced to constitute mobile courts to dispose of land disputes. According to the *Searchlight* 50,000 maunds of paddy was harvested from several villages of the district of Santhal Parganas. In both these districts several tribals succumbed to bullet injuries. Huge demonstration took place and meetings were held. It was a rare show of tribal solidarity.

Another notable feature of the movement was the common cause the tribals made with non-agricultural labourers. During the first week of January 1974 nearly 1500 tribals associated themselves with the struggle of the institutions of cases against 150. Again on February 1975 when some henchmen of the management of Khaskuina colliery attacked labourers, several hundred tribal peasants from the neighbouring villages resisted. Again in the same year, anti-social elements in the pay of management fired at the Sijua Colliery workers. The tribal peasants in the vicinity also fought side by side with the workers. The victims were both workers and peasants. Annual Meet of Jharkhand Mukti Morcha is held every year on 4th February from 1973 to 1976 when lakhs of workers with red flags and peasants with green flags attended it. The tribal movement to secure lost lands, repudiate debts, and get back pledged articles reached its climax with the end of 1974 and beginning of 1975. While the movement had engulfed Dhanbad, Giridih, and Santhal Parganas Districts, its impact over the entire area was not uniform.

Kumar Suresh Singh in his paper "Agrarian Dimension of Tribal Movement" has also discussed the land question and forest issue undertaken by Jharkhand Mukti Morcha and its consequences. This radicalization was also due to the influence of the Naxalite movement, infiltration of tribal organizations by extremist elements and the entry of the leftist parties in the region, in a big way. The latter had generally kept themselves out of tribal politics, and their interest had thus far been limited to the sections of the workers engaged in mining and industries. The leftist orientation to tribal politics meant a greater stress on the political education of workers and agrarian issues, a linking up of local and all-India politics, violence and militancy of means, and a better organization. There was also commitment by all-India leftist parties to the concept of tribal autonomy as distinct from that of formation of tribal State. The *morcha* has launched an operation to recover alienated land from moneylenders and big peasants during the last three years. There have been 120 violent incidents including looting of crops or forcible harvesting of crops standing on lands in illegal (2) and murder (28). In the process there have been 5 incidents of clash with the police. The largest number of incidents (69) occurred in 1974. Since then the number of incidents has declined.

The Agrarian Land Movement was followed by Forest Movement in the dense Saranda Forest Area of Singhbhum District where the resistance to the plantation of teak became the symbol of movement. While *sal* plantation in this region is about a hundred years old, the Forest Development Corporation during the last two years undertook to plant teak in 2000 hectares in the *sal* forests. Rumours were spread that teak was replacing *sal*, a sacred tree and that nothing grew under teak, not even grassroots and tubers, on which wildlife and the tribal people subsist. As elephants did not eat the leaves of the teak, they destroyed teak trees and their depredations in areas under crops increased. The agitations also contended that fruits bearing trees were being cut down to establish teak nurseries, thus depriving the tribal people of the source of food.

It was mainly in the areas where the Forest Development Corporation operated that the agitation grew intense; the agitationists cut-off all communications to this region by blocking roads and damaging bridges. They turned to destroy nurseries, 11 of which were damaged in the two divisions of the Forest Development Corporation, causing a loss of about Rs. 6 lakh. Felling of *sal* trees has been justified by the agitationists on the ground that they enjoyed the traditional right to reclaim land for cultivation. They contended that his traditional right to reclaim land as Mundari Khunkhattidar had been given by the former *zamindar* of Porhat, but was not recorded as such during the last survey and settlement operations. They also claimed that all forest areas constituted the Jharkhand and so they had right to fell trees to reclaim land. Felling of trees of the protected forests occurred over an area of about 300 acre entailing a loss of Rs. 4.10 lakh.

As the agitators collected in large numbers to fell trees and cut-off communications, the police resisted and there was a confrontation. This was a reason for the first firing on 6th November, 1978 in Goelkira. Another problem was to round up agitators who were wanted in various cases. It was difficult to locate them and when they were arrested, there was resistance, which often turned violent. This led to the second firing on 25th November, 1978. The most serious incident was the firing on a tribal crowd at Gua on 8th September, 1980 in which 13 tribals lost their lives. The Jharkhand Mukti Morcha has emerged as a major political force in the industrial and mining belt of Chhotanagpur, and in State politics in the 1980 General elections. It seeks to broad base the separatist movement by including within its ambit the peasant and the working classes. As Jharkhandis are producer irrespective of caste, tribe or nation residing in Jharkhand. The Jharkhand is described as an internal colony which is being exploited by outsiders. The Jharkhand must turn into Lalkhand, that is, the movement of political separatism and struggle of the working classes should go together.

The above scenario indicates the nature and extent of dispossession and displacement due to Forest and Land Acquisition which intensifies the anger and vengeance of the tribals in Jharkhand. It would be appropriate to understand the extent of displacement which has taken place in Jharkhand due to different type of development projects (see Table 5.23).

Table 5.24 shows that 75.2 per cent of the persons displaced by projects related to water resources were tribals. In the same way, the percentage of persons displaced by the establishment of industries and quasi-industries was 34 per cent. Nearly 29.6 per cent of those displaced by mining industries were tribals. Similarly, 89.7 per cent, 15.8 per cent and 27.7 per cent tribals were displaced by defence

Table 5.23: Land Alienation in Jharkhand due to Various Projects

Sl. No.	*Type of project*	*Total displaced*	*No. of rehabilitated*	*Persons not rehabilitated*	*Percentage of displaced not rehabilitated*
1.	Mines	2550000	630000	1920000	75.29
2.	Dams	16400000	4100000	12300000	75.00
3.	Industries	1250000	375000	875000	70.00
4.	Wildlife	600000	125000	475000	79.00
5.	Others	500000	150000	350000	70.00
	Total	**21300000**	**5380000**	**15920000**	**73.86**

Source: Lourdusamy, 1997:25.

Table 5.24: Total Tribal Lands Alienated in Jharkhand due to Various Projects (1951-1995)

Sl. No.	*Project name*	*Total displaced*	*Scheduled Tribes*	*Percentage*
1.	Water resources	232968	175127	75.2
2.	Industries/quasi-industries	66087	22473	34.0
		21809	7415	
3.	Mining: coal/non-coal	268588	79568	29.6
		134294	3975	
4.	Defence establishment	264353	237147	89.7
5.	Wildlife/national park	509918	80867	15.8
6.	Infrastructure development	50000	13800	27.6
	Grand Total	**1548017**	**620372**	**45.32**

Source: Ekka and Asif, 2000:95.

establishment, wildlife sanctuaries and infrastructural development, respectively. Thus according to the study by Ekka and Asif (2000:95), the total percentage of tribals displaced by various enterprises in Jharkhand from 1951 to 1995 was 45.32. The figures clearly indicate that the Adivasis are the worst sufferers of all the so-called development projects.

The magnitude of displacement by some of the major projects can be evinced from the data given in Table 5.25.

Projects varying from multi-purpose dam, reservoirs, power plant or any other industries have led to large scale displacement, destruction of livelihood, cultures and also physical environment. In Jharkhand, the impact of these development projects have been on the dalits and tribals and among them women, who suffer even severe forms of discrimination. The impact has rarely been on a positive direction as

Table 5.25: Magnitude of Alienation by Development Projects

Sl. No.	*Name of the Project*	*Magnitude of Displacement*
1.	TISCO (1907)	3564 acre of tribal land
2.	Heavy Engineering Plant (1958)	9200 acre, 25 villages and 12,990 tribal
3.	Bokaro Steel Plant	46 villages and 12,487 tribals
4.	Coal Mining (1981-1985)	1,50,300 acre
5.	CCL-ICL (1981-1985)	1,50,300 acre
6.	Icha Dam	21,000 acre in Bihar 10,500 acre in Odisha 5,600 families
7.	Chandil Dam	43,495 acre
8.	Koel Karo	16,350 families (70% of tribals)
9.	Jambir/Baura Dams and Expansion of Haldia	5,980 acre submerged
10.	Netarhat Firing Range	2,24,900 (78% tribals)

Source: *Adivasis Yuva Sangh* (1994), Update from Delhi: Issue No. 74, (April 1994), New Delhi, Update Collective.

repeated/multiple displacement, migration and drastic change in livelihood patterns have socially and culturally denuded the status of women, increasing violence and abuse against them. The benefits arising out of these projects have only occurred to the big business houses and the displaced people have been provided manual labour required by these projects.

Subarnarekha Dam Project also displaced a large number of tribals and other marginalized people from the villages of the district of Saraikela, East Singhbhum and West Singhbhum. The total area acquired by them for the entire Subarnarekha Project was 8222.20 acre comprising 76 villages. The process of rehabilitation for this project is almost in the process of completion. (Special Land Acquisition Officer, Subarnarekha Project Adityapur 14-10-16). During the Globalization era the Government of Jharkhand passed the Jharkhand Industrial Policy 2001 under the Chief Ministership of Babulal Marandi. The State Government constituted a "Land Bank" at District Level to make available the required land to intending entrepreneurs to overcome the delay in land acquisition process. The Chhotanagpur Tenancy Act, 1908 has been amended to facilitate setting-up of any unit for industrial purpose for the purpose of mining.

5.14 Present Status of Land Holding Pattern in the State of Jharkhand

The present land holding pattern as revealed from the statistical profile 2005 of Government of Jharkhand shows that the total operational holding in the State is Rs. 24.69 lakh and the total operated areas was 39.05 lakh. The marginal holdings constituted 62.60 per cent, the small holdings 17.50 per cent holdings, the semi-medium holding were 14.03 per cent, medium holdings were 4.50 per cent and the large holdings were 1.10 per cent. The operated area held by the marginal holding were only 21.44 per cent, small holdings were 15.99 per cent: the semi-medium had more operated area consisting of 26.72 per cent and the medium holdings were having 26.51 per cent: the large holdings consisting of 10 hectares and above were having 9.34 per cent of the total operated area. This would be clear from the data presenting in the following Table 5.26:

Table 5.26: Land Holding Pattern in the State of Jharkhand as on 2005

Sl. No.	*Size of holding (in hectares)*	*Holdings*		*Area*	
		Number (in lakh)	*Per cent*	*Lakh Hectares*	*Per cent*
1.	Marginal (0–1)	15.45	62.60	8.03	21.44
2.	Small (1 to 2)	4.32	17.50	6.56	15.99
3.	Semi-Medium (2 to 4)	3.54	14.30	9.94	26.72
4.	Medium (4 to 10)	1.11	4.5	10.06	26.51
5.	Large (10 and above)	0.27	1.10	4.46	9.34
6.	All holdings	24.69	100.00	39.05	100.00

Source: A Statistical Profile 2005, Government of Jharkhand.

It is in this background that we have to understand the status of operational holdings in the sample districts of Ranchi (Khunti), East Singhbhum, West Singhbhum, Saraikela-Kharasawan. The operational holdings of these four districts are given in the Table 5.27.

It is evident from the Table 5.27 that the pattern of operational holding at the State level in Jharkhnd is also reflected in the sample districts. The largest operational holdings are held by the marginal holding which is nearly over 60 per cent of the total operational holding

Table 5.27: The Operational Holdings of the Four Sample Districts of Jharkhand

Sl. No.	District	Marginal (0–1)		Small (1 to 2)		Semi Medium (2 to 4)		Medium (4 to 10)		Large (10 & above)		Total No. of holdings in (000) hectares
		No.	%	No.	%	No.	%	No.	%	No.	%	
1.	Ranchi	143.52	51.27	69.70	24.90	46.69	16.68	16.05	5.73	3.98	1.42	279.94
2.	East Singhbhum	114.02	64.98	30.49	17.38	20.87	11.89	9.52	5.42	0.56	0.33	175.46
3.	West Singhbhum	110.19	63.24	25.55	14.66	22.20	12.75	14.25	8.18	2.04	1.18	174.23
4.	Saraikela Kharasawan	46.06	63.27	10.76	14.65	9.36	12.75	6.00	8.17	0.85	1.16	73.43
5.	Total of Sample Districts	1544.85	57.96	431.95	16.21	488.92	18.34	173.10	6.49	26.32	1.00	2605.14

followed by the small farmers who have between 14-16 per cent of the total operational holding, the semi medium control between 20 per cent of the total operational holding but it was only 9.36 per cent in the Saraikela-Kharasawan district, the medium holdings operate between 6-8 per cent of the total operational holding and large farmers operate only around 1 per cent of the total objectional holding. It could be inferred from the above data that the major cultivator are the marginal farmers followed by small and semi-medium farmers. The medium and large farmers constitute only 7 per cent of the total operational holdings in the State and in the studied sample districts.

Table 5.28: The Operated Area of the Four Sample Districts in Jharkhand

Sl. No.	District	Marginal (0-1)		Small (1 to 2)		Semi Medium (2 to 4)		Medium (4 to 10)		Large (10 & above)		Total No. of operated area in (000) hectares
		No.	%	No.	%	No.	%	No.	%	No.	%	
1.	Ranchi	94.29	19.58	100.81	20.93	125.56	26.07	94.38	19.59	66.61	13.83	481.65
2.	East Singhbhum	66.90	28.80	45.28	19.31	59.42	25.34	53.56	22.84	9.35	3.99	234.51
3.	West Singhbhum	1.76	0.83	35.84	16.71	62.38	29.08	82.33	38.38	32.18	15.00	214.49
4.	Saraikela Kharasawan	22.25	20.04	14.20	12.78	26.30	23.69	34.71	31.26	13.56	12.22	111.02
5.	Total of Jharkhand State	752.06	19.51	655.14	17.00	993.94	25.79	1006.60	26.12	445.98	11.58	3853.72

Source: Agricultural Census Publication.

The operated area in the State shows that the marginal farmers control only 19.51 per cent of the total operated areas, small farmers control 17 per cent of the total operated area whereas semi-medium farmers control 25.79 per cent and the medium farmers control 26.12 per cent and the large farmers control 11.58 per cent of the total operated area. It indicates the agrarian inequality in the Jharkhand State. Those the marginal holdings have nearly 57.96 per cent of the total operational holding whereas they control only 19.51 per cent of the total operated area followed by 17 per cent controlled by the small farmers of the total operated area the maximum area is controlled by semi-medium farmers (25.79%) and the medium farmers (26.12% of the total operated area) and the large farmers those have only 1 per cent of the total operational holdings but control 11.58 per cent of the total operated area indicating the predominance of the semi-medium, medium and large holdings. This pattern is also reflected in the districts of East Singhbhum, Saraikela-Kharasawan and West Singhbhum. The marginal farmers control 29.08 per cent and the medium holding controls 38.38 per cent followed by the large holdings who control 15 per cent of the total operated area. In the 4 sampled districts, West Singhbhum is characterized by more agrarian inequality than in the districts of East Singhbhum, Saraikela-Kharasawan and Ranchi district (Khunti). The Ranchi district also subsumed district of Khunti which has been bi-furcated from the Ranchi district.

5.15 Highlights of Land Issues in Jharkhand

- The tribals are still sanguine to their traditional leadership of village headmen like Munda, Manjhi, Manki, Baisi, Perha system which are the traditional source of their identity and strength.
- The traditional ingredients still continue to be the major source of strength for the tribals to preserve and protect their land and forest.
- The adivasis in Jharkhand have militant tradition of land struggle since the colonial period.
- They have preserved the integrity of Land and Forest Issues as important ingredients of their cultural identities.
- The Private Property Right in land, the undermining of Communal Rights, the Colonial Land Acquisition Law of 1894 have been the major precipitants to promote the lands struggle among tribals as a live issue.
- The welfare laws like Schedule V Area, the favourable features of PESA have hardly been enacted in the State of Jharkhand to safeguard the Land Rights of the tribals.

- The Chhotanagpur Tenancy Act, 1908, the Santhal Pargana Tenancy Act, 1949, The Khuntkatti Rights make them alive to the traditional cultural identity.
- The Land ceiling laws, Gair-mazarua land distribution and Bhudan land distribution have been a major failure in the State of Jharkhand.
- The Land Acquisition laws are inimical to the traditional CNT Act, 1908 and Chhotanagpur Tenancy Act, 1949.
- The protection of Marginal and Small landholdings through proper Land Policy is a necessary prerequisite.

References

"Baseline Report on Restoration of Land to the Allottees of Ceiling Surplus and Government Wasteland", Study undertaken by RCDC with support from NIRD, Hyderabad in Koraput district of Odisha, November 2006.

Ekka, Alexius and Mohammed Asif, (2000). *Development induced Displacement and Rehabilitation in Jharkhand: A Database on its Extent and Nature*, New Delhi: Indian Social Institute.

Jena, Manas (2013). "Land Rights", Odisha Jami Adhikari Abhiyan, Bhubaneswar, Mineral Resources, "The Opportunity in Jharkhand", Minsitry of Mines and Geology, Government of Jharkhand, 2003.

Marandi, Babulal, Chief Minister of Jharkhand, "The Industrial Policy of 2001", Government of Jharkhand, Ranchi.

Ministry of Coal and Mines, Department of Coal, letter no. 47011/1(4) 2000-CPAM dt.26-12-2001, Pachwara Central Block, Santal Pargana.

Munda, Arjun, Chief Minister of Jharkhand, "Industraial Policy of 2012", Government of Jharkhand, Ranchi.

Pattnaik, Sanjay (2008). "Director Research and Advocacy", Regional Centre for Development and Co-operation, Bhubaneswar, Odisha Copyright, UNDP 2008 "Status Report—Land Rights and Ownership in Odisha" August 2008, New Delhi.

Reddy, T. Prabhakar (2015), "Tenancy Laws and Land Licensed Cultivators in Andhra Pradesh: A Study", In: Faizi, Iyer and Kaur, *Tenancy Laws and Practices: Emerging Issues*, New Delhi: Manak Publications.

Report of the Expert Group on Prevention of Alienation of Tribal Land and its Restoration, Ministry of Rural Development (2006).

Report of the Panchayat Extension to Scheduled Areas Act, 1996 (PESA) Enquiry Committee, Ministry of Panchayat (2006).

Report of the Sub-Committee on Land, Planning Commission (2006).

Roy, R.N. Pandey (2002). *Hand Book on Chhotanagpur Tenancy Laws*, 4th edition, Allahabad: Rajpal and Company.

Singh, S.K. (2005). *A Series on Self-Governance for Tribals: Tribal Lands and*

Indebtedness, National Institute of Rural Development, Ministry of Rural Development, Government of India, Hyderabad, vol. 1, pp. 226.

Swain, M. (1998). *Peasant Agriculture and Share Tenancy in Odisha*, New Delhi: Commonwealth Publishers.

Swain, M. (1999). "Tenancy Structure in Odisha: Implication for Agricultural Growth," *Artha Vijnana*, 41 (3): 245-61.

Swain, M. (2015). "Changes in Incidence of Tenancy in Rural Odisha: Implications for Second Generation Tenancy Reforms", Paper presented in National Institute of Rural Development, Hyderabad in 2015 in a National Seminar on Tenancy Situation in India.

The Scheduled Tribes and Other Traditional Forest Dwellers (Recognition of Forest Rights) Act, 2006.

6

Significance of Non-Timber Forest Produce in the Livelihood of Adivasis in Jharkhand and Odisha

6.0 Coverage of NTFP in the State of Jharkhand and Odisha

In this chapter an attempt is made to discuss the significance of Minor Forest produce in the Livelihood of the Adivasis in Jharkhand and Odisha. The data for the study has been collected during 2014-16 in the four districts of Jharkhand and four districts of Odisha. The districts covered in Jharkhand include West Singhbhum, Khunti, Saraikela-Kharsawan and East Singhbhum. The Districts covered in the State of Odisha include Sundargarh, Kalahandi, Koraput and Rayagada. The significance of minor forest produce in Jharkhand is discussed initially followed by the importance of NTFP in Odisha.

6.1 Forest Produce as a Source of Livelihood for Rural Poor in Jharkhand

Jharkhand is blessed with many Non-Timber forest produce of economic value. Tradionally, these resources only cater to the rural economy. Some of NTFPs traded most are—*Harra, Bahera, Chiraunji, Karanj*, *Jamun, Chiraita*, Bamboo shoots, Tamarind, *Mahua*, *Dori*, *Sal* seeds, *Neem* seeds, Honey, *Satabri* etc.

6.2 Major Non-Timber Forest Produce (NTFP) in Jharkhand

NTFP plays an important role in the livelihood support of tribal and forest dwellers in terms of subsistence and income generation. NTFP sustains millions of tribals by providing an alternate source for food and income. *The dependence is maximum on produce like kendu leaf, mahua, lac, char, tamarind, sal seed, amla etc. (Source:* Jharkhand

State Minor Forest Produce Co-operative Development and Marketing Federation Limited. Medicinal plants are found in abundance in Jharkhand. *Amla, Harra, Bahera, Karanj* and various other herbs and shrubs over hundred species not only can be grown but also processing units both at rural and urban centres can be set up.

Table 6.1: Major Non-Timber Forest Produce (NTFP) in Jharkhand

Sl. No.	*Name of NTFP*	*Annual Production (app in MT.)*	*Value Added Products*
1.	Chiraunji	2000	Dry fruit, used in confectionary
2.	Karanj	5000	Antibiotic oil, ointment, spray etc.
3.	Harra	2000	Harra powder and Triphala churna
4.	Amla	2000	Amla powder, Triphala churna and morabba
5.	Bahera	2000	In Triphala churna
6.	Jamun Pulp and Kernel	5000	Jamun syrup and Jamun powder
7.	Chiraita	2000	Antibiotic chiraita powder
8.	Bamboo Shoots	2000	Pickle and vegetables
9.	Tamarind	200000	Packed without seed, paste
10.	Mahua	2,00,000	Wine
11.	Dori	20,000	Oil / Soap
12.	Sal seeds	1,00,000	Oil / Feed
13.	Kusum	10,000	Oil / Feed
14.	Hill broom	200	Broom
15.	Thorn Broom	200	Broom
16.	Satabari	200	Medicine
17.	Adda leaves / Mahulan Patta/ Siali leaf	500	Plate
18.	Mahu/Honey	100	Food
19.	Baividang	N.A.	Medicine
20.	Kalmegh	N.A.	Medicine
21.	Dhawai Phool	N.A.	Medicine
22.	Neem Seed	500	Oil / Soap
23.	Sarpagandha	500	Medicine
24.	Aswagandha	500	Medicine
25.	Palas / Tesu Phool	1000	Colour
26.	Kendu leaf	N.A.	Biri
	Other important Minor Forest Produce include honey, medicinal plants, herbs gums, and resins.		

Source: Jharkhand State Minor Forest Produce Co-operative Development and Marketing Federation Limited.

6.3 Major Issues in NTFP Collection, Trade and Value Addition

The livelihoods of the poor rural and tribal families depend on a range of forest produce such as, tassar, lac, honey *mahua, chiraunji,* medicinal plants and a number of NTFPs. *Key issues and challenges related to NTFPs in the State of Jharkhand are lack of marketing focus.*

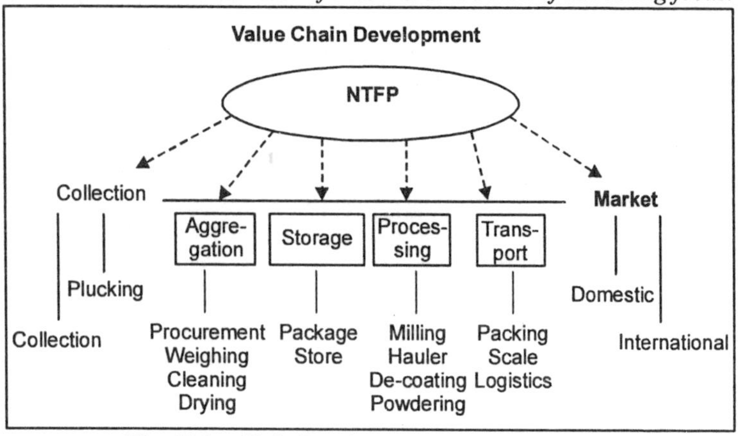

Fig.: Value Chain Development

Seasonality of NTFP Collection and Trading

Name of the NTFP	*Jan*	*Feb*	*Mar*	*Apr*	*May*	*Jun*	*Jul*	*Aug*	*Sep*	*Oct*	*Nov*	*Dec*
Tamarind		C	C									
		PT	PT	T								
Mahua Flower			C	C								
			PT	PT	T	T						
Mahua Seed						C	C					
						PT	PT	T	T			
Sal Leaf	C	C			C	C	C	C	C	C	C	C
	T	T			T	T	T	T	T	T	T	T
Siali Leaf						C	C	C	C	C	C	C
						T	T	T	T	T	T	T
Char Seed				C	C							
				PT	PT	T	T					
Kusum Lac						C	C			C	C	C
						PT	PT			T	T	T

Note: Abbreviations

C Collection Season
PT Peak Trading Season
T Trading Season

Source: NTFP Survey Report, Strengthening NTFP based Livelihood Systems through a market-led Approach, MART, NOIDA.

Majority of the forest produce is sold in the raw form and are traded in the same form (without any value addition except for certain trivial functions).

Kendu leaf is an important Forest Produce but this is still handled by the State and particularly by the Forest Department in Jharkhand. During the past 2-3 years particularly from 2014-15 and 2015-16 the *Kendu Patta collection in the State of Jharkhand has considerably declined due to the strong Left Wing Extremism* particularly in the districts of West Singhbhum, Khunti, Latehar and Palamau. The contractors are not coming forward to participate in the tender of Kendu leaves as the Left Wing Extremism activist are demanding heavy amount from them from their profit.

Normally, the Jharkhand State Forest Development Corporation Limited, Ranchi invites auctions from the contractors to participate in the biddings in different Forest Divisions on the specified dates and they have to submit special amount as demand draft in favour of Jharkhand State Forest Development Corporation Ltd. on lump sum basis. The place of receiving tender are located at Ranchi/Jamshedpur/ Hazaribagh/Giridih/Daltonganj and Garhwa. The bank draft is payble at Ranchi only. The rate of collection cost of Kendu leaves payable to the primary collectors of Jharkhand decided by the State Government should be acceptable to the tenderers. There are several Minor Forest Produce project circle and the most important circles are Ranchi, Daltonganj, Garwha, Hazaribagh and Giridih. The name of the MFP Project Division and various ranges under them are given below.

Table 6.2: Kendu Patti Collection from 2002 to 2014 and Price paid to Pluckers

Year	*Rate paid to labour per bag of Kendu leaf (In Rs.)*	*Collection in lakh bags*	*Price paid to KL Pluckers in crores*	*Gross premium to corporation*	*Total Sale (in lakh amount)*
2002	401	5.09	20.413	7.680	28.093
2003	426	3.87	16.491	6.484	22.975
2004	431	4.74	20.423	6.416	26.839
2005	451	3.48	15.692	5.619	21.311
2006	456	3.06	13.978	7.538	21.516
2007	471	7.50	35.311	15.298	50.609
2008	501	5.65	28.326	14.862	43.188
2009	551	5.68	31.299	16.463	47.762
2010	601	5.68	34.164	20.757	54.921
2011	651	4.19	27.307	28.256	55.563

(Contd.)

Year	Rate paid to labour per bag of Kendu leaf (In Rs.)	Collection in lakh bags	Price paid to KL Pluckers in crores	Gross premium to corporation	Total Sale (in lakh amount)
2012	701	7.69	53.906	41.244	95.150
2013	901	4.13	37.211	23.105	60.316
2014	901	4.13	37.211	23.105	60.316
2015	**1066**	**3.01**	**32.035 (62.11%)**	**19.130 (37.38%)**	**51.165 (100.00%)**

Source: Forest Corporation, Forest Department Government of Jharkhand.

The filled data for the present study was collected during 2014-16 by the Research Team in the districts of Khunti, Saraikela-Kharsawan (Tables 6.3 and 6.4).

It can be deduced from the Abstract that throughout Jharkhand 7.96 lakhs of standard bags are the notified yield as per the figures given by the Jharkhand State Forest Development Corporation Ltd. The maximum extent is from the Hazaribagh division but from other divisions like Dhalbhum, Ranchi, Daltonganj, Garhwa and Giridih is around above 1 lakh standard bags each based on the figure of 2015. However, field investigations suggested that during the year 2015-16 most of the contractors did not participate in the tender submission because of the influence of left extremism and so the actual Kendu leaf collectors at the grassroots also did not venture the procurement of the Kendu leaf from the forest. This deprived the tribals of an important source of their economic family earning.

6.4 Review of Studies on NTFP in Jharkhand

There are paucity of studies on NTFP as a source of livelihood in Jharkhand. Here an attempt is being made to review couple of available studies on NTFP in Jharkhand. These are Ashish K. Gharai and Sheela Chakrabarti (2009) and another study is by Md. Ajaz-ul-Islam, *et al.* (2013).

Gharai and Chakrabarti (2009) have made a study of the commercialization potential of selected NTFP in the three districts of Jharkhand, mainly Gumla, Hazaribagh and Simdega. All the NTFPs available in each area were studied, but the main analysis is based on four major NTFPs, i.e. *Mahua*, *Lac*, *Karanj* and *Chiraunji*. Sample size was approximately 30 per cent of total number of households in each village.

Table 6.3: Collection of *Kendu Patta* in major MFP Project Divisions in Jharkhand State

Sl. No.	*MFP Project Division*	*MFP Range*	*Notified Yield (In standard bags)*	*Remarks*
1.	Dhalbhum	Anandpur	11,000	Presently located in West Singhbhum district
		Goelkera	15,850	
		Chaibasa	17,450	
		Chakradharpur	14,850	
		Chakulia	20,450	
		Mango	20,800	
		Total	**1,00,400**	
2.	Ranchi	Lohardaga	9,200	Ranchi District
		Ranchi	24,800	
		Gumla	32,300	
		Simdega West	18,200	
		Chandwa	26,200	
		Total	**1,36,900**	
3.	Daltonganj	Manatu	22,000	Palamau District
		Daltonganj	20,650	
		Kundri	26,900	
		Manika	20,450	
		Latehar	24,400	
		Nagar	27,450	
		Garhwa–I	18,800	
		Garhwa–II	15,550	
		Ranka	26,800	
		Bhawanathpur	23,275	
		Bhanbaria	24,700	
		Mohammadganj	12,550	
		Total	**2,63,525**	
4.	Hazaribagh	Champaran	23,600	Hazaribagh District
		Kodarma	16,350	
		Hazaribagh–I	16,150	
		Hazaribagh–II	14,550	
		Vishnugarh	27,500	
		Hunterganj–I	13,850	
		Hunterganj–II	45,000	
		Chatra	26,450	
		Simarig	11,200	
		Kunda	11,200	
		Total	**2,05,850**	
5.	Giridih	Satgawan	9,800	Giridih District
		Gawan	11,350	
		Jamua	11,350	
		Dumri	16,000	
		Sahebganj	24,800	Babhagalpur District
		Pakur	9,200	Pakur District

(Contd.)

Sl. No.	MFP Project Division	MFP Range	Notified Yield (In standard bags)	Remarks
		Deoghar	8,250	Deoghar District
		Dumka	15,900	Santhal Pargana
		Godda	9,750	District
		Total	**1,16,400**	
		Grand Total	**8,23,075**	

Source: Jharkhand State Forest Development Corporation Ltd., Ranchi, 2015.

Table 6.4: Abstract of Notified Yield (in Std. bags) of *Kendu Patta* in Jharkhand

Sl. No.	Name of Division	No. of MFP Range	No. of Units	No. of Territorial Range/Part territorial range	Notified Yield (in Std. Bag)
1.	Dhalbhum	6	95	46	102400
2.	Ranchi	7	110	44	105900
3.	Daltonganj	5	92	39	116200
4.	Garhwa	7	137	36	149125
5.	Hazaribagh	11	146	69	205850
6.	Giridih	9	106	66	116400
	Grand Total	**45**	**686**	**300**	**795875**

Source: Jharkhand State Forest Development Corporation Ltd., Ranchi, 2015.

The study found that Simdega has many NTFP resources, but lack of proper market and infrastructure for processing various items, makes NTFP related livelihoods less profitable as stated below:

- In Gumla, nearly half of the households surveyed were found to be involved in agriculture and the rest were marginal farmers, who engaged themselves in NTFP collection.
- Simdega district is rich in NTFP resources and almost all the household surveyed were involved in NTFP collection along with agriculture and allied activities.
- *Mahua* generates maximum income followed by *Karanj* and *Chiraunji*. *Mahua* is widely collected across all these studied villages for which they spend on an average of 23 days in the summer season. During this period they collect an average of 2264 kgs of *Mahua* per village.
- More than 85 per cent of Mahua collected is used in making alcohol and thus storage of raw and processed material becomes a huge problem. Oil extraction from *Mahua* is not widely practiced.

- Value addition is done only for *Mahua* and *Karanj* (with *Karanj* they prepare pickle). As *Mahua* is used for preparing wine, they generally use a specially designed indigenous machine for this purpose.
- Women play a very important role in collection of NTFP. Here, taking all the NTFPs that are being collected in all the house hold surveyed into consideration, it was found that around 83 per cent of women are involved in NTFP collection.
- Transportation of NTFPs related problems. Transport is one of the most crucial factors which decide the fortune of NTFP trade. In Jharkhand, lack of proper roads and transport facility in the rural areas affects the trade. During peak season, NTFP products are procured by them 3-5 times a month. Each trader covers around 35-40 villages for procurement of NTFPs.

Chiraunji is collected for 26 days on an average, during summer season. *Karanj* is mostly found in Gumla. The villagers sell seeds directly to small traders at cost of Rs. 7 to Rs. 8: on an average 415 kgs are collected per day. Lac is available mostly in Simdega district. Lac is sold at around Rs. 100 to Rs. 120: on an average 1840 kgs. of lac are collected each day. *Mahua* is available in abundance in Simdega district but major problem in collection is that the area is affected by Naxalite activities. The average days of collection in a season is 23 days. *Mahua* generates maximum income after value addition followed by *karanj*. The additional income from value addition comes to Rs. 4400.

Women play an important role in the collection of *Mahua* and *Kendu* leaves (*Diospyros melanoxylon*). They not only collect the *Kendu* leaves, but also make bundles of 50/100 leaves and sell it in the market. They also make leaf plates from these leaves and sell those at the market. Thus, women play active role in collection as well as in marketing of *Kendu* leaves. *Karanj* is also available in good amount in local forest. The local women are involved in the collection of *Karanj* which are then dried and seeds are squeezed to get oil. The entire process from collection to selling of oil is done mainly by women. *Chiraunji* (*Buchanania lauzan*) which are found in very small amount are also collected by some households. Female members of these households are mainly involved in collection and selling of *Chiraunji*. Forest fringe villages in the selected study areas are not solely dependent on NTFP collection, processing and selling. Most of them, especially in Hazaribagh district are engaged in agriculture and allied activities, with NTFP collection being mostly a subsidiary occupation.

Mohammad Ajaz-ul-Islam, *et al.* in their study on "Livelihood Contributions of Forest Resources to the Tribal Communities of Jharkhand" have analysed the livelihood contribution of forest resources to the Tribal Community of Bundu block in Ranchi district of Jharkhand. *Sal* leaf fetched highest earning (₹ 2,08,000 per annum) among surveyed households in the area followed by lac (₹ 1,00,500 per annum), fuel wood (₹ 89,600 per annum), tooth brush (₹ 67,200 per annum), fodder (₹ 64,000 per annum), *mahua* flower (₹ 56,760 per annum), mango (₹ 31,000 per annum), *chiraunji* (₹ 25,200 per annum), *ber* (₹ 24,000 per annum), *mahua* seed (₹ 17,424 per annum), *jamun* (₹ 16,800 per annum), tamarind (₹ 13,000 per annum), *koinar* tender leaf (₹ 9,600 per annum), *bhelwa* (₹ 9,600 per annum), bamboo corn (₹ 7,200 per annum), *kachnar* flower (₹ 7,200 per annum), *kusum* seed (₹ 5,850 per annum), *chiraita* (₹ 4200 per annum), *phutkal* leaf buds (₹ 4,000 per annum), *tendu* fruit (₹ 3,500 per annum), *toot* (₹ 3200 per annum), *bel* (₹ 2,991 per annum), jackfruit (₹ 2,625 per annum), *sal* seed (₹ 2,250 per annum), *rugra* and *khukhri* (₹ 2,250 per annum), *karanj* seed (₹ 2,200 per annum), *jirhul* flower (₹ 1,800 per annum), *harra* (₹ 1,500 per annum), *bahera* (₹ 1,200 per annum) and *barhar* (₹ 1,100 per annum).

The extraction and marketing of fodder generated highest unpaid employment opportunity of 6041 man-days/annum among the people in the study site followed by fuel wood (4326.46 man-days/annum), *sal* leaf (2421 man-days/annum), tooth brush (532.80 man-days/annum), lac (505.63 man-days/annum), *mahua* flower (133.32 man-days/annum), *ber* (71.00 man-days/annum), mango (57.20 man-days/annum), *jamun* (40.32 man-days/annum), *mahua* seed (32.04 man-days/annum), *tamarind* (31.00 man-days/annum), *chiraita* (30.00 man-days/annum), *rugra* and *khukhri* (28.20 man-days/annum), *koinar* tender leaf (27.20 man-days/annum), *bel* (22.94 man-days/annum), *kachnar* flower (21.50 man-days/annum), jackfruit (21.30 man-days/annum), *bhelwa* (19.80 man-days/annum), *sal* seed (18.00 man-days/annum), *kusum* seed (15.60 man-days/annum), bamboo corn (10.52 man-days/annum), *toont* (9.70 man-days/annum), *karanj* seed (8.80 man-days/annum), *chiraunji* seed (8.40 man-days/annum), *tendu* fruit (8.40 man-days/annum), *phutkal* leaf buds (8.20 man-days/annum), *barhar* (6.85 man-days/annum), *jirhul* flower (5.60 man-days/annum), *harra* (3.00 man-days/annum) and *bahera* (2.40 man-days/annum). The percentage of households involved in collection of various NTFPs varied from 1.83 per cent to 100 per cent while household's percentage involved in NTFPs marketing was 1.83 per cent to 80.49 per cent in the study villages. Income and unpaid employment generated through NTFPs based self-employment for the surveyed population in the area were computed to the Policies.

The NTFP markets are by and large imperfect and the aboriginal people do not get a fair return for their labour. The poor marketing infrastructure and lack of storage facilities compels them to sell off their produces to the first market contact that is generally the haat or the petty trader. The middlemen invariably exploit collectors of NTFPs on account of prevailing malpractices, forced and distress sales. The present situation reflects that all the major NTFPs are available for around 2-3 months except for fuel wood, fodder, sal leaf, lac and tooth brush and bulk (peak) trading seldom goes beyond 3-4 months.

Sanjay Kumar Verma and Sujit Kumar Paul (2016) in their study "Sustaining the Non-timber Forest Products (NTFPs) Based Rural Livelihoods of Tribals in Jharkhand: Issues and Challenges" found that income contribution from crop cultivation is higher than that from NTFPs. To make NTFPs collection by tribals sustainable various issues and challenges need to be addressed.

Dependency on Market forces for MFP in Jharkhand:

- Limited marketable surplus at the individual level and thus organizational effort is needed.
- Dependency on local intermediaries for market information related to price of produce.
- Heavy dependency on local trader for accessing easy credit. By providing the credit the local middleman controls the fate of produce.
- Direct access to terminal market and organized private players etc.
- Idea of stakeholders involved in the value chain.

6.5 NTFP Management and Trade in Jharkhand

Generally, the rights admitted inside the forest are:

- Right to take firewood. An average family is allowed 168 cft. of stacked firewood which is subjected to change depending on the capacity of the annual coupes and can be limited or reduced.
- Right to graze cattle in the forests except in coupes up to 5 years of age. Besides the above rights a number of concessions have been admitted from time to time and they are:

— Concession to take head load of dry firewood by the poor and landless people without any payment, for their own use, sale or barter, *vide* Revenue Department, Government of Bihar, letter No. C/F-5076/54-67-RT dated 9th May, 1954.

— Concession to remove all edible flowers and fruits free of any royalty. Concession to remove "Jhanti Jhuri" of thorny species for "Gherawan" purposes. Turis (a community engaged in making of bamboo based products) are to be given bamboo at concessional rate *vide* Government letter No. 226/69-1669 dated 6th June, 1969.

The first major policy level shift for the State Government had taken place a year before in the form of The Bihar Kendu Leaf (Control of Trade) Act, 1972. This Act was the first to initiate the nationalization of NTFP in the State of Bihar. The Kendu Leaf became a big revenue earner for the State. *Secondly its aim to check the exploitation of the tribal and give them their due share of the price, also was achieved to some extent.* The Bihar Forest Development Corporation was created in the year 1975 to basically look after the management, marketing and trade related issues of the Forest Department. The result was that the process of Bihar State Forest Development Corporation trading in *Sal* seeds (Nationalized in 1977 itself) was initiated in the year 1977.

Under the provisions of Bihar Forest Produce (Regulation of Trade) Fourth Ordinance, 1977, the Bihar State Forest Development Corporation was appointed as an agent for the purchase and trade of *Mahua* fruit and seed, *Karanj* fruit and seed and *Kusum* fruit and seed with effect from 1st April, 1978. Again under the provisions of the Bihar Forest Produce (Regulation of Trade) Third Ordinance, 1980 the preview of the Bihar State Forest Development Corporation was extended to include *Harra* fruit and seed, *Palas* fruit and seed, *Aonla* fruit and seed and *Bahera* fruit and seed.

- An Act was framed in the year 1984 known as the Bihar Forest Produce (Regulation of Trade) Act, 1984. The Act talks of appointing one or more than one agent for all or any specified Forest produce. It visualises greater role of Gram Panchayats, LAMPS, PACS, Vyapar Mandal or the Bihar State Tribal Co-operative Development Corporation Ltd. or

The Bihar State Forest Development Corporation or any similar Corporation is being appointed as an agent for one or more forest produce.

- This Act restricts the purchase or transport of specified forest produce. An officer of the Government is authorised in writing in this behalf. An agent in respect of the unit in which the specified forest produce grown or found, shall purchase or transport or import or export such specified forest produce in and from such area.
- The Act also expanded the range of products coming under the State's purview. The new addition to the list were: Fruit and seeds of *Maula, Kamla, Chiraunji, Kacheria,* Flowers of *Mahua*, Gums and Resins of *Karaya, Katila, Dhaura, Sal* resin, *Salai* resin, *Sabai* grass, lac, *Tasar, Mahulan* and *Sal* leaves, *Khair*, bamboo and medicinal and Fibre yielding plants.
- Earlier Bamboo along with *Sabai* grass was leased out to paper mills and private companies but at present no product is as such leased out due to Naxal activity. However, *Sal, Mahua* seed, *Mahulan* and *Kendu* leaf are given to private traders for collection and marketing under the *Ek Musht Pranali*. This is not exactly leasing, but here also the specified products are given to private traders for collection and marketing for a certain period of time, on advance payment with other terms and conditions.
- The major markets trading in various NTFP/NTFP based products in the State are: Daltonganj, Garhwa, Latehar, Chatra, Hazaribagh, Gumla, Giridih, Ranchi, Jamshedpur, Chaibasa and Chakradharpur. The main traders of these markets get collected NTFP from sub-trader/regional wholesaler/agents and depending upon the utility and demand of a particular NTFP it is traded in the domestic or export market.
- There is a general disenchantment among the next generation of primary collectors, towards taking up NTFP collection as their source of income. The naxalite movement in the interiors is also a great problem for the primary collectors because they are the ones who get directly affected.

NTFP in West Singhbhum District of Jharkhand

The potential of *Kendu* leaves are very high in the Kolhan division.

Collection by Forest Development Corporation could not do justice with the potential and needs efficient management. Usually, 50 leaves half bundled in one direction and half in other direction constitute a "*pola*".

Table 6.5: Time Spent in Collection and Processing of Different Forest Produces

Finished Products	*Raw Products*	*Time Consumed in collection, processing and marketing (hours)*						
		Collect	*Dry*	*Clean*	*Crush*	*Work*	*Market*	*Total Time*
Sal Seed	*Sal* Fruit	8	1	1	4	4	8	26
Karanj Seed	*Karanj* Fruit	8	—	—	6	6	2	22
Mahua Flower	*Mahua* Flower	8	4	—	—	—	4	16
Dola	*Mahua* Fruit	8	—	—	—	—	8	32
Kusum Seeds	*Kusum* Fruit	8	—	—	2	3	8	21

Source: From Field Survey.

The tribals of local village bring their commodities to the nearby haats for selling. These commodities undergo various commoditization processes.

Sal Leaves

The *sal* ('*sarjom*' as locally named by the Ho tribes of the region) tree holds a special position in the socio-economic life of tribals in Jharkhand as each part of the tree (wood, seed, leaves, young shoots) is used everyday by forest dwellers. For many poor households, *sal* leaves are the only utensil used for serving food. This forest product is distinctive in that it is extracted throughout the year for both domestic consumption and sale. These leaves are mainly collected from the forests. Many poor tribal families are involved only in the collection of '*sal*' leaves for the sale in *haats*.

Khajur

Khajur (*Khijur*) leaves come from bushes which are found in abundance in open forests and on dry land with moderate tree cover. In West Singhbhum they are common on the plains than in the hills or forests. The branches are used for fences and the leaves for roofing. Sleeping mats made from *khajur* leaves are used in most rural areas of West Singhbhum and are also exported to Bihar and West Bengal.

Vegetables and Flowers

Tribals living close to the forest supplement their food intake by collecting forest-based food. They collect a number of different wild vegetables, tubers and flowers which they are sometimes unable to differentiate. For convenience, therefore, these are referred as wild vegetables. Example of such wild vegetables include *pitalu, masia kand* and Bamboo shoots (*helta*). In West Singhbhum district at least seven types of wild and leafy vegetables are regularly collected from local forest areas by tribal women gather. Although most wild vegetables are of herb and shrub origin a few such as *futkal* and *koinar-aa* are from trees. Other vegetables like tomato, lady's finger, brinjal and cucumber are also sold in the *haats* by the tribals which they grow in their farms. These vegetables are cultivated in winter season and include extensive labour as there is no irrigation facility and so they used to irrigate it physically using tins carrying on their shoulders. Once these vegetables get ready then they are taken to the local *haats* by the women on their heads and sold in a minimum price. Most of them are illiterate, because of which they are unable to fix the price and sold it by '*keja*'. One *keja* resembles a unit of handful quantity. Generally, they do not have weighing scale (*taraju*), thus, they use this unique means for measuring their commodities.

The *Mahua* tree has a very important place in the socio-economic and cultural life of tribals of West Singhbhum as it has variety of uses including the provisions of timber, food, liquor and shade. In the region, *mahua* trees are found on homestead and farm land as well as in the forest and on government wastelands. There is a lot of market demand for both the fruits and seeds of the tamarind tree. Whereas tamarind fruits has a very good market in South India, tamarind seeds is locally used by millers to produce tamarind flour. Almost all tribal households in West Singhbhum villages have tamarind trees on their homestead land. Tamarind collection takes place primarily in February and March, although the pods may be left on the trees for later collection. The sale of tamarind fruit and seeds is major source of income in West Singhbhum district.

Oil Seeds

The main tree borne oilseeds in Kolhan are *sal, kusum, neem, karanj* and *mahua*. Oil seeds of tree origin are quite important for the income needs of tribal households in remote locations of West Singhbhum. The oil content of *mahua* seed (known locally as '*madkam*') varies from 33-43 per cent which is higher than for most other oil seeds. Most tribals obtain *mahua* oil using rather inefficient home-made wooden crushers which often extract as little as 12 per cent of the seed oil content. *Mahua* oil is used for good quality soaps as well as edible oil and *mahua* seed cake is used as fertilizer. In West Singhbhum, *Mahua* seeds are one of the main sources of income and subsistence during the lean summer months (April–July) for many poor tribal families. *Kusum* is a large deciduous tree, the fruit of which contains one or two seeds which contain nearly 33 per cent oil. In West Singhbhum, almost all of the *kusum* seeds collected are sold to local traders. *Kusum* trees are particularly abundant in forests and farm and homestead land in West Singhbhum. The *Neem* tree (*Azadirachat indica*) is a tropical evergreen tree native to India. It is also known as "the village pharmacy" because of its healing versatility. In the West Singhbhum districts, *neem* trees can be found in large number in its villages and in enormous numbers in the forests. The tribals of the villages basically use the *neem* seeds for extracting oil and *neem* twigs for *datun* (toothbrushes). They also use the *neem* leaves and *neem* barks for curing certain diseases.

Sal Leaves

Sal leaves are used for domestic consumption and increasingly (among the poorest families) for the manufacture of *sal* leaf plates for sale in urban markets. *Sal* leaves are collected throughout the year at weekly or sometimes at monthly intervals and generally speaking, it is women and children who undertake the share of leaf collection. The leaves are collected mostly by the women belonging to different age right from children to old age. They spend whole day in the forest for collecting the leaves. They move in a group of 4-8 and collect an average of 5 kg of leaves by one person. Once the branches are removed, the leaves are than arranged and tied with climbers and brought to the home. *They walk a long distance back again having heavy bundles of leaves on their head. Once they reach the home, the leaves are again arranged and re-tied with the climbers and prepared to be taken to the market for sell.* Each bundle of leaves weighs around 1 to 1.5 kg. *The male and female both participate in taking these leaves to the market. The male generally uses bicyle for this purpose but females usually carry it on their head and again walk a long distance from their home to the rural haats and town markets.* They sit at the road sides or even in a small corner in the market place or *haat* to sell these. *The buyers bargain them to the very extent and they lastly sell them in the minimum prices of Rs. 3 to 5.*

Khajur Leaves

The women roam through the farmlands and collect the leaves cutting it with *datrom* (*hasua*). Once brought to the home is further sorted and kept in the water for few days. Once it gets soft, it is used for making mats. The process of making mats is quite time-consuming and it takes 5 to 6 weeks to prepare a mat of a standard size (7 × 3 ft.). The prepared mats are generally used for the household's activities but they are also sold in the market. These mats are sold in the market at a price ranging from Rs. 200 to 400. The leaves are also sold in the local haats in the raw condition in the form of bundles. Each bundle of 15 kg (approx.) is sold in Rs. 20-30. Of course, they face extensive bargaining by the buyers. They walk a long distance to make it to reach the market and again bringing it back on their heads if unsold. One more important point here is, the price is not decided by the sellers, instead the buyers have the power to decide the price and he pays the most appropriate price according to him.

Karanj Seed

Karanj oil is used widely in West Singhbhum as a source of oil for lamps, body massage and occasionally for cooking and medicinal purpose. The oil is also used commercially in the manufacture of soap. Collection takes place primarily in March and April and the tribals need not have to spend long travelling to collect *karanj* seeds, i.e. around half an hour as most *karanj* trees are situated on homestead and farm field land rather than in the forest.

Mahua (Madhuca latifolia) Flowers and Seeds

It is a rich source of edible oil. The seed is collected between June and July and as there are a large number of *mahua* trees on homestead and farm land, the average travelling time required to collect *mahua* seeds tends to be relatively short (about half an hour). The processing of *mahua* seeds is quite labour intensive and the time consuming with drying taking an average of just under 25 hours and oil extraction taking around 4.5 hours. Similar to the leaves, these oil seeds are also collected by the tribal women and children. They are usually collected in the form of fruits; later the seed is separated from the fruit and further processed to produce oil from it. This whole process requires a long lime and labour, which can be examined.

Tamarind (Tamarindus indica)

Most households in West Singhbhum have tamarind trees on their homestead or farm land and there is lot of domestic and market demand for tamarind fruits which are used as a source of food. Tamarind collection takes place primarily in February and March, although the pods may be left on the trees for later collection. The tamarind fruits have its importance for household subsistence and cash income among the tribals. The average journey time for tamarind collection in West Singhbhum was quite short half an hour as a result of the widespread availability of tamarind tree on homestead land. On the one hand, there are products which the tribes bring to the market with lot of effort and on the other side, there are *haats* which are controlled by the non-tribals and non-local persons and are highly competitive and impersonal. This results in exploitation of these tribal products as well as the tribal people who produce products. In this process of capitalist encroachment to the tribal economy, the local tribes of Kolhan get entangled in the vicious circle of capitalist structure of this market system. In this sense, they are at the 'tail-end' of the capitalist value chain. They are already dependent on the markets for their livelihood and now they become more vulnerable to this exploitation. [*Source*: Bace Buriuly (2013) *Tribal Weekly Markets* (*HAATS*)—*A study In West Singhbhum District of Jharkhand*, Mumbai: Centre for Social Entrepreneurship, School of Management and Labour Studies, Tata Institute of Social Sciences].

6.6 Lac Cultivation and Processing in Jharkhand

Lac is a natural resin secreted by an insect Kerrialacca (Kerr), which thrives on the tender twigs. The raw lac is the source of three valuable, natural and renewable products, i.e. resin, dye and wax. Rangeeni and Kusumi are the two strains of lac insect which are classified based on the preference of the insect for specific host plants. Lac cultivation is an important source of income for livelihood of the forest dwellers in Jharkhand. Besides, it had high potential for generating employment for both men and women in forest and fringe areas of Jharkhand.

Jharkhand State ranks 1st in production of lac followed by

Chhattisgarh, Madhya Pradesh, Maharashtra and West Bengal. These five States contribute around 97 per cent of the national lac production. Regarding share of different crops *jethwi* ranks 1st (32.60%) followed by the *baisakhi* (27.25%), *aghani* (24.32%) and *katki* (15.82%) in national lac production. In the year 2012-13, the production of all the crops in comparison to previous year production has increased. Major Lac producing districts in Jharkhand during 2012-13 were Ranchi, Simdega, Gumla, West Singhbhum, Palamau, Latehar.

Lac Processing Scenario

On the basis of surveys conducted at different lac processing centres in the country, the total quantity of sticklac processed during 2010-11 was 13,600 tons which also included the imported lac in India. There are twenty eight lakh processing units in Chhattisgarh, 15 units in Jharkhand, 6 units in Maharashtra, 2 units in Madhya Pradesh and 143 units in West Bengal. West Bengal ranked 1st (42.7%) followed by Chhattisgarh (26.5%), Jharkhand (25.7%), Maharashtra (5.1%) and Madhya Pradesh (0.7%).

Table 6.6: Amount of Sticklac processed in India during 2010-11

States	*Quantity processed (tons)*	*Percentage share in lac processing*
West Bengal	5800	42.33
Chhattisgarh	3600	26.28
Jharkhand	3500	25.55
Maharashtra	700	5.11
Madhya Pradesh	100	0.73
Total	**13700**	**100.00**

Source: Indian Institute of Natural Resins and Gums, Namkum, Ranchi, 2010-11.

Almost 75 per cent of lac produced in India is exported to different countries of which the main customers are USA, UK, Germany, Italy, France, Japan, China, Sweden, Brazil, Argentina and Russia. The total export of lac and its value added products during the year 2010-11 was 6339.05 tons valued Rs. 211.13 crore (Table 6.7).

Though Jharkhand produces 56.88 per cent of sticklac in the country, it processes only 25.74 per cent of the lac. Rest of the lac produced in Jharkhand is despatched to the neighbouring States, mostly West Bengal, for its processing and State lose revenue by supplying lac as a raw material to these States.

Table 6.7: Export of Lac and its Value added Products from India during 2010-11

Sl. No.	*Name of the product*	*Export in 2010-11*	
		Quantity (tons)	*Value (Rs. lakhs)*
1.	Shellac	4616.18	13565.14
2.	Seedlac	1089.55	3659.44
3.	Dewaxed shellac	200.125	1051.68
4.	Bleached lac	336.13	1598.86
5.	Aleuritic acid	64.00	1118.13
6.	Gasket lac	4.32	6.62
7.	Shellac wax	28.75	113.05
	Total	**6339.05**	**21112.92**

Source: Indian Institute of Natural Resins and Gums, Namkum, Ranchi, 2010-11.

6.7 Role of Indian Institute of Natural Resins and Gums

Indian Institute of Natural Resins and Gums, Namkum, Jharkhand has played yeoman service in promoting the lac cultivation in Jharkhand, Bihar, Uttar Pradesh, Odisha, Chhattisgarh, West Bengal, Rajasthan and other States in India. It is located in Ranchi from where it imparts In-campus Orientation programme, Demonstration of lac cultivation technologies in different States, field visit programmes to different districts and States, impetus to production, marketing including export, conducting workshops and seminar, having direct face-face interaction with the lac farmers, promoting shellac industry and monitoring scientific lac cultivation, processing and utilization. It has been of seminal benefit to the tribals of the Jharkhand and other States. There have been some success stories of the tribal cultivator in Jharkhand due

MARKETING CHANNELS OF LAC

Private Channels

Lac Growers Agent Paikars Rakhiwals Arhatdars Wholesaler Manufacturer

Cooperative Channels

Farmers Agent Purchase Committees LAMPS; PACS; VMSSS Marketing of Lac—A Cooperative Approach to the intense effort of the Indian Institute of Natural Resins and Gums, Namkum, Jharkhand. These case studies were mainly from the district of Ranchi and Khunti.

Lac Cooperative in Jharkhand

There are a good number of important *haats* in the lac growing areas where lac is grown in abundance. As it is a non-nationalized item, it is being handled by very many intermediaries. Big manufacturers distribute money to the *paikars* on the basis of individual purchasing capacity in the morning of each *haat* day. These *paikars* purchase sticklac in the *haat* at price dictated by the principal buyers. In the evening, they bring purchased stock to the buyer and take their commission, the commission is generally Rs. 5 to Rs. 7 per maund (40 kg): the commission also includes transport cost from *haats* to buyer's godowns.

Some *paikars* bring the stock to manufactures in the areas and negotiate the rates with them. If the rates are acceptable to *paikars* they deliver the stock and receive commission at the rate of Rs. 10 to Rs. 20 per maund. There are also some *arhats* in some towns. These arhats are in Ranchi, Chandwa, Daltonganj and Ranka (Garwah). The function of these *arhats* generally is to arrange sticklac for the potential buyers. The buyers approach these arhats and indicate their requirements. Then *arhatdars* contact *paikars* or lac traders in locality for the required stock. Commission of the *Arhatdars* is 3 per cent of the value of the stock transacted at these places. They charge commission from both the buyers and sellers. In most of the *haats*, lac growers bring sticklac for sale, but there are *haats* where *paikars* collect sticklac from the interior areas and bring the stock on Horseback for sale. These haats are at Ranka (Palamau district) and Tamar (Ranchi district).

At present, *arhatdars* in Ranchi town have gradually become practically non-functional. *Paikars* and other lac traders in Dudhi area in Uttar Pradesh collect sticklac from *haats* in the area. Presently, there being no processing unit in Uttar Pradesh, the entire stock of sticklac produced is smuggled to Jharkhand. The rates are also very cheap in these areas. The field study has revealed that Ranka *Haat* situated on the borders of Uttar Pradesh, is dominated by middleman who collect sticklac from the surrounding villages bring stock in the *haat* and sells it.

Role of JHASCO LAMPS

JHASCO LAMPS operates in lac growing areas by giving support price to the farmers through Vyapar Mandals and multipurpose agricultural societies. There are about 178 affiliated societies with the JHASCO LAMPS in the whole of Jharkhand, basically in Palamau, Ranchi and Chaibasa, but about 50 to 60 societies are actually doing the lac marketing. The presence of JHASCO LAMPS the price of sticklac in the market was only Rs. 30 (thirty) per kg in 2002. But when JHASCO LAMPS declared its rate of Rs. 50 per kg. of sticklac were enhanced by the traders also. The lac growers are getting good price through the LAMPS, PACS and VMSS.

The primary multipurpose agricultural cooperative societies are called LAMPS, (Large Area Multi-Purpose Cooperative Society). There are about 1000 members in each of the LAMPS which covers 15 to 20 square kilometres area. There are 834 LAMPS in Jharkhand, but only 152 LAMPS are affiliated to JHASCO LAMPS. Most members of the LAMPS depend upon the farming of minor forest produces like lac, tamarind, *mahua* etc. But among these, lac is an important produce of the tribal farmers. Primary Agricultural Cooperative Societies are called PACS. There are 476 PACS in Jharkhand and 152 are affiliated with the JHASCO LAMPS. 16 PACS are doing lac marketing with it in the area of Palamau and Garwah.

Vyapar Mandal Sahyog Samitis are existing at block level. These are basically the marketing societies. The JHASCO LAMPS gives 3 per cent commission to the societies to encourage the working of LAMPS, and PACS and VMSS to safeguard the interests of the rural tribal lac farmers. All societies purchase sticklac from the farmers. Purchase committee of the society fix the price of lac on the basis of the support price of JHASCO LAMPS. Therefore, JHASCO LAMPS is trying to eradicate the exploitation of farmers by the middleman. [J. Kumar, "Marketing of Lac—A Cooperative Approach", K.K. Sharma and R. Ramani (ed.), 2011, "*Recent Advances in LAC CULTURE*", Ranchi: Indian Institute of Natural Resins and Gums, Namkum].

In order to help and assist the primary producers in lac in Jharkhand, the procurement agencies particularly Lamps have played an important role in the procurement of lakh from the primary producers, giving them the assured price, procuring the quantities and handing them over to JHASCO LAMPS for example during the year 2015 nearly 15 primary LAMP organizations at the grassroots level in the Khunti and Saraikela-Kharsawan districts had procured 558.78

quintals of seed lac from 597 beneficiaries and paid them Rs. 1,78,81,837 (i.e. 1.788 crore) rupees paid to the beneficiaries. This was in fact a significant contribution of JHASCO LAMPS. The kusum emporium located in Ranchi has also live contact with several SHGs in Ranchi, Khunti and other districts of Jharkhand and purchasing their lac product and doing creditabl service. In the same way the Jharkhand State Co-operative Lac Marketing and Procurement Federation Ltd., Namkum has also been procuring lac from the beneficiaries and is marketing the lac produce. It tries to operate based on MSP and its procurement prices from 2010-11 to 2014-15 have been as follows:

Table 6.8: Status of Jharkhand State Co-operative Lac Marketing and Procurement Federation Ltd., Namkum (Ranchi)

Sl. No.	*Year*	*Prevailing Procurement price of Sticklac (Rs. per kg)*		*Brood Lac (Rs. per kg)*		*Quantity (in MT)*	*Value (Rs. In Lakh)*
		Kusumi	*Rangeeni*	*Kusumi*	*Rangeeni*		
1.	2010-11	100-150	70-100	250	300	6339.05	21112.90
2.	2011-12	150-180	120-150	660	315	6858.21	36461.30
3.	2012-13	200-800	150-600	650	435	4361.30	48027.60
4.	2013-14	460-750	200-450	425	350	8153.10	56853.60
5.	2014-15	210-350	150-200	290	310	6569.17	32249.70

Source: DGCIS, Kolkata, Shexil, Kolkata.

The Jharkhand State Co-operative Lac Marketing and Procurement Federation, Namkum, have been extending adequate support to the lac cultivators and lac growers by procuring their lac produce. However, they have been themselves on a losing ground because their procurement price based on the minimum support price is much lower than the prevailing market price. One of the important reason for this is the gap between the prevailing market price and MSP. For example, the prevailing Market price for the *Kusumi* lac during 2015 June was Rs. 100-130 per kg as against Minimum Support Price (MSP) of Rs. 320 and for *Rangeeni* lac prevailing market price was Rs. 90-110 per kg as against MSP of Rs. 230 per kg fixed by Government of India which is almost three times higher than the prevailing market price.

Lac Cultivation as Rural Enterprises

Lac is cultivated mostly in rural area of Jharkhand. For this purpose extensive training of farmers is necessary in their fields. Indian Institute of Natural Resins and Gums have undertaken rural enterprise training for the lac cultivating farmers in different districts of Jharkhand and other States. A brief account of the activities of India Institute of Natural Resins and Gums, Ranchi including the Capacity Buildings of Farmers and Entrepreneurship Development is given below:

- Extensive training programme on scientific lac cultivation, processing and utilization were organized for farmers, trainers and students. A total of 1256 farmers from different districts of six States *viz.* Jharkhand, Odisha, Chhattisgarh, West Bengal, Madhya Pradesh and Maharashtra participated in the programmes.
- Under Trainer's training programme on "Scientific method of lac cultivation, production processing and utilization", 211 participants were trained as Trainers through 10 different courses.
- Educational training on production, processing and uses of natural resins and gums imparted to 119 students through four courses of ten days duration each.
- Special Trainer's programme on "Advance technology of lac production, processing and utilization" were conducted on the request of NABARD, Pune and 28 persons from different districts of Maharashtra participated in the training.
- Short term training of three days duration on "Natural resins and gums" was organized for 11 forest officials (DFO, SDO and RO) of Gadchiroli, Maharashtra.
- Subject specific training for 12 participants on "Plantation raising and lac cultivation on Flemingia semialata" and "Scientific lac cultivation on Butea monosperma".
- Sixteen camps on farm-training on "Scientific cultivation of lac" organized in collaboration with other organizations in Jharkhand and Uttar Pradesh to train 1670 farmers.
- Under On-farm, Motivational/Supplementary training programme on lac cultivation, 25 camps were organized in collaboration with NGOs and GOs of different States. About 3454 persons (mainly farmers) representing twelve districts of six States benefited from the programme.
- Under In-campus Orientation programme on lac cultivation in collaboration with NGOs and GOs of different States, 63 batches (3163 farmers and students) were sensitized on natural resins and gums.
- Monitoring of *kusumi* lac crop, technical guidance remedial measures for pest attack, demonstration of inoculation

spraying etc. were conducted in the State of Jharkhand, Chhattisgarh, West Bengal and Andhra Pradesh at 25 places.

- A total of 19 *Kisan Gosthis* organized by the Institute in Jharkhand and West Bengal. The Institute participated in nine *Kisan Melas* organized by different institutions in West Bengal, Jharkhand, Odisha, New Delhi, Maharashtra and Bihar.
- New linkages have been developed with District Planning Office, Collectorate, Khunti with the sanction of new project entitled "Lac cultivation and processing unit establishment" for development of lac in Khunti district of Jharkhand in partnership with "Torpa Rural Development Society for women" and "Bioved Research Institute for Agriculture and Technology".
- A research project entitled "Cluster based on-farm participatory research in farming system perspective" at Saraitoli Rampur, Ranchi was initiated with ICAR-Research Complex for Eastern Region, Research Centre, Ranchi. During the period from January to December 2012, the Institute has earned Rs. 11,53,650 as training charges.

In-Campus, Orientation Programme on Lac Cultivation

In-Campus, Orientation programme on Natural Resins and Gums were organized with GOs and NGOs of different States and 3275 farmers and students visited the Institute for the purpose.

Table 6.9: In-campus One Day Orientation Programme on Lac Cultivation by the Indian Institute of Natural Resins and Gums, Namkum

States	District	No. of Batches	No. of Stakeholders
Jharkhand	Khunti	5	157
	Ranchi	37	2180
	Simdega	1	20
	West Singhbhum	2	86
	East Singhbhum	1	28
	Dhanbad	6	307
	Gumla	3	176
	Latehar	1	16
	Jagdalpur	1	10
Bihar	Katihar	2	49
	Siwan	1	35
Uttar Pradesh	Allahabad	2	55
	Varanasi	1	44
Total		**63**	**3163**

Source: Indian Institute of Natural Resins and Gums, Namkum, Ranchi, 2014.

Other Activities

Monitoring of *kusumi lac* crop, technical guidance, remedial measures for pest attack, demonstration of inoculation, spraying etc. at different locations were carried out by the institute. These were conducted in the States of Jharkhand, Chhattisgarh, West Bengal and Andhra Pradesh at 25 places (Tables 6.10-6.12).

Table 6.10: Transfer of Technology Activities related to Lac Production

Sl. No.	*District-State*	*Venue (Village Block)*	*Collaborating Agency*	*Date*	*Purpose*
1.	Latehar, Jharkhand	Pesrar, Latehar	TRIFED	04.05.11	*Rangeeni* lac on *Palas* and *Ber*
2.	Manika, Latehar	Manika, Latehar	TRIFED	05.05.11	*Rangeeni* lac on *Palas* and *Ber*
3.	Ranchi, Jharkhand	Lapung, Ranchi	TRIFED	10.05.11	*Baisakhi* crop on *Akashmani*
4.	Saraikela-Kharsawan, Jharkhand	Kuruspur, Sraikela-Kharswas	KVK, Saraikela	14.07.11	Inoculation of *rangeeni* lac
5.	Ranchi, Jharkhand	Beradih, Ranchi	NCS, Ranchi	28.08.11	*Kusumi* lac on *Ber*
6.	Ranchi, Jharkhand	Sorha, Ranchi	NCS, Ranchi	28.08.11	*Kusumi* lac on *Ber*
7.	Khunti, Jharkhand	Khunti, Ranchi	NCS, Ranchi	28.08.11	*Kusumi* lac on *F. semialata*
8.	Ranchi, Jharkhand	Gutidih Ranchi	Udyogini, Ranchi	31.08.11	*Kusmi* lac on 400 *Ber* trees
9.	Ranchi, Jharkhand	Jaradih, Ranchi	Udyogini, Ranchi	31.08.11	*Kusumi* lac inoculated on *Ber* trees
10.	Latehar, Jharkhand	Lalli, Latehar	IINRG	03.09.11	*Kusumi* lac on *Ber* trees and *rangeeni* lac on *palas* trees.

Source: Indian Institute of Natural Resins and Gums, Namkum, Ranchi, 2012.

Table 6.11: Demonstration of Lac Cultivation Technologies

Sl. No.	*State*	*District*	*Technologies*	*Host plants utilized*	*Linkages*
1.	Jharkhand	Latehar	*Kusumi* lac on ber *Rangeeni* lac on palas	*Ber*-50 *Palas*-70	Progressive farmers
		Ranchi	*Kusumi* lac on ber	*Ber*-150	KVK Divyayan
2.	Chhattisgarh	Raigarh	*Kusumi* lac on *F. semialata*	*F. Semialata* 1,000	NGO (Janmitram)
3.	Bihar	Patna	Raising of F. *Semialata*	–	ICAR-Research Centre for Eastern Region (RCER)
4.	West Bengal	Paschim Midnapur	*Kusumi* lac on *F. semialata*	*F. Semialata* 1,000	NGO-International Mass Awarerness Programme (IMAP)
5.	Odisha	Mayurbhanj	*Kusumi* lac on *F. semialata*	*F. Semialata* 900	Progressive Farmer
6.	Uttar Pradesh	Allahabad	*Kusumi* lac on *F. semialata*	*F. Semialata* 1,000	NGO-BIOVED Research Institute of Agriculture, Science and Technology

Source: Indian Institute of Natural Resins and Gums, Namkum, Ranchi, 2012.

6.8 Lac Cultivation and Processing Unit Establishment in District Khunti

This project has been initiated by District Planning Office, Collectorate Khunti, Jharkhand during the year 2014-15 to address the major issues of the poor resource constraint faced by the people inhabiting in forest and sub-forest areas through scientific interventions and utilization of locally available natural resources. Lac cultivation is one of the viable interventions in this direction to provide livelihood support for sub-forest and forest dwellers with additional opportunity of employment at industry level and better utilization of degraded land with biodiversity conservation. District Planning Office, Collectorate, Khunti has taken the initiatives and provided funds through the District Innovative Fund to Indian Institute of Natural Resins and Gums, Ranchi for developmental activities in Khunti

Table 6.12: Details of Crop Output (Brood lac Yield)

Sl. No	*Location*	*Input*	*Output*	*Yield Ratio*	*Remarks*
1.	Badpurunapani (Mayurbhanj, Odisha)	15 kg	75 kg	1:5.06	*Kusumi* broodlac provided by the Institute Crop: *Kusumi* lac on *F. semialata* (*Aghani* 2011-12)
2.	Baihamunda (Rayagarh, Chhattisgarh)	20 kg	120 kg	1:6	Input facilitated by NGO Crop: *Kusumi* lac on *F. semialata* (Aghani 2011-12)
3.	Lalli and Nadbelwa (Latehar, Jharkhand)	50 kg (Kusumi)	200 kg	1:4	*Kusmi* broodlac provided by the Institute Crop: *Kusumi* lac on *ber* (*Aghani* 2011-12)
		75 kg (Rangeeni)	–	–	Crop utilized for self-inoculation Crop: *Rangeeni* lac on *palas* (*Baisakhi-cum-Katki* 2011-12)
4.	Putadag, Kuturloba and Jhiki (Ranchi, Jharkhand)	150 kg	585 kg	1:3.9	*Kusumi* broadlac provided by the Institute Crop: *Kusumi* lac on ber (*Aghani* 2011-12)

Source: Indian Institute of Natural Resins and Gums, Namkum, Ranchi, 2012.

district. Three institutions, namely District Planning Office (DPO), Torpa Rural Development Society for Women (TRDS), Torpa and Bioved Lac Resource Training Centre, Khunti, has come forward to work together in collaboration with IINRG, Ranchi under the project to demonstrate improved technologies of lac cultivation on existing lac host trees (kusum, ber and *palas*) and establish *Flemingia semialata* farms as well as small scale lac processing unit and imparting skill development for preparation of lac based handicraft items. *The work will be carried out in Torpa and Rania Blocks of Khunti district through formation of SHGs (31) and total 415 families will be covered under the project.* Six farmers across three villages of Khunti district were idenitifed and 1200 seedlings of quick growing bushy lac host, *Flemingia semialata* were distributed for planting in farmer's fields.

Some *Butea monosperma* (*palas*) trees were identified in nearby villages for raising *rangeeni* summer season (*baisakhi*) lac crop. Two quintals of rangeeni broodlac have been distributed to 93 members of 8 SHGs across six villages in two blocks of Khunti district. Demonstration of bundling and inoculation of broodlac as well as monitoring and technical guidance in five villages of Torpa block was conducted. The Institute is Consortium partner and Birsa Agriculture University, Ranchi is the lead centre. The project was concluded in March 2012, but again revived during November 2012.

Performance and Output from Rangeeni Summer Crop

The data have been collected from farmers who raised rangeeni lac crop on *Butea monosperma.* A total of 21 households of Jamtara and 20 from Dumka districts has produced 481 and 516 kg *rangeeni* broodlac, respectively during July 2012. *An income of Rs. 1,20,250 and Rs. 1,29,000 have been generated from marketing of broodlac by the households of Jamtara and Dumka districts respectively.* It is worthy to note that lac insect survived well in most of the areas despite increase in maximum temperature during summer and also there was no pre-summer mortality as in other areas of Jharkhand. Two spray of indoxacarb and fipronil was carried out on lac culture as per schedule of spray. Around 108 man-days were generated by intervention of this activity in the adopted villages.

Performance and Output from Rangeeni Rainy Season Crop

A total of 165 and 179 kg *rangeeni* broodlac was produced from Jamtara and Dumka districts, respectively from *rangeeni* rainy season crop harvested during November 2012. An estimated income Rs. 86,000 generated from marketing of 344 kg broodlac. Two spray of indoxacarb was carried out on the rainy season crop. Broodlac was successfully marketed by the farm families to the farmers of adjoining villages. *Around 112 man-days generated by intervention of this activity in the adopted villages.*

Marketing of Scraped Lac

A total of 87 kg lac obtained as Phunki scraped has been marketed by 41 households of 16 villages to traders. An estimated income of Rs. 26,100 has been generated after marketing. The total income generated from lac production by 41 households is to the extent of Rs. 3,61,350 in 16 villages of Dumka and Jamtrara and average income comes to around Rs. 8,813 per household.

Field Visit and Crop Monitoring

More than 25 field visits were undertaken by the faculty of the Institute for interaction with farmers and monitoring of lac crop time-to-time in adopted villages of Jamtara and Dumka districts. A total of 900 kg of *rangeeni* broodlac was inoculated on 1600 trees of *B. monosperma* in Novembr, involving 53 households of nine villages in Jamtara and Dumka districts. A total of 10 demonstration was carried out for *rangeeni* lac cultivation on *B. monosperma* tree, one in each village namely Badamanjhiadih, Saurimundu, Kasitand, Karmatand, Chaina in Jamtara district; Karmatand, Jiyathar, Guhiajori, Bhounraand, Amra villages in Dumka District. A total 30 farmers from Jamtara and Dumka district have successfully completed three days training on Scientific Lac Cultivation at IINRG, Ranchi from 5th to 7th March, 2012.

Table 6.13: Production of Lac from Rangeeni Summer and Winter Crop during 2012

Block	*No. of House-hold*	*Production of broodlac in July 2012 (kg)*	*Production of broodlac in October 2012 (kg)*	*Production of scraped lac (kg)*	*Total production (kg)*
Jamtara District	21	481	165	51	697
Dumka District	20	516	179	36	749

Source: Indian Institute of Natural Resins and Gums, Namkum, Ranchi, 2012.

Table 6.14: Inoculation of *Rangeeni* and *Kusumi* Summer Lac Crop on *Palas* and *Ber* Tree

Block	*No. of House-hold*	*Quantity of rangeeni broodlac used (kg)*	*No. of palas tree inocula-ted*	*Quanity of kusumi broodlac used (kg)*	*No. of ber tree inocula-ted*	*Total No. of trees inocula-ted*
Dumka District	24	400	825	35	50	875
Jamtara District	29	500	775	—	—	775
Grand Total	**53**	**900**	**1600**	**305**	**50**	**1650**

Source: Indian Institute of Natural Resins and Gums, Namkum, Ranchi, 2012.

Training Conducted

A total of 61 farmers, research scholars and Research Associate have been trained on "Scientific lac cultivation processing and uses" under one-week training programme at IINRG, Ranchi. Twelve on-farm training camps organised at different villages in Kanker, Jagdalpur and Narayanpur districts for 1133 farmers. A training programme on forecast of larval emergency and assessment of broodlac quality was conducted for Research Association, consortia partners and officials of forest department at S.G. College of Agriculture, Jagdalpur where more than 35 persons participated.

Technical Guidance and Advisory

Technical guidance was given to R.K. Mission, Narayanpur for demonstration of *kusumi* lac cultivation on kusum, ber and *Flemingia semialata.* Six demonstrations have been conducted at Brehmebera and Palki village. More than 200 farmers have seen these demonstrations. More than 20 farmers have succesfully adopted *kusumi* lac production technology on *kusum* tree and six farmers each earned around Rs. 20,000 and three farmers around Rs. 10,000 from lac production.

6.9 Income Generation through Kusumi Lac Cultivation: Success Story—Case Study

Description of the lac cultivation activity: Shri Jagdish Hansda came into contact with the Joydeb Mahto (Master trainer under capacity building programme at IINRG, Ranchi) in 2011. He was inspired to join the occupation of lac cultivation. But, he was not able to do this in the absence of host trees with him. Hence, he took the 75 host plants of *ber* on lease from the locality during 2011. He is doing the scientific lac cultivation by adopting the technologies for pruning of lac host, selction of good quality broodlack, bundling of broodlac and inoculation on plan, phunki removal, spraying of recommended pesticides and use of synthetic net.

Impact: Shri Jagdish Hansda has purchased good quality *kusumi* broodlac (31 kg) and inoculated on 75 ber plants in June-July 2011. He got 3.12 quintal *kusumi* lac production. This produce (broodlac) was again inoculated for *jethwi* crop on 34 *kusum* trees. In June-July 2012, he purchased 6.17 qt (Rs. 4.31 lakh) broodlac for inoculation on 217 *ber* and 21 *kusum* trees. On 4th February, 2013 he harvested the bumper crop of *kusumi* lac (about 20 qt). *At the current price of Rs. 700/kg he earned the gross income Rs. 14 lakhs and thus, net profit about Rs. 9 lakh.* Out of this, he also shared the 25 per cent with his partners (14 farmers who have given the host plants on lease). In addition, he also developed two acre land with 14,000 *F. semialata* host plants. This improved the living standard of himself along with the farmers in his locality. Lac cultivation on 100 tree of *palas* resulted into generation of 35 man-days for women out of a total of 80. For producing one quintal of broodlac: women can contribute around 43 per cent of the total manpower involved. Similarly, on 100 trees of *ber*, out of a total of 157 man-days, 110 man-days are generated for women. For producing one quintal of sticklac 14 man-days for women are generated which constitute 70 per cent of the total manpower. Similarly, for trees of *kusum* out of a total 192 man-days, 85 man-days are generated for women. Production of one quintal broodlac from *kusum* tree will result into generation of 6 man-days for women out of a total of 14 man-days which constitute around 44 per cent of the total manpower.

Female Labour-days for *Palas*, *Ber* and *Kusum* cultivation the are quite substantial and in *ber* lac cultivation in particular the female labour days are much higher than male labour days (K.K. Kumar, 2011). *Lac resin is such a versatile product that it makes its presence felt in most of the sectors like varnish, paints, inks, adhesive, food, cosmetics, leather, electrical, pharmaceutical industry, besides some miscellaneous uses.* The wax obtained from lac insect also finds its uses in shoe. Automobile and floor polish, bottle sealer, tailor's chalk, crayon, lipstick and fruit coatings. From a very small-scale cottage unit consisting of 3-5 persons to a very big lac based unit of more than 100 person, can be established.

6.10 Manufacture of Lac-Bangles and Ornaments

The lac Bangle unit can be started with only Rs. 10,000 as a capital investment. At present many units are being run exclusively by women in many parts of the country. Like lac bangles, women can run this unit also many such units are already working. A unit of 3 women can give earning of about Rs. 100 per woman per day in sealing wax. The simple method of preparation of varnish for wooden furniture and its application can involve women also in this particular field. Besides these, there are many big lac based units manufacturing bleached lac, de-waxed decolourized lac, lac-dye etc. which involves women at various steps. A few lac-based products are easy to manufacture and women can be involved in such units.

LAC CROP CALENDAR

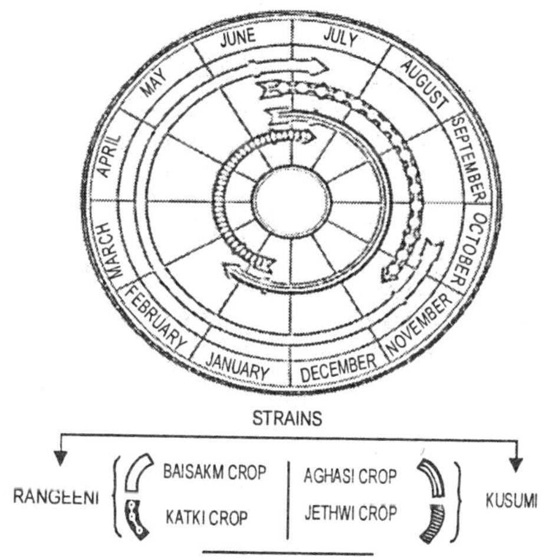

Field Visit/Demonstration/Training to Farmers

Twenty five field visits were undertaken for interaction with farmers and monitoring of lac crop time to time in adopted villages of Jamtara

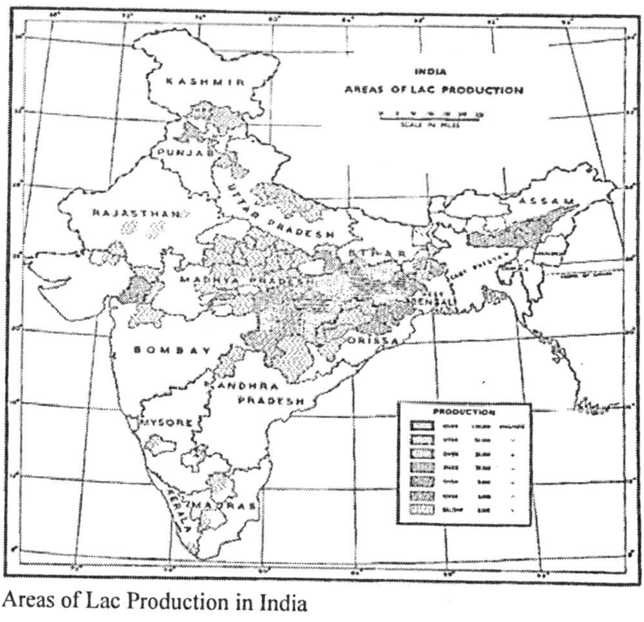

Fig.: Areas of Lac Production in India

and Dumka districts by the experts of IINRG, Namkum (Ranchi). With assistance of IINRG, Namkum 57 families were trained from Dumka and Jamtara Blocks of Santhal Pargana which generated income for the farmers ranging from Rs. 5400 to Rs. 9300. District Planning Officer, Khunti, Jharkhand made a tieup with IINRG, Namkum during the year 2014-15 to address the major issues of the poor resource constraint faced by the people inhabiting in forest and sub-forest areas through scientific interventions and utilization of locally available natural resources. Lac cultivation is one of the viable interventions in this direction to provide livelihood support for sub-forest and forest dwellers with additional opportunity of employment.

The lac cultivation, productivity and marketing has considerable scope in Jharkhand in the context the role of Indian Institute of Natural Resins and Gums, Namkum, Ranchi plays a potential role in the advancement of this crop in entire Jharkhand. It has also important policy implications, which are not only relevant for Jharkhand but also other adjoining States like Odisha, Chhattisgarh, West Bengal etc. *We list below some of the policy implications for the Government of Jharkhand to promote the lac cultivation in a more vigorous ways.*

Indian Institute of Natural Resins and Gums, Namkum, Ranchi is technically competent to promote lac cultivation in the important districts of Jharkhand were lac cultivation is already taken place like the district of Khunti, Ranchi, Simdega, Palamau, Latehar, Goomla, Garhwa and other adjoining districts. Already IINRG have providing on-farm training programme "Scientific lac cultivation" in some of these districts during 2012 due to which 1670 farmers benefited from this programme.

IINRG is not only providing training to the tribal farmers but also collaborating with various government departments of Jharkhand like Forest Department, Tribal Welfare Department, JHASCO LAMPS as also with various NGOs like R.K. Mission, Ranchi, SEEDS, Sarjamdih Kisan Club, Ranchi, Manohar Bhai Patel Academy, Gondia, District Industrial Centre, Purulia, Arouse, Lohardaga, KVK Saraikela-Kharsawan, KVK, Kodarma, ATMA, Ranchi, Jadavpur University, LDO Purulia and District Administration Purulia, V.C. Educational and Social Welfare Society, Ambikapur.

IINRG also undertakes in-campus, orientation programme on lac cultivation with different stakeholders with includes the government and NGOs of different States including farmers. For example during 2012-13 it had organized one day oriented programme for 3163 stakeholders which included several NGOs like PRADAN, R.K. Mission, Ranchi,

Udyogini, Ranchi, AROUSE Society, Simdega, Firayalal Public School, various ATMAs, Marwari College, Ranchi, St. Xavier College, Ranchi, BHU, Varanasi, Guru Nanak Higher Secondary School, Ranchi etc. Most of the stakeholders are from Jharkhand.

Apart from the established NGOs there are also various educational institutions like Kolhan Mahila Sangathan, Chaibasa, D.A.V. Public School, Dhanbad, St. Joseph Degree College, Torpa, Vegetable Growers Association, Jharkhand, S.H.I.A.T.S. Allahabad, Adivasi Mahila Samaj Seva Kendra, Gumla, Krishi Vigyan Kendra, Saraikela, Bishop's School, Ranchi, Central School, Namkum, SARA B.Ed. College, Irba, Ranchi, Kasturba Gandhi Balika Vidyalaya, Ranchi, Mahila Samaj Seva Kendra, Khunti, Bihar Pradesh Yuva Parisad, Latehar etc.

Other activities of IINRG includes demonstration of inoculation spraying etc. at different locations particularly in Jharkhand, Chhattisgarh, West Bengal and Andhra Pradesh at 25 places during April 2011 and the important collaborating agencies were Forest Department Jharkhand, TRIFED Jharkhand and prominent NGOs of Jharkhand and other neighbouring States. IINRG also undertakes demonstration of lac cultivation technologies under farmer field condition in Jharkhand and other adjoining States. It is of particular significance that TRIFED of India Ltd., Ministry of Tribal Affairs, Government of India, New Delhi had conducted six State participants of Jharkhand, Odisha, Chhattisgarh, West Bengal, Andhra Pradesh and Madhya Pradesh in which 666 SHGs comprising 6600 tribal members are covered.

It is useful to find that the District Planning Office, Khunti has initiated programmes during the year 2012-13 to address the major issues of the poor resource constraint of the tribal through lac cultivation to provide livelihood support for the tribal of Khunti district which also include Torpa Rural Development Society for women in collaboration with IINRG, Ranchi. Two quintals of *rangeeni* broodlac have been distributed to 93 members of 8 SHGs across six villages in two blocks of Khunti district. Demonstration of bundling and inoculation of broodlac as well as monitoring and technical guidance in five villages of Torpa block was conducted. It is recommended similar initiative should be undertaken by the other district planning office in different districts of Jharkhand. Beside this the Government of Jharkhand should take up a consolidated step with the inclusion of Forest Department, Department of Rural Development, Department of Planning and IINRG to undertake on policy initiatives for the

Cultivation, Training, Production and Marketing of the lac crop in the entire State of Jharkhand to enhance the livelihood option of the tribals and other marginalized groups.

Though the Ministry of Tribal Affairs, Government of India, has undertaken the policy of MFP through Minimum Support Price of 24 MFP items from the year 2013-14 as a measure of social safety for MFP gatherers who are primarily member of Scheduled Tribes. However, the procurement and marketing benefits have yet to be availed in the State of Jharkhand. The State of Odisha has procured some of the MFP under the State procurement agency for the total value of Rs. 163.20 lakh. This is a good initiative and the State Government of Jharkhand should also try to procure MFPs under MSP scheme at the earliest shows as to provide a substantial livelihood source for the tribals. Most of the MFPs are located in the Left Extremist districts of Jharkhand which would also alienated the Adivasis from the Maoist influence.

Presently, the policy of the Jharkhand Government for the procurement and marketing of different MFPs is very weak. During our field study we could find that in the Saranda forest area the tribals women in large numbers are procuring *sal* leaves, *siali* leaves, *mahua* seeds etc. and selling it in the village *haats* which are several kilometres away from the villages and they sell it to the local traders who fleece them by providing only 20-30 per cent of the prevailing market price. The local tribal women also travel by train to the adjacent markets of Odisha like Rourkela to sell their products were also they are cheated by local traders. This is a neglected area of Government of Jharkhand and they should actively try to promote marketing facility of the tribals so that they could get adequate remunerative price for their NTFP.

Though IINRG is helping the adivasis of Jharkhand in promoting cultivation of lac and providing training in scientific method, motivating women to involved in lac cultivation but they have no mechanism for promoting lac marketing. This field is left open to be exploited by the local traders lac factory owners and other enterprising people to profit out of the lac produce which does not reach the tribal farmers. The Government of Jharkhand and the District Administration should fill this gap.

6.11 Analysis of Non-Timber Forest Produce in Odisha

A.K. Maharana, H.S. Mishra, K.K. Mohati (ed.) (SCSTRTI), Bhubaneswar (2004) have studied Two tribal pockets of Odisha inhabited by two different tribal communities—one chiefly depending on shifting cultivation and the other on forest collection, i.e. the Kutia Kandha and Hill Khadia. The Hill Khadia of Jashipur area do not inhabit in Uni-ethnic villages. In Belghar area (Rangaparu and Tuakela) 50.89 per cent of the Kutia Kandha working population depend upon the collection and sale of minor forest produce as their subsidiary occupation. Next to it comes wage earning which engages 20 per cent of their working population. In Jashipur area (Podagada and Ramjodi) Hill Khadias who mostly depend upon collection and sale of minor forest produce (61.74%) as their principal occupation, have cultivation (66.09%) as their favourite subsidiary occupation. But all other communities except Hill Khadias of Jashirpur area (Podagada and Ramjodi) have collection and sale of minor forest produce and wage earning as their subsidiary occupations.

Out of 233 total surveyed households 150 (64.38%) are land owning and 83 (35.62%) are landless households. The maximum number of are marginal farmers. The average land holding per marginal farmer is calculated at 1.30 acre. *Next to Hill Khadia stands Kutia Kandha with 40.50 per cent landless households. All the Bhumij, the Munda and the Gond households are land owning households.* Next to these communities stands the Kolha and the Santhal with 91.30 per cent and 83.33 per cent land owning households respectively. All Kutia Kandha households of Belghar area (Rangaparu and Tuakela) possees both house and house-site.

All the Minor Forest Produces (MFPs) obtained from the forest can be categorized under fibre and flosses, grasses, bamboos, reeds and canes, essential oils, oil seeds, tans and dyes, gums, resins and oleoresins, drugs, spices, poisons and insecticides, leaves, edible products, lac and its products and other products. Much of the above MFPs are allowed to be removed free or at a concessional rate by the tribal people. The people living near forest collect MFP for own consumption and value addition. The perishable items of MFP, like fruits, green leaves and mushrooms are collected by the tribal people for own consumption. In case of surplus, fruits like mango, jackfruit, tamarind and non-edible MFP, like bamboo and cane are sold to others either with or without value addition. MFP of the industrial importance like *Kendu* leaf, *Sal* seed, *Pulang* seed etc. are collected by the forest communities for the purpose of sale only. They do not put additives and preservatives to raise the value of highly perishable items due to ignorance of the techniques involved. Certain MFP items like arrowroot, mango pulps are always put on the sale after value addition.

Mahua flower, *Sal* seed, ripen fruits etc. are collected from the tree bottoms. The simple method followed to collect these MFP items is to sweep the ground clean and wait leisurely for the bounty to fall. No labour is incorporated in this operation. Certain MFP items like leaves of *Sal*, *Kendu* and *Siali* are plucked when they are green. These items are then dried under the sun to expel the moisture and then processed for different uses. No tools or implements are necessary in both the cases. A few bamboo baskets are only required. The knife and axe is required for felling and debarking the tree for dry matters like bar and sap etc. For collection of resin, gum and honey much labour is necessary. The usual knife, axe and climbing rope accompany a collector of these items. It is always noticed that collected items are removed from the forest either by carrying poles or head loads.

MFPs are collected mostly from common lands (Ibid.: 87, 90). The distance covered by the collectors for collecting the MFP varies from tribe to tribe. *The nomadic/semi-nomadic tribes cover greater distance in their pursuit. Agrarian tribes collect MFP near their village or agricultural land.* In the study villages their area of foraging operation is within 2 kms. from their habitats. For the shifting cultivators the felled areas,—generally the hill slopes located two to six kilometre away from their habitats, are the collection grounds. Their collection activity is within the area of their agricultural activity or within one kilometre from their shifting cultivation fields (the felled areas). The agrarian tribes of Jashipur area, such as the Gond, the Bhumij, the Kolha and the Santal collect MFP near their habitats or agricultural fields. They do not go deep into the forest. They also exploit the roadside and riverside woodlots where tree species, like *Mahua*, *Karanj*, *Kusum, Polang*, jackfruit, mango, and *Kochila* are found. The semi-nomadic Hill Khadia usually go deep into the forests—sometimes more than 10 kms. in groups and collect a variety of MFPs and return to village a day before the commencement of the local weekly market to dispose of their collected MFP. *During group collection they spend several nights inside the forest. The inhabitants of the study villages collect as many as 64 varieties of MFP.* Out of it, 55 items are collected by Hill Khadias to sustain themselves throughout the year.

The shifting cultivators—Kutia Kandhas, collect as many as 37 items of MFP. The agrarian tribes of Jashipur area such as the Kolha, the Santhal, the Munda, the Bhumij and the Gond have similar choice for their items of MFP and they collect 18 varieties of MFP. They collect oil seed of tree origin, Siali bark and grass. According to the data the collection of listed items as per one Hill Khadia family is more compared to other ethnic groups. *Per household per annum MFP items collected comes to 17.58 kgs. of honey, 59.5 kgs. of resin, 40 kgs. of Mahua flower, 62 kgs. of Kusum seed, 50 kgs. of Mahua seed, 85 kgs. of Sal seed, 2.75 kgs. of arrowroot, 3050 kgs. of gum, 100 bundles of Siali bark, 90 kgs. of Paja bark and 1.97 kgs. of Patalgaruda.*

6.12 Social Economic Livelihood Issues

It is widely recognized that non-timber forest products (NTFPs) provide substantial inputs to the livelihoods of forest dependent population. In 1986 NTFPs accounted for almost 40 per cent of forest department revenues, 75 per cent of net export earning from forest produce. NTFPs perhaps account for substantial engagement of wage labour force in the tribal belt. This sector provides enough opportunity for self-employment. About 70 per cent of NTFP collection in India takes place in the Central Indian Tribal Belts. *Women are the main thrust of most of the small-scale forest based occupation.* One of the largest employer of women is the *bidi* industry. Women are employed to collect *Kendu/Tendu* leaves and to roll them.

Gender and NTFP

Gender focused studies on NTFP highlight the higher incidence of women's involvement in NTFP activities (Falconer, 1990) and higher income from products of the commons was found to represent 27 per cent of women's local non-farm income, as compared with 10 per cent for men (Hopkins *et al.*, 1994). In Odisha, among the 1.7 million (approx.) pluckers (to include at least one associate of the registered pluckers) of almost are women/girls.

It has been estimated that many village communities in India derive as much as 17-35 per cent of their annual household income from sale of NTFP (Tewari, 1994). In Odisha, up to 40 per cent of the income of the rural poor comes from the collection of forest products. NTFP provide about 40 per cent of total official forest revenue, 55 per cent of forest based employment and nearly 400-500 million people living in and around forest of India depend on NTFPs for their sustenance and supplementing their meager income. Investigations in NTFP trade-channels in eastern Indian States have revealed that intermediaries pay only 16-20 per cent of the market price to collectors and quite often, such prices turn out be just 20-25 per cent of their prevailing minimum daily wages. A bundle of 50 *sal* (*Shorea robusta*) leaf plates, which is procured at source in Odisha, at less than Rs. 12, are exported from Kolkata at Rs. 932 (Satapathy, 2001). Similarly, the *Sal* resin procured at Rs. 20 per kg is sold at Rs. 80 per kg. This reflects the deplorable status of the poorest NTFP gatherers, who usually end up with very low returns, which is often much less than the minimum daily wage, though NTFP trade channel beyond the gatherers and State revenue often corner higher share.

6.13 Decentralizing of NTFP

VSS members have normally been entitled for collection of NTFPs from Reserve Forest and other forest lands excluding PA, their counterparts in the Protected Areas (PA), which are known as Eco-Development Committees (EDC) hardly enjoyed this privilege chiefly because the norms are different for Protected Areas. State of Odisha has gone ahead during the year 2000 to not only denationalize most NTFPs of the State (except bamboo and *kendu* leaves), but to put their transport and trade under the control of the Panchayati Raj Institutions (PRIs). Other Indian States have also passed similar laws and orders, but the number of item covered by State intervention in Odisha in March 2000 was one of the highest in India (Saxena, 2003).

A study on "NTFP and Rural Livelihoods" (Vasundhara, 1998) in Bolangir district of Odisha found a correlation between average income from NTFP and land holding status. In forest rich areas, landless and marginal farmers have higher incomes from NTFP than the next higher land holding class. Thus, the equity enhancing capacity of NTFP is greater in areas with large public forests. According to a study carried out by RCDC in Baikumpa village of Phulbani district in Odisha in 1998, one household gets around Rs. 280 per month (from July to October) from Siali plates. In similar study in Talapalaput village of Koraput district, the income per household varies between Rs. 1100-1200 from unprocessed tamarind excluding domestic consumption during the February-April period air pricing would undoubtedly double this income.

The poor of the lower income groups particularly the landless labourers and marginal farmers derive largest share of their total income from forest produce. According to the study, which was done in 5 undivided districts of Odisha, the dependence of NTFP is distinct and visible varying from 27 per cent in individual Koraput district to 52.2 per cent in undivided Kalahandi. The average income from all types of NTFP was Rs. 1941.81 for the study area.

6.14 Thrust of NTFP Policies

In spite of strong dependency of tribal and forest dwelling communities on NTFP, their access to these valuable resources has been unfortunately deteriorated due to several factors. Absence of proper regulatory framework, large forestland diversion to different developmental activities, nationalization of NTFP, exploitation by government owned agencies and contractors in marketing of NTFP are some of the major factors. Although there are some progressive Central Acts likes PESA and FRA, which clearly speak about the ownership of MFP to Gram Panchayats and Gram Sabha, but some States still do not have any exclusive and comprehensive policy for management of NTFP. States have been exercising monopoly rights for procurement and tradeoff products like *Kendu/tendu* leaf, *sal* seed; bamboo etc. for several years.

Panchayats (Extension to Scheduled Areas) Act, 1996

Panchayats (Extension to Scheduled Areas) Act, 1996 commonly known as PESA is a historic move by the Union Government, which clearly endows Gram Sabha or Panchayats at appropriate level to own, control and manage MFP in Scheduled V areas. An expert committee constituted by MoEF made the following observations to confine the term '*Minor Forest Produce*'.

Minor Forest Produce is the produce, other than timber, harvestable on a non-destructive basis. The term 'forest produce' and 'timber' will have the same meaning as in the Indian Forest Act, 1927. Regarding 'ownership' the Committee felt that in accordance with the spirit of the Act (PESA), the Gram Sabhas/Panchatyat, should be endowed with usufructory rights rather than ownership of MFPs available from all lands except Wildlife Sanctuaries and bio-sphere reserves, because ownership might create many complications (GoI: MoEF, 1998).

Table 6.16: State Provision of Ownership Rights of MFP

State	*State Provisions*
Odisha	The Odisha Act 15 of 1997, the Odisha Gram Panchayats (Amendement) Act, 1997, Section 44 and sub-section 2b vested the power to Gram Panchayat.

Source: The State Institute of Rural Development Bhubaneswar Odisha.

It may be mentioned here that both *sal* seed and *kendu* leaf business had significant political implications for the State. In 1990s, TDCC, Agency Marketing Cooperative Society, OFDC and Utkal Forest Product Limited (UFPL) were given the leases to collect forest produces in different divisions as below:

- TDCC was given the right to MFP items, viz. tamarind, hill broom, honey, and *mahua* in all the 27 divisions of the State.
- UFPL, a joint sector company was given the exclusive right to collect 29 NTFP items in all the forest divisions of the State.
- AMCS was given lease to operate in 3 divisions for all produces except the ones given to TDCC and UFPL.
- TDCC was additionally given rights over all the produces except those given to UFPL in 19 divisions.
- OFDC was given rights over all produces in 5 divisions (not allocated to AMCS and TDCC) except those given to TDCC and UFPL (Patnaik, 2005).
- The policy ensured that there was only one buyer for a produce in a division but at the same time there was no onus on the agencies to buy the produce collected by the primary gatherers. Hence, the illegal trade flourished due to various reasons.
- The policy of March 2000 recognized the importance of MFPs in the forest dwellers' life. It also recognized the importance of sustainability of resources. As per the requirement of PESA, it gave ownership rights over 'MFP's to GPs in Scheduled Areas, and only regulatory rights to rest of the GPs. MFP was defined under this policy in vague way, creating a pseudo-category of "Minor Forest Produce" (term used in PESA) under NTFP: initially 60 items were declared as MFPs (later the number rose to 69). Monopoly leases were no more allowed, and commercial lease was to be allowed for items not under the MFP list.
- On 26th May, 2000, the Panchayati Raj Department, in exercise of power under section 152 of the OGP Act, issued an administrative order prescribing the manner in which the rights transferred to the GPs shall be dealt with. Since, royalty was withdrawn, a token amount of Rs. 100 was fixed as registration fee per each produce that is to be given to the GP in which the traders intend to procure. There is no restriction on the traders on number and volume of produces that they

want to trade and transact provided they pay the registration fee.

- In matters of collection, primary gatherers will be subject to reasonable control by the Divisional Forest Officer through imposition of temporary ban if collection method is found to be harmful.
- The DFO reserves the right to set a minimum target for procurement for respective items for the dealer(s).
- VSS will continue to enjoy rights of ownership over MFP and NTFP in reserve forest areas.

Odisha Gram Panchayats (Minor Forest Produce Administration) Rules, 2002

- The GP shall have the power to regulate procurement and trading of MFP, whether produced in government lands and forest areas within the limits of Gram (village) or collected from the Reserved Forests and brought into the Gram.
- Priority would be given to the VSS and its members for collection and trading of MFP.
- Price fixation would be done by the Panchayat Samiti (PS) in September and would be circulated to different offices of district administration and to all the GPs.
- The Gram Sabha would ratify prices fixed and necessary changes can be made based on the local needs.
- If Panchayat Samiti fails to fix the price then the District Collector would call a meeting of PS preferably in October to fix-up the minimum procurement prices.
- The trader registered to procure MFP from the GP shall furnish monthly return and also annual return in a prescribed format.
- The GP shall furnish an annual return on the procurement and sale to the Forest Range Officer.

State Specific Issues

In Odisha at present, apart from OFDC, which is dealing with *kendu* leaf and bamboo, other institutions have very limited role in NTFP procurement and trade. There are about 1 million pluckers (officialy much less) dominated by women and adolescent girls, whereas the plucker's cards are sometimes issued in the name of male head of the family, *thereby depriving the female members of the family of the benefits of social security measure since only a cardholder is eligible to get the benefit.*

Legal Issues

After the enactment of PESA the Odisha Government has handed over ownership rights of MFP to Gram Panchayats. Out of them, only a few are procured commercially as neither the primary collectors nor the traders have thorough knowledge on domestic and commercial use of many items. Further, there is hardly any attempt to develop the marketability of currently obscure items.

6.15 Role of Intervening Institutions

TDCC and OFDC in Odisha

TDCC suffered huge financial losses but it was not compensated by the Government. TDCC has a number of branches in the State, and procures from the traders and primary collectors (or their groups) directly. It had to diversify its business activity to petrol pumps, fertilizer trading, and some processing units have also been added to its infrastructure.

Table 6.17: Interventions by Different Institutions for Promotion of NTFP Enterprises in the Project Area

Institution	*Intervention in NTFP Enterprises*	*Remarks*
DSMS/ ORMAS	CFC-common facility centers have been established for collection and value addition on NTFP such as neem and *mahua* seeds for oil, and *Badhun*. Oil expellers have been provided to SHGs in for processing of oil from *neem* and *mahua* seed. SHGS have been provided with revolving fund under special SGSY programme and income generation fund.	DSMS is supporting SHGs for setting up enterprises on agriculture and forest produces. Earlier DSMS had supported for processing of Hill Brooms and now it is concentrating on processing of *Kandula* dal.

(Contd.)

Institution	*Intervention in NTFP Enterprises*	*Remarks*
TDCC	It was engaged in procurement and trade of Hill Brooms, *Sal* seed, tamarind, *Sialui* leaf etc.	From this year there is no substantial involvement in procurement and trade of NTFP because of internal restructuring etc.
OFDC	Procurement and marketing of *kendu* leaf, harvesting of bamboo and collection and sale of *sal* seed. Each division has been suggested to take-up other NTFP procurement and trade and each division has been allocated a sum of Rs. 1,00,000 as revolving fund.	The trade in *sal* seed has declined significantly and from the current year OFDC may not procure *sal* seed. In case of other NTFP nothing visible has been done by OFDC.
MART as a partner of WORLP	In 2004 MART did an extensive study for WORLP for developing businesses promotion and market development strategy in Bolangir. It strongly suggested for collective action for procurement and trade of *Mahua* flower, *Badhun*, *Char* seed, and processing of *Mahua* seed and *Neem* seed for oil and processing of *sal* leaf and cups in Bolangir district. It is providing support service to PIAs and SHGs for collective action for *Char* seed and *mahua* flower, and also to improve the quality of the produce through proper drying and storage. It has demonstrated drying platforms in 5 places. It is also assessing the status of infrastructure in the rural *haats* and developing strategies to strengthen *haats* for trading of forest and agricultural produces. SHG members have been taken on exposure to markets and trained to negotiate with the traders.	MART has provided a detailed operational strategy for WORLP to proceed further in enterprise development on NTFP. This covers the economics of the different enterprises. Because of collective interventions in *Mahua* flower and *Char* seed procurement price was increased and SHGs earned profits after paying higher than the market price to the primary collectors. But the volume of trade through collective action is very low.

(*Contd.*)

Institution	*Intervention in NTFP Enterprises*	*Remarks*
NGOs including PIAs	Sabuja Viplab purchased *Neem* seed and *nagarmotha* from different areas and supplied to traders and industries in huge volumes. Vikalpa procured *neem* seed with a higher price and supplied it to some processing units. The humanity is providing training to the primary collectors and 10 SHGs on good harvesting and primary processing on *myrabolans* oil seeds etc. One of the groups has started producing *triphala* and *pachnan amla*. RCDC is building capacity of the Gram Panchayats, SHGs and Forest Protection Committees for collective interventions in management and trade of NTFP. It is promoting cooperatives to procure and trade NTFP. It is promoting trade in *badhun*, *mahua* flower, tamarind, *siali* leaf, amla, *harida* etc. Srsti—an NGO is promoting enterprised through SHG especially on *myrabolans*. Lokdrusti has promoted a women's federation and a social bank with thier membership of more than 700 SHGs. Now some of the SHGs are into collection and processing of honey, which is sold locally and the turnover is very low. Antyodaya, Charm and Parivartan are engaged in collective action for trading of tamarind, siali leaf, hill brooms, harida, amla etc.	18 SHGs in Turekala-project area of WORLP with the support of MART and Livelihood Support Team procured and sold 388 quintals of a *mahua* flower and earned a profit of Rs. 150-165 per quintal after paying the primary collectors one rupee higher than the prevailing market price. Similarly, there is appreciation of price of *Mahua* flower in other project areas in Bolangir and Nuapada districts.

Role of MART in Odisha in TSP Areas

MART's quest for innovative solutions has repeatedly proven the need to marry the learning from the ground to the scientific knowledge and management principles available in public and private domains. Over the past 7 years, MART has intensively worked in Odisha by deeply involving the community and finding space for their voiced needs. So far MART has experimented with and established various models and mechanisms that are accepted as durable solutions to the development challenges posed in Odisha in particular. Under the "Western Odisha Rural Livelihood Project", MART has developed and established the "pro-poor value chain" concept wherein private sector is engaged as an equal business partner with the community to ensure a win-win situation. This model is termed simplistically as the "Collective Marketing Model". This model has been furthered to include the government towards better fulfilment of its development objectives and was replicated under the "Odisha Tribal Empowerment and Livelihood Programme" to cover 396 villages. The relevance and success of this model is reflected in its adoption for project design, pilot and upscale for the "Odisha Forestry Sector Development Project" under which 68 clusters have been developed in 9 forest divisions of the State. *For the present research study we have selected the product cluster of 11 crops which include Maize, Ginger, Chilly, Turmeric, Tasar, Hillbroom, Lac, Sabai, Sal leaves, Siali leaves and Tamarind, which are mostly located in tribal blocks.*

Maize

In Papadahandi block, nearly 20,500 (80%) farmers belonging to 22 Gram Panchayats (GPs) were involved in maize cultivation and producing around 33,500 MT from 6,700 hectares in *Kharif* season with an average productivity of 5 MT per hectare. Similarly, in *Rabi* season, production of 3,500 MT is achieved from 650 hectares with an average productivity of 5.5 MT per hectare. Although the productivity is higher in *Rabi,* lack of irrigation facilities forces most farmers to cultivate maize in *Kharif* season only. The total production of maize in the block in both seasons is 51,925 MT from 7,350 hectares (sourced from Department of Agriculture). Uplands are used for maize cultivation in *Kharif* and medium land of *Rabi.*

It is proposed to promote a block level maize cluster at Papadahandi. Focusing on the geographical location and large production of the area it is planned to promote two sub-clusters at Mokiya and Semala. The Mokiya sub-cluster covers 1,720 households cultivating over 620 hectares and producing 3,220 MT. Semala sub-cluster covers 1,960 households cultivating over 590 hectares and producing 2,950 MT. Market for maize is available in local, town, terminal and national levels. The local and town level traders directly procure maize from farmers. Town level traders, supply them to regional markets, processors and higher level market players of Odisha. The higher level market players process the produce for different kinds of products like cattle feed, poultry feed, corn flakes and popcorn.

Table 6.18: Community Institutions engaged in Cultivation of Maize Crops in District Nabrangpur

Trend	*Farmers Activity*	*Supporting factors*	*Constraints*	*Opportunities*
The last 5 years trend shows that, coverage of land under maize cultivation is increasing in the block.	A common producer has to plough the land 4-5 times by: he has to incur around Rs. 1000-1,200 per acre.	Availability of hybrid seeds, fertilizer, pesticides and credit at the door step.	Rate of interest is high. Lack of irrigation facility. Low productivity.	Formal credit linkage with MFIs and banks will reduce interest rates.

Sub-cluster Selection of Ginger in District Koraput

Trend	*Highlighting features*	*Household coverage*	*Production Volume*
Ginger is cultivated as a traditional commercial crop in Pottangi block of Koraput district for a long time.	More than 90 per cent of farmer households are involved in ginger cultivation including tribal farmers.	310 households	202.50 MT Ginger cultivation contributes significantly to the households income of these tribal farmers.

In the six villages selected for the cultivation of the ginger the total number of households is 406 and the number of SHGs involved is 58. The total area under ginger is 230 acre and the average yield is 525 quintals per acre. The ginger is procured by the local traders of the area who have been already identified by MART. Ginger cultivated in the cluster is of native variety (*Suprava*) developed by the High Altitude Research Station (HARS) located at Pottangi and a few High pungency and demand in the market. Farmers of the cluster do not convert their produce into any other form and sell them as it is in markets. No entrepreneur at the cluster level is processing ginger into any other form. The variety of ginger produced in Pottangi has high market demand in urban and local as well as outside markets of the State due to its quality. Major markets for the product are located at Berhampur, Bhubaneswar, Cuttack, and some parts of Andhra Pradesh.

Sub-cluster Selection of Chilly

Chilly Plant	*Households Coverage*	*Production Volume*	*Input and Yield*
Chilly (*Capsicum annum*) belongs to the genus capsicum under *Solanaceae* family	12,496	2177 MT	Lime powder, *Neem* cake, Organic Manure, Paper Slus: average yield per acre are10-12 qtl.

Sub-cluster Selection of Turmeric

Kandhamal is the largest turmeric producing district of the State. Block level turmeric is being to be promoted at Darinbadi, with two sub-clusters at Bamunigaon and Simanbadi. The Bamunigaon sub-cluster 15 villages of 3 GPs, were 1120 households cultivating over 420 hectares and producing 315 MT of the turmeric, Likewise, Simanbadi cluster covers 1450 households are cultivating over 550 hectares and producing 413 MT. Turmeric is the most dominant crop in the block, in which about 50 per cent of the total households are involved. The total number of households involved are 3230 and the number of SHGs are 90. The area involved is 2425 acre and the yield per acre is 4.5 quintals. The marketable surplus is 72,800 quintals. The NGO associated in coordinating the SHG and the households working in the area is known as KASAM.

Issues and Constraints at the Farmer's Level

Farmers are using traditional rhizomes as seeds, which over the years have degraded drastically, yielding turmeric with low curriculum content. Repetitive turmeric farming on the same tract of land also leads to decline in productivity. Farmers neither use hybrid seed rhizomes nor apply appropriate compost, fertilizer and pesticides. Surprisingly, there are no traditional returns for the product being organic. Individual marketing and pre-production credit linkage with local traders restrict better price realization.

Sub-cluster Selection of Tasar

Tasar culture is an age-old practice in the State and is found in hilly districts, namely, Mayurbhanj, Balasore, Keonjhar, Sundargarh, Deogarh, Sambalpur, Dhenkanal, Angul, Jajpur, Boudh, Sonepur, Kalahandi, Nuapada and Nabarangpur. Years ago, tribal farmers used the natural forest grown tasar food plants *Asana* and *Arjuna* for tasar silkworm rearing. Farmers practise tasar cultivation because it is a traditional crop, highly labour intensive and grown with very low capital investment with very high return in a very short time (45-60 days). It is mostly grown in roughed and upland areas with *Asana/Arjuna* plantation. There are 763 households in 7 villages and out of them about 95 per cent belong to ST category, 3 per cent belong to SC and the rest belong to OBC category. There are 92 such households who primarily practiced tasar cultivation in the last season. The total number of households cluster involved in block in cultivating tasar are 765 and 31 SHGs. The local traders procured the tasar from the farmers directly and pay them according to the prevailing market price. There is no government machinery for fixing the market price: as a matter of fact it should be included under MSP by the Ministry of Tribal Affairs, Government of India instead of leaving the farmers to be exploited by the traders. In fact, Jharkhand also has major cluster producing Tasar particularly in the district of Saraikela-Kharsawan district and these two clusters can be combined for the mutual benefits of the farmers growing tasar. The TRCs takes the cocoons from the farmers at a rate fixed by SERIFED based on the quality parameters. Mostly, the segregation is made for two types of cocoons, the poorer quality is called Gicha (Non-reeling cocoon) and the superior quality called Daba (Reeling Cocoon) with further grading within. SERIFED providing additional incentive of Rs. 400 per Kahana for the best variety to encourage quality practices in rearing of tasar. The cluster does not have any reeling and spinning society and hence, there is no production of silk at the cluster-level. But, the process is being practiced in societies established in the blocks of Bangiriposi and Kuliana. However, there are TRCSs in the district along with SHGs that are involved in making yarn from cocoons.

Sub-cluster Selection of Hill Broom

Hill Broom is mostly found in Rayagada district, where it grows in the hilly slopes of forests. It is one of the major sources of livelihood of the tribal people in these areas. The inflorescence of the plant is used to sweep floors as brooms. The tribals collect the grasses and immediately sell them to traders, as their economic condition is poor and are always on the brink of survival. But, the traders after getting the produce from the tribal people, process and sell them at a much higher price and margin. Unfortunately, the poor tribals are deprived of the same as they are not only unable to make any value addition to it but are also not selling the produce to the traders at a fair price. Hill Broom is mostly used for clearing the floor at household level. With a bit of innovation and creativity, it is also used for decorating hotels and restaurants. Hill broom collection is done at Kashipur, K. Singhpur and Rayagada TSP Block in Rayagada ITDA. Kashipur has a major share—40 per cent to the total production and 50 per cent families of 8 GPs are involved in collecting 3000 quintals of Hill broom. It is focused to promote a block level cluster at Kashipur, with two sub-clusters at Mandibishi and Sikarpai (K. Singhpur). The total number of households engaged in the Hill Broom occupation is 229 and the total collection is 495 kgs, which has the total market surplus of 6125 kgs. In this cluster SHG godown are providing to the households engaged in this activity. The NGO guiding the hill broom household is AGRAGAM, Ama Sangathan. The main challenge, however, lies in organizing the supply availability of raw-material, augmenting skill set of the community members and developing a time bound marketing system.

Sub-cluster Selection of Lac

Lac is natural polymer (resin) produced by a tiny insect, *Kerria lacca* (Kerr). The insect is purposefully cultured on the shooters of several tree species such as *palas*, *kusum* and *ber*. Lac cultivation is a subsidiary source of income for a large number of farmers mainly in Jharkhand, Chhattisgarh, West Bengal, Odisha and North-Eastern States of the country. India, which is the highest producer of lac, contributes around 55 per cent of the world's requirement and exports around 80-90 per cent of its production. In Odisha, it has a special importance in bangle making. More than 500 households from Tartari cluster are engaged in the activity. Though seasonal changes in the current fiscal have led to losses with poor productivity, lac cultivation is still regarded a profitable business. The brood seed usually comes from Ranchi and reaches to the farmer. The cooperative society based at Tartari with support from ITDA, Nilgiri facilitates the farmers in availing the seeds. On an average, the access to host plants ranges from

3-5, with each farmer requiring 30-35 kg of brood seed. Farmer has to apply pesticides at regular intervals, three times per season. The produce of sticklac per farmer is 20-25 kg on an average. The farmer either directly sells the produce at local hats as in Chhatrapur or moves to the cooperative societies for sale. The produce in small volumes also moves to traders based at Udala and other markets from where it directly goes to large markets in Balrampur and Jhalda. Places like Balrampur have big traders with own processing units to form Shellac and Button lac. These products finally move for further processing for its various industrial usages.

One of the biggest concerns in lac cultivation is fluctuation in production. Despite good unrealized demand for lac (both domestic as well as overseas), the production growth has not been very healthy. This can be attributed to fluctuation in yield due to lack of use of scientific cultivation techniques and prevailing marketing practices. The seed (broodlac) cannot be stored as it is very short lived. Therefore, whenever, there is a dip in lac production due to adverse climatic conditions in an area, resilience in production is constrained by broodlac supply. At present, more than 90 per cent of broodlac comes from Ranchi. The price varies with the conversion of stick lac to shellac. The cost of raw stick lac costs Rs. 140 per kg, while that of shellac is Rs. 550 per kg, increasing the price by more than 15 per cent. However, due to demand of raw lac in the local area and poor access to primary processing unit (just one primary processing unit in Tartari), the producer sells it in raw form only. At present, the major problem lies in procurement. Farmers do harvest the immature seeds from the trees and sell to meet their immediate cash requirements. This results in poor quality of stick lac. There is a gradual movement of stick lac from the village hats of markets in Udala and Sarat and then to large markets like Balrampur, Jhalda and Ranchi for processing. Less than 10 per cent of stick lac processing is carried out at the cooperative. Stabilization of production through intervention in technology coupled with backward (broodlac produces) and forward linkages (community based lac procurement agents) would be the key. Thirdly, the cluster has over 30 SHG women who have knowledge of making bangles and small crafts from lac.

Sub-cluster Selection of Sabai

Sabai grass is practically considered "The Money Plant" in Mayurbhanj district, which ensure cash throughout the year. The industry is associated with various activities of raising production of grass and processing of consumer goods such as ropes, mats, carpets, sofa sets, wall hangings and other sophisticated fashionable articles. *Sabai* grass industry also has tremendous export potential. Artistically designed *sabai* products are very popular in foreign countries which earn precious foreign exchange for the country. The industry helps in the growth of entrepreneurship amongst villagers. This also ensures economic development through modernization and innovation of industrial culture in rural areas.

More than 3,500 households from the cluster panchayat of Khunat block are engaged in this activity. The average annual production of *Sabai* from the cluster is estimated to be 1400 MT. *Sabai* is perennial grass. Hardly any cost is involved in the process of *sabai* grass production except sowing and harvest. The cultivation is purely organic with no prevalent usc of pesticides or fertilizer. This sowing is done during June. The nursery is available from local sources, relatives and other farmer at nominal prices. There is no such organized seed supplier available for *sabai*. The harvesting starts from mid-September and goes up to December. Price of *sabai* can be fetched either in the form of grass, rope or crafts. Handicrafts of *sabai* need specialized training and are limited to a small number of artisans. Paper industry has also a great demand for *sabai* grass in raw its raw form. From the local area, direct procurement of *sabai* grass has increased its demand. The major markets for *sabai* grass are Mayurbhanj and it is sent to the paper mill for paper making and also for making sabai rope. The markets for *sabai* rope are Varanasi, Firozabad, Patna and Ajmer. The *sabai* rope is used for cot making, glass binding, roof making and furniture. The *Sabai* craft has major market in Kolkata and it is used for artistic handicraft.

Sub-cluster Selection of Sal Leaf

Mayurbhanj is a tribal dominated district and has 26 Tribal Sub-Plan (TSP) Blocks in Odisha. About more than 80 per cent of the total geographical area of the district is covered by forest. So, the economy of the district, to a large extent is forest based. A large cross section of the population depends on the collection of Non-Timber Forests Produces (NTFPs) for livelihood. One of the main NTFPs abundantly available in the district is *sal* leaf, available almost for 8-9 months a year. More than 70 per cent of the population derives their livelihood from *sal* leaf collecting, stitching and selling as observed from villager of *Kutchilaghati and Ambadali sub-clusters in Samakhunta Block.* Samakhunta has 64.38 per cent tribals out of the total population as per 2001 census. Women collect *sal* leaves by hand using sticks and dry them keeping on roftop, village roads beside railway lines. They bundle them unto *chhaki* (100 Pali means, two leaves and three jointed leaves) and sell them in the local hat. A family produces around 60 bundles per month getting about Rs. 1500 month for 3-4 months a year. In lean season, this income is reduced to Rs. 500 per month. *About 60 per cent of households are engaged in collection of sal leaf and making the two patri and three patri in villages.* Town traders buy the *Palis* and *Tini patri* from village level collectors. Some Bentanati traders have pressing machines and makes different types of cups, plates and supply them to institutional traders. As the villagers are unaware of the markets and demand of the product, the big traders often take advantage of this and procure at very lower price. Also, there is lack of adequate storage facilities in the village level. The *sal* leaves collection in the village of Kutchulaghati and Ambadali are done by 225 households assisted by 14 SHGs and the collection per household is 4200 row leaves per day: the marketable surplus is 8000 quintals which are sold to the local traders.

Role of Primary Collectors

Collect the leaves from the forest by using a small sharp knife. In a day one male/female used to collect approximately. 8 to 12 kg wet raw leaves. After collection they used to put it in sunlight for a day or two for drying. Generally, drying is made in the road near to their house or in their homestead land. After the leaves get dried, they used to sort the leaves in order and put a heavy stone or wood on the top of the leaf bunch to make it even. Once the dried raw-leaves are properly pressed for a day they used to make it in bundle. The bundle is then pressed and tried with the help of ropes made of thick Siali creepers. Some household used to pin the dried leaves in pins, extracted from bamboo and palo stick to make it semi-stitched plates. After the *Pali, Tini patri* and plate are made, they used to make customized pack of 100 no per Chhaki. The village level traders operate on weekly basis. The primary collectors bring Leaf *Pali, Tin Patri* and plate to a village point for Transaction.

Leaf products rate differ after accessing the quality (Small size, black coloured, leaves with holes etc. are considered as of poorer quality) of those leaf plates. Storing the leaf bundles in temporary storage points in and out of the villages. Primary collectors get the money at a sale point and get advance from the Trader for leaves for the next week. The trader inform the regional Traders (Town Trader) about the quantity procured village-wise to enable them make necessary planning for lifting from the storage point.

At village level traders does not do any processing.

Town Traders/Block Level Trader

Open the collected bundles for quality checking of leaves. Sorting grading of those leaves, some of the town and traders do pressing according to the demand of various terminal markets. Re-bundle the graded leaves into 45-50 kg average pack with the help of a iron angle ring by experienced workers for easy transportation in trucks. Preparing for forest gate passes for inter state transportation. Identify the right Traders in the terminal markets for linkage of the produce. The buyer to sewing and pressing with procured leaves to make plates, tray and cups. Adding 40 per cent more price to the cost of production for exporting that to outside. Hording the product for off-season. Sometimes fixation of base prices for regional markets as per the demand and supply of the market. Order/supply to the various stitching units.

Sub-cluster Selection of Siali Leaf

Siali is commonly called by names such as *Siali patra, Madrasi patra, khali patra, patrol, Adda* leaves etc. in various parts of the country. The leaf is used in huge quantities for various purposes like the marriage parties, religious parties, for wrapping and for packing items. Due to its strength and flexibility, the stem of *siali* leaf is often used as rope. In general, the primary producers/collectors of *siali* leaves are women. Almost 60-70 per cent of women in Kandhamal district are engaged in this activity. There are 11,274 households in this TSP Block. *Siali* leaf is one of the most common and important NTFPs, which provides income opportunities for about 9 months to the people of Khajuripada Block. Usually, the women collect leaves using sticks, and dry them on the rooftops. Rough stitches of 14 inch, 16 inches and 18 inches by taking 7 to 9 leaves and bundling them into *Chhakki* (100) before selling in the local *haat* is done by them. A family is able to stitch up to 3 *Chhakkis* per day and 90 *Chhakkis* per month. They get about Rs. 8 per *Chhakki*, which means for monthly 90 *Chhakis* (4.5 Bundles), they earn about Rs. 720 per/month for 3-4 months in the peak season and

Rs. 480/month in the lean season. In Khajuripada village 776 households are organized under 11 SHGs and the total marketable surplus for them 2700 quintals. They are guided by local NGO and the product is bought by the local traders of the area. Similarly, in the village Sudrukumpa 8 SHGs are engaged in *siali* leaves activity involving 120 households and the total marketable surplus is 2700 quintals; they are guided by 1 NGO who facilitates the sale of *siali* leaves to the local traders in the market so that they are not heavily exploited. *Siali* is mostly found in *sal* forests and grows well in places with good moisture content; hence, the concentration is around perennial water sources like streams, seasonal falls and other water bodies. It is a creeper plant with high regeneration capacity; this creeper is found in abundance in Khajuripada and Sudrukumpa forest regions under Khajuripada TSP Block of Phulbani ITDA. The plant has a seasonality pattern growth and has best growth during the rainy season (May-November). The product features during the period are tender, soft, good green colour, without holes and big in size. From December onwards, the quality starts deteriorating. During autumn the product moves through the lean period, when the availability of the product decreases drastically.

Activities of Primary Collector

Collect the leaves from the forest by using a small sharp knife. In a day one male/female used to collect approximately 10 to 20 kg wet raw leaves. After collection they used to put it in sunlight for a day or two for drying. Generally, drying is made in the road near to their house or in their homestead land. In bad weather they used to chain those leaves in rope and hang it on roof of their living room. Some used to hang the leaf chains in the kitchen.

After the leaves get dried, they used to sort the leaves in order and put a heavy stone or wood on the top of the leaf bunch to make it even. Once the dried raw-leaves are properly pressed for a day they used to make it in bundle. The bundle is then pressed and tied with the help of ropes made of thick *siali* creepers. Some household used to pin the dried leaves in pins, extracted from bamboo and palo stick to make it semi-stitched plates. Finally, the prepared dried stitched leaf bundles are ready for sale by the primary collectors. The price ranges between Rs. 8 per *Chhakki*.

Village Traders Commission Agents

The village level traders operate on weekly basis; where the date and time for lifting the same from the villages is fixed. The primary collectors bring all the bundles to the village point for transaction. Leaf rate differs based on assessing the quality (size, colour, leaves with holes etc.).

Storing the leaf bundles in temporary storage point. Payment to the primary collectors and advance given to them if necessary for the next week. Inform the Regional Traders (Town Trader) about the quantity procured village-wise and making necessary planning for its lifting to the trading point. At these level, village traders do not do any processing. The Village Traders sell at the rate of Rs. 8.40.

Town Traders/Block Level Traders

Opening the collected bundles for quality checking of leaves. Sorting and grading of those leaves according to the demand of various terminal, markets. Re-bundle the graded leaves into 45-50 kg average pack with the help of a iron angle ring by experienced workers for easy transportation in big trucks. Preparing for forest gate passes for inter-state transportation. Arrangements of economic mode of transport. The different temples are purchasing the *Siali* plate from the Odisha traders. Identify district level Traders, Institutional buyers and State level Traders and selling them after value addition. Cost ranges from Rs. 9 to Rs. 9.50. The Institutional buyers add value doing sewing and pressing and sell adding 40 per cent more price of the cost of production outside the State. Hoarding the product for off-season sale. Sometimes fixation of base prices for regional markets is done based on the demand and supply of the market.

Sub-cluster Selection of Tamarind

Tamarind is slow growing, long lived marine tree, which reaches a height of 80-100 ft. (20-30 m) with a trunk of circumference 25 ft. (7.5m). The leaves are normally flattish, irregular curved and bulged. Pods vary from 2 to 7 inches in length. They may be brown extremely and at first are tender-skinned with grey, highly acidic flesh and soft, whitish under developed seeds. As they are matured, the pods fill with somewhat juicy and the pulp turns brown or reddish-brown. Thereafter, the skin becomes brittle, with easily cracked shell and the pulp dehydrates naturally to a sticky paste. Tamarind seeds are hard, brown, square in form, 1/8 to ½ inch (1-2.5 cm) is diameter and each is enclosed in a parchment lime membrane. Tamarind is produced in all seven TSP Blocks in Malkangiri ITDA, with Mathili block having a share of 40 per cent in the total production. Nearly 60 per cent of families in 20 GPs are involved in tamarind collection and are producing 32,000 quintal. The three sub-clusters are Mathili, Kiang and Nayakuda. The tamarind trade in the five selected villages is being carried out by 28 SHGs involving 353 households each household is collecting 21 kgs of tamarind on average: the total marketable surplus is 4350 kgs which is being coordinated by an NGO known as ODC. They are selling it to the local private traders already identified by them.

6.16 Role of TDCC in Sundargarh District

The Sundargarh Branch of TDSS started functioning since 1973 with an object to serve the tribals covering the following area by catering them essential commodities and their needs through fair price shop and collect minor forest product from them. This goal has been successfully achieved by Sundargarh branch in the past 27 years.

The area of operation of this Branch consists of following forest divisions, such as:

- Sundargarh Forest Division
- Bamara Forest Division
- Redhakhol Forest Division
- Sambalpur Forest Division.

The State Government has adopted new policy for procurement of MFP items during the year 2000-01. Since 2000-01 TDCC has not been able to collect a sizeable quantity of MFP items from the open market by competing to the private traders due to non-availability of prospective buyers. The collection of MFP by TDCC during 2012-13 for *Siali* leaves, *Sal* seeds and chilly has been for Rs. 8.53 lakhs and during 2013-14 it has been for Rs. 8.93 lakhs.

Table 6.19: MSP fixed by Government of Odisha of NTFP Items

Sl. No.	*Name of the Items*	*MSP fixed by the Government per K.g.*
1.	*Sal* Seeds	Rs. 10.00
2.	*Mahua* Seeds	Rs. 22.00
3.	*Harida*	Rs. 11.00
4.	Lac (A. Kusumi Variety)	Rs. 320.00
	(B. Rangeeni Variety)	Rs. 230.00
5.	*Sal* Leaves	Rs. 21.00
6.	Tamarind (Seeded)	Rs. 22.00
7.	Forest Honey	Rs. 132.00
8.	Genduli Gum	Rs. 108.00
9.	*Chargutuli*	Rs. 100.00
10.	*Karanja* Seeds	Rs. 21.00

Source: Tribal Development Co-operative Corporation of Odisha Ltd., Sundargarh Branch Manager TDCCOL, Sundargarh, 18-04-2015.

Table 6.20: Product-wise Profit Made by Traders from Tribals in Sundargarh District (2015-16)

Sl. No.	*Name of Traders*	*Name of Products*	*Total Quantity Sold (in Quintals)*	*Net Profit (In Rs.)*	*Per Quintal Profit (In Rs.)*
1.	Sahoo RGP	Mahua	120.200	3900.00	448.419
		Vegetable	6.000	5000.00	833.333
2.	Ehitu RGP	Mahua	138.1500	69400.00	502.353
3.	Local RGP	Paddy	356.000	188000.00	528.089
		Fishery	12.410	71900.00	579.371
		Mahua	31.000	21000.00	677.419
		Tomato	2.000	1600.00	800.000
		Vegetable	164.000	69800.00	425.610
4.	Local Bisra	Vegetable	83.800	77500.00	924.821
		Hotel	–	2500.00	–
		Paddy	15.000	2700.00	180.000
		Fishery	–	6800.00	–
5.	Local Panposh	Tailoring	3290.000	79850.00	24.271
		Vegetable	195.000	51500.00	264.103
		Stationery	–	4000.00	–
		Fishery	–	4000.00	–
		Mushroom	0.060	480.00	8000.000
		Paddy	11.000	15000.00	1363.636

(Contd.)

Sl. No.	Name of Traders	Name of Products	Total Quantity Sold (in Quintals)	Net Profit (In Rs.)	Per Quintal Profit (In Rs.)
6.	Local Birmitrapur	Vegetable	568.000	437600.00	768.838
		Moong Business	26.000	54600.00	2100.000
		Grocery	10.000	21000.00	2100.000
		Mahua	110.000	182606.00	1660.054
		Tomato	8.000	16800.00	2100.000
		Paddy	48.000	100000.00	2083.333
		Bodi business	44.000	90,600.00	2059.091
		Char processing	28.000	2,80,000.00	10,000.000
		Goat business	26.000	54,600.00	2,100.00
		Petty business	18.000	36,000.00	2,000.000
7.	Local Banki	Vegetable	286.000	3,85,600.00	1348.251
		Grocery Shop	3.000	13,700.00	4566.667
		Petty business	34.000	23,000.00	676.471
		Paddy	219.000	1,09,100.00	498.174
		Moong	32.000	8,600.00	268.750
		Piggery	1.000	700.00	700.000
		Mahua	77.000	57,800.00	750.649
		Goat business	20.000	4,000.00	200.000
8.	Local Kuarmunda	Mahua	4.000	2,400.00	600.000
		Vegetable	754.000	4,24,500.00	562.997
		Tomato	16.000	8,800.00	550.000
		Paddy	17.000	3,400.00	200.000
		Petty business	31.000	38,400.00	123.871
		Bodi business	26.000	6,200.00	238.462
9.	Deepak Sahu	Char processing	66.000	1,62,000.00	245.454
10.	Kalinga Herbal Fair	NTFP	–	2,500.00	–

(Contd.)

Sl. No.	*Name of Traders*	*Name of Products*	*Total Quantity Sold (in Quintals)*	*Net Profit (In Rs.)*	*Per Quintal Profit (In Rs.)*
11.	Kiti Campus	NTFP	0.400	700.00	1,750.000
12.	Adibasi MLA Bhubaneswar	Dal, Bidi etc.	3.000	9500.00	3166.667
13.	Nuagaon	Tomato	280.000	195000.00	696.429
14.	Jai Kishore RGP	Siali Leaf	11.000	2100.00	190.909
15.	Rahim Akhtar	Char processing	214.000	375000.00	175.234
16.	Nuagaon	Vegetable	55.000	5500.00	100.000

Source: Based on field data collection during 2014-15 in Sundargarh District for ICSSR Project (K. Gopal Iyer).

Table 6.21: Abstract of Income for SHG (in Rs.) from Different Products in Sundargarh District

Sl. No.	*Product*	*No. of SHGs*	*Quantity Procured (In Qtls.)*	*Per SHG Quantity Procured (In Rs.)*	*Per SHG Sold price (In Rs.)*	*Remarks (In Qtls.)*
1.	Mahua	73	608.50	8.366	15481.00	6.438 In SHG Quantity sold
2.	Paddy	40	210.00	5.250	22518.00	14.850 In SHG Quantity sold
3.	Fishery	17	10.93	0.643	7091.00	10.93 In SHG Qty Sold
4.	Vegetable Cultivation	178	2295.513	12.896	19255.00	8.823
5.	Tailoring	37	3060 (Pieces)	83 (Pieces)	5314.00	8383 Pieces for SHG sold
6.	Charcoal Processing	27	201.5	7.463	51485	3.481 for SHG
7.	Bodi (Vegetable)	4	60.00	15.0	12325	Sold per SHG
8.	Petty business	7	95	13.571	19628.00	
9.	Goat business	2	25	12.500	2050.00	

(Contd.)

Sl. No.	Product	No. of SHGs	Quantity Procured (In Qtls.)	Per SHG Quantity Procured (In Rs.)	Per SHG Sold price (In Rs.)	Remarks (In Qtls.)
10.	Piggery	1	1	1.000	1400.00	
11.	Arisa Honey	1	—	—	2000.00	
12.	Tomato Cultivation	5	—	62.000	86840.00	
13.	Siali Leaf	1	310	11	12100	
14.	NTFP	2	11	30	6000	
15.	Dal, Bidi etc.	6	60	10.500	17883.00	
16.	Hotel	1	63	—	—	

Source: Based on field data collection during 2014-15 in Sundargarh District.

With the liberal policies/devolution of power to Gram Panchayats to manage NTFP there are now many players—both private and government in NTFP procurement trade. TDCC, DSMS, FDA/VSS, SHGs, NGOs, NABARD, PRIs, medicinal plant growers, traders etc. are into different kinds of interventions in NTFP procurement, enterprises and marketing but hardly there is any coordination among them for addressing the challenges in the NTFP.

6.17 Role of ORMAS

Genesis

Odisha Rural Development and Marketing Society (ORMAS) was established by the Government of Odisha in Panchayati Raj Department as an autonomous body in the year 1991 under Societies Registration Act, 1860. At present, it is functioning in all the 30 Districts of the State under the Chairmanship of Collector and District Magistrate to strengthen the economic status of the artisans and other marginalized sections.

Objectives

ORMAS is promoting several activities successfully like Incense Stick Production (*Agarbatti*) in several districts of Odisha by SHG women groups. MKSP Agriculture covers 9 tribal districts of the State. MKSP (tasar) functions into Left-wing Blocks of Keonjhar district.

6.18 Role of MART

MART's quest for innovative solutions has repeatedly proven the need to marry the learning from the ground to the scientific knowledge and management principles available in public and private domains. This paradigm is reflected in business approach and activities in Odisha that has grown. Over the past 7 years, MART has intensively worked in Odisha by deeply involving the community and finding space for their voiced needs. So far MART has experimented with and established various models and mechanisms that are accepted as durable solutions to the development challenges posed by rural India in general and Odisha in particular. Under the "Western Odisha Rural Livelihood Project", MART has developed and established the "pro-poor value chain" concept wherein private sector is engaged as an equal business partner with the community to ensure a win-win situation. This model is termed simplistically as the "Collective Marketing Model". This model has been furthered to include the government towards better fulfillment of its development objectives and was replicated under the "Odisha Tribal Empowerment and Livelihood Programme" to cover 396 villages. The relevance and success of this model is reflected in its adoption for project design, pilot and upscale for the "Odisha Forestry Sector Development Project" under which 68 clusters are being developed in 9 forest divisions of the State.

Sub-cluster Selection of Sal Leaf

Mayurbhanj is a tribal dominated district and has 26 Tribal Sub-Plan (TSP) Blocks in Odisha. About more than 80 per cent of the total geographical area of the district is covered by forest. So, the economy of the district, to a large extent is forest based. A large cross-section of the population depends on the collection of Non-Timber Forests Produces (NTFPs) for livelihood. One of the main NTFPs abundantly available in the district is *sal* leaf, available almost for 8-9 months a year. More than 70 per cent of the population derive their livelihood from *sal* leaf collecting, stitching and selling as observed from villages of Kutchilaghati and Ambadali sub-clusters in Samakhunta Block.

6.19 VSS Management in Sundargarh District of Odisha—A Case Study

The Odisha Forestry Sector Development Project is being implemented with the objectives of restoring degraded forests and improving the income level of villagers by promoting sustainable forest management including JFM plantations and community development, thereby improving environment and alleviating poverty. These forestry based community institutions are termed as Vana Samrakshana Samiti (VSS) in the peripheral reserve forest area and Eco-development Committee (EDC) in the case of protected areas. Vana Samrakshana Samitis an independent, formal, democratic "village based community institution" comprising inhabitants of a village constituted for the development/management of earmarked forests as per the Odisha JFM Resolution. Here an attempt is made to discuss the functioning of VSS in Rourkela Forest Division including the number of SHGs formed as also the income generated from the VSS.

Table 6.22: Rourkela Forest Division

Name of the District	*Sunder-garh*	*Name of the Forest Division*	*Rourkela Forest Division, Rourkela*
Total Subdivision covered	3	Total Forest Management Unity	6 Forest Ranges
Total CD Blocks Covered	8	Total GP covered	59
Forest Division	1	Total VSS	174 VSS under OFSDP 92 VSS under Ama Jangal Yojana (Started recently)
Total No. of SHGs	**463**	**Total Cluster**	**6**

Source: DFO, Forest Division, Rourkela.

Table 6.23: Operational Area under Ama Jangala Yojana (AJY-VSS)

Range	*No. of VSSs*	*Area (in Ha.)*		*Total*
		RF	*PRF/DPF*	
Banki	13	375.00	596.20	971.20
Bisra	26	1919.40	0	1919.40
Kuarmunda	26	1110.00	750.00	1860.00
Biramitrapur	5	320.00	70.00	390.00
Panposh	7	935.00	0	935.00
Rajganpur	15	1272.00	0	1272.00
Total	**92**	**5931.40**	**1416.20**	**7347.60**

Source: DFO, Forest Division, Rourkela.

Income Generation Activities

NTFP-based Small Income Generating activities undertaken by SHGs by 147 VSS and 305 VSG's Rourkela division. The SHGs in Rourkela Forest Division made a net profit of Rs. 24.56 lakhs in trading in different products.

Impact of the Programme

- Community based organization like—VSS and SHGs strengthen.
- Leadership quality among tribal women is increased.
- Solidarity among villagers is enriched.
- Articulation power of the SHG members improved.
- Annual income of households is raising among the SHG members.
- Managerial potential of the tribal women has been developed.
- Bargaining power of tribal women has been increasing.
- Social dignity is increasing.
- Wider business network is established. Out-migration is going to be reduced.
- Healthy cooperation and kinship among villagers is upgrading.
- Cluster cooperative is strengthened.
- The Income Generation Activities is inspiring and encouraging the other SHG members.
- Leading to the socio-economic and political empowerment of the tribal people in general and women in particular in Forest Division, Rourkela.

Source: Information furnished by DFO-CUM-DMU-CHIEF, OFSDP, ROURKELA FOREST DIVISION *vide* letter no. 6938/OFSDP/ Dt.16-10-2015.

Result of NTFP Survey and Analysis done in Rourkela Forest Division

Sample survey has been conducted in 100 sample plots. Its analysis is presented below:

A total of 77 trees species with a total number of 3770 have been enumerated in 100 sample plots out in which the maximum number per ha has been recorded for *Sal* (951) followed by *Chara* (494) and *Asan* (283) etc. and the lowest being represented by Barang, Genduli, Barakoli. Accordingly, the percentage distribution per ha is highest for *Sal* (25.22%) followed by *Sidha* (10.2%), *Asan* (7.5%), *Bheru* (6.6%) so on so forth.

NTFPs Inventory Data (Climber) of Rourkela Forest Division

A total of climber species have been enumerated in 100 sample plots out of which the maximum number per ha has been recorded for *Atundi* (147) followed by *Dudhia* (131), *Budilaha* (64) etc., and the lowest being represented by *Kirkichi, Kaincha, Kunduru*. Accordingly, the percentage distribution per ha is highest for *Atundi* (32.7%) followed by *Dudhia* (29.18), *Budhilaha* (14.45).

Potential NTFP Inventory Data (Tree) of Rourkela Forest Divisions

Seven trees species out of total enumerated tree species of 77 have been categorized as potential species which are having potential to play a pivotal role in the livelihood of forest fringe dwellers. A close look on the statistical result reveals that total potential NTFP trees species contributes 71.3 per cent of total tree species enumerated per ha basis. *Sal* is the predominant Tree NTFP contributing 95.1 per ha out of the total 377 stems per ha of all trees species. Next to *sal* comes *Chara, Sidha, Asan* etc.

6.20 Policy Implications of the Study in Odisha and Jharkhand

The Government of Odisha has entrusted provision of the ownership rights of MFP to the Odisha Gram Panchayat as per (Amendment Act, 1997) and vested the power of MFP to Gram Panchayat. This is in accordance with the PESA Act of 1996 of giving ownership right over MFP in the Gram Panchayats in Scheduled areas. It has entrusted 69 items of NTFP to Gram Panchayats. On 26th May, 2010 the Panchayati Raj Department in exercise of power under Section 152 of the OGP Act issued an Administrative Order prescribing the manner in which the rights are transferred to the GPs. Further Rs. 100 was fixed as registration fees for each produce to be given by the traders who intend to procure. There is no restriction on the traders on number and volume of produce that they want to trade and transact.

The State Government of Odisha made rules in November 2002. The GP shall have the power to regulate procurement and trading of MFP, whether produced in government lands and forest areas within the limits of Gram (village) or collected from the Reserved Forests and brought into the Gram. Priority would be given to the VSS and its members for collection and trading of MFP. Price fixation would be done by the Panchayat Samiti (PS) in September and would be circulated to different Offices of District Administration and to all the GPs.

The Gram Sabha would ratify prices fixed and necessary changes can be made based on the local needs. If Panchayat Samiti fails to fix the price then the District Collector would call a meeting of PS preferably in October to fix-up the minimum procurement prices. The trader registered to procure MFP from the GP shall furnish monthly return and also annual return in a prescribed format. The GP shall furnish an annual return on the procurement and sale to the Forest Range Officer.

After the enactment of PESA the Odisha Government has handed over ownership rights of MFP to Gram Panchayats. Out of them, only a few are procured commercially as neither the primary collectors nor the traders have thorough knowledge on domestic and commercial use of many items. Further, there is hardly any attempt to develop the marketability of currently obscure items. The panchayat members are not yet conversant of the rule and prices of Minor Forest produce. Hence, the traders are still ruling the roost and exploiting the primary producers. There needs to be awareness generation of primary producers in which the gram panchayat have to play the primary role along with the experts of the State Rural Development Institute, Bhubaneswar have to impart training to the elected panchayat members so that they are capable to fix the remunerative price for the commodities and able to tackle the traders for reduced exploitation. They should also be able to create awareness among the grassroots producers the market prices and appropriate market where they can get remunerative prices.

The expert group constituted by MoEF made the following observations to confine the term "Minor Forest Produce". Minor Forest Produce is the produce, other than timber, harvestable on a non-destructive basis. The term "forest produce" and 'timber' will have the same meaning as in the Indian Forest Act, 1927. *Regarding 'ownership' the Committee felt that in accordance with the spirit of the Act (PESA), the Gram Sabhas/Panchayat should be endowed with usufructory rights rather than ownership of MFPs available from all lands except Wildlife Sanctuaries and bio-sphere reserves, because ownership might create many complications* (GoI: MoEF, 1998). The policy of March 2000 recognized the importance of MFPs in the forest-dwellers' life. It also recognized the importance of sustainability of resources. As per the requirement of PESA, it gave ownership rights over "MFP"s to GPs in Scheduled areas, and only regulatory rights to rest of the GPs. MFP was defined under this policy in vague way, creating a pseudo-category of "Minor Forest Produce" (term used in PESA) under NTFP, and initially 60 items were declared as MFPs. VSS will continue to enjoy rights of ownership over MFP and NTFP in reserve forest areas.

The policy of government of Odisha relating to NTFP also has given roles to some of the intervening institutions in marketing of NTFP particularly to TDCC, OFDC, ORMAS and MART. TDCC procures MFP items from the grassroots procurers by fixing MFP and SHGs have also been associated with revolving fund and they are playing useful supplementary role in procurement and trade. Similarly, MART has also involved a good strategy for collective action in procurement and trade of important NTFP by selecting suitable clusters and marketing facility particularly in the scheduled areas. These are good examples on Value Chain Analysis and feasibility strategy of product cluster in TSP areas of Odisha. They have made successful product cluster of few crops like *maize, ginger, chilly, turmeric, tasar, hillbroom, lac, sabai grass, sal leaves, siali leaves and tamarind.*

The Government of Jharkhand need to take up several policy measures on NTFP learning from Odisha experience. After the enactment of PESA the Odisha Government has handed over ownership rights of MFP to Gram Panchayats. The Government of Jharkhand should have similar initiative. The GP shall have the power to regulate procurement and trading of MFP, whether produced in government lands and forest areas within the limits of Gram (village) or collected from the Reserved Forests and brought into the Gram. Priority would be given to the VSS and its members for collection and trading of MFP. Price fixation would be done by the Panchayat Samiti (PS) and would be circulated to different offices of district administration and to all the GPs. The Gram Sabha would ratify prices fixed and necessary changes can be made based on the local needs. If Panchayat Samiti fails to fix the price then the District Collector would call a meeting of PS preferably in October to fix-up the minimum procurement prices. The trader registered to procure MFP from the GP shall furnish monthly return and also annual return in a prescribed format.

The TDCC in Odisha procures several items of NTFP from the grassroots procurers and SHG for few items based on Minimum Support Price. It may be mentioned in this context, that the Ministry of Tribal Affairs, Government of India has announced marketing support for Tribal Produce for 24 MFP items, which is introduced in Odisha,

Chhattisgarh and Andhra Pradesh, but not in Jharkhand. The Government of Jharkhand should connect itself with the marketing support for tribal produce being extended by Ministry of Tribal Affairs.

The Government of Jharkhand has acquired the reputation of *primus interpares* in Jharkhand in lac cultivation and lac production. It has the facility of IINRG, Namkum for promoting training cultivation and production facilities. However, marketing is a causality for which the Government of Jharkhand should take appropriate step in the procurement, collection and marketing of lac products. The IINRG does not have the mechanism of marketing facility; the Government of Jharkhand should intervene in promoting lac production cluster area for procurement of lac by fixing MFP and procuring MSP rate from the tribal farmers. Women and SHGs play a prominent role in the procurement, cultivation of lac and selling it in the local haat and market. This system should be replaced by an institution similar to JHASCO LAMPS/TDCC so that there is proper livelihood promotion of the tribal farmers. During our field study in Saranda forest area we could find that *Sal* leaf, *Mahua, Siali* leaf, *Tamarind, Karanj*, and other NTFPs are procured by the women groups and taken to the local *haats* for selling it to the traders where they are fleeced. There is enough scope for farming clusters of MFP production area for bulk procurement at prices fixed by Gram Sabha or Gram Panchayat on the line of the working system in the State of Odisha. Already the Government of Jharkhand has found few clusters in Saranda, Porahat, Goilkera, Sonua, Manoharpur and other adjoining areas which can also be suitably utilized for NTFP procurement. They can be given trading at the Gram Sabha and Gram Panchayat level to get acquainted with the entire process of NTFP procurement and marketing.

R.K. Yogi, R.K. Singh, *et al.* (2016) have discussed New Policy Interventions in the lac sector in Jharkhand. Their policy interventions include creation of a revolving fund to be provided for procurement of NTFP for the gatherers at the prefix MSP. The revolving fund requirement shall be accessed based on an Annual Procurement Fund. Subsidy is required for the State to compensate for loses that may be incurred during the MSP operation. This is essentially an anti-poverty measure, as it addresses the livelihood of some of the poorest communities in the country. The scheme shall provide training on sustainable harvesting and value addition activities including facilitation for the marketing of the produces to one hundred thousand tribal MFP gatherers.

The existence and dissemination of complete and accurate market information is the key to achieve both operational and pricing efficiency. Therefore, a nationwide information network portal MFPNET dedicated to NWFPs is being established to implement Information and Communication Technology (ICT) based schemes for speedy collection and dissemination of information and data for its efficient and timely utilization. In many States, purchase and sale of NWFPs in local weekly markets is done in the open and thus buyers and sellers have to face a lot problems during the rainy and hot summer seasons. In order to improve the condition of these places, formal structures where trading can take place in a systematic manner need to be established. The stock procured by the State designated agencies in each weekly market may be too small and therefore, would need to be transported to the the aggregation centres from where bulk quantity can be transported to the centrally located warehouse/cold storage. Therefore, it is essential to establish a warehouse of 50 metric tonnes at the block level to aggregate the stocks procured at each local market.

References

Arnold, J.E.M. (1995). "Socio-economic benefits and issues in Non-Wood Forest Product use". In *Report of the International Expert Consultation of Non-Wood Forest Products*. Rome: Food and Agriculture Organization of the United Nations.

Buriuly, Bace (2013). "Tribal Weekly Market (HAATS): A Study in West Singhbhum District of Jharkhand (Unpublished report)", Centre for Social Entrepreneurship, School of Management and Labour Studies, TISS, Mumbai.

Falconer, J. (1990). "Non-Timber Forest Products in Southern Ghana: Main Report", Republic of Ghana Forestry Department and Overseas Development Administration, Natural Resources Institute, Chatham.

Ganguli, R. (2007). "Minor Forest Produces feel the heat of Rising Rupee", *The Economic Times*. 16th July, 2007.

Gharai, A.K., and Chakrabrati, S. (2009). "A study on NTFP related Livelihood dependency and people's perception of the commercialization potential of Selected NTFPs in selected Locations of Gumla, Hazaribagh and Simdega Districts of Jharkhand". Secunderabad: Central for People's Forestry.

Hopkins, J.C., Scherr, S.J. and Gruhn, P. (1994). "Food Security and the Commons: Evidence from Niger", *Draft Report to USAID*. Washington: IFPRI.

Islam, M.A., S.M.S. Quli, R. Rai and Angrej Ali (2014). "Exploration of Variables Predicting Livelihood Assets Status of Tribal Communities subsisting in Forests of Jharkhand", India, *J. Hum. Ecol.*, 47(3): 241-249 (2014).

Khare, A. (1989). "Small Scale Forest Enterprises in India with special reference to the Role of Women", *Wasteland News*. November, 1989-January 1990.

Khare, A. and Rao, A.V.R. (1993). "Products of Social Forestry: Issues, Strategies and Prioritie", *Wastelands News*, 6 (4): 7-17.

Kumar, J. (2011). "Marketing of Lac—A Cooperative Approach", pp. 269-273. In: Sharma, K.K. and Ramani, R. (eds.) (2011), *Recent Advances in Lac Culture*, Indian Institute of Natural Resins and Gums, Ranchi. pp. i-x, 1-319.

Kumar, S. and Ankita Chaudhary (2016). "Enhancement of Livelihood Activities through non-Timber Forest Products: A Study in Jharkhand's Ranchi and Simdega Districts", *Jharkhand Journal of Development and Management Studies*, XISS, Ranchi, Vol. 14, No. 1, March 2016, pp. 6919-6930.

Kumar, K.K. (2011). "Lac as a Rural Enterprise for Women", pp. 274-281; In: Sharma, K.K. and Ramani, R. (eds.) (2011). *Recent Advances in Lac Culture*. Indian Institute of Natural Resins and Gums, Ranchi. pp. i-x, 1-319.

Satapathy, R., (2001). "Forest Gives Pittance to Tribals, Huge Profits to Traders", *Times of India*, Eastern India Special, 26 March, 2001, New Delhi.

Saxena, N.C. (2003). "Livelihood Diversification and Non–Timber Forest Products in Odisha: Wider Lessons on the Scope for Policy change", ODI Working Paper No. 223. London, U.K.: Overseas Development Institute.

Tewari, D.D. (1994). "Developing and Sustaining Non-timber Forest Products: Policy Issues and Concerns with Special Reference to India", *Journal of World Forestry Resource Management*.

Vasundhara and Vikalpa (1998). "NTFP Policy in Odisha and a Comparative Analysis of NTFP Policy and Prices with Neighbouring States", Vasundhara, Bhubaneswar.

Verma, Sanjay Kumar and Sujit Kumar Paul (2016). "Sustaining Non-timber Forest Products (NTFPs) based Rural Livelihoods of Tribals in Jharkhand: Issues and Challenges", Ranchi; *Jharkhand Journal of Development and Management Studies*, XISS, Ranchi, Vol. 14, No. 1, March 2016, pp. 6865-6883.

Yogi, R.K., R.K. Singh, A. Bhattacharya, A.K. Jaiswal and Alok Kumar (2016). "Current Scenario and New Policy Interventions in the Lac sector", Indian Institute of National Resins and Gums, Namkum, Ranchi, *Jharkhand Journal of Development and Management Studies*, XISS, Ranchi, Vol. 14, No. 1, March 2016.

Appendix-I
Lac Culture—Time Table in Jharkhand

Months	*Kusumi*	*Rangeeni*
January	Forecast of larval emergence from winter crop (*aghani*). Pruning of new *Kusum* trees.	Cleaning of termite from *palas* and *ber* trees. Spray of intesticide in last week (Before male emergence)
February	Pruning of new *Kusum* trees. Harvesting of aghani crop and simultaneously pruning of trees. Inoculation of summer crop (*jethwi*) using nylon net. Phunki removal and scraping. Pruning of *ber* trees for inoculation in July or August.	Partial harvesting of inolucated trees of *palas*.
March	First spray of ethofenprox on lac culture.	Estimation of yield of sticklac from *baisakhi* ari.
April	Seond sprays of ethofenprox, if attack of *chrysopa* is seen (but not between 65-90 days of inoculation)	Crop harvesting in *baisakhi* ari sticklac coupe and simultaneously pruning of trees. Pruning of trees in broodlac coupe and also collection of ari lac (left during October/November six months before).
May	Spray of ethofenprox, if attack of Chrysopa is seen (but not between 65-90 days of inoculation).	Scraping of arilac from sticks and its marketing.
June	Forecast of larval emergence and estimation of yield from *jethwi* crop. Estimation of boodlac requirement for inoculation of *aghani* crop.	Forecast of larval emergence and estimation of bodlac yield from *baisakhi* crop.
July	Harvesting of *jethwi* crop partially or fully as per requirement after observing	Leave *baisakhi* crop in broodlac coup for self-colonisation.

Months	*Kusumi*	*Rangeeni*
	yellow spot. Inoculation of *aghani* crop. *Phunki* removal and scraping	Partial harvesting of excess broodlac in broodlac coupe.
August	First spray of insecticide ethofenprox, after 30th days of inoculation	First spray of intesticide emulsion (thofenprox) and fungicide (bavistin) one month after inoculation.
September	Second spray of intesticide and fungicide emulsion between 37-40 days of inoculation.	Second spray of insecticide ethofenprox (if necessary) Forecast of larval emergence in broodlac coupe. Estimation of broodlac requirement in ari and second broodlac coupe.
October	Third spray of insecticide and fungicide emulsion between 60-65 days of inoculation.	Harvesting of broodlac when a few crawlers appear on encrustation. Inoculation of broodlac in ari coupe and in a broodlac coupe.
November	Make arrangement to prevent theft of *aghani* crop.	*Phunki* removal, scraoing and disposal of scraped lac. Estimation of incidence of predators and parasitoids. Spray of intesticide (ethofenprox) on lac culture.
December	Estimation of yield from *aghani* crop Estimation of broodlac requirements for *jethwi* crop.	Second spray of insecticide on lac culture (if needed).

Source: "Lac Culture Operations—When, Why and How?" Indian Institute of Natural Resins and Gums, Indian Council of Agricultural Research, Namkun, Ranchi (Jharkhand), 2011, p. 13.

Appendix-II

Total NRG Production, Export and Import During 2012-13

Particulars	*Production (Tons)*	*Export*		*Import*	
		Quantity (tons)	*Value (Rs. lakh)*	*Quantity (tons)*	*Value (Rs. lakh)*
Guar gum	807541.68	331497.58	2114672.40	460.35	2573.72
Lac	19575.00	4361.30	48027.58	NA	NA
Karaya um (Indian Tragcanth)	212.50	5764.40	2220.80	71.92	197.86
Other NRGs	10251.78	3949.48	11197.83	89214.06	75763.32
Total	**837580.96**	**345572.76**	**2176118.61**	**89746.33**	**78534.90**

Source: Indian Institute of Natural Resins and Gums, Namkum, Ranchi, (Jharkhand), *Annual Report*, 2013-14.

Appendix-III

Marketing Support for Tribal Produce by Mota

Mechanism for the marketing of Minor Forest Produce (MFP) through Minimum Support Price (MSP) and development of Value chain for MFP.

Tribal Ministry has introduced from the year 2013-14, a centrally sponsored scheme of "*Mechanism for Marketing of Minor Forest Produce (MFP) through Minimum Support Price (MSP) and development of value chain MFP*" as a measure of social safety for MFP gatherers who are primarily member of Scheduled Tribes. The scheme seeks to establish a system to ensure fair monetary returns for their effort in collection, primary processing, storage, packaging, transportation etc. It also seeks to get them a share of revenue from the sales proceeds with cost deducted. It also aims to address other issues for sustainability of process. The scheme envisages fixation and declaration of Minimum Support Price for the Selected MFP Procurement and Marketing operation at pre fixed MSP will be undertaken by the designed States Agencies. The MORD has fixed MFP for 24 items, namely:

Item No.	*Item Name*	*Price in Rupees per kg.*
1.	*Puwad* Seed	8
2.	*Kusum* Seed	18
3.	*Mahua* Seed	20
4.	*Sal* Leaf	21
5.	*Sal* Seed	10
6.	Lac	
	Rangeeni	100
	Kusumi	150
7.	*Chiraunji*	60
8.	Wild Honey	150
9.	Myrobalan	8
10.	Tamarind (with seed)	18
11.	Gums (Gum Karaya)	108
12.	*Karanj* Seed	10
13.	*Neem* Seed	12
14.	*Baheda*	15
15.	Hill Broom Grass	10
16.	*Shikakai*	30
17.	*Guggul*	700
18.	*Bael*	15
19.	*Nagarmotha*	25
20.	*Palash*	8
21.	*Shatavari*	40
22.	*Madhunashini*	35
23.	*Kalmegh*	15
24.	Tamarind (de-seeded)	40

Source: *Annual Report,* 2016-17, Marketing Support for Tribal Produce (pp. 87-92), Ministry of Tribal Affairs, Governmnet of India, New Delhi.

To implement the Scheme, Ministry has initiated the following action: Operational Guidelines for procurement and sale of identified MFP under the scheme have been issued on 03-01-2014. Minimum Support Price for 10 MFP namely, Tamarind, Honey, Gum *karaya*, *Karanj* seed, *Sal* seed, *Mahua* seed, *Sal* leaves, *Chiraunji* pods, Myrobalan, Lac (*Rangeeni* and *Kusumi*) has been announced.

Appendix-IV

Areas of Lac Production in Bihar and Jharkhand

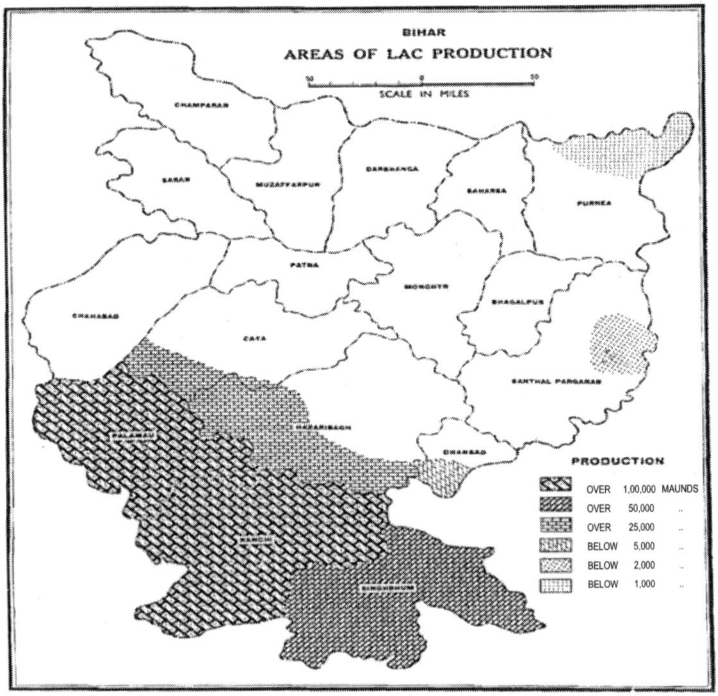

7

Labour Migration from Odisha and Jharkhand

7.0 Objectives of the Study

The present chapter examines the Seasonal Labour Migration of the Marginalized Section from Odisha and Jharkhand to other States of India for earning as labourers in different industries. The specific objectives of the study are as follows:

Labour Migration from Odisha

- Nature of Seasonal Migration
- Social Groups Characteristics of Migrant Labour
- Migration from Kalahandi District
- Migration from District of Koraput
- Bondage of Migration in Destination States
- Role of NHRC in Release of Bonded Labourer
- Child Labour and Bonded Labour
- Combating Distressed Migration.

7.1 Nature of Seasonal Migration from Odisha

Deepak K. Mishra (2016) has analysed Seasonal Migration from Odisha as a response of the poor to extreme poverty, lack of employment and limited livelihood options. He observes that while migration is opted as a livelihood strategy by both the poor and relatively better off sections of the rural society, but seasonal migration is mostly the strategy of the relatively marginalized groups. Persons belonging to deprived social groups have greater chances of migrating seasonally based on low earning occupations at Origin. The urban construction sector in particular has employed a large number of seasonal migrants accompanied with several sub-contractors and middleman. *The incidence of seasonal migration is relatively higher from the regions with low levels of development and land productivity* (Keshri and Bhagat, 2012; Mishra and Bose, 2013).

Odisha is not only the poorest State in India, but it is also at the bottom in terms of many indicators of social and economic development. Odisha has the highest IMR among the major States. On many other aspects of social sectors of development its performance has been dismal but in recent years *there has been drastic decline in the levels of poverty in Odisha*; however, the overall context of poverty and deprivation continues to be worse than the average for the country. As per 2009-10, Odisha has registered a poverty percentage of 37 per cent. There are distinct regional patterns in the concentration and inter-temporal trends in the incidence of poverty. *Poverty in Coastal Odisha has declined to comparatively low levels while that the in the North and South Odisha it is continuously remained high. The regional and social concentration of poverty indicates that SCs and STs have higher rate of poverty than others. It is rooted in the historical processes of economic transformation and stagnation. Northern and Southern Regions of Odisha are very poor where an overwhelming majority of SCs and STs population lives.* The Northern and Southern Odisha has been the home of a tribal groups which were brought under the political control of British colonialism.

The process of land alienation through debt bondage continued unabated (Sara, 1991). *Gradually a stage came where Kalahandi, Bolangir and Koraput (KBK Region) came to be recognized as synonymous with mass poverty, starvation and hunger deaths.* Seasonal migration from interior Odisha needs to be viewed as an outcome of cumulative disposition, marginalization and exploitation. The extent of out migration has increased in recent decades which highlights the deepening of these processes of disposition. Region-wise the highest percentage of short term migration in Odisha is found in the Southern Region which is clear from the following Table 7.1.

Table 7.1: Seasonal Migration, Region-wise Odisha (Rural)

Sex	*Coastal*	*Southern*	*Northern*	*Total*
Male	(11.76) [97.37]	(72.72) [84.11]	(15.51) [68.66]	(100) [82.55]
Female	(1.50) [2.63]	(64.99) [15.89]	(35.50) [31.34]	(100) [17.45]
Total	(9.97) [100]	(71.38) [100]	(18.65) [100]	(100) [100]

Note: Figures in parentheses refer to the percentage to row totals and those in square brackets refer percentages to column totals. Seasonal migrants by social category, Odisha (Rural).

Source: Unit level Data, NSSO, 64th Round Migration.

Table 7.2: Percentage of Social Groups

Social Category	*In Per cent*
ST	40.83
SC	23.58
OBC	23.49
Others	12.11
Total	**100.00**

Source: Unit level Data, NSSO, 64th Round Migration.

Table 7.3: Seasonal Migrants (by UPAS) of those in Labour Force at Origin (Rural)

Usual Principal Activity Status	*Male*	*Female*	*Total*
Self-employed	28.14	11.63	25.73
Regular Wage/salaried	2.96	0	2.53
Casual Wage	66.05	88.37	69.3
Unemployed	2.85	0	2.44
Total Labour Force	**100**	**100**	**100**

Source: Unit level Data, NSSO, 64th Round Migration.

Short term migration is highest among households engaged in agricultural labour (38%) and other non-farm labour (28%). Households that are self-employed in agriculture constitute 20 per cent of the total migrants. Such households, though possessing land, belong to the category of small and marginal farmers. Over 80 per cent of short term migrants belong to households possessing land less than or equal to just an acre. Although, the percentage of migrants out of total population is low, and a large percentage of land poor have not migrated, what is clear is that the incidence of short term migration declines sharply among those who have more land. *Landlessness, thus, appears to be a vital push factor for migration.*

The characteristics of land poorness, low literacy levels, engagement in casual wage labour (both aricultural and other labour) together reflect the poverty vulnerability of short-term migrants of Odisha. *The distribution of migrants across industries shows that they are mostly engaged in construction (36%) and manufacturing (38%). More females (25%) than males are also seen to participate in agricultural activities at destination places.* There is a neat correspondence between the spatial and social concentration of poverty on the one hand and that of seasonal migration, on the other. It is precisely in those regions where poverty ratios are higher and seasonal migration is more prevalent. Similarly, it is the SCs and STs of Odisha who have a higher share both in the population below the poverty line and also among the seasonal migrants. Seasonal migrants typically belong to the marginalized sections in terms of land ownership and employment patterns and also they are over represented among the poor. In other words, unlike the case with migrants, in general, *seasonal migrants are, by and large, a more vulnerable and disadvantaged group. The migration process starts in the month of September and October, during the Nuakhai festival. Labour contractors, sardars and their agents start advancing small sums of money as advance to labour families in exchange for their promise to migrate.* Generally, the advance is given to a household group called *pathuria*, consisting of a man, his wife and a young child. In the last one year, there has been an increase in the amount of old debts on account of social ceremonies, like marriages, and in repairing and construction of houses. Seldom money being spent in acquiring new productive assets such as land or bullocks.

7.2 Social Groups Characteristics of Migrants

Available data indicates that *SC and ST families lead the pack of migrants*. Around 41.44 per cent SC families migrate to other places in search of casual labour, followed by ST and OBC families. However, 37.40 per cent ST families have been reported to have migrated to other places in search of work. Among OBCs, 33.71 per cent families migrate to other places in search of employment.

Large farmers constitute only 0.68 per cent of the total. Around 46.50 per cent of the total area of the district is the net sown area, whereas the net irrigated area is only 36.66 per cent. The average agricultural productivity of 1,043 kg per ha for *Kharif* and 1,524 kg/ha for the *Rabi* crop is much below the State average. However, the cropping intensity of 159.98 per cent is slightly above the State average. A large number of families (84.20%) are indebted, their borrowing being mainly from informal sources and for consumption purposes. Migration is also an important source of livelihoods in the district. Percentage of families living below the poverty line has declined from 85.77 per cent (BPL Census, 1997). With the growth of employment, the real GDDP of Kalahandi has grown at the rate of 3.59 per cent per annum with a compound annual growth rate of 2.68 per cent from 1999-2000 to Rs. 10,319 in 2004-05 at a compound annual rate of 1.27 per cent. This indicates that the district economy and per capita district income have been growing, though the pace of growth is relatively slow. The real NDDP per employed person shws an increasing trend compared to 1999-2000. Looking at the emerging trend, it is apparent that the district economy has been diversifying slowly. Secondly, the work participation rate shows an increasing trend with regard to participation of females in different sectors of growth. With the exploration of growth potential in other sectors, the proportion of the population that directly depended on agriculture and allied activities has declined from 86.66 per cent in 1971 to 80.00 per cent in 2001. Along with that, the proportion of the work force engaged in the non-farm sector has increased from 14.34 per cent in 1971 to 20.00 per cent. *This indicates that the workforce has been diversifying from the farm sector to non-farm sectors.* With the improved financial services, availability of credit for enterprise and growth of production sectors, scope of employment and income generation has increased in the district. Due to the increasing scope of investment, private players have started entering the District. It is expected that with the sector growth and increased investment, unemployment will reduce in the district and so will extreme poverty and hunger. Various development interventions have significantly contributed to poverty reduction and employment generation. The increasing scope of irrigation and Government Policy of at least 35 per cent irrigation in all the blocks is further going to contribute to higher production growth and thereby availability of foodstuff. *With better scope of employment, Government PDS, special discounted rice at Rs. 2 per kg and increased pension for the vulnerable segment, the district is expected to minimize the incidences of malnutrition.* [*Source: District Human Development Report, Kalahandi*, Planning and Coordination Department, Government of Odisha, pp. 49-51.]

7.3 Migration of Inter-State Labour from the District of Kalahandi to Other States

Most of the workmen after the paddy season go to South India like undivided Andhra Pradesh, Karnataka and Tamil Nadu to work in the brick kiln either through middle man or *suo motu.* Workers going to Raipur area are doing rickshaw pulling, engaging in restaurant, civil construction work etc. The labourers working outside the State are enrolled as building constructions workers. *A survey was conducted from 15th October to 31st October, 2014 by the Anganwadi workers under the guidance of State Labour Institute, Bhubneswar* to work out the labour migration. The survey indicated that the migrants who went to different States are as follows.

Table 7.4: Labour Migration from Odisha to Other States

Sl. No.	*Name of the States*	*No. of Migrant Workmen*
1.	Gujarat	7,333
2.	Maharashtra	4,368
3.	Tamil Nadu	3,870
4.	Kerala	3,681
5.	Chhattisgarh	3,592
6.	Andhra Pradesh	3,268
7.	Karnataka	2,072
8.	Goa	1,682
9.	Uttar Pradesh	422
10.	Other States	2,482
	Total	**32,770**

Source: Labour Department, Government of Odisha, Bhubaneswar.

The survey indicates tentative figure on labour migration which fluctuate from season to season and in reality it is much higher. The Assistant Labour Officer, Bhawani Patna had written to a labour recruiting agent named Mojib Khan of village Latur, district Bolangir of illegally recruiting 51 labourers (28 adult and 23 children) from villages Ballipada and Arjun Gaon of Narla Block in the district of Kalahandi and drafted to Pedapally area of Karim Nagar District (in Telangana) to be engaged in Brick Kiln Industry named as M/s. SVG Brick without obtaining labour licence. One of the migrant labour from among them was physically asolted by the employer Suryabag W/o Jitender Bag belonging to Bhanpur village and met with death on 3rd December, 2015 at the work cite. He also did not obtain labour licence. The Assistant Labour Officer demanded a show cause notice from him. A letter addressed to Labour Commissioner, Odisha from Dy. Lab. Commissioner, Kalahandi bearing No. 2974 of 8th December, 2015 of returned 293 persons from Karim Nagar of Telangana and arrangements were made to bring them to Nodla Railway Station on 4th December, 2015. Two buses were arranged for transportation of the migrant workmen to their native places. Of the 116 migrant workmen who returned 65 were from Balipada village and another 51 were from Arjun Gaon village. Of these 51 adult and 65 were children. [*Source*: District Labour Officer, Kalahandi, Bhawani Patna.]

7.4 Migration from District of Koraput

The District Labour Officer Jeypore has provided information on migration of workmen of Koraput district to outside State through licence contractor. During 2011, licencee was provided to 8 contractors for 215 workers. The migrant labourers were taken to Gujarat, Bangalore, Karnataka and Andhra Pradesh. During 2012-13 also workman who went outside the States were 215 and the Contractors were the same 8 persons who were in 2011. *During these years also the workers were taken to Gujarat, Bangalore, Karnataka, Andhra Pradesh, Maharashtra, Tamil Nadu and Madhya Pradesh.* However, the actual number of migrant workman is much larger as they are taken by un-licensed contractors. The State and District Administration also received complaints on migration of workmen from Koraput District who were taken by un-licenced contractors to others States, viz., Kerala, Karnataka, Rajasthan and Madhya Pradesh and Maharashtra. The complaints were received by the administration for which 7 prosecution were filed by the administration. And all the workmen returned to their villages. During 2012, compensation were paid to 4 workers amounting to Rs. 28,000. During 2013, compensation were paid to 55 workers amounting to Rs. 66,092 *besides this 2 workers died* for which employees compensation cases filed; similarly during, 2015 also 2 workers died and employees compensation cases have been filed for them. As per the Statement of District Labour Officer 11 migrant workmen of the Dashmantapur Block were repatriated from Bangalore by District Administration during the year 2014; similarly, 1 missing workman of Dashmantapur block was repatriated from village Mahindral of Hoshiarpur district of Punjab by the District Level Machinery in the year 2015.

A comprehensive study on the impact of migration in the district of Koraput was conducted by SOVA with the support of local NGOs in Koraput. The study focused on existing pattern or migration from rural areas of the district of Koraput to other parts of Odisha. In Koraput more than 50 per cent of the total population comprising STs. Out of 62 tribes in the State of Odisha, 51 are found in the district of Koraput. The numerically large tribes in the district are Khond, Paraja, Godaba, Bhumia and Bondas. Some of the tribal groups are still cultivating podu cultivation (shifting cultivation). During the 1950s people from tribal regions were recruited by Tea States to work in the tea gardens of north-eastern States. A large number of tribal persons were also engaged in the laying of the railway line between Koraput and

Vishakhapatnam. The phenomenon of migration is believed to have taken root in the aftermath of the severe drought of the 1960s. Currently, large number of people in the district leave their village and flock to the brick kilns and stone quarries in Andhra Pradesh and construction sites of the towns and cities. The labour migration have emerged as one of the main alternatives for tribal people who meet the demand for unskilled labourers in States like Andhra Pradesh, Tamil Nadu, Mumbai and other location. *The study points out that almost all the 13 blocks are experiencing migration in varying degrees and intensities*. They migrate to Andhra Pradesh from other blocks of Koraput; the migration is mostly city driven. In most cases the adult head son or daughter moves in search of employment to other areas it has also been observed that families of the other migrant also move with the migrants which is called family migration. As per the study only 17 per cent of the respondents moved with families to destination point whereas 83 per cent move singly. *Out of the total migrant families 44 per cent migrate to Andhra Pradesh, Tamil Nadu; 9 per cent migrant to Kerala, 5 per cent to Karnataka and Maharashtra.* There are also smaller percentage of migration to the States of Goa, Gujarat, Assam, Rajasthan and Chhattisgarh. Mobility of the people from their villages to the destination point is *influenced by an advance sum of money* being offered by the labour contractor. An organized network of middle man moneylenders and labour contractors operate without any hindrance and recruit poor tribal people as migrant workers. Jeypore, Lamtaput, Potangi and Koraput were the most popular areas of experiencing migration mostly to Andhra Pradesh. 82 per cent of the migrant belong to SCs and more than half of them belong to younger age group. In 90 per cent cases the migrant move along and 10 per cent move with the family; 43 per cent are seasonal migrant 41 per cent short duration migrant, while the remaining 16 per cent migrant throughout the year.

Around 82 per cent of the migrant families belong to STs followed by SCs who contributed 10 per cent of total migration and OBCs make up for 4 per cent. Generally, 90 per cent of the persons migrate alone and only 10 per cent migrate with their wife and children. The study reveals that 59 per cent of migrants are in the age group of 16-35 years and 31 per cent is above 35 years and 10 per cent are children up to the age of 15 years. The majority of migrant families have agriculture land which is most upland and with low productivity. They perceive migration as a simple solution to meet their livelihood needs. According to the Sova Study 42 per cent of migrants hold annual income between 10,000-20,000, 24 per cent have income between Rs. 5000-10,000, their income is in combination of subsistence agriculture and wage labour. The study observed that 58 per cent of the households mortgage their lands at the time of taking loan and some of them also mortgage other assets and ornaments with the moneylenders. Delay in payment was the major problem with the working of MGNREGA. Those who are engaged in MGNREGA contribute to the decrease in migration flow. People migrate during October/November and returned back prior to monsoon during the months of May-June. The study finds that 46 per cent of respondents know about the destination points through middle man. The labour contractors were operating in all the blocks to facilitate migration. People take advances as commitment for jobs about 35 per cent of the migrant receive advance wages. *Ranging from Rs. 1000 to Rs. 5000 in Koraput district only four labour contractors and 40 labourers are registered with the district labour office.* The migrant work in stone cutting, construction earth work and farming. The majority of workers live in temporary huts in the work side. Their health care is neglected. The study reveals that 26 per cent of them reported that they were physically abused and with excess work load. Violence take place also against the women workers. The children face health problems which are not addressed. The media reports estimates that the inter-state migrants from the district of Koraput is above 1.50 lakh.

7.5 Migration of Inter-State Labour from the District of Kalahandi to Other States

Most of the workmen after the paddy season go to South India like undivided Andhra Pradesh, Karnataka and Tamil Nadu to work in the brick kiln either through middleman or *suo motu*. Workers going to Raipur area are doing rickshaw pulling, engaging in restaurant, civil construction work etc. The labourers working outside the State are enrolled as building constructions workers. A survey was conducted from 15th October, 2014 to 31st October, 2014 by the Anganwadi workers under the guidance of State Labour Institute, Bhubaneshwar to work out the labour migration.

The survey indicates tentative figure on Labour migration which fluctuate from season to season and in reality the migration is massive extending to over two lakh. The Assistant Labour Officer, Bhawani Patna had written to a labour recruiting agent, named Mojib Khan of village Latur, distrect Bolangir of illegally recruiting 51 labourers (28 adult and 23 children) from villages Balipada and Argun Gaon of Narla Block in the district of Kalahandi and drafted to Pedapally area of Karim Nagar District (in Telangana) in the Brick Kiln Industry named as M/s. SVG Brick employed migrant workers without obtaining labour licence. *One of the migrant labour from among them was physically assaulted by the employer Suryabag belonging to Bhanpur village and met with death on 3rd December, 2015 at the worksite.* The Brick Kiln owner also did not obtain labour licence. The Assistant Labour Officer demanded a show cause notice from him. A letter addressed to Labour Commissioner, Odisha from Deputy Labour Commissioner, Kalahandi bearing No. 2974 of 8th December, 2015 indicates the number of returned migrants as 293 persons from Karim Nagar of Telangana and arrangements were made to bring them to Nodla Railway Station on 4th December, 2015. Two buses were arranged for transportation of the migrant workmen to their native places. Of the 116 migrant workmen who 65 returned were from Balipada village and another 51 were from Arjun Gaon village. Of these 51 were adult and 65 children.

7.6 Continuity of Seasonal Labour Migration from Odisha and their Bondage in the Destination States

The complaints on bondage of the seasonal workers from the destination States like Andhra Pradesh, Karnataka, and Tamil Nadu as also from several other States continue to appear in the mass media and are also being reported to the National Human Rights Commission particularly from 2007 onwards. In this Section attempt is being made to refer to the cases which have been reported to NHRC recently to establish the phenomenon that the seasonal labour migration continues unabated from Odisha and the incidence of bondage also galore. The important destination States of the seasonal migrant labourers from Odisha are Andhra Pradesh, Karnataka, Tamil Nadu followed by Maharashtra and other States. The NHRC obtains Half Yearly Report on Status of Rehabilitation of Bonded Labourers from some of these destination States in the prescribed proforma about the number of such incidences taking place during recent years.

It is estimated that more than two lakh labourers from Odisha migrate to the Brick Kilns of Andhra Pradesh every winter after completing the harvest operation. In Andhra Pradesh they mostly migrate to the Brick Kilns adjacent to the city of Hyderabad, Secunderabad, Vidya Nagram, Vishakhpatnam etc. The labourers from Maupada district migrate to the Brick Kilns of Faizabad and other districts of Uttar Pradesh. The history of migration is related to the two major droughts, one in 1964-65 and the other during 1996-97. The process of migration starts during November/December and continues up to May-June. The contracts are finalized between the contractors and the workers usually for six months. Of late, apart from Andhra Pradesh they are also migrating to Chennai and Bangaluru. There are also internal migration within Odisha to Brick Kilns in Coastal Odisha such as Bhubaneswar, Cuttack, Jagatsinghpur and Puri. They also migrate to the irrigated districts of Bargarh, Sambalpur and in the adjacent district where Hirakud Dam Project has facilitated intensive cultivation. Some of them also migrate to the adjacent Chhattisgarh State to cities like Raipur and Bilaspur to work as rikshaw-pullers and migrant workers. One of the recent phenomenon is the establishment of large horticulture and agriculture farms in Chhattisgarh by farmers from Rajasthan, Gujarat, Punjab and Haryana who supply vegetables to the cities of Nagpur and Raipur. Due to the latest spate in construction work seasonal workers have also started working in the construction sector in cities like Chennai, Mumbai, Delhi, Bangaluru and Thiruvananthapuram.

The seasonal migrants consider it as a compulsion in spite of being aware that they have to work for very long hours (10-14 hrs.) and they have to work for pittance. They have to migrate every year as the alternative is unemployment and even hunger. There has been attempt to arrest migration by providing employment under MGNREGA and distributing rice of pittance at subsidized rates, but still the flow of migrants continues. Several elements of bondage in the seasonal migration contracts are the following:

(a) Migrants take money in advance which are monitored by labour contractors and their agents.

(b) The migration contracts are very short term and mostly seasonal confined to the rates per thousands of brick. After reaching the destination, the migrants have to work at the rates specified by the employers.

(c) Migrant workers are taken from the origin to the destination place by the labour contractors or their agents. The destination place is usually unknown to the migrant workers.

(d) If the workers are unable to work due to illness or other problems, they have to suffer worst form of coercion including violence. They forfeit their right to seek other alternative employments.

The workers employed in the Brick Kilns are often subjected to these elements of bondage. There is intimate linkage between seasonal migration and poverty. The advances and cycles of debt continued for meeting the daily consumption needs expenditure for social ceremonies for their basic household survivals. Their only way of repaying the debts is through work in bonded conditions. The poverty is ingrained due to low agriculture productivity, subsistence, single crop agriculture and prevalence of high incidence of landlessness. Sometimes, marginal and small farmers also migrate due to distressed conditions. The Government of Odisha has tried to implement MNREGA to arrest migration which has limited success. In village Tentulimunda 20 landless families have stopped migrating with the assurance of 100 days of work. According to the observation of Deepak Mishra, "As a large number of labour households have found a source of sustenance during the lean season, they have been able to free themselves from the clutches of exploitative moneylenders and employers in agriculture" (page 283). Deepak Mishra has also observed changes in the life style and consumption patterns of the seasonal labourers. Mobile Phones and jeans have become a marker of change in the social status of the migrants. Dr. Mishra also critiques observation that seasonal "migration can act as poverty reduction strategy" as he observes that even after years of seasonal migration, the conditions of migrating households have not improved much. Only those migrant labourers who have become labour agents and have been able to break the cycle of debt that induced migration have become really better of and those migrating to construction sector are much better than those migrating to the Brick Kilns.

The seasonal migration has also led to several adverse outcome for the migrants and their families. One of the worst victims are old parents, children and women. The seasonal migration has disrupted the studies of the children forcing children to depend on seasonal migration. Women have not only to face long hours of work but sexual violence as well. The State Government have initiated some sporadic arrests of agents and labour contractors, but there has been no systematic attempt to implement the Inter-state Migration Act. *The rehabilitation of the freed bonded labourers has no significant desirable effect for stopping migration as the rescued workers are again migrating to work in the bondage conditions.* One of the interesting observation by Deepak Mishra is "The local political economy of accumulation is deeply entrenched in the seasonal labour process. Although, Kantabanji has emerged as a key trading centre, the labour migration network has already been established as a key aspect of the local economy" (page 285). Labour circulation has become a preferred arena for rent seeking and accumulation for some of them.

One of the crucial findings of Deepak Mishra is that seasonal migration is more likely to be distressed-driven-coping strategy against poverty and limited options of livelihood. The pre-capitalist enteritis are getting reconfigured in the age of globalization. There are strong linkages between migration and production relations in agriculture in the areas of origin. The seasonal migration has become an institutionalized phenomenon to networks of kinship, reciprocity and bondage. "The author's succinct observation is the adverse incorporation of migrant labour into the global production networks signals the continuing significance of un-freedom under global capitalism" (page 286). (Deepak K. Mishra, 'Seasonal Migration from Odisha: A view from the field', In Internal Migration in Contemporary India, Chapter 10, pp. 263-290, Sage.)

7.7 Role of NHRC in the Release of Bonded Labour

The complaints on bondage of the seasonal workers from the destination States like Andhra Pradesh, Karnataka, and Tamil Nadu as also from several other States continue to appear in the mass media and are also being reported to the National Human Rights Commission particularly from 2007 onwards. In this Section attempt is being made to refer to the cases which have been reported to NHRC recently to establish the phenomenon that the seasonal labour migration continues unabated from Odisha and the incidence of bondage also galore. The important destination States of the seasonal migrant labour from Odisha are Andhra Pradesh, Karnataka, Tamil Nadu followed by Maharashtra and other States. The NHRC obtains Half Yearly Report on Status of Rehabilitation of Bonded Labourers from some of these destination States in the prescribed proforma about the number of such incidences taking place during recent years (*see* Table 7.5).

As per the Report of the National Human Rights Commission, the status of bonded labour in Odisha, who were identified at the destination place in Andhra Pradesh between January 2001 and December 2015 where 10,042 of whom 8751 persons were male, 1138 were females and 153 were child bonded labourer. Of the total bonded labour 9593 were released (inclusive of male, female and children) and 7852 were released on certificates. The number of bonded labour rehabilitated with a grant of Rs. 20 thousand were only 3151; besides this 1317 bonded labourers were rehabilitated by the State Government in the State of Origin and the rest 2181 are yet to be rehabilitated. This

Table 7.5: Consolidated Statement of Bonded Labour Identified, Released and Rehabilitated in Andhra Pradesh for the period January 2011 to December 2015 (1/2011 to 12/2015)

Sl. No.	*Descriptions*	*Consolidated Status*				*Reporting Period*
		Male	*Female*	*Children*	*Total*	
1.	No. of Bonded Labours Identified	8751	1138	153	10042	1/2011 to 12/2015
2(a)	No. of Bonded Labours Released	8487	953	153	9593	-do-
2(b)	No. of Bonded Labours Released on Certificate	7056	643	153	7852	-do-
2(c)	No. of Bonded Labours Released without Certificate	1233	00	00	1233	-do-
2(d)	No. of Bonded Labouis awaiting Release	00	00	00	00	-do-
2(e)	Language of Release Certificate	00	00	00	00	-do-
3(a)	No. of Bonded Labours transferred to other States for their Rehabilitation	1946	433	91	2470	-do-
3(b)	No. of Bonded Labours Transferred with Police Escort	1507	247	91	1845	-do-
3(c)	No. of Bonded Labours Transferred without Police Escort	7227	00	00	7227	-do-
3(d) to 4(c)	Specific Information	00	00	00	00	-do-
5.	No. of Bonded Labours Received on Rehabilitation Grant of Rs. 20,000	2552	525	74	3151	-do-
6.	No. of Bonded Labours Rehabilitated by the State	834	409	74	1317	-do-
7.	No. of Bonded Laboutrs yet to be Rehabilitated	1760	328	93	2181	-do-

Source: Data collected from National Human Rights Commission, New Delhi.

shows that 40.13 per cent of the bonded labourers were rehabilitated by paying Rs. 20,000 which is a pittance for proper rehabilitation. Besides this, the rehabilitation of 13.73 per cent cases were undertaken by Government of Odisha, but the nature of rehabilitation is not mentioned which raises issues relating to proper rehabilitation. The worst are the cases of 2181 bonded labourer constituting 22.74 per cent who have not been rehabilitated and are required to fend for themselves.

7.8 Bonded Labour in Karnataka

The figures in Table 7.6 indicate that information with respect to State of Karnataka is available only from 2012 to 2015. However, the figures of State of Karnataka indicate lower levels of incidence of bonded labourers. During the years between 2012-15, the number of labourers identified was 2583 which is much lower than the State of Andhra Pradesh. However, all the 2583 bonded labourers were also released and rehabilitated. The number of bonded labourers transferred to other State was 71 and number sent back to different States with police escorts was 432. The number of bonded labourers who are yet to be rehabilitated.

Table 7.6: Half Yearly Report on Status of Rehabilitation of Bonded Labourers (January 2012 to June 2015)

State: Karnataka

Sl. No.	*Descriptions*	*Status of Current Year*	*Consolidated Status of Preceding Years*	*Reporting Period*
		Total	*Total*	*January, 2015 to June, 2015*
1.	No. of Bonded Labours Identified	583	2583	-do-
2(a)	No. of Bonded Labours Released	583	00	-do-
2(b)	No. of Bonded Labours Released on Certificate	583	00	-do-
2(c)	No. of Bonded Labours Released without Certificate	00	00	-do-
3(a)	No. of Bonded Labours transferred to other States for their Rehabilitation	361	00	-do-
3(b)	No. of Bonded Labours Transferred with Police Escort	361	432	-do-
4.	No. of Bonded Labours Received on Rehabilitation Grant of Rs. 20,000	00	1127	-do-
5.	No. of Bonded Labours Rehabilitated by the State	00	3	-do-
6.	No. of Bonded Laboures yet to be Rehabilitated	881	759	-do-

Source: Data collected from National Human Rights Commission, New Delhi.

Specifically in the State of Odisha, 101 bonded labourers were identified all of whom were released and rehabilitated. The number of bonded labourers who were rehabilitated in the State is 72. It appears that NHRC has sensitized the Government of Odisha on the bonded labourers issue. The figures for January-June 2015 for the State of Odisha indicate that during this year 409 bonded labourers were identified, out of whom 350 were provided with release certificate. Among them 131 were transferred from other States and 107 were transferred to few States without police support. However, all the 409 labourer are yet to receive the benefit of rehabilitation.

The number of bonded labourers identified in the State of Odisha during 2014 was 1520 and 2167 were identified during the year 2015. Most of the identified bonded labourers during 2014 and 2015 were provided with release certificates and smaller amount were rehabilitated. The sensitivity of the Government of Odisha on bonded labourers is a welcome indicator.

As per the report of the National Human Rights Commission, the status of bonded labour in Odisha, who were identified at the destination place in Andhra Pradesh between January 2001 and December 2015 were 10042 of whom 8751 persons were male, 1138 were females and 153 were child bonded labourer. Of the total bonded labour 9593 were released (inclusive of male, female and children) and 7852 were releasaed on certificates. The number of bonded labour rehabilitated with a grant of Rs. 20 thousand were only 3151; besides this 1317 bonded labourers were rehabilitated by the State Government in the State of Origin and the rest 2181 are yet to be rehabilitatated. This shows that 40.13 of the bonded labourers were rehabilitated by paying Rs. 20,000 which is a pittance for proper rehabilitation. Besides this, the rehabilitation of 13.73 per cent cases were undertaken by Government of Odisha, but the nature of rehabilitation is not mentioned which raises issues relating to proper rehabilitation. The worst are the cases of 2181 bonded labourer constituting 22.74 per cent who have not been rehabilitated and are required to fend for themselves.

However, even these steps of identification, release and rehabilitation were quite un-common things by the Government of Odisha and the recent measures are welcome addition to the relief work being undertaken. This is just the beginning and it needs a much more systematic attempt on the part of both Government in the State of Origin and in the State of Destination to systematically eradicate the phenomenon of bonded labour.

7.9 Bonded Labour in Odisha

The NHRC identified a total of 2583 cases between July 2012 to June 2015 of bonded labourers who had migrated from the State of Odisha during the previous five years. Of these bonded labourers, all the 2583 cases were also released and certificates were also issued to all of them which is a unique achievement. Out of 2583 cases of bonded labourers the number rehabilitated in other States includes nearly 432 cases and 1127 of the released bonded labourers were rehabilitated by receiving a grant of Rs. 20,000. However, the number of bonded labourers rehabilitated by the Karnataka State were only four cases which is a very poor outcome. Besides this, the number of bonded labourers yet to be rehabilitated account for 1540 cases which indicates that they could not get justice within the provision of the Bonded Labour Act. However, this is a break through to the earlier cases of impasse when the bonded labourers did not receive justice either at the destination State or at the State of Origin. This is also happening because of the active intervention of the voluntary organizations acting both at the destination State and also at the State of Origin. In spite of this, the phenomenon of bondage is still being continued in perpetuity between the State of Origin which is State of Odisha and the destination State where Karnataka is one of them. Without the intervention of the voluntary organizations even this success would have been difficult to imagine. This only shows that the State Agencies and District Agencies which are entrusted with the responsibility of the task of identification, release and rehabilitation are not taking their work seriously.

The State of Odisha which is one of the States with very high incidence of bondage has also become little active during the current period in the task of identification, release and rehabilitation of bonded labourer which is reflected from the figures collected from the National Human Rights Commission in this regard. The data shows that between the year January 2014 to June 2015 the number of bonded labour cases identified by the Government of Odisha with own efforts is 2167 of which the males are 1252, the females 664 and the children 251. Further, of this, bonded labour identified the major number of 2146 have also been released indicating very marginal gap between the identification and release of bonded labour within the State of Odisha. Out of the bonded labour released the maximum number of 2132 have also been given released certificate which entitles them to rehabilitation grant. The figures of rehabilitation grant of Rs. 20,000 have been

Table 7.7: Half Yearly Report on Status of Rehabilitation of Bonded Labour (January-June, 2015)

State: Odisha

Sl. No	*Description*	*Consolidated Status of Preceding Years*				*Reporting Period*
		Male	*Female*	*Children*	*Total*	
1.	No. of Bonded Labours Identified	1252	664	251	2167	January-June 2015
2 (a)	No. of Bonded Labours Released	1241	654	251	2146	-do-
2(b)	No. of Bonded Labours Released on Certificate	1241	652	239	2132	-do-
2(c)	No. of Bonded Labours Released on without Certificate	00	02	12	14	-do-
3(c)	No. of Bonded Labours transferred without Police Escort	11	12	00	23	-do-
4(a)	No. of Bonded Labours received on transfer from other State	476	403	232	1111	-do-
4(b)	No. of Bonded Labours received on transfer with Police Escort	17	04	02	23	-do-
4(c)	No. of Bonded Labours received on transfer without Police Escort	243	210	59	512	-do-
5.	No. of Bonded Labours received Rehabilitation Grant of Rs. 20 thousand	302	237	78	617	-do-
6.	No. of Bonded Labours Rehabilitated by the State	302	237	78	617	-do-
7.	No. of Bonded Labours yet to be rehabilitated	939	417	173	1529	-do-

Source: Data collected from National Human Rights Commission, New Delhi.

received only by 617 freed bonded labourers and a major figure of 1529 released bonded labourers are yet to received the rehabilitation grant which is a poor rate of success of Government of Odisha.

The NHRC has been receiving complaints from NGOs and other Civil Society Activists on the Migrant and Bonded Labour involved in the Brick-Kiln and other industries in Southern States of Andhra Pradesh, Karnataka and Tamil Nadu. Some illustrative cases are mentioned below:

NHRC Case Studies

Case No. 631/10/1/2013-BL dated 24-6-2016

The NHRC received a reply from the Deputy Commissioner, Bangaluru, Urban District dated 28-10-2015 that out of 20 Bonded Labourers, Smt Basanti Chand and three others were released on 6-12-2013; necessary release certificate had also been issued in their favour and the labourers were shifted to their home town by train. There was some mistake in the release certificate which needed to be corrected. The Commission observes, "It is very disturbing to note that poor bonded labourers who had been released way back in 2013 are still in dark as to when they shall be entitled to get the rehabilitation assistance from the Government".

Case No. 1187/10/1/2015-BL Dated 24-06-2016

The Commission has received a complaint from one Biranchi Narayan Mahapatra an NGO on behalf of one Baburao Sabar and his wife who were residents of Kidinaga, Block Kashinagar, District Gajapati, Odisha alleging that he along with other labourers are being held as bonded labourers in a brick kiln at Pillappa, Mallure region of Bangaluru, Karnataka. It has also been alleged that they are being exploited and assaulted by the brick kiln owner and his men. A prayer has been made of payment of their wages and rescuing from bondage. The District Magistrate, Bangaluru, Karnataka was directed to depute an officer subordinate to him for an immediate on the spot enquiry for identification of the bonded labourers, if any, and to take further action in accordance with the provisions of law.

Case No. 1008/1/15/2014-BL dated 24-6-2016

Subsequent to the initiative of the NHRC, a report dated 13-3-2015 was received from the Collector and District Magistrate, Bargarh relating to 62 labourers for the rehabilitation by the State Government *vide* DRD letter No. 713 dated 13-3-2014. No sanction of funds were received by PR Department, Odisha. However, as per the direction of the NHRC, rehabilitation assistance of Rs. 20,000 each was handed over to 59 released labourers from the DRDA Fund. The BDOs were also instructed to cover all eligible released labourers under various social security, livelihood and shelter security schemes to prevent their further relapse into bondage. Similarly, 45 other labourers of Bolange District were released and rehabilitated. Actions were also taken to released and rehabilitate 32 other labourers of Puintula and Bonga Munda Block.

Case No. 547/22/12/2016-BL dated 24-06-02016

A case was received by NHRC relating to 550 bonded labourers on 7th March, 2016. The labourers were from Odisha and Chhattisgarh and were rescued from a Brick Kiln in Tiruvallur District of Tamil Nadu. They were working under inhuman conditions at Pondavakkam in Ponneri Taluk. They were forced to work from 3 a.m. onwards on a weekly wages of Rs. 400 per family. They were paid advance before they move to Tamil Nadu. The families were brought from 6 districts of Odisha and some from Chhattisgarh. It raises a serious issue of violation of human rights of the victim labourers. The NHRC issued notice to Secretary Labour Department, Government of Tamil Nadu calling for a factual report within two weeks indicating the steps taken for the rehabilitation of bonded labourers and payment of released amount.

Case No. 271/1/15/2015-BL dated 24-06-2016

NHRC considered the complaint by Activist A.K. Basheer, Secretary, Association for Rural Development, Nellore, Andhra Pradesh. He enclosed release certificates of bonded labourers who had been released between 2012-2015 and requested for permanent rehabilitation of the released labourers. The Project Director DRDA, Nawapuda received a report from the Commission on 8th June, 2015 and subsequently it was intimated that the freed bonded labourerrs have been provided work under MGNRES and they have also been included in Rural Housing Scheme. The Panchayati Raj Deptartment, Government of Odisha had received the rehabilitation assistance for the released labourers. A total of 225 labourers were released between 16th April, 2012 to 4th February, 2015 by Sub-Collector Gudur. It was found that 132 migrant labourers belongs to Odisha. Each of the labourers have been paid Rs. 11,000 by the owner of the Brick Kiln and another sum of Rs. 6000 was paid to cover their travel expenses to their native place. They belong to District of Bargarh, Bolangir and Sambalpur Districts.

Case No. 402/1/0/2014-BL dated 24-6-2016

The NHRC came across a distressing report (*The Hindu* dated 7-3-

2014) that the bonded labourers from Odisha working in Brick Kilns may forfeit vote. The Hindu report brought out that because of debt bondage more than 3 lac migrant workers from Western District of Odisha were tied to bricklens in Andhra Pradesh, TN and Karnataka and will miss out on voting on the Lok Sabha polls likely to take place in two phases in April, 10 and April, 17, 2014. The Principal Secdretary Labour Deptt. Government of Andhra Pradesh submitted that the willing labourers were allowed to visit their native places and cast their votes. The Labour Commissioiner, Government of Tamil Nadu also Stated in his communication dated 8-10-2015 that a meeting with Employe3e Association was held on 17-3-2014 and the migrant labourers were allowed to go to the places on their own expenses on leave to exercise their Panchayats. The Karnataka Government stated that the labourers can avail leave to exercisxe their votes in Odisha. The NHRC wanted the complete report in this matter by 4th March, 2016.

Case No. 308/1/0/2014-BL dated 24-6-2016

Fourteen workers from Odisha, including women and children, were released from bonded labour at Kokkirapalli near Elamanchili following a raid by Revenue Divisional Officer of Anakapallei and the police, on Friday. Following the intervention of former Union Secretary E.A.S. Sarma and complaints received by the NHRC and the International Justice Mission, Collector N. Yuvaraj directed RDO Padmavathi to investigate and get the workers released. "She along with local tehsildar and a Sub-Inspector went in search of the brick kiln in a private vehicles and found them engaged as bonded labourers," Mr. Yuvaraj said. The labourers—five men, six women, and three children—are from Karla in Bolangir district of Odisha. A compensation of Rs. 1.5 lakh was handed over to them. They were given tickets and put in train to their village. A constable was accompanying them.

7.10 Analysis of Cases in which Concrete Action has been taken by NHRC

The author has not only been able to collect the secondary data from NHRC about the identification, release and rehabilitation of bonded labourers but also could collect some case studies of the interventions of the State Governments both at the State of Origin and the State of Destination to take some concrete steps to provide relief to the bonded labour based on the complaints filed to them from the voluntary agencies and from the other stake holders. In this study few such cases have been highlighted to signify the role played by NHRC. These cases related mainly to the migrant labour from Odisha which is the State of Origin to the destination State of Andhra Pradesh, Karnataka and Tamil Nadu to work as bonded labourers in the brick kilns. These cases also provide us the ignominy faced by the bonded labourers in the process of release and rehabilitation. In one case of the release of 20 bonded labourers getting release certificate from Dy. Commissioner, Bangaluru, the Commission had to observe that the poor bonded labourers who have been released way back in 2013 are still in dark about their entitlement to rehabilitation assistance.

There is also another case in which the bonded labourers from Odisha were exploited by the Brick Kiln owner in Bangaluru District, Karnataka where the bonded labour was assaulted by the Brick Kiln owner. The NHRC directed District Magistrate, Bangaluru to conduct spot enquiry and to provide remedy to the bonded labourers. The cases of complaints received by NHRC indicate that while efforts are made to release and rehabilitate the bonded labour but rarely any legal action is taken against the labour contractors. The monitoring of NHRC consistently through the process of release and rehabilitation also results in the bonded labourers receiving the rehabilitation grant. There is a case of 62 labourers from Bargar district of Odisha in which due to the persistence of NHRC, the bonded labourers were able to get the rehabilitation amount of Rs. 20,000 each. Similarly, there is another case of complaint received by NHRC in which 132 migrant labourers belonging to Nuapada District of Odisha where working as bonded labour in Nellore District in Andhra Pradesh and due to the intervention of NHRC each of the labours were paid Rs. 11,000 by the owner of the brick kiln including an additional payment of Rs. 6000 by the Brick Kiln owners.

These are some of the sample cases to suggest the relief being received by some of the bonded labours due to the intervention of NHRC. However, an important question is have stopped the perpetuity of bondage in Odisha. However, acute cases of bondage is still prevalent in the State of Odisha due to their migration to the Southern States particularly in the Brick Kiln Industry. This phenomenon of continuity in bondage has been cited through case studies which depict the contemporary situation of prevalence and perpetuity of bondage from KBK District of Odisha due to the sustained prevalence of poverty.

Bondage in Odisha is continuing unabated which is a matter of concern. The effort of NHRC in providing rehabilitation ends the movement an amount of Rs. 20,000 is paid to the rescued labourers. Even in the State of Origin there is enough opportunity under the MNREGA scheme for these bonded labourers to get work and get freedom from bondage. Though, the thrust of the government is to provide relief and rehabilitation to the bonded labourers but in the absence of any deterrent step being taken against the labour contractors, the bondage continues without break. There have been very acute pathetic cases of bonded labour including child labour being subjected to severe exploitation including beating and facing violence. The typical case is one of Susanta Kumbhar aged 12 who was maimed by his employer as he wanted to study instead of working as bonded labour. In another case a bonded labour named Dayalu Nial who refused to work as bonded labour was caught by his neck in a forest and one of his kidnappers slashed his hands with the help of an axe on the plea that he refused to work as a bonded labour after taking a bonded debt. This incident took place during December 2004. His injured hand was thrown in to the Jungle. This news was flashed in Media across the country. These are examples to suggest that refusal to work as bonded labour after taking debt bondage, there is often threat to life of the male, female and even child bonded labour. In fact, migration has become one of the major source of survival in KBK District in Odisha. This is happening in spite of several streams of Rural Development work being undertaken by the Government of Odisha in different districts including KBK District.

The railway station at Kantabanji, from where agents traffic labourers to several States. (Left) Dura Mahananda, 50, says her family got trapped into the slave trade because they needed to clear their debts. (Photo: Samir Jana/HT)

During the migration season, Kantabangi station remains so crowded, there is no space for one to walk on the platform. The trains to Karnataka, Andhra and Tamil Nadu are mostly at night. Often trains are forcefully stopped for hours here by the labour contractors to facilitate the transfer of workers. Everyone has their share. The cops are paid Rs. 5,000 to Rs. 10,000 per group for their support. Poaching is common and fights often break out and people get killed by agents in a bid to get the maximum number of labourers.

Case Study-2

The problem is not isolated to Odisha, "Activists and academics estimate that some 10 million bonded labourers are working in India's key industries. Odisha, Bihar, Uttar Pradesh, Jharkhand and West Bengal are the main source areas. While inter-generational bonded labour has decreased with time, the number of chronically poor and landless workers that enter debt bondage is increasing. There are certain sectors where bonded labour system is more widely prevalent, like in agriculture, brick kilns, weaving etc. Lack of action taken against those employing bonded labourers adds to the difficulty in checking the problem. The District Magistrates or the authorities having powers to enquire into complaints do not prosecute the owner. After the rescue of bonded labourers, in 99 per cent cases, prosecution is not launched. Even if it is launched, there is hardly any conviction or sentence under the Act.

'What will I do with just one hand?'

We only get work for two months during the rains. I would earn Rs. 100 per day, my wife Bhanumati would earn Rs. 80 per day. We are a family of five. Two months of proper work can not sustain us for the year. For the rest of the time, we would do odd jobs when we could. Then in 2013, a contractor came to the village to look for people to work in the brick kilns in the south," says 40-year-old Santosh Kumbhar.

The sardar promised Rs. 5,000 for six months of work plus an additional Rs. 100 per person per week to buy food. He also bought their train tickets and off went the entire family. "But the sardar disappeared after taking us there and we never got any money. Sometimes we were given Rs. 100 to buy food. If we asked for money, the malik would threaten to sell us off. My 12-year-old son Susanta was made to do the work of turning the bricks. One day, he was not well. The malik would beat him up. One day he beat him on the hand with an iron rod so badly that he was seriously injured. But he was not given any proper treatment. Two months after he was hit, we were rescued by the social workers and Susanta was treated in a hospital in Cuttack, but he has been maimed for life," rues Santosh saying,

Maimed by his employer, Susanta Kumbhar, 12, is unsure of his future now. (Photo: Samir Jana/HT)

"All this is my fault. If I hadn't gone there in the hopes of finding a better life, my son wouldn't have lost his hand". Poverty teaches these people a strange kind of stoicism. Susanta is attending the local school now. But ask him what he wants to do with his life and he says with a strange calm, "I don't know. What will I do with one hand?" Susanta was not the only one in the family to be harassed. The boy's 14 year old sister, Jayanti, remembers, "He used to abuse me and say dirty things to me. His men would guard us all the time".

Care Study-3

Injustice

It is important to note that even labour trafficking and bonded labour, though a pervasive and long functioning concept in our country, experience changes in pattern. The traffickers have been quick to adapt and continue with their operations. For instance, it is my experience that from Odisha migration caused by everyday desperation has been on the decline. For example, starvation is no longer a pressing issue in Odisha as opposed to a decade or so ago and is contributing less to labour trafficking on account of strong economic growth and robust social safety net programmes for the poor. However, there is still a paucity of higher paying livelihoods, providing leverage for traffickers to nudge people to explore opportunities in nearby States. In light of this change, traffickers now extend a lump sum payment of around Rs. 13,000 per family member. For a family of five members to receive Rs. 65,000 in one payment is a lot of money, and helps to cover major expenditures such as marriages, building a house, medical emergencies etc. Such is the new tactic to induce unwitting labourers.

Moreover, the financial gain that labourers are induced with quickly falls apart if one takes a look at the calculations carefully. Labourers receive a weekly allowance and they only receive a full settlement of their wages at the end of the season (usually five-seven months), which is deceptive. The labourers are charged interest for the upfront lump sum payment and the weekly allowance, which is then deducted from their wage earnings. In sum, the net payment received by the labourer is lower than what was promised/expected. Moreover, this net value is below the minimum wage set by the State. Labourers do not have any recourse besides fearing for their and their families' lives if they choose to speak-up.

I do not need to elaborate on the injustices committed as there is sufficient evidence to demonstrate how labourers are exploited, forced to live in hovels, denied minimum wages and their basic human rights. Indeed I have heard of such injustices first hand. I hope our enforcement mechanism would be strengthened in consideration of the adversarial consequences that are imposed on those forced in to bonded labour.

Case Study-4

Punished by axe: Bonded labour in India's brick kilns

India's economy is the 10th largest in the world, but millions of the country's workers are thought to be held in conditions little better than slavery. One man's story—which some may find disturbing—illustrates the extreme violence that some labourers are subjected to.

Dialu Nial's life changed for ever when he was held down by his neck in a forest and one of his kidnappers raised an axe to strike.

He was asked if he wanted to lose his life, a leg or a hand.

Six days earlier, Nial had been among 12 young men being taken against their will to make bricks on the outskirts of one of India's biggest cities, Hyderabad. (*Source:* Humphrey Hawksley, BBC News).

During the journey, they got a chance to escape and ran for it—but Nial and a friend were caught and this was their punishment. Activists and academics estimate that some 10 million bonded labourers are working in India's key industries, indirectly contributing to the profits of global Indian brands and multinationals that operate in the country and have helped to transform India into an economic powerhouse. Nial struggles to wind the cord, his brow creasing. His brother works quickly, outpacing him. Then the spool flips out of Nial's hand. Rahaso gives it back him. Disappointment and anger flood through Nial's face. It was in early December that Nilamber, a friend from a nearby village told Nial about a job in brick kiln for which he would supposedly get 10,000 rupees ($165; £98) up front. It was all being organised by one of Nilamber's neighbours, Bimal, who was trying out working as a broker.

On the sixth day, his kidnappers were drinking heavily. The contractor and five of his men drove them to remote woodland. First they were held down and beaten. Then, they were made to kneel and mutilated. "They threw my hand into the woods," he says. "I wrapped my left hand around my wound and held it tight. I squeezed it to stop the bleeding until the pain became too much and I released it. Then I had to grip it again". A basic survival instinct took over. They followed a stream to a village, where they were able to bind their wounds and cover them with a plastic bag. Then they took a bus to a nearby town to seek hospital treatment. Nial stiffens as he tells the story. Often he stops to gather his thoughts. He has now begun a two-year programme run by a charity, the International Justice Mission (IJM), to help him recover from his ordeal. As part of his rehabilitation, he joins a group of more than 150 people at a counselling session in Odisha—all of whom have been freed from bonded labour in the past few months, mostly in brick kilns. Among them are dozens of children. Most of the men have been badly beaten. There are women who have been raped, and two who were kicked in the stomach while pregnant—the husband of one was thrown to his death from a train.

7.11 Child Labour and Bonded Labour in Odisha

Though child labour is prohibited under the law, children continue to work in various sectors. According to Human Development Report, 2011, published by Planning Commission, Government of India, child labour is more prevalent in rural areas than in urban areas and is higher among boys than girls. Boys are traditionally and economically more active in labour market. The Agriculture Sector employs the majority of child labour. Gender disparity and rural urban gap has been reduced in recent times.

According to 1991 census, the number of working children in Odisha was reported 4,52,394, which was 5.9 per cent of total child population in the age group of 5-14 year. The corresponding figures in 2001 census stood at 3,77,594 and 4.7 per cent respectively. As per 2001 census, highest number of child labour was reported in Ganjam district (38,947) followed by Mayurbhanj (32,994), Keonjhar (31,983) and Bolangir (15,242), while Jagatsinghpur reported the lowest (2,448). Out of total 3,77,594 child workers in 2001 census, about 71 per cent were marginal workers.

During 2004-05, 4.9 per cent of the State's child population in the age group 5-14 year was reported as working children while the corresponding figures for rural and urban areas stood at 5.3 and 1.7 per cent respectively. This problem is more acute among ST communities, in case of which about 8.0 per cent children are engaged in various economic activities. During 2004-05, 5.2 per cent of total, 5.6 per cent of rural and 2.2 per cent of urban male child population was reported as working children while the corresponding figures for female child workers stood at 4.5, 5.0 and 1.3 per cent respectively. However, the magnitude of child labour has sharply declined to 3.4 per cent in Odisha by the end of 2007-08 as against 2.4 per cent at All India level. Twenty four National Child Labour Projects (NCLP), one in each district except Nuapada, Bhadrak, Boudh, Jagatsinghpur, Kandhamal and Kendrapara, are operating in the State with an objective of eliminating child labour from hazardous occupations through providing non-formal education and vocational training to identified child labourers and to bring them into the mainstream of formal education system. During 2012-13, 39,409 child labours were admitted into 812 special schools opened under NCLP. They are provided with textbooks, educational and vocational materials, mid-day meal and Rs. 100 per month per child.

During 2001-02, a survey on bonded labour was conducted in 10 districts, i.e. Koraput, Malkangiri, Rayagada, Sundargarh, Cuttack, Kalahandi, Kandhamal, Mayurbhanj, Bargarh and Keonjhar districts through which 19 bonded labours were identified in Malkangiri district. Out of these 19 bonded labourers, 17 were rehabilitated and two others could not be traced due to migration or death. During 2006-07, 35 bonded labourers of Odisha were released from Tamil Nadu (18 of

Subarnapur, 13 of Jaipur, 2 each from Sambalpur and Ganjam districts) and rehabilitated under different poverty alleviation programmes. During 2008-09, 14 bonded labourers form Bolangir district were released in Karnataka and sent to their native villages in Odisha and State Government released Rs. 2.40 lakh to DRDA Bolangir for their rehabilitation. Similarly, 384 bonded labourers (Bolangir—214, Nuapada—100, Nabarangpur—14, Rayagada—13, Kalahandi—3, Koraput—9, Subarnapur—17 and Puri—14) were released in 2011-12 and an amount of Rs. 76.80 lakh including Rs. 34.80 lakh central share was utilized for their rehabilitation through the concerned DRDA.

The ingredients of bonded labour are:

1. Existence of a bonded debt, i.e. an advance obtained, or presumed to have been obtained, by the labourer from the creditor.
2. Forced labour in consideration of advance obtained, or for any economic consideration received by the labourer.
3. Working for the creditor for a specified or unspecified period, either without wages or for nominal wages, i.e. less than the minimum wages fixed by the Government.

7.12 Combating Distress Migration in Odisha

The western part of Odisha is considered to be a drought prone region. This has compelled more than 2 lakh people migrate from this region every year to Andhra Pradesh and other States to work in brick kilns (UNDP Report, 2009). The reason for high levels of migration in the area is due to collapse of livelihoods in agriculture and related occupations. Social, political and economic disadvantages along with ecological disturbance in the area also contribute for high levels of migration in the region. The bad show in agriculture resulting from continuous droughts uneven land distribution, loss of forest, poor performance of the government schemes have been the push factors forcing people migrate to other States in search of employment.

During the year 2012 a strategy was developed to productively engage the migrant families in MGNREGS. The strategy was piloted in 8 high migration prone GPs of Bolangir district with close collaboration of Bolangir District Administration covering about 2100 families prone to distress migration. Need based plans were prepared for the area for execution under MGNREGS. *Rozgar Diwas* (Employment Day) was introduced to register the left out families and record their demands for work. At least one ongoing community project in each village round the year was ensured. Barefoot engineers were introduced to speed-up the works measurement process. Electronic Fund Management System (EFMS) was strictly implemented in the area to ensure timely disbursement of wage payment. Regular health camps, access to PDS commodities and other social security schemes were strictly ensured.

The pilot had significant impact at the ground. The collective effort put in the area retained about 70 per cent families from migration during the year. This was possible because of the increased access of the migrant families to MGNREGS. Timely engagement and timely wage payment encouraged them to work in the scheme. With the success of the pilot Hon'ble Chief Minister of Odisha declared 150 days of employment in a year for migrant families (additional 50 days to be borne by the State Government), State Government also declared to organize Rozgar Diwas across the State. Also a high level decision was taken at the government level to provide 150 days of job assurance under MGNREGS to migrant households in the beginning of the year which would encourage them to work under the scheme.

The issue is now being approved by the State Government in a project mode. Based on the pilot strategies, a Detailed Project Report (DPR) has been prepared for 3 years which has been operational since July 2013. Following outputs are expected from the project.

- Fifty per cent households prone to distress migration are employed for 100-150 days under MGNREGS.
- Under MGNREGS average person days per household in the project area is increased by 40 per cent.
- Fifty per cent of the works created under MGNREGS are linked to livelihood activities in the project area through convergence with Line departments.
- One institution at the Block level in each Block of the project area function as Independent institution and get into livelihood interventions.
- Fifty per cent increased in coverage of beneficiaries (elderly, widow etc.) under social assistance schemes.

[*Source*: MGNREGS in Odisha—The Path, Panchayati Raj Department, Government of Odisha, pp. 35-36.]

7.13 Special Plan for KBK Districts

The State Government, in consultation with the Government of India, has formulated a Long Term Action Plan (LTAP) for speedy development of the KBK districts. The special plan has focused on improving productive infrastructure strengthening livelihoods of the marginalized communities, improving literacy levels and accelerating the pace of development in this region. Special Central Assistance to the extent of Rs. 2,593.95 crore has been received from 1998-99 to 2013-14 and an amount of Rs. 2,509.17 crore has been utilized by the end of March 2014.

The implementation of the special plan has brought several benefits to this region. As per the Tendulkar Committee methodology, rural poverty in this region came down by 25.40 per cent points from 73.40 per cent in 2004-05 to 48.00 per cent in 2011-12. Enrolment rate in primary's schools in KBK districts has gone up to 98.5 per cent during 2011-12 from 75.89 per cent in 1996-97. Similarly, the enrolment rate in upper primary schools has risen from 56.39 per cent in 1996-97 to 103.58 per cent in 2010-11. The dropout rate in primary schools in KBK districts has been reduced to 3.57 in 2011-12. Female literacy rate has also increased to 45.49 per cent in 2011 while the overall literacy rate has increased to 57.17 per cent in 2011.

In order to fill critical gaps in development of the KBK region, a scheme Biju KBK Plan was launched during the year 2006-07 in the KBK districts out of the States own funds. An annual outlay of Rs. 120 crore has been envisaged for the region. The scheme initially focused on *Bijli, Sadak* and *Pani*, i.e. village electrification including street lighting, construction of concrete roads within the village or any other form of connectivity and creation for irrigation/drinking water source. However, the focus of this scheme has been revisited in 2013-14 to improve human development indicators in the KBK region. An outlay of Rs. 120.00 crore has been proposed for this scheme in the Annual Plan 2014-15.

The Government of Odisha has also tried to combat distress migration through the implementation of MNREGA scheme in the villages of Origin. A systematic effort in this direction was taken-up by a voluntary organization named OMEGA to productively engage the migrant families in the MNREGA work during the year 2012. The strategy was piloted in 8 high migration prone Gram Panchayats of Bolangir District. The Government report claims that it had a significant impact on the ground. It was instrumental in retaining about 70 per cent families from migration. Besides this the State Government of Odisha in consultation with GoI have formulated a long term action plan for speedy development of KBK District. The special plan has focused on improving productive infrastructure, strengthening livelihoods of the marginalized communities, improving the literacy level and accelerating the case of development. In spite of such concentrated efforts, the high incidence of bondage in KBK District perpetuates which attracts systematic attention of the Government of Odisha to ease the phenomenon of distressed bonded labour from Odisha.

7.14 Resume of Migration from Odisha

The present study is to understand the process of high incidence of migration taking from KBK Districts in Odisha to the Southern States of India particularly Andhra Pradesh, Karnataka, Tamil Nadu and Kerala. The State of Odisha is one of the highly migration prone States and particularly the KBK Region which has been recognized for perpetual poverty and accompanying bondage. The poverty in KBK Region is one of the highest in Odisha though the overall poverty ratio has minimized in the State. This region has attracted the national and international attention due to its acute poverty and bondage. In this study, attempt has been made to understand the prevalence of bondage both through the secondary data as also through the primary data. There is very strong tie-up between the grassroots recruiter and contractor and the flow of migration to the Southern States. The districts of origin which are prone to bondage are the districts of Kalahandi, Koraput, Bolangir and Rayagada as also some of the other adjacent districts. It is the rock bottom among the caste and class hierarchy who are victims of bondage and it is the upper echelon who are the employers and perpetrator of bondage. The prevalence of bondage has been in existence in the KBK Region particularly from the mid-1960s to the globalization era. The poor implementation of the Rural Development Programme have also enormously contributed to the prevalence and sustainable of bondage in this region. There has been also severe neglect on the part of Government of Odisha and the District Administration to ignore the phenomenon of bondage in this region. One of the important rationale for highlighting the high incidence of bondage in the region must be attributed to the active intervention of the voluntary organizations who have yielded pressure on the State and District Administration to intervene into the situation. The KBK Plan and other measures like MNREGA have partly been able to minimize the incidence of bondage in this area. However, the recruiting agents and other vested interest are so deeply entrenched into the social routes of the region that it is only through a serious concerted effort that this phenomenon can be tackled. The Government of Odisha claims that through the implementation of MNREGA programme they have been able to tackle the phenomenon of migrant labour in the region. However, the continued prevalence of bondage and the interventions by NHRC lend evidence to the high incidence of bondage still perpetuating in this region. The social activism has been able to make a difference into the situation. The overall development scenario in KBK Region last 20-25 years have reduced the incidence of poverty, still lot of efforts is needed to address the phenomenon of perpetuation of migration and bondage in this region. The author has tried to substantiate through the secondary data as also through the primary date of the enormity of the problem still persisting and sustained efforts needed of the major stake holders to address the situation.

In fine, the following aspects can be highlighted with respect to the status of seasonal migrant workers from Odisha to other States:

- The high incidence of migration is taking from KBK Districts in Odisha to the Southern States of India particularly Andhra Pradesh, Karnataka, Tamil Nadu and Kerala. KBK Region has been recognized for perpetual poverty and accompanying bondage.
- There is very strong tie-up between the grassroots recruiter and contractor and the flow of migration to Southern States.
- It is the rock bottom among the caste, class and the tribals who are the victims of bondage and it is the upper echelon of the employers who are perpetuating bondage.
- The prevalence of bondage has been in existence in the KBK Region from the mid-sixty's to the present globalization era.
- The poor implementation of rural development programme and tribal development programme have also enormously contributed to the prevalence and sustainable bondage in the region.
- There is also the incidence of child labour among the migrant workers. During 2004-05, 4.9 per cent of the State child population in the age group 05-14 years was reported as working children; among the STs 8 per cent were child labour.
- One of the strong interventions have been undertaken by the voluntary organizations who have yielded pressure on the State and District Administration to initiate action into the otherwise dormant situation. They are also instrumental in

activating NHRC to strongly intervening into the situation for the identification, release and rehabilitation of the migrant bonded labour.

- In spite of continued intervention the bonded labour situation in Brick kilns of labourers from Odisha to Southern Region is continuing unabated.
- The Government of Odisha also has intervened to improve the socio-economic situation in the KBK Region during last 20-25 years which have reduced the overall incidence of bondage and poverty.

7.15 Labour Migration from Jharkhand

The objectives of this research study on Jharkhand focuses on the following issues:

- To identify the factors that contribute to their option for domestic work and continuing with this occupation.
- To examine the process of migration and continuous inflow of Tribal Women to be employed as domestic workers in urban sectors.
- The explore the nature of work, living conditions, relations with their employers and problems faced by the women domestic workers.

The study has largely drawn on the base line study of Marianus Kujur and Shri Vikas Jha on "Tribal Women Domestic Workers in Delhi" (2008). In their study they covered 320 women from Jharkhand, 141 from Odisha, 40 from Chhattisgarh and the rest from other States of Assam, West Bengal, Madhya Pradesh etc. This study was based on samples of tribal domestic workers from Delhi. Out of the 586, tribal women included in the sample, 54.78 per cent of the tribal women domestic workers in Delhi were from Jharkhand, 24.06 per cent from Odisha and rest from other States. About 85 per cent of the migrant labours in Delhi were from the Districts of Simdega, Gumla and Ranchi in Jharkhand and Sundargarh and Mayurbhanj Districts in Odisha. The highest number of sample workers were from Simdega and Gumla District of Jharkhand contributing to 28.35 per cent of the migrant women district workers and 23.99 per cent were from Ranchi district. These are among the backward districts of Jharkhand. In Odisha majority of the domestic workers, i.e. 62.41 per cent were from

Sundargarh district and remaining 33.33 per cent were from Mayurbhanj district. Political economy of migration to Delhi reveals that exploitation takes the form of isolation, land alienation, appropriation of resources and development induced displacement leading to migration. Tribal women domestic workers are predominantly young, single women who seek domestic work due to poverty, low levels of education and lack of vocational training. Kin Chain Migration/village chain migration also contributes to the proliferation of tribal domestic workers. The domestic work fulfils some of the economic needs of the domestic workers, but the marginalization suffered by them has a lasting impact on the community. Some of these features of marginalization are:

- Alienation and up rootedness from their own culture.
- Illiteracy and further marginalization.
- Constant fear of losing job and being sexually abused.
- Victimization on suspicion.
- Work being considered as of menial character.
- Their vulnerability; and
- Problem of marriage.

The study on domestic workers shows that the working condition of domestic workers in Delhi is highly unsupportive and unhygienic. Their entire continuity of work and subsistence depends upon the benevolence of their masters who are rarely humane in their approach towards domestic workers. Most of the domestic workers are dependent on their employer not merely for wage but also for few favours like loans, old clothes, food and in some cases shelter too. There are no educational facilities. Medical treatment is provided only in extreme cases. Sexual harassment at work place is omnipresent in this informal and unorganized sector and in most cases such incidences go unreported due to subservient position of the worker. There is no question of any leave and other tangible benefits in terms of bonus, promotional prospects, stability in job and good and hygienic physical work environment at the work place. When they fall ill or needed a leave for emergency, they are expected to bring in a substitute. As there is no written contract between the employer and the domestic worker there is immense scope for exploitation, particularly in the case of minor girls, who are employed as domestic workers, are 'disciplined' with iron rods, so that, they work better. Owing to their unorganized natu2re of work they are also not protected by labour laws and statutory provisions. Even for a trivial reason, the Tribal Domestic Workers (TDW) can lose her job. Similarly, there are minimal chances for any increase in her salary.

The socio-economic condition of women domestic workers is rather sad and deplorable in urban centres. They came from very poor families, with the majority of them being illiterate or having studied only up to the primary school level. In most cases, the husbands of women domestic workers are either unemployed or underemployed. Their family is marked by frequent quarrels and disorganization. Women domestic workers invariably live in slums or tents. The surroundings of their dwelling is equally depressing and unhealthy. Most women domestic workers suffer from several health problems. They suffer from anaemia, malnutrition, bodyache and general weakness. They develop cracked hands and feet, which become sore due to continuous work in water, using strong abrasive detergent and soaps.

7.16 Recruitment Process and Agents

The recruitment procedure for hiring domestic worker is not fair and well defined. It is very difficult to find jobs without any contacts. The entire sector of domestic workers is managed by the agency of relatives, co-villagers and the agents. The easily available agency for this sector are the relatives. In most of the cases, the women come along with their relatives who are already working as domestic helps and are inspired/allured by them to come and join them. The other agency is that of the co-villagers who seeing their pathetic conditions invite them to the city and work as domestic help. In this process of recruitment and supplying domestic workers, kinship usually act as the focal point. *The modus operandi* of such people is very simple. They operate in slum clusters having a substantial inhabitation of domestic workers. They invite people from the villages to the city and provide them with all the boarding and lodging facilities in Delhi. Subsequently, they get some job for these people and thus complete the chain of recruitment and supply of domestic workers.

On the other hand, because both men and women in the middle class families are employed, it necessitates an extra hand to take care of the household chores. It is here that tribal women become handy as domestic workers. Thus, the increase in tribal women becoming domestic workers is not just limited to pull and push factors as argued by some social scientists but it is also directly connected with the globalization process. As many as 44.03 per cent of the domestic workers interviewed in Delhi were Oraons, mainly from Gumla, Simdega, Jashpur and Sundargarh districts of Jharkhand, Chhattisgarh and Odisha. The data also revealed that of the total respondent, 26.96 per cent were Mundas mainly from Ranchi district and 12.80 per cent were Kharias from Simdega and Sundargarh districts. Thus, while these three tribes constituted 83.79 per cent of the total TDWs interviewed in Delhi, the Oraon, Munda, Kharia and Santhal put together, constituted 89.93 per cent.

As many as 80.21 per cent domestic workers are in the age group of 15-25. If we expand the age group to another five years, that is 15-30, the percentage of the domestic workers shoots upto 91.13 per cent of the total respondents; 38.91 per cent of TDWs belonged to the age group of 15-20 years. 41-30 per cent of the age group of 21-25 years, 10.92 per cent to the age group of 26-30 years, 6.66 per cent to the age group of 31-40 years, and 1.02 per cent to age group of above 41-50 years. Less than one, that is, 0.34 per cent was found to be above 51 years of age. Thus, the figures demonstrators that a substantial section of the tribal women domestic workers belonged to the age group of 15-25 years. This implies that the demand for the domestic workers in Delhi took a big jump from 0.85 per cent in the age group of 9-14 to more than 91 per cent in the age group of 15-30 years. However, the demand for domestic workers in the age group 31-40 came down drastically to 6.66 per cent only. What the survey shows is that there was demand for young domestic workers and the employers did not prefer ageing domestic workers. There was further decrease in the percentage of the age group of 41-50 years to 1.02 per cent only. The domestic workers in the age group of above 51 years had only 0.34 per cent demands in the *kothis* (middle class and upper class residences) of Delhi.

As many as 94.20 per cent domestic workers were school drop-outs and with no formal education or had been somehow able to complete education at the primary level only (45.22%). The tribal girls in the age group of 15-20 were normally found to be the students of high school or above. There were large number of middle school dropouts. There were also many cases of failure in high school examination. In either case the girls seemed to want a short break—first, by spending some months in Delhi as a time pass, and second, by earning some quick money before going back to their place of origin, either to pursue their study or to carry on with their routine life. It was observed that the low level of literacy among the tribal women domestic workers directly affected the working conditions. For instance, the recruitment policy of the placement agencies, choice of the girls for household work, facilities provided to the girls, such as accommodation, salary, working hours, signing of contract etc. were decided based on TDWs qualification. The placement agencies took advantage of the illiterate or poorly educated tribal women when contracts were signed.

In the present study the data show that 13.99 per cent matriculate, 2.56 per cent intermediate and 0.51 per cent graduate. However, the percentage of the illiterate (without formal education) and primary education dropouts put together (34.99%) was much higher. The present study shows that nearly 72.01 per cent of TDWs were unmarried. Nevertheless, tribal boys in the village do not show any preference for these girls. However, exodus *en masse* of the tribal boys now to Delhi has changed the scenario. The tribal men in diaspora seem to be developing an understanding of the situation of TDWs. Hence, they have no problem entering into conjugal relationships when they go back home. The families of both the parties do not have any difficulties either.

Our study demonstrates that the large migration of the tribal women is taking place from the few pockets of Odisha, Jharkhand and Chhattisgarh. It is important to note that significant number of tribal women is migrating from Gumla, Simdega, Jashpur, and Sundargarh districts of these three States to work as the domestic help. Moreover, the tribal women mainly belong to four tribes of the Oraon, the Kharia, the Munda and the Santhal. The study also suggests that nearly 23.04 per cent of the tribal women are without any formal education, which make them prone to the exploitation of unscrupulous agents and the employers. Lack of education and poverty places them in a very weak bargaining position and they are not able to insist on work contract with the employers. The low level of literacy among the tribal women domestic workers directly affects the working conditions, that is, recruitment policy of the placement agency, choice of the girls, facilities provided to the girls, such as accommodation, salary, working hours, signing contracts etc. The profile also highlights that majority of TDWs are unmarried. With the institution of joint family breaking down due to various processes of change, the nuclearization of family is very much visible among tribals. This social transformation has its bearing on the migration of TDWs from their villages to cities. Thus, illiteracy, poverty and lack of any support in the urban centres make them vulnerable to all kinds of exploitation.

The profile of women domestic workers from Jharkhand reveals that as many as 44.03 per cent of the domestic workers were from the tribal community of Oraon mainly from Gumla, Simdega, Jashpur and Sundargarh districts of Jharkhand, Chhattisgarh and Odisha. Of the total domestic workers 26.96 per cent were from Munda Tribal Community mainly from Ranchi district and 12.08 per cent were Kharias from Simdega and Sundargarh districts. These three tribes, i.e. Oraon, Mundas and Kharias constitute 83.79 per cent of the total women domestic workers studied in Delhi. It was interesting to note that as many as 91.47 per cent of the domestic workers were Christians and only 1.63 per cent were non Christians. The age composition of women domestic workers reveals that 80.21 per cent of them were in the age group of 15-25; if the age range increased from 15-30, the percentage of the domestic workers shoots up to 91.13 per cent. The study shows that the substantial section of the tribal women domestic workers belong to the age group 15-25 years. The young girls were preferred to the older ones for domestic work. The educational status of the domestic workers shows that as many as 92.20 per cent were school dropouts and with no formal education. The tribal girls in the age group of 15-20 normally found to be the students of High Schools or above. There were large number of middle school dropouts. The data also reveals that 72 per cent of the domestic workers were unmarried and only 21.84 per cent were married. The unmarried domestic workers belong to the age group of 15-25 years.

The unmarried girls who are of marriageable age are treated as outsiders in their village of origin. This was because the migrant domestic workers had picked up some urban mannerisms which was not liked by the local village residents. However, the exodus of tribal boys to Delhi has changed the scenario. Hence, the marriage age of the migrant domestic workers have become easier than earlier. The data also reveals that 65 per cent of the household in Jharkhand and 73 per cent from Odisha had sent their women out to earn and support their households. The basic reason for migration appears to be earning money for their families. The unavailability of work, uncertain agriculture and family distressed in tribal areas of eastern India are the main reasons for migration. At the destination place the domestic migrant workers had their monthly income between Rs. 2001 and 3000 for 23.38 per cent monthly income, only 4.61 per cent had monthly income between 3001 and 4000 and 2.56 per cent had monthly income above Rs. 4000. The study shows that 85.75 per cent of the domestic workers had a monthly income ranging from Rs. 1000 to Rs. 3000 and rest had monthly income ranging from 3000 to 4000 and above. One of the important factors which influenced the decision making of the tribal women workers to migrate was the social networks (ties of kin, friends and village). The data shows that a large section of the migrants consisting of 54 per cent migrated through their friends, 31 per cent migrated through the help of relatives and rest with the help of placement agencies and others. The data reveals that nearly 91 per cent of the tribal women had migrated to Delhi with the help of close acquaintance like friends, relatives, husbands as their own. Agents and Social networks played a key role in providing information to domestic workers about job to the cities. Many of them said that they have taken due permission from their guardian for taking-up domestic work in Delhi. The data also reveals that many of the domestic workers left from home without the knowledge of parents and guardians. Majority of the domestic workers interviewed says that they had taken permission from the family members. The working conditions were very exploited as they had to work from 10 hours to 14 hours a day. Sunday was a day of rest for some of them. The interview with few of the domestic workers shows that the working condition of migrant tribal domestic workers were highly exploited. Long hours of work, poor, irregular and non-payment of remuneration, dismissal without notice and non-existence of any contract between the employer and the women workers clearly point out that working conditions are far from satisfactory. Ill treatment and sexual harassment of the tribal women domestic workers also took place at their work place. It makes the working conditions of the tribal women domestic workers as not only exploitative but also dangerous.

Only 43 per cent of the tribal women saved the money in bank and another 32 per cent kept the money with themselves. This indicated that 75 per cent had savings. Majority of the women workers had money to send back home and few of them did not have this capacity. Nearly 64 per cent of the domestic workers have been sending home money up to Rs. 2000 per month. The domestic workers accepted that the financial status of the family have improved and their remittances were used to the household expenses and to educate their children. However, there is an important problem of socio-culture alienation in the process of migration. When they go back to their home, they find themselves out of place and face serious adjustment problems. The social life of the tribal women in Delhi were centred around meeting the acquaintances of friends and relatives. The culture and social identities of the tribal women were maintained through meetings during the week ends or the months ends. Such meeting provided relief to the drudgery of domestic workers. Tribals boys in the place of origin did not prefer the domestic female workers for marriage. Many had crossed their normal marriageable age and there was also suspicion of their sexual exploitation in their work place. The social consequences like disintegration in the families and social isolation in the urban centres have the great consequences on the psyche of tribal domestic workers. Majority of them did not want to settle down permanently in Delhi. The tribal women domestic workers continued to be relegated to the position of second class citizen.

The reason behind migration of tribal women according to the study seems to enough to ensure their own advancement and that of the household members. The survival of the household members was the most important cause of tribal women domestic workers to migrate in such large number to cities. In Jharkhand nearly 83 per cent and in Odisha about 84 per cent of the tribal families owned more than one acre of land. The land was unproductive due to the vagaries of nature. Poor agriculture production-*cum*-apathy of the government to develop irrigation facilities absence of rural employment programmes were reasons to migrate. The tribal women domestic workers are migrating with the help of relatives, husbands, friends and on their own. Many of them get their contacts from the relatives and also from the placement agencies. Many of the domestic workers have very low education. The domestic workers are heavily burden with work and they have to do major part of household activities like cleaning of pots, utensil and floor of the house, cooking, child care nursing the elderly, purchase of provisions and vegetable. Some of them are driven away from the working home after being accused of theft and other complaints. A large number of women have reported other form of exploitation like scolding and beatings. The exploited working conditions prevail due to illiteracy, irresponsibility of placement agencies and absence of any legal aid. The migration continues despite severe form of exploitation faced by tribal women. One of the reason for continued migration is that they have benefited economically from migration. The tribal families at the place of origin have utilized the remittances for managing expenditure on food and education, for buying land and paying for the mortgage land as also for purchasing bullocks. There is good percentage of Christians among the women migrants. They easily have access to education facilities as being primarily tribal Christians to get primary and higher school education as also contribution of the local churches. The study recognizes the complexity and multi-dimension aspect of migration of tribal women in urban centres.

The study shows that the domestic workers send a substantial portion of their earning to support their families. Their income is utilized mostly for meeting the daily expenses of the family, settling the debts and education of the siblings. The dependence of the family on the domestic workers has enhanced their status in the families. They have now started taking decisions on the family, education of siblings, marriages of siblings and fixing their own marriages. Increased role in decision-making in the family matters reveals the enhanced status of the women in the families.

In fine, the reason for the continued migration of the young tribal women from the districts of Jharkhand in general and Odisha in particular is that their economic condition is poor. The programme on the upliftment of the socio-economic conditions of the tribal families is not been properly implemented at the grassroots level. The programme on women empowerment also does not generate income for the less educated girls and women. It is necessary that both governments of Jharkhand and Odisha should undertake special income earning programmes and vocational education for the girls and women who are educated up to Matriculate or Secondary level so that they can depend for their livelihood at the local level and need not have to spend and uncomfortable life at the place of migration.

References

Das, Kalpataru (2014). "*MGNREGS in Odisha—The Path*", Panchayati Raj Department, Government of Odisha, Bhubaneshwar.

Kujur, Joseph Marianus and Vikas Jha (2008). *Tribal Women Domestic Workers in Delhi*, New Delhi: Indian Social Institute.

Shalini, S.C.N., Gita Rana, *et al.*, (1993). *Tribal Domestic Worker at the Crossroads*, Programme for Women's Development, New Delhi: Indian Social Institute.

Singh, R.V. (2012). "District Human Development Report Kalahandi", Planning and Coordination Department, Government of Odisha, Bhubaneswar.

Srinivas, Injeti (2014). "Odisha Economic Survey 2013-14", Planning and Coordination Department, Government of Odisha, Bhubaneswar.

Thakur, Rameshwar (2004). "*Human Development Report 2004*", Planning and Coordination Department, Government of Odisha, Bhubneswar.

Upadhyaya, B.K., (2011). "*District Statistical Handbook, Kalahandi*", District Planning and Monitoring Unit, Kalahandi, Directorate of Economics and Statistics, Odisha, Bhubaneswar.

8

Conclusion

8.0 Thrust of the Research Study

The main focus of the present research study is the comparative analysis of the Tribal Land, Forest and Identity Issues in Odisha and Jharkhand. The following issues were examined in this study in the States of Jharkhand and Odisha:

- The State policy with respect to land and forest during the Colonial and Post-Colonial period in the States of Jharkhand and Odisha.
- One of the basic assumption of the study is that Land and Forest has been the major source of Cultural Identity for the Tribals and the Marginalized people historically and continues to be so.
- The Social and Tribal Movements have been rooted in resistance against Land and Forest Rights during Colonial Period and continues to be so during Globalization era.
- The Transformation of the Tribal Communal Property and Forest Rights into Private Property and State Property have been the major blow to the Tribals; this could be attributed as the principal cause of their revolt against the Forest Policy during the Colonial period and Globalization period. Accordingly one of the important objectives of the present study would be to establish the linkage between Land and Forest with Tribal Identity in Jharkhand and Odisha.
- The second major predicament faced by the tribals both during the Colonial period and Post-Colonial period have been the Land Acquisition Policy which was the outcome of Land Acquisition Act, 1894. Due to the implementation of this Act considerably area of Tribal lands particularly those containing Mineral were acquired for the purpose of industrialization and

also for Development purpose. The tribals were reduced to the status of pauperization and proletarianization during last two centuries. Accordingly, the present research study would examine the impact of Development Induced Displacement during the Colonial and Post-Colonial period in the States of Jharkhand and Odisha.

- Since Forest Rights are an important identity issue for the tribals and hence, the study would also examine the nature of Forest Rights Struggles of the Tribals and the marginalized both during the Colonial and Post-Colonial period.
- The tribals heavily depend upon the Non-Timber Forest Produce for their day-to-day survival and hence, the present research study would also examine the extent and nature of dependence of the tribals on the Non-Timber Forest Produce.
- Due to the process of pauperization and proletarianization, the tribals are required to migrate to other States as Migrant Labour for their Wage Labour and Subsistence. Consequently, the present research study would also examine the impact of migration on the livelihood and living conditions of the tribals in Jharkhand and Odisha.
- The Tribal States in Central and Eastern India are becoming the theatre of vulnerability of the Adivasis and they are placed in a predicament to face the violence perpetrated by the Corporate Groups, States and the Maoist [Sharma, B.D., 1995) *Globalization: The Tribal Encounter*, Har-Anand Publication, New Delhi.]

8.1 Hypothesis

- The violation of land rights and forest rights of tribal community during the Colonial and Post-Colonial period would be igniting ingredient for generating tribal movement and tribal identity.
- Development Induced Displacement would be a basic precipitant for the pauperization and the proletarianisation of tribals in Jharkhand and Odisha.
- Poverty is likely to contribute migration of tribal labourers and marginalized communities from Odisha and Jharkhand to other States.
- Social injustice may be attributed as the primary cause of Naxalite violence in Jharkhand and Odisha.

8.2 Methodology

The above research questions have been examined in the States of Jharkhand and Odisha in different districts. In the State of Jharkhand, the empirical study has been conducted in the districts of Khunti, Saraikela-Kharsawan, West Singhbhum, East Singhbhum and Dalma Sanctuary. In Odisha the study has been undertaken in the tribal districts of Sundargarh, Koraput, Kalahandi, Rayagada and in the two coastal districts of Jagatsinghpur and Jajpur. In each district in both the States 3-4 villages have been selected for empirical study. One of the important objective has been to select the districts mainly from the Vth Schedule Area. The study is based both on the secondary statistics, published sources and empirical study. A structured questionnaire has been constructed to collect the basic information, supplemented by non-directive interviews and case studies.

8.3 Factors Contributing to the Growth of Jharkhandi Identity

The following attributes are considered as the key to understand the factors contributing to the growth of Jharkhandi Identity:

- Land as the essential ingredient of identity
- Concept of DIKU
- Forest as an Important Ingredient of Identity
- Development Induced Displacement—Internal Colonism
- Traditional institutions as a basis of Identity.

Land as the Essential Ingredient of Identity

The identity of the *Adivasis* is closely linked to the natural resources and the environment amidst which they live. They have the total right on that part of the 'Mother Earth' as they call her bequeathed to them by their ancestors. The land (*zamin*), water (*jal*) and forests (*jungal*) which constitute their habitat belong to them as part of cultural heritage. They have developed various norms, values, beliefs and practices which regulate the use of the natural resources around them in such a way that nature always remained bountiful to them. The *Adivasis* have a special relationship to the land they hold. To them land is not simply a factor of production, but a source of spirituality as well. The land provides assurance for their continued survival. It is the land, more than anything else, that gives life and meaning to their whole being; for it is in their land that their history and identity are contained. The traditional land base holds important symbolic and emotional meaning for them as the repository of ancestral remains (*sasans*), clan origin sites, and other sacred features important to their religious system. *Ownership of land for the tribals of Jharkhand, is vested in the community.* No individual has the right to permanently alienate the land from the community. *The community is the trustee of the land it occupies. The community includes not only the living members but also the ancestors and future generations.* Jharkhandi Identity has been the basis of the Jharkhand political movement from time to time (Mullick, Basu, S., 2002). The outsiders who migrated to this region also sharpened the tribal identity; *it is the self-definition that matters first, the perception by others does lend credence to it and make it further pronounced.* The British introduced the Permanent Settlement in 1793 *thereby imposing private property right of ownership of land* in the tribal areas of Jharkhand which had earlier communal ownership of property. The tribals of Jharkhand strongly resisted this imposition of private property right in land and launched militant tribal movements, notable among them being *Kol Rebellion of 1832-33, Santal Hul of 1855-56* and *Birsa Munda Uprising of 1895-1900.* These movements were led by the leaders of different tribal ethnic groups mainly belonging to Ho, Munda, Santhal, Oraon and Kharwar. Hence, the simultaneous spread of the movement within a span of 70 years among the major tribal ethnic community became the real basis of the formation of Jharkhand identity, i.e. *Pan Tribal Identity*. Such a strong resistance by different tribal groups of Jharkhand even compelled the British subsequently to recognize the indigenous system of land tenure and governance which was promulgated as Chhotanagpur Tenancy Act, 1908, Santhal Pargana Tenancy Act, 1949 and Wilkinson Rule, 1833. The recognition of the indigenous system of land tenure strengthened the foundation of Jharkhandi Identity in the administrative and political parlance.

They also recognize the Communal Property Right of Khunt-Kattidari which has been protecting the tribal interest on land till today and has also become important part of the tribal identity. The Chhotanagpur Tenancy Act, 1908, recognized "Khunti-katti rights" which means (1) "Raiyat having Khunt-katti Rights" means a raiyat in occupation of or having any subsisting title to land reclaimed from *jungle* by the original founders of the village or their descendants in the male line, when such raiyat is a member of family which founded the village or a descendant in the male line of any member of such family.

This Act also ascribes a special meaning for the word "Mundari Khunt-kattidar". Mundari Khunt-kattidar means a Mundari who has acquired a right to hold jungle and for the purpose of bringing suitable portions thereof under cultivation by himself or by male members of his family, and includes the male heirs in the male line of any such Mundari when they are in possession of such land. Their rent of a tenure holder or village head man is liable to enhancement during the continuation of his tenancy; such enhancement shall be made only by an order of the Deputy Commissioner. The Act also defines who is a 'settled raiyat'. Every person who for a period of 12 years after the commencement of the Act has continuously held raiyati land situated in any village shall be deemed to have become on the expiry a settled raiyat of that village. The Act also recognizes under section 18 that Bhuihar and Mundari Khunt-khatidar are to be settled raiyats in certain cases. Every person who is a settled raiyat of a village have a right to occupancy in all land held by him as a raiyat in that village. When the immediate landlord of an occupancy holding is a proprietor or permanent tenure holder, such person shall hold the land as a proprietor or permanent tenure holder as the case may be. The provisions of the Act relating to occupancy raiyats shall also apply to a Khunti-katti raiyat. The Act also makes it specific as to who is a non-occupancy raiyat; once a raiyat is admitted in the occupation of such land, he becomes liable to pay such rent as may be agreed between himself and the landlord. The Act also specifies the conditions under which the land can be converted into a Korkar with the Deputy Commissioner's permission and such rights extends to every cultivator for landless labourers. When a record of rights and obligations of raiyats having Khunt-katti rights has been prepared, no land shall be recognized as lands in respect of which Khunt-katti can be acquired.

One of the most important provision is to protect the alienation of tribal land; it is the incorporation after Section 71, the following "A power to restore possession to member of the Scheduled Tribes over land unlawfully transferred". The Act also gives unusual powers to the Deputy Commissioner to evict the transferee from such land without payment of compensation and restore it to the transferred or his heir. It is important to mention that many of the provisions of the Chhotanagpur Tenancy Act, 1908 have also been incorporated in the Santhal Pargana Tenancy Act.

The British realized the ingenuity of the traditional land system of the Jharkhandi tribals and accordingly they introduced the Chhotanagpur Tenancy Act, 1908, Wilkinson Rule of 1833 in Kolhan

Area, the recognition of *Manjhi* system of the Santhals in the Santhal Pargana Settlement (Amendment) Regulations of 1908. These legislations not only provided legitimacy to the tribal land tenure system, but also recognized the communal land ownership system like the Mundari Khuntkatti Dari system (Areeparampil Mathew, 2002 : 39) which are still preserved in the districts of Khunti, Saraikela along with the traditional Munda Manki system among the Ho and Munda community, Parha system among the Oraon and the Manjhi system among the Santhals. These have become the symbols of the tribal and Jharkhandi identity and are the strength for the continuing militant resistance against the exploiters whom they term as *Dikus*. It would be apt to quote Mullick here "The colonial rule thus prepared the ground for a territorial identity of the region in accordance with the demand of their political autonomy. The leaders of the Adivasi Mahasabha may be subsequently credited for having picked up the cultural name of Jharkhand to identify the region politically and giving it an institutional form by forming the Jharkhand party in 1950 (Munda and Mullick, 2003). The Jharkhand Coordination Committee in its Memorandum to the President of India on 10th December, 1987 had also emphasized the fact that Land is life in Jharkhand Cultural heritage; Land is given by God and Jharkhandis made it habitable and therefore, Jharkhand people have inalienable rights on the land and forest, hills and mountains of Jharkhand.

Concept of DIKU

One of the important indigenous cultural epithet "DIKU" was ingrained with emotion, sentiment and vengeance which signified essentially 'exploiters' who alienated the tribal land and forest rights during the British period and continued to do so during post-independence period as well. The British generated new class of exploiters in the form of landlords, moneylenders, police, State bureaucracy, liquor contractors and their ilk. The vengeance with which the tribals confronted them in the nineteenth century is a testimony to the strong tribal ethos of identity and militant movement. (Areeparampil Mathew, 2002: 161). The process of land alienation by upper caste—class combine during the post-independence period was also responsible to keep the phenomenon of DIKU alive which was noticed in its most intense form in the agrarian struggle led by *Jharkhand Mukti Morcha* during the period 1974-77 (Singh, K.S., 2004). The Jharkhandi identity had the inclusive connotation of all the Jharkhandis who are exploited either by the landlords or capitalist cum industrialist or moneylenders—liquor contractors-*cum*-bureaucrats. The alienation of Jharkhandis lands were done not only by the upper class but also by the class of industrialists who acquired the tribal land for the mining and industrial purposes. This also included the immigrants from Bihar (inclusive of North Bihar) and other parts of India who not only constituted the landlord and the category of capitalists, but were also lumpen category who squeezed the developmental benefits of Jharkhand. The mafia of the mines is drawn from the notorious ABC (Arrah, Ballia, Chapra districtrs of Bihar) where cultural backwardness matches junker brashness. The aggression of these immigrants is unleashed on tribal workers and peasants [Das, Arvind J., "Jharkhand's Roots: Tribal Identities in Indian History". In P.C. Chatterji (ed.) *Self-Images, Identity and Nationality*, Shimla: Indian Institute of Advanced Studies, 1989].

The Jharkhand movement got a new lease of life with the radicalization of the agrarian movement. With the effort of the Sivaji Samaj unity was forged among the Mahatos and the Santals which ultimately led to the emergence of the Jharkhand Mukti Morcha (JMM) in 1973, with Binod Behari Mahato as its President and Sibu Soren as the General Secretary of the Organization. The Marxist Coordination Committee of A.K. Roy also lent adequate support to the Morcha. Some of the Naxalite groups, operating in the Dhanbad area, also provided moral support to the movement. Thus, radicalism found a new expression under the banner of the Jharkhand Mukti Morcha and the movement got transformed significantly on many counts [Maharaj, R.N. and Iyer, K.G., "Agrarian Movement in Dhanbad". In Sengupta, N. (ed.) *Fourth World Dynamics*: *Jharkhand*, New Delhi: Authors Guild Publications, 1982).

8.4 Jharkhand Mukti Morcha: Radicalization of Jharkhand Movement

Radicalism found its expression with the formation of the Jharkhand Mukti Morcha under the leadership of Shibu Soren in 1972. This was yet another significant development on two counts firstly, it catered to the needs of the mining and industrial labour and secondly, it made a headway into a non-tribal (mainly Kurmi-Mahtos) population which so far had been lukewarm to the cause of the Jharkhand movement. In Bihar it developed special relationship with the Jharkhand Mukti Morcha which continued to the next General Election (in 1985) when the JMM won 14 seats thus again becoming a major opposition party in the Bihar Legislature, (Dr. Ram Dayal Munda, "The Jharkhand Movement Retrospect and Protest," Report submitted to Buta Singh, Jharkhand Coordination Committee, June 1990, p. 5).

Agrarian radicalism was best seen among the Santhals who were more sensitive to the agrarian question. The JMM launched an operation to recover alienated land from money-lenders and big peasants in North Chhotanagpur consisting of the tribal pockets of Giridih, Dhanbad and Hazaribagh districts, an area which was not the stronghold of the Jharkhand Party. There were 120 violent incidents including looting of crops or forcible harvesting of crops standing on lands in illegal possession of moneylenders, attacks on exploiters, arson and murder. The largest number of incidents (69) occurred in 1974 and since then the number of incidents has declined sharply. The Kurmi Mahtos alliance with Santhals gave the JMM an extra ethnic dimension; there was the possibility of the Santhal movement developing into a pan Santhal awakening cutting across the Santhal areas of Bihar and West Bengal. The Hul Jharkhand supported it. The Santhals of Hazaribagh, Giridih and Dhanbad formed a common front with those of the Santhal Parganas, Cultural revivalism as an elements of the ancient tribal self-government was revived. The Baisi (assembly) in the Santhal Pargana functioned as a court without fees or pleaders and renders simple justice.

In the course of this phase of the movement there were 46 confrontations from October 1977 to June 1978 for the formation of a separate State mostly confined to South Chhotanagpur. The issues against which the leaders of the movement agitated were (a) acquisition of land for large irrigation projects and firing ranges; (b) survey and settlement operations; (c) collection of loans, rent and cooperative dues; (d) nationalisation of forest produce and collection of *Kendu* leaves; and (e) panchayat elections based on 73rd Amendment. This phase of the movement for a separate State reached its culmination in Ranchi on 12 May, 1978.

The mafia of the mines is drawn from the notorious ABC—Arrah, Ballia, Chapra districts of Bihar, where cultural backwardness matches junker brashness. The aggression of these immigrants is unleashed on tribal workers and peasants [Das, Arvind N., "Jharkhand's Roots: Tribal Identities in Indian History". In P.C. Chatterji (ed.) *Self-Images Identity and Nationality*, Shimla: Indian Institute of Advanced Studies, 1989]. The process of internal colonialism of the tribals and *sadans* continued during the post-independence period and the liberalization era. It needs to be specially mentioned here that the gradual penetration of migrants into the tribal areas of Jharkhand gradually reduced the position of the tribals to a minority and today they are only 27 per cent of the total population. This has weakened the process of Jharkhandi Identity and also a transformation of Jharkhand identity from *ethnicity to regionalism* (Singh, K.S., Alloysius, 2003). The Jharkhand movement also acquired greater degree of radicalism because of leftist leadership and ideology. In fact A.K. Roy termed Jharkhand Identity as *Lal Khandi* (Roy, A.K., 1981). *The concept of DIKU became an emotionally and sentimentally surcharged concept which has been intrinsically motivating the Jharkhandis to resist their land and forest.*

8.5 Forest as an Important Ingredient of Identity and Ethnicity

The tribals in the Jharkhand area considered land and forest as twin plinth of their economy which is also important source of their identity. *The British had made forest as the property of the State thereby seriously violating the forest rights of the tribals*. This has also promoted discontent and conflict among the tribals. The forest are also associated with the concept of *sacred grove* which are important landmarks of historical and religious symbols for the tribal which they strongly identify and any destruction of the sacred place also enrages the tribals with the feelings of vengeance (Areeparampil, S.J., 2002: 6-8).

The causes of Forest *Andolan* in West Singhbhum district was the encroachment by the Forest department on Adivasi Community Forest, exploitation and harassment of Adivasis by Forest officials, Commercialization of forest and the resulted pauperization of Adivasis and Destruction of Forests by Contractors in Collusion with Forest officials. The Tribals also waged militant struggles on *Forest Issue* in Singhbhum district of Jharkhand during 1978-1985 *known as Jungle Kato Andolan* (Areeparampil Mathew, 1992 in Narayan, S. (ed.), *Jharkhand Movement: Origin and Evolution*, New Delhi: Inter-India Publications, pp. 144-189). One of the major reasons for launching such movement was the attempt of the British Colonial Power to convert the Khunt-katti villages into Reserve Forest. The *Andolan* took the form of felling of trees in these forests by the Adivasis as a symbolic protest against the threat to their livelihood and identity. The State's reaction against this movement was one of increased repression. [Areeparampil Mathew, 1992 in Narayan, S. (ed.), *Jharkhand Movement: Origin and Evolution*, New Delhi: Inter-India Publications, pp. 144-189]. *The hypothesis proposed here is that the violation of forest rights kindled the emotion and identity of the tribals and precipitate further militant movement. During the nine years of the Andolan there were more than eighteen police firings on Adivasis in which many innocent people were killed. Hundreds of adivasi houses were looted and burned down by the police and the forest officials. Thousands of Adivasis were implicated in false cases just for the purpose of harassing them.*

Inclusiveness of Identity

The electoral politics has also placed the tribals in the open fray politics with *Sadans* and other non-tribal groups. In Jharkhand apart from the Scheduled Tribes, there are various other indigenous groups who have been sharing similar culture and language with the tribals. These are Scheduled Castes, Backward Class communities which includes Kurmis, Koeris, Gwala, Momins etc. These communities are grouped under the generic category of *Sadans* and have been actively participating in the political process of the State and identify themselves as Jharkhandis specially during the post-independence period (Kesari, V.P.,1992).

Hence, in the process of identity formation of Jharkhand, the Jharkhand identity consist of the following:

- Scheduled Tribes known locally as *Adivasis* (the *Autochthon).*
- *Sadans* also called in local parlance as *Mulniwasis*, coterminus with the indigenous people of Jharkhand.
- Exploited classes of peasants, working class and other deprived and discriminated communities have now been included under the concept of Jharkhandi (Sengupta, Nirmal, 2003 : 338-339).

Jharkhandi Identity is thus inclusive which not only subsumes Adivasi and indigenous groups but incorporates those who are also exploited people. Apparently, the category of (*Dikus*) are excluded from the category of Jharkhandi Identity which has a special connotation within the Jharkhandi culture and *lingua franca*. It needs to be specially mentioned here that the gradual penetration of migrants into the tribal areas of Jharkhand gradually reduced the position of the tribals in a minority and today they are only 27 per cent of the total population. This has weakened the process of Jharkhandi Identity and also a transformation of Jharkhand Identity from ethnicity to regionalism (Singh, K.S.: Alloysius, 2003).

The continuous struggle of the tribals and the electoral politics culminated in the formation of a State called Vananchal synonymously equated with Jharkhand. This new State of Jharkhand was constituted on the 15th November, 2000 under the direction, guidance and leadership of BJP. In this new political formation, the BJP have co-opted the various Jharkhandi factions. They have promoted new Industrial Policy in the era of globalization and liberalization by opening the mines of Jharkhand for the multinationals and corporate sectors. This signifies the continuation of the policy of internal colonialism in which the key tribal leaders like Sibu Soren, Babulal Marandi etc. played a key role. The groups and organizations and particularly the tribals are strongly opposed to the acquisition of tribal lands in the liberalization era and they are resisting any changes in the Chhotanagpur Tenancy Act, 1908 and Santhal Pargana Tenancy Act. It is as a result of the formation of strong Jharkhandis Identity both during the colonial and post-colonial era that the Jharkhandis are able to resist land alienation and land grabbing during the Globalization era. This is the achievement and the heritage of tribals of Jharkhand which is continuing as one of the major saviours of their survival and continued existence.

Gradually, the tribal heritage dimension was getting diluted in the movement and the regional aspect became the predominant character of the Jharkhand movement. This definition of the nature and character of the movement became the dominant point of view across the political spectrum. *Thus, the whole question of the autonomy of the Jharkhand region came to acquire more geographical, regional and development related overtones.* The issue of the tribal identity of the region was lost in the emphasis on the development problems both by the government agencies as well as the political groups of the region.

8.6 Formation of Ethnicity and Identity in Odisha

S.N. Tripathiy (2016) has undertaken "An Analysis of Tribal Movements in Contemporary Odisha". He has described the heroic roles played by some distinguished tribal leaders like Laxman Naik of Koraput, Ratan Naik of Keonjhar, Dora Bisoyee and Chakra Bisoyee of Ghumsur and Veer Surendra Sai of Sambalpur. They protested against the British and the British could not dare to enter into the remote hilly areas of the Khonds. The tribal communities had an extensive history of struggle against the British during the colonial period. The tribes had their own cultural, religious and social identity, their own taboos and any inroad into the tribal society was resisted by the tribes with all their individual and collective might (Pande, 1989b). The second aspect of the resistance movement could be attributed to immigrations of the chain of resourceful peasants, moneylenders and scribes from the costal planes to the tribal hinterland and the process of forced assimilation of the tribes with the economic policies pursued by the immigrants. Alienation of Land Ownership of Tribal Raiyats and eviction of tribal tenants was the direct and inevitable outcome of this process of invasion of unscrupulous traders and moneylenders and prosperous peasants from the planes into the tribal areas and forced induction of the tribes into their ways. The most dominant characteristic of the tribal resistance movement was that it was fundamentally an uprising against the foreign rulers and in that sense could be constructed to be the precursor of the national liberation movement which took a distinct shape and gathered momentum under the inspiring leadership of Mahatma Gandhi nearly one century later. The new policy introduced brought a radical change in the concept of land ownership. Tradition had conferred ownership or title to land on the basis of membership of a clan or tribe. The new policy put an end to this; it also put an end to attempts at land grabbing by the leaders of a clan or tribe by force.

If alienation of tribal lands in favour of non-tribal immigrants constituted an important factor of tribal unrest and uprising in the early part of the nineteenth century, it is no less today. It has no doubt enacted laudable legislative enactments like the Tribal Land Alienation Regulation of 1956 to arrest the process of grabbing of land of tribes by non-tribes but the process is going on unabated and often unnoticed. The crafty and resourceful members of the non-tribal community are responsible for such land grabbing. Land alienation coupled with denial of a fair and equitable return on the products of their hard labour have been responsible for misery and deprivation of members of the Scheduled Tribe community on an increasing scale. For the last few decades and more particularly since 1990s, the issue of human rights—violation of rights to life and livelihood of tribal people—is a central concern. Therefore, the discourse on tribal movements and issues of tribal livelihood revolved around securing their self-defined rights on land and forest resources. The experience in Odisha shows that tribal people's protest movements, however well organized, have to take cognizance of the powerful interests of economic elite and industrial capital—both domestic and foreign—that wield considerable political power. Protest movements by the tribal people of Odisha in different pockets have attracted the attention of policy-makers, bureaucrats, academic and activists across the world. Laws like Land Acquisition Act and the Indian Forest Act etc. legitimize the continuing decline in access and control over forest resources that are considered as the basis of their subsistence economy. Historically speaking, the inevitable sequel of all projects was displacement and displacement has been a saga of marginalization. The Land Acquisition Act, 1894 has the provision that the government is not bound to provide a displaced person anything, but cash compensation if the concerned person can show the evidence of his land title, unfortunately, the tribes could not produce the same and as a result of which, they are usually deprived of the compensation.

8.7 Development Induced Displacement—Internal Colonialism in Jharkhand and Odisha

The British also violated the tribal land rights by promulgating the colonial land legislation known as the Land Acquisition Act of 1894 which gave unrestricted power to the British colonialists (eminent domain) to acquire tribal lands which were containing mines and other natural resources. The British acquired huge areas of tribal lands covered with minerals, like Coal, Iron, Manganese, which were mostly located in tribal lands of Chhotanagpur. Even during the colonial period, the tribals were displaced from these lands without adequate compensation and rehabilitation. *The land acquisition thus became a distinct marker of tribal discontent and cumulative resistance (Ekka and Asif, 2000). The uneven development of the area and of the different segments of the society is creating the problem of internal colonialism. The uneven development of the different region of Jharkhandi society is inbuilt ingredient of the internal colonialism and deformed capitalism.* The State possesses 37 per cent of the total minerals of India. Among these came up huge number of establishments on Damodar River basin and the famous Jharia Coalfield in Dhanbad district, one of the richest treasure house of India's metallurgical coal. Damodar river basin is very important because of the coal mining industry; 46 per cent of the total reserves of coal in India lie in this region. The Singhbhum—Odisha border known as Iron Ore series and Kolhan series constitute one of the richest iron belts in the world. Copper is another very important mineral. Total reserves of this area is about 153 million tonnes with 2.5 per cent copper content. Similarly, the area is also rich in copper, bauxite, mica, limestone and Kyanite too. The Uranium Corporation of India Ltd., a public sector undertaking has its main mining centres in Jadugora, Bhatin, Narwapahar, Turamdih and other areas in Singhbhum. Hydro power, Thermal power projects and Dams are the other big reasons for displacement. These hydel-power projects, as roughly estimated has a total of 5,07,952 acre of land occupation in the State. It has displaced as many as 2,32,968 persons. An additional 6026.87 acre of land has gone against setting up of thermal power stations.

The Development of industries during the British period has been rooted in the capitalist production system which has also been continuing during the post-independence period culminating in the liberalization era in the form of *market-led capitalism*. The studies on *development induced displacement* have been conducted by several scholars (Fernandis and Asif, 1997), Jharkhand (Ekka and Asif, 2000) who have shown that mining industries, dams, reservoirs, power plants etc. have led to large scale displacement in Jharkhand estimated to be 1.5 million people of whom 41.27 per cent are Adivasi, 14.16 per cent dalits and the rest 44.57 per cent from other communities. Between 1951 and 1995, 155 lakh acre land have been alienated to various schemes. Involuntary displacement has become a human right issue. The tribals and Ethnic minorities became the first victim of conquest and colonization. *This has been called ethnocide or cultural genocide. Ethnocide entails two principal aspects—economic and cultural* (Basu, Sajal, *Jharkhand Movement: Ethnicity and Culture of Silence*, Shimla: Indian Institute of Advanced Study, pp. 46-47). Several prominent scholars have emphasized that Impoverishment leads to landlessness, houselessness, powerlessness, marginalization and so on.

There were strong resistance to land acquisition for various developmental projects in Jharkhand which culminated in several violent movements against the construction of the big dams like Koel-Karo, Subarnarekha Project and Kutku, involving the large scale alienation (both legal and illegal) of tribal lands. On 4th April, 1982, Gangaram Kalundia, a retired Army person was killed in the police firing as he was leading the resistance to the Dam being built over the river Kharkai as a part of Subarnarekha Multipurpose Project (Report of the Delhi Unit of PUCL, March, 1979). The above resistances against past land acquisition is very much fresh in the minds of the Jharkhandis and they are sensitive to further land acquisition.

Globalization was accompanied with land acquisition of mines and industries which developed resistance both in Jharkhand and Odisha. It would be necessary to mention here that Jharkhand Government has signed well over 100 MoUs with corporate sectors during the globalization era. Notable among them are Corporate giants, namely Arcelor, Mittals, Jindal, Essar, Tata, Hindal, Abhijit Group etc. Among the MoUs signed by the State Government 74 are for setting up steel plants and 24 for power plants with the estimated investment of Rs. 4,67,240 crore requiring approximately 2 lakh acre of land. Due to the liberalization policy foreign companies have been allowed 100 per cent participation in mining projects (Ekka, Alex, 2003). The strong roots of tribal identity in Jharkhand are facilitating them to resist land acquisition for mining and industrial purpose in the liberalization era. The hypothesis emerging from this is as follows: "The land acquisition by the State and corporate agencies in the era of globalization would be met with stiff resistance in areas imbued with strong Jharkhandi Identity".

There was turmoil against displacement in the Jharkhand State on October 1, 2008; the villagers attacked the Kohinoor Steel Plant near Jamshedpur, seized 70 trucks and stopped the work. The Jindal Steel, Essar, and CESE were forced to leave the areas; as a result, the Government of Jharkhand is not able to execute several MoUs at the grassroots. The strong resistance by the tribals in the liberalization era has made land acquisition difficult. The Jharkhandis are very sensitive to forcible acquisition of land for mining and developmental purpose. *The strong roots of tribal identity in Jharkhand are facilitating them to resist land acquisition for mining and industrial purpose in the liberalization era. The hypothesis emerging from this is as follows: The land acquisition by the State and corporate agencies in the era of globalization is being met with stiff resistance in areas imbued with strong Jharkhandi Identity.*

Since a decade, the thickly forested and riverine region of Lanjigarh in Kalahandi (Odisha) is under severe pressure from mining development for bauxite deposits and alumina processing, by the British Vedanta Group, in collaboration with State of Odisha, Odisha Mining Corporation and also the Ministry of Environment and Forests. The proposed mining will severely degrade the Niyamgiri hills ecosystem which is a rich wildlife habitat and an important and recognized elephant corridor, endanger the Dongaria Kondh's self-sufficient forest-based livelihoods, and lead to the extinction of their culture over a period of time. More than 7 sq. km. of the sacred undisturbed forest land on top of the mountain that has been protected for ages by the Dongaria Kondh as sacred to their deity, Niyam Raja, and essential for the region's fertility; will be stripped off its vegetation, soil and rendered into a vast barren exposed land.

The Supreme Court of India imposed conditions on Vedanta Aluminium project to make a comprehensive plan for rehabilitation and all-round development of project affected tribal families before their displacement, which are to be monitored by the Government of Odisha. It has been observed that with the latest unanimous rejection from the Gram Sabhas of the tribes who resisted allowing the Niyamgiri for mining Vedanta, the concerned Land Acquisition has been stopped. The prominence of tribal people's concerns stems from the realization that they have not benefited from development projects while the mainstream societies have prospered at their expense, pushing them deeper into the poverty trap. The Panchayat Extension to Scheduled Areas (PESA) Act, 1996 has made it mandatory for the States having Scheduled Areas to make specific provisions for providing wide range of powers to the tribes for their development. There is no denying that what goes in the name of 'naxalism' is to a large extent a product of collective failure to assure to different segments of society their basic entitlements under the Constitution and other protective legislation.

Felix Padel and Samarendra Das (2008), in their paper, "Odisha Highland Clearance: the reality Gap in R & R" have examined anguishly about the grim reality of displacement taking place in contemporary Odisha and have also explained them in strong culture terms. Their aim in this paper is to draw attention to a number of very grave aspects of what is term "Development Induced Displacement". The social construction of reality in tribal culture is world away from mainstream culture and it is a real challenge for the bureaucratic technology focus mind set which guide development projects to comprehend the enormity of what is involved when tribal people are approved it from their land and villages to a resettlement colony. It is because of this reality gap that resistance to projects is so intense. What is happening in terms of *Cultural Genocide—the extension of people communities and social structure—which largely explains why they fight so strenuously to resist displacement.* Displacement arises out of a clash of ideology. On one side the value systems of traditional culture, relationship with land and community are more important than money. On the other hand ideology of industrialization as development in which market forces and financial profit take precedence over other rights and values have deleterious effect on the marginalized. The police firings that killed tribal people at Maikanch village in December 2000, and Kalinganagar industrial area in January 2006 are the key symbols of this struggle in Odisha. Cultivators look on industrial projects that lower their standard of living and destroy their communities as the opposite of real development. This divide and rule legacy of British colonialism is bearing fruit now, in internal colonialism carried out through large scale privatization of resources and takeovers of huge tracts of cultivated land by mining and construction companies in Odisha and neighbouring States.

Most of Odisha's first wave of industrial projects have been notorious for their lack of adequate R & R, such as the Rourkela steel Plant, the Hirakud, Upper Kolab and Indravati dam projects and also NALCO in Koraput, sometimes cited as a model of good practice. So, the present situation in Odisha involved several high profile struggles of people opposing displacement in Odisha. Three companies in particular face protracted opposition, in a series of projects some of which have already caused displacement or are currently causing agitation, while others, e.g. iron ore mines have yet to be finalized. Tata at Kalinganagar and Gopalpur (steel plants), Naraj (thermal power plant near Cuttack. Dhamra (port) and north Odisha (iron-one mines), and Vedanta at Lanjigarh alumina refinery, Niyamgiri (planned bauxite mine), Jharsaguda district smelter and giant power plant, near Puri university-*cum*-business centre and Gandhamardan another bauxite deposit.

The Land Acquisition Act, 1894 is an expression of the doctrine of 'eminent domain' which invess power in the State to take over private land for a *public purpose* (Usha Ramanathan, 2008, *Social Development Report*, p. 27). The development projects in India have displaced over 60 million people over last 70 years most of whom have not been properly rehabilitated (Harimohan Mathur, 2008, *Social Development Report*, p. 3). Impoverishment is the most consistently visible impact on the life of those forcibly displaced. This has followed impoverishment relating to landlessness, joblessness, houselessness marginalization, in security, morbidility and mortality, loss of access to common property and social disarticulation. Sekhar Singh (2008) observes that forcible displacement is perhaps among the worst forms of violence that the innocence can be legally subjective to. There is growing opposition to displacement and its impact. Strong opposition to displacement that cause impoverishment also leads to resistance against displacement which happened at Kalinga Nagar, Kashipur and Nandigram. They triggered massive solidarity across the country. T.K. Oomen (2008) has indicated that institutionalization of protest and mobilization can be discerned from the formation of People's Forum to Oppose Displacement (2008). According to Fernandes and Asif

(1997) Displacement induced for the period 1951-1955 in Odisha and Jharkhand was 14.65 lakh and 15.48 lakh respectively. By 2004, the total DP/PAP's in Jharkhand and Odisha went up to 30 lakh each. (Fernandis, 2008: 91). The Hirakud Dam in Odisha displaced 1.10 lakh; the percentage of tribal displaced in Jharkhand and Odisha is over 40 per cent each while the Dalits constitute 13.75 per cent of the displaced in Jharkhand, 11.64 per cent in Odisha. The proportion of private and common land acquired in Odisha and Jharkhand is given below:

Proportion of Private and Common Land Acquired in Jharkhand and Odisha

(In per cent)

States	*Private*	*Common*	*Forest*
Jharkhand	55.46	22.56	22.32
Odisha	41.81	27.99	30.20

Source: Social Change, 2008, p. 97.

8.8. The Highlights of Land Acquisition and Displacement in Jharkhand

- The Adivasis in Jharkhand have a militant tradition of land struggle since the Colonial period.
- They have tried to preserve the integrity of Land and Forest issue as an important ingredient of their cultural identity.
- The Private Property Right in Land, the undermining of communal rights, the colonial law of Land Acquisition of 1894 has been the major precipitant to promote the land struggle among tribals as a Live issue.
- The Land Acquisition has been invariably forceful as the welfare law like Schedule-V provision, the favourable feature of PESA have seldom been implemented to safeguard their possession.
- One of the shortcomings of the tribals has been that they have been reduced to the status of minorities in their own State which was a constraint to preserve their cultural identity. In the emerging contest, the Adivasis have rightly united with *Moolnivasis* and the Proletariates.
- The Chhotanagpur Tenancy Act, 1908, the Santhal Pargana Tenancy Act, 1949, the Khutkatti Rights make them alive to the Traditional Cultural Identity and Traditional Ingredient.

> The Amendment to CNT Act, 1908 and SPT Act, 1949 liberalizing the acquisition of land for the Corporate Sector has generated great anger and protest among the Adivasis of Jharkhand which is directly affecting their social and cultural identity. They have strongly protested against such amendment.

According to K.B. Saxena (*Social Change*, 2008, pp. 715-716), the absolute nature of the power of the State through the use of Eminent Domain for compulsory acquisition of land should be abandoned. Gram Sabha of the village should be mandatorily consulted whether in areas covered by PESA or outside for their consent to the acquisition. The acquisition of land, where absolutely necessary for public purposes, should be undertaken after consultation with the Gram Sabha and on terms which they collectively settle with the acquisition authority. The scope of public purpose should be drastically narrowed down to projects covered by the Directive Principles of State Policy and where the project provides to the affected persons direct, tangible and demonstrable benefits. Prof. K.B. Saxena has compared the National Rehabilitation and Resettlement Policy 2007 with the Odisha Government rehabilitation and resettlement policy of May 2006.

He points out the following favourable points for the marginalized community in the Odisha Policy:

- If the process of negotiation includes land procured/purchased directly by the corporate/private parties, as seems to be the case, since the definition of project area includes land which is acquired/alienated/purchased, it is certainly more equitable, just and humane in its applicability. On the issue of coverage, unlike the National Policy which restricts it to those affected by projects satisfying the specified numerical benchmark of the level of displacement, the Odisha Policy does not place such a barrier and is, therefore, more liberal.
- This coverage of displaced persons in Odisha Policy has been well formulated as compared to other policies.
- The definition of 'family' is more inclusive in the Odisha Policy than in the National Policy. It recognizes unmarried daughters and sisters over thirty years of age, a widow or a woman divorcee as a separate family for the benefit of rehabilitation and is, thus, gender neutral. Additionally, it empowers physically and mentally challenged persons and minor orphans by conferring the status of a separate family.

- The Odisha Policy has also provided for dovetailing of normal development programmes with the resettlement and rehabilitation package to be made available to the displaced community on a priority basis.
- The Odisha Policy clearly stipulates that no physical displacement shall be effected before the completion of resettlement work while the National Policy is less equivocal on this issue. It merely requires 'adequate progress' in the rehabilitation and resettlement to be ensured before physical shifting of the affected persons and therefore, shows less sensitivity to the inconvenience faced by the displaced persons.
- The Odisha Policy recognizes the harassment involved to the affected persons who have gone through the experience before and, therefore, provides for, at least, additional 50 per cent compensation over and above the normal compensation to mitigate it. The Odisha Policy also requires steps to be taken by the rehabilitation and resettlement agency to acclimatize the resettled people in the new habitat including development of a cordial relationship with the host community in the resettlement site.
- The Odisha Policy marginally scores over the National Policy in some respects. It classifies projects into five types: (a) Industrial, (b) Mining, (c) Water Resources/National Parks, (d) urban and linear projects, and (e) Any other projects. It makes provision for employment only in Type (a) and (b) projects.
- The other important provision is that one time cash compensation ranging from Rs. 1 to 5 lakh where employment cannot be provided has been added in the Odisha Policy.
- A mandatory provision has been made for allotment of 2½ acre of irrigated agricultural land or five acre of non-irrigated agricultural land to each ST displaced family in type (c) projects while the displaced families of all other social categories would be provided with two acre of irrigated or four acre of non-irrigated agricultural land.
- On the provision of homestead land and house building assistance, the Odisha Policy is more liberal than the National Policy.
- It is in respect of benefits to the landless and the homestead less encroachers that the Odisha Policy shows greater

sensitivity than is to be found in the National Policy. The landless encroachers will get *ex-gratia* equivalent compensation admissible under the Land Acquisition Act for a similar category of land provided the encroachment is of ten years duration continuously and unobjectionable.

- This includes the mandatory Social Impact Assessment, gamut of physical amenities and social infrastructure to be provided at the resettlement site. Neither of the two policies assure replacement of land for land lost not even to STs or a durable, sustainable and dignified employment.
- The massive resistance to land acquisition throughout the country created an atmosphere for the Central Government to enact the Land Acquisition Amendment Act of 2013 which has brought some positive dimension to the Forcible Land Acquisition Act of 1894. "The Right to Fair Compensation and Transparency in Land Acquisition, Rehabilitation and Resettlement, 2013" has provided higher compensation for land acquisition (at least four times of market prices in rural areas and twice the market price in urban areas) and makes consent of 80 per cent and 70 per cent of affected land owners as imperative for acquiring land for private and public-private partnership projects. It has compensation provisions for landless households like tenants, farm workers, who depend on farming activity on acquired land, and automatic rehabilitation and resettlement (R & R) package is applicable if the acquired land is more than 100 acre in rural areas and 50 acre in urban areas. Further, irrigated and multi-cropped land can be acquired only as the last resort and only up to a small percentage of total such land in a given areas, for example, not more than 5 per cent in multi-crop districts. It also includes annuities, land for land, transportation allowance, a portion of capital gains from resale and construction of alternative housing and communal amenities in the even of loss of homestead, tightens the definition of public purpose, and provides for social impact assessment (SIA) (Ghatak & Ghosh, 2011; Raghuram & Sunny, 2015). For the first time, land acquisition and R & R provisions have been brought together in one law RECTLARRA, 2013 [(Nielsen & Nielsen, 2015). Sukhpal Singh (2016), "Land Acquisition in India: an Examination of the 2013 Act and options", *Journal of Land and Rural Studies*, Special Issues—Land Acquisition,

Rehabilitation and Resettlement in India (LARR), Vol. IV Issue 1, January, 2016, pp. 66-78.]

- The Land Acquisition Act, 1894 was comprehensively amended in 2013 which, among others, provided for prior consent of land owners in cases of acquisition for private companies and public partnerships, social impact assessment of all projects requiring land acquisition and restrictions on acquisition of irrigated agricultural land to accommodate some of the concerns of people affected by land acquisition. Chapter II of 2013 Act deals with determination of SIA and public purpose. The insertion of SIA in Chapter II in the 2013 law was the first of such objectives was to ensure that the entire document could be weighed against the benefits that were claimed to accrue to the people in the project report. The second objective was to examine whether the activities to be undertaken by the project would qualify for being called 'Public Purpose'. This exercise was to examine whether the extent of land to be acquired is necessary. The most important purpose was to make it participatory one. It was also intended to identify the extent of displacement it would cause of those dependent on agricultural land. It was intended to identify the livelihood losers. It also prevents the acquisition of irrigated multi-cropped land Saxena, K.B. (2015), "The Ordinance Amending the Land Acquisition Law (2013): Farmers Lose out in the Unequal Contest of Power", *Social Change*, 45(2), pp. 324-336, CSD 2015, New Delhi: Sage Publications].
- The major issues with the proposed Amendments in the 2013 Act and implemented through ordinances (now withdrawn) are as follows: The proposed amendment removing SIA was aimed at completely doing away with the SIA. It is important to recall that there were several reasons for which SIA was brought in, which included ensuring that both positive and adverse impacts of the proposed project could be investigated and documented to establish the overall utility of the project to the people while taking a decision on acquisition of land; examining whether the activities to be undertaken by the project qualified for being called "Public Purpose"; ascertaining whether the extent of land proposed to be acquired was necessary and, if so, was the barest minimum needed for the project and, whether it could be met from the unutilized land already available with the government or an

alternative land so as to avoid acquisition of land and consequent displacement of people. The 2013 Act had excluded private hospitals and private educational institutions from the ambit of infrastructural projects for which land could be acquired without the consent of the affected persons. The ordinance omitted these exclusions implying that there two purposes have also qualified for being considered 'infrastructure' for which compulsory acquisition could be undertaken by the State, and therefore, the obligation for obtaining a prior consent of the affected people for such acquisition would not have been necessary. The 2013 legislation also had land acquisition provisions only for government or private companies while the amendments from ordinance made it for any entity by replacing private company with private entity (Ramesh, 2015a). This change had extended the facility of acquisition of land by the State even to registered societies, cooperatives, trusts, proprietorships, partnerships, non-profit organizations etc. and enormously expanded the ambit of acquisition and therefore, had potentially increased the displacement of people manifold (Saxena, 2015) although this kind of definition of public or State was there in the LAA of 1894 as well (Verma, 2015) and, therefore, the new Act (2013) is as regressive as the LAA of 1894.

- It would be now pertinent to examine the adverse impact of the latest amendment to Land Acquisition Act, 2013 on the persons from whom lands are acquired. The National Democratic Alliance (NDA) government proposed amendments in 2014 (enforced through an ordinance which now stands withdrawn) in the 2013 Act which included removing land owner consent clause and the mandatory SIA for projects in five areas, that is, defence, rural infrastructure, housing, industrial corridor and social infrastructure. It also changed the term 'private company' to 'private entity' and definition of public purpose to include private hospitals and education institutions. A new chapter was proposed to be added to the 2013 Act which empowered appropriate government to exempt five categories of projects from the obligation of obtaining consent of the families affected by acquisition of land which include: projects vital to national security or defence of India, rural infrastructure, including electrification; affordable housing for the poor people, industrial corridors and infrastructure, including social and public private partnership projects (Saxena, 2015).

- The 2013 legislation also had land acquisition provisions only for government or private companies while the amendments from ordinance made it for any entity by replacing 'private company' with 'private entity' (Ramesh, 2015a). The change had extended the facility of acquisition of land by the State even to registered societies, cooperatives, trusts, proprietorships, partnerships, non-profit organizations etc. and enormously expanded the ambit of acquisition and therefore, had potentially increased the displacement of people manifold (Saxena, 2015) although this kind of definition of public or State was there in the LAA of 1894 as well (Verma, 2015) and, therefore, the new Act (2013) is as regressive as the LAA of 1894.

8.9 Implementation of Forest Rights Act, 2006 in Jharkhand and Odisha

Here attempt has been made to discuss the findings on the implementation of the Forest Rights Act, 2006 in the Sampled Districts of Jharkhand and Odisha. The Sampled districts covered in Jharkhand are the Districts of West Singhbhum, East Singhbhum, Saraikela-Kharsawan, Khunti and Dalma Sanctuary. The Sampled Districts covered in Odisha are the Districts of Koraput, Rayagada, Kalahandi and Sundargarh.

The figures in Table 8.1 indicate a gist of the implementation of Forest Rights Act, in the sample districts of empirical study of Jharkhand. From the consolidated figure, it can be evinced that the approved claims by DLC in these four districts are 6888 out of which 6358 beneficiaries have been given titles which constitutes 92.31 per cent of the total claims approved. The total area of titles given in the Four districts is 12751.03 acre which comprises 1.37 acre per beneficiary. However, the figures also clearly indicate that the average area per beneficiary assigned is 4.30 acre in West Singhbhum district followed by 1.09 acre in Saraikela-Rajkharsawan district and is much below One acre in the district of East Singhbhum and Khunti. The highest average area assigned to the beneficiaries in the West Singhbhum district can be attributed to the impact of Left Extremist Movement in the district. The beneficiaries in the West Singhbhum

Table 8.1: Implementation of Forest Rights in the Five Districts of Jharkhand

Sl. No.	*Name of the sample district*	*No. of claims approved by DLC*	*No. of beneficiary given titles*	*Total Area Titles given (in Acres)*	*Average area per beneficiary (in Acres)*	*Remarks*
1.	West Singhbhum	2475	2475	10643.09	4.30 acre	Intense Left Extremist affected area
2.	Saraikela-Rajkharsawan	571	571	626.22	1.09 acres	Moderately affectted Left Extremist area.
3.	East Singhbhum	3430	2900	1267.00	0.44 acre	Bordering Odisha and West Bengal.
4.	Khunti	231	231	152.47	0.66 acre	Covered by khunt khanti community rights.
5.	Dalma Sanctuary Area	181	181	62.25	0.34 acre	This sanctuary is located in East Singhbhum and Saraikela.
	Total	6888	6358	12751.03	1.37 acre	

Source: ICSSR Study.

district can much more usefully utilize the assigned land for cultivation purpose than in district of East Singhbhum and Khunti. *The lessons learnt from the Saranda Action Plan is now being implemented also in the other districts of Jharkhand affected by Left Extremism.*

Jharkhand is an important State for FRA implementation, with a large forest area and a very large tribal and non-tribal forest-dependent population. However, by 10th October, 2014, the number of individual claims received in Jharkhand was only 48,900; and of these, only 18,516 titles were distributed covering an area of 44,387.60 acre. This is one of the lowest figures among the States of Central and East India which is a cause for concern about the manner of the implementation of the Act. Moreover, very few claims for Community Forest Rights have been received; those listed as CFR claims are mostly for diversion to non-forest activities or minor claims for graveyards and threshing grounds. Hence, the main objective of giving community rights to forest resources has not been achieved.

The reasons for this situation in Jharkhand include:

- A number of potential claimants appear to be left out of the process entirely, due to lack of awareness and information, non-supply of forms etc.
- A large number of applications have been rejected due to

wrongful interpretation of the Act.

- A number of cases of inordinate delays in processing claims, providing support to Gram Sabhas to process claims, and tenable allegations of corruption by the implementing staff and village leaders have emerged.
- Several cases of the Forest Department illegally initiating plantation activities in the land for which cultivation claims have been filed (or could be filed).
- Several deviations have taken place from the process of implementation laid down in the law, including less involvement of the Gram Sabha, wrong attribution of rejection made by the officials to the Gram Sabha, no communication of rejection to the claimants etc.
- Where claims have been granted, the process of mutation of land records is incomplete; and in the case of community claims, the titles issued are defective.
- Several communities believe that applying under the Act will weaken their claim for full forest rights as per earlier Acts, for which they have been agitating since a long time.

Table 8.2: Consolidated figures of implementation of Forest Rights Act, 2006 (individual) in the Sample District of Rayagada, Kalahandi and Koraput in Odisha

Districts	*No. of Claims approved by Gram Sabha*	*No. of claims approved by SDLC*	*No. of claims approved by DLC*	*No. of Certificate of titles distributed*	*Area (in acre) Total*
Rayagada	33677	23283	22077	19498	35684.43
Kalahandi	11185	10530	10520	10077	15299.71
Koraput	29910	27804	27676	25742	40086.42
Total of the Three districts	**74772**	**61617**	**60273**	**55317**	**91070.56**

Source: ICSSR Study.

It can be noticed from the above comparative table of the three sampled districts that SDLC approved 82.37 per cent of the claims sent by Gram Sabha and DLC approved 97.86 per cent of the claims. The number of Certificate of titles distributed was 55,317 constituting 91.78 per cent of the total claims approved by DLC. The area distributed constitutes 91,070.56 acre, i.e. 1.65 acre per title. The area distributed can be utilized for cultivation purpose with convergence programme. The SDLC needs to again probe into the 17.63 per cent of the claims which have not yet been approved.

Table 8.3: Consolidated Status of Implementation of Community Rights in the Sampled Districts of Koraput, Rayagada and Kalahandi in the State of Odisha

Sl. No.	*Items of information on Community Rights*	*Implementation of Community Rights in Districts*			*Remarks*
1.	**No of claims received**	**Koraput**	**Kalahandi**	**Rayagada**	In the District of Koraput 309 claims under Form B and 140 claims under Form C are still pending.
	Form B	466	405	191	
	Form C	158	206	8	
	Total B+C	**624**	**611**	**199**	
2.	**Total claims settled (B+C)**				
	Number	169	178	193	
	Area in Acres	11044.2	3789.20	2372.40	
3.	**Total claims distributed**				
	Number	58	146	172	
	Area	**2780.87**	**3201.6**	**23081.35**	

Source: ICSSR Study.

It can be seen from the above table that in the three sampled districts of Koraput, Rayagada and Kalahandi, the total number of claims received in Form (B + C) are 624, 611 and 199 respectively. Altogether in the three districts the total number claims received are 1434 and the total claims settled inclusive of three districts are 540 and the total area in which claims settled in the three districts is 17,205.8 acre. However, the total claims distributed is highest in district Kalahandi consisting of 23,081.35 acre whereas it is much lower in the district of Koraput (2780.87 acre) and Rayagada (3201.60 acre). In the State of Jharkhand the Sampled Districts are West Singhbhum, East Singhbhum, Sariakela, Khunti, and Dalma Sanctuary, but the Community Forest Rights has been located by the District Administration only in the District of West Singhbhum where the number of claims filed at Gram Sabha level is 1691 and 39 of them have been recommended. This is a very low figure as compared to the Community Rights claims settled and distributed in Odisha.

Table 8.4: FRA Beneficiaries covered under Different Government Schemes in Convergence Programme during 2015 in the Districts of Kalahandi and Rayagada in the State of Odisha

Sl. No.	District	No. of certificates of titles distributed to individual claimants	No. of rights holders covered under various Government Schemes for their benefit					
			IAY	Mo Kudia	Mo Pokhari	Land Development Under MGNREGS	+Other Programmes	Total
1.	Kalahandi	10077	3494	03	38	3200	310 (143-Wadi and 167-Land Levelling by OTELP)	**7045**
2.	Rayagada	19498	9435	65	313	1521	2043	13377

Source: ICSSR Study.

It is a healthy sign that in both the Districts of Kalahandi and Rayagada the Forest Rights titles have been converged with different Government Schemes which include Government of India Scheme of House Construction, MNREGA programme for land development and productivity State Housing Rights Programme etc. These are input augmentation programmes which will give additional benefit to the FRA beneficiaries; it will not only make the FRA land productive, but also generate additional income to the beneficiaries. It may be mentioned that in the State of Jharkhand there is no Provision of any convergence programme to be associated with Forest Rights Programme. In this respect the District Administration and State Government of Odisha are trying to take a forward and progressive step relating to the implementation of Forest Rights programme.

Table 8.5: Forest Rights Distributed in the State of Jharkhand and Odisha for the Period Ending 31-12-2015

States	No. of claims received			No. of titles distributed up to 31-12-2015			Extent of Forest land for which titles distributed (in acre)		
	Individual	Community	Total	Individual	Community	Total	Individual	Community	Total
Jharkhand	80819	2734	83553	41691	1434	43125	87989.80	NA	87989.80
Odisha	603271	12866	616137	349400	5004	354404	550912.53	179663.50	730576.03

Source: ICSSR Study.

The number of individual claims filed in the State of Jharkhand is 89,345 whereas in the State of Odisha 6,03,271 claims have been filed which is much larger as compared to Jharkhand. The community claims filed in the State of Odisha is 12,866 against only 2,862 claims filed in Jharkhand. It is clear that both individual and community claims in the State of Jharkhand are much lower as compared to Odisha. The number of titles distributed in Jharkhand is 51.58 per cent of the total claims received indicating a very large number of claims still pending at Gram Sabha, SDLC and DLC level. The figures of Odisha indicates that 57.91 per cent of the total claims received have been distributed up to 31st December, 2015 which is higher than the figure of Jharkhand. The extent of forest land distributed to the individual beneficiary is 87,989.80 acre which is 1.77 acre per title in Jharkhand as against 1.58 acre per title in Odisha. The per acre area distributed per beneficiary is higher in the State of Odisha as compared to the State of Jharkhand. The figure of community rights issued in the State of Odisha is 1,79,663.50 acre but figure of Jharkhand is much lower. The Eighteenth Report of Committee on Petitions (Sixteenth Lok Sabha, as on 31st December, 2015) mentions that, 43,125 titles (41,691 individual and 1,434 community titles) covering nearly 88,000 acre of forest land has been granted in Jharkhand. In nutshell it can be stated that the performance of the implementation of Forest Rights Act, 2006 is much better in Odisha as compared to Jharkhand.

Nearly 13.1 per cent individual claims in Odisha and 23.1 per cent claims in Jharkhand are pending. 38.2 per cent claims in Jharkhand and 26 per cent individual claims in Odisha are rejected. Rejection is high in Chhattisgarh and pending cases are high in Jharkhand among the study States. In spite of several efforts, the picture depicts the low level of importance given to community claims in comparison to individual claims. The percentage of individual claims rejected in Jharkhand is 38.2 per cent while it is only 26 per cent in Odisha. The Community claims rejected in Jharkhand is 2.7 per cent as against 5.6 per cent in Odisha. The Goilkera block is located deep inside the Saranda Forest Division which is part of West Singhbhum district. This area is one of the *Epi-centre of Jangal Kato Andolan (of Adivasis)* during 1979-1985 *and presently the primary theatre of Left Extremist movement.* The tribals had launched a militant movement during 1980-86 in which the forest lands were felled and transformed into the cultivable land. Those felled forest areas have also been included in the assignment of forest rights to the local tribals mostly comprising the tribal community of Mundas and Hos. The average area of land assigned per beneficiary is 6.56 acre which is one of the highest area assigned in any Jharkhand Block. This is also part of the area of Saranda Action Plan formulated by the Government of

India during UPA Government. Even in the villages of Sonua Block the average area assigned per beneficiary is higher than most of the other blocks in the State of Jharkhand. Sonua Block is also part of the Saranda Action Plan. Hence, the forest rights have been more effectively implemented in the Maoist affected area of Saranda Forest Division as compared to other Forest divisions of Jharkhand.

As per the Forest Reserve Survey, 2006 the Adivasis had forcibly occupied 2770.79 hectare land between 1980 and 1988 which constituted 3.24 per cent of the total Saranda Forest area. In Saranda Forest the individual *pattas* accepted claims is 416 and the distributed *pattas* are 394 covering 315.74 acre and the average land per family is 75.8 decimal (Letter No. 594, DC West Singhbhum). The Total Community Pattas distributed in Saranda Forest is 3558.32 acre (*Source:* Letter No. 594, DC Office, West Singhbhum). The total lease area given to different Companies like SAIL, Rungta Mines, Usha Martine, Tata Steel, and other Companies include 14,410.09 acre (Answer given by the Steel Minister on Rajya Sabha Unstarred Question No. 436 on 15th March, 2012). Besides this, another 9337.54 acres have been given to 22 Mining Companies in 2012.

The PTG households have also been provided titles under FRA 2006 in Rayagada District. The PTGs are located in 3 blocks of Rayagada District, namely, DKDA Parsali (K. Singhpur Block), DKDA Chatikona (Bisam Cuttack Block), and LSDA Putasangi (Gunupur Block). There are 3006 number of PTG households in the district out of which claims were received by FRC numbering 3131 and all these were sent to Gram Sabha and the number of claims approved by Gram Sabha was 2697; *the certificate of titles were also issued to 2697 numbers involving an area of 4395 acre in the entire district of Rayagada.* It is quite appreciable that so many individual Titles have been conferred to PTG families. It may be mentioned that the Total number of individual titles approved in the entire Rayagada District was 19,498 and the area assigned was 35,685 acres and the area of titles assigned to PTGs was 4395 acres *constituting 22.5 per cent of the total district. This is indeed a good augury in the implementation strategy of Government of Odisha.*

As on 30-11-2016, the total number of claims filed under FRA is 42,43,668 out of which 36,88,859 claims have been disposed of and 17,30,729 titles have been issued. Odisha has the distinction of issuing highest number of titles which is 4,05,509 (3,99,996 individual titles and 5,513 community titles). Madhya Pradesh has the distinction of having highest forerst area over which titles have been issued under this Act. The total forest area over which title has been issued in Madhya Pradesh is 21,10,991.87 acres.

8.10 NTFP in Jharkhand and Odisha

The major NTFPs in the State of Jharkhand is *Sal, Karanj, Mahua, Chiraunji, Tamarind* and *Gum Karya*. The *Kendu Patta* collection is done through Forest Department in Jharkhand. The total price paid to *Kendu* pluckers in the year 2014 was Rs. 37.211 crore but during 2014-15 to 2016-17 the collection of *Kendu Patta* has considerably declined due to strong Left Wing Extremism particularly in the Districts of West Singhbhum, Khunti, Latehar and Palamau. The contractors are not coming forward for participating in the tender of *Kendu* leaves as the Left Wing Extremism activists are demanding heavy amount from them from their profit. The important NTFP collected in West Singhbhum District are *Sal* leaves, *Khajur* Leaves, *Karanj* seeds, *Mahua* seeds and flowers and *Tamarind*. The studies on NTFP in Jharkhand in the Districts of Gumla, Hazaribagh and Simdega reveal that the four major NTFPs are *Mahua*, *Lac*, *Karanj* and *Chiraunji*. The average percentage of annual income from NTFP in the villages surveyed was in the range of 10 per cent to 31 per cent. In the district of Simdega NTFP resources lack proper market and infrastructure for processing various items of NTFP. It was found that *Mahua* was widely collected across all the studied villages for which they spent 23 days in the summer season. Women play a very important role in the collection of NTFP. *Karanj* is mostly found in Gumla district. In the Bundu block of Ranchi district *Sal* leaf fetched highest earning followed by lac, fuel wood, tooth brush, fodder, *Mahua* flower etc. The NTFPs markets are by and large imperfect and the aboriginal people do not get a fair return for their labour. The poor marketing infrastructure and lack of storage facilities compel them to sell off their produce to the first market contact that is generally the *haat* (local village market) or the petty trader. The selling of almost all the forest resources is predominantly done in the local weekly markets where transaction takes place on a mutually agreed price quoted between vendors and petty traders. The middlemen invariably exploit collectors of NTFPs on account of prevailing malpractices, forced and distress sales. The present situation reflects that all the major NTFPs are available for around 2-3 months except for fuelwood, fodder, *Sal* leaf, lac and tooth brush and bulk (peak) trading seldom goes beyond 3-4 months.

8.11 Lac Cultivation and Processing in Jharkhand

Lac Cultivation as one of the major NTFPs, is an important source of income for livelihood for the forest dwellers in Jharkhand. It has also high potential for generating employment for both men and women in forest and fringe areas of Jharkhand. Jharkhand State ranks 1st in production of lac followed by Chhattisgarh, Madhya Pradesh, Maharashtra and West Bengal. These five States contribute around 97 per cent of the national lac production. *Jethwi* ranks first (32.60%) followed by the *Baisakhi* (27.25%), *Aghani* (24.32%) and *Katki* (15.82%) in national lac production. In the year 2012-13, the production of all the crops in comparison to previous year production has increased. The major districts producing lac in Jharkhand are Ranchi, Simdega, Gumla, West Singhbhum, Palamau, Latehar and Garhwa. On the basis of surveys conducted at different lac processing centres in the country, the total quantity of sticklac processed during 2010-11 was 13,600 tonnes which also included the imported lac in India. There are twenty eight lac processing units is Chhattisgarh, 15 units in Jharkhand, 6 units in Maharashtra, 2 units in Madhya Pradesh and 143 units in West Bengal. West Bengal ranked first (42.7%) followed by Chhattisgarh (26.5%), Jharkhand (25.7%), Maharashtra (5.1%) and Madhya Pradesh (0.7%). The amount of sticklac processed in India during 2010-11 was 13,700 tonnes of which 42.33 per cent was processed in West Bengal, 26.28 per cent in Chhattisgarh, 25.55 per cent in Jharkhand, 5.11 per cent in Maharashtra, only 0.73 per cent in Madhya Pradesh. Almost 75 per cent of lac produced in India is exported to different countries of which the main customers are USA, UK, Germany, Italy, France, Japan, China, Sweden, Brazil, Argentina and Russia. The total export of lac and its value added products during the year 2010-11 was 6339.05 tonnes valued at Rs. 211.13 crore. Jharkhand produced 56.88 per cent of sticklac in the country, but it processes only 25.74 per cent of the lac. Rest of the lac produced in Jharkhand is despatched to the neighbouring States, mostly West Bengal, for its processing and State loses revenue by supplying lac as a raw-material to these States.

Indian Institute of Natural Resins and Gums, Namkum, Jharkhand has played yeoman service in promoting the lac cultivation in Jharkhand, Bihar, Uttar Pradesh, Odisha, Chhattisgarh, West Bengal, Rajasthan and other States in India. It is located in Ranchi from where it imparts in-campus-orientation-programme, demonstration of lac cultivation technologies in different States, field visit programmes to different districts and States, impetus to production, marketing including export, conducting workshops and seminar, having direct face-to-face interaction with the lac farmers, promoting shellac industry and monitoring scientific lac cultivation, processing and utilization. It has been of seminal benefit to the tribals of the Jharkhand and other States

Lac cultivation generates women employment on a considerable scale. Hundred tree of *palas* resulted into generation of 35 man-days for women out of a total of 80. For producing one quintal of broodlac: women can contribute around 43 per cent of the total manpower involved. Similarly, on 100 trees of *ber*, out of a total of 157 man-days, 110 man-days are generated by women. For producing one quintal of sticklac 14 man-days were generated by women which constitute 70 per cent of the total man-power. Similarly, from trees of *kusum*, out of a total 192 man-days, 85 man-days are generated by women. Production of one quintal broodlac from *kusum* tree result into generation of 6 man-days for women out of a total of 14 man-days which constitute around 44 per cent of the total manpower. Overall, in the indigenous methods, women contribute 59-55 per cent of the physical input in terms of labour up to preparation of seedlac stage. The lac bangle unit can be started with only Rs. 10,000 as a capital investment. At present many units are being run exclusively by women in many parts of the country. A unit of 3 women can give earning of about Rs. 100 per women per day in scaling wax. Twenty-five field visits were undertaken for interaction with farmers and monitoring of lac crop time to time in adopted villages of Jamtara and Dumka districts by the experts of IINRG, Namkum (Ranchi). An innovative project of lac cultivation has been initiated by District Planning Office, Collectorate Khunti, Jharkhand during the year 2014-15 to address the major issues of the poor resource constraint faced by the people inhabiting in forest and sub-forest areas through scientific interventions and utilization of locally available natural resources. The work is carried out in Torpa and Rania Blocks of Khunti district through formation of SHGs (31) and total 415 families will be covered under the project. The role of IINRG, Namkum in imparting training, demonstrating lac cultivation in the field of tribal farmers, associating Forest, Tribal Development, Rural Development and NGOs in the training and research programmes has greatly augmented the knowledge and cultivation of lac culture in Rural Jharkhand as also in the neighbouring States like Odisha, Chhattisgarh, West Bengal etc. It is suggested that the Government of Jharkhand should associate most of the tribal districts in the cultivation and training programme of IINRG to promote a very important source of NTFP livelihood in Jharkhand.

8.12 NTFP in Odisha

The present study also analyses the role of NTFP in the State of Odisha. Initially, a review of study on NTFP in Odisha is being undertaken to understand the background. A research conducted by A.K. Maharana, H.S. Mishra, K.K. Mohanti (ed.), (SCSTRTI), Bhubaneswar (2004) have studied two tribal pockets of Odisha inhabited by two different tribal communities—one chiefly depending on shifting cultivation and the other on forest collection. According to this study, in general, the people living near forest derive income from (a) agriculture, (b) collection of Minor Forest Produce (MFP), (c) wages, (d) live-stock rearing, (e) salary, and (f) other miscellaneous sources. Agriculture stands as the main source of livelihood for the agrarian tribes—the settled cultivating tribes such as the Kolha, the Santal, the Bhumij, the Munda and the Gond as well as the shifting cultivating tribe, such as Kuntia Kandha. Wage earning is mostly confined to the landless families—the 'Sukhbasis', belonging to all the ethnic groups living in the study villages. The collection and the sale of MFP remain as the main source of income for the Hill Khadia. As high as 90.33 per cent of total income of this ethnic group is derived from the collection and sale of MFP (p. 63).

Forest dwellers are more dependent for their livelihood on NTFPs than for (1) earning cash income; (2) satisfying household needs such as fodder, medicine, shelter and other household goods; (3) sourcing traditional agricultural inputs; and (4) obtaining supplementary foods such as roots, tubers, vegetables, fruits and grains for the family. Studies in States of Odisha, Madhya Pradesh, Himachal Pradesh, Bihar and Jharkhand have also indicated that over 80 per cent of forest dwellers depend entirely on NTFP. Nearly 17 per cent landless depend on daily wage labour mainly on collection of NTFP and 39 per cent people are involved in NTFP collection as a subsidiary occupation (Negi, 1993). Many of them get 50 per cent or more income from NTFP and next important source for 20 to 30 per cent of the rural labour force. The dependence on income from NTFPs has been shown to be inversely related to the size of landholdings in Odisha. In Odisha, about 10-12 million poor tribals and forest dwelling community, who are landless or marginal farmers mostly belonging to Scheduled Caste and Scheduled Tribe communities also depend critically on forest for subsistence and much needed cash during the lean summer months.

Forest Rights Act, (FRA) 2006 clearly defined the MFP. VSS members in Odisha have normally been entitled to collection of NTFPs from Reserve Forest and other forest lands. Their counterparts in the Protected Areas (PA), hardly enjoyed this privilege chiefly because the norms are different for Protected Areas. A study on NTFP and Rural Livelihoods (Vasundhara, 1998) in Bolangir district of Odisha found a correlation between average income from NTFP and landholding status. Panchayats (Extension to Scheduled Areas) Act, 1996 commonly known, as PESA is a historic move by the Union Government, which clearly endows Gram Sabha or Panchayats at appropriate level to own, control and manage MFP in Scheduled V areas. Regarding 'ownership' the Committee felt that in accordance with the spirit of the Act (PESA), the Gram Sabhas/Panchayats should be endowed with usufructory rights rather than ownership. It may be mentioned here that both *Sal* seed and *Kendu* leaf business have significant political implications for the State. The nationalization move is partly seen as a step to check the influence of traders of these NTFPs.

In 1990s, TDCC, Agency Marketing Cooperative Society, OFDC and Utkal Forest Product Limited (UFPL) were given the leases to collect forest produces in different divisions. The policy of March 2000 recognized the importance of MFPs in the forest dwellers' life. It also recognized the importance of sustainability of resources. As per the requirement of PESA, it gave ownership rights over MFPs to GPs in Scheduled Areas, and only regulatory rights to rest of the GPs. MFP was defined under this policy in vague way, creating a pseudo-category of 'Minor Forest Produce' (term used in PESA) under NTFP; initially 60 items were declared as MFPs (later the number rose to 69). Monopoly leases were no more allowed, and commercial lease was to be allowed for items not under the MFP. On 26th May, 2000, the Panchayati Raj Department, in exercise of power under section 152 of the OGP Act, issued an administrative order prescribing the manner in which the rights transferred to the GPs shall be dealt with. Since royalty was withdrawn, a token amount of Rs. 100 was fixed as registration fee per each produce that is to be given to the GP in which the traders intend to procure.

The State Government of Odisha made rules in November 2002, which has following salient features:

- The Gram Panchayat shall have the power to regulate procurement and trading of MFP, whether produced in government lands and forest areas within the limits of village or collected from the Reserved Forests and brought into the Gram.
- Priority would be given to the Van Suraksha Samiti (VSS) and its members for collection and trading of MFP.

- Price fixation would be done by the Panchayat Samiti (PS) in September and would be circulated in different offices of District Administration and a to all the GPs.
- The Gram Sabha would ratify prices fixed and necessary changes can be made based on the local needs.
- If Panchayat Samiti fails to fix the price then the District Collector would call a meeting of PS preferably in October to fix-up the minimum procurement prices.
- The trader registered for procuring MFP from the GP shall furnish monthly return and also annual return in a prescribed format.
- The Gram Panchayat shall furnish an annual return on the procurement and sale to the Forest Range Officer.

In India, *Sal* seed finds uses in food processing industries like Chocolates, Ice Creams, Vanaspati etc. Domestic food laws remain a bottleneck in further diversification of the uses of *Sal* seed. *Mahua* has always been controlled by the State excise laws in Odisha except for a brief period when it was nationalized.

In Odisha there are of *Intervening Institutions in Marketing NTFP like TDCC, OFDC, ORMAS and MART*. TDCC has a number of branches in the State, and procures from the traders and primary collectors directly. It is engaged in procurement and trade of Hill Brooms, *Sal* seed, *Tamarind, Siali* leaf etc. from the tribals and other marginalized people. DSMS/ORMAS have been established by the Government of Odisha for collection and value addition on NTFP such as *neem* and *Mahua* seeds for oil. Oil expellers have been provided to SHGs for processing of oil from *neem* and *Mahua* seed. OFDC is engaged in procurement and marketing of *Kendu* leaf, harvesting of bamboo and collection and sale of *Sal* seed. MART as a partner of WORLP has done an extensive study for developing business promotion and market development strategy in Bolangir. It strongly suggested for collective action for procurement and trade of *Mahua* flower, *Badhun*, *Char* seed, and processing of *Mahua* seed and *Neem* seed for oil and processing of *Sal* leaf and cups in Bolangir district. It is providing support service to PLAs and SHGs for collective action for *Char* seed and *Mahua* flower, and also to improve the quality of the produce through proper drying and storage.

The Government of Odisha has taken several initiatives for strengthening the procurement of NTFP in different districts of Odisha. It has also established linkage of SHGs with traders in different districts of Odisha and particularly in Sundargarh district where the present author conducted field study. The SHGs are trading in different products like *Mahua*, Charcol processing, vegetable cultivation, goat business, piggery etc. and making good annual income. The VSS in Sundargarh district has been able to promote and manage large number of SHGs in the Van Samrakshana Samiti (VSS) and promote good income particularly in Rourkela Forest Division through *Ama Jangala Yojana*. The number of VSS in Rourkela Forest Division is 147 and the number of SHGs 305. They are involved in income generating activities like *Mahua* business, Bamboo basket-making, *Sal* seed, *Char* selling, leaf plate making, vegetable cultivation, paddy cultivation and lac business. These are indeed progressive step undertaken by the Government of Odisha. The Government of Jharkhand does not have sound policies to procure different type of NTFP. Lac cultivation and lac culture, however, is onc of the most attractive NTFP activity which is carried out during all the months with the active support of the Indian Institute of Natural Resins and Gums located at Ranchi (Jharkhand) under the overall supervision of the Council of Agricultural Research, Namkum.

The Government of Jharkhand need to take up the following policy measures on NTFP learning from Odisha experience:

- After the enactment of PESA the Odisha Government has handed over ownership rights of MFP to Gram Panchayats. The Government of Jharkhand should have similar policy initiative.
- The Gram Panchayat shall have the power to regulate procurement and trading of MFP, whether produced in government lands and forest areas within the limits of *Gram* (village) or collected from the Reserved Forests and brought into the Gram.
- Priority may be given to VSS and its members for collection and trading of MFP in Jharkhand on the same pattern as it is done in Odisha.
- Price fixation of NTFP items are done by the Panchayat Samiti (PS) in Odisha; similarly steps should be taken by the Government of Jharkhand to introduce measures for the price fixation of NTFP items at the grassroots levels through Gram Sabhas.
- The TDCC in Odisha procures several items of NTFP from the grassroots procurers and SHG for few selected items based

on Minimum Support Price. The Ministry of Tribal Affairs, Government of India has announced marketing support for Tribal Produce for 24 MFP items, which is introduced in Odisha, Chhattisgarh and Andhra Pradesh, but not in Jharkhand. The Government of Jharkhand should connect itself with the marketing support for tribal produce being extended by Ministry of Tribal Affairs.

The Government of Jharkhand has acquired the reputation of *primus inter pares* in Jharkhand in lac cultivation and lac production. It has the facility of IINRG, Namkum for promoting training cultivation and production facilities. However, marketing is a casualty for which the Government of Jharkhand should take appropriate step in the procurement, collection and marketing of lac products. The IINRG does not have the mechanism of marketing facility; the Government of Jharkhand should intervene in promoting lac production cluster area for procurement of lac by fixing MFP and procuring MSP rate from the tribal farmers. Women and SHGs play a prominent role in the procurement, cultivation of lac and selling it in the local haat and market. This system should be replaced by an institution similar to JHASCO LAMPS/TDCC so that, there is proper livelihood promotion of the tribal farmers.

During our field study in Saranda forest area we could find that *Sal* leaf, *Mahua*, *Siali* leaf, *Tamarind*, *Karanj*, and other NTFPs are procured by the women groups and taken to the local haats for selling it to the traders where they are fleeced. There is enough scope for forming clusters of MFP production area for bulk procurement at prices fixed by Gram Sabha or Gram Panchayat on the line of the working system in the State of Odisha. Already the Government of Jharkhand has found few clusters in Saranda, Porahat, Goilkera, Sonua, Manoharpur and other adjoining areas which can also be suitably utilized for NTFP procurement. They can be given trading at the Gram Sabha and Gram Panchayat level to get acquainted with the entire process of NTFP procurement and marketing. The Government of Jharkhand has already formed clusters for procuring *Kendu* leaves from the different pockets of the State.

R.K. Yogi, R.K. Singh *et al.* (2016) have discussed New Policy Interventions in the lac sector in Jharkhand. Their suggestion for policy interventions include creation of a revolving fund to be provided for procurement of NTFP for the gatherers at the prefixed MSP. The revolving fund requirement shall be accessed based on an Annual Procurement Fund.

Subsidy is required for the State to compensate for losses that may be incurred during the MSP operation. This is essentially an anti-poverty measure, as it addresses the livelihood of some of the poorest communities in the country. The scheme shall provide training on sustainable harvesting and value addition activities including facilitation for the marketing of the produces to one hundred thousand tribal MFP gatherers. The existence and dissemination of complete and accurate market information is the key to achieve both the operational and pricing efficiency.

8.13 Analysis of the Left Extremist Affected Areas in Jharkhand and Odisha

The analysis of the impact of Left Extremist Movement in the States of Jharkhand and Odisha is based on:

- Report of the Planning Commission, Government of India, (2008)—"Report of an Expert Group to Planning Commission—Development Challenges in Extremists affected Areas" (2008);
- Santosh Mehrotra, (edited), "Countering Naxalism with Development—Challenges of Social Justice and State Security" (2014);
- Saxena, K.B., "Militant Left Radicalism, State and Civil Society: The Centrality of Tribal Land Rights, Recommendations of a National Seminar", (*Social Change*, Volume 41, Number 3, September 2011).

As per Planning Commission Report, the intensity of unrest resulting to extremist methods and effort to resolve issues through violent means is a challenge to state authority. It is in response to the gathering of unresolved social and economic issues for long durations. It creates the impression that policy-making and administration responds to extreme means. The more recent development is in the emergence of CPI (Maoist) after the merger and consolidation of two powerful Naxalite streams in September 2005. Due to Union Government's attention to the CPI (Maoist) [formed by the merger of CPI M-L (Peoples War) with Maoist Communist Centre (MCC) in September 2004] and its association to the Naxalite phenomenon, that party and its method of functioning have started defining the official understanding of the Naxalite movement.

According to the authors, however, the fact that the Naxalites employ methods of violence in tackling these issues has other consequences, which include injury, fear and disruption of normal life. It is also a fact that Naxalite activity is not confined to solving people's grievances. They are engaged in a violent fight against the State for overpowering and overthrowing it. So, though the aspiration of "land to the tiller" continues to be given, the focus of the Naxalite movement is on trying to provide land. The Naxalites seem to have had greater success in opposing land acquisition policies of State Governments and Government of India. Internal displacement caused by irrigation, mining, industrial projects, resulting in landlessness and hunger, is a major cause of distress among the poor, especially the Adivasis. It is well known that 40 per cent of all the people displaced by dams in the last seventy years are forest dwelling Adivasis. The Naxalite movement has come to the aid of such victims of enforced migration in the teeth of the law. Landlessness, extremes of poverty and social oppression can also be cause of displacement. Moreover, through this process of forced migration, many tribals have left their villages and even State and migrated into neighbouring States. The Minimum Wages Act remains an Act on paper in much of rural India. Dissatisfaction with improper and other mal-governance created anger among the suffering population. The Naxalites exploit the situation for their own political gain by giving the affected persons some semblance of relief or response; thereby they tend to legitimize in the eyes of the masses their own legal or even illegal activities. However, the Naxalite movement itself brings further police repression on the poor as a matter of State policy.

The Ministry of Home Affairs (MHA)'s *Annual Report* for the year 2006-07 mentions the spread of Naxal movement across 12 States of the Union. The profile of violence during the last few years has been shown in Table 8.6.

The Naxal problem has to be tackled in a multipronged approach. Some of the ameliorative measures like National Rural Employment Guarantee Act (NREGA), 2005, The Scheduled Tribes and Other Traditional Forest Dwellers (Recognition of Forest Rights) Act, 2006, National Rehabilitation and Resettlement Policy, 2007 have been introduced. The State's response to continued unrest and social dissension in areas predominated by Scheduled Castes and Tribes was to formulate three protective laws and a major policy decision. These Acts are the provisions of the Panchayats (Extension to Scheduled Areas) Act, 1996, the National Rural Employment Guarantee Act, 2005, The Scheduled Tribes and Other Traditional Forest Dwellers (Recognition of Forest Rights), Act, 2006, and the National Rehabilitation and Resettlement Policy, 2013.

Table 8.6: Naxalite Violence between 2003 and 2006

Head	*2003*	*2004*	*2005*	*2006*
No. of Incidents	1597	1533	1608	1509
No. of Civilians killed	4100	1466	524	521
No. of Policemen killed	105	100	153	157
No. of Naxalites killed	216	87	225	272

Source: The Ministry of Home Affairs (MHA), *Annual Report*, 2006-07, Government of India.

Acquisition of land has emerged as the single largest cause of involuntary displacement of tribals and turning them landless. Indiscriminate land acquisition should be stopped and land acquisition for public purpose should be confined to public welfare activities and matters of national security. SCs and STs are the two groups that have truly taken advantage of the employment being offered under NREGA. One of the major causes of rural poverty identified in the report was disappearance of Common Property Resources (CPR). The new legislation, i.e. the Scheduled Tribes and other Traditional Forest Dwellers (Recognition of Forest Rights) Act, 2007 conferring forest rights on the Scheduled Tribes and other Non-Tribal Forest Dwellers is a step in the right direction and will serve to reverse the "historical injustice".

Santosh Mehrotra's (ed.) (2014), *Countering Naxalism with Development—Challenges of Social Justice and State Security*, (Sage) states that of the 83 districts that are reorganized by the Ministry of Home Affairs, Government of India as LWE affected, the majority are in five States of Andhra Pradesh (16), Bihar (22), Chhattisgarh (16), Jharkhand (21), and Odisha (19). In other words, these five States account for 90 per cent of the total number of affected districts. The implication from a security perspective is that without a very high degree of inter-state, combined with inter-governmental collaboration (between centre and State, and between States), there is precious little likelihood to any success in the long run against the Maoists. In these poorer States of India, the SCs and STs constitute a high proportion of marginalized. Another important fact is that the STs in these States usually live in highly forested, relatively hilly, rugged terrain. These very forested districts also have high concentrations of major reserves of minerals. The mining by private and public enterprises in these areas became another source of conflict with the Adivasis. While these are the root cause of the conflict, over the last decade or so, the Maoist insurgency has become extortionate and survives upon such extortion.

Meanwhile, the number of violent incidents continued to grow between 2001 and 2010 as did the number of deaths.

Table 8.7: Year-wise Incidents and Deaths due to Naxalism in Different States (2001-2011)

Years States		*Andhra Pradesh*	*Bihar*	*Chhattisgarh*	*Jharkhand*	*Odisha*
2001	Incidents	461	169	105	355	30
	Deaths	180	111	37	200	11
2002	Incidents	346	239	304	353	68
	Deaths	96	117	55	157	11
2003	Incidents	577	250	256	342	49
	Deaths	140	128	74	117	15
2004	Incidents	310	323	352	379	35
	Deaths	74	171	83	169	8
2005	Incidents	535	186	385	312	42
	Deaths	208	96	168	119	14
2006	Incidents	183	107	715	310	44
	Deaths	47	45	288	124	9
2007	Incidents	138	135	582	482	67
	Deaths	45	67	369	157	17
2008	Incidents	92	164	620	484	103
	Deaths	46	73	242	207	101
2009	Incidents	66	232	529	742	8
	Deaths	18	72	290	208	2
2010	Incidents	100	307	625	501	61
	Deaths	24	97	343	157	1
2011	Incidents	54	314	465	517	1
	Deaths	9	62	204	182	0

Source: Ministry of Home Affairs (2012).

According to Santosh Mehrotra, it is critical that peace talks are initiated soon between the States on one hand and the extremists on the other. The focus of left-wing extremists has been on the slogans "land to the tiller". LWEs have tried to provide land that is surplus of ceiling to the landless, in situations where the State Government has failed to distribute ceiling surplus or Bhoodan land. The left-wing extremists tend to target landlords who have large holdings or are oppressive in their conduct (even if they are not big land owners); the State police, in such situations, intervene often on behalf of the landlords. It is estimated that in the development process, 60 million persons have been displaced between 1947 and 2004 on account of a variety of development projects: irrigation, mining, and industrial projects. In three States—Odisha, Jharkhand and Chhattisgarh—which are rich in minerals, mining projects have threatened the livelihoods of the Adivasis, since they live in forests under which are buried these minerals. Proper implementation of the PESA Act, requires giving the rightful role of governments to Gram Sabhas and through them to Gram Panchayats (the village council elected by the village assembly).

State needs to address the development challenges in the States where Left-Wing Extremist violent is concentrating. Santhosh Mehortra refers to the Integrated Action Plan (IAP) implemented under the leadership of each District Collector. Such Integrated Action Plans has been conceived by Planning Commission in different States including Jharkhand and Odisha. Till 2014, there were 17 Districts in Jharkhand and 18 districts in Odisha where such Integrated Action Plan were undertaken. In Jharkhand it covered 3162 Panchayats and 18,239 villages. In Odisha it covered 3767 Panchayats and 30,223 villages. Bhatia (2005), Bal Gopal (2006) and Sundar (2006) have observed that the Rural Poor understood the objectives of the Naxal movement 'change' not 'revolution' in the context of Bihar, Jharkhand, Andhra Pradesh and Chhattisgarh. There are some authors who have argued that finding a solution to the security problem is problematised due to the fact of the existence of Mineral resources as a major factor behind the continued conflict. Santhosh Mehrotra observes that the overall security-centric approach has proved to be less successful.

Prakash Singh and Ajit K. Doval (2014), in their paper entitled "Development to Deal with Causes of Discontent, Unrest and Extremism", have observed that the Naxal movement has been recognized as the single biggest threat to internal security in the country by no less a person than by the Ex-Prime Minister of the Country Sh. Manmohan Singh. Violence was also at peak in 2010 when 2119 incidents took place in which 960 persons were killed. The Socio-economic problem are related to poverty, land reforms, unemployment, corruption, tribal rights and governance. Unemployment registered an increase between 1993-94 to 2004. The Planning Commission figures show that out of a total of 3,75,000 cases of tribal land alienation registered till 2002, covering 8,55,000 acre of land, only 1,62,000 cases could be disposed of in favour of the tribals, covering a total area of only 4,47,000 acre. The author observe that there is sharp increase in the ranks of Naxal cadres, estimated to be nearly 12,000, with nearly 1,000 new recruits joining every year. Constant-up gradation in weapons and training has led to higher firepower, acquisition of skills in fabrication of improvised explosive devices, field tactics, intelligence trade craft, and communications. The authors also observe that money has emerged as one of the main prop sustaining the movement. The sources of fund raising include the cuts from civil contractors; levies on road transporters; levies on forests, coal, iron ore, and other mining products; protection money from businessmen; and collection from quarry and mill owners.

According to the authors, the Naxal problem would need a comprehensive multi-pronged approach involving:

- Strengthening the law enforcement agencies;
- Mobilizing the support of the people;
- Addressing the grievances—improving governance; and
- Developing the areas affected by Naxal activities.

K.B. Saxena (2011), in his analysis of "Militant Left Radicalism, State and Civil Society: The Centrality of Tribal Land Rights" (*Social Change*, 2011) is critical of the Security-centred approach to Militant Left Radicalism, which he says is not a sudden eruption. It is also not primarily a law and order problem created by an unlawful political formation challenging the legitimate democratic government. It is a political movement which needs to be contextualized in the objective overall current situation of the people involved which creates conditions for its emergence. The tribes are at the centre of this conflict which arises from a deep discontent and neglect with a long history and multiple dimensionality in its underlying causes. These include, among others, loss of land so integral to their existence, deprivation of access to other natural resources, forest and water, unimplemented laws which protect their interests, failure to factor in and counteract extremely adverse implications of the pattern of national development for them and threats perceived to their identify and culture.

According to him the security-centric view outlined suffers from questionable assumptions, untenable logic, and has disturbing implications for public policy. The context of Naxalite violence has to be related to the acute socio-economic and cultural exploitation of these groups, the failure of the State to implement its own progressive laws, developmental policies, and protective measures, and the widespread social discrimination and bias against them in institutions of governance. It is rooted in genuine, social and economic demands and political aspirations Prof. K.B. Saxena *specifically mentioned that the social discrimination and social injustice are the primary causes for the prevalence of the Naxalite violence.* Hence, he suggests that the states. should address the progressive law, Development Policies and

Protective measures. He also points out that the role of Civil Society Group is important to reflect the Human rights approach towards the solution of this problem.

8.14 Naxal Violence in Jharkhand

According to partial data complied by the South Asia Terrorism Portal (SATP), Jharkhand recorded a total of 97 fatalities, inclusive 43 civilians, 12 Security Force (SF) personnel and 37 left wing extremist (LWE) cadres in 2014. In 2013, the State registered fatalities, including 48 civilians, 26 SF personnel and 57 LWE cadres. A decline in Maoist activities in the State is evident while civilian fatalities remain at the same level, SF fatalities have reduce more than half from 26 to 12, between 2013 and 2014. LWE fatalities have also come down from 57 to 37 indicating that extremists are carefully avoiding active engagement with the SFs.

Maoist cadres, including an area commander at Nayanpur in Giridih District on September 12, 2014, the Maoists engineered a big revenge attack on the Tritiya Pra Committee (TPC) on August 9, 2014, killing at least 14 cadres of this splinter group at Choti Kauriya village under Vishrar Police Station limits in Palamu District. Maoists also killed three civilians each on two occasions, on June 3 and July suspecting them of acting against their interests. PLFI was responsible for one major incident, killing seven persons, including special police officers and two members of the Shanti Sena (Peace Army), a vigilance formation operating in the State. Geographically, fatalities were recorded in Gumla, Palamau, Khunti, Dumka, Giridih, Hazaribagh, Ranchi, East Singhbhum, Simdega, West Singhbhum, Latehar, Lohardaga, Seraikella-Kharsawan, Bokaro Chatra, Daltonganj, and Garhwa. Among other patterns of violence recorded by SATP, the Maoists engaged in at least 12 incidents of arson in eight district, namely: Gumla, Lohardaga, Chatra, Dumka, East Singhbhum, Khunti, Latehar and Ramgarh. In 2013 LVE groups were involved in 12 incidents of arson in six districts, eight recoincidents of abduction and eight incidents of explosions.

However, in a significant security lapse, 55 under trials, of whom 26 were in jail on charges of Maoist activities, made a escape from the Chaibasa District when they found the main gate open as soon as the vehicle in which they were taken to court returned to the jail premises. As a part of the Ulgulan movement, villagers hold day-long meetings called "Shanti Sabhas" to mobilize support against extremists, convince the youth against joining them.

8.15 Saranda Action Plan in West Singhbhum District, Jharkhand

Saranda forest has been one of the densest forest in India and it was also an important abode. Government of India had sent a team of senior officers from Ministry of Rural Development and other institutions who visited the Saranda Forest Area from October 18-20, 2011. They had a very intensive interaction with the District Administration and sent a report to Shri Arjun Munda, Chief Minister, Government of Jharkhand on 25th October, 2011. The team had submitted a recommendation which was developed in consultation with the district officials of West Singhbhum District. Saranda forest is a very rich *Sal* forest of 800 sq.km. lying in the trijunction of Jharkhand, Odisha and Chhattisgarh States. It is of strategic importance and has been under the control of Maoists for many years. The Eastern Headquarters and many training camps of the Maoists were located in Saranda forest. Recently, the CRPF has conducted operations and cleared the area. The Ministry of Rural Development is keen on implementing a focused development plan in Saranda forest through the Jharkhand Government as the tribal inhabitants have been victims of long years of official apathy and isolation from the development process due to Maoists' presence. There are around 7000 tribal households with population of 36,500 in Saranda Forest in 56 villages. It is home to the Ho tribals who speak the Ho dialect. Of the 56 villages. It is home to the Ho tribals who speak the Ho dialect. Of the 56 villages, 14 are forest villages, around 10 are unsurveyed Jharkhandi villages and the rest are Revenue villages.

The area has 25 per cent of the known iron ore deposits in the country and the reserves are exploited by more than 12 mining companies with 50 mines. Chiria, the biggest iron ore deposits in Asia is also located in Saranda. The Saranda Mining Plan has 44 iron ore mining leases in West Singhbhum District comprising 12,374 (ha). The proposed mining products which includes 18 mining projects include 16115.80 (ha) (*Source:* Buletin of mining leases and prosecting licences, 2010, Indian Bureau of Mines). Presently, the administration does not have its presence in Saranda and there is no information about the implementation of the government schemes in Saranda. The Saranda Action Plan proposed interventions which are categorized both a short term and a medium term. The short term interventions include the following:

- *Solar Lamps*—To be provided to all the 7,000 families living in Saranda Forest.

- *Bicycles*—Distribution of Bicycles to 7,000 families for school girls.
- *Transistors and Musical Instruments*—These will be provided from IAP funds.
- *Those Excluded from BPL List*—Out of 7,000 households in Saranda around 3,000 households are eligible to be included in BPL and they are entitled to the schemes like IAY, NSAP Pensions, Ration Cards etc.
- *Provision of IAY Houses*—Around 4,000 IAY houses will be needed to provide all the households with IAY houses.
- *NSAP Pensions and Community Certificates*—OAP Pensions, Widow Pensions and other pensions to be provided to all eligible persons.
- *Forest Right Titles*—The coverage at present is estimated to be less than 5 per cent of eligible families. The titles can be distributed very quickly in the forest villages where the position and ownership are well established.
- Much emphasis was given for Employment under MGNREGA as it signaled the initiation of the development process. It is essential to employ a strong team of local tribal youth who can deliver all the services. Around 30 tribal youth can be engaged as Rozgar Sahayaks and paid the wages of unskilled/semiskilled workers. It is better that the administration makes weekly cash payment which can be made in front of a payment committee. The State Government may relax the qualifications of JEs to the District Collectors in case of 6 Gram Panchayat in Saranda.
- Most of the tribal have land holdings in Saranda and these lands can be developed by taking works under MGNREGA.
- *Employment linked skill training for youth*—There is good potential for providing skill training to youth who can be absorbed in the mining and other sectors. There are nearly 12 big mining companies operating in the area. The JSLPS project in Jharkhand is working with 12 organizations which are providing employment linked skill training including L&T, *Don Bosco* and IL&FS. Many of the youths were provided skill training and employed in various vocational skills not only within Jharkhand but also in far of places like Bangaluru, Karnataka, Chennai, Andhra Pradesh etc. This has been an important scheme for alienating the youth from the influence of the Maoist. The local tribals also were angry with

the Maoist and also attacked them with bows and arrows not only in Saranda Forest, but also in the adjacent Dalma Forest Sanctuary. This was a major unprecedented event in which the Maoist had to directly encounter the tribals and they had to escape from the hilly and forest region.

- *Mobile Health Units/Health Camps*—The health volunteers were appointed to check the health status of the tribals and to provide medicines to them. This scheme was very popular with the women.
- *Watershed Programme*—Forest Department and Watershed Agency are involved in construction of watersheds for providing irrigation facilities to the cultivating fields of the Adivasis which is considered as a good entry point activity.
- *PMGSY Roads*—The District Administration has identified 11 roads and also capacity building activity for the PRI functionaries.
- Livelihood in Saranda, promotion of improved agriculture and horticulture, development of animal husbandry and poultry, collection of NTFP and skill trainings leading to employment in mining sector have been activated.
- *Integrated Development Centres (IDC):* To be set up in temporary structures where security and civil officials can be put up to deliver various government schemes.

The present author undertook field visits in the few villages comprising Saranda Forest Area along with Researchers. He could see and visualize that forest right pattas had been distributed to the Adivasis and they were trying to make it productive. They were also using simultaneously the facilities being provided by MGNREGA scheme to make the forest lands productive. The Mundas village headman was also active in the Gram Sabha villages. The young lady health workers used to visit the villages regularly for checking-up the status of health of the women workers including the children. The MGNREGA employment has a positive impact on the youth of the villages. The vocational guidance facility provided to the educated girls and boys had s salient effect in alienating the youth from the impact of the Maoist. However, the Maoist could easily cross over to their Odisha and Chhattisgarh Border from the Jharkhand villages for getting refuge; however, the Saranda Action Plan had the immediate effect of the decline in the Maoist influence from the West Singhbhum area. They could find ways to escape to Saraikela and

Khunti area where their presence became strong. The Adivasis had also constituted Shanti Sena to minimize the impact of the Maoist but the Naxalites are deeply penetrated in the Arki Block of Khunti District. During the year 2015-16 there were several encounters between the Police and the Maoist in the Khunti area resulting in violence in both the sides. Though the Government of Jharkhand boast itself of the success of the Saranda Action Plan but its long term impact is yet to be observed. It has also become difficult for them to procure NTFP because of the intervention of the Maoist. It is suggested that both development oriented work and security centre approach should be employed jointly by the Government of Jharkhand, Government of Odisha, Government of Chhatisgarh and Government of West Bengal. Special measures need to be taken to convert the forest villages into revenue villages and also initiate functioning of schools as also vocational centres in the Manoharpur, Goelkera, Sonua and adjoining areas.

8.16 Maoist Movements in Odisha

According to Rajat Kumar Kujur (2006), the iniquitous development agenda pursued by successive governments at the centre and the State has rendered several tribal groups in Odisha, who reside in some of the poorer, more inaccessible districts of the State, largely marginal to the governance process. Arguably, it is this alienation and under development that has afforded a fertile ground to several Naxalite groups to set up base in these districts. Suranjita Ray in his paper "Maoist Killiongs in Malkangiri", *Mainstream*, Vol. IV, No. 51, December 10, 2016 has observed that increasing inequalities, deprivations and disparities have made the interiors of the rural areas more vulnerable to the forces of the Maoist movement. Violations of the people's rights have seen the escalation in Maoist activity in vast areas of Telangana and Andhra Pradesh, Chhattisgarh (Southern), Odisha (Western) and Jharkhand. While the present Odisha Government expects the Naxalites to come to the negotiating table without any preconditions, the irony is that the response of the government has been primarily to address the movement as a major law and order problem.

Naxalites are spreading their influence across Odisha and there are reports that they have established a corridor through the State with Jharkhand at one end and Andhra Pradesh on the other. The merger of the People's War and the Maoist Communist Centre culminating in the birth of the Communist Party of India (Maoists) and the failure of the peace talks between the extremists and the Andhra Pradesh Government appear to have contributed towards the growth of the Naxalite movement in the remote districts of Odisha. (*Frontline*, Volume 22, Issue 14, July 2-15, 2005) (*The Hindu*). In the past two decades the Naxal movement has strengthened itself in almost fifty per cent of the districts of Odisha. Besides Malkangiri, the Naxalites have spread in several districts such as Koraput, Nabarangapur, Rayagada, Gajapati, Ganjam, Sundargarh, Mayurbhanj, Keonjhar, Sambalpur, Kandhamal, Deogarh, Jharsuguda and Jajpur. The Chashi Mulia Samiti, a frontal organization of the CPI (Maoist), has led several land capture programmes in the tribal villages of the south-western districts which experienced illegal transfers of land from the tribal people in particular.

Anshuman Behera (B10-2016), NIAS Backgrounder, Bengaluru, has identified few flash points which have accentuated the Maoist Movement in Odisha:

- Chitrakonda Police Station Attack, 1968.
- The biggest ever strike of its kind in Odisha took place on August 9, 2001, when approximately 230 armed Naxalites of the PWG launched simultaneous attacks on Kalimela and Motu Police Stations in Malkangiri district. They killed six police personnel and injured approximately 22 others, and took away a huge quantity of arms and ammunition.
- Since, then, the Andhra-Odisha border areas have become increasingly vulnerable. On December 5, 2002, an estimated 18 police personnel belonging to the Odisha Special Armed Police (OSAP) were injured in a landmine blast triggered by the PWG near Kolnara on the Rayagada-Behrampur State highway.
- Koraput town stormed by the Maoists, 2004.
- 14 police personnel killed in Maoist attack in Nayagarh, 2008.
- 38 Security personnel killed inside Balimela Reservoir Ambush, 2008.
- Landmine blast claimed 17 lives of police personnel in Malkangiri, 2008.
- Kandhamal Riot, 2008.
- Foreign tourists abducted, 2012.
- Odisha Maobadi Party formed, 2012.

- Odisha Police in the early hours of October 24, 2016 killed twenty-four Maoists on the outskirts of Malkangiri along the Andhra-Odisha border which have exceeded the earlier killings. The death toll rose to thirty Maoists the next day.

Precipitants to Autonomous Tribal Movement in Odisha

The Land Acquisition in Odisha had adverse effect on the Adivasis and it generated autonomous tribal movements as also precipitant to the Maoist Movement in Odisha as indicated below:

- The tribals in Odisha have a prolonged history of militant resistance against land alienation and land acquisition.
- They have again demonstrated this in the contemporary land acquisition process and particularly during the globalization era.
- The noteworthy militant resistance have been demonstrated in Kalinganagar Episode and in POSCO struggle.
- The Activists including the radicals have actively supported the tribal movements in different parts of Odisha.
- The women have played a crucial role in resistance movement everywhere and their participation in POSCO Movement have been exemplary.
- The environmental experts like Shri N.C. Saxena have played significant role in clearly pointing out that the Forest Rights Act, 2006 were violated in case of POSCO Project and Acquisition of Land by Vedanta from Niyamgiri Hills.
- The Dongaria Konds could adequately resist their sacred and religious significance of Niyamgiri Hills and even the Supreme Court pronounced positive decision protecting the land rights, forest rights and religious rights.
- The State Government of Odisha violated most of the protective legislations like the PESA Act of 1996, provision of Scheduled V Area, Forest Rights Act, 2006, role of Gram Sabha and liberally used Brutal Police Force to protect the Corporate Interest.
- The tribal and the marginalized sections amply demonstrated that the militant protest movement, their collective solidarity, their cultural identity with land and forest are their major strength.
- On the aftermath of the Kalinganagar Massacre the Government of Odisha was compelled to enact the Odisha Resettlement and Rehabilitation Policy, 2006.

- The Land Acquisition and Land Alienation Policy is a continuity of Colonial and Post-Colonial Policy.
- Felix Padel and Samrendra Das (2008) have rightly characterized the police firing in Maikanch Village in December 2000 and in Kalinganagar Industrial Area in January 2006 as "Cultural Genocide," the intrusion into peoples' community and social structure. They have also termed it as "Internal Colonialism" carried out through large scale privatization of resources and takeover of huge tracks of cultivable land by corporates.
- They have also significantly observed that mining bauxite from Niyamgiri Hills is an assault on Kond Religion as they recognize mountains as sacred entities and source of life. "Cultural Genocide" and the sacrificing people's quality of life make-up their cultural and community life. According to Felix Padel and Samrendra Das, the present situation in Odisha involves sacred high profile struggles of people opposing displacement in the State. "Physical Genocide" meaning the extermination of all members of a tribe often went alongside "cultural genocide": "The Killing of Cultures"—"Cultural Genocide" most clearly apply to tribal cultures which differ markedly from mainstream orientation in their life style grounded in the nature.
- It would be necessary here to mention the case of MCL, Sundargarh as the Land Acquisition here became controversial. The land was acquired in the 1980s and compensation was not paid for several years. The displaced people had complained to the High Court and the Supreme Court to fix-up a fair compensation based on the latest market rate. Accordingly, the Supreme Court appointed a Claims Commission to fix-up the latest market rate to the displaced persons by MCL. Hon'ble Supreme Court approved the scheme *and the claims Commission was formed by the court in July, 2010*. The Claim Commission recommended that the compensatory value of the acquired land of village Gopalpur be assessed on the average market rate. The Claims Commission decided the following average market rate for the displaced persons in village Gopalpur taking September 2010 as the cut-off period. The following average market rate were fixed by the Claims Commission for the displaced persons in Gopalpur village.

Other Major Land Acquisition in Odisha

Land Acquisition by MCL in Sundargarh district of Odisha has been one of the major bickering in the area of land acquisition which lingered for quite a long time and agitated the minds of the Activists and the displaced persons for quite a long time culminating in a series of negotiations and conflict between the people and the Government of Odisha.

Table 8.8: Average Market Rate of MCL Land Acquisition in Gopalpur

Nature of Land	*Approximate value of the land per acre*
Gharabari	Rs. 12 Lakh
Mal and Goda	Rs. 8.5 Lakh
Behal and Berna	Rs. 10 Lakh
Others categories	Rs. 3.5 Lakh

Source: District Administration and Field Study.

The largest land acquisition in Sundargarh district is for Basundhara Gajan Bahal Area of MCL in which land is being acquired from 14 villages from land owners as indicated below:

Table 8.9: Village-wise Land Acquired for MCL in Sundargarh District (Odisha)

Sl. No.	*Name of the Village*	*No. of Land Owners*	*Remarks*
1.	Sardega	99	The rehabilitation package includes a plot of 10 decimals or Rs. 3 lakh house building assistance, of Rs. 2.55 lakh maintenance allowance for 12 months. The claim commission increased the land compensation from Rs. 8.50 lakh per acre to Rs. 12 lakh per acre.
2.	Gopalpur	42	
3.	Tikilipara	142	
4.	Bolinga	199	
5.	Bankibahal	55	
6.	Gopalpur	545	Compensation has already been assessed by Claims Commission.
7.	Tikilipara (P)	167	*Note:* The rates for different *kisams* of private land were assessed for the purpose of land acquisition for KOCP and Basundhara.
8.	Garjanbahal	202	
9.	Kuida	49	
10.	Karlikachhar	69	
11.	Sarmal	92	
12.	Bangarkela	88	
13.	Jhupiranga	501	
14.	Kiripsira	216	

Source: District Administration and Field Study.

Table 8.10: Market Rate of Different Assets fixed by MCL Sundargarh

Sl. No.	Name of the Villages	Rate of different kisam of land
1.	Sardega and Gopalpur (P) (Two Villages)	Goda–11,779.00 Masa–15,313.00 Besa–21,202.00 Basa–24,736.00 G.B.–43,592.00
2.	Tiklipara (P), Balinga and Bankibahal (Three Villages)	Goda–15,227.00 Masa–19,795.00 Besa–27,409.00 Basa–31,977.00 G.B.–36,957.00
3.	Gopalpur, Tikilipara (P), Garjanbahal, Kuida, Karlikachhar, Siarmal, Bangurkela, Jhupurange, Kiripsira, Tumulia and Ratansara (Eleven Villages)	Goda–8.50 lakh Masa–8.50 lakh Besa–10 lakh Basa–10 lakh G.B.–12 lakh Others 3.5 lakh

Source: District Administration and Field Study.

Table 8.11: Status of Land Acquisition of B.G. Area of MCL in Sundargarh District (IB block–VIII under B.G. Area)

Sl. No.	Villages	Notified Land in Acre				
		Forest	GNF	Tenancy	Total	Total Acquired
1.	Sardega	328.77	240.51	290.90	860.18	Full
2.	Gopalpur (P)	382.41	1549.84	1127.97	3060.22	Part
3.	Ratansara	472.25	370.33	1007.17	1849.75	Full
4.	Jhupurunga	133.97	344.71	1384.10	1862.78	Full
	Sub-Total	**1317.40**	**2505.39**	**3810.14**	**7632.93**	**3089.00 Ha**

Source: District Administration and Field Study.

Table 8.12: Lands Acquired and Leased Out to MCL-IB Block–VIII under B.G. Area

Sl. No.	Villages	Notified Land in Acre				
		Forest	GNF	Tenancy	Total	Total Acquired
(1)	(2)	(3)	(4)	(5)	(6)	(7)
1.	Tiklipara	1056.87	204.83	482.15	1343.85	Full
2.	Siarmal	423.45	198.02	240.87	862.34	Full
3.	Gopalpur (P)	—	125.59	15.08	140.67	Full

(Contd.)

(1)	(2)	(3)	(4)	(5)	(6)	(7)
4.	Tumulia	312.58	436.62	1632.12	2381.32	Full
5.	Karlikachar	102.41	90.65	318.88	511.94	Full
6.	Kulda	149.01	162.15	231.66	542.82	Full
7.	Bankibahal	435.93	159.19	241.21	836.33	Full
8.	Balinga	236.18	451.25	547.21	1234.64	Full
9.	Garjanbahal	135.92	255.55	406.88	798.35	Full
10.	Bangurkela	279.29	246.01	530.66	1055.96	Full
11.	Kiripsira	505.91	395.73	779.47	1681.11	Full
12.	Lalma RF	420	0	0	420	Full
	Sub-Total	**4057.55**	**2197.15**	**4688.09**	**11809.33**	
TOTAL IB BLOCK–VII and XI IN AC		**5374.95**	**5230.98**	**9236.33**	**19,842.26**	
TOTAL IB BLOCK–VII and XI IN HA		**2175.212**	**2116.949**	**3737.892**	**8030.053**	

Source: District Administration and Field Study.

Table 8.13: Summary of Employment and Resettlement under B.G. Area in MCL (as on 31-03-2015)

Sl. No.	*Project Head*	*Villages*	*PAF's Category (A to E)*	*Eligible for Employ-ment*	*Employ-ment Provided*	*Eligible for Resettle-ment*	*Plot Provided and shifted*
1.	KOCP	Banki Bahal	153	87	72	118	67
		Balinga	289	187	187	272	NA
2.	BWOCP	Gopalpur	58	31	29	39	—
		Sardega	240	133	127	159	124
	BEOCP	Tiklipura	258	186	179	132	132
Grand Total			**998**	**624**	**594**	**720**	**323**

Note: Cash compensation is provided as an alternative to employment and some of the workers are opting for this alternative. Similarly, for resettlement also there is provision of cash compensation instead of opting for plot. These options are responsible for variations in the ultimate figure.

Source: District Administration and Field Study.

8.17 The Status of Migrant Labour in Odisha and Jharkhand

There is the process of high incidence of migration taking from KBK Districts in Odisha to the Southern States of India particularly Andhra Pradesh, Karnataka, Tamil Nadu and Kerala. The State of Odisha is one of the highly migration-prone States and particularly the KBK Region which has been recognized for perpetual poverty and accompanying bondage. The poverty in KBK Region is one of the highest in Odisha though the overall poverty ratio has minimized in the State. This region has attracted the national and international attention due to its acute poverty and bondage. In this study, attempt has been made to understand the prevalence of bondage both through the secondary data as also through the primary data. There is very strong tie-up between the grassroots recruiter and contractor and the flow of migration to the Southern States. The districts of origin which are prone to bondage are the districts of Kalahandi, Koraput, Bolangir and Rayagada apart from some of the other adjacent districts. It is the rock bottom among the caste and class hierarchy who are victims of bondage and it is the upper echelon who are the employers and perpetrator of bondage. The prevalence of bondage has been in existence in the KBK Region particularly from the mid 1960s to the Globalization era. The poor implementation of the Rural Development Programmes have also enormously contributed to the prevalence and sustainable of bondage in this region. There has been also severe neglect on the part of Government of Odisha and the District Administration to ignore the phenomenon of bondage in this region. One of the important rationale for highlighting the high incidence of bondage in the region must be attributed to the active intervention of the voluntary organizations who have yielded pressure on the State and District Administration to intervene into the situation. The KBK Plan and other measures like MNREGA have partly been able to minimize the incidence of bondage in this area. However, the recruiting agents and other vested interests are so deeply entrenched into the social roots of the region; it is only through a serious concerted effort that this phenomenon can be tackled. The Government of Odisha claims that through the implementation of MNREGA programme they have been able to tackle the phenomenon of migrant labour in the region. However, the continued prevalence of bondage and the interventions by NHRC lend evidence to the high incidence of bondage still perpetuating in this region. The social activism has been able to make a difference into the situation. The overall development scenario in KBK Region for last 20-25 years have reduced the incidence of poverty, still lot of efforts are needed to address the phenomenon of perpetuation of migration and bondage in this region. The author has tried to substantiate through the secondary data as also through the primary data of the enormity of the problem still persisting and sustained efforts needed of the major stakeholders to address the situation.

The incidence of seasonal migration is relatively higher from the regions with low levels of development and land productivity (Keshri and Bhagat, 2012; Mishra and Bose, 2013). The regional and social concentration of poverty indicates that SCs and STs have higher rate of poverty than others. It is rooted in the historical processes of economic transformation and stagnation. Northern and Southern Regions of Odisha are very poor where an overwhelming majority of SCs and STs population lives. The process of land alienation through debt bondage continued unabated (Sara, 1991). Gradually, a stage came where Kalahandi, Bolangir and Koraput (KBK Region) came to be recognized as synonymous with mass poverty, starvation and hunger deaths. Seasonal migration from interior Odisha needs to be viewed as an outcome of cumulative disposition, marginalization and exploitation. The extent of out-migration has increased in recent decades which highlights the deepening of these processes of disposition.

Short term migration is highest among households engaged in agricultural labour (38%) and other non-farm labours (28%). Households that are self-employed in agriculture constitute 20 per cent of the total migrants. Such households, though possessing land, belong to the category of small and marginal farmers. Over 80 per cent of short term migrants belong to households possessing land less than or equal to just an acre. Landlessness, thus, appears to be a vital push factor for migration. The characteristics of land poorness, low literacy levels, engagement in casual wage labour (both aricultural and other labour) together reflect the poverty vulnerability of short-term migrants of Odisha.

The distribution of migrants across industries shows that they are mostly engaged in construction (36%) and manufacturing (38%). More females (25%) than males are also seen to participate in agricultural activities at destination places. The migration process starts months before the actual migration takes place, in the month of September and October, during the *Nuakhai* festival. Labour contractors, sardars and their agents start advancing small sums of money as advance to labour families in exchange for their promise to migrate. Most of the workmen after the paddy season go to South India like undivided Andhra Pradesh, Karnataka and Tamil Nadu to work in the brick kiln either through middle man or *suo motu*. In Andhra Pradesh they mostly migrate to the Brick Kilns adjacent to the city of Hyderabad, Sikandarabad, Vijyanagram, Vishakhapatnam etc. The labourers from Maupada district migrate to the Brick Kilns of Faizabad and other districts of Uttar Pradesh.

As per the report of the National Human Rights Commission, the status of bonded labours in Odisha, who were identified at the destination place in Andhra Pradesh between January 2001 and December 2015 were 10,042 of whom 8751 persons were male, 1138 were females and 153 were child bonded labourer. Of the total bonded labours 9593 were released (inclusive of male, female and children) and 7852 were released on certificates. The number of bonded labours rehabilitated with a grant of Rs. 20 thousand were only 3151; besides this 1317 bonded labourers were rehabilitated by the State Government in the State of Origin and the rest 2181 are yet to be rehabilitated. This shows that 40.13 per cent of the bonded labourers were rehabilitated by paying Rs. 20,000 which is a pittance for proper rehabilitation. Besides this, the rehabilitation of 13.73 per cent cases were undertaken by Government of Odisha, but the nature of rehabilitation is not mentioned which raises issues relating to proper rehabilitation. The worst are the cases of 2181 bonded labourer constituting 22.74 per cent who have not been rehabilitated and are required to fend for themselves. To specifically 2683 workers were identified in 3025 in the State of Karnataka of whom 1127 were rehabilitated in the State of Odisha and 759 bonded labourers are yet to be rehabilitated. The NHRC identified a total of 2583 cases between July 2012 to June 2015 of bonded labourers who had migrated from the State of Odisha during the previous five years. Of these bonded labourers, all the 2583 cases were also released and certificates were also issued to all of them which is a unique achievement. Out of 2583 cases of bonded labourers, the number rehabilitated in other States includes nearly 432 cases and 1127 of the released bonded labourers were rehabilitated by receiving a grant of Rs. 20,000. Approximately, 40.13 per cent of the bonded labourers were rehabilitated by payment of Rs. 20,000. Besides this, the rehabilitation of 13.73 per cent cases were undertaken by Government of Odisha, but the nature of rehabilitation is not mentioned which raises issues relating to proper rehabilitation.

The author has not only been able to collect the secondary data from NHRC about the identification, release and rehabilitation of bonded labourers, but also could collect some case studies of the interventions of the State Governments, both at the State of Origin and the State of Destination to take some concrete steps to provide relief to the bonded labourers based on the complaints filed to them from the voluntary agencies and from the other stakeholders. In this study few such cases have been highlighting to signify the role played by NHRC. These cases related mainly to the migrant labour from Odisha which is the State of origin to the destination State of Andhra Pradesh, Karnataka and Tamil Nadu to work as bonded labourers in the brick kilns. These cases also provide us the ignominy faced by the bonded labourers in the process of release and rehabilitation. In one case of the release of 20 bonded labourers getting release certificate from Dy. Commissioner, Bengaluru, the Commission had to observe that the poor bonded labourers who have been released way back in 2013 are still in dark about their entitlement to rehabilitation assistance.

The present study is to understand the process of high incidence of migration taking from KBK Districts in Odisha to the Southern States of India particularly Andhra Pradesh, Karnataka, Tamil Nadu and Kerala. The State of Odisha is one of the highly migration prone States and particularly the KBK Region which has been recognized for perpetual poverty and accompanying bondage. The poverty in KBK Region is one of the highest in Odisha though the overall poverty ratio has minimized in the State. There is very strong tie-up between the grassroots recruiter and contractor and the flow of migration to the Southern States. The districts of origin which are prone to bondage are the districts of Kalahandi, Koraput, Bolangir and Rayagada as also some of the other adjacent districts. It is the rock bottom among the caste and class hierarchy who are victims of bondage and it is the upper echelon who are the employers and perpetrator of bondage.

The study on "Domestic Workers from Jharkhand to Delhi" shows that their working conditions is highly unsupportive and unhygienic. Their entire continuity of work and subsistence depends upon the benevolence of their masters who are rarely humane in their approach towards domestic workers. Most of the domestic workers are dependent on their employer not merely for wage but also for few favours like loans, old clothes, food and in some cases shelter too. There are no educational facilities. Medical treatment is provided only in extreme cases. Sexual harassment at work place is omnipresent in this informal and unorganized sector and in most cases such incidences go unreported due to subservient position of the worker. The socio-economic condition of women domestic workers is rather sad and deplorable in urban centres. They came from very poor families, with the majority of them being illiterate or having studied only up to the primary school level. In most cases, the husbands of women domestic workers are either unemployed or underemployed. Their family is marked by frequent quarrels and disorganization. Women domestic workers invariably live in slums or tents. The surroundings of their dwelling is equally depressing and unhealthy. Most women domestic workers suffer from several health problems. They suffer from anaemia, malnutrition, bodyache and general weakness. They develop cracked hands and feet, which become sore due to continuous work in water, using strong abrasive detergent and soaps. It is very difficult to find jobs without any contacts. The entire sector of domestic workers is managed by the agency of relatives, co-villagers and the agents. The easily available agency for this sector are the relatives. In most of the cases, the women come along with their relatives who are already working as domestic helps and are inspired/allured by them to come and join them. The reason behind migration of tribal women according to the study seems too enough to ensure their own advancement and that of the household numbers. The survival of the household members was the most important cause of tribal women domestic workers to migrate in such large numbers to cities.

8.18 Resume

The basic assumption in the present study has been that the violation of Land Rights and Forest Rights have been the primary causes for generating identity issues and the reasons for militant tribal movements both in Jharkhand and Odisha. The discussion in Chapters 1, 2 and 3 has tried to establish this strong association. The Land Rights were not only related to the transformation of Communal Property Rights into Private Property, but also the conversion of Communal Forest Rights into State Property. The protest of the tribals are reminiscences of both forms of militant education in the two States of Jharkhand and Odisha. The Land Acquisition Act of 1894 facilitated the acquisition of land for various public purposes and for companies. The mines, both in Odisha and Jharkhand, became the property rights of the government and there was wholesale exploitations of tribals in this process.

The Land Acquisition Act is often criticized as draconian, undemocratic and inegalitarian for the following reasons:

- It is anti-people Act and is weighed in favour of the government.
- The Act is draconian and lot of claims have been made on the grounds of public purpose with only partial utility.
- In most of the cases it is acquired at well below the market value of the properties. There is a considerable difference between the market value of the property and the value that the land acquisition officer pays to the land owners.
- State retains its right to assert the domination over the private and public land on the grounds of public exigencies and for public good which is a disputed issue.
- It is also argued that the relocation and rehabilitation of land owners displaced by the actions of the Act, is not followed

adequately, and that this is not covered comprehensively in the framework of the Act.

- The Act uses compensation without even once mentioning rehabilitation.

The Government of Odisha brought out a Rehabilitation and Resettlement Policy in May 2006. It has been appreciated by experts as one of the effective peace of legislation in providing provisions for the effective rehabilitation of the displaced policy. The process of negotiation includes land procured/purchased directly by the corporate/private parties as seems to be the case, since the definition of project area includes land which is acquired/alienated/purchased. It is certainly more equitable just and humane in its applicability (Saxena, K.B., 2008). The definition of 'family' recognizes unmarried daughters and sisters over thirty years of age, a widow or a woman divorce as a separate family for the benefit of rehabilitation is, thus, gender neutral. Additionally, it empowers physically and mentally challenged persons and minor orphans by conferring the status of a separate family. The Odisha Policy has also provided for dovetailing of normal development programmes with the resettlement and rehabilitation package to be made available to the displaced community on a priority basis. This is intended to be in addition to the benefits which a displace is entitled to under the Policy. The National Policy does not make any mention of it.

The Odisha Policy clearly stipulates that no physical displacement shall be effected before the completion of resettlement work while the National Policy is less equivocal on this issue. It merely requires adequate progress in the rehabilitation and resettlement to be ensured before physical shifting of the affected persons and, therefore, shows less sensitivity to the inconvenience faced by the displaced persons. In matters of providing employment the Odisha Policy mentions that where employment is not provided, one time cash compensation ranging from Rs. 1 lakh to 5 lakh would be provided. A mandatory provision has been made for allotment of 2½ acre of irrigated agricultural land or five acre of non-irrigated agricultural land to each ST displaced family in type (c) projects while the displaced families of all other social categories would be provided with two acre of irrigated or four acre of non-irrigated agricultural land. On the provision of homestead land and house building assistance, the Odisha Policy is more liberalized than the National Policy.

It is in respect of benefits to the landless and the homestead less encroachers that the Odisha Policy shows greater sensitivity. This includes the mandatory Social Impact Assessment, gamut of physical amenities and social infrastructure to be provided at the resettlement site detailed enumeration of rehabilitation benefits, norms of compensation assessment, unutilized acquired land. However, the Odisha Policy does not assure replacement of land for land lost not even to STs of a durable, sustainable and dignified employment. The absolute nature of the power of the State through the use of Eminent Domain for compulsory acquisition of land should be abandoned. Gram Sabha of the village should be mandatory consulted whether in areas covered by PESA or outside for their consent to the acquisition. The acquisition of land, where absolutely necessary for public purposes, should be undertaken after consultation with the Gram Sabha and on terms which they collectively settle with the acquisition authority. These terms would reflect the social cost of land. This is the only democratic and humane method for acquisition of land. The referendum carried out by the Maharashtra Government in Rayagada for acquisition of land for SEZ shows the way in this regard. The scope of public purpose should be drastically narrowed down to projects covered by the Directive Principles of State Policy and where the project provides to the affected persons direct, tangible and demonstrable benefit.

The definition of the word "occupiers" should include all those who are in possession of any land and tare engaged in its cultivation other uses but have not been able to obtain valid rights on it prior to the issue of notification under Section 4(1) of the Land Acquisition Act. The residence on the date of notification for acquisition of land should suffice or this purpose. Appropriate adjustment in the entitlement of benefits can be made in the case of person falling in this category. Such a person may not be resettled in the new location but may be provided cash compensation for loss of his/her livelihood.

Environmental Impact Assessment and social impact assessment should be mandatory in all cases irrespective of the size of the project or the nature of purpose for which land is acquired. This exercise should be carried out through a participatory mode. The social impact assessment should specifically focus on the impact of the project on people, their economic conditions, social status, cultural values, identity and access to resources and benefits and not merely on infrastructure and institutions. Landlessness should be neutralized by allotment of land, joblessness should be tackled through provision of employment. Homelessness should be eliminated by provision of housing. Marginalization should be addressed by measures which restore the community and its support system. Morbidity and mortality should be overcome by provision of adequate health services right from the day the displaces are shifted to the new site.

The present research study has formulated few hypotheses to be tested. The first hypothesis has been that the Violation of Tribal Communal Land Rights and Forest Rights during the Colonial and Post-Colonial period would be igniting ingredient for generating tribal movement and tribal identity in Jharkhand and Odisha. This hypothesis has been tested in Chapter-2 entitled "Identity and Ethnicity in Jharkhand and Odisha". The second hypothesis relates to Development Induced Displacement as a basic precipitant for the pauperization and proletarianisation of the tribals. This hypothesis has been exhaustively tested both in the context of Jharkhand and Odisha in Chapter-3. The third hypothesis relates to the contribution of poverty to migration of tribal labourers from Odisha and Jharkhand to other States. This hypothesis has been tested in Chapter-7. The fourth hypothesis is that Social Injustice may be attributed as the primary cause of Naxalite Violence. This hypothesis has been briefly tested in the concluding chapter.

The continuation of the Land Acquisition Policy during the colonial period continued with the same basic ingredient of the State as "Eminent Domain" and the private landed property free for acquisition by the State went unchallenged and resulted in militant protest in Kalinganagar and Jharkhand. This resembles a basic contradiction between the State and the Tribals in spite of massive structure changes and social transformation. The only resilience is the amendment to the Land Acquisition Act during 2013 which inducted two important safeguards, namely, "Environmental Assessment", "Social Impact Assessment" and "Consent of the People" before land acquisition as envisaged in the PESA Act, 1996. In spite of such an official position the Government of Jharkhand has again tried to bring amendment to Chhotanagpur Tenancy Act, 1908 and Santhal Pargana Act, 1949. The struggles are in continuing process both in Jharkhand and Odisha.

References

Alloysius, G. (2003). "Ideology and Hegemony in Jharkhand Movement", In: R.D. Munda and S. Bosu Mullick (eds.), *Jharkhand Movement: A Historical Analysis*, Copenhagen: IWGIA and Birsa, Document No. 108, pp. 206-15.

Areeparampil, M.S.J. (2002). "Struggle for Swaraj", Chaibasa, Jharkhand: Tribal Research and Training Centre (TRTV).

Balagopal, K. (2006). "Maoist Movement in Andhra Pradesh", *Economic & Political Weekly*, XII (29): 3183-87.

Behera, Anshuman (2016). "Maoist Conflict in Odisha", National Institute of Advanced Studies, Bengaluru, NIAS Backgrounder, B10-2016.

Bhatia, Bela (2005). "The Naxalite Movement in Central Bihar", *Economic & Political Weekly*, XI (15), pp. 1536-43.

Das, Kalpataru (2014). "MGNREGS in Odisha—The Path", Panchayati Raj Department, Government of Odisha, Bhubaneswar.

Das, Prafulla (2005). "A Naxalite corridor", *Frontline*, Vol. 22, Issue 14, July 2-15, 2005, *The Hindu*.

Kesri, Visveshvar Prasad (1992). "Jharkhand Ke Sadan", Ranchi: Chhotanagpur Sanskritik Sangh.

Maharaj, R.N. and K.G. Iyer (1982). "Agrarian Movement in Dhanbad", In: N. Sengupta (ed.), *Fourth World Dynamics: Jharkhand*, New Delhi: Authors Guild Publications.

Mehrotra, Santosh (2014). (ed.) *Countering Naxalism with Development: The Challenge of State Security with Social Justice*, New Delhi: Sage Publications.

Mehrotra, Santosh (2014). "*Human Development in India's Tribal Areas: Peace to Secure Development or the Other Way Round*", New Delhi: Sage Publications, pp. 1-24.

Mohanty, Manoranjan (2015). *Red and Green—Five Decades of the Indian Maoist Movement*, Kolkata: Setu Prakashani.

Padel, Felix and Samarendra Das (2008). "Odisha's Highland Clearance: The reality gap in R and R", *Social Change*, Vol. 38, No. 4, December, pp. 576-608.

PUCL (1979). "Repression in Singhbhum", New Delhi: "Report of the Delhi Unit of People's Union for Civil Liberties and Democratic Rights", Delhi in Bihar, March.

Ray, Suranjita (2016). "Maoist Killings in Malkangiri", *Mainstream*, Vol. LIV, No. 51, New Delhi, December, 10, 2016.

Roy, A.K. (1982a), "Jharkhand: Internal Colonialism", *Frontier*, 17 April, 4-7.

Saxena, K.B. (2014). "The Naxalite Movement and State Policy", In: Mehrotra, Santosh (ed.) (2014). *Countering Naxalism with Development*, Sage Publications, New Delhi.

Saxena, K.B., (2011). "Militant Left Radicalism, State and Civil Society: The Centrality of Tribal Land Rights", *Social Change, Journal of the Council for Social Development*, Volume 41, Number 3, September, 2011, pp. 473-484.

Sen, Arindam (2010). "Anarchism or Revolutionary Marxism", *Seminar*, 607 (March): 2010.

Singh, K.S. (2004). "Ecology, Ethnicity, Regionalism and State Formulation: An Exploration of the Jharkhand Movement", In: Balakrishnan, Rajiv, "Jharkhand Matters", Konark Publishers, pp. 116-142.

Singh, Prakash and Ajit K. Doval (2014). "Development to Deal with Causes of Discontent, Unrest and Extremism", *op. cit.*, Mehrotra, Santosh, 2014, pp. 55-70.

Singh, R.V., (2012). *District Human Development Report Kalahandi*, Planning and Coordination Department, Government of Odisha, Bhubaneshwar.

Srinivas, Injeti (2014). "Odisha Economic Survey 2013-14", Planning and Coordination Department, Government of Odisha, Bhubaneswar.

Sundar, Nandini (2006). "Bastar, Maoism and Salwa Judum", *Economic & Political Weekly*, XLI (29): 3187-92.

Thakur, Rameshwar (2004). *Human Development Report 2004*, Planning and Coordination Department, Government of Odisha, Bhubaneswar.

Tripapthi, S.N. (2016). "An Analysis of Tribal Movements in Contemporary Odisha" in Chaudhary, S.N. (ed.), *Social Movements in Tribal India*, pp. 76-98.

Upadhyaya, B.K., (2011). "*District Statistical Handbook, Kalahandi*", District Planning and Monitoring Unit, Kalahandi, Directorate of Economics and Statistics, Bhubaneswar, Odisha.

Vasundhara and Vikalpa (1998). "NTFP Policy in Odisha and a comparative analysis of NTFP policy and prices with neighbouring States", *Vasundhara*, Bhubaneswar.

Index